The Strikers of Coachella

Justice, Power, and Politics

COEDITORS
Heather Ann Thompson
Rhonda Y. Williams

EDITORIAL ADVISORY BOARD
Peniel E. Joseph
Daryl Maeda
Barbara Ransby
Vicki L. Ruiz
Marc Stein

The Justice, Power, and Politics series publishes new works in history that explore the myriad struggles for justice, battles for power, and shifts in politics that have shaped the United States over time. Through the lenses of justice, power, and politics, the series seeks to broaden scholarly debates about America's past as well as to inform public discussions about its future.

A complete list of books published in Justice, Power, and Politics is available at https://uncpress.org/series/justice-power-politics.

The Strikers of Coachella
A Rank-and-File History of the UFW Movement

CHRISTIAN O. PAIZ

The University of North Carolina Press
Chapel Hill

This book was published with the assistance of the Authors Fund of the University of North Carolina Press.

© 2023 Christian O. Paiz
All rights reserved

Set in Minion Pro by Westchester Publishing Services
Manufactured in the United States of America

Complete Library of Congress Cataloging-in-Publication data for this title is available at https://lccn.loc.gov/2022043911.

ISBN 9781469671697 (cloth)
ISBN 9781469672144 (pbk)
ISBN 9781469671703 (ebook)

Cover illustration: Sand dunes from Walter C. Mendenhall, *Ground Waters of the Indio Region, California, with a Sketch of the Colorado Desert* (Washington, D.C.: Water Supply and Irrigation Papers of the Unites States Geological Survey, 1909), 28. Courtesy of the Internet Archive (identifier: watersupplyirrig224unit).

How clever time works, overlapping people's lives at certain stages, and as some eyes are waking up, others are already closing, securing the continuity of the world.
—Rigoberto Gonzalez

To my parents,
and to my students

Contents

List of Illustrations, ix

Introduction, 1
In a Small Place

PART I The Rancher Nation and Its Discontents

Chapter 1 The Law of the Jungle, 25
Power and Society in the Coachella Valley, 1945–1965

Chapter 2 The Known World, 47
Fragments and Fissures in the Coachella Valley

PART II To Make the World Anew

Chapter 3 A Flash Flood in Red, 73
On the Farmworkers' Many Movements, 1965–1970

Chapter 4 In a Field of Flowers, 102
The UFW Offensive against the Rancher Nation

Chapter 5 Chicana/o Coachella and the Civic Retreat of the Rancher Nation, 127

PART III Politics in a Precarious Present

Chapter 6 Insurgent Frailties, 153
Errors, Setbacks, and Fissures, 1970–1973

Chapter 7 The Battle for Coachella, 1973–1974, 174

Chapter 8 Overlaid Tenses and Trajectories, 205
Movements In and Out of the Coachella Valley, 1974–1977

PART IV Denials and Afterlives

Chapter 9 Sparks at Dusk, 231
   Elections and the (Denied) Promise of Utopian Futures, 1977–1983

Chapter 10 Here Is Where We Meet, 255

Acknowledgments, 281

Appendix. Oral History Project: United Farm Worker Movement in the Coachella Valley, 285

Notes, 291

Index, 389

Illustrations and Maps

Illustrations

"The Strikers of Coachella," 2

Editorial cartoon about how bosses suppress farmworkers, 14

"Pilgrims in Search of Justice," 78

"Members of the Historic Bagdasarian Sit-In," 97

Richard Chavez, 99

The Farm Worker in the 1970s, 103

"Farm Worker Women for Equality . . . What about Us," 118

"Teamsters Have the Growers, We Have the People," 192

Excerpt from Cesar Chavez's speech, 199

"For What Are We Fighting," 268

The Manongs, 275

Maps

Southern California, 13

Midcentury Coachella Valley, 13

Coachella Valley after 1970, 169

The Strikers of Coachella

Introduction
In a Small Place

In the summer of 1969, the United Farm Workers (UFW) newspaper, *El Malcriado*, published an eight-photo spread titled "The Strikers of Coachella": two of Mexican women, two of Filipino men, and four of other farmworkers and children.[1] Some captured earnest moments, like a young mother gazing blankly out of a car window while her bothered toddler looked at the camera, rubbing his eye. Another framed a sitting man with elbows on knees and clasped hands, leaning forward expectantly, listening to a speech amidst others. A third angled upwards to a striker with microphone in hand and eyes near closed, exhorting an out-of-view audience. The photos also showed laughing, smiling faces—of older men and women, of children, in lighthearted and quotidian moments, comforting even, without the attrition inherent to most rebellious acts, like joining a farmworker strike.

The photos appeared at the end of the UFW's 1969 Grape Strike in the Coachella Valley, a small desert near California's U.S.–Mexico border. There, Filipino and Mexican farmworkers harvested the country's earliest table grapes and, there, the UFW sought an early victory to press the larger San Joaquin Valley grape ranchers into signing contracts. By then, the UFW counted four years since its 1965 Delano Grape Strike, when Filipino and Mexican grape workers, demanding higher wages and a union contract, led one of the largest interracial farmworker strikes in California's history. For Delano strikers, the next four years brought social ruptures, interracial solidarities, leadership opportunities, and unexpected, often far-removed allies. To overcome their strike's limited visibility in rural California, the UFW deployed creative tactics, like a Pilgrimage to Sacramento in 1966 and a twenty-five day fast by the UFW leader, Cesar Chavez, in 1968. As it gained national prominence, the UFW extended its Delano Grape Strike to the Coachella Valley in 1968–69, and mounted an extraordinarily successful National Consumer Grape Boycott, which pressured California's table grape ranchers into UFW contracts in 1970. In these efforts, *El Malcriado* served as a cultural–political bridge connecting white, middle-class consumer allies to the UFW and its membership. To these readers, the newspaper offered the 1969 photospread as a testament of their shared fight for farmworker justice, inviting them to gaze solemnly, almost reverently, at their comrade-in-arms: "The Strikers of Coachella."

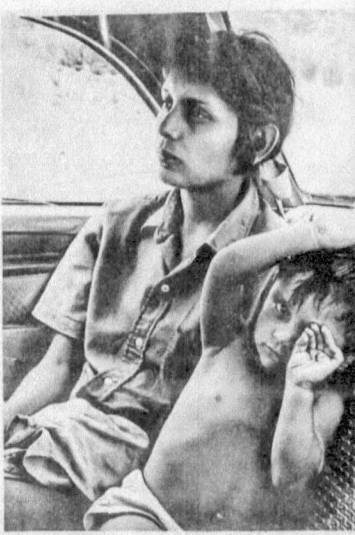

THE STRIKERS OF COACHELLA

photos by Bob Thurber

El Malcriado, July 1, 1969, 8. Walter P. Reuther Library, Archives of Labor and Urban Affairs, Wayne State University.

And yet, the newspaper provided no captions; it gave no names, quotes, or backgrounds—nothing on what people saw, what they said, much less on what they hoped for, yearned for. The textual austerity is especially surprising given the photospread's visual splendor, its diversity of photographed figures, its community of feelings and stories. Arguably, the austerity reduces the grape strikers to silhouettes and story placeholders, to a homogeneous Other that serves as the readers' empty canvas, readers who could then project any fantasy and desire, any version of their wishful thinking, including the notion that they knew and understood the Coachella Valley grape strikers of 1969.

Many years have since passed, but the wishful thinking remains. Schools and streets are named after UFW leaders, while classrooms, museums, and public agencies routinely cover it.[2] In this spirit, the Postal Service unveiled a commemorative stamp of a key UFW leader, Cesar Chavez, in 2002, while the National Park Service named the UFW headquarters a national monument in 2012.[3] Some have adopted the UFW's tenacious optimism and slogans as part of their political lexicon, such as *si se puede, boycott grapes* and *huelga!*[4] In 2008, presidential candidate Barrack Obama used *si se puede*'s translation—Yes We Can—to encapsulate his unprecedented, and successful, campaign.[5] In the last fifteen years, the UFW movement has also been the subject of *at least* ten books, a motion picture, and two documentaries.[6] The tally grows further when we include the titles before 2005.[7] Collectively, these accounts cover many aspects of the UFW, including its broad and interracial leadership, its deep roots in transnational labor history, its eclectic, almost festive tactics, its visionary politics, and its self-inflicted wounds. And yet, like *El Malcriado*, the collective portrait has presented UFW farmworkers in their very absence—as background to leaders, or as vague figures of political virtue, or as mute witnesses to the actions and voices of others, especially white liberals.[8] Few have eschewed this absent frame.[9]

This book is an attempt to return to the UFW's rank-and-file members. It traces their intersecting lives in the Coachella Valley and their aspirations, politics, and actions in and out of the UFW movement. It draws inspiration from historians of forgotten peoples—those everyday women, men, and children, students, teachers, and workers, from rural towns and impossibly large cities, who joined in the anonymous, but no less daunting or significant effort, to build life-affirming worlds.[10] Like these historians, I ask modest questions. Who, for instance, joined and sustained the UFW movement in the Coachella Valley? What lives had they lived, and how did their past shape their relationship to the union? What did farmworkers want and what costs were they willing to bear? Who did they meet; what ideas and politics did they gain; how did they transform their work, communities, and families, and, in the process, themselves? In turn, who did not join the UFW, and why? How did farmworkers relate to social, cultural, and political differences, whether pro- or anti-UFW? How did they respond to UFW demands or understand its decline? Finally, what remains of their efforts? I ask: Who were these people? What did they see and hear, desire and experience? How did they move the world and how did the world move them?

Of *El Malcriado*'s photographed Coachella Valley strikers, these questions have been largely impossible for me to answer. But of the multiple communities who led, sustained, and defined the Coachella Valley's UFW movement from the 1960s to the 1980s, much can be said, as I discuss in the next two sections. For now, I want to briefly state the book's assumptions. It assumes all people are poets, philosophers, and visionaries; that they calculate the possible against the real and see glimpses beyond the marginality shaping much of their lives; that social, political, cultural, and personal differences always exist, even amidst talk of unity and shared histories; that joy, frustration, and uncertainty lace all social and personal efforts that promise, empower, challenge, and disappoint; that nothing is permanent, neither structures nor movements; and that nothing is ever in vain, even if shadowed by failures. At its most ambitious, *The Strikers of Coachella* aims to move in rhythm with farmworkers' steps and gazes—to consider the weight of life lived in shaping choices, or the felt precariousness in the gamble that is to strike while poor and non-white, or the palpable quality of holding aspirations for changes that feel always impossible and yet, occasionally, possibly real. *The Strikers of Coachella* narrates a history of the UFW movement that transcends its leaders and shows how everyday people were of utmost historical significance: they initiated and propelled forward movements, and they helped determine our present fortunes. History often sits among forgotten peoples.

A Field of Stories

A central argument in *The Strikers of Coachella* relates to how it approaches the UFW as a subject. In history, unions and social movements can sometimes appear as cohesive vehicles moving on a single timeline to a preestablished and ideal future, much like a train on tracks.[11] Here, the questions center on what the subject did or did not do to get to the a priori endpoint—questions, I suspect, that attempt to address the perennial concern of why unfreedom remains and how freedom can be gained.[12] Though much can be learned from this historiographic model, it also carries significant shortcomings. It risks, for example, collapsing into a single subject, the multiple subjectivities and desired futures driving a union or social movement. The collapsing also tends to privilege the views of leaders and/or the members reiterating the historian's claims, which are then offered as representative of an otherwise diverse community. Lastly, it presumes a maximum level of transparency and shared presence in an organization, in which all participants can see each other, the means for their shared endpoint, and the fair distribution of collective burdens. In doing so, this historiographic model understates the opacities shaping social life and takes for granted concerns to be historicized, such as participants' distinct, often incommensurable, and always evolving desires, discourses, and calculations.

Like *El Malcriado*'s photographs, the train-on-track model risks misrepresenting the history of the UFW movement—for there were simply too many people from too many places in too many moments to speak of a singular subject. The Delano Grape Strikers of 1965, for example, belonged to two distinct organizations: the American Federation of Labor-Congress of Industrial Organizations (AFL-CIO) affiliated Agricultural Workers Organizing Committee (AWOC) and the nonaffiliated National Farm Workers Association (NFWA). The former was led by older Filipino bachelors, who migrated to the United States in the early twentieth century and built resilient, if deeply marginalized, co-ethnic communities on the Pacific West's migrant labor circuit. The NFWA, in contrast, was led by Mexican families, including grandparents and children, inspired by the Mexican Revolution and by southwestern strikes. The two organizations encompassed different languages, cultural practices, migration patterns, social positions, and ages. They also claimed different histories of social marginality and organizing, and lived in distinct present worlds, as shaped by their networks of dependents and caretakers, their relations to places outside the United States, and their visions of near and distant futures. Many Mexican families, for instance, were just starting their adult lives in 1965, while most Filipino bachelors were entering the twilight of theirs.

This collective difference grew after the Delano Grape Strike's first year. In August 1966, the two organizations merged to form the AFL-CIO's United Farm Workers Organizing Committee (UFWOC), which then expanded the Delano Grape Strike beyond the San Joaquin Valley. In four years, UFWOC marched along California's agricultural spine and rallied in Sacramento; declared strikes in other table grape-growing regions, such as the nearby Arvin-Lamont and the further south Coachella Valley; courted and won the support of national political leaders and civil rights organizations, like the Mexican American Political Association (MAPA), the United Mexican American Students (UMAS), the Brown Berets, and the Black Panther Party; founded consumer boycott houses in U.S., Canadian, and European cities; participated in national, regional, and local elections, government hearings, and news programming. Its membership diversified further when it won grape contracts in 1970. Pro-UFW farmworkers in the 1970s and early 1980s included Mexican lettuce workers in the Imperial and Salinas Valleys; Mexican farmworkers in dates, tomatoes, and vegetables in California; Yemeni, Filipino, and Mexican grape workers in the San Joaquin and Coachella Valleys; African American farmworkers in Florida and Mexican farmworkers in Texas, Washington, Wisconsin, and Arizona. The UFW movement also attracted a large community of religious, labor, and political allies, especially Chicana/o activists, each of whom carried differences amidst their similarities, and each of whom played key roles in the UFW's evolving meanings and fortunes.

Finally, the UFW's history is at least two decades long—from the early 1960s to the mid- 1980s. In these years, the social, political, economic, and cultural contexts for joining an agricultural union shifted in dramatically different ways. These shifts, in turn, shaped the risks involved in striking and/or unionizing, the goals considered possible by multiple communities, and the available allies and resources when in crisis. In California, these shifts included: from a small harvest strike in rural Delano in 1965 to a national, interracial movement leveraging civil rights discourses to mount a grape boycott in the late 1960s; from farmworkers striking for a contract when such contracts were unheard of in agriculture to striking when they had become possible, even if uncommon; from demanding union recognition with a strike to doing so with an election, as mandated by California's Agricultural Labor Relations (ALRA) Act of 1975; from joining a movement buoyed by the many rebellions of the 1960s to joining one in the late 1970s and early 1980s, when social progress appeared to collapse into the black hole of U.S. politics. Like its members and allies, the contexts in which the UFW operated came in many forms and fundamentally shaped its fortunes. To add further complexity, specific populations entered and left the UFW in distinct places and periods—thus creating experiential distance between pro-UFW farmworker communities and different views of UFW campaigns.

There was, in short, no single UFW train, nor a single set of UFW train tracks. Instead, the UFW represented a union of many peoples and many contexts intersecting in complex and contingent forms, which collectively produced and moved on multiple timelines and spaces. To study its history, and to avoid the absent frame of *El Malcriado*'s farmworkers, historians must attend to its plurality. To do this, we need to abandon the historiographic model of a single subject moving on a shared timeline to a preestablished endpoint—where the main questions are: who derailed the subject and how can it be retracked?

The Strikers of Coachella offers a UFW story of plurality in the Coachella Valley. There, pro-UFW farmworkers included women and men, migrants and residents, adults and children, the ardent and the reluctant. Some were Filipino men who traced their labor in the region to early twentieth-century migration circuits and post-World War II (WWII) desert grape cultivation. Others were Mexican families who settled in the Coachella Valley soon after white arrival in the early twentieth century, many fleeing political turmoil. More came from post-WWII Mexican im/migrant communities, those who settled in the United States after years as braceros, or caravanned from Texas, Arizona, and California, or daily crossed the southern border. Most pro-UFW farmworkers counted decades in agriculture, but some only a few years, or none at all. The latter joined as allies, as people who shared farmworkers' marginality through familial, ethnic, and social ties. A few members joined after long union histories, but most translated histories of nonlabor dissent into agricultural social unionism. Almost no one worked only in grape fields, and many, if not most, followed harvests throughout the U.S. West—though their migration patterns varied significantly. Like the UFW, the "Strikers of Coachella" encompassed a plurality of histories, positions, and desires. In a union of many people, each person carried their own material for making sense of their lives, the lives of others, and the potentials of a union.

To hold this plurality, the book presents a UFW movement with multiple beginnings and endings, one of overlaid trajectories and shifting visions. It sees the UFW movement as a *field* of stories—as a figurative and literal field where farmworker stories merged, pulled apart, and blurred into new forms, much like a kaleidoscope. These were stories about self and others, past and future, hope and reality. They spoke about what was right and wrong, what was owed, what could be gambled, what had to be held dear, and what could be lost. They were variously vague and specific, shared, contested, and/or misunderstood. They also gained new forms through and against the stories of others, which simultaneously reshaped the speakers and field anew. In the UFW's field of stories, multiplicity shimmered, syncretism and community jostled next to division and misrecognition, and beginnings and endings remained plural and in flux.

With this approach, the book begins with the Coachella Valley's post-WWII agricultural expansion and the submerged farmworker politics before turning to the UFW's local history. The latter begins with the initial Coachella and Delano Grape Strikes of 1965 and continues with the UFW's campaigns of the late 1960s, its 1970 victory over California's table grape ranchers, and its three-year tenure in the Coachella Valley grape fields. It then pivots to the UFW's early contract failings, the 1973 Coachella Grape Strike, the mid-1970s farmworker union elections, and the UFW's subsequent membership decline. The book does not present these events as points along a shared timeline. Instead, it sees them as changes in the field of stories, as if turning the knob on the UFW kaleidoscope. These changes pertained to what was considered possible, who was involved, what was contested, how victory and losses were understood. They also reflected key changes in local, regional, national, and transnational contexts, as well as within the UFW leadership. The UFW's field of stories in the Coachella Valley moved in ambivalent, nonlinear ways.

Consider, for instance, the life of the labor leader Pete Velasco, who migrated from the Philippines to the United States in 1930 for greater social and educational opportunities.[13] Like other Filipino men, however, Velasco found a Great Depression haze of low farm wages and racial hostility, conditions that prevented his schooling, segregated him, and limited his marriage prospects. He did find a close Filipino community in Los Angeles, and after serving in WWII he settled in the San Joaquin Valley to work in the nearby grape and vegetable fields. There, he saw white rancher wealth produce Filipino poverty. And there, he saw daily displays of racial inequality and denigration, such as ranchers' choice term for older Filipino men: "my boys." Velasco also joined multiple unions and, in 1965, he helped lead AWOC's Delano Grape Strike. After AWOC and the NFWA merged in 1966, Velasco took greater leadership roles in the new union, including organizing UFWOC's Coachella Grape Strike of 1969, which *El Malcriado* attempted to portray. He was nearly sixty years old by then, a bachelor still, and a skilled laborer with decades of farming and union experience. He was also an American war veteran with more years in the United States than in his childhood home in the Philippines.

In the Coachella Valley in 1969, Velasco organized Filipino migrant grape workers by framing UFWOC through Filipino history. The union, he said, could redress past marginality and shape how others saw them at the end of their lives. "We will become trusted and earn favor to our children," Velasco wrote, "our children will praise us, even the Ranchers." For him, the Coachella Grape Strike of 1969 offered older Filipino men a moralized visibility, one that perhaps spoke of a desire to be known as they knew themselves: as militants who fought exploitation; as men who fulfilled their obligations; as a people to be respected and remembered.[14]

Among ethnic Mexican farm laborers, the UFW appeared considerably different. They were two-thirds of the Coachella Valley's grape workers and the great majority of those in the region's fifty other harvests. Most arrived after WWII and faced pervasive marginality—from camp shacks and poverty-ridden *colonias* to racist schools, violent police officers, and negligent politicians. Like Filipino farmworkers, they drew from specific histories to engage the UFW. For many, it echoed the Mexican Revolution's egalitarian politics, which they had carried across the U.S.–Mexico border and now deployed against the region's racialized dichotomy of white ranchers and Mexican farmworkers. For many women farmworkers, furthermore, the UFW represented the means for contesting white ranchers' and Mexican farmworkers' overlapping patriarchies, while Chicana/o activists credited the UFW's 1968–69 grape strikes with igniting a local Chicana/o movement—one that fought the racial inequities outside of, but fundamental to, the region's agriculture exploitation.

For nineteen-year-old Amalia Uribe Deaztlan, these threads converged with UFWOC's Coachella Grape Strike of 1969. Her family had moved to Coachella in the late 1950s and lived in an abandoned, windowless house. She was ten years old and attended a racially segregated school, where she learned Mexicans were "expected" to be farmworkers. In 1964, she left school after the eighth grade and joined her parents in field work to replace her older brothers' wages, who enrolled in college to escape the military draft. For the next five years (1964–69), Deaztlan labored next to her mother and listened to her stories of the Mexican Revolution and aiding poor families. Her brothers also shared stories about a Chicana/o movement in their colleges. When UFWOC initiated the 1969 Coachella Grape Strike, Deaztlan drew from her family's stories to envision a previously inconceivable future for her. She joined the strike, she said, to escape a life of farm labor, to discover a new world. "I wanted to see and explore and see what was there for me," Deaztlan explained, "[to] understand my world . . . live in a little town . . . walk the streets and see what's life [there]." She wanted more, she said, a more embodied in the open-hearted, unbounded sojourner discovering "little towns."[15]

Velasco and Deaztlan played central roles in the Coachella Grape Strike of 1969.[16] But their approach to and visions of the UFW movement reflected their differences of age, gender, ethnicity, aspirations, and movement experience. Another thousand farmworkers joined UFWOC's 1969 Coachella Grape Strike and just as many chose against it. Each drew from distinct histories and politics, from what they considered reasonable, possible, and necessary—and each used these to make and explain their choices. More did the same under UFW grape contracts (1970–73), in the Coachella Grape Strike of 1973, and throughout local union elections in 1975–77. In each instance, farmworkers told stories to themselves and others in a shifting context—as did others in other places. Like the UFW as a whole, the Coachella Valley's union and social movement encompassed many peoples and many contexts intersecting in unpredictable ways for approximately two decades.

The field of stories frame helps us see the UFW as a collection of contingent meetings. These were meetings to talk about the project at hand, to direct efforts and learn about others; meetings of glances and laden memories, yearnings, and calculations; meetings to keep the faith, meetings that frustrated and dragged on; meetings to make choices that affected the contexts for future choices. In such meetings, farmworkers came across others and moved together, or moved together only to move apart, or moved together (or apart) without recognizing it. Many also chose against unionization's inherent risks, and their reasons, shape-shifting and multiple, affected the UFW movement as much as its strikers. Lastly, most people moved in meandering ways: in and out of regions and campaigns, in and out of desires and aspirations, in and out of believing and disbelieving, strikebreaking and striking, being central and marginal to the organization. They all moved, in short, in a plural present tense, where potential existed and could be seized, but where the future remained unpredictable and daunting.

Such a reframing suggests a rather sobering view of agency.[17] That farmworkers resisted their marginality is clear. What is key is that in a two-decade-long social movement of thousands of people and dozens of locations, agency overflowed individual intentions. Resistance was never direct effect, much less freedom. For most, instead, life remained tenuous yet compelling, precarious and promising, near calculatable and always not. Victories were also momentary and often arrived as surprises—as a field of stories converging in unexpected ways and shaping the shared-enough material world. Potential dissipated unexpectedly, too. To me, it is unclear what to do with such a limited sense of agency, or how to leverage UFW history to create a roadmap for a better future—as historians are inclined to do. In fact, *The Strikers of Coachella* provides little in the form of social and political strategy. It only pays close attention to farmworker stories and their collective efforts to uphold the skies of better worlds. Through this fidelity, I hope we can forge our own stories of new tomorrows, stories without guarantees or reassurances, but with enough promise to afford us to meet each other and to see, in Deaztlan's words, "what [is] there for [us]."

The Rancher Nation in the Coachella Valley

The Coachella Valley is a small place, tiny even, a mere forty-five miles long by fifteen miles wide. It is nestled in California's sparse interior, between Los Angeles to the northwest and the U.S.–Mexico border to the south. It is part of the Colorado desert, and its balmy falls and winters yield to warm springs and stunningly hot summers. Today, it is known for its conspicuous consumptions—for its resort hotels, luxury dining, golf courses, and caravan-like cultural events, like the widely recognized, Coachella Valley Art and Music Festival, or, more colloquially, *Coachella*. The Coachella Valley is also the ancestral home of the Cahuilla people, a people who, generation after generation, adapted the desert and adapted to it, and connected it to other Cahuilla bands and the broader mosaic of Indigenous nations in what is today the U.S. Southwest.[18] In the early to mid-twentieth century, the Coachella Valley was primarily a collection of irrigation-based and white-owned farming settlements. Today, it continues to grow million-dollar harvests, but—and much like its militant labor history—its farmworker communities rarely appear in the self-promotion or sun-draped views.[19]

Though the book prioritizes farmworker stories, the chapters are structured according to the Coachella Valley's social world and the UFW's impact on it. To do this, I adopted the UFW's "Rancher Nation" metaphor for midcentury agricultural California, which saw the latter's social, political, and cultural life as overdetermined by ranchers. In the Rancher Nation, one UFW member recalled, "the *patron* is like the absolute monarch. He is the king. He has his own private security guards. He has his own private judges and enforcement system. His rule is law, and nobody challenges him. He is life and death."[20] To the UFW, mid century California ranchers held expansive powers through their private property and a collection of allies in government and nongovernment institutions, such as county and city councils, police officers, schools, churches, courts, newspapers, farming research centers, state and national agencies, and transnational labor and consumer markets. With these resources and, with various levels of violence, California's ranchers secured a malleable workforce, grew profitable harvests, and built the state's rural economic foundations, including its secondary industries and tax base. In the process, ranchers claimed to have made modern life possible in their rural lands, where they ruled with impunity and as the final authorities—much like a king.[21]

Predictably, farmworkers existed in the Rancher Nation's social, cultural, and civic margins, where they faced poverty wages, job insecurity, structural under/unemployment, sexual harassment, and relentless humiliation. Most moved through contractors and supervisors—each carving their own subsovereignties in the rancher-king's name, each one guarding and inflicting more violence for him. The Rancher Nation also produced and relied on farmworkers' cultural and civic marginality, such as school and housing segregation, racial discrimination in public and private spaces, political disempowerment, absent social services, and police abuse. At its core, the UFW Filipino leader Philip Vera Cruz noted, the Rancher Nation was violent precarity. "To deny a man decent wages and job security," he wrote in *El Malcriado* in 1970, "making it impossible for him to live in dignity and peace with himself and his family, this too is a form of violence. To be subject to the overt racism and bigotry so common . . . these are forms of violence. When a farm worker's wife in labor pains is turned away from a county hospital, and her baby subsequently dies—this is a form of violence."[22] With decades of experience, Vera Cruz knew of the needless death in farmworker communities and its origins in rancher "greed, indifference and a belief that life is a battlefield." "If a [rancher] could get someone to do a job for nothing," he wrote, "he would do

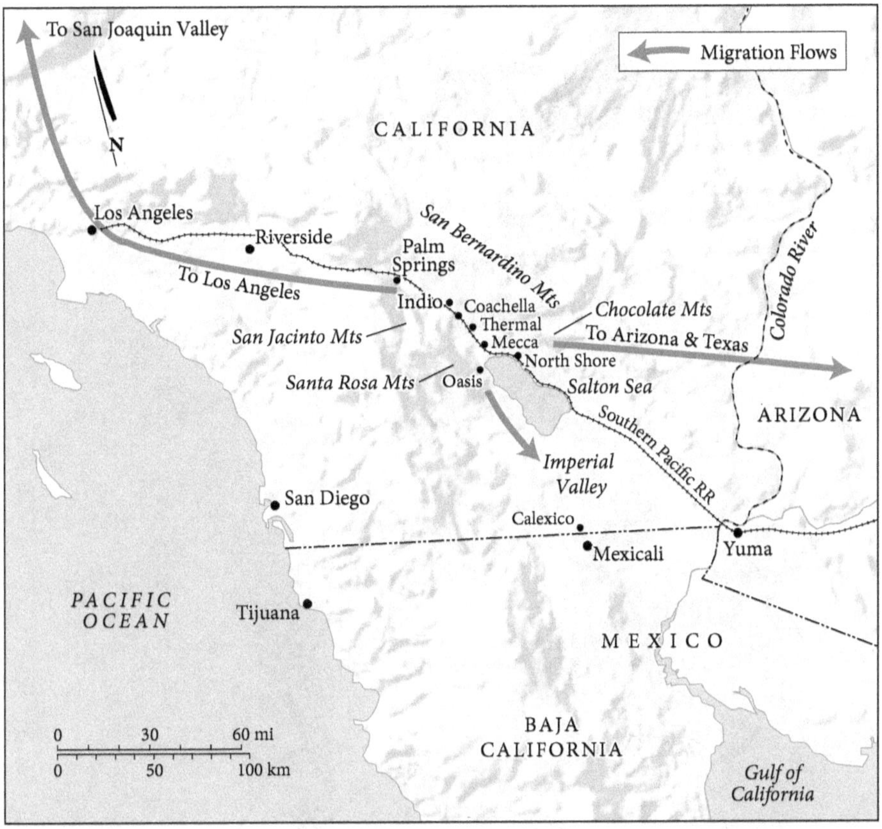

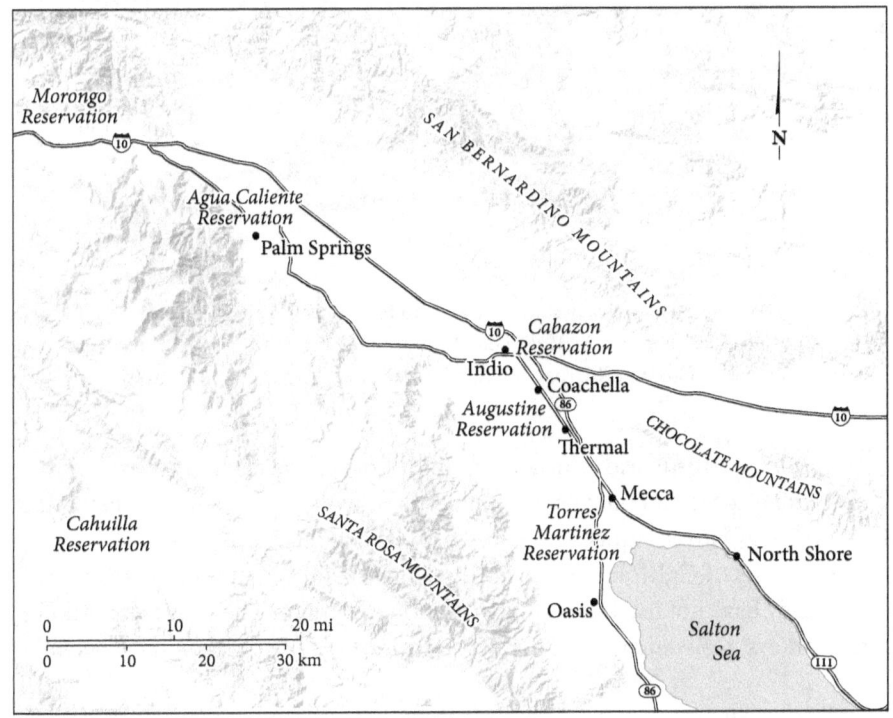

Southern California and midcentury Coachella Valley

"Patrones," or bosses, use their laws, judges, and police officers to sit on top of "campesinos," or farmworkers. *El Malcriado*, June 30, 1966, 12. Walter P. Reuther Library, Archives of Labor and Urban Affairs, Wayne State University.

that, too."²³ In this world, workers "[could] not talk sense to his boss"; only a union and a contract could "promote better relations between [ranchers] and workers" and "surely squeeze justice from [their] big money bags."²⁴

Historians of Californian agriculture have long documented this world, even if they have not used the Rancher Nation metaphor. They have also studied farmworkers' resistance to it.²⁵ Drawing from them, *The Strikers of Coachella*

14 Introduction

traces the Coachella Valley's "Rancher Nation" and the UFW's attempt to abolish it. There are four parts to this history. The first, encompassing chapters 1 and 2, presents the Rancher Nation before the UFW movement. The first chapter begins in the early twentieth century when white pioneers claimed to civilize the country's last frontier. They called the Cahuilla a near-extinct race and spoke obsessively of seeding a feminine "wasteland" to make it "bloom." By 1940, these settlers counted ten thousand irrigated acres, several million-dollar harvests, including the entire national date fruit, and a string of Orientalist-inspired towns on the Coachella Valley's eastern half: a couple thousand residents in Indio and Coachella; several hundred in Thermal, Mecca, and Oasis; decidedly less in the ghost town of Araby.[26] This early white settlement relied on a diverse workforce that included Cahuilla, South Asian, Filipino, and Mexican laborers. By the 1920s, however, Coachella Valley ranchers settled on Mexican families, who they controlled and repressed through racial segregation, deportations, and the migration circuit's frenetic exhaustion.[27]

The Coachella Valley underwent dramatic transformations after WWII. On the western half, luxury development extended the Hollywood-tied Palm Springs model with new cities.[28] On the eastern half, in contrast, the completed All-American Canal (1948) triggered a stunning expansion of irrigated production: in two decades, over fifty thousand acres of undulating desert soil became ordered fields for fifty harvests, including the region's "money maker": first-to-market table grapes.[29] Ranchers again relied primarily on ethnic Mexican farmworkers, including Mexican American residents and migrants, new Mexican immigrants, and short-term contract laborers under the Bracero Program (known as braceros). The exception was in grapes, where Filipino men from the San Joaquin Valley counted for a third of harvest workers. Most, if not all, farmworkers faced immiserating conditions and lived in a society that Chicana/o activists described as nothing less than feudal. Lastly, local ranchers found farmworker allies through patriarchal relationships, which would complicate future UFW campaigns.

Chapter 2 turns to three sets of submerged stories contesting the Coachella Valley's Rancher Nation.[30] The first two traced specific histories of rebellion to make citizen-based claims. Mexican American residents, for instance, who were largely not farmworkers, used their citizenship to demand greater political representation, equal social and municipal services, and education reforms. Similarly, Filipino American AWOC grape workers, who were largely not Coachella Valley residents, demanded the wages and benefits other U.S. workers took for granted. Neither substantively engaged the ethnic Mexican farmworker community, whose stories of rebellion and possibility were primarily rooted in early twentieth-century revolutionary Mexico. Even if they all appeared in the Rancher Nation's margins, in other words, these three sets of submerged stories reflected significant historical and social differences. Other social cleavages included different migration patterns, ages, and genders. They may have moved in a shared space and faced subjection under the Rancher Nation, but Coachella Valley farmworkers (local and migrant) and residents (farmworkers and not) still led different lives without a unified political front. The chapter closes with AWOC's 1965 Coachella Grape Strike, which preceded and encouraged the Delano Grape Strike of 1965, but which was largely unregistered by Coachella Valley residents or ethnic Mexican grape workers.

The book's second part spans chapters 3 to 5, which collectively traces the multiple and often intersecting rebellions undermining the Rancher Nation from 1965 to 1973. These eight years included the UFW movement's five-year grape campaign for union recognition and labor contracts (1965–70) and the three-year grape contract period in the Coachella Valley (1970–73). Chapter 3 covers the former, when dissident stories coalesced unexpectedly in the mid- to late 1960s and, to rancher surprise, culminated in 1970 with UFWOC's unprecedented contract victory. In the Coachella Valley, the fight began with non-farmworker Mexican American demands for political representation in city councils. It then blossomed into an early Chicana/o movement through the UFW's Coachella Grape Strikes of 1968 and 1969. Collectively, the two mobilizations shook the Coachella Valley's economic, political, and discursive foundations. And yet, contingencies and ambiguities remained, as did misrecognitions, shortcomings, and tensions. These dynamics exemplified the plurality and politics inherent to a "field of stories," and they hinted at the trials the two movements would face in the 1970s.

Chapters 4 and 5 overlap the first three years of the 1970s and trace the UFW and Chicana/o attempts to undo the Coachella Valley's Rancher Nation. This process was ambitious, multifaceted, and successful in many regards. It was also inchoate, contradictory, and dialogic. Chapter 4 shows how farmworkers curbed grape rancher power and instituted what one UFW organizer called a "constitutional monarchy," where ranchers, supervisors, contractors, and farmworkers existed and worked under a shared contract-based framework. Women farmworkers also used UFW contracts to challenge workplace sexual harassment and discrimination and to reshape gender relations in their families and communities. For some Filipino UFW members, these were years of cross-country campaigns and the completion of a farmworker retirement home. In parallel form, chapter 5 shows how Chicana/o activists in the Coachella Valley won police and education reforms, led local political campaigns, and created a critical counter public. For many movement participants, these years held much promise, as modest improvements rippled into seismic transformations and spurred new visions of better futures.

Here, it might be useful to pause and reflect on the book's structure. Though the book uses the Rancher Nation as a metaphor to describe the Coachella Valley's social relations and to measure the UFW's impact, I am not suggesting UFW or Chicana/o activists used this metaphor or held a common view of a shared-enough material world. Instead, the many people involved drew from distinct histories, politics, and social positions to articulate limited, complicated, and evolving stories about their worlds. These stories were shaped by neighbors, organizations, and strangers, who themselves were in mid- and co-constitution. No one, furthermore, predicted the events between 1965 and 1973; few spoke about a preestablished path or about uncontested end goals; most discovered/created an evolving politics as circumstances, organizations, and they themselves changed. At the same time, many dynamics and factors remained outside their purview and control, even when they ardently attempted to reshape their world.

The book's third part, encompassing chapters 6 to 8, covers the years from 1970 to 1977 and foregrounds the two movements' nonlinear and unpredictable qualities. While chapters 4 and 5 considered the UFW and Chicana/o movements' visions and reforms, chapter 6 to turns their inability to consolidate wins in the Coachella Valley. The UFW's weaknesses included a poorly managed office, a tardy union drive in non-grape fields, and an ineffective response to Filipino alienation. These weaknesses were exacerbated by rancher hostility, anti-UFW state campaigns, and an increasingly critical national environment. Similarly, Chicana/o movement successes were vulnerable to conservative backlash, white flight, and divisive politics. Both movements weakened further after the Teamsters Union—at rancher request—raided UFW grape contracts in 1973 and disrupted local insurgent momentum.

Chapter 7 focuses on the UFW's response to the Teamster-rancher raid and its failure to interrupt the Rancher Nation's reconstitution. As in previous chapters, chapter 7 takes a rank-and-file perspective and prioritizes a plurality of people and spaces. Lastly, while chapter 6 cautioned against a triumphant narrative, chapter 7 avoids a declension story. Though significantly weakened, both movements continued to attract new participants and continued to foster visions of a post-Rancher Nation world.

Chapter 8 covers the mid- to late 1970s period, when contradictory trajectories and overlaid timelines produced simultaneous declension and ascension. Some people left, often in bitterness, disappointment, and/or exhaustion. Others joined for the first time or deepened their participation, took leadership roles, and expanded earlier goals. In these years, potential was neither fully realized nor extinguished. For example, though the UFW failed to recover its Coachella Valley grape contracts in 1973, its 1973 Coachella Grape Strike still created new leaders and pushed California to legislate farmworker labor rights in 1975. The latter allowed the UFW to return to the Coachella Valley in 1975–76 with state-administered union elections among citrus and vegetables workers, some of whom encountered the UFW in 1973. These elections provoked new rounds of farmworker resistance, while Chicanas/os turned to public institutions: they became teachers in schools serving the farmworker community; they became health workers in new low-income clinics; they took roles as public officials distributing aid. Some returned to the Coachella Valley after years away in regional colleges to lead new UFW campaigns.[31] All moved, furthermore, in a shifting national context that was increasingly hostile to any egalitarian politics. Collectively, these chapters stress a contingent and precarious set of developments, of victories mixed with defeats, and vice versa, of potential and not, of hope, bitterness, ambivalence, and vulnerability.

The book's final part, chapters 9 and 10, traces the UFW's decline and aftermath, a subject of considerable debate in the recent UFW scholarship. This book rejects the argument that Cesar Chavez imploded the UFW in the late 1970s and early 1980s. In this rendering, the UFW became increasingly antidemocratic, which allowed an erratic, punitive, and mentally unsound Chavez to attack dissident union leaders and members. If earlier historians fawned over a saintly Chavez, the new generation castigates in disillusionment, charging him with pulling defeat "from the jaws of victory," reproaching him for farmworkers' present marginality.[32] But as *The Strikers of Coachella* argues, this leadership-driven argument requires readers to ignore the local, regional, and national contexts, when nearly *all* unions and progressive movements collapsed under the weight of reactionary politics and economic transformations. Non-elite and non-white communities had few resources to stem the changes militating against them, much less to transform Californian agriculture. As Lane Windham concludes about union decline in 1980s America: "It is not enough to blame lousy . . . leaders."[33] As a rule, moreover, scholars would do well to pause before attributing white supremacy's resilience in the United States to non-white peoples—including their exceedingly flawed leaders.

Chapter 9 focuses entirely on the 1977 farmworker elections in the Coachella Valley's grape fields, which would become the UFW movement's last significant organizing burst in the desert. As in other ALRA campaigns, these elections offered farmworkers spaces for articulating visions of a unionized future. But the elections were also fundamentally undermined by ranchers' pervasive and egregious unfair labor practices (ULP), including the use of false employee lists, the surveillance of pro-UFW workers, pervasive threats of violence, verbal and physical attacks, bribes for anti-UFW votes, election fraud, and retaliatory firings—often of entire pro-UFW crews. The UFW contested rancher hostility and illegal behavior with ALRA's bureaucratic procedures, but the latter only provided final decisions three, if not four, years after the 1977 grape elections. By then, like most U.S. unions, the UFW found itself with dwindling resources, a disgruntled and vulnerable workforce, an even more hostile political context, and an ineffective labor law. Even if Chavez had been on his best behavior, in other words, the UFW still faced an overwhelmingly reactionary opposition, one that was concurrently devastating established and far better resourced organizations. And yet, even then, as chapter 10 argues, the UFW's field of stories in the Coachella Valley, and those of the intersecting Chicana/o movement, continued to produce afterlives and the potential for new social ruptures.

Ultimately, *The Strikers of Coachella* narrates how a collection of marginalized peoples in a small desert valley offered alternatives—plural, contingent, evolving—to the Rancher Nation in the mid-twentieth century, and how such alternatives became increasingly untenable by the late 1970s and early 1980s. Arguably, this period's restructuring has also forced most U.S. workers to live in their own Rancher Nation, where bosses rule by fiat and precariousness collapses into premature death; where there is only the relentless rhythm of economic exploitation and political marginality; where the insistence that alternatives do not exist jostles against the insistence that nothing is wrong. Tellingly, the Coachella Valley is now known for enabling conspicuous consumption, a consumption-based familiarity that hides its race-laced social inequality and its rich history of resistance—its feast of brief hopes. In that final respect, the Coachella Valley offers us a vision of twentieth-century America distilled.

On Archives and Literatures

This book builds on the intellectual labors of others—a union, so to speak, of historians, archivists, interviewers, librarians, and theorists. It draws from scholars in Filipino American Studies and Chicana/o/x Studies, and from the histories of U.S. social movements, labor, settler-colonialism, and agriculture. It uses the official UFW collections in the Archives of Labor and Urban Affairs in Detroit (Michigan); the new collections in the Welga Archive-Bulosan Center for Filipino Studies at the University of California, Davis, and the digital Farmworkers Movement Documentation Project. For regional and rancher histories, the book draws from the archives at the Coachella Valley History Museum, the Palm Desert Historical Society, and Riverside County's

Public Library. The book also uses census data, local, regional, and national newspapers, the collections of key movement figures, such as the pro-UFW priest and social scientist Victor Salandini and the Filipino UFW leader Philip Vera Cruz, and the trove of documents produced by farmworker strikes, lawsuits, and elections.

The book's evidentiary heart, however, is nestled in oral history. From 2013 to 2021, I conducted two hundred hours of oral history interviews with seventy Coachella Valley residents and movement participants, which I discuss at length in chapter 10.[34] The interviews were largely unstructured, focused on participant stories, and in dialogue with my evolving understanding of this history. In some cases, interviews with specific participants continued for almost a decade. I met most participants through local community leaders and by happenstance: a fortuitous visit to a bar, a local protest, an offhand comment inviting questions. Some participants were not involved in either the UFW or Chicana/o movements, but their recollections of the Coachella Valley still offered critical context. Without these participants' trust and candor, I could not have written this history. Lastly, I paired my interviews with oral interviews conducted by other scholars and institutions, especially of Filipino strikers, Mexican braceros in the Coachella Valley, and Mexican American pioneers.[35] I am indebted to and grateful for these scholars' contributions to oral history, and I hope my book will contribute in return to our shared intellectual endeavors.[36]

Close readers will notice I have limited my commentary on the UFW literature. I avoid discussing it in depth to re-center the UFW and Chicana/o movement participants who remain largely unknown in academic circles. For now, I will note that I see this literature's shortcomings as rooted in its insistence on faulting Cesar Chavez for the UFW's fortunes in the 1980s. In this insistence, it places disproportionate attention on UFW leaders and white volunteers and marginalizes the very farmworkers who sacrificed for and powered the union. It also inappropriately psychologizes Chavez's actions and decontextualizes the UFW in the late 1970s and early 1980s. This has been a missed opportunity.

We still know very little about the UFW movement. We know little about the strikers and their communities, much less about the gendered and racial dynamics shaping their politics. We know little about their quotidian hopes and dreams, and about their transformations and visions in movements. We know little about their perspective on the UFW's decline in the 1980s, little about the union's afterlives, little of much, much more. As scholars build archives, however, and as they move past histories of union leaders, I expect we will see a new wave of UFW scholarship—one that moves with farmworkers' concerns, desires, and regrets; one of specific spaces, like the packed earth of agricultural rows, or the tight, dilapidated quarters of poverty, or the many small towns in rural California; one that stresses human nobility, fallibility, and frailty, the qualities that inspire and grate, reassure and threaten, unravel and reassemble; and one that speaks of actual contingency and the interplay of people in multiple spaces with multiple desires and multiple calculations. From the bottom up, and from every possible vantage point, I hope this scholarship immerses us in all the humanity that is the attempt to build new worlds.

PART I

The Rancher Nation and Its Discontents

Chapter 1

The Law of the Jungle

Power and Society in the Coachella Valley, 1945–1965

It is unclear what farmworkers thought while commuting to work in the dark hours of the desert's early mornings. Perhaps they spoke of their families and neighbors, the harvest and their aspirations and worries. Perhaps the car radio played the Spanish station, or perhaps they all sat quietly in a rambling vehicle moving southeast to the Coachella Valley's fields. From Indio and Coachella *barrios*, the drive would cover long stretches of two-way backstreets—unlit and uninterrupted, neither empty nor filled—along a mountain-ringed backdrop and a still-dark sky. Some cars likely stopped for gas or coffee, for that bit of morning bread in the small townships of Thermal, Mecca, and Oasis, where green fields hugged mountains marked by the ancient Lake Cahuilla. After sleepy banter with the cashier, another rumbling stretch took them to the fields. If work fell eastward enough, the drive ended with the dark twinkles of the Salton Sea, the large body of water that separates the Coachella Valley from its larger, southern cousin, the Imperial Valley.

Through the morning and afternoon, these farmworkers would toil among grapes, citrus, dates, and vegetables. Most did so under authoritarian labor contractors and supervisors and in crews that earned a pittance, enduring conditions that hurt the body and humiliated the spirit. Labor wounds also bled into spaces outside the fields—into the poor, segregated neighborhoods or the barrack-like camps where farmworkers lived, and into the local and regional social, political, and cultural institutions controlled by ranchers and their allies. Farmworkers held almost no political power, and nearly all were without medical and social services. They faced police abuse, as well as derision or erasure in pro-rancher newspapers. Most had no choice but to send their children to schools that stunted them. For those with a rebellious streak, the only options were exile, subjugation, or resigning to dreaming of better futures on those long morning drives.

This was the Coachella Valley that farmworkers faced in the 1950s and 1960s—a world the United Farm Workers (UFW) movement described as a "Rancher Nation," where ranchers ruled like "absolute monarch[s]" and overdetermined the "life and death" of farmworkers, whose exploitation enriched the kingdom.[1] Yet as the pages that follow will show, the Coachella Valley's Rancher Nation was not without complexities. Drawing from settler colonial scholars, this chapter argues that local ranchers identified as civilizing pioneers in a "reclaimed" desert frontier, where their farmworkers could hold no presence, much less make demands. This settler identity explains ranchers' ferocious hostility toward the UFW in the 1960s and 1970s. Among ethnic Mexican farmworkers, furthermore, marginality came in differentiated forms. Women, migrants, and/or noncitizens faced the worst conditions and often subsidized the lives of others, especially husbands and families closely associated with labor contractors. Additionally, Filipino and Mexican grape workers lived apart from each other, an issue discussed further in chapter 2, while some residents existed outside the rancher's barking authority—whether Mexican American families in nonagricultural industries or wealthy "winter birds" in the valley's westside cities—which further complicated social relations in the region.

To understand the UFW movement's history in the Coachella Valley, in short, we must first reckon with the complicated social fault lines structuring this world. Life in the Rancher Nation could not be reduced to a two-sided fight between rancher-kings and insurgent peasants. The battle was real, but easy certainties or politics were not.

All Hail the King

In the white summer heat of 1950, the editors of the *Desert Rancher* presented the new monthly as their answer to the "long-felt need expressed in countless ways by Valley ranchers, packers, shippers and businessmen. 'Give us more farm news . . .'"[2] The editors also published the local weekly, *Desert Barnacle*, a booster platform covering community concerns. With the *Desert Rancher*, they planned to focus on the agricultural industry: on its multiple harvests in elongated seasons; on the best practices learned through trial and error and university labs; on fluctuating markets for labor, commodities, and credit; on the benefits of farmer associations and dangers of unionism; on the bustling businesses luring outside investors; and on the ranchers who made it all possible—self-made white men of dedication and civic leadership.

In such a spirit, the monthly profiled ranchers and showcased their contributions. In the first issue, the *Desert Rancher* wrote on Horace Hagerty, the child of Coachella Valley pioneers and the proud owner of "Mesquite Ranch" in Thermal.[3] Hagerty purchased the 120 acres with his mother in 1924, when it was "forbidding desert," and transformed it into "one of the Valley's best" ranches. He completed "the development work himself," using an "old Fresno scraper [to] level the first 50 acres" and plant a "balanced load": dates for fall, grapes for summer, sweet corn and spinach in between. The choices reflected his expertise in farming (the crops "provid[ed] nutrients for each other") and local weather patterns. He eradicated weeds, used "low, brush-covered sand dunes" to protect crops from winds, and built a basketball court, a baseball diamond, and several "roomy, clean, comfortable" houses. The ranch was "shaded by large trees and attractively landscaped" and included a seventy-acre "quail and wild game refuge." So when Hagerty described himself as "a plain dirt farmer," the *Desert Rancher* tacked the description to his modesty, for he "seem[ed] to turn every ill wind into a gentle breeze that blows good." In this respect," it wrote, "he is most typical of Valley ranchers—who have carved a livelihood out of a once forbidding desert—with patience, hard work and water."

In three decades, Hagerty's private wealth circulated as a public good and epitomized the frontier's putative egalitarianism. His children and neighbors made use of the ranch's many spaces, while his wife offered domestic warmth to the wider community: "On any cool summer evening you're apt to find a group of oldsters and kids on the front lawn enjoying a church picnic. They may be listening to Mrs. Hagerty playing the accordion—or eating some of her good date nut bars and drinking iced tea."[4] The family also organized school fundraisers and church socials, employed two families, and supported local businesses.[5] Hagerty's many years of self-driven labor, of his patience and hard work, had thus built a life of "gentle breezes" for an entire community in a former "forbidding desert."

This pioneer story appeared in Coachella Valley histories,[6] novels and memoirs,[7] in newspapers,[8] booster tracts and county fairs,[9] in the built environment and oral histories.[10] In it, white American settlers found the region in the early twentieth century. It was surrounded by the San Jacinto and Santa Rosa Mountains to the west, the San Bernardino and Chocolate Mountains to the east, and the Salton Sink, soon to be Salton Sea, to the south. Home to the Cahuilla people, what is today the Coachella Valley had long held dozens of Cahuilla villages. Some clustered the valley floor near water sources or ringed along the mountain foothills and aquifer-fed wells. Others sat on the San Jacinto and Santa Rosa Mountains, or further west still. The Cahuilla were also well connected to other Indigenous Nations through trade networks, religious practices, and kinship ties.[11] But, and much like other pioneers, the new white settlers claimed nothing had existed in California's deserts, nothing civilized at least, only a prehistoric "backwardness" and a ferocious "wasteland" of heat, sand, and shrubs. Settlers associated the latter with Indigenous decay and racial inferiority. The Cahuilla, one settler wrote, "had lost much of their hardiness and [had] become indolent."[12] Another compared "ancient" palm trees to Cahuilla's purported existential passing: "restless heads of the old warriors . . . bent together in the night breeze, talking in sibilant whispers of the decades that had come and gone, of a vanished race and the coming of strange new men."[13]

In contrast, the pioneer story marveled at the settlers' labors and "the remarkable destiny of a desert wasteland ... made to bloom."[14] They "discovered" the region's aquifer, it said, that gave biblical water eruptions for newly tilled soil, as if God, a white man himself, had sanctified their presence. They "reclaimed" ten thousand acres, built an agricultural economy centered on palm dates, and founded small towns with modern amenities, such as electricity, phones, roads, schools, and houses, even ice machines for ice-cream socials. By 1940, the adjacent cities of Indio and Coachella—on the valley's geographic center—counted several thousand settlers, a railroad depot, packing sheds, housing and commercial districts, multiple schools, churches, and parks. Outside the cities, date palms covered what had been "virgin" desert land. Further east, three small towns appeared: the nine hundred residents in a Thermal of cotton, vegetables, and cattle; the six hundred settlers in Mecca, which tied its visibility to the region's Orientalist discourse; and Oasis, a settlement of a couple hundred vegetable ranchers. The Salton Sea shimmered past these towns. The land to the west of Indio, in contrast, alternated between sand dunes and date trees until its westernmost point, where the small resort city of Palm Springs catered to Hollywood tourists.[15]

There was nothing particularly original about the Coachella Valley pioneer story. The U.S. West at mid century was littered with the self-aggrandizing racial historicism of Frederick Jackson Turner's "Frontier Thesis."[16] In "The Significance of the Frontier in American History" (1893), Turner claimed U.S. culture formed on the frontier's brawny transformation of "savage" wasteland into civilization's progress, where pioneer men cleared land and built homes, formed associations, and nurtured egalitarian cultures. In the visceral intimacy with untouched land and self-governance, European excesses yielded to Americanism. The country's repeated westward migrations withered class distinctions in sending communities, while spreading U.S. dominion over spaces that were virginal yet untamed, inert yet expectant. Turner spoke directly to, and of, the American heart; by then, his country had already engaged in a centuries-long parade of theft and genocide, where crimson ribbons spoke of progress and civilization, of the white man's destiny.[17]

As in Hagerty's profile, agriculture played a seminal role in this parade. The plowing of fields and harvesting of bounty, and the related town construction, embodied progress against wild nature. In the 1880s and 1890s, California was the land of most stunning progress—a produce-laden landscape stamped with technological modernity. As in past frontiers, the lands' transformation indicted Mexicans and Indigenous Nations as lazy, unintelligent, and backwards. It also justified violence against both.[18] At the turn of the century, Turner's settler heart entered Southern California's deserts and heralded the "reclaiming" of the "barren" and "uninhabitable" through irrigation. In their stories, canals would flow like lacework on the desert mother's reawakened bosom; abundant fields would stand on formerly parched earth; homes would appear in what had been nowhere, life in what had been desolation; even young leaves would flutter to comfort during searing summers.[19] California's Imperial Valley was the center of this desert pioneer story.[20] But, further north, white pioneers told the same for a land they now called the Coachella Valley.

These settlers sought to build and narrate a society that Native Studies has labeled settler colonialism, a colonial project that aims to create a permanent society on Indigenous land, where Indigenous erasure and white birth occur simultaneously, inevitably, and innocently.[21] In the Coachella Valley's pioneer story, life began with the masculine rancher. *He* settled the region. *He* chose the produce. *He* sold successful harvests. *He* laid the ground for secondary industries. In almost all instances, male ranchers spoke in and for the Coachella Valley's settler society.[22] He embodied the region's frontier identity, historicity, and security, which shaped all other social positions, including his demurring wife and appreciative children, his community and business partners, and the racialized Others who served as a contrast to whiteness.

This story, already established before World War II (WWII), framed the Coachella Valley's agricultural growth after the completion of the Coachella Extension to the All-American Canal in 1948. In two decades, ranchers turned 18,000 acres of "reclaimed" desert (the majority for dates, cotton, and vegetables) into an expanding checkerboard of green fields against brown desert: 35,516 acres in 1951, 55,000 in 1957, over 65,000 in the early 1960s.[23] Three harvests structured its years: dates in September to December; citrus from October to May; table grapes from May to July.[24] In between, another fifty harvests, plus nurseries, livestock chicken farms, packing sheds, and secondary industries, like shipping and marketing. In 1954, Coachella Valley ranchers grew *six* million-dollar harvests and produced a total valuation of $24.5 million, a tenfold increase from 1940.[25] In 1964, they grew *ten* million-dollar harvests, a "whopping" total valuation of $42 million, and another "$20 to $30 million [in] livestock and nurseries."[26] To the *Desert Rancher*, "Coachella Valley magic" extended the early pioneer's vision: the "lure of the desert," it wrote, "[had] appealed only to a few botanists, artists and hardy pioneers who saw the wasteland as a challenge. Today, thousands of once arid acres are now lush growing farms."[27] Even if Coachella Valley residents were without this data, the changes were still seen and felt, for each new field made the former "wasteland" increasingly hearsay, its lingering memory serving to evidence progress achieved.[28]

In the post-WWII Coachella Valley, table grape production was particularly significant, and it would play a central role in the UFW and Chicana/o movements of the 1960s and 1970s. In 1964, local grape ranchers counted seven thousand acres of Thompson grapes, three thousand acres of Perlette grapes, and more acres in a collection of niche varieties. Collectively, grapes represented nearly a fourth of the Coachella Valley's irrigated acreage, a concentration that reflected the fortuitous alignment between the desert's early summer heat and the national table grape market. California produced nearly all table grapes in the United States and the great majority were harvested in central California's San Joaquin Valley from September to November. With an early desert cache, local grape ranchers could thus earn first-to-market premium prices. For this reason, Perlettes were especially popular, as they ripened weeks before the early Thompsons.[29] Some San Joaquin Valley grape ranchers took advantage of the early summer harvest by planting vineyards in the Coachella Valley, such as Richard Bagdasarian, who brought his twenty-five years of experience to Mecca in 1948.[30] These ranchers, along with men with no prior farming histories, joined pre-WWII grape pioneers.[31] Together they worked the "June moneymaker," while others tended to dates, citrus, fruits, vegetables, and cotton.[32]

As with Hagerty, male ranchers and their labors were credited for the region's *collective* prosperity. When the *Desert Rancher* celebrated a $35 million crop valuation in 1958, for instance, it stressed that rancher life was not "all gravy" because total valuations did not mean individual rancher profits. A "winning crop" meant year-long "hard work" and diligence, heavy costs in labor and other inputs. It was not individual wealth, but *shared bounty*.[33] Harvests meant wage receipts and secondary industries in shipping, packing, marketing, and financing. They helped build local commerce, filled tax coffers and fueled tourism, and paid for "modern classroom[s]." The small settler cities also gained new city halls, libraries, and a junior college, as well as all the amenities expected in postwar, white America. Even their homes were smartly designed and filled with the newest features. "Today," the *Desert Rancher* announced in 1955, "the Valley farmer or rancher ties modern conveniences and styling of urban living to up-to-date methods of agriculture."[34] The region's agricultural base arguably induced more investments from newly settled ranchers.[35] By 1964, Indio was a "real life boom town" of fifteen thousand residents and sixty-five thousand tourists.[36] In Coachella and the eastern townships, where sluggish commerce barely grew, boosters still predicted an agriculture-based commercial and demographic boom.[37] If the good life, in short, meant new homes and churches, or sports and arts for the young; if it meant sidewalks, pools, and lamps, or the in-migration of "city boys" looking for a farming life; if it meant businesses and tax credits, or a string of modern housing projects—then, it originated in the rancher's clearing of the land and subsequent harvests.

The ranchers' identity as modern-day pioneers was self-evident and visceral. It shaped their relationship to self and others, and it served as the local language to make sense of itself. White ranchers brought civilized law to a former wasteland, they said; they built the kingdoms they now ruled. Before the rancher become a king, in other words, he had already been a successful settler–colonizer. It was the latter's supposed completion that strengthened his claim to the former's status. Armed with such an origin story, few rancher-kings tolerated challenges to their authority, however justified or rational. In the late 1960s, the UFW movement would do exactly that and provoke their self-righteous fury.

Of Silences and Violence

This pioneer story required silences, and the latter's elaboration underscores the Rancher Nation's innate social violence. These silences included the government's role in the region's white settlement, the persistence of Cahuilla resistance to white encroachment, and the role of racialized workers in all agricultural production. White settlement, for instance, took place only after state intervention. Federal armies stole Indigenous lands, while federal engineers and scientists surveyed for railroads and canals, encouraged date orchards, and "discovered" the Coachella Valley's aquifer. After WWII, the Boulder Canyon Project, a federal dam-and-irrigation system, succeeded where pioneer enterprise had failed. As water arrived, the ever-reliant rancher benefited from more public aid. They received fruit grafts, horticultural practices, and unlimited, vulnerable labor with the Bracero Program (1942–64)—a collection of U.S.–Mexico agreements that contracted Mexican nationals in U.S. fields. The program allowed for the region's expanded acreage and empowered ranchers to unilaterally lower wages and replace "troublesome" workers.[38] If this was not enough, they also received a postwar consumer class in Southern California's suburbia, which benefited from subsidized mortgages and education, and from an unrivaled military-industrial economy. The Rancher Nation was less pioneer bootstrap independence, in short, and more welfare colonialism—a quality common to the U.S. West.[39]

The Cahuilla also challenged white settler claims. In the nineteenth century, Cahuilla resistance secured reservations in the eastern Coachella Valley, Palm Springs, the Cabazon mountain pass, and the western side of the San Jacinto Mountains. Despite U.S. colonial disruptions—such as diseases and environmental destruction in mid nineteenth century gold rushes, or land theft in the 1870s and 1880s, or federal attempts to break up reservations through allotment in the 1890s and early 1900s—the Cahuilla kept effective pressure on federal agents. In the early twentieth century, multiple Cahuilla reservations in and adjacent to the Coachella Valley were in open rebellion against U.S. officials.[40] In later decades, they fought encroachment on their lands and against abusive federal agents who disregarded tribal authority. They also demanded a "square deal, that's all, . . . [for] a certain degree of self-government."[41]

Such resistance continued in the mid-twentieth century. In 1919, Southern California tribes formed the Mission Indian Federation (MIF), which played a key role in their opposition to Palm Springs' 1930s expansion into the Agua Caliente Cahuilla reservation. Characteristically, the early rancher newspapers, the *Coachella Valley Submarine*, lamented the Cahuilla's success in protecting their land with causal racism: "Pale face officials," read one headline, "capitulate to demands of Palm Springs Redskins."[42] In the Great Depression, furthermore, Cahuilla leaders used traditional desert foods to fight community hunger, and after WWII they debated Indian "termination," kept contact with other reservations, and nurtured cultural affirmation.[43] Alvino Silva, for instance, recalled asking his father for advice on how to deal with white racist bullies in his school. His father told Silva: "when they come here, they stole everything of ours; and now they refuse to know us. They don't really want to know us. That is why they are calling you those names." Silva's father then recounted Cahuilla history to show his son "the Cahuilla [have] a great history," a history that then shaped Silva's adult life as a Cahuilla leader in the mid- to late twentieth century.[44]

Like California, the Coachella Valley's white settlement depended on a diverse workforce of Cahuilla, Japanese, South Asian, Filipino, and Mexican laborers. They toiled in railroads, a salt plant, and early irrigation construction. They cleared land, plowed, and planted, harvested and packed. In the late 1910s, ethnic Mexicans were the principal labor source, and in the early 1960s, the Coachella Valley Farmers Association (CVFA) estimated its workers as 8,232 "domestic workers from California," an "excess" of 1,000 "domestic Filipino[s]," 1,500 "gate hires," and 2,947 braceros.[45] The "domestic workers" were ethnic Mexican locals who arrived in the Coachella Valley in the 1910s to 1920s or in the 1950s. The latter were usually Tejano families. "Domestic workers" referred to ethnic Mexican migrants from California, Texas, or Arizona. The "gate hires" were Mexican farmworkers who regularly crossed the U.S.–Mexico border, while braceros were Mexican nationals on short-term contracts. The exception to ethnic Mexican farmworkers in the Coachella Valley were Filipino migrants from the San Joaquin Valley, who represented a quarter of the desert's early grape harvest workforce.

Despite their significance, the Rancher Nation's booster pamphlets, pioneer memoirs, and newspapers seldom made references to these people. In local histories, farmworkers appeared only briefly, such as in brief allusions to Cahuilla and Mexican men rerouting the Colorado River after an engineering accident flooded the Salton Sink and threatened agricultural interests in the Imperial Valley. They appeared in ranch property descriptions noting "farm labor quarters," or in construction histories—"Mexicans made the adobe in the ranch"—and critiques of "gentleman farmer[s]" who "supervised the ranch but [do] not soil [their] hands."[46] The *Desert Rancher* published *no* articles on farmworkers in the 1950s and early 1960s—nothing on where, how, and with whom they lived. The few articles discussing labor did so to refute criticism of the Bracero Program's exploitation and/or to portray farmworkers as a rancher-utilized commodity.[47] To the *Desert Rancher*, ranchers secured labor for frenetic harvests, wielded farmworkers, tools, and seeds for optimal yields, and solved problems when labor, like all commodities, occasionally malfunctioned.[48] Farmworkers only became visible when the Bracero Program was terminated in 1964; panicked newspapers shrieked over looming labor shortages, insisting on the program's value and "domestic" labor's inferiority to "imported" labor.[49] The *Desert Rancher* similarly carried a two-page sketch of disembodied hands holding tomatoes, titled: "These Hands are Important to You! . . . They Belong to a Mexican Bracero!"[50] In these articles, farmworkers were never people, never more than hands to be used by the pioneer ranchers.

Arguably, farmworkers could not exist in the Coachella Valley's Rancher Nation—not as contributing to the region or as members of its civic community. Just as no one credited the short handle hoe for an agricultural "miracle," no one credited the hoe wielder.[51] This erasure sustained the rancher story—for to admit farmworkers as part of the civic community questioned white ranchers' claim of self-sufficiency and racial civilization. Ranchers needed to erase laborers; anything less challenged their settler-colonial claims. Despite appearing like separate projects, the erasure of Indigenous people and the erasure of non-white laborers were two sides of the same coin: that of the white settler singing himself a deluded love song.

For most farmworkers in the Coachella Valley, the laboring day began before dawn and continued well past hot afternoons—hours spent bent and crouched, picking and thinning, hoeing and packing. Most moved to supervisor orders and at the frenzied pace of younger men, those who could be lured by masculinity and bigger paychecks. Few breaks broke the day, and once at home pain accrued and morphed. To Maria Marron, fifty years later, the effects were obvious in the men and women walking stiffly in town squares, "completely bent over . . . unable to straighten up." "That is the farmworkers' inheritance," Marron said, "injured knees . . . curved backs, arthritis in the knees, fingers, hands," and cancer from pesticides.[52] Arguably, Marron erred

The Law of the Jungle   33

optimistically for, in the 1960s, farmworker lifespans counted less than fifty-five years; many would not live long enough to gain their inheritance.

Despite the physical impact, farmworkers only earned abject poverty. Postwar wages ranged from 65 cents to $1 an hour, if not less.[53] Most faced structural underemployment, which forced families to chase harvests for necessities. Some spent mornings wandering back roads looking for work with the sinking feeling they would not earn for daily needs.[54] Collectively, low wages and structural underemployment congealed into racialized and region-wide poverty. In a 1966 dissertation on Coachella Valley farmworkers and migrant education, Uvaldo Palomares found that farmworker families that ranged between six and eight persons earned annually an average of $2,800 to $3,200.[55] In 1960, the official poverty line began at $4,000 for a rural family of six. Similarly, in the 1960 Census district encompassing the eastern townships of Mecca, Oasis, and Thermal, 82 percent of households were listed as agricultural laborers, and 12 percent were listed as ranchers. Of all households, 50 percent earned $2,000 or less per year, while another 31.5 percent earned $2,000 to $4,000—which is to say *every* farmworker household toiled in poverty.[56]

To be a Coachella Valley farmworker at mid century was to live a life of pervasive, structural precarity. In oral history interviews, precarity arrived as hunger, or as heat and cold in the hovels pretending to be homes, or as the hand-me-downs that barely draped over one's body. It came in the lack of medical care that accentuated life's ever-present frailty or in the familial turn to child labor to make ends meet, or in the tempo of harvest restlessness, of moving from one substandard camp to another, from one emaciated paycheck to another, from one barking contractor to another—those who simultaneously repelled, subjected, and denied escape. None of this was a private matter, as the teacher, Margaret MacKaye, wrote in her 1954 master's thesis on the Bracero Program in the Coachella and Imperial Valleys: "the [farmworkers'] obvious poverty made many [white] Americans jump to conclusions about their intelligence and morality that were not warranted." One white woman, MacKaye wrote, evidently surprised, "was scared to death of them!" Her ethnic Mexican students also regularly missed class, because "they lacked what we consider the necessities of life and were not eager to advertise the matter."[57] It is likely her students also missed school to help their families by working in the nearby fields, work that failed them the "necessities of life" and narrowed their futures to that of precarity.[58]

Still, there is *more* to precarity than material deprivation. The ranchers' violence meant a child's hunger pangs, the fear of sexual harassment, and the humiliating choice (in absence of work restrooms) of urinating and defecating in public or attempting to discipline one's body. For some, precarity felt like entrapment and suffocation, as Clementina Olloque recalled: "There was no way to leave [the fields], there was no way to leave ... [I felt] a desperation ... [like] not finding the key to the door of the house you're in."[59] For Max Huerta, it meant denial of decent schools, food, and goods, which metastasized into racial shame: "It's like you are in a hole.... It does not take long before it gets inside you.... When you hear, 'You are just a Mexican, you are just a dumb Mexican,' then you start to believe that you are a dumb Mexican."[60] And for most, resistance risked blacklists and banishment. As the future UFW leader Philip Vera Cruz wrote in 1970, no farmworker could talk "sense" into the rancher; unchecked powers had encouraged his moral devolution; "his conscience," he wrote, "is always submerged by greed, indifference and a belief that life is a battlefield in which he either wins or loses."[61] In the Rancher Nation, workers could only secure "peace and harmonious living" with an effective counterweight against ranchers' profound social violence.

The Mexican Peasants

The rancher-king's power was most prominent in his fields, and his impact was greatest among farmworkers. But the Rancher Nation also needs to be understood as including a repertoire of government and nongovernment institutions, such as city councils, county boards, police departments, Border Patrol agents, rural courts, school districts, churches, and newspapers, state organizations, and politicians. Collectively, this repertoire advanced the rancher-king's interests in and out of his fields, defended against critics, and supplemented the ranchers' property-based powers. With these figures and resources, rancher-kings combined their "private security guards" with their "own private judges and enforcement system" to ensure "nobody challenge[d] [them]."[62] The fact that judges and officers were not, in fact, "private" was only in name. In the Rancher Nation, public powers aligned with private rancher interests, while rancher production sustained the economic foundation for all in the repertoire, including the judges and officers. More than just agricultural social relations, in other words, the Rancher Nation refers to the rancher-king's near-seamless sovereignty across public and private spaces, one fortified precisely by the exchanges between them.

This nation covered the communities of the eastern Coachella Valley, where ranchers and their allies created a deeply unequal and racialized world—one that attempted to allay the contradictions of a white settler society with its insatiable need for cheap, and thus usually non-white, wage labor. What, in fact, can a white-loving people do with so many non-white workers, so cheap and so necessary, yet so racially disagreeable, too? The answer was rather simple and unsurprising: racial segregation, aggressive policing, and the occlusion of non-white residents and their demands, including for basic social services and humane working conditions. The answer was also the occasional removal of surplus labor through deportation and/or racial violence.

This racialized world took root at the beginning of the region's white settlement. And though the initial workforce was racially diverse, by the 1920s nearly all Coachella Valley farmworkers were Mexican families who had recently migrated to the United States. Most found housing in the poor *colonias* of Indio and Coachella or in shacks along the rancher property's periphery. Most sent their children to schools with Mexican classrooms that prohibited Spanish speaking, practiced corporal punishment, and ignored culturally relevant teaching.[63] Most of these families existed in the migrant circuit's cycle of labor, poverty, and unfulfilled dreams for much of their lives.[64] Before WWII, they also likely saw "No Mexicans," signs, experienced job discrimination, and lived in segregated communities, which extended to cemeteries.[65] These ethnic Mexican residents had no co-ethnic and/or political leaders in city and county councils, school and water boards, state and federal offices.[66] Newspapers routinely presented ethnic Mexicans as irrational, violent, and alcoholic men,[67] or as unsupervised children on the brink of death,[68] or as families in "sordid" homes filled with "ignorant care, filthy surroundings, improper feedings."[69] When local white residents fretted about increasing "Mexican storks" in the late 1920s, a columnist for the *Coachella Valley Submarine* naturally called for the eugenicist favorite: "to evolve a legal way to decrease the Mexican birthrate."[70]

Such calls encapsulated the Rancher Nation's ambivalent relationship to ethnic Mexican laborers—simultaneously needing them and repulsing them. The balance lay in Mexicans "prov[ing] satisfactory" to the economy, a standard implying wage suppression in the Great Depression and continued threats of removal.[71] So, when California in 1931 offered daily relief of $3.20 per family or a minimum work wage of $4 a day, Coachella Valley ranchers fought state officials and lowered the wage to $2—halving farmworkers' income.[72] Moreover, when the Great Depression deepened, white residents pushed for "repatriating" ethnic Mexican families on public relief.[73] Another local graduate student, Louisa Sprenger Ames, found white "prejudiced feelings" lowered public aid to unemployed Mexican families during the Great Depression.[74] Writing against such prejudiced feelings, Ames could only offer a paternalist, and racist, alternative: "Mexicans are by nature childishly improvident with regard to future needs. . . . It is only fair that any community which depends upon a certain group for its economic soundness should accept the responsibility of caring for the needy of that group during lack of employment."[75] These dynamics were evident to the teacher, Margaret

MacKaye, whose study I referred to earlier. Quoting an "old timer," Mackaye referred to Mexican families living in "some kind of a shack or tent... with materials found around the ranch."[76] In this world, she observed, "the rancher tended to be 'king,' the Mexican farm families his 'peasants,' with all the resultant social problems."

After WWII, when the Coachella Valley underwent rapid economic, demographic, and spatial changes, its general racialized contours remained mostly in place. The labor required for the agricultural expansion was met with Mexican braceros,[77] Mexican immigrants,[78] and Mexican-Tejano families.[79] Nearly all earned poverty wages, lived in dilapidated housing, if not worse, and had little political, economic, and cultural power in the Coachella Valley.[80] The white rancher class, in contrast, earned more than $10,000 a year and embodied the local elite: in 1960, the one hundred wealthiest people in Coachella and eastern townships were all ranchers. Other white residents worked in year-long, skilled positions in agriculture, such as managers, foremen, machine operators, and mechanics, or in secondary industries, like construction, commerce, schools, and the water district. White poverty existed, but it remained an invisible minority that did not challenge the region's social structure of wealthy white ranchers and well-off white partners, and of poor Mexican farmworkers and their racialized, working-class neighbors.

The Rancher Nation's work-based hierarchies, in short, had parallel dynamics outside the fields. In Coachella, for instance, ethnic Mexicans made up two-thirds of the population in 1960, of which only 22 percent were farmworkers. But the relative significance of other industries did not undercut the city's biracial structure: ethnic Mexicans were still three times more likely to be in poverty than whites, while only 5 percent graduated from high school and none from college. For whites, the latter rates were 20 and 12 percent, respectively. The Mexican majority also did not have representation in the city council or in local and regional institutions.[81] This lack of political power allowed white leaders to ignore their demands, including equal infrastructural funds for the city's *colonia* in the 1950s.[82] The Coachella council also ignored ethnic Mexican complaints about police abuse and rejected a farmworker housing project in the city.[83] Its local schools still segregated ethnic Mexican students and disproportionately tracked them in remedial classes, all while school districts refused to hire Mexican American teachers.[84] For farmworker families, moreover, the migrant cycle dashed hopes for their children's upward social mobility through education, as migration often impeded student learning.[85]

Similar dynamics existed in Indio despite its diversified economy and population. In the two decades after WWII, the city doubled its total population (to fifteen thousand in 1960), gained a tourism sector, and grew secondary agricultural industries. In 1960, white residents accounted for 70 percent of the city's population, while Mexicans made up the rest. Of the latter, 90 percent lived in just two neighborhoods: the prewar *colonia* in the city's old downtown and the peripheral Farm Labor Camp. In the former, residents lived in crumbling buildings and concentrated poverty and reported low educational attainment. In the labor camp, farmworkers found obscenely substandard housing that was originally meant to be temporary when it was built in the Great Depression.[86] Both came with failing, abusive, and decrepit schools that segregated most ethnic Mexican students from the entire city's white student population.[87] One such student, Margarita Carrillo, recalled her third-grade teacher hitting her for "stealing" classroom paper. Carrillo said another student told their teacher that "Margarita" took paper without the teacher's permission. Carrillo did not speculate why this was a grave offense or why the teacher thought a slap to a girl's face was an appropriate punishment. Whatever the rationale, the teacher learned she had three "Margaritas" and had slapped the wrong girl. To keep all quiet, she paid each twenty-five cents and renamed them "Margie," "Margaret," and "Maggie." Carrillo only reclaimed her name a decade later, when she met a group of Chicana college students in a theater troupe.[88]

There were other non-white people in the Coachella Valley's Rancher Nation, but these did not trouble the region's overall racial dichotomy. Japanese families, for instance, settled in Oasis in the early twentieth century and built small vegetable ranches. They did not work for white ranchers and appeared sparingly in local newspapers; there was almost nothing, for instance, on the internment of Japanese American families during WWII. But after the war, Japanese Americans embodied postwar opportunity and were regularly contrasted positively against ethnic Mexican workers' racialized poverty. The *Desert Rancher* profiled three Japanese American ranchers, including Ed Kono, who traced his local history to the early 1920s (making him "practically a native of Coachella Valley") and spoke of his postwar success as "typif[ying]" local "growth."[89] Japanese American ranchers also joined local rancher associations, participated in rancher-led social events, and sent their children to white-tracked classrooms. Some ethnic Mexican farmworkers spoke of Japanese American ranchers as exploitative and hostile, while some conservative Mexican Americans saw them as models to emulate: "Chicanos" should have "the courage and pride," wrote one to the local newspaper, "to get out of our little nooks [and] work to obtain an education . . . like the Japanese."[90]

Filipino migrant grape workers were another non-white population in the region, having initially arrived in the late 1920s. But, a few years later, a white vigilante attack ended their in-migration. Local whites justified the attack in their newspapers by contrasting Filipinos to Mexicans: Mexicans were well established, served as cheap, reliable labor, and bought goods from local merchants, while Filipinos did "not conform to our ways of livings" and were "holed up" in "conditions that would be a disgrace for a well-bred pig."[91] This white preference, however, did not reduce Mexicans' precarious position in the Coachella Valley, for six months after the anti-Filipino vigilante attack white locals successfully pushed for Mexican repatriation to solve the Great Depression's strain. Filipino migrants returned to the Coachella Valley only after WWII, when San Joaquin Valley ranchers relied on their expertise to expand the desert's vineyards. Despite their significance to the region's most lucrative harvest, Filipino grape workers remained relatively invisible in the local racial landscape. They never appeared in newspapers or local organizations, did not interact much with ethnic Mexican workers and did not tax white public institutions. Arguably, their erasure signaled a key source of their racialization.

Lastly, after WWII, the land between Indio and Palm Springs—date orchards and sand dunes—gained a flurry of new millionaire country clubs, golf courses, and winter resorts promising a "gracious desert living" of modern amenities and unspoiled nature. In the new city of Palm Desert, the Silver Spur Country Club trumpeted emblematically: "the valley's newest and finest ranch home community: secluded, restricted, sheltered ... and with magnificent views."[92] This westside region was almost universally white by the early 1960s. In the few non-white pockets, white supremacist policies continued to shape non-white lives, such as in Palm Springs' campaign to displace Mexican Americans and African Americans living on Cahuilla reservation land near the city's downtown, which white city officials identified as central to its resort-based economy.[93] Though complementing the region's agricultural economy, the west-side racial dynamics appeared to be largely removed from the eastern Coachella Valley.

In the latter, to conclude, a collection of public institutions reified the economy's racialized hierarchies and extended the rancher-king's power into spaces beyond his fields. Exceptions certainly existed. Some ethnic Mexican residents made their way out of *colonias* and some, especially if phenotypically light, sent their children to white schools. Some experienced social mobility after WWII and a few may have felt no racial hostility—despite the segregation, political underrepresentation, and racist newspapers. Exceptions, of course, are precisely that. The overall social structure remained as MacKaye described—where "the rancher tended to be 'king,' [and] the Mexican farm families his 'peasants.'"[94] Any future challenge to these rancher-kings would have to consider the social institutions shaping and containing the farmworkers' social, political, and cultural worlds.

Whom to Guillotine?

The temptation, here, is to write only of a dichotomous world—of peasant workers and rancher-kings, and of the former's uniform oppression and shared oppressor, in the form of the latter. But this was not the case. Though most farmworkers faced alienating conditions, their lived experience spoke of great diversity. If scholars still imagine a social movement groundswell as ending with a guillotined king, then the Coachella Valley's history presents a sobering reality. In practice, determining who to fight, and with whom, was never easy.

The labor contractor, for instance, upended the dichotomy. Generally male, he gathered workers, distributed pay, and established wages, conditions, and expectations.[95] He undercut union organizing by monitoring workers, blacklisting rebels, and hiring strikebreakers from the large transnational labor force. For personal profits, he engaged in parasitic entrepreneurialism, such as selling goods at work, providing rides to and from ranches, and renting spare housing to migrant farmworkers, all at exorbitant prices.[96] Most also charged a "job fee" of approximately 10 percent of farmworker wages.[97] As such, the contractor was arguably thriving in his position: he usually owned the neighborhood's biggest houses, drove the newest cars, and lived in visible comfort. He also gained goods unavailable to other farmworkers—from everyday forms of deference to the fulfillment of the patriarchal prerogatives to provide and protect. Some even bought homes in white neighborhoods and sent their children to white classrooms.[98]

For these reasons, labor contractors can appear as mini kings sitting above and outside the laboring class, embodying the Rancher Nation's intermediary glue.[99] But this image also simplifies his presence *within* the laboring population.[100] His children and siblings also worked in the fields, as did his cousins, compadres, and neighbors. Even the general workforce reflected his intimate touch: his farmworkers included camp residents under the contractor's management; the friends of a brother-in-law's sister; the parents of a son's friend. Each had asked for a job, and each gained through him. Instead of a social class pyramid, in other words, the agricultural workforce's structure better resembled a large social web with multiple concentrated clusters, where clusters represented a labor contractor circled by his closest relatives and associates. The rest tethered outward in wider concentric circles, reflecting their relative levels of privilege and subjection. Along the farthest peripheries existed loosely associated farmworkers who were often outside the contractor's good graces and/or new to the region's labor market. Beyond this group, the concentric circles tightened once more into another dense cluster—signaling yet another labor contractor and his social network.

This social web distributed wages and alienation in differentiated forms. To relatives and friends, the labor contractor offered higher paying positions and lucrative harvests. Both meant, at minimum, greater income and job security in an otherwise unforgiving and sporadic industry. For these farmworkers, furthermore, the labor contractor sometimes forgave the job fee and limited his practice of wage theft to those farther out. For the distanced mass, in contrast, he lowered wages, instituted job fees, stole work hours, and assigned farmworkers to poor fields and to fewer job hours. Social distance also meant greater exposure to nonmaterial alienation, like public denigration and humiliation, the routine sexual harassment of women workers, and the public-enough undercounting of boxes picked.[101] A farmworker's relationship to the labor contractor, in short, shaped their experiences in the fields and, by extension, in the Coachella Valley. For those closest to him, farmworker life could mean social security, respect, and occasional luxury—a life from which some even imagined attaining "progress" and "belonging."

Oral history participants estimated that the labor contractors' close circle ranged from 10 to 20 percent of the farm working population. Presumably, in a revolutionary (and rather optimistic) moment, the 80 percent could neutralize the privileged minority on the way to dethroning the king. But this also simplifies the gendered relationships within that 80 percent and overlooks the critical role of patriarchy in the workforce's constitution, in its distribution of marginality, and in the formation of farmworker politics.

Of the women farmworkers interviewed, all but one spoke of patriarchy shaping their lives as much as wage exploitation and white supremacy.[102] They spoke of husbands and fathers dominating families, of men's commandments serving as familial law, and of pervasive domestic violence.[103] The latter cannot be overstated. Virginia Ortega labeled farmworker "machismo" as "brutal," while Guadalupe Carrizales described marriage as "a new form of government" for women.[104] Interviewees also spoke of gender norms that contained women in submissive mother and wife roles and tied their presence outside their homes to sexual impropriety. They stressed the rampant sexual harassment from supervisors *and* coworkers, and the gendered dimensions of farmworker exploitation. For example, the lack of restrooms in Coachella Valley fields can be seen as a symbol of the workforce's profound commodification and of the ranchers' collective disregard of farmworker humanity. But for women farmworkers, the lack of work restrooms also meant they occasionally had to crowd around each other in a hyperpublic effort at privacy-against the leering eyes of the surrounding men, whether bosses or underlings.[105]

Furthermore, some women said male workers commonly used their wages to spend nights in bars, where they found gambling, sex workers, and alcohol-laden sociability. These luxuries mimicked the unequal gains found among contractor-adjacent families: both found a less-than alienated existence at the expense of farmworker women and children.[106] In the most extreme cases—though not necessarily rare—men compelled spouses and children to work in agricultural fields to confiscate their wages. "Many times," recounted Virginia Ortega, "men controlled their sons' and daughters' checks. That is as true as the sun shining during the day."[107] Gender inequality even shaped the audible workday: women said very little and almost never spoke to each other, Maria Marron recalled, while Maria Serrano speculated that women were not allowed to talk by their husbands. The men, in contrast, spoke incessantly of "partying . . . about how much beer they had the previous night, about having gone to the bar. There were a ton of bars in Indio. And well, they spoke of such things, of playing cards and who had won and how much they had won in previous times. Well! They spoke of that."[108] This was a public world of male bravado—even if glinted by labor exhaustion, poverty, and racial deference. If some have emphasized familial solidarity, these women farmworkers stressed their families' patriarchal constitution, in which men's politics could not be assumed to be opposing a political economy that subjugated their families.[109]

Lastly, women spoke of familial patriarchy as interwoven with agricultural social relations, where the latter's gendered discrimination and exploitation sustained the former, and vice versa. Common hiring discrimination against women—supervisors said women workers were incapable of enduring supervisor-imposed conditions—secured greater dividends to ranchers and contractors, who squeezed greater profits from masculinity.[110] Male workers also gained extra opportunities through gender hiring discrimination: they, too, earned a larger wage receipt and could thus credit themselves with the family's survival, and turn the work fields into spaces for performing the daily practice of masculine protection (of family) and authority (over family). In contrast, women farmworkers' reduced resources also meant limited abilities to gain economic independence from their husbands and fathers, whether abusive or not. Even when working, women farmworkers recognized that the low wages and male-based contractor system made them economically dependent on men.

Farmworkers, of course, did not have exclusive ownership of patriarchy. The Coachella Valley's heroic white ranchers also radiated patriarchal self-celebration. They, too, ruled their families with impunity and arrogance. All *Desert Rancher* profiles retold the same scenario of patriarchal normativity; wives cooked, hosted socials, and spoke of their husband's foresight in bringing them to a small desert community; the children, like gendered trophies of racial longevity, told of helping in the ranch; the husbands, sitting above and apart, spoke directly about the future. The profiles also included portraits of their nuclear families, all smiles, no deviations. Amidst all the celebration, however, tacit references to the patriarch's authority and violence punctured through. Rancher spouses repeatedly said they sacrificed careers, gave up family and friend networks, and/or faced desert solitude when their husbands unilaterally decided to settle their family in the Coachella Valley. Their husbands ignored their protests, the rancher wives added, almost uniformly, and derided their questions and concerns. Some male ranchers even used their spouse's savings without their permission to buy desert land—a stunning, and impressively larger, equivalent to the farmworkers' familial wage theft. Once settled in the desert, however, rancher wives were expected to parrot the same conclusion, which they did to the *Desert Rancher*: their husbands had been right all along and they were grateful for it.[111]

The Coachella Valley's economy thus incorporated differently positioned families through a racialized structure of patriarchal privileges and exchanges. Reflecting the most power privileged, white male ranchers and their allies lived in the imagined center with stories of pioneering fatherhood. The male, non-white labor contractor served the dual roles of supplying non-white labor to white ranchers and jobs to workers, distributing the various levels of spoils and violence through a gendered lens. Like a patriarchal father, labor contractors also provided for and punished his dependents, trickling wages downward and away from the center in unequal and patriarchal terms and inflicting greater violence along the peripheries. In the Coachella Valley, white ranchers leveraged Mexican farmworker patriarchy to exploit labor, secure pioneer profitability, and, relatedly, fortify their patriarchal authority over *their* white families. Meanwhile, Mexican farmworker men relied on white ranchers' blind eye to rule their families with impunity, which then served as a crutch for the otherwise unmanly submission to rancher exploitation. At the nexus of the exchange stood ethnic Mexican women and children—the very foundation of the Coachella Valley's fantasies of Indigenous disappearance and of a modern, reclaimed desert, of embodying America itself.

Adding further complexity, the farmworker class included temporary contract laborers under the Bracero Program, southwestern ethnic Mexican migrants, undocumented Mexican immigrants, Filipino grape workers, and newly settled Tejano families. They worked different harvests, lived in often disparate spaces, and held distinct histories and relationships to the region and to the United States. For example, while braceros worked multiple harvests in short-term periods and lived in camps removed from Mexican barrios or segregated from Filipino camps, Filipino migrants arrived in the Coachella Valley annually for the early grape harvest, stayed in the same camps near Mecca, and claimed a long history of labor organizing in the United States. Even among the local farmworker communities, such as

Tejanos and long-established Mexican Americans, different histories and social positions served to create misrecognition and hostilities. For some farmworkers, Coachella Valley wages meant remittances for conditions in home countries and regions. For others, Coachella Valley dynamics appeared no worse, and sometimes even better, than other places—a comparison the sociologist Patricia Zavella termed "peripheral vision."[112] As such, social conditions *elsewhere* often framed farmworkers' relationship to local realities and politics. The result was a proliferation of farmworker calculations and few class-wide collective efforts.

Coachella Valley's Filipino farmworkers stand apart in some telling of this history. Historians of early twentieth century Filipino farmworkers have portrayed Filipino labor contractors as empowering figures who served the seemingly uncontradictory role of ethnic organizer, labor contractor, and union leader. They secured jobs when Filipinos were denied employment. They negotiated higher wages for all to share. They dealt with issues arising from pervasive anti-Filipino prejudice. Many doubled their personal financial success as racial pride for a bourgeoning Filipino community in the United States. For instance, Jerry Paular recalled, "The contractors enabled our families to survive. Without their willingness to accept the responsibility of our welfare and to bargain on behalf of the people they represented, we would have no one to represent us before the landowner. They were men of substance. . . . They'd go broke before they'd see a family starve."[113] Like Paular, historians have rightly recognized the empowering role Filipino labor contractors could play in their communities. In comparison to the Coachella Valley's Mexican workforce, Filipino crews can appear as particularly egalitarian.

But, some Filipino labor leaders have expressed skepticism about these contractors' goodwill. Philip Vera Cruz's biography, for instance, recounted the "many incidents where one Filipino had ripped off another, causing Filipinos to be suspicious of their own people. I learned quickly in this country that when people are poor and hungry they will turn even against their own."[114] Filipino community leaders, he added, enriched themselves through "rackets"—from the "bars for the disgusted and the despondent, to the gambling for the unjust and greed and the dance halls for the lonely and the unhappy."[115] Speaking in the late 1970s, Vera Cruz noted Filipino farmworkers' mistrust of the UFW in the mid-1970s, which he felt originated in Filipino fears they would lose their jobs if the union ended the contractor system in agriculture.[116] Yet, Vera Cruz insisted on the UFW's anti-contractor push: "The UFW wanted to make the hiring of the worker a more equitable and clear-cut process that was controlled by the union and not by some easily manipulated or bribed individual who would be under the direct influence of the grower."[117] Vera Cruz's Filipino contractor resembled less a figure of community adulation, and more as a potential extension of the ranchers' power. Oral histories of Filipino leaders in the San Joaquin Valley suggest a similarly vexed relationship between Filipino labor contractors and their workers.[118]

Over and over again, farmworker difference and complicity defied simplicity and stability. For many, the enemy came in intimate form—as the father/husband, relative and neighbor, as people who brought workers to fields, surveilled dissent, and provided a semblance of stability to an otherwise unequal and unstable social and economic structure. While distinct, Filipino farmworkers also existed in entangled relationships with labor contractors and their ranchers. The Rancher Nation was riven by complexities that shaped farmworkers' experiences in ways that likely safeguarded the structure's overall stability. If anyone hoped to eliminate the Rancher Nation, they would have done well to consider such differences and complications, and then move deftly through them, and with them, to offer ways out to the multiple entangled communities.

Conclusion

At the end of the workday, as farmworkers drove to their small homes, they may have noticed the squat, desert-bare Chocolate and San Bernardino Mountains on the Coachella Valley's eastern boundary (see book cover). Unimpressive when compared to the much larger, regal San Jacinto Mountains, these smaller ranges nonetheless dance with a subtle magic, gained each day with the passage of light. The mountains are full of crevices, canyons, and wrinkles, swirling lines of arroyos, textured in shrubs. They are also often underneath desert-white clouds, spotty and woolly, solitary or massed. Most importantly, the mountains always face the setting sun after a long workday. As the sun migrates across the sky, these humble, almost non-mountains shift in colors, textures, and depth—from dark browns and light greens to the most unlikely blues, purples, and reds; from sunlit alleys and swirls to lurking cloud shadows; from dusty shrubs to the monsoon gray curtains blurring mountain with sky. Even if singular and material, in other words, these mountains appear as a shifting plurality. Perhaps farmworkers, covered in dirt and feeling the pain and pleasures of physical exhaustion, saw this shimmering dance, wondered about what more could be seen.

The Rancher Nation mimicked such flux. Rooted in a settler colonial story, it credited the white male rancher for the Coachella Valley's agricultural transformation in the early to mid-twentieth century. In doing so, it leveraged a deep national obsession with the racialized frontier and deployed the pioneer's gendered labors as metonyms for citizenship, race, and community. It did so only by erasing the evident realities on the ground: that white civilization was predicated on settler violence; that it relied on federal welfare; that it produced an immoral exploitation of racialized labor. The laborers in question included ethnic Mexicans and Filipinos, the migrant and settled, women and men, the young and the older. Each person, family, and community negotiated local and nonlocal social conditions, calculated their resources and risk thresholds, identified enmities, identified friends. Each also held a distinct standpoint from which to see the Rancher Nation's structure, each a distinct color inflection to the material reality that was, on the varied worker relationships and their collective relationship to the rancher-king. Much like the mountain's shifting colors and textures, the Rancher Nation gained its magic of stability through movement and time—the movement and time of labor and harvests, the movement imposed to make ends meet, the time accrued as the frailties of a human person. The Rancher Nation was an ordering rhythm, a discursive, material, and political rhythm enveloping differences and attempting to drown out the stories of and for an alternative world—stories that refused to die.

Chapter 2

The Known World

Fragments and Fissures in the Coachella Valley

In the early 1960s, the Coachella Valley's agricultural annual tempo moved to its searing summer. The season began with the summer's end—from hot Septembers and warm Octobers to balmy winters of crisp blue days. In April, warmth stirred once more, and then climaxed in May and June, when hot mornings prickled skin and sweetened grapes. In July and August, however, the summer heat was furious enough to still even the rancher-king's confidence. Little moved, little grew, little promised. If irrigation canals and railroads had solved the region's aridity and isolation problems, its summers burned wild and unruly, as if intent on defying the white ranchers' racial reclamation of the forbidding desert.

And yet, not all was still in these summer months. In the evenings, surprising cool breezes could still be felt. A subtle swirl around a boulevard of tall native pines, a whorl next to an elementary school. The heat may have been stultifying, but stirrings of breath remained and signaled a potential change in the near future.

In the early 1960s, such winds appeared from two fronts to challenge different aspects of the Coachella Valley's Rancher Nation: from non-farmworker Mexican American residents and from migrant Filipino grape workers. The former traced their local history to the early twentieth century, when they built family ranches, sent their children to local schools, and fostered self-sustaining, even when impoverished, *colonias*. In the post-World War II (WWII) economic boom, the majority found jobs outside most alienating farm labor. But they still faced racial inequality and political disempowerment. In response, Mexican American residents highlighted their U.S. citizenship, led local political campaigns, and contested the Rancher Nation's racial underpinnings. Filipino grape workers, in contrast, claimed an ambivalent presence in the region. Most had permanent homes in the San Joaquin Valley, where the grape harvest was twice as long as in the Coachella Valley. In the latter, most lived in rancher-owned camps while harvesting for two months. Many also belonged to the Filipino-led Agricultural Workers Organizing Committee (AWOC), which prepared for a string of California harvest strikes in late 1964 and early 1965. Like Mexican Americans, Filipino farmworkers framed their labor organizing as seeking the markers of U.S. citizenship, which had been denied to them.

Both fronts troubled the solidity and stability of the Rancher Nation's claims and futurity in the Coachella Valley. But neither offered an assured trajectory out of the rancher's dominion nor could have predicted the seismic transformations the region would experience in the late 1960s and early 1970s. Both were led by small minorities and both mounted limited critiques that overlooked populations outside their citizen-based politics. Their critiques, for example, struggled to incorporate the Coachella Valley's largely invisible, ethnic Mexican farmworker community, which did not use a U.S. citizenship discourse to situate themselves within and/or fight against the Rancher Nation. The Coachella Valley's farmworkers, given their vulnerabilities and distance from citizen-based campaigns, did not have many social vehicles for improving their living and working conditions. For some, the stories of the possible drew from Mexico's revolutionary past and often pointed to a future in Mexico.

The postwar Coachella Valley, in short, held a collection of rebellious stories, stories that overlapped and diverged or moved through unseen proximity, stories that drew from shared or distinct pasts, stories from a shared present with lives that were never commensurable enough. The difference drawn hinted at the multiple and vague futures sought by those on the Rancher Nation's margins. This chapter turns to the Coachella Valley's insurgents. It stresses social differences and ambivalent potential, a combination that would set the stage for the late 1960s social movement crystallizations. The latter was never linear; it was always contingent in a precarious present, made visible only by the very naming it facilitated.

Not Even the Dogcatcher

Isabel Reyes was born in a ranch house in Thermal in 1927, the fifth in a migrant farmworker family that, like many others, traded Mexico's civil war for the Southwest's agricultural circuit.[1] When Reyes's mother died unexpectedly in 1930, her father settled the family on his relative's Thermal ranch, where cousins, aunts, and uncles jostled together on a small plot of land, and where Reyes found mother figures in older cousins and made friends with nearby children. For the next decade, her family would weather the Great Depression and racial prejudice on this ranch, growing much of their food and joining the town's mutual aid societies, sports leagues, music bands, and churches. There, she found a close-knit community that felt far removed from the ranchers' pioneer stories.[2]

Reyes's experiences in the Coachella Valley embodied the cultural mixtures and inequalities that defined the borderlands in this period. She attended segregated schools that prohibited Spanish speaking and with teachers who relied on corporal punishment. But she also made friends with rancher children among many others.[3] She learned English and embraced U.S. cultural practices even as she read about her family's home country, which she grew to see as her own. By adolescence, Reyes was bilingual and bicultural, immersed in a blending that did not dissolve the social limits on her life. By then, she hoped for a profession outside field labor, her son said in the early twenty-first century, but these aspirations evaporated in a community tied and subjected to farm labor. Like most ethnic Mexican children in the Coachella Valley, Reyes knew her family depended on her labor. And like other ethnic Mexican students, she left school at fourteen (1941) to thin, pick, and pack, while her rancher friends attended theirs.

Reyes's life in postwar Coachella Valley carried similar limitations and opportunities. She met and married a young bracero named Jose Ceja. In the 1950s, she had a family and a lucrative job in Cal Date's packing shed, while her husband worked year-round as an irrigator.[4] Reyes also moved her family out of Indio's Farm Labor Camp, an insultingly decrepit complex, and bought a new house in a housing tract promoted by a childhood rancher friend. She used similar contacts in 1962 when she bought a home in Coachellita, the city's Mexican colonia a mile from the city center. Her postwar life moved with a semblance of upward social mobility in an ethnic Mexican community. Her children even attended high school and entertained a future outside agriculture. And still, Reyes remained a couple of paychecks away from poverty, struggled with a domineering husband, and had no illusions as to who held local power: to her children, she instructed, learn English and do not make enemies.

Much like Isabel Reyes, the Coachella Valley's Mexican American community inhabited ambivalent social positions—where racial slights coexisted with economic opportunity and where blended cultural practices grew from the ground of U.S. citizenship.[5] Almost all emigrated before the 1930s and most found early work in the desert's bourgeoning fields. Some built entire ranches for absentee owners. A small number bought land and grew food for themselves and the market. Others worked in nearby mines, packing sheds, and railroads. Some settled in poor colonias that combined vague autonomy with municipal powerlessness. Others made homes in unincorporated towns or along ranch edges. Parents enrolled children in segregated schools and families joined civic, religious, and social organizations. They overcame the Great Depression and repatriation.[6] And, much like Reyes, the postwar era offered a variegated landscape of social opportunities and indignities, of cultural hybridity and social–political exclusions.[7]

Significantly, by WWII, most of the adult immigrants had lived half their lives in the Coachella Valley, while the second generation only knew the desert as their home. This latter generation answered the war's call for democratic sacrifice and embraced the "Americans of Mexican descent" identity—both of which appeared tentatively reciprocated by local relations: newspapers began to abstain from explicit racism and occasionally recognized Mexican American contributions to the region and country. The Coachella Valley High School also saw an increase in ethnic Mexican students, while the postwar boom opened positions without the worst conditions of unskilled, migrant farm labor.[8] Those jobs went to thousands of Mexican braceros, who lived in the region's isolated labor camps under short-term contracts. They also went to Tejano and Mexican families, who arrived in the 1950s and early 1960s. Both braceros and newcomers provided a cultural contrast to Mexican Americans' cultural and political citizenship and local residency, while supporting Mexican American businesses, like restaurants and bars.[9] Though originating in migrant farm labor, and though still racialized as non-white, the Coachella Valley's Mexican American community had nonetheless carved out an intermediary social, political, and cultural presence in Indio, Coachella, and the eastern townships.

Obvious racial inequality, however, remained. The region's racialized poverty was structural: white rancher profit relied on Mexican exploitation and produced MacKaye's rancher-king and Mexican-peasant dichotomy. On the political realm, Mexican Americans in 1960 held no elected offices in local and regional governing bodies—even though they accounted for two-thirds of Coachella's population and represented a significant minority throughout the region. The political underrepresentation led to Mexican colonias receiving less local and state funds for infrastructural development, while facing extra scrutiny from police officers and blight-adverse agencies. Local schools still segregated students and employed racist teachers. When Indio built a new high school in 1960, it drew white students farther away from the older, and now Mexican-concentrated, Coachella Valley High School. Local newspapers still noted Mexican American contributions to the region, but they also focused on Mexican drug use and criminality, mocked large, unruly Mexican families, and profiled drunk Mexican men who failed to elude the police.[10] Most tragically, Mexican American oral histories sometimes speak of white friends in warm tones of conviviality, but white residents never mentioned them in the local newspapers' interest sections at mid century.[11]

The Rancher Nation, in other words, simultaneously attracted and repelled the older Mexican American community. It called on them to share in citizen sacrifices while fulfilling less than promised. In an increasingly civil rights minded nation, the Coachella Valley's social inequalities remained legitimated. This ambivalent social position shaped Mexican American politics, which coalesced around two poles in the early 1960s. In the first, and the most visible in archives, a collection of professionals and business owners joined Coachella's white-dominated Chamber of Commerce and the under-thirty Jaycee. They also built chapters of the League of Latin American Citizens (LULAC) and the American GI Forum and focused on charity projects, such as distributing clothes and shoes to farmworkers, on fundraisers, and on Catholic Church-related events.[12] In the city of Coachella, Mexican Americans also formed social groups, such as the Progresista Lodge (PL) and the Civic and Patriotic Committee (CPC). The former hosted dance fundraisers for local public projects, such as the installation of park benches in Coachella's central park, while the latter organized annual celebrations for *Cinco de Mayo* and Mexican Independence Day.[13]

Critically, in local and English language newspapers, these groups never broached the subject of racial inequality or protested their political underrepresentation, the related under-allocation of public funds, or the local economy's reliance on farmworker exploitation. Instead, they reiterated the Rancher Nation's stories of a self-made, egalitarian community. For them, citizenship appeared to be earned by performing the dominant rancher stories, which secured their political visibility as worthy for potential inclusion. Citizenship did not exist a priori or provide the basis for contesting social inequality. Instead, Mexican American groups adopted the white showcasing of charitable projects, such as giving aid to poor people across the border or poor people in, but not of, the region—a spectacle that identified unfortunate need at the edges of an already-just society.[14] When the CPC began to organize Mexican events in the early 1950s, for instance, it characteristically emphasized their U.S. citizenship and presented the annual celebrations' shared activities as evidence of social equality: they invited all valley citizens ("of Anglo as well as Mexican origin"), stressed white appreciation of Mexican culture, and aptly photographed white and Mexican residents smiling together.[15]

Perhaps these efforts reflected Mexican Americans' postwar social mobility and their genuine desire to build a multicultural and multiracial community, still feeling the good war's afterglow. But these efforts also reflected a politics that smothered all social critique, one that denied the Coachella Valley's structural inequality precisely to secure citizenship's visibility: as good Americans, they appeared to tell white neighbors, they knew they had it good.[16] In an explicit example from 1954, several Mexican American leaders endorsed Coachella and Indio council candidates with the unambiguous title, "To Our Good Neighbors of Coachella Valley." "We, the undersigned property owners," they announced, "residents and Americans of Latin extraction justly, proud of and sincerely interested in the welfare and development of the City of Coachella, desire to publicly acknowledge, with an expression of gratitude, the effective efforts of the present city administration on behalf of the health and growth of our community."¹⁷ To their credit, Mexican American organizations did not reproduce white pioneers' anti-Indigenous racism. But they shared the settler–colonial preoccupation with development and communal self-sufficiency, and they insisted on a myopic stance toward the region's anti-Mexican racism.¹⁸ As mentioned earlier, a 1964 letter to the *Coachella Valley Sun* from one such leader mocked "Chicanos" for lacking "the courage and pride to get out of our little nooks" and "work to obtain an education . . . like the Japanese." Unlike him, he added, Chicanos voted for Democrats' "free lunch," "cr[ied] discrimination," and blamed "gringos" for their lives.¹⁹

But as the 1964 letter indicated, conservative Mexican Americans faced opposition from other activists. In the early 1960s, the opposition came from Coachella Valley residents who formed the Voters League (VL) and the Mexican American Political Association (MAPA). Like conservative residents, these latter activists spoke English and emphasized their U.S. citizenship. They proudly traced their history in the Coachella Valley and U.S. Southwest, and some brandished their national roles in WWII and afterwards. They knew they had built the region's economy and that they remained an integral part of its wealth production. But they also argued that Mexican Americans held a second-class status locally and regionally. This status produced a mounting of political grievances, which the VL and MAPA would begin to fight through local elections and, increasingly, social protests in the mid-1960s.

Based in Coachella, the VL initiated this challenge in elections for city council and county supervisor. One VL member was Angela Salas, who was born in the late 1920s to a miner–union family from Arizona and who, as an adult, worked as a skilled carpenter and in a date packinghouse. If she "thought there was an injustice," her son recalled, "she was there to try to help resolve [it] . . . if it meant politics, organizing, campaigning, she had no reservation about doing that. . . . She always felt you needed to have representation, to physically participate yourself and try to get others as well." Salas's social justice commitments and participation was partly rooted in her socially conscious Catholicism.²⁰ Some of the other VL members included Isabel Reyes's brothers and husband, and the large families Reyes had known since childhood. These members saw the VL as a vehicle for political empowerment, as Reyes's son explained: "there were no Latino office holders in the whole city of Coachella. Not on the water board, not on the city, not on the council . . . not even the dogcatcher was Mexican."²¹ Reyes's husband, Jose Ceja, joined the VL despite being an immigrant. His own history as a militant *Cardenista* in Michoacan, Mexico, told him that only political contestation, not charity, would solve the community's pressing issues.

This contestation materialized in the 1964 Coachella city council elections, when the VL organized a candidates' town hall, registered voters, and endorsed a slate of three—of whom two were Mexican American. One of these candidates, Nabor Rodriguez, framed the election as rectifying Mexican Americans' civic marginality: "We have problems," the *Coachella Valley Sun* quoted him in halting speech, "I'm speaking [of] Anglo American[s], and there has been unflattering publicity about law enforcement."[22] The newspaper did not explain his reference to Anglo Americans, but noted Rodriguez's vow for better communication between Coachella and its Mexican American residents, which was "lacking in the past." The other candidate, Ben Saiz, rejected the VL's endorsement because, as he explained, he did not want to be seen as serving only "one faction."[23] Tellingly, when Rodriguez lost and Saiz won in April 1964, the *Coachella Valley Sun* celebrated "the most successful" election and presented it as "proof" of American freedom, where "anyone can effectively participate in local politics . . . and make a real impression on any community."[24] In October 1964, the VL again lobbied for the appointment of one of its members to an open council seat. In response, the newspapers lectured them in condescending tones on democratic processes while conservative Mexican Americans lambasted "Chicanos" and their victim claims.[25] The VL had hit a political nerve. In fact, as early as 1965, it faced increasing police harassment for its purported communist sympathies.[26]

In tandem, Mexican Americans also formed MAPA chapters in the Coachella, Imperial, and Palo Verde Valleys. Each drew together an eclectic group of civil servants, educators, small business owners, and independent contractors. In the Coachella Valley, the members were male and non-farmworker, and its leaders largely recent transplants with long histories of labor and race justice activism.[27] From Blythe, California, for instance, Alfredo Figueroa traced his family to Joaquin Murrieta and recalled childhood memories of miner strikes. As a young adult, he serenaded braceros, campaigned for John F. Kennedy, and sued Blythe's Police Department for a beating that left him unconscious.[28] From Arizona miner towns, Ray Rodriguez and Raul Loya grew up in spaces dominated by white power figures. But, Rodriguez said, unionized Mexican American families still fought for labor contracts and taught their children to do the same; both led their own wildcat strike before their twentieth birthdays.[29] Lastly, Alfredo Fuller came from Nogales, Arizona, a border community that eloquently mirrored his family: with an African American father and a Mexican mother, the young Alfredo lived on the bridge in-between. He recalled a pleasant if poor childhood and protective parents and neighbors. In a telling memory, he described walking Nogales's rolling hills, past houses with open windows playing the same song from the town's only radio station; as if linked by each house, he moved to the unbroken community rhythm.[30] In 1964–66, Rodriguez, Loya, and Fuller arrived as teachers. They were the first in their families to earn college degrees, and they intended to use them to aid others.

To these MAPA members, especially the recent transplants, the Coachella Valley's social relations were nothing less than feudal, a stark reality only outdone by what they saw as social paralysis among its ethnic Mexican communities. MAPA connected local conditions to broader experiences in the U.S. Southwest. To change local conditions, they argued, activists needed a federated group that fought on multiple scales—both across the country and along various levels of governance. For them, the VL's focus on city elections was too limited; they instead preferred a buffet-like view of resistance: there was no key site, just a relentless assault against injustice. They advocated education reforms, picketed the Post Office for discriminatory hiring, and aided local political campaigns. They would also support the AWOC–National Farm Workers Association (NFWA) Delano Grape Strike in early 1966, publish a bimonthly newspaper, and distribute college scholarships. They did so without decorum. Most were in the masculine hubris called the mid-twenties and early thirties, and most believed that social justice required crossing the arbitrary lines of civility. Their tactics included pickets, marches, public accusations, local boycotts, rallies, and aid to still-fledging unions.[31]

By early 1965, the Coachella Valley's Mexican American communities counted on multiple civic organizations engaging and/or challenging the discursive, political, and social underpinnings of the Rancher Nation outside the fields. They demanded recognition of and/or compensation for their local and national contributions and they presented a collection of social grievances. They competed for political leadership and advanced social policies that threatened rancher allies. In explicit and implicit forms, they rejected the permanence of the Mexican peasant status.

Things Are Different Now

In the late 1970s, Willie Barrientos recounted his history in the United Farm Workers (UFW) with his birth and childhood family: he was born in 1908 in Ilocos Sur, Philippines, and raised by an anti-imperialist family who taught him to fight for Filipino independence. "When I was young," Barrientos said, "I was a fighter. I was *born* that way. My mother raised me that way." Like other Filipino youth in the early twentieth century, he learned of a bountiful United States from white colonial teachers and labor contractors, envisioning migration to the United States as an escape from poverty.[32] But expectations soured as soon as he arrived in the late 1920s. In Hawaii, ten hours paid one dollar—

"worse than highway robbery," he said—while in Los Angeles and Seattle, residents called him "monkey" and barred him from attending public schools.[33] To earn a living, Barrientos joined Stockton's Filipino asparagus crews, but he chafed at the low wages and grueling regimen, and ultimately settled in late 1930s San Francisco, where he found janitorial work and a gradually older community of Filipino bachelors. Together, they weathered racial discrimination, anti-miscegenation laws, and low wages that suppressed their remittances. This early denial stayed with Barrientos and shaped entire his life: "This all hurt me," he said, "We cannot marry. We cannot buy land, until we fight [in WWII]. That's all hurt me. That's why I get old in my head and in my heart and in my hand."[34] After WWII, he joined Filipino crews on the Pacific West's circuit, migrating along an archipelago of harvests and labor camps, and stringing together a community despite the dire conditions.

Like Barrientos, the Filipino migrants who arrived in the Coachella Valley to harvest grapes in 1965 had already lived an entire life. Born in the Philippines at the turn of the century, most came from peasant families in the land-scarce and migration-driven Luzon and Visayas regions. They grew up under U.S. imperialism, an impoverishing, export-oriented economy, and a cultural politics that heralded the United States as a land of modernity, education, and security. Many heard as much from white teachers and Christian missionaries or from the films, novels, and newspapers saturating the islands. They learned it, too, from early Filipino letters speaking of rose-tinted arrivals, or from returnees' stunning transformations, all with new clothes and new selves, and thick rolls of dollar bills.[35] Most Filipino migrants had made a life-changing choice in the 1920s and 1930s when they signed labor contracts from Hawaiian and Pacific West ranchers. Most imagined a temporary sojourn—a chance to gain security for their families and a bit of the adventure allowed to them as young men.[36] For some, migration may also have signaled moving to another cultural home, for many had learned English and read about U.S. heroes and pledged to a flag that claimed to pledge in return.[37]

For many, arrival brought days of magic; days of new freedoms, clothes, skyscrapers, and inventions; of Chinatown gambling houses, camp cockfights, and company with women in red-light districts, often as their first experience.[38] These early days also spoke of nearby farm work and a social mobility that required only bodily exertion, as if golden futures laid in their recent adolescent metamorphosis.[39]

But these were also days of reckoning. Most moved under the newly invented political category of U.S. "Nationals." The category allowed them to circumvent racist bans against Asian immigration, but it denied them the possibility of gaining U.S. citizenship.[40] It also failed to counter racial hostility in Hawaii and the Pacific West, where they faced housing segregation, job discrimination, and depictions as unassimilable aliens and disease vectors, as yet another sexual threat to the always-vulnerable white woman. In the late 1920s and early 1930s, racial hostilities metastasized into murderous mob attacks in multiple states.[41] "Everywhere I went," wrote the Filipino writer, Carlos Bulosan, "I saw white men attacking Filipinos. It was but natural for me to hate and fear the white man."[42] Western states reacted to these attacks by adding Filipinos to anti-miscegenation laws, which then criminalized Filipino sexuality, thwarted future marriage prospects, and fortified racial tropes about Filipino gender and sexual deviance. In 1934, Congress also unilaterally "granted" the Philippines a ten-year path to independence to end Filipino migration, all while pushing for Filipino repatriation. Locally, county officials denied unemployed Filipino workers Great Depression aid, thus assuring that the young men faced the period's social misery alone.[43]

On the agricultural circuit in the U.S. Pacific West, they entered an industry based on a cheap, pliable labor. With ethnic Mexicans, they replaced the previous workforce of Chinese, Japanese, and South Asian migrants, totaling approximately fifty-six thousand in the West Coast in 1930.[44] Like former generations of farmworkers, they were critical for many harvests but endured poor conditions, poverty-level wages, employer surveillance, and long days spent bent over tending to crops. For fifteen-year-old Magnos, the grueling pace paid misery: ten hours earned him $2.75 in 1927 and "pain in my body . . . my back, my arm . . . after I got to my bed I'd be crying."[45] Wages fell further in the Great Depression, while conditions in decrepit camps worsened. The future UFW leader Philip Vera Cruz described these as "stinking" "bunkhouses" resembling "chicken coops with mosquitos all over," where "roof holes" offered the bittersweet chance to "count the stars" in the evening.[46] To survive, the young men migrated in Filipino-led crews to harvests in Montana, Idaho, Washington, Oregon, California, and Arizona. Some worked Alaska's canneries in the summer, but even here wages did not improve substantially or offset the supervisor rackets that ate away at earnings.[47] Few found the America they had heard of in their hometowns. From their vantage point, the Rancher Nation was a colonial space between the United States and Philippines and along the Pacific West's migrant circuit.

Despite these conditions, Filipino migrants stayed in the United States and cobbled together enough food and warmth to build a sense of community. They helped friends, coworkers, neighbors, and relatives through an ethic of reciprocity in times of need.[48] They built cultural, civic, and labor groups, distributed songs, newspapers, and greetings on the circuit, and raised agricultural wages with well-timed harvest strikes. They also placed bets on prized roosters in cock fights, cheered Filipino boxers as paragons of ethnic masculinity, and sent hard-earned remittances to their extended families in the

Philippines.⁴⁹ These efforts created surrogate families, provided material support, and built an increasingly shared identity as Filipinas/os—whether on the migrant circuit and in cities like the luminescent Stockton, where much could be found after a harvest; camaraderie and respect in pool halls, restaurants, and sidewalks; affection in dancehalls and private rooms; sophistication in the weight of a McIntosh suit over an immaculately groomed body.

In this community formation, unions played a central role. In 1920s Hawaii, Filipinos joined Japanese strikers, and in California they went on strike in 1933, 1934, and 1939 as members of the Cannery and Agricultural Workers International Union, Filipino Labor Union, and Filipino Agricultural Labor Association, respectively.⁵⁰ In Alaska, they fought contractors, while in Seattle they built several radical union locals.⁵¹ Though repressed, these efforts produced partial victories, militancy, and a pantheon of leaders, such as Larry Itliong, Cipriano Delvo, Chris Mensalvas, and Ernesto Mangaoang.⁵² Arguably, Filipino unionism claimed the very qualities denied by a racist society. If Hawaiian growers expected pliant workers to weaken Japanese militancy, then Filipinos stood "shoulder to shoulder" with strikers.⁵³ If whites justified murderous mobs by claiming Filipinos lowered wages, then Filipino strikers aimed "to uphold and EMULATE the STANDARD OF AMERICAN WAGES" and be "the most desirable types of people ... beyond reproach."⁵⁴ If forced bachelorhood fueled emasculating discourses that racialized them as outside U.S. norms, then their union demands doubled as masculine claims to a normative American citizenship—as the citizen's right to strike and "get a man's wage and not a horse's wage."⁵⁵ As "union men," they built a Filipina/o community of resistance and self-assertion, and gained a history to leverage in future struggles.⁵⁶

Like the Mexican American residents of the Coachella Valley, migrant Filipino workers drew from a long history of social and labor contestation. During and after WWII, furthermore, their fortunes in the United States changed significantly. They suddenly appeared as wartime allies in American films and newspapers, often contrasted positively against the purportedly disloyal Japanese Americans.⁵⁷ Some found themselves in starched military uniforms, in the Philippines for the first time since their migration to the United States, sometimes as newly minted U.S. citizens. Some married Filipinas while on military tours and built late families after their return to the United States. Others found lucrative jobs in military industries and in labor-starved agriculture, or they built businesses in internment-vacated Japanese American districts. Still others "fulfilled obligations" by paying their siblings' education in the Philippines, ensuring their family's social security and completing a major reason for their initial migration.⁵⁸ After WWII, many also pointed to military service and the country's racial democracy claims to call for U.S.

citizenship and the repeal of anti-miscegenation laws. A few even accepted white dinner invitations, where hosts were "pleasantly surprised to learn that Filipinas were civilized."[59] Once hounded, they appeared to have found in postwar America a vague and hesitant acceptance—for if not entirely repentant of its vigilante days, the country could not afford its worst racial impulses during the Cold War.

But the embrace was bittersweet. Much older bodies, most no longer moved with the springy masculinity of their youth. Most toiled in insultingly substandard conditions—no water, no restrooms, no benefits—with ranchers who *still* called them "my boys." To Lorraine Agtang, a Filipino farmworker's child, these conditions demonstrated the ranchers' status as "kings of the [San Joaquin] valley, [with] their big cars . . . their big homes out in the farms, their kids going to college."[60] To the UFW leader Philip Vera Cruz, California's agricultural towns never gave up their earlier racial exclusions and denigrations: "you could always feel," he recalled in the late twentieth century, "[whites'] sense of racial superiority."[61] Even the end of anti-miscegenation laws spoke of residual marginality—for many never married and grew into older age alone in a country that never felt enough like home, moving (still) from camp to camp, pausing briefly in the cities of their youth: there, they saw old friends and tended to personal matters; there, they rented rooms and paid for companionship; there, they made a furtive bet and walked the streets of many years past.[62] Old scars are always slow to fade.

In this context, Filipino migrants began working in the postwar Coachella Valley. They arrived as highly skilled grape workers and at the behest of their San Joaquin Valley employers, who expanded their grape acreage in the newly irrigated desert.[63] For the next twenty years, 1,500 Filipino grape workers incorporated the Coachella Valley into their migrant circuit. They arrived after the Sacramento and Salinas harvests and stayed for approximately ten weeks (from May to early July) in rancher-owned camps at the edges of the Mecca township, about thirteen miles east from Coachella. Most worked in Filipino crews and under Filipino contractors as part of a Filipino circuit. Once the local "money maker" ended, most turned to Delano and the longer San Joaquin Valley table grape harvest season. For them, the Coachella Valley was a small point in a geographically expansive and historically deep landscape. Their contacts with the ethnic Mexican resident community were scarce and usually limited to Filipino contractors who hired Mexican farmworkers. And, like in other parts of California, Filipino farmworkers saw the Coachella Valley's ranchers become "millionaires" through Filipino labor and expertise: "Filipino blood," Fred Abad said many years later, "Filipinos made [ranchers] rich."[64]

Drawing from early organizing efforts, Filipino workers continued to join unions and tend the fires of discontent. In 1948, the Stockton-based Filipino American Labor Union led four thousand asparagus workers on strike for higher wages, better conditions, and instant payment for their labor.[65] Some were veterans of past strikes, while others, like Claro Runtal, traced his future UFW membership to lessons he learned in the 1948 strike: only unions offered workers the "power to demand better living conditions, and above all . . . justice."[66] Arguably, this lesson stayed with him despite the 1950s repressive climate. As Arlene de Vera argued, the anti-labor Taft–Hartley Act (1947) and attempts to deport radical Filipino leaders undercut some Filipino organizing.[67] But it did not end all efforts. Philip Vera Cruz still led the National Farmworkers Labor Union in Delano, Larry Itliong still built labor and political organizations in Stockton, and Cipriano Delvo and Chris Mensalvas still organized the Pacific Northwest.[68] And many unseen farmworkers, like Barrientos and Runtal, still remembered their family's values and their past strikes, using both to challenge ranchers through daily acts.

Some of these Filipino farmworkers began to organize under the AWOC in 1959. The latter was the AFL-CIO's attempt to capitalize on the Bracero Program's termination.[69] AWOC's national leadership relied heavily on Filipino organizers and crews. Itliong would play the most famous role, but others included Cipriano Delvo, Chris Mensalvas, Ben Gines, Pete Manuel, Pete Velasco, and Sammy Torda. Like guides on well-worn paths, they moved on the migrant circuit and spoke of their past efforts and their new possibilities. They visited Filipino camps in the valleys of Sacramento, Coachella, and San Joaquin; they secured jobs, defended wages against rancher pressure, and collected union dues; they targeted Filipino contractors, who could be pressured to ally themselves with their union; occasionally, they helped get jailed coworkers released.[70] Perhaps some felt the optimism that Delvo shared with Mensalvas in 1959: "Things are different now . . . Our mistakes taught us a lesson and this time . . . it is going to be us to designate the time, place and the kind of weapon."[71]

As in the past, Filipino AWOC leaders presented unionism as a means for eliminating agriculture's powerless subject-worker, whose vulnerability and impoverishment racialized him as outside the community of U.S. citizens. For AWOC, race equality, unionism, masculinity, and citizenship were coconstituting: as union men, they refused to return to a time when white ranchers, white police officers, and white workers did what they wished with them. Instead, as union members, they stood up collectively and laid claim to their long-denied citizen rights.

This vision appeared in AWOC organizers' activity summaries. In their retelling, unionism exemplified an ideal Filipino masculinity that fought

The Known World   59

histories of gendered racialization and social marginality. They confronted ranchers, spoke as aggressive equals, and made them yield to agreed terms. In July 1963, for instance, Gines, Torda, and Manuel visited the Coachella Valley to address a wage dispute. They had to do little, Gines wrote with satisfaction, because the rancher "learned that we were coming, so he raised the wages."[72] He knew enough, so he changed his tune to avoid AWOC. The organizers then "visited other camps, collected dues and signed members." Similarly, Salvador Benzon spoke of AWOC to a thousand men in front of pro-rancher officials before sauntering into a rancher office to say: "You know, if the wage is right and [there are] good conditions, I am your friend and I'll bring the people."[73] The recruiter appeared startled, unused to Benzon's directness and replied hurriedly: "No, no, you can't do anything for me until my manager arrives." If ranchers had ignored Filipino demands and grew their wealth through Filipino labor, or if ranchers called them "monkeys" and "boys" and paid them "highway robbery," as men like Barrientos, Abad, Runtal, and Gines said, then AWOC's ability to secure agreed-upon wages or address ranchers as equals exemplified the unions' masculine promise to recalibrate the Rancher Nation's social hierarchies.

Unionization also meant the ability to foster social parity with other U.S. laborers and gain the material markers of equal citizenship. It arguably entailed the masculine performance of demanding these rights. In early 1965, for example, Riverside County, where the Coachella Valley is found, held a public hearing on the Bracero Program's termination and its estimated exacerbation of agricultural farm labor shortages. All fourteen speakers echoed the ranchers' call for the program's resumption. Tellingly, no labor representative or farmworker leader was invited to speak. And yet, AWOC intervened. "Why," one asked, "should the farm worker be a second-class citizen" without social services or security, living in "hunger and fear?" Of all Americans, AWOC said, only farmworkers lacked union rights and job protections, a lack that it then tied to the Bracero Program's debilitating effect on agricultural unions. "We are not asking for anyone to give us something," AWOC stressed, "and we don't want anything taken away from us. We are just asking what we are entitled to have."[74]

This unionism shaped Filipino organizing in the first year without the Bracero Program. In March 1965, AWOC led a successful harvest strike in Sacramento Valley's asparagus fields. The union then pivoted to the Coachella Valley, where Sammy Torda found widespread grape worker militancy. In April meetings, he set a common wage demand (from $1.25 to $1.40) and secured pledges from Filipino crews to participate in a surprise harvest strike. They expected the surprise to grant AWOC a bargaining upper hand: "There has been no meeting between Union and employer," he said, "it is our belief that only thru work stoppage and a firm determination can the desired result be obtained."[75] Reflecting farmworker knowledge, AWOC knew ranchers would refuse to negotiate until necessary. With a well-timed strike, AWOC planned to thrust necessity on grape ranchers and gain the higher wages it would demand in later grape harvests. Here, finally, Filipino farmworkers appeared poised to strike at the Coachella Valley's grape ranchers and win what they were "entitled to have." Perhaps some felt the keen precision of Bulosan's words—"I had struck at the white world, at last; and I felt free"[76]—as Torda wrote: "There is no better time than the present. Conditions and circumstances are in our favor."[77]

Venimos a Trabajar

During the Coachella Valley's postwar agricultural expansion, the labor force grew from waves of ethnic Mexican laborers. These workers differed from each other and from Mexican American residents and Filipino American migrants. In 1962, they included 8,232 migrant farmworkers from the Imperial, San Joaquin, and Sacramento Valleys, Tejano families from the Rio Grande Valley, and Mexican immigrant families who recently settled in the Coachella Valley. Another 3,000–4,000 workers were braceros, Mexican nationals under short-term contracts who lived in military-style barracks on rancher land, and who had limited interactions with ethnic Mexican residents. Another 1,500 farmworkers were "gate hires" who crossed the border every morning and rode contractor busses for nearly two hours to reach the fields.[78] In addition to different pasts and positions, farmworkers also held different relationships to the Coachella Valley. Some intended to stay for a couple months, some a bit more; others sought to settle permanently, even if precarity undermined certainty. Some came as single men, with or without official sanction; others came as families, whether as racialized citizens or as former bracero families.

Despite their diversity, they fitted tetris-like in a rancher-led world.[79] They entered the region's social bottom of lower wages, greater underemployment, and fewer public resources. These conditions, in turn, shaped their politics and relationships to Mexican American and Filipino American campaigns: most were relatively untouched by the latter's organizing and citizen discourses. Instead, most farmworker politics turned to Mexico and the possibilities they associated with it. For some, laboring in the Coachella Valley promised upward social mobility for themselves and their families *in* Mexico; for others, their positions in Mexico served as a basis for critiquing Coachella Valley conditions, or, even, for embracing local conditions as "not the worst." For many, if not most, popular histories of the Mexican Revolution provided a significant, everyday politics without a clear outlet for organizing in the region.

We can begin with the bracero population—a quarter to a third of the labor force from 1943 to 1964—and their testimonies in the Bracero Oral History Project (BOHP).[80] Conducted in the early twenty first century, these oral histories covered bracero lives before, during, and after the program. The BOHP has nearly eight hundred oral history interviews, including sixty accounts of braceros in the Coachella Valley. Of these interviewees, most were born in the 1930s to small landowning or landless families in rural towns in Mexico's north-central highlands. Most spoke of growing up in a postrevolutionary world of instability and scarcity, of absent educational opportunities, of multiple war-related traumas, such as a parent's death, clusters of political violence, and regional displacement. Many worked in agriculture and menial labor as children to help their families cobble together the bare necessities. And in adolescence in the mid- to late 1940s, most came to the same realization: Mexico's national economy and government policies offered few options to escape their poverty, debt, or uncertainty.[81] When word came of U.S. contracts that paid multiples of Mexican wages, they and their families calculated the program's costs and benefits—and many then opted to make the trek northward.[82]

Significantly, bracero oral histories rarely spoke of contesting rancher power in the Coachella Valley.[83] Some made the occasional complaint to a supervisor and a few organized to alleviate specific concerns, such as food quality. But no one spoke about unions, strikes, or the end of the Rancher Nation. This should not be surprising. Braceros held vulnerable positions in the United States and the program's design explicitly militated against challenges. Program officials, for instance, rejected politicized workers *in* Mexico and kept worker organizers in the United States under close surveillance. In the Coachella Valley, the Coachella Valley Farmers Association's bracero barracks director, Porfi Bazua, had a reputation for "taking care [of] . . . any troublemakers," his assistant and a life-long Mexican American resident of the Coachella Valley, Louise Neely, recalled. If braceros "cause[d] any trouble," she added, "they'd be sent back." When asked how quickly, she said, "Oh, right away! They would be kept for a day or two, but they'd get a bus where they would be sent back."[84]

The braceros' labor discipline also reflected the relationship they had to the region via the Bracero Program, for their short contracts aimed for transformed lives in Mexico. A contract could mean a debt paid, land acquired, extra income offered to aging parents, an education for younger siblings. It could mean social rehabilitation, escape from racialized marginality, or the fulfillment of patriarchal prerogatives as the male breadwinner. To engage in this project of social transformation via the Bracero Program, entire Mexican families adopted a sacrificing stance, especially bracero spouses: they labored in family harvests and state-mandated programs, dealt with the public glare as bracero families, and borrowed money to pay for the administrative costs associated with the Bracero Program. And because one contract was not enough to reach their aspirations, many bracero families engaged in disciplined labor to secure future contracts.[85] Braceros thus existed in a web of people and choices across two countries in search of social gains *in* Mexico. Recognizing the sacrifices and labors undertaken by their families, Coachella Valley braceros uttered the same refrain: *venimos a trabajar*.[86]

In tandem with the Bracero Program, the Coachella Valley saw a wave of undocumented immigration—usually young, single men who crossed the border without authorization after failing to secure a bracero contract. This dynamic was typical for the country in the late 1940s and the early 1950s, when undocumented immigration ranged from half to one million a year.[87] In Margaret MacKaye's study on Southern California's Bracero Program, Coachella Valley ranchers repeatedly said they preferred undocumented laborers over braceros and proudly practiced "widespread disobedience of immigration laws." When asked why, one rancher told MacKaye: "Why bind yourself to the regulations of the Farmers Association when you could hire a better man at your door and pay him what you pleased?"[88] "Wets," another said, "worked better" than "lazy" braceros—who "knew they were protected by their contracts and complain[ed] to the Farmers Association if they didn't like their treatment." When Border Patrol officials attempted to tighten immigration-labor regulations in the mid-1950s, Coachella Valley ranchers merely participated in the descriptively named ritual, "drying out the wetbacks," which involved "hauling their prize Mexican laborers down to the border in station wagons or trucks, get them 'legalized' and bring them triumphantly back."[89]

Limited archives make it difficult to determine undocumented immigrants' relationship to the Coachella Valley, their perception of local dynamics, or their everyday acts of contestation. Most likely shared in bracero desires for life-changing employment and for migration's implied adventures, much like young Filipino men in the 1920s and 1930s. But undocumented immigrants also faced greater threats from local ranchers and immigration officials. Immigrants could not, as the rancher answers above implied, be "lazy," "make complaints," or rely on a "contract." Even when MacKaye noted the Coachella Valley consensus that local ranchers took care of their undocumented immigrants, she admitted that some did not "play square" and used immigrants' status to steal wages and re-enforce their authority.[90] Increased deportations in the late 1940s and early 1950s exemplified this social vulnerability. During the 1954 "Operation Wetback," white residents reported seeing "several hundred wetbacks being herded on a train for the border . . . several times during the week," all "shuffling" in chains. One can imagine that with eyes on Mexico amidst rancher greed and state removal, these young immigrant men focused on gaining wages from desert harvests before their homebound journeys.

Significantly, and despite exceptions, braceros and undocumented immigrants reported strained relationships with local Mexican Americans, who routinely called them "wetbacks" and "alambristas." The latter terms referred to the metal fence "wires" that immigrants presumably jumped over to cross the U.S.–Mexico border. Similarly, if braceros and immigrants spoke of any discrimination it usually stemmed from Mexican Americans. Bar fights and muggings, again, had the local population playing in the aggressor role.[91]

In contrast to these farmworkers, the region also received entire families in the 1950s—a flow which continued in the 1960s and 1970s. Exact numbers are elusive, too, but oral histories considered the migration significant to the region's demographics and noticeable to residents. Most visible were Tejano families from the border-adjacent Rio Grande Valley, a racialized agricultural land with a long history of violent repression. These newcomers reportedly came as migrant farmworkers displaced by white Texan ranchers' turn to cheaper and more malleable labor—thus fleeing the state in what one historian has called a Tejano diaspora.[92] Those who arrived in the Coachella Valley usually had little more than what they could pack in a car and a determined ambition to find better ground. The other newcomers were Mexican immigrant families. Most had former bracero husbands who gained permanent residency for themselves and their families through their agricultural employers. The rest came from northern Mexico, as part of the never-ending borderlands trickle across a fictional line. Like braceros, these families had worked in Mexican agriculture and usually on land gained through the Mexican Revolution. But few had previously experienced the frenetic migrant labor spanning vast landscapes, as was characteristic of U.S. agribusiness.

As with other migrants, Tejano and Mexican newcomers came to the Coachella Valley for higher wages and consistent employment. In Texas, agricultural wages were half what could be found in California; in Mexico, the wage differential was even greater. Israel Huerta's family, for instance, heard from other Tejano families that California offered a bounty of jobs paying $1 an hour—a marked contrast from their poor and segregated town of McAllen, Texas, and its cotton and vegetable fields that never moved beyond the fifty-cent mark. In 1963, when Huerta was fourteen years old, his family trekked westward in search of "a land of gold," "milk and honey." They soon realized their naïveté, but for a family who had worked for two cents per cotton pound, the Coachella Valley still offered many harvests and higher wages, where the promise of getting ahead through hard work stood as self-evident.[93] Similarly, Mexican families considered the higher wages abundant reason for making a permanent move to the United States and, like previous generations, for moving swiftly into the Southwest's agricultural labor market.

And yet, in most aspects of life, the Coachella Valley remained a place of difficulties and insecurities. Local Mexican Americans had already taken the most lucrative jobs, which meant newcomers earned less money and had less consistent employment. In the summer, most migrated to harvests in Central and Northern California and returned in early October—much later than the school year's start. In 1962, AWOC organizers also discovered that "unorganized locals" received lower wages than Filipino grape workers ($1 versus $1.10), while being charged more for camp housing ($2.10 a day versus $1.75).[94] Those in Indio's Farm Labor Camp lived in literal shacks of corrugated tin; they burned in the summer and froze in the winter in a space that could only fit a couple of twin beds and a small burner.[95] Those less lucky had less. When Amalia Uribe Deaztlan's family of eight settled in Oasis in 1960, they rented a near-abandoned house with window-less frames.[96] Similarly, when Huerta's family arrived in 1963, they found neither housing nor jobs, and spent shelterless nights in the desert—a reality other families faced, if the local news articles on homeless families and overcrowded homes are any indication.[97]

The region's racial inequality, in other words, was accentuated for these families. Police officers harassed their adolescent children and schools subjected them to abusive teachers.[98] Given their recent arrival, Mexican children struggled more with English-only classrooms, while some ended in "Trainable Retarded Education" classes.[99] These families' ground position in the economy, and the related need to migrate to multiple harvests, meant their children enrolled in schools late in the year and nixed potential for a school-based escape from farmworker poverty.[100] Lastly, oral histories shared that newcomer families, especially Tejanos, faced everyday hostility from local Mexican Americans. Some locals even identified Tejanos through their poverty and dislocation, and referred to them as "Tejanitos," a diminutive, paternalistic term. Others said Tejanos "had a chip on their shoulder"—a surprising assessment—and thus did not know how to *behave* in a region without South Texas's racial inequality and violence. In turn, Tejanos portrayed locals as whitewashed and/or as socially conceited (uppity, one said).[101]

Given this reality, newcomer families remained outside the region's citizen-based contestations for power. To conservative Mexican Americans, they represented charity projects or wayward populations in need of disciplining—especially their delinquent-described youth, who, they implied, refused the rigors of education-based social mobility.[102] Similarly, the VL's electoral efforts and MAPA's drive against hiring discrimination were peripheral to newcomer lives or outside their political capacity. Most, for instance, were not Coachella Valley residents or U.S. citizens and thus did not join in the VL's insurgent candidacies or MAPA's election campaigns. MAPA also saw farmworker families as objects for liberation and alternated between sympathy and derision, which hardly invited coequal participation. Lastly, the Filipino-led AWOC made only minimal efforts to reach local Mexican farmworkers, usually under pressure from Filipino members who complained about Mexican underbidding. To organizer surprise, even minimal efforts elicited considerable pro-union enthusiasm among Mexican families, but the language barriers remained and impeded organizers' ability to expand AWOC. Subsequent requests for Spanish-speaking organizers went unfulfilled and the initial meetings in 1962 and 1963 had no follow-ups. Instead, each year AWOC simply migrated out of the desert once the grape harvest ended, following Filipino members to other harvests across California's agricultural landscape.[103]

Lastly, many newcomers existed as if in suspended flux. Amalia Uribe Deaztlan's father, for instance, imagined earning enough money to return to his Mexican *ejido* with a new tractor, achieving a long-awaited upward social mobility. In contrast, Israel Huerta's family moved to Delano a couple years after arriving in Indio—where they hoped for better opportunities but only found more of the same. Other families split in two, even if temporarily: Manuel Arredondo and his brothers, for instance, returned to Texas to finish their education, while their family remained in Coachella. These families lived a precarious present—amidst a difficult even if occasionally promising labor market and along the peripheries of organizing efforts. For them, agency appeared in a near-obvious form: work to find a break.

This does not mean that Mexican farmworkers remained apolitical, as if merely pecking away at meager offerings. Though distinct from Mexican Americans and Filipino Americans, Mexican and Tejano families carried vibrant justice stories—stories that may not have had the focus of the citizens but could nonetheless offer breezes to a suffocating summer.

Amalia Uribe Deaztlan's mother, Amalia Becerra, was emblematic. An indigenous Purepecha woman from Michoacán, Becerra gained an ejido through President Cardenas' land reform program. She referred to herself as an "ejidataria," as a woman who fought wealthy landowners and now owned her land. She was also the family "rebel" who taught her children about the Mexican Revolution and "defended and supported poor people."[104] When the family migrated to the border city of Mexicali, Baja California in the 1950s, she made her home into a base for relatives and hometown residents planning to cross into the United States.[105] Similarly, when the family settled in the Coachella Valley in 1960, her rebellious spirit guided her relations with neighbors—usually by finding ways to aid families in need. By 1964, her college-attending sons had transformed Becerra's class-conscious and service-oriented politics into a militant Chicano identity, which inspired their involvement in civil rights campaigns on campus. By 1965, Deaztlan said, her brothers regularly spoke to the Mexican students in Coachella Valley "High School, [about] organizing, and being proud of our history,"[106] lessons for a racially just future in the United States, one that strained against her father's wishes to return to their Mexican ejido. "I would be thinking," Deaztlan said of her younger and increasingly politicized self, "what will I do with that ejido and tractor?"[107]

There was also Pablo Carrizales from Tamaulipas, Nuevo Leon. In the early 1940s, he married Guadalupe when both were teenagers. By the time they met, Guadalupe Carrizales recalled, he had gained a political philosophy from a local doctor, who spoke about the Mexican Revolution and took him to political gatherings.[108] "With that doctor," she said, "[Pablo] taught himself many things about politics . . . about what was happening [in Mexico]."[109] This teaching fueled Carrizales's gendered militancy, in which masculinity and radicality represented two sides of the same coin. For him, the biggest compliment was being compared with Mexico's male revolutionaries, those who demonstrated their manhood through social justice. After a decade as a bracero in Texas, where poor conditions led to losing four molars in one day, his family joined him in the United States, and together in the early 1960s they migrated to California, where they had relatives in the Central Valley farming town of Merced. They drove, Guadalupe Carrizales said, a dilapidated car across white supremacist towns. They had no money, their children grew sick, and then their car broke down in Coachella. Luckily, they met a family who knew another family who lived in Indio's Farm Labor Camp. The latter hosted them until they secured their own corrugated unit in 1964—by which time they worked in the nearby fields.

Politics could also point inward, toward the hierarchies structuring farmworker families. Maria Marron, for instance, spoke of forced migration from her native Guadalajara, where she was a teacher in a private Catholic elementary serving underprivileged girls. Her father had been a bracero in the Coachella Valley for most of her life, though he sent little money home. As a result, Marron and her mother created a woman-led world that, in turn, built her sense of accomplishment and autonomy. In 1963, however, Marron's father compelled the entire family to migrate to Coachella, where they promptly joined the labor force. To Marron, the desert was a far cry from Israel's "milk and honey." It was ugly, she said, hot and dry and ugly. She also discovered the patriarchal practice of familial wage theft. She labored for hours in endless fields under a searing sun, she said, all so her father could take her wages and spend them as he saw fit, while white ranchers showcased their profits.

Angry with him—for ending her autonomous life, for his submissiveness to bosses—she engaged in daily acts of rebellion against his authority.[110] She even married to escape her home, she said, but only found another patriarchal man in her young husband. Feeling like she had lost everything since leaving Mexico, Marron searched for something that made her feel "util"—useful, purposeful, meaningful.

Like Deaztlan and Carrizales, Marron's story reflected the region's daily struggles and resistance stories. These families and farmworkers remained largely removed from the rising campaigns of Mexican American residents and Filipino American unionists, but they would eventually foster a farmworker movement in the late 1960s and, for a brief a moment, help dethrone the Coachella Valley's rancher-kings.

Conclusion: AWOC's Coachella Grape Strike in 1965

To live in the Rancher Nation without a crown meant living in a world defined by its very diversity—one of different histories, experiences, and politics. For local Mexican Americans, their history and postwar social mobility led to a citizen-based politics that critiqued their marginality in the Coachella Valley. For Filipino Americans, labor organizing was a means for improving their three-month work stay in the desert and, in related fashion, for claiming the U.S. citizenship's material conditions. Lastly, ethnic Mexican farmworkers juggled daily survival and political invisibility with stories and actions that upheld their claims to dignity and potential. To be part of the desert's non-rancher class was to be part of a social singularity only in abstraction; experiences told of fragments and fissures—even when moving in shared spaces, like a small desert valley of fields and towns.

Such difference cannot be understood as simple cultural dissimilarity or chauvinism, nor reduced to singular social fault lines, such as Mexican–Filipino, citizen–foreigner, or local–migrant. Instead, differences originated in their combination and produced more than distrust amidst the jockeying for coveted social crumbs. Instead, these communities largely did not *know* each other. How, for instance, could braceros understand Filipino lives? How could Coachella Valley locals *not* misrecognize Texan migrants given their experiential gulf? Or how exactly could someone like Ben Gines understand the life and politics of someone like Maria Marron? Could they all find common ground without the common spaces that facilitated a multifaceted exchange? Thus, the qualities of the Rancher Nation insurgents: from radically different origins and with different positions in the local political economy; without a common political language to translate life differences, and with almost no public spaces for inventing it. In the Coachella Valley, in short, class and race were experienced through fissures—fissures that militated against self-recognition and made common fronts against the Rancher Nation unlikely and rare.

But, of course, possibilities always remain. In 1964, such a possibility materialized when the Bracero Program was terminated. For the first time in two decades, California ranchers faced a potential labor shortage. Filipino AWOC organizers knew as much and led a successful harvest strike in Stockton asparagus in early 1965. Two months later, they led a ten-day strike against Coachella Valley grape fields and demanded a fifteen-cent wage raise. The pro-rancher, local newspapers, *Coachella Valley Sun*, presented the AWOC strikers as impulsive and violent, and attributed the stoppage to farmworkers' misunderstanding of the Labor Secretary's push for higher *date* farmworker wages as "a mandatory minimum wage for all agriculture." When grape farmworkers learned otherwise, the newspaper continued, they struck the largest grape rancher and unleashed a torrent of violence, including attacks on workers and the burning of a car. To further delegitimize the Coachella Grape Strike of 1965, the *Coachella Valley Sun* used square quotes to refer to the strike, as if its reality were in doubt. The accusation of misunderstanding, moreover, denied Filipinos' long history of agitation for citizenship-based rights and placed them outside the community. At the end, the newspaper credited grape ranchers for the ensuing peace after ranchers, on their own accord, they said, raised wages to avert greater violence. It did not consider the possibility that AWOC organizers had predicted this very result.[111]

To the labor leader Vera Cruz, the Coachella grape strikers were neither "angels nor devils." They went on strike out of conviction, responded to rancher violence with self-protection and "believed they were fighting for their right to live and to have an opportunity for betterment. It was as simple as that."[112] This belief spoke of Filipinos' shared context of older age, farmworker poverty, and a history of deferred dreams. And it spoke, in its success, of the organizers' ability to make demands on the world and live in "betterment," one rooted in past struggles and one harkening to new vistas—vistas of how "things are different now." Once the Coachella Valley grape ranchers agreed to higher wages, AWOC members celebrated their victory and then worked the grape harvest. They did not demand union recognition but they planned strikes in Central California's grape harvests—plans in which AWOC leaders and rank-and-file members engaged each other to consider long-shot odds against powerful ranchers, as if holding a somber conversation on how to live their last years of life. From Coachella, they migrated to Arvin-Lamont and then Delano, where Larry Itliong had organized an AWOC strike meeting in late August 1965.[113]

Filipino AWOC strikers had achieved a remarkable feat against the Coachella Valley's Rancher Nation, but it did not have a major impact on ethnic

Mexican farmworkers or on local Mexican American organizations. I have placed this strike in the conclusion for this very reason—to suggest its ambiguous value in the moment of its articulation, especially among the Coachella Valley's peasant class, and to note that AWOC's local insurgency could very well have ended here. The AWOC Coachella Grape Strike in 1965, in short, represented an enlivening breeze against the Rancher Nation's furious heat. But it did not suggest a natural, inevitable turn of the season.

PART II

To Make the World Anew

Chapter 3

A Flash Flood in Red

On the Farmworkers' Many Movements, 1965–1970

During the Coachella Valley's monsoon season, flash floods appear suddenly and unexpectedly after many false alarms. On some days, for instance, grey clouds may collect above the desert floor only to dissipate into warmth and bright humidity; on others, they may give soft rain before returning to a quiet suspension. Then, there are days of gray skies the color of milky lead; days of slow swirling against faded purple mountains and illuminated browns: darker for soil, lighter for green-speckled brush, near white for sand dunes. On such days, rain may fall abundantly and accumulate suddenly, and then, again, stop—as if both impulsive and bored. But on days of a flash flood, thick concrete clouds crackle with the visceral intimacy of a torn sky. For those walking or driving, or eyeing the swirling gray with interest and trepidation, the downpour is enveloping. It pours on and pours through. It clatters rooftops and moistens walls with color, rippling gutters and dusty streets. With each flash of thunder, the water falls with greater weight, heralding the flood's arrival after the fact. In a handful of hours, it can tear away at the built ground—damaging homes, drowning ranches, threatening lives—and wash away a past to expose an uncertain future.

Perhaps for this reason, early pioneers saw flash floods as characteristic of the frontier's dangers and took pains to document the Coachella Valley's ecological history. Their later infrastructure-based "taming" further illustrated the white settlers' racialized modernity: once, their pioneer stories said, aridity and floods alternated in a lawless wasteland; now, white men managed both.

The last four years of the 1960s can be understood as culminating in a flash flood, a political storm that surprised the Rancher Nation and threatened to wash it away. It began with Mexican Americans' fight against social and political inequality and grew amidst an already-brewing national storm: from national civil rights and Chicana/o agitation to anti-Vietnam War protests and a popular-political culture that stressed the calm *after* the storm. Delano's ragtag army of Filipino and Mexican grape strikers reinforced the whirlwind. But like so many past turbulent skies that evaporated into summer's drunken heat, these clouds threatened but did not burst until 1968 and 1969. In these years, the United Farm Workers (UFW) led two multiracial grape strikes and a devastating National Consumer Grape Boycott. For Chicanas/os and Mexican farmworkers, the UFW strikes served as political synergy; it drew rebellious currents, provided a common-enough rebel discourse, and looped the strike's energy into other race-justice campaigns. Grape ranchers and their allies, in turn, appeared overwhelmed by a storm they did not expect or even considered possible. Quite suddenly, in fact, it forced grape ranchers into UFW contracts (1970), precipitated a domino effect throughout agricultural California, and signaled a new era for the Coachella Valley.

Most celebratory UFW histories end in this moment and imply a contract augured a new world. But, as with all flash floods, this political storm did not end the Rancher Nation. It could only weaken it and, at most, provide grist for future struggles. These struggles would be heavily shaped by the ranchers' near-irrational hostility toward the UFW, as well as by the farmworkers' unresolved fissures, Filipinos' mounting suspicions of a Mexican-dominated union, and a fast-changing political climate in California and the United States.

A Gathering of Rainmakers, Part I

In late August 1965, Larry Itliong led two Agricultural Workers Organizing Committee (AWOC) meetings in Delano's Filipino Hall to discuss the upcoming grape harvest in the San Joaquin Valley. Accounts of the meetings speak of kinetic energy, of "standing room only," of Ilocano, Visayan, and Tagalog voices merging into a cacophony of defiance. Many of those in attendance had gone on strike in the Coachella Valley grape fields. Now, three months later, AWOC called for better working conditions and Coachella's higher wages. Itliong began the first meeting by speaking "about the low wages, bad housing facilities, lack of protection from labor law, [and] antiquated working conditions."[1] Others reiterated the lack of protections "workers have taken for granted for a long, long time." Some pointed at their bodies, aged with labor, and at the ranchers who "become what they are today because of us," "richer while we still remain poor and wanting." They warned against retiring in "shameful" dependency and spoke of missed chances: "If we had a union contract with the [ranchers] when we were still young, we could also be enjoying what other workers have. But since we failed to do so, we need to work even though our bones and bodies are aching."[2] Finally, Felicing Ytom expressed what the majority felt: they would strike Delano's table grapes if ranchers did not agree to the Coachella Valley's wages, giving ranchers a week to respond to their written demand.

When the next meeting arrived, few could have been surprised by the news: the ranchers returned AWOC's letters unopened. Thirty grape workers immediately lined up at the microphone to speak. The crew-leader Jimmy Aimes called for a harvest strike like in the Coachella Valley. Another crew-leader, Bob Armington, stressed the rancher's implicit insult: "when they ignore our written demands it only means they do not respect or care about us." "They call us 'boys,'" said another, "we should teach them a lesson." George Catalan followed—"it is time we stand up for our demands"—as did more, speaking of their "frustrat[ion] [with] the treatment and attitude of the [ranchers]." To the skeptics, Johnny Pader reassured by recounting the Coachella Valley strike and promising a quick Delano resolution: grape ranchers "learned their lessons" and "will not want to lose money here, too."[3] When Fred Abad called for a strike vote, "everyone in the hall stood up with their hands in the air," cheering the start date of September 8, 1965.

On that date, one thousand Filipinos at ten labor camps refused to board the busses that took them to work.[4] "The bosses figured," Itliong reflected two years later, "Let them stay. In five days, these guys will be hungry and begging to go back to work. Well they were wrong." Delano ranchers visited camps to threaten strikers when they did not return. "They came to the camp," recalled Nick Yap, "and told us, 'if you don't go back to work tomorrow, we'll cut off the electricity.'" By 1965, the sixty-plus Yap counted thirty years in labor organizing, including the Industrial Workers of the World (IWW) and the Filipino Agricultural Labor Association's (FALA) 1937 asparagus strike. Yap settled permanently in Delano after World War II, when "most [ranchers] had small ranches, only forty to fifty acres." In two decades, he saw ranchers gain "thousands of acres" and heard their talk of financial difficulties. "If they are so broke," he asked, "how can they be constantly buying more land?"[5] So, when his employer threatened to cut the power to their camp, Yap returned to his defiant past and "went downtown and bought some candles." "We have used that kind of light for years," he said, "It won't hurt us again."

To AWOC's Filipino strikers, the Delano Grape Strike of 1965 was an opportunity to speak back to ranchers and envision a better world. Willie Barrientos, for instance, said his employer asked him, "Willie . . . you've been working for me for ten years. But now you are [one of] the leaders against me? What's wrong?" Perhaps Barrientos thought of his mother's lesson to fight injustice, or his anti-imperialist grandfather's admonitions to fight for Filipino independence, or perhaps of early Hawaiian farmworker strikes and a subsequent life of struggle, when he retorted, "You don't know? I am going to tell you. *Me*, I build you up from your head to your feet, with all my pals, with all my brothers here. Where are you today without my brothers here? Now, I want *my* share. We want *our* share to live as a human being, so we can also send our children to school and be educated like your children."[6] When the rancher mistakenly sensed fear, Barrientos corrected him: "I look him in

[the] eye, 'No, I'm not scared of you. I build you up, and you think I don't know it, huh? My brothers are here. That's why we had the strike this day . . . because we want a higher wage, and better conditions. Because we have been exploited for centuries and centuries."[7] Like his brothers, Barrientos had known decades of poverty and loss amidst bounty, and he welcomed the Delano Grape Strike like an existential arrival that tended past traumas. "Here is the time," he said, "I have been waiting for this time."

When Delano grape ranchers began to evict Filipino strikers from camps and replace them with Mexican farmworkers, AWOC convinced the Mexican-led National Farm Workers Association (NFWA) to declare a solidarity strike. The NFWA was founded in 1962 by Cesar Chavez, Dolores Huerta, and Gilbert Padilla, all Mexican Americans who previously organized the civil rights group, the Community Service Organization (CSO). From 1962 to 1965, the three built a base of ethnic Mexican farmworker families whose politics drew from the Mexican Revolution and southwestern strikes. For some, like Esther Uranday, the NFWA offered key resources for her family, such as death insurance. Born in nearby Earlimart, Uranday spent her young life in fields and migrant housing with a family of fourteen siblings, two parents, and several extended relatives. She married young and had three children on the migrant circuit, the last one sickly and without medical care. At eleven months, Uranday said, her son was "really sick . . . so we took him to the hospital and on the way to the hospital, in between Earlimart and Delano, I felt like he was going . . . [that he] gave his last breath and passed away. I was blowing in his mouth and he passed away in my arms. He was eight months old . . . I was nineteen, nineteen years."[8] Uranday and her husband, both young, spent days and nights after their baby boy's death collecting money from their poor farmworker neighbors to pay for the funeral. "I vowed [to] never again . . . go through something like that," she said, so she joined the NFWA.

From September to November 1965, approximately two thousand grape workers like Uranday, Barrientos, and Yap picketed their employers' fields. Many spent days roaming the San Joaquin Valley's country roads, speaking to farmworkers and disrupting ranch operations. They demanded higher wages, union recognition, and a labor contract, all improvements on AWOC's Coachella Valley demands. Both AWOC and NFWA found allies in California's labor, civic, student, and religious groups, most of them based in coastal cities. When Delano's grape harvest ended in November 1965, the strikers turned to these allies to bring their demands to the U.S. public. The campaign would last five years.[9] In popular accounts today, and in some academic histories, the two groups appear as insurgent and intrepid in these years, as leading an unlikely and yet inevitably triumphant social movement. These years also serve as a narrative shorthand for everyday people's power to affect their world for the better, one that shares in the era's civil rights political optimism.[10] But several qualities need to be stressed to understand the UFW movement, especially to appreciate its reception in the Coachella Valley in the late 1960s.

First, the 1965 Delano Grape Strike lasted longer than participants expected and demanded sacrifices that most felt they could not offer. Even before Delano's harvest ended in 1965, many grape strikers wanted to return to their fields to earn the harvest's lucrative wages.[11] When AWOC and NFWA leaders rebuffed them, many strikers became newly minted strike breakers—a dynamic that grew with each year. As early as spring 1966, the NFWA leader Cesar Chavez recalled, most strike participants were non-farmworker students who answered their call for aid.[12] Workers' wish to return to the fields reflected agriculture's social qualities, such as rural isolation, rancher resources, absent worker savings, and the lack of labor protections. "Who," the Filipino striker, Rudy Reyes, asked, "wants to hear about the 'Great Farmworkers' Struggle,' when your wife and kids are asking for money?"[13] The NFWA and AWOC responded to the strike's challenging demands with social movement tactics that infused the strike with a sacrifice ethos.[14] In a 1967 profile of Luming Imutan, for instance, *El Malcriado* listed her lost possessions, for no one had "bills paid, or [received] the $5 a week that we get now," and told of how they "ate at Filipino Hall" because striker families could not buy groceries, "except once a month when we sometimes got a donation." She also took "the insults that people give you . . . who called us a 'disgrace' to the public."[15] Nonetheless, Imutan picketed for the "good . . . of all farmworkers" and chose to bear sacrifices for early contract victories.[16]

Second, while Filipino and Mexican strikers spoke of and practiced interracial solidarity—most emblematically in shared Filipino Hall meals—tensions remained. In 1965, for instance, NFWA leaders refused to follow white AWOC leaders, while AWOC leaders refused to share AFL-CIO funds with the NFWA. Filipino and Mexican farmworkers' segregated lives in the San Joaquin Valley had made them strangers to each other and susceptible to rancher-propagated stereotypes.[17] From the strike's start, furthermore, many Filipino strikers suspected a Mexican majority in a union or labor market meant a future of Filipino disempowerment.[18] When the two organizations merged in August 1966 into the United Farm Workers Organizing Committee (UFWOC), these concerns led to Filipino labor leader defections, including AWOC organizers Ben Gines and Pete Manuel.[19] According to Philip Vera Cruz and Andy Imutan, these organizers spread misinformation among Filipino workers, which led to further Filipino rank-and-file alienation in the merged union.[20] This topic, I should note, is understudied. There are likely many ways to understand Filipino concerns about being a "minority within

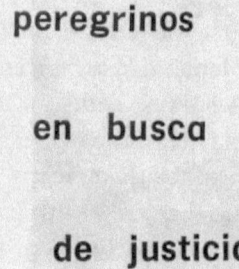

peregrinos en busca de justicia

NFWA and AWOC members participating in the NFWA's 1966 Pilgrimage to Sacramento. Translation: "Pilgrims in Search of Justice." *El Malcriado*, April 10, 1966, 8–9. Walter P. Reuther Library, Archives of Labor and Urban Affairs, Wayne State University.

a minority union."[21] What is clear now is that these concerns remained in 1966–67 and were likely exacerbated by white coverage of the Delano Grape Strike. As Philip Vera Cruz noted in 1972, "seldom a writer took notice of the Filipino farmworkers and their union activities."[22]

Third, Filipino and Mexican strikers blamed new immigrants for undermining their strike.[23] In October 1966, Texas strikers associated with the UFW picketed Immigration and Naturalization offices with signs that read "Join our union or stay in Mexico" and "Stop Mexican Nationals from breaking our strike." The union's editorial noted, "grape strikers in Delano have the same problem."[24] A year later, Vera Cruz's union meeting notes summarized similar worries among Delano strikers: how does a movement continue, he asked, when flooded with "wetbacks, green cards, out-of-state workers?"[25] In most cases of these critical references to immigrants, the pro-union concerns came with an interracial veneer: the UFW movement, increasingly identified as an ethnic Mexican union in national newspapers, insisted on presenting itself as a multiracial coalition of U.S. citizens fighting racist white ranchers, who relied on undocumented immigrants to uphold an undemocratic rural society. The UFW's newspaper, *El Malcriado*, made this direct argument in a serial cartoon that ran from December 1966 to August 1967, in which three Mexican immigrants unwittingly broke a fictional 1967 Filipino grape strike in the Coachella Valley.[26] Even if three immigrant characters had known of the Filipino grape strike, the cartoon implied their vulnerable positions, aspirations for lives in Mexico, and alienating migrant experiences made solidarity impossible. In its somber final frames, the cartoon showed white ranchers expelling Filipino strikers while Mexican immigrants labored in a militarized field bordered by date palms, where "nobody has yet heard of . . . Delano."[27]

By early 1968, in short, the UFW in Delano reflected the qualities stressed in this book. As a social movement and union, it asked rank-and-file farmworkers to make choices about their lives and potential futures, choices laced with morality amidst grape ranchers' overwhelming power. In these choices, tensions, fissures, and differences swirled with syncretism and coalitions—producing a shifting field of stories that occasionally threatened the San Joaquin Valley's Rancher Nation. The early UFW movement, however, remained ambivalent—not ascendant but alive—an unprecedented potential without a clear and realistic trajectory.

A Gathering of Rainmakers, Part II

Another social storm brewed in the Coachella Valley. Unlike Delano, it found expression in spaces outside the fields: in local elections, protests against racial discrimination, and calls for equal citizenship. The storm's distinct streams—the Voters League (VL), the Mexican American Political Association (MAPA), the UFW—moved near, and occasionally riffed off, each other, providing potential for attacking the Rancher Nation. But, as before, potential mixed with uncertainty, agency with contingency, as multiple actors and circumstances interacted simultaneously, ambiguously.

In early 1966, for example, the VL-led campaigns for city and county elections in April and June, respectively. Resident grievances again centered on police abuse, insufficient infrastructural funding, and the city's dismissal of key community projects, like affordable farmworker housing.[28] Unlike earlier years, the VL purportedly "went underground" and held secret meetings where it endorsed two Mexican American candidates, Nabor Rodriguez and Roger Perez. If victorious, they would be the city's first ethnic Mexican leaders without ties to ranchers.[29] The candidates spoke of developing the city with "fresh ideas" and of their neighbors' encouragement to serve their community.[30] Still, white residents reacted by calling the VL an undemocratic threat: "Is the candidate a 'tool,'" asked a *Coachella Valley Sun* columnist, "for some specific group or special interest? Unless a candidate has convinced you he'll work for the ENTIRE community and EVERYONE in it, watch out!"[31]

Despite the warning, the VL candidates won by big margins and augured a new era of Mexican American leadership. The VL then invited county supervisor candidates to vie for its endorsement. Having won Coachella's first Mexican American council seats, the VL now seemed poised to shape county policies in the Coachella Valley's eastern towns, where ethnic Mexican farmworker families lived and where Riverside County held jurisdiction. Through both campaigns, Mexican American leaders were suddenly ascendant and targeting their political marginalization in the Rancher Nation. Local newspapers responded by accusing the VL of "selling out" democracy that turned elections into a bidding game, wondering about Mexican Americans' political maturity: "If this is the caliber [of] men our own Valley Americans of Mexican descent have for political leader," wrote a *Coachella Valley Sun* columnist, "then they're in bad trouble."[32] The VL rejected the racialized charges of political illegitimacy and immaturity, and framed their victories in relations to the Coachella Valley's hierarchy: the VL aimed to "raise [their] people 'above their second-class status,'" its president Uvaldo Palomares declared, "and mold them into an 'effective political force by democratic means.'"[33]

Concurrently, the local MAPA chapter endorsed candidates for Coachella and Indio, picketed the Post Office for discrimination, and distributed college scholarships to Mexican American students. It also endorsed the fledging Delano Grape Strike before anyone else and led local pro-striker actions, like picketing Frank Sinatra's Palm Springs house, where the state's governor fled in April 1966 to avoid the NFWA's Pilgrimage to Sacramento.[34] In

May 1966, it organized a fundraiser for Delano that drew 350 people,³⁵ while the radio owner and MAPA member, James Caswell, promoted the strike and interviewed Gilbert Padilla. Most dramatically, MAPA confronted the *Coachella Valley Sun* for, as they alleged, ignoring farmworker conditions and misrepresenting Delano strikers. The confrontation resulted in an unusually hostile and public altercation, which the outraged editors compared to "something that might have come from the Berkeley campus, or from some Communist group—but certainly nothing like this would happen in... the *Coachella Valley Sun*."³⁶ While the Rancher Nation had attempted to relegate Filipino AWOC strikers to the community's civic margins in 1965, it now appeared to struggle with MAPA's unprecedented attack.

And yet, much like a swirling grey sky without thunder, the desert's political storm dissipated repeatedly. In 1966, the *Coachella Valley Sun* celebrated the desert's grape harvest and made few references to Delano strikers.³⁷ Rancher allies claimed MAPA's May fundraiser was poorly attended and failed "to show Chavez how much he was appreciated by the local citizenry." "The great majority of good, clean, hard-working people in Coachella Valley," they insisted, "are going to think for themselves and not be taken in or pressured by a lot of hot air from outsiders and a few local kooks."³⁸ Other efforts also budded little rebel fruit. The VL won two Coachella city council seats in 1966 but only held a minority vote. Their county candidate lost the June election and then the VL underwent a takeover by "responsible" conservative leaders in October 1966. A month later, Ronald Reagan won California's gubernatorial race in a campaign explicitly opposing Delano strikers. In early 1967, local elites celebrated the lack of unrest then sweeping the rest of the country, and in December 1967, the *Coachella Valley Sun* recapped the year's fortunes—a growing economy, minimal protests, "delinquents" fined—to forecast a bountiful 1968: "If we were to make a prediction based on what we are fairly certain is coming this way next year, we'd have to say it should be the most exciting year we've seen in the valley yet."³⁹ Even Chavez was far away thunder, fading after a September hurricane literally flooded a UFW-aligned strike in South Texas.⁴⁰ By then, the former gray clouds spelling potential appeared to lose much of their menace.

Still rebel undercurrents remained. The conservative VL spent 1967 advocating for Mexican American teachers, participating in school boards, and preparing candidates for 1968 elections. In February, Mexican Americans protested unequal infrastructural funds again and won a city commitment to disburse more money by September.⁴¹ In March 1967, Coachella approved low-income housing in an about-face from 1966.⁴² MAPA organized families to participate in elections for the Community Action Committee, which would play a role in distributing "war on poverty" funds.⁴³ The *Coachella*

Valley Sun even complained that formerly uninvolved residents casted votes for a MAPA majority. In oral history interviews, MAPA leaders explained they paired their anti-poverty drive with a push for education reform. They approached local leaders to "tell them, 'You have problems.'"[44] When leaders ignored them, insisting "our children are fine. They're getting a good education," MAPA turned to mentoring students.[45] Of the MAPA's Jim Caswell, the young Henry Perez said: "All I know is that he affected my future. He was the one that motivated me to go to college. He was the one who made me go to law school."[46]

These developments also existed amidst less visible undercurrents. Oral histories speak of everyday solidarity actions among ethnic Mexican residents. Amalia Uribe Deaztlan's mother still spoke of "defending the poor," and Guadalupe Carrizales remembered the aid her family received from farmworker locals in 1964. Calisto Ramos, a high school student in the mid-to-late 1960s, said his mother regularly "offer[ed] assistance to people who were single parents and were poor and struggling.... She would tell me, 'Take this pot of food to a family over there.'"[47] She also led a group of women to pick already harvested fields to distribute produce to families in need. These actions were common, mitigated marginal conditions, promoted social justice values, and echoed national justice campaigns.[48] They also fostered a younger generation to engage their world. Like Ramos's mother, for instance, Deaztlan's mother instilled her social values in her sons, who attended the University of California, Los Angeles (UCLA) and joined Chicana/o groups.[49] With other college students from the Coachella Valley, such as the artist Ramses Noriega, they also encouraged high school students "to study to get out that ... squalor type [of] poverty.... Education was the only hope that there was for us."[50]

Two more undercurrents appeared in 1967. The first was the Vietnam War and the numbers of young men returning in flag-draped coffins.[51] MAPA's Ray Rodriguez recalled, "everyone had somebody who had gone to Vietnam. I had a brother who went. He was in the Marines.... [Young people] were afraid that their time was going to come. That someone from their families was going to get drafted."[52] The war affected everyone in myriad ways. Some left school to work and make up a missing brother's wages.[53] Others left to attend college and avoid the draft. The national calls to end the "unjust war" filtered locally and mixed with the fear of "get[ting] that call." The casualties further stressed their racialized position in the country and, in the process, politicized more young men and women.[54] "You're seeing and experiencing going to funerals for friends, classmates, that got killed in Vietnam," Calisto Ramos said, "I was attending them. I said, this is not right. You draft people, you take them, for an unjust war, I just did not agree with it."[55] Many others also attended those funerals, practiced the same rituals. And for some, like Ramos, the Vietnam War fostered an overt anti-war and anti-racist politics and, by 1967, pushed local Chicanas/os to initiate demonstrations.

Second, the Coachella Valley's Mexican farmworkers began hearing of the Delano Grape Strike while on the migrant circuit. Some even became supporters, like Virginia Ortega, who immigrated with her husband to Coachella in 1965. Ortega's father had organized in Mexico for small farmers, fought railroad land grabs, and taught her to stand up against all social injustice. When Mexican authorities jailed her father and other community men for squatting on railroad-claimed land, Ortega recalled, her mother and other community women defended their families' land claims. Similarly, her grandmother ("a fighting woman, a role model")[56] told Ortega stories of "rebellion,"[57] which largely ended with the same lesson: "never let them take away from you what is yours."[58] This childhood shaped how Ortega navigated the world; she even chose her husband only after seeing him help a stranger in need.

In 1966, Ortega and her husband immigrated to the United States and found work at Delano's grape harvest, unaware of UFWOC's ongoing, if anemic, strike. She noticed a rowdy group ("una gritadera") near the fields and next to a truck with candles, flags, and the Virgin of Guadalupe.[59] When she asked her supervisor about them, he simply called them troublemakers who would soon be removed. But, Ortega then met a young woman striker, who asked her and another farmworker to "support" them. "We want a contract with more justice," the striker said, "We want rights for the worker. We want days of festivities. We want so many things, friend." When Ortega asked how they could support, the striker presented them with a petition: "your signature, just your signature, supporting the idea." Ortega and her coworker signed eagerly, and then she fetched her husband to sign.[60] To her surprise, he chastised her. "You are so dumb, love," he said, "Don't you know they can jail you, that they can take away your green card and leave me here alone?" She initially felt confused and conflicted by his response, but later she confronted him: "I remember my father," she told him, "and he taught me that people must have dignity, and fight for a better life." When he relisted the risks, she reassured him "there are so many people" involved. Then, she added: "What's more, we must support."[61]

In 1967, Ortega's family moved to Indio's camp, where they met farmworkers who also crossed paths with Delano strikers, most without meeting any prominent leaders. Most pro-striker neighbors shared Ortega's moralized politics and drew from their lives in, and stories from, Mexico to speak about what must be done. Pablo Carrizales, the Texan bracero introduced in chapter two, wrote to *El Malcriado* in 1967 about his feelings of solidarity that compelled action despite the sacrifices: "By radio, the newspaper, I found out about the suffering, sacrifices, the work and troubles of the people in Delano in their battle against injustice, and the voice of my soul won over my condition as an immigrant ... the hunger, the coldness, the sadness and the sufferings ... became mine, and I turned myself into one of you."[62] In early 1967, the UFW remained far removed from Carrizales's new desert home, and any publicized pro-union politics risked employer retribution. Still, his "soul won over" his fears and transformed him into a striker: "as far as my strength lets me, up to the limits of what can be done within the law ... I will help you, even financially, as far as my poverty lets me."[63]

By late 1967, in short, the Coachella Valley had its own movement of VL electoral campaigns, MAPA's multiple fronts, student activism, and farmworkers' growing awareness of Delano strikers. Though challenges remained, and the Rancher Nation exuded optimism, a storm churned beneath the surface. In this context, UFWOC expanded its Delano Grape Strike to cover the Coachella Valley. It also strengthened its National Consumer Grape Boycott, calculating it would starve the ranchers' opposition.[64] When Cesar Chavez visited the Coachella Valley in late 1967, he asked MAPA to connect him with a farmworker leader. They brought him to Carrizales and the two spoke privately. After Chavez left, Carrizales told his MAPA friends, all non-farmworkers, to get ready for a farmworker strike.[65]

La Llegada de Cesar Chavez al Valle de Coachella

In late 1967, MAPA members Alfredo Figueroa and Bernie Lozano composed a *corrido* predicting a farmworker rebellion in the Coachella Valley grape fields. Titled, "Cesar Chavez's Arrival to the Coachella Valley," the corrido used Mexican history to frame the union and its leader.[66] "In all struggles," it began, "there have been great men/ of identical likeness/ identical to Zapata/ also Hidalgo/ not forgetting Juarez." Like them, the "caudillo" Chavez spent years "seek[ing] out injustices/ to conquer," such as the "latifundistas" he defeated in 1966 and 1967. The song did not need to introduce Emiliano Zapata, Miguel Hidalgo, or Benito Juarez; their last names were enough to evoke Mexican history, all national heroes who sacrificed their lives to protect Mexican liberty. Now, Chavez planned to do the same in the Coachella Valley, where he would "arrive with enthusiasm/ to see his people/ that he finds here" and spark freedom, much like Mexico's revolutionaries.[67]

In interviews, Figueroa described the song as a tongue-in-cheek tool for educating farmworkers about the upcoming strike. It was playful and hopeful, he said, not naïve about the future. And yet, the song provides a revealing artifact of 1968 Coachella, when ethnic Mexican activists mounted a multifaceted rebellion against the Rancher Nation. Like the corrido suggested, locals drew from personal and collective stories about rebellion to lead race justice and farmworker union campaigns. Their efforts gained strength from civil rights victories, anti-Vietnam War protests, and the rising Chicana/o movement, much like a political storm with multiple currents. But as in previous years, 1968 still failed to produce the corrido's linear path of emancipation—of arrival met with a communal uprising, of shared goals and timelines, of sacrifices borne easily. Instead, local insurgent visions and stories were diverse, vague, and shifting-in-action, while rancher strength remained formidable. Lastly, by framing the Coachella Grape Strike of 1968 as a fight against the local dichotomy of white rancher and Mexican farmworkers, locals risked overlooking Filipino migrants. Even if unprecedented, the year's rebellion was uncertain and contingent, interchangeably catalyzing and deflating.

The year began inauspiciously. The VL, MAPA, and United Mexican American Students (UMAS) campaigned in council elections, against hiring discrimination, and among students. But national events shifted opportunities. In January, the Tet Offensive belied claims of a near peace and triggered more anti-war protests. News then filtered of Chavez's fast to recommit UFWOC to nonviolence, which introduced the union to more Coachella residents. In March, Mexican American students in Los Angeles stormed out of schools to protest conditions, marching unapologetically and speaking of a new movement. Soon afterwards, an exhausted Chavez broke his fast while next to Robert F. Kennedy, both flanked by Filipino and Mexican workers. The moment's moral fortitude endowed UFWOC with early civil rights movement optimism and launched Kennedy's presidential candidacy.[68] Then the storm quickened: Johnson withdrew from the presidential election to focus on Vietnam; King was assassinated while campaigning for Black worker rights; rebellions engulfed cities; students took over campuses; fury raged.

In these months, local activists joined a presidential campaign, protested the Vietnam War, pushed for education reforms, and supported UFWOC's grape strike. MAPA played a critical role. It led Kennedy's Riverside County campaign, registered new voters, and mobilized Mexican Americans.[69] To their surprise, students came out of the "woodwork" to join them. Some had formed UMAS, while others had VL parents who taught them about politics or had seen enough of their parents' advocacy to become activists. For many, the Kennedy campaign also echoed their parents' enthusiasm for John F. Kennedy and offered a tangible project for building a local movement. Much like a storm, multiple currents swirled into potential.

Additionally, MAPA organized farmworkers for the grape strike. They met them in homes, visited camps, distributed flyers, cajoled the recalcitrant. Because UFWOC focused on Kennedy, it sent no organizers until June 1968.

This had three effects. First, MAPA built the strike's infrastructure by relying on its members' union pasts and their contacts with local families. As non-farmworkers, they said they struggled to "understand" farmworker views, so they turned to the friend, Pablo Carrizales, who served as a cultural bridge. Second, most local farmworkers remained skeptical of the strike—easily calculating the lopsided risks and noting it was led by a non-visible union and by visible, but non-farmworker professionals. Some questioned organizer intentions: who could believe that some people simply wanted to help others out of the kindness of their hearts?[70] Third, the farmworkers who did join MAPA's early strike campaign expressed a moralized politics of solidarity, one encapsulated in Ortega's retort to her husband ("we must support") and one that echoed UFWOC's Delano core.

This third point warrants elaboration because it highlights a central quality of UFWOC's multiyear grape strike: workers *chose* to join a precarious campaign with personal–political stories of toil and poverty that compelled them to help others. For instance, Armando Sanchez grew up in Zacatecas, Mexico, where he worked in agriculture since childhood and "suffered" landowner abuses. He never attended school or learned to read, his son said, but "he was intelligent," brave, and ambitious. At fourteen, Sanchez migrated alone to the California border and found the usual indignities: fields without rest, water, or restrooms; low wages and wage theft; constant supervisor denigration. In 1968, he was in his thirties, recently married, and a father, working in the Coachella Valley's grape fields. It is unclear when he learned of UFWOC or the exact reasons for joining the early strike, for he died before I began conducting interviews. His son, however, said his father became an early strike committee member as it reflected his father's morality and biography: he, too, had known the suffering of farmworkers, and he wanted to end it. "One sees . . . the suffering of people," his son said, and some, like his father, felt compelled to act—a compulsion that "one carries in their heart, inside, like an inheritance."[71]

Similar stories abound. The Coachella Strike Committee included Pablo Carrizales, Ramon Melgoza, Tereso and Vivian Rendon, Mary Lou and Rafael Torres, Nicasio Campos, Irene and Emiliano Treviño, Mr. and Mrs. Esquivel, and a coterie of adolescent workers, such as Amalia Uribe Deaztlan and Irene Reyes. Some joined without official positions, such as Juanita Martinez, who said she spent 1968 organizing meetings, encouraging workers to strike, and picketing *seven* ranchers. She was an immigrant, married with children, possibly near middle age. For her, striking risked wages, blacklists, and immigration retaliation. Still, she "help[ed] the movement voluntarily and talk[ed] to the people, explain[ed] to them the union, and what it was we were fighting for and why we wanted the union, to strike all the ranchers who did not want to sign a contract with the union."⁷² In staccato, near breathless form, Martinez explained how she fought "voluntarily" when victory was uncertain, when one did so for more than the promised material benefits. "I have never stop[ped] helping organize people," she wrote, reflecting who she was and expected others to be.⁷³

As with the corrido, farmworkers like Martinez and Sanchez drew from life in Mexico and along the border to trace vague outlines of union life. But, unlike the song, the Coachella Grape Strike of 1968 signified a story fundamentally about self and others, about what one was called to do. The strike meant a choice; no one was poor enough or confident of victory enough to produce the non-choice of mere reaction, as the corrido sang. Such choices became acutely visible in UFWOC meetings, the organizer Tony Lopez recalled. The farmworkers he spoke to expressed fury, fear, and exhaustion.⁷⁴ Most were supportive, but they doubted the strike's odds and asked about repercussions: "And if they fire me?" "Yes," he would reply, "that's a possibility. But if you don't fight, what will happen? You will always be subjugated in whatever they tell you. Jump, you jump. Run, you run. You must fight." For those unconvinced, Lopez painted a union future for their children: "Let's hope your children don't have to work in the fields, but if they have to" then a union will make sure "they can work comfortably, without the pressure."⁷⁵ Like others, Lopez closed his 1968 meetings with the same message: be ready in June, when Chavez's union (as it was increasingly referred to) will take a vote for a harvest strike in the Coachella Valley grape fields.

The desert's grape ranchers knew of the strike's difficult choices, too. When UFWOC telegrammed them early in 1968 to hold elections and negotiate a contract, the ranchers quickly rejected both, fearing elections would grant an easy victory to UFWOC ("Cesar has a lot of charm for those people") and predicting an ineffective strike.⁷⁶ They knew the obvious: voting a union into existence under an agreement of noninterference differed from a protracted struggle with few promises and many immediate costs. Much like waiting out a storm, grape ranchers relied on sober worker calculations to withstand the union's assault.⁷⁷ Some ranchers probably noticed that the local organizing did not include Filipino farmworkers, who would arrive in May and, thus, may be less responsive to yet another strike. Rancher allies simply ignored the union. The *Coachella Valley Sun* even reported on "elated" ranchers, whose early grape harvest promised higher returns than the previous record.⁷⁸

While the strike challenged the Rancher Nation's economy, the VL and MAPA led parallel political fights. The VL won two seats in Coachella, and MAPA organized Kennedy's campaign. Less visible, MAPA also mentored students, some of whom were also participating in UFWOC's strike.⁷⁹ On June 5, 1968, these efforts culminated with Kennedy's California victory.

For UFWOC and MAPA, it meant standing next to a candidate with a clear path to the White House—an unimaginable feat at the beginning of the year. Local activists immediately pivoted to the Coachella Grape Strike of 1968 in a one-two punch against the Rancher Nation—as if finally bringing forth a flash flood.[80] But then, news arrived of Kennedy's assassination, only minutes after a victory speech that "singled out Cesar Chavez and Bert Corona and the Mexican American community," and that referred to the UFWOC leader, Dolores Huerta, as "my old friend." He smiled at her as she stood next to him, thanked her for her tireless labor.[81]

The *Coachella Valley Sun* speculated the "Kennedy shooting may have stopped Chavez's 'Parade,'" hoping the "young men from out of town" with "'La Raza con Kennedy' stickers" had lost their storm.[82] But MAPA and other activists simply converted the march into a mourning procession and pro-Chavez rally. With both, UFWOC finally arrived in the Coachella Valley, though hardly with the corrido's self-confidence. With less than four weeks left in the harvest, UFWOC organizers moved in with local leaders and met with families. On June 13, the union held a press conference to speak on working conditions and publicize their "height of harvest" strike, which would target the harvest's final three weeks. Three days later, on June 16, the corrido-singing Alfredo Figueroa met his MAPA crew at 4 A.M. in Indio, from where he rode with others in the back of a truck—all packed in, each with a fluttering red flag. He knew other picketers drove that morning, too, that they all headed into the expanse of desert and fields, that they, too, saw the ribbon of red and orange creasing the mountains' silhouettes—a fitting backdrop for holding up a bullhorn and announcing a strike: "Hermanos y Hermanas . . ."[83]

For the next three weeks, the strike remained uncertain—much like the events leading to it. The workforce had already declined from a 3,000 peak to 1,500–2,000. Of these, UFWOC said, 1,000 honored the strike, with most skipping the picket line to work elsewhere.[84] Local news pegged the number at a modest 600—which nonetheless reflected substantial support. These workers honored the strike despite the risks and the near certainty it would not lead to union recognition. Like previous strikers, they engaged in a principled strike and for reasons beyond immediate material concerns. But, challenges remained. Court injunctions limited pickets and placed them away from ranches.[85] Strikers alleged ranchers turned to Mexican immigrants to complete the harvest.[86] In late June, *El Malcriado* argued the injunction undercut their ability to block immigrant strikebreaker busses—echoing the 1967 cartoon. Less mentioned were Filipino workers. For them, the strike meant losing lucrative work and souring relations with ranchers—all without a victory. Many also worried about being replaced by Mexican immigrant workers. As the Filipino organizer Willie Barrientos reported in April 1968, Filipinos asked him: "If we strike, who will stop the g.c.'s [green card holders]?" Facing the Mexican farmworker population, Barrientos reflected, "We Filipino workers are beginning to look more and more like a needle in a haystack."[87] To ranchers, these challenges meant the strike was "unsuccessful" and only managed to "slow down the work somewhat with continued harassment."[88]

But the region's largest and longest strike made itself impossible to ignore. For three weeks, strikers convened nightly in Coachella's central park, listened to striker leaders, and watched plays by fellow strikers. They chanted union slogans, held up their eagle-emblazoned flags, and marched in the city. Even critical or unconnected residents noticed the strike-in person and/or in local newspapers and radio updates. For Flora Mendoza, whose family had long lived in Indio's colonia, the strike made her "afraid of shootings, of dead people, because we had never—actually, *I* had never seen a strike before, or anything like that."[89] For Louise Neely, who also came from an old Mexican American family and managed the Coachella Valley Farmers Association's bracero barracks, the strike "surprised [her] . . . These people were desperate to get attention, to make awareness about the conditions of the workers and to finally have a voice. . . . But, at first, I just thought [Chavez] was a troublemaker."[90] Both shared views common among conservative Mexican American residents.[91]

The strike peaked in Coachella's Fourth of July rally, where congressman John V. Tunney was slated to speak, and where one thousand strikers and their allies mixed with the valley's residents, many neither ethnic Mexicans nor farmworkers. Claiming neutrality, Tunney painted the strike as a private matter and ignored the farmworkers in the crowd. Whispers grew, Figueroa recalled, and when he raised the union flag, strikers spontaneously erupted into a chant: *Huueelllggaaa, Huueelllggaaa, Huueelllggaaa.*[92] Tunney attempted to speak over them, while Coachella's mayor raised the speaker volume. Both failed to drown them out, and when the speakers gave out, the acoustic chant remained—repeated over and over, as Tunney supporters left and Tunney reprimanded strikers' lack of gratitude for the country's freedoms.

After the UFW migrated north, the Coachella Valley's Rancher Nation mocked the strike as ineffective and unpopular, as mere "harassment" in a good harvest,[93] an "invasion of riff raff" on law-abiding people.[94] It called Chavez a failed organizer and cynical troublemaker, who used Coachella as a proxy for his war on Delano.[95] The Tunney "Clap Down," it added, were only thirty outsiders and newcomer "kooks,"[96] who they accused of widespread criminality. The latter included "rock throwing, broken windows and slashed tires," unverified rape charges, marijuana possession, and the surreal pattern of picketers throwing themselves in front of cars.[97] The ranchers, in contrast, expressed concern about their workers' harvest income,[98] while some conservative Mexican Americans wrote public letters in opposition to UFWOC and MAPA.[99]

There was some truth to these claims. The strike was late, brief, and erupted with little previous UFWOC presence and almost no Filipino support. And yet, the strike still affected the Rancher Nation's self-serving narratives. If the latter presented white patriarchal rancher-kings as civilizing a former wasteland, then strikers accused ranchers of the opposite: of being social parasites and government dependents, whose racial arrogance placed them outside mid century U.S. norms. If all subjects in the Rancher Nation gained their visibility through the rancher, and led to the workers' mute commodification, then the strikers' marches, pickets, rallies, and meetings pointed to a future shaped by farmworker subjectivities. The strike and Chicana/o mobilization threatened more than ranchers' material base. Its public visibility targeted the region's claim of white civility. It ruptured past racial decorum and repressed stability and signaled a growing storm.

Outside the fields, in fact, the strike produced a social crisis. A young Chicano picketed a conservative Mexican American storeowner, earning a disturbing-the-peace charge for calling her a "son of bircher."[100] Coachella's district attorney charged five men for the Tunney "clap down," including MAPA's Loya, Caswell, and Figueroa. Businesses complained to the police of "an unidentified woman and two unidentified teenage girls" who threatened to picket them if they did not pressure the city and *Coachella Valley Sun* to support UFWOC.[101] A white social worker from the adjacent Desert Sands Unified School District (DSUSD) charged the district with "white racism" and led a "pray in" to advance MAPA's education reforms.[102] In August, a new group, "Citizens United for Social Justice," announced plans to primary Tunney,[103] while another picketed the *Coachella Valley Sun* (again) for not printing their "side of the story." In the fall of 1968, as young men formed a Brown Berets chapter and provoked white panic over a potential race riot,[104] a local court sentenced MAPA's "clap down" men to four months in jail, a rancher victory that spoke volumes of its desperate power practices. A month later, the grape thinning season began, and, with it, the prospects of yet another UFWOC strike.

UFWOC's 1969 Coachella Grape Strike

The temptation, at this point, is to write a linear story of movement intensification in the 1969 Coachella Grape Strike and a climax with 1970 contracts. Certainly, there is reason for it. After the 1968 strike, UFWOC mounted an unprecedented boycott in the United States and Europe, gained endorsements from civil rights groups, labor councils and politicians, and caused $3–4 million in rancher losses.[105] By late 1968, the national press reported on UFWOC'S "significant victory" of "finally [having] made its cause a national major issue [and] forced politicians to take sides."[106] Chavez wrote as much in a letter to the Desert Grape Growers League (DGGL) in 1969, when he called for negotiations and pointed to their thirty-one boycott offices—a "machinery" of "labor, church, civil rights and other groups." "Surely," he taunted the DGGL's president, Mike Bozick, "it must seem to you at times that you are only running away from the inevitable."[107] In parallel fashion, the Chicana/o movement appeared ascendant as it joined the Poor People's Campaign, established new organizations (such as the Mexican American Legal Defense and Education Fund and Center for Autonomous Social Action), and advocated for insurgent academic departments.

But, as with preceding years, the ground dynamics remained complicated. Pro-rancher locals, for instance, closed ranks and fought the boycott in late 1968 and early 1969. They wrote letters to journals and newspapers, produced anti-UFWOC documentaries, and led grape "buy-in" stunts.[108] Most Coachella Valley grape ranchers sold their harvest before the boycott's effect and relied on a large labor pool and greater financial resources to withstand a future strike.[109] In 1968, rancher allies also won in local, regional, and national elections.[110] Nixon's presidential win even encouraged state politicians to introduce bills to undercut UFWOC.[111] Chicanas/os also struggled to convert their rising visibility into tangible wins. MAPA, for instance, was stalled in its school desegregation and war on poverty campaigns, while four of its members faced jail sentences for the Tunney protest.[112]

Challenges also faced the two movements. In its national profile, for instance, UFWOC presented white Americans with an enticing political narrative: of brave, nonviolent farmworkers confronting a Mississippi-like, white rancher class, and of white consumers joining the farmworkers' heroic struggle through the boycott. In the United States, UFWOC argued, all citizens had the right to make and answer a boycott. National economic prosperity and political egalitarianism came hand-in-hand—for unlike other countries, U.S. factory workers could afford luxuries like grapes and could join farmworker co-citizens to root out the vestiges of an un-American and feudal-like inequality.[113] UFWOC claimed it did not win the 1968 grape strikes because federal officials refused to close the border with Mexico, thus giving ranchers strikebreaking immigrants.[114] Through the boycott, UFWOC told consumers, white Americans could aid their Filipino American and Mexican American co-citizens by undermining white rancher profits, whose use of immigrant workers upheld a racial apartheid in Civil Rights America.[115] To UFWOC, a shared citizenship bridged distinct histories and connected farmworkers and consumers in a common American campaign.

But the actual the discourses utilized by strikers could not have been more different. Fissures remained between Delano and Coachella leaders, Mexican and Filipino workers, and racialized farmworkers and white consumers. Coachella Valley grape strikers, for instance, still framed UFWOC through local power realities and ethnic Mexican history. They prioritized local conditions, challenged Delano's authority in Coachella, and ignored the National Consumer Grape Boycott. Delano leaders, in fact, could only convince two local strikers, Tony Lopez and Pablo Carrizales, to move to boycott cities in 1969.[116] The rest agreed with Ramon Espinoza, who considered the boycott unrelated to the Coachella Valley and refused to subject his family to boycott sacrifices.

The Coachella Committee also continued to include only ethnic Mexican workers, who remained oblivious of Filipino strikers. The latter dynamic reflected the differences discussed in chapter two. The committee member Irene Reyes, for instance, joined the UFWOC because she felt farmworkers needed higher wages and better conditions. Born in 1947, she was the youngest of five in a Tejano family; she did not like school, she said, and like others had worked as a child. When UFWOC arrived, Reyes joined organizers in house visits and then led her own. It was unlike her, she said, but the organizing "made me grow more, and gave me more assurance of myself, more confidence."[117] The strike also felt historical: "I knew . . . it was the first time [the Mexican community] had done something like this. So, it was a big one." When asked about non-Mexican strikers, Reyes only recalled a "handful" of white Delano organizers.[118] For her, the 1969 Coachella Grape Strike targeted her community's conditions and was driven locally by ethnic Mexican farmworkers. She did not speak of white boycotters and Filipino workers—which makes sense given the gulf separating her from white consumers and older Filipino men, and the 1968 convergence of Mexican farmworker and Mexican American activism.

These dynamics appeared when UFWOC returned to the Coachella Valley in March 1969, four months before the harvest began. Its organizers held meetings, distributed flyers with demands, and coordinated with local leaders.[119] It found support from 1968 strikers and by April held a rally in Indio's fair grounds with five hundred farmworkers.[120] But challenges appeared early, as the Filipino leader Pete Velasco wrote to Gilbert Padilla, Coachella's strike director. Local farmworkers still saw UFWOC as a "Mexican union," Velasco noted, which was solidified by local news.[121] This view threatened their ability to organize Filipinos and, given their harvest numbers, endangered UFWOC's strike.¹²² To "Win Filipinos," UFWOC had to create a Filipino-run office near Mecca's camps, use Filipino history and conditions to shape union remarks, and stress Filipinos in local and UFW history.¹²³ Filipinos were pro-union, he added, even if many struggled to join the strike.¹²⁴ A typical Filipino foreman likely thought: "I have joined the strike with AWOC. I was foreman at Marco Ranch. I was paid good. We (with his boys) were shut off our camp. I lost everything, car, TV, furniture, my boy didn't go to college, my wife cried. Now, you ask me to do the same thing." Velasco reminded Padilla Filipinos had already endured strike sacrifices and would likely pause before considering similar risks—even if pro-union. UFWOC should "persuade [Filipinos] to: 1. Act and think together; 2. Agree to pull out of field together; Mexican foremen too; 3. It will not take long to make the growers to surrender [sic]."

We can understand Velasco's letter as an intervention in Coachella's Mexican-inflected movement. To its credit, UFWOC adopted his recommendations and assigned him as Coachella's strike director. In mid-April, it also organized mixed Filipino-Mexican pairs to visit Filipino camps in Mecca and Mexican camps in Coachella and Indio. These pairs were to help communication and trust between workers, as well as provide evidence of the union's interracial commitments to white consumers.¹²⁵ Lastly, organizers were to speak on the "Filipino situation," such as, "why no wives . . . what the [ranchers] have done to Filipinos. Two laws on the books that hindered Filipinos: one limited immigration to men only. . . . Second, forbade marriage of Filipino with other races. Not till 1949 was this law stricken down."¹²⁶ Through Velasco, UFWOC argued rancher racism imposed a life of unwanted bachelorhood on Filipino workers. But through the 1969 strike, Filipinos could have the final say.

And yet, challenges persisted. UFWOC organizer notes from late April found interracial mistrust among migrant farmworkers who shared the same camp, usually expressed as one group doubting the other group would strike. Among ethnic Mexican residents, the problem was not mistrust but Filipino invisibility: few knew of or spoke about Filipinos in 1969, even if MAPA leaders celebrated Filipino militancy or ethnic Mexican strikers, like Amalia Uribe Deaztlan, interacted with Filipino leaders. Having framed the strike as a fight against Coachella Valley's racial inequality, ethnic Mexican locals also saw it as *supported*, but not *determined*, by Delano.¹²⁷ They demanded local control, pressing UFWOC to "get more involvement from the [Coachella] committee," and pushed Velasco to accept a compromise in late April: Delano organizers would visit Filipino camps while locals took "charge of the campaign to sign up workers in Coachella." The committee's meetings then continued in Spanish and included sign-up sheets with "Zapatistas y Chavistas" headings—echoing (again) MAPA's 1968 corrido.¹²⁸

Unwittingly, Coachella's demand for local authority blunted UFWOC's multiracialism and produced two parallel strike tracks. In the first, ethnic Mexican farmworkers fought their racialized exploitation, used Mexican history to frame UFWOC, and gained aid from Chicana/o activists who saw farmworker exploitation as foundational to Mexican Americans' subjected status in the U.S. Southwest. Almost serendipitously, the Coachella Valley gained two social movements against the Rancher Nation—the red flags of farmworker strikers and the Chicana/o fight against racial inequality. They pivoted off each other, leveraging each unlikely eruption to facilitate their own campaign. In the second, Delano UFWOC organizers reached out to Filipino migrant workers, speaking of masculinity and citizenship, of rectifying a racist, colonial past. In early May, Velasco instructed organizers to read his letter, in which he stressed "Filipinos [as] the key" to UFWOC's success and predicted a ranchers' "surrender" through unified action.[129] "When," he asked, "will our lives change if we don't bind together?" With the strike, Filipinos could gain "a better state and better job" and a moralized visibility: "we will become trusted and earn favor to our children," Velasco wrote, "our children will praise us, even the Ranchers." In the twilight of their lives, perhaps such visibility spoke of a desire to be seen militants who fought their marginalization, as men who fulfilled their obligations, as people to be respected and known. To the skeptical, he asked they "trust" him, consider their "obligation," see the opportune moment. Unlike earlier years, this strike would be interracial and widespread, quickly force ranchers into contracts, and militate against further Filipino erasure.[130]

The UFW movement also maintained its citizen-based boycott narrative, telling white consumers of fellow citizens expanding U.S. egalitarianism to a retrograde region. In mid-May, *El Malcriado* followed Coachella Valley grape strikers in their "100 Mile March" to the border city of Calexico, where they met Mexican unions and encouraged "Mexican Nationals" to join their strike. The same issue carried a political cartoon of transnational agribusiness personified as the giant in *Gulliver's Travels*—tied down by cross-border solidarity—and a Chavez quote: "the real enemy of the US farm worker is not the Mexican farm worker, but rather the [ranchers] who refuse to pay decent wages."[131] In both speech and cartoon, UFWOC claimed to be in solidarity with its southern neighbors, while defining itself as a U.S. movement emblematic of American racial democracy. In contrast, Coachella Valley grape ranchers lacked American qualities. They "ignored wage laws," stole wages, and lived outside respectable behavior.[132] When the strike erupted in late May, *El Malcriado* detailed ranchers' nonnormative desperation: they lashed out at strikers, furiously attacked with cars and guns, escaped arrests through outsized power, and saddled farmworker desperation with shame: "grown men break down and cry and say that they are ashamed to be working."[133] Presenting strikebreaking as a symptom of a broader illness—agribusiness's dramatic inequality—UFWOC framed white consumers as the key population to an emergent farmworker world, one without the desperate choice between fear and shame, or ranchers' privileges and impunities, or the apt-name of "Mississippi in California."

Arguably, the UFWOC illustrated its claims in July when Filipinos from five camps went on strike and refused to leave. The strikers then "raided" other camps and forced startled workers into the desert night: "*campesinos* and ranchers," *El Malcriado* wrote, "became groggy and chaotic, [and] unwillingly crew after crew walked out like zombies." One striker, Claro Runtal, recalled "Sheriffs, policemen, security guards, lawyers of the company came down to our labor camp . . . we were guarded like ex-convicts." When a reporter asked Runtal if he "worked for" Chavez, he replied, "Not exactly working for him sir, but I am working for the policy of our Union."[134] UFWOC quickly framed the "Filipino sit-in" as the moment that "shook the whole valley wide" and forced ten ranchers into negotiations.[135] It also evidenced UFWOC's multiracial politics, for Filipino Americans saved the strike, and with it, their Mexican American co-strikers, by undermining white ranchers' power to exploit immigrant laborers. If there was a moment that represented the UFW's success, and the rearticulation of UFWOC as a Filipino and Mexican union, then it was here.

But, divisions remained. The strike committee member Deaztlan, for instance, recalled Filipinos "came from a different place; they lived in a different place. They were pretty much secluded from the rest of the population." As a result, Mexican and Filipino farmworkers only "interacted," but did not "socialize," while working. She and local strikers knew little about Filipinos. Nonetheless, she insisted there was no tension between the two communities, adding: "[Velasco] would always be part of what we were doing. . . . He was always in the forefront with us."[136] As a committee member, she was best positioned to know Filipino strikers.[137] But her reassurance pointed to the fissures. In her quote, the "we" and "us" alluded to local Mexican strikers, which placed Velasco as an ally-outsider. She also recalled the "sit-in" as a reaction to *her* mistreatment by police officers when she walked into a Filipino camp—a solidarist act she presented as testament to UFWOC's multiracialism. But her memory of Filipino solidarity also functioned as erasure, for it missed the specificity of Filipino grievances and Velasco's interventions in UFWOC's self-identity. The tenacious distance between Mexican and Filipino strikers reflected the region's segregation and its pervasive marginalization of local Mexicans. It also reflected tensions between Coachella and Delano leaders,

Filipino grape strikers during the UFW's 1969 Coachella Grape Strike. Pete Velasco is in the first row, far right, with an infectious smile. *El Malcriado*, July 15–31, 1969, 2. Walter P. Reuther Library, Archives of Labor and Urban Affairs, Wayne State University.

and the Chicana/o movement's catalyzing role in UFWOC's Coachella strikes.

To white America, *El Malcriado* maintained its story of worker unity,[138] of a heroic humanism that pivoted on and identified with white consumers. By late June, it gleefully wrote on boycott-suppressed prices: "The strikers describe Bozick as a desperate man, frantically trying to hold together his little empire, furious at his fellow growers who have already agreed to negotiate . . . but also watching . . . prices for grapes go down, down, down."[139] Velasco also spoke of a boxer-like national body—of arms moving in sync, swinging at backward vestiges: "The Coachella strikers are the first to remind [consumers] that the strike and boycott are like a boxers' left and right arms, both necessary to win the struggle for a decent life for the farm worker."[140] In his rendition, boycotters and strikers found unity and mutual recognition despite their varied backgrounds and profoundly different relations to rancher power. Guided by a common gaze, they served a one-two punch for U.S. egalitarianism in rural California.

And so, it was. A few Coachella Valley grape ranchers opened negotiations as the harvest closed. When these did not produce contracts, UFWOC wielded the boycott as a weapon. By January 1970, Chavez "favor[ed] send[ing] top people on [the] boycott" over another strike. But he would not have to make this choice. Before the harvest began, the once-proud rancher-kings came to UFWOC in clusters, asking for the contract's black eagle. A couple months later, Chavez forced Delano ranchers to sign contracts in UFWOC's union hall—five years after the Delano Grape Strike in 1965, all surrounded by the chant: *huelga, huelga, huelga.*

Conclusion: The Nature of Victories

In early 1965, the rancher-king subject bounded the Coachella Valley's imagined community: as proud builders of a civilized world in the reclaimed desert; as independent and entrepreneurial by nature in an unforgiving market; as sophisticated in modern techniques, yet intimately tied to the land; as businessmen who alchemized profit into public wealth. The settler-colonial Coachella Valley depended on the rancher-king's success and existed within his grammar of the self-made and homespun, where there was no need to actively exclude the laboring subject, for the tenets of racialized property did this naturally. The rancher's community was a moral one by definition: its very existence was a heralding monument to the living tissue of America.

But, in just five years, a collection of forces arrived like a flash flood, threatening all. Mexican Americans joined political contests, held secret meetings, ran their own slates. They organized parents, accused white leaders of racism, riffed off the national tenor—off its bitter antagonisms, its questioning of established relations, its auguring of a new world. And then, a rag-tag army of unionists claimed the ranchers' workers, meeting menacingly in public, forcing ranchers and their allies to take note. The combined group orchestrated Tunney's clap down, harassed pro-rancher residents, swerved from one demonstration to another. Ranchers fought back, but by late 1969 the Rancher Nation's material base, democratic discourse, and racial deference appeared fundamentally disturbed, if not broken. A few months later, grape ranchers finally buckled and accepted unionization.

But all was not well with the insurgents either. In 1968 and 1969, UFWOC was in the Coachella Valley for a total of five months. Many farmworkers participated in its strikes, but many people did not. Some remained skeptical of UFWOC chances; others felt threatened by a UFWOC-determined world. The 1970 contracts also only covered a third of Coachella Valley's fields, which meant UFWOC needed to organize the rest as it established a permanent Coachella office. Unsurprisingly, Delano leaders continued to struggle with Coachella leaders, who saw the contract victory as theirs. By late 1969, UFWOC even disbanded a local strike committee in favor of their own hand-picked farmworkers.

Richard Chavez, Cesar Chavez's brother and an early NFWA leader, pointing to unionized table grapes harvested in the Coachella Valley. *El Malcriado*, June 15, 1970, 1. Walter P. Reuther Library, Archives of Labor and Urban Affairs, Wayne State University.

The most pressing issue, however, remained the lack of substantive solidarity between Mexican and Filipino farmworkers. Coachella Valley local strikers continued to miss Filipino strikers as they framed UFWOC as a Mexican fight against local exploitation. When the strike committee underwent changes in October 1969, it still lacked Filipino members, most of whom had migrated to the San Joaquin Valley. Local Chicanas/os continued to see UFWOC as a fuse for a larger Chicana/o movement. When students organized a Coachella Chicano Conference in support of UFWOC in June 1970, they again reduced the union to Mexican farmworkers. For many Filipino workers, this framing substantiated fears that they could be sidelined by a strike they initiated. They remained "a minority within a minority union," and UFWOC's 1970 victory offered no reassurances. Arguably, a year is simply not enough time to undo a lifetime of differences and distances.[141]

The Rancher Nation was also more than the grape fields. It was a social, political, and cultural edifice that secured the Coachella Valley's political economy and the white ranchers' patriarchal authority. This edifice did not disappear after UFWOC's victory. In fact, in late May 1969, the MAPA's clap down men began four-month jail terms, in which time James Caswell's health would deteriorate drastically and lead to his early death. MAPA's Raul Loya faced censure from his school district and almost lost his teaching credential. In the 1969 summer, Coachella even set a youth curfew for the first time, in what critics claimed was a repressive measure. In October, conservative Mexican Americans helped kick MAPA out of anti-poverty programs.

A measure of the Rancher Nation's strength took placed on the day the largest grape rancher, Lionel Steinberg, signed UFWOC contracts in 1970. On that evening, the conservative Mexican American Progresista Lodge held a fundraiser dance in Coachella's park, were people paid to dance to live music.[142] A group of Chicana/o students from nearby colleges, who had earlier attended a Brown Beret rally against the Vietnam War, approached the dance excitedly without understanding the need to pay. They interpreted the fundraiser's insistence as a form of racial hostility. One young man reportedly took a microphone and lectured the crowd to stand up against injustice, ending with, "Chicano Power! Que Viva la Raza! Que Viva Cesar Chavez!"[143] When the fundraisers called the police, accusing them of disturbing the dance, the students attempted to rally their friends. But the station was only a hundred yards away; the police quickly surrounded the students, pepper sprayed them, dragged them down the stage steps. One man yelled, "ASI NOS TRATAN MI GENTE, ASI NOS TRATAN!," while another cried out, "Don't let them take me away."[144] More people arrived, having heard the commotion; some were local Chicana/o youth in "el movimiento," others were nearby residents. The police later claimed the crowd swelled to five hundred, all yelling profanities and throwing rocks and bottles. When more backup arrived, one hundred cops surrounded the entire group of Chicano activists and conservative Mexican Americans, all riot-ready with tear gas, batons, and sirens.

Those who arrived late to the scene, having heard of a homegrown riot, saw the police block *every* entrance into Coachella's main street center. They could see a lot of people running, including the conservative Progresistas, trying to flee the police attack.[145] In the next morning, the riot's effects included three to four city blocks of broken windows and several overturned police cars, one smoldered into ash. Away from the action, the mayor's *home* was lit on fire.[146] For witnesses, the story was obvious: "if you're brown, you're a wetback."[147] Even if the Chicana/o movement could claim a victory with UFWOC's contracts, and even if those pink-cheeked, liberal whites sighed with relief that justice was finally done, locals knew the Coachella Valley remained under enemy rule.

Chapter 4

In a Field of Flowers

The UFW Offensive against the Rancher Nation

In January 1970, *El Malcriado*'s cover presented a woodcut portrait of a lone, barefoot farmworker garbed in the cotton trousers and straw sombrero reminiscent of Mexico's early twentieth century peasantry. Standing upright in an expansive field, the farmworker held a long-handled hoe and shielded his face from a midday sun showering the sky and surrounding hills. In the background, a shawled woman held the hands of her child and walked toward the worker. Underneath the portrait, the title read: "The Farm Worker in the 1970's: Review of the Past . . . Hopes for the Future . . ."[1]

The portrait captured the United Farm Workers' (UFW) sense of epochal transition in 1970. According to its newspaper, farmworkers of the past had faced the "basic poverty," "malnutrition," and "racial, social and economic injustices" characteristic of agricultural California. But the previous five years proved "things can be changed [and] the seemingly endless cycle of poverty can be broken." Already the UFW's early labor contracts offered the "highest wages," "decent working conditions," bans on "pesticide poisoning," and access to medical care. As in the woodcut portrait, these benefits meant rest from exertion, a laboring solitude amidst familial love, and fields without the stooping demands of the short-handled hoe or a supervisor's barking presence. Upright and unsupervised, the UFW's future farmworker embodied a humanist promise, where even the shielding from the midday sun—hand to temple with closed eyes—conveyed existential contemplation, as if drawing inspiration from the very sun that once bore down on farmworkers. More than material benefits, the UFW argued, its labor contracts represented a "blueprint for building a new society for farmworkers, a society that value[d] the worker as a human being."

Within months after this issue, Coachella Valley grape ranchers succumbed to the UFW's demand for union recognition and labor contracts. One by one, a domino effect took hold in the spring and summer of 1970—concentrating strikes and a growing consumer boycott to squeeze all holdouts.[2] In July 1970, *El Malcriado* memorialized the last surrender with a political cartoon of a farmworker bowler whose "Huelga" ball struck against rancher pins.[3] No longer taking "their poverty, their hunger and their dreary hopeless existence for granted," *El Malcriado* wrote, the UFW's new Coachella Valley members

El Malcriado, January 31, 1970, 1. Walter P. Reuther Library, Archives of Labor and Urban Affairs, Wayne State University.

moved "to chip away at the old foundations of the rural farm economy." The decade began with a "ray of hope," the UFW proclaimed, that early morning dawn of a new era, one that promised to finally eliminate the "endless cycle" of "birth, death, fruition, harvest, then the dead and cold of winter."[4]

Such predictions would be premature, unfortunately. For most Californian farmworkers, the UFW's table grape contracts lasted only three years (1970–73). And yet, while they were in effect, the UFW's contracts in the Coachella Valley raised wages, improved working and living conditions, organized farmworker committees, and fostered independent farmworker leadership. They also provided a string of formerly unheard of benefits for farmworkers, such as job security, union seniority, health insurance, pensions, *vacation days*. Most importantly, they established grievance procedures and a union-controlled hiring hall that tempered the rancher-king's foundational source of power: his ability to fire and hire at will. These seemingly quotidian contract specificities represented the beginnings of a seismic shift in rancher–farmworker relations—a shift that can be easily overlooked in the drive to indict the union for its shortcomings. In these three years, Coachella Valley UFW members used the "machinery of unionism" and their "new sense of dignity and power" to "build a better future." They contested the rancher-king's former impunity, pressed against the Rancher Nation's power relations, and carved out lives outside rancher-created precarity, even if the shelter was only temporary.[5]

A Constitutional Monarchy

Tony Lopez lived in a UFW boycott house in a Chicago suburb in early 1970, about an hour trip by train to the city center where Eliseo Medina coordinated the local boycott campaign. In a matter of three years, Lopez had moved from Coachella migrant life to full-time striker and volunteer in the effervescent Delano—and then to boycott organizer in a city far removed from his childhood home. As with other UFW worker volunteers, Lopez found in the UFW movement's whirlwind a collection of new possibilities, experiences, and relationships. Like the Coachella Valley after two years of grape strikes, Lopez had by 1970 already lived the potential embedded in the UFW—for the mere attempt to end the Rancher Nation shook established forms and offered new possibilities, even if not promises. When news arrived of the first Coachella Valley grape contracts in April 1970, he learned of yet more transformations: assigned to return to the Coachella Valley, Lopez would serve as the region's first contract enforcer.[6]

Nearly fifty years later, in an oral history interview near the very fields he struck, Lopez told a typical union story. Early in the 1970 grape harvest, a pro-UFW supervisor came to the Coachella UFW office to report that a field manager for a UFW-contracted grape field fired his entire forty-person crew. The farmworkers, incensed, refused to leave and sent their supervisor to get the UFW's support. Lopez quickly drove to the field and spoke to the manager, who said (in anger) that one of the crew members did poor work. Lopez took this moment, he recalled, to *teach* the field manager on what he should have done: fairness, Lopez said, required the manager to speak to the farmworker in question and then touch base with him later in the day. In Lopez's lesson, the farmworker would reply to the manager, "Yes, yes, I must have overlooked that"—an understanding that simultaneously addressed the conflict and reflected worker dignity and constrained managerial power. When the field manager protested Lopez's lesson by saying he still could not work with this employee, Lopez remained firm: "to fire one person," he said, "you have to have justification. But, to fire 40, just because you felt like it?" Before the manager could answer the nonquestion, Lopez added, "We all make errors. You just committed one. Firing a whole crew just for one person, just because you thought that was fair."

Lopez then ordered the field manager to reinstate all forty employees, at which point the UFW crew supervisor immediately shouted to his workers to begin the day. In Lopez's story, the field manager remained silent—a far cry from the pre-UFW world when ranchers and managers fired farmworkers for any reason, often entire families for issues involving a single person. They were "used to this power," Lopez recalled, and sometimes they fell back into "those times before the contracts." His job was to help union members bring ranchers up to the UFW present.

Lopez's rendering of work life in the Coachella Valley's grape fields suggested the scale of the changes wrought by UFW contracts. To Lopez, the latter provided a common set of rules that allowed farmworkers to respond to rancher misbehavior and create a new social equilibrium. The contract included a union-controlled hiring hall, worker-elected grievance committees, and legally binding arbitration procedures. The first limited the rancher's ability to hire and fire at will, and arguably provided a space for dissent without risking livelihoods. The grievance committee heard farmworker complaints and served as an intermediary between farmworkers, the UFW, and Coachella Valley grape ranchers. Lastly, the arbitration procedures meant that unresolved contract violations could result in grievances filed against the violating party. If these remained unaddressed, a neutral party delivered a legally binding decision, which risked literally bringing ranchers "to court" for violations—whether these were denied breaks, banned pesticide use, or absent work restrooms.

Months after Lopez's arrival in the Coachella Valley, Philip Vera Cruz echoed Lopez's experiences in a series of *El Malcriado* articles. In "Union

Protection and Power," Vera Cruz presented the UFW as the only counterweight to outsized rancher power and its obscenities: "His conscience is always submerged by greed, indifference and a belief that life is a battlefield in which he either wins or loses."[7] Given this context, farmworkers could not expect rancher self-discipline or rationality ("a worker cannot talk sense to his boss") to facilitate "peace and harmonious living." Instead, they had to build a union and secure a contract to doubly "promote better relations" and "squeeze justice from [ranchers'] big money bags." The UFW organizer, Doug Adair, also saw the 1970 table grape contracts as a seismic power shift between ranchers and farmworkers. In the Rancher Nation, he said, farmworkers depended on rancher wealth and were vulnerable to rancher greed. Farmworkers could not even acquire the most basic needs, such as bodily privacy. But union members could now use the UFW contracts to equalize labor relations: "It was like you're changing [the absolute monarchy] to a constitutional monarchy," he said, and "the union contract is the constitution."[8] The UFW's most militant members used it to construct a new world: "[They] picked up that contract and said . . . we're equal and we have the right to life, liberty, and the pursuit of happiness. They wanted everything they could possibly get out of that ranch contract and they pushed it to the limits."[9]

Lopez, Vera Cruz, and Adair understood the UFW movement's commonly celebrated gains—wage increases, cold water, clean restrooms, work breaks, pesticide bans—as by-products of a greater power transformation, what Adair named a constitutional revolution. No one thought of this power transformation as a passive phenomenon, in which born-again ranchers suddenly respected farmworkers' humanity and recognized their former inhumanity. Instead, they argued, the contracts augured a new context for worker–rancher struggles in places like the Coachella Valley's grape fields, where new UFW members used the union-controlled hiring hall, grievance committees, and legally binding procedures to make themselves heard and to improve their lives in concrete ways.

We can see the contract's implications to the Rancher Nation in grape workers' response to ranchers' egregious behavior. While rancher-kings had once been powerful enough to make all labor struggles invisible in the public sphere, farmworkers now inaugurated a period of increased visibility. In three short years, nearly every Coachella Valley grape rancher earned a collection of worker grievances for substandard working and living conditions, for disrespecting workers, firing without cause, and hiring nonunion members. When UFW grievances remained unaddressed, farmworkers pressured the union to arbitrate. And when grape ranchers continued to flaunt contract violations in 1972 and 1973, they pushed the local UFW office to use its hiring hall to force them into settlements: wayward ranchers, the UFW announced, would be the targets of labor bans until outstanding grievances were addressed. If in former times the rancher-king had determined life and death, such UFW bans illustrated the contract's profound implications for a labor-hungry class—the contract meant that social death could be distributed in egalitarian forms.

Mike Bozick, the self-titled "Mr. Grape" and the militant anti-union president of the Coachella Valley Grape Growers Association, provides a useful entrance point to these changes. In 1971, UFW organizers visited his fields and housing camps and rated both subpar. They found camps with "one filthy toilet [for] 50 to 60 workers" and "no toilet paper."[10] In his grape fields, the violations included "suffocating toilets," "water not iced," lack of mandatory breaks, a shortened lunch, missing first aid kits, and the employment of non-UFW workers. In the 1972 grape harvest, the UFW office again cited Bozick for subpar camp conditions—"there were no facilities for hot water for showering or for washing of clothing and dishes"—and demanded their immediate rectification.[11] These conditions represented holdovers of—or a falling back into, as Lopez said—a pre-UFW rancher time when they could refuse to provide hot water in camps and disregard its effect in icy mornings or when they could express their contempt with suffocating, filthy toilets and lukewarm water in 110 degree summer weather. In refusing even the most basic standards, Coachella Valley grape ranchers like Bozick harkened to an era when farmworkers warranted *nothing*.

Such rancher contempt appeared most in grievances related to farmworker treatment. In the 1971 harvest, for instance, the Coachella UFW office filed a grievance against Bozick's supervisor, Rudy Silva, who yelled at Mohammed Murshed for missing "special grape bunches" and "challenged Murshed to fight."[12] The UFW organizer's notes summarized the rest: "[Silva] swung at Murshed. But, missed and fell. Murshed held him down. Mrs. Silva (Rudy's wife) attacked [Murshed] from behind and scratched his back. Later [Silva] went to camp (11:30 A.M.) armed with a pistol and evicted Murshed from labor camp." Less than a year later, the UFW office cited Bozick's foreman unpaid union dues and completing contract-covered work. When confronted, Bozick's foreman "disparage[d], denigrate[d] and/or subvert[ed] the Union" and told his workers they did "not [have] to report to the Local Office."[13] The UFW office also cited Bozick's foreman, Henry Alterado, for firing Juan Rodriguez for "singing" at work. The grievance noted Alterado "warned" Rodriguez to stop singing and when Rodriguez did not, Alterado fired him.[14] It is likely Alterado attempted to dismiss Rodriguez for a previously inconceivable public defiance, not so much for the singing itself.

In these instances, Coachella Valley grape ranchers' behavior embodied and pined for the precontract world when they fired and hired at will and their supervisors ruled crews like fiefdoms. But, under UFW contracts, unionized farmworkers reported rancher contract violations to their grievance committees and brought complaints to the Coachella office. In the first two grievances, the UFW's organizers demanded the supervisors' termination, while in the third the UFW pressed the grievance into arbitration and argued "singing [was] not just cause for discharge." They further required "that Mr. Rodriguez be immediately reinstated and be paid full back wages since the day he was terminated."[15] In these cases, the paper trail ended before there was a settlement, thus foreclosing making conclusions about the union's effectiveness. Still, the point remains: UFW grievances reflected a newfound farmworker assertion against egregious rancher behavior and signaled rank-and-file contestation that had previously assured dismissal. In pressing Mr. Rodriguez's case, for instance, the Coachella UFW office fought supervisors' unmitigated power to determine farmworkers' livelihoods and sought to achieve an unthinkable pre-contract scenario: the whistling return of a swaggering-defiant farmworker despite the patriarchal orders of rancher-serving supervisor.

The most striking quality of these grievances, however, were their pervasiveness. They appear *everywhere*. At a Karahadian labor camp in 1971, farmworkers cited unclean restrooms ("es un cochinero"), women's broken showers (which forced them to use men's showers), broken windows in the main hall, and the abrupt end to rancher-provided transportation to fields, a standard practice prior to unionization. Other Karahadian farmworkers, primarily Filipino men, reported being called to work only to be dismissed without compensation because of unexpected rain.[16] At Freedman and H&M, UFW members reported on supervisors hiring nonunion workers. They also reported on substandard living and working conditions. One worker leader, Ramon Serrano, added: "[we] want gas to go to work, or rancher-provided transportation."[17] At KK Larson, farmworkers confronted an anti-union supervisor; though "turmoil seemed to be the order of the day," the UFW organizer reported, "but everything turned out for the best . . . the forewoman, Josefina did not have her way."[18] Lastly, at Coachella Imperial Distributor, farmworkers collected a petition against the foreman after he "insulted several workers," "used profanity in the presence of women and minors," and refused to give workers their contract-mandated breaks.[19] Only *one* Coachella Valley grape rancher, a former machine unionist, avoided a collection of UFW grievances in three years, illustrating both rancher anti-UFW hostility and farmworkers' constant pressure on rancher behavior. As UFW organizer notes made apparent, pro-UFW farmworkers also pressured the union by asking: "what is happening with this issue?"

Indicative of the newly visible power struggle, most grievances dealt with rancher refusals to honor the UFW hiring hall. In 1971, the Coachella UFW office filed three grievances against Bozick for hiring nonunion farmworkers: on April 26 for three workers, May 6 for eight workers, and May 11 for refusing to accept dispatched workers and for a supervisor's demand that the UFW office dispatch "his" workers.[20] The UFW filed similar grievances against the rest of Coachella Valley's grape ranchers, including Karahadian,[21] Coachella Vineyards,[22] Henry Moreno,[23] Herbekian,[24] Oasis Gardens,[25] Tenneco,[26] and the especially anti-UFW David Valdora.[27] For each violation, the UFW demanded pay for the union members who lost working hours. Much has been written about the UFW's disorganized hiring hall and worker dispatches under its three-year grape contracts.[28] Coachella Valley ranchers later alleged the disorganization led to frustrated harvests and used it to oppose contract renegotiation in 1973. But, as the Bozick examples shows, hiring hall grievances dealt with a small number of farmworkers and never enough to imperil harvests. These grievances also originated because ranchers and supervisors insisted on hiring workers outside the hiring hall—a choice oral history interviewees related to bosses hiring relatives and/or favorite, and dependent, employees. Reflecting the period's power struggles, the UFW used its hiring hall and member grievances to fight Coachella Valley grape ranchers, who repeatedly attempted to regain their ability to hire and fire at will, and, by extension, diminish the UFW's power in rural California.[29]

The clearest example of these struggles involved the grape rancher Harry Carian, who held out against UFW unionization until 1971. Even as a latecomer, Carian racked up large number of grievances, including for poor camp conditions in August 1971, for bypassing the UFW hiring hall on October 1971 and January 1972, and for employing farmworkers in bad standing with the union. In late January 1972, the Coachella UFW office also filed three grievances for hiring nonunion farmworkers, contracting out UFW-covered work, and failing to provide farmworkers with restrooms or cold water in the workday.[30] These problems led to a "very constructive" meeting between the UFW and Carian on February 1972, in which (among other issues) both parties clarified the UFW's dispatch system and agreed, per the UFW demand, that Supervisor Lorenzo Santos "will change his attitude toward 'workers' and UFWOC [United Farm Workers Organizing Committee]."[31] But, tensions and violations persisted in later months and, again, led to reconciliation efforts by Carian's labor relations lawyer, who deflected Carian's behavior by speaking of both parties' alleged hostility: "the allegations do indicate a hostile attitude on the part of the union which may have been caused by poor attitude on Mr. Santos' part."[32]

Whatever reconciliation was reached, it was short lived. On May 10, 1972, Carian (again) hired ten workers outside the hiring hall and the UFW (again) filed a grievance. A series of angry phone calls followed, as did a vaguely threatening Coachella UFW letter demanding the grievance's resolution.[33] The threat became more direct in October 1972 when Carian ignored a Coachella UFW meeting to address yet another grievance for an unjustified worker dismissal. "Mr. Carian," wrote the Coachella UFW office, "will find that if it is impossible for him to cooperate with us in settling grievances and respecting the contract he has signed with the UFW, that it will be impossible for us to cooperate with him in the coming work season." Sure enough, when grape work began in December 1972 and Carian again incorrectly filed a dispatch order, the UFW organizer wrote back: "A complete package of our dispatch procedure forms were sent to your office with sufficient time for discussion. These forms were disregarded. Your request is not being acknowledged until the proper forms are used."[34] What became apparent to Carian in 1972 also characterized Coachella UFW tactics with other local grape ranchers: the hiring hall became a resource for securing contract observance, pithily shown by Coachella's report to the UFW headquarters in La Paz in December 1972: "Bozick didn't want to settle some 4 grievances, so [we] didn't dispatch anyone and they were settled."[35]

To address this situation, several Coachella Valley grape ranchers called for a meeting with the UFW in January 1973. The Coachella UFW office agreed to the meeting but brought along the union's grievance committee members for each rancher, which surprised and bothered the ranchers' labor relations lawyer: "he would give [the ranchers'] position," he said, "and leave." The rancher position was simple: they did not want to follow the UFW's new hiring hall procedures, which had been implemented in October 1972, arguing they were not part of the 1970 labor contract. The Coachella UFW office, however, did not bend to their demands and instead told the present grape ranchers to follow UFW procedures if they wanted to safeguard their harvests. Carian, who had ignored previous meetings, quipped with the paternalism of the rancher-king: he would use the UFW dispatch forms, he said, "as a courtesy," but emphasized ranchers "do *not have* to follow this procedure" (emphasis in original).[36] As if to challenge the spectacle of their employees' presence in the meeting, the grape ranchers added: "Contract procedures suggests how many people shall be present in grievance meeting. Next time, if Union insists on having so many workers present, advise in advance. A larger hall will be needed. Union should pay for the hall." The UFW's response was as succinct as it was telling of the world they wished to construct: "We'll bring as many people as we want, and we don't have to advise."

As previously discussed, the rancher-king's power laid in his ability to determine who ate and who did not, and in his ability to wield resources and institutions to sustain this choice. As a monarch, he played the patriarch's role—distributing jobs, privileges, and marginality, imposing terms of employment, and enforcing conditions with unemployment's existential threat. As Philip Vera Cruz argued in 1970, *el patron* represented "life and death." But, with the UFW's contract-based hiring hall, grievance committees, and arbitration procedures, the Coachella Valley's union members could literally bring grape ranchers to court. When more proved necessary, the local UFW office simply threatened to starve ranchers of their life/labor force, a threat that finally brought them to concede to UFW demands. Despite union errors and rancher recalcitrance, in other words, the Coachella Valley's unionized grape workers moved in these three years as if to dethrone the rancher-king and institute a world beyond the rancher's whims, greed, or barbarity. They wanted "their rights," as Adair noted, the "little things, that is contract enforcing," as the self-effacing Lopez remembered, "to talk sense to their bosses," as Vera Cruz predicted.

A New Sense of Dignity and Power

Though the UFW's 1970 grape contracts did not signal a fully transformed agricultural landscape in the Coachella Valley, they did provide a plane on which farmworkers could begin, as Adair recalled years later, to "exercise their rights and defend their rights."[37] At first sight, these union grievances imply a rather limited set of demands. But, when taken collectively, they represented power negotiations for an expansive, if vaguely defined, future egalitarianism. Some local union members even imagined the Coachella Valley's grape fields as potential spaces of sustenance for them and for their families.

This expansive egalitarianism appears in the oral history of Maria Serrano, who joined the migrant circuit with her husband and children after they immigrated from Mexico in the mid-1960s.[38] She immigrated, she said, because she met six young women (all between nineteen to twenty-three years old) near the U.S.–Mexico border, who spoke of working in a "field of flowers" in the United States. Seemingly happy and autonomous, the women workers embodied the independence and fulfillment she wished for her adolescent daughters. "I daydreamed," she said, "of being next to my daughters, being very happy cutting flowers, passing our days very happily."[39] In Serrano's vision, her daughters would have "their own money" and the chance to "go to night school and learn the language." Most conspicuously, her vision had no quotas, no bosses barking orders, not even male coworkers. "The reality," Serrano added quickly, "was so different, like you can't even imagine." Instead of a field of flowers, she found fields paying poverty wages and stretching as far as the eye could see, where farmworkers moved hunched over for hours at the supervisor's fast clip—only to then feel debilitating pain and exhaustion once at home. The absent restrooms, the disgusting lukewarm water, and migration's precarity only accentuated how wrong Serrano had been in her vision.

When the migration circuit brought her to Stockton, California, in 1966, however, she met the UFW leader Gil Padilla, who spoke to her about the bourgeoning UFW movement and their contract demands for better working conditions and higher wages. Whether or not Padilla knew it, Serrano interpreted his vision of an empowered farmworker population through her transnational and gendered lenses. She joined immediately, Serrano said, and while laboring on the migrant circuit she kept repeating Padilla's message: cold water, clean restrooms, worker power. In 1968, Serrano and her family settled in Coachella, where she again heard of the UFW, this time leading a harvest grape strike. Though she was not a grape worker, Serrano became an active supporter. When asked why, she said Padilla helped her see the empowering potential in unionization—a potential she had been striving toward to for many years already.[40]

Given her UFW membership since 1966, Serrano had enough union seniority to secure her a position in Freedman Ranch after the UFW and Steinberg signed labor contracts in 1970. Suddenly, Serrano recalled, she entered an altered workspace. She noticed first her coworkers' joy: "they were euphoric, with joy, because finally they had gained the first contract with the farmworker union."[41] When Serrano's family started to work at a fast clip, as they had learned under the Rancher Nation, the other farmworkers stopped them and said: "hey, hey, hey, what is going on? Calm down, go calmly, little by little."[42] Paid hourly, they learned, allowed them to work without the desperate daily rush and sinking feeling "that we were not even going to make for the daily food."[43] She noticed the camaraderie too, of crews sharing jokes while working or singing to the nearby portable radio: "They would put the radio on their vine," she said, "and they would move and bring it along. All were very happy."[44] The grape workers also received their first ten-minute break by mid-morning and then a lunch and a second break—all respected by supervisors who no longer yelled at them. She also learned about the contract-mandated bans on pesticides, the cold water for thirst, and the new portable restrooms at the vineyard's outer edges.

Arguably, those workplace restrooms most succinctly embodied the UFW contract's significance and its effect on farmworkers' lived experience in the fields. Serrano remembered them as clean, stocked with paper, and paired with a water station for hand washing. Seemingly trivial, their presence spoke to the everyday humiliation and discomfort once faced as a farmworker:

> Everything was different. Different. Ay . . . I even go to the restroom, and ay, I even sit down very comfortably because it was clean. It smelled of *Piño Sol*, or something like *Piño Sol*, it even smelled nice [deeply breaths in the aroma]. And I say, if only I had had this when I was working with the short-handled hoe. I was even embarrassed [to have to use a restroom], we would even hold it in so that we would not have to go to the restroom—because we were embarrassed. No no, we didn't have a way to do our necessities because we were all mixed [with men] and there just wasn't anywhere to go. What would cover us? The plant was this small [two inches]. Well where? Well where? There were no trees, nothing.[45]

Those restroom portables, so suddenly visible, marked grape ranchers' pre-UFW callousness as much as their restrained powers under the UFW contract. With such contracts, Serrano could be more than labor exerted in the Coachella Valley's fields. She could be a person, a body, and claim her right to privacy and comfort. Not since crossing that imaginary line on the sand had Serrano felt free from the daily choice between humiliation and humiliation—for what is to be forced to "hold it," like a desperate child, but merely a privatized form of humiliation?

Unexpectedly, then, Serrano's union membership brought her to a space like the vision that propelled her immigration. She now earned more money through the contract's higher wages and the elimination of the labor contractor's 10 percent cut. The UFW's hiring hall also curtailed exposure to labor contractor sexual harassment; employment no longer required sexual "favors" from women workers. She felt "incredibly happy," Serrano said, "mostly for my poor daughters, who did not have to be working so hard."[46] When asked if others noticed the altered realities, she exclaimed: "Of courrrssseee! . . . The other workers would say, 'That is the old man.' And well, they no longer had to be careful around him. [Steinberg] would pass us and look at us menacingly, with killer eyes. But, well no, we were now happy. And we were harvesting." To Serrano, Freedman remained "rebellious," still "angry" for being "practically forced" to sign a contract. But she and her co-unionists did not have to be careful around the boss, or live in the power relations implied by such cautious measures. Instead, grape workers could speak to each other, point to the old man, and know that though "killer eyes" remained they undoubtedly had to "pass." When asked if she had finally found her "fil de flores," that initial dream that had convinced her to cross the international border, she replied, "a little, a little."[47]

Serrano's oral history interview, as well as the union grievances discussed above, challenged grape ranchers' common claims of worker satisfaction in their pre-UFW world. They also contested ranchers' subsequent assertions of UFW disorganization, ineffectiveness, and abuse. Throughout the contract period, in fact, Coachella Valley grape ranchers argued the local UFW office mishandled seniority, broke up families when distributing crews, and charged cash-strapped farmworkers for unpaid dues prior to providing a job dispatch. In early 1973, these ranchers would speak of UFW-victimized farmworkers to unilaterally end contract negotiations with the UFW and sign contracts with the Teamsters Union, which had almost no previous ties to the Coachella Valley's grape workers. UFW errors certainly existed, as chapter six will discuss, but rancher assertions of widespread UFW disorganization and abuse, and their related claim of defending farmworkers, stretches credulity and belies their interests to delegitimize farmworker power. Fortunately the pro-UFW Catholic priest Victor Salandini surveyed forty-two Freedman farmworkers in 1974 on their experiences working under a UFW contract, including newly gained work benefits and altered rancher behavior. At least six interviewees were Filipino and twenty-two were women; most had been farmworkers for many years, and nearly all had worked under UFW contracts since 1970. Most reported working for Freedman with and without UFW representation. Though mediated, the survey provides a rich view of farmworkers' relationship to unionism in the early 1970s.[48]

In the survey, people spoke as adults and adolescents, as men and women, as Filipino, Mexican, migrant and settled, as parents and partners or neither. Most workers did not speak of the UFW by referencing a distant horizon, but instead of immediate life transformations. Maria Sanchez, for instance, shared her a husband underwent a hernia operation with the UFW insurance ("he was very happy"), noted transformed ranchers ("growers and foreman no longer bawl us out," "they used to fire us for any reason"), and identified with the union's leadership ("Chavez is one of our people").[49] Enriqueta Simo's diabetic husband was "being cared for in the union clinic in Calexico," while Edmundo Ramirez used the health plan for his daughter's "medical services" and wife's recent pregnancy.[50] Guadalupe Ortega, a "small woman" and single mother of seven, lived near the border and took her children "to the doctor specialist . . . many times." Chavez "understands us," Ortega added before requesting affordable, union-provided transportation from Imperial Valley.[51] For Estella Gonzalez, the UFW meant being "happier" and losing her "fear [of] the growers." For Miguel Ramirez, it meant a world transformed: "Before a worker was treated like a mule" and "had no breaks."[52] Similarly, Porfiria Rodriguez spoke of workplace improvements and union benefits, and then said she wanted the union to advocate for affordable housing. Elodia

Servin, who echoed her co-unionists, said the UFW also meant "there is also no discrimination of sexes."[53]

Of the forty-two workers interviewed, all but two wanted to keep the UFW as their union. This may not be particularly revealing given that Freedman workers were known to be ardent UFW members. But even the eight workers who shared strident criticism of UFW shortcomings spoke of its contract-based improvements. In interviews with the Filipino migrant workers Carlos Masip, Themistocles Abeno, and Vicente Tijan, for instance, Salandini asked about the union's tenure in the Coachella Valley, Masip began with a blunt appraisal of the local office, "illiterate people have been placed in charge of administration." These people had imposed fines for late dues and held poorly organized meetings. On the margins, Salandini noted he had attended such meetings, as if adding credence to Masip, who added: "People should be treated better . . . there should be *no fines*" and the dispatch should end its 'preference to Mexicans'" (emphasis in original). Eight other workers shared similar criticisms of the union.[54] But most also pivoted at the end, as like Masip: "Despite all, the union has improved our lives," he said, "having worked with the [ranchers] under no contract, we realize the many benefits of a union contract." For him, the contract meant union seniority, job security, better treatment, and respect from ranchers who had previously called Filipino farmworkers, "my boys."

Salandini also noted the dissent from Masip's two coworkers, who speculated that the Teamsters Union, who raided Coachella Valley grape fields in 1973, could do a better job.[55] These two workers were alone in this speculation. The rest emphasized the UFW benefits. The Filipino workers Fred Abad, Felix Ytom, and Herman Murello spoke of the higher wages, the improved working conditions, and the UFW's health insurance. Abad shared he underwent a free hernia operation and his wife had "a major operation" in a "good hospital" in San Francisco, per the UFW's suggestion. Both experiences stood in sharp contrast to the lack of health care coverage prior to unionization, which had grown in significance with their ages. In fact, all three farmworkers had been part of the Delano Grape Strike in 1965. In one pre-strike meeting, their co-unionists spoke of their generation-specific needs for a labor contract: "If we had a union contract with the growers when we were still young," one pro-striker said, "we could also be enjoying what other workers have. But since we failed to do so, we need to work even though our bones and bodies are aching."[56] Abad, Ytom, and Murello all disregarded the Teamsters Union as rancher pawns who did not represent their interests before closing the interview by specifying the UFW's impact on their lives: "I joined the union because I believe it is good for all farm workers"; "Generally speaking the union has improved my life"; "The clinics have benefitted us"; "The union is fighting the growers"; "There have been grievances but they have been resolved"; "The union has made us feel more like human beings."

While the interviews' are still a mediated source, they still show how UFW members clearly saw the union's shortcomings. But they also saw that unionization had already initiated a profound break from their past experiences in the Rancher Nation. In this break, Adair stressed, "the [UFW's] end goal . . . was a radical vision. It wasn't an extra nickel. It wasn't an extra dime. It was justice. It was dignity. It was the growers treating us with respect. That was the bottom line."[57] Coachella Valley grape ranchers remained "rebellious," as Serrano observed, but few UFW members in 1974 appeared to doubt that the pre-UFW and precontract days of rancher impunity and callousness, for the time being, were partially over.

In the process, some farmworkers spoke of a personal transformation through the union. Maria Serrano, for instance, said she took on union leadership positions in Freedman ranch committees. When her co-unionists elected her committee president, she was responsible for bringing union member complaints to their supervisors and filing grievances when supervisors or ranchers ignored them. Though Serrano's life story up to the 1970s had been one of consistent assertiveness, she said she was initially very afraid to approach the field bosses, who were almost uniformly male and English speaking. When asked how she managed to overcome this fear, Serrano said she was not sure, that she had to "pull power/force out from where I did not have it—I had to report to the union."[58] In the process, Serrano found a power she had not formerly recognized. As a union leader, she also attended many union training meetings, where she learned to respect, but not fear, the rancher. All farmworkers, she said, had to learn to use "definitive and confident words."[59] For Serrano, these trainings and union roles reiterated what she saw on her first day in the UFW grape field: that the UFW movement's 1970 victory meant a profound transformation of labor power relationships, one that impacted farmworkers' lived experiences in the fields, and, relatedly, their sense of self.

Similarly, one of Serrano's co-unionists, Maria Marron, told of an epistemological transformation because of her UFW membership.[60] In her interview, Marron recounted the transformation with an allegory, in which a man approached a boy selling newborn and still blind puppies. When the man enquired on their selling price, the boy said, "five dollars." The man said they were too small to be worth five dollars but said he would return for them once they opened their eyes. Three weeks later, the man returned with his five dollars and asked the boy for one puppy. But the boy replied, "No, [the puppy] is worth more now." Incredulous, the man asked "why?!" and the boy said, "Because it opened its eyes." Marron laughed when telling this story, adding: "That's what happened with us. We didn't have anyone to open our eyes. We had this wish to have justice, to have freedom.... But we had no one to aid us. And here came Cesar Chavez and he opened our eyes, and so we were worth more."[61] For Marron, the UFW contracts meant more than transformed relationships between coworkers and supervisors; it also shaped how she saw the world. We may be cautious of attributing this effect to only Cesar Chavez, as she did. But we would do well to consider her emphasis on the union's epistemological impact: she no longer felt blind.

Here, No One Walks Over No One

Though Coachella Valley farmworkers held onto distinct visions of the UFW movement, as did their non-farmworker allies, two political visions deserve extra attention. The first, espoused by women union members, understood the UFW as advancing for what can be described as a feminist world inside and outside the Coachella Valley's working fields. The second, espoused by Filipino members, envisioned the UFW as providing social welfare in the form of a retirement home, one that broke away from the American West's colonial and racist history of labor. Both visions reiterated the expansive politics found in the everyday "machinery of unionism," as visible through grievances, oral histories, and survey interviews.

We can begin the discussion on women farmworkers with Petra Ruiz, who joined the UFW movement after she witnessed a UFW funeral procession for Imperial Valley farmworkers killed in a 1971 bus accident. The procession, Ruiz explained, echoed her mother's deep humanitarianism; it moved her, she added, and "there" she "join[ed] Cesar, in the caravan taking the bodies to Mexicali, and there I never let him go ... that was the beginning." A few months later in 1971, Ruiz began working in Freedman Ranch under a woman leader she referred to as her *"commandante,"* Rosario Pelayo.[62] Ruiz would work for Freedman for the next two decades and serve in various UFW leadership capacities in the Coachella Valley. When asked about the UFW's goals in the early contract years, Ruiz began her answer with abstract concepts—of worker respect, equality amongst workers, of wide-ranging notions of justice. In her rendition, each value marshaled the next: "respect—fighting against being egoists or only for oneself ... that we be for everybody, all us even, for everybody.... Equality—that is what we were searching, for everybody."[63] "Here," Ruiz restated UFW goals in succinct terms, "no one walks over no one." When asked about "justice," she echoed other pro-UFW farmworkers: "to demonstrate that what the foreman said was not true. And us, well, to fight to help for our own people."[64]

But for Ruiz, these values also highlighted the gendered specificity of farm labor exploitation and of women's fight against farmworker patriarchy.

Pro-UFW women members elaborate on unionization's gendered implications. *El Malcriado*, April 20, 1973, 2. Walter P. Reuther Library, Archives of Labor and Urban Affairs, Wayne State University.

Coachella Valley grape fields, Ruiz explained, remained the domain of male supervisors and farmworkers who sexually harassed women and mocked their labor capacities.[65] These men said women unionists should stay at home so other men could take their union grape jobs, advocating for normative gender roles (male breadwinners) and assumptions (stronger male bodies). When the UFW's women members defied them, Ruiz said, they spread rumors about the women's sexual improprieties and referred to them as "bitches." When asked to clarify who made these offensive remarks, she pointed to her male supervisors *and* coworkers, even some pro-UFW worker-leaders. Her son, who was also present in the interview, added that the local community saw the husband as the family's source of authority. If a woman and wife wanted to participate in a public event, even if the event was associated with the UFW and the husband was pro-union, she had to ask for her husband's permission. And these men, interjected Petra, always wanted their wives at home. When women defied their husband's authority, continued her son, they ran the risk of being physically assaulted by their husbands.[66]

In Ruiz's account, pro-UFW women challenged such politics in three ways. First, women defied the frail female trope by working faster than male-dominated crews. In doing so, women union members contested the faux-biological argument for a gendered separation of space: of a masculine laboring public and of a private feminine space of presumed leisure. By claiming their union jobs, women members also safeguarded a potential source of economic independence from men. Ruiz said the fight for women's access to UFW jobs continued in the 1970s, often against the intransigence of pro-UFW men.[67] Second, women participated in many UFW activities in both local and nonlocal campaigns, including trips to Los Angeles and Orange County (where they joined lettuce boycott picket lines), leadership-training retreats at the UFW headquarters in La Paz, and political lobbying drives in Sacramento.[68] The UFW publicized these events and often cajoled members to participate further. For Ruiz, women's public participation challenged the patriarchal limits imposed on their mobility and autonomy; the usual male refrain, Ruiz said, was "Why isn't she in her house?" Such union activity participation also secured women members' seniority status in the UFW and, by extension, their opportunity to work in unionized grape fields—where they continued to challenge male co-unionists.

Third, and lastly, when male supervisors and farmworkers continued to sexually harass women farmworkers in UFW-contracted grape fields, Ruiz and others turned to the UFW contract's grievance system.[69] Ruiz remembered that in 1972 she and other women unionists filed a grievance against a supervisor for tolerating male farmworker sexual harassment, arguing the latter violated the contract's nondiscrimination clauses. Soon after the filing, Ruiz said the supervisor met with her and her coworkers to ask that they speak with him directly to avoid future grievances. In her recounting, the supervisor spoke sheepishly, almost pleadingly: "No, don't be ungrateful," he told them, "Never go to the office to complain. Better to just tell me."[70] Whether the supervisor spoke in such tones is irrelevant—for Ruiz's memory reflected her understanding of the UFW contract's potential to re-shape relations between men and women in a Mexican farmworker community. The women's reply to the supervisor even conditioned the supervisors' good standing with the UFW on fighting farmworker patriarchy: "'But, are we going to have more complaints?' they asked the supervisor, 'We will not complain [to the Union], but you *have* to teach the same workers that we are not what they say.' Because, they would say that we were, you know, bitches" (emphasis in original).[71]

In her oral history interview, Ruiz also shared a pre-UFW life of fighting for her and other women's safety and respect, usually from male violence and sexual harassment. This was also the case for other pro-UFW women, like Maria Serrano and Maria Marron. The difference at Freedman Ranch in the early 1970s was simply that the union's grievance-based power granted Ruiz an *extra* tool for actualizing her already-held politics and principles. For Ruiz, in short, the UFW movement's 1970 victory in Coachella Valley grape fields provided a new means for demanding respect, equality, and justice. The UFW contract meant men had to learn to respect and share spaces with women. They had to see women as skilled workers with rightful access to union jobs, and they had to check their impulse to control women's movement and autonomy. For those who could not learn this politics, unionists like Ruiz could turn to the contract's antidiscriminatory clauses and grievance procedure. With both, former patriarch supervisors could be forced to speak in pleading tones and, perhaps more importantly, lecture recalcitrant male workers to relinquish their patriarchal fantasies-or else face the union's arbitration powers. In Ruiz's recounting, the supervisors followed their demands only to keep their jobs, because the patriarchal grape rancher already recognized *his* economic vulnerability under a UFW contract; they were thus less amenable to grievance-accumulating supervisors. For Ruiz, in short, to be a *Chavista* was to be for farmworker empowerment and for women's rights.[72]

Despite this rank-and-file feminist unionism, the UFW's newspaper did not identify patriarchy as a significant force in farmworker communities, nor recognize women's presence independent of their husbands and fathers. In *El Malcriado*'s first two years of publication—and thus before its makeover to serve the consumer boycott and its white liberal readers—the drama of farmworker oppression involved only male actors, usually in a trinity cluster: the obese and racist white male rancher, the sly and predatory labor contractor, and the always-emasculated farmworker who repeatedly fails to protect and provide for his family.[73] Embodying different objectionable masculinities, the three figures jointly contributed to farmworker marginalization, especially of women and children. When the UFW movement adopted its boycott strategy and turned its newspaper into a white story machine, the union exchanged the trinity for a dichotomous world of racist white ranchers and bewildered-but-cohesive farmworker family units who collectively fought poverty with familial solidarity and built a visionary and progressive movement.[74] The UFW movement presented these untroubled, valiant families as "the farmworkers," a term that conveniently vacated all internal power struggles and allowed white consumers to see the key culprit behind farmworker marginalization: the obese and regressive white rancher class. In such portraits, Ruiz's critique of male farmworkers and supervisors—as sustaining gendered hierarchies—had little resonance.

And yet, the UFW's contract and general policies did provide for empowered actions. Its family approach to organizing meant that women farmworkers were half of its membership and often in leadership positions. In the Coachella Valley, for instance, women members powered the UFW campaigns in the 1960s, such as Amalia Uribe Deaztlan and Irene Reyes, the two young women who sat in the UFW's Coachella Strike Committee. Women also served as union stewards, such as Maria Serrano in Freedman Ranch and Maria Marron in Karahadian Ranch.[75] For some women, the UFW provided opportunities to use specific skills, such as Evangelina Mendoza, who contributed her literacy skills as a meeting secretary.[76] Second, the UFW contract's antidiscrimination provisions represented real union commitments gender equality. In late 1973, Serrano brought a complaint to the central UFW leadership about the all-male crews for grape pruning, which was considered too arduous for women. She explained that women's exclusion from these crews guaranteed they would always lack enough annual work hours to maintain their union seniority or benefits. Cesar Chavez agreed with her and opened these jobs to women members, though it nearly provoked a revolt among male members.[77] Lastly, the UFW's hiring hall meant women no longer gained jobs through labor contractors, who discriminated against women and mixed job provisions with sexual predation.[78]

Women members also paired these union commitments with their own initiatives. Meetings and demonstrations, for instance, provided common spaces for discussing poor conditions, forming new friendships, and resisting patriarchal violence.[79] Virginia Ortega described an instance of such violence when she recounted a 1973 UFW meeting on wage theft: in mid-session, she said, a male farmworker arrived unexpectedly and threatened his wife with physical violence for having disobeyed his prohibition against attending UFW meetings. His threat did not go uncontested, Ortega explained. His wife chastised him publicly and marked a shift in the family's power dynamics: "I came because I also have my work hours," Ortega quoted her, "and I have my check and my daughters' checks. That is why. You are not going to keep everything. So, I had to come."[80] The "brave Paulita," as Ortega remembered, may have contested her husband's authority prior to the UFW movement, as many women had contested their patriarchal husband. But, in the UFW world, "Paulita's" defiance also came with her co-unionists' collective chiding when he threatened her again: "What is thhaaaat? What is thhaaaat?," they said in unison, shaming him until "he closed his beak."[81] To Ortega, the UFW's rank-and-file women members built spaces and solidarities to challenge their husbands and pointed to a future where men "did not keep everything."

Lastly, the contract's wages, benefits, and antidiscriminatory hiring clause promoted women's economic independence from men. With the latter, they could challenge the patriarchal men in their lives. Evangelina Mendoza, for instance, said her husband repeatedly attempted to prohibit her from participating in UFW activities and would respond to her defiance with anger and threats of abandonment. Regarding the latter, Mendoza's reaction betrayed no concern for her family's well-being. With unionized wages, she could respond to her husband's threat: "'Ay, God bless him!' And then I went to sleep."[82] When asked about the source of her husband's generalized anger, she replied, "I made more money than my husband. That was his rage, that I earned more money than him." He mocked her repeatedly, Mendoza added, alleging that she "'[didn't] even do anything' for her income. 'That's what you think,' she would snap back, 'but I do work.'"[83] Like other women, Mendoza leveraged UFW benefits to resist her husband's control and belittling. Through *her* union, she also challenged a central patriarchal presumption: that within marriage, the husband as principal breadwinner was the family's law.

Away from Coachella Valley, Delano-based Filipino members also associated bread-and-butter union goals with aspirations that transcended farm work. Like Coachella Valley women members, pro-UFW Filipino men understood the UFW as addressing multiple forces entangled with exploitation. One such force was the long shelf-life of California's anti-miscegenation laws. For many, the state's anti-miscegenation laws meant a lifetime of bachelorhood and, by the early 1970s, limited resources and family networks in their last years of life. For some, older age meant poverty and loneliness, and the looming prospect of losing rancher camp housing once they were unable to work. In this context, and after several years of Filipino pressure, the UFW open[ed] the Paulo Agbayani Village in Delano, California.[84] Conceived in the late 1960s and finalized in late 1973, the Paulo Agbayani Village was to be a retirement community for aging farmworkers, most of whom would be Filipino. A rather humble structure, the village had fifty-nine rooms, a small dining hall, and a small community center. Its residents, *El Malcriado* reported, would live in a "collective" of individual rooms and a shared dining hall and community room. For social activities, land was reserved for "a collective garden" and for "rais[ing] chickens." Residents could also volunteer in the village's upkeep or serve as guard duty in the UFW's former headquarters, which was adjacent to the village. All decisions were to be made democratically, the paper added.

In explaining the significance of Agbayani Village, *El Malcriado* printed two photos: one of eighteen "original" Filipino strikers of the 1965 Delano

Grape Strike and another of six aging Filipino men, all playing cards around a small wooden table, a couple with cigars.[85] Under the latter photo, the caption read: "they will have their own home and will enjoy the life of recreation and rest they have earned with their sacrifices in the fields and in the fight for dignity and justice."[86] For Bob Armington, a Filipino "UFW foreman," the "building of this village [was] a monument to the working people" who spent lives in California's labor camps—a condition that had been imposed by white supremacy, labor exploitation, and American imperialism in the Philippines. Rebelling against this twentieth century condition, Filipino men triggered the 1965 Delano Grape Strike, "the first heroic page in the history of the liberating strike against the grape industry." To *El Malcriado*, the village thus embodied Filipino farmworkers' life of resistance against marginalization, as well the UFW attempt to actualize a historic turning point: for men long denied a home in the United States, the village promised to offer rest and belonging. It was most appropriately named after Paul Agbayani, an original grape striker in 1965 who died while on the picket line in 1966.[87]

These political visions for the village were evident when it was originally envisioned in 1969 and 1970. In August 1969, *El Malcriado* reported on the "first concrete steps . . . towards Filipino Retirement Village" and summarized Philip Vera Cruz's argument for its construction: "Filipinos, more than any other ethnic group in farm labor, were trapped by an inhuman system which in effect denied them the right to have families. . . . Today, thousands . . . are reaching 65 or 70, with no families, no security, nowhere to settle down. After working in this country for 40 years or more, providing the labor that made hundreds of growers into millionaires, the Filipinos are now being thrown out of the camps, denied jobs, tossed aside like a piece of rusty old machinery."[88] For Vera Cruz, the village was a response to a history of Filipino racialization and objectification that continued to haunt them in older age, in their lack of families and networks of support, in their frailer bodies and impoverished livelihoods. It fought rancher commodification of Filipino labor, where men were "tossed aside like a piece of rusty old machinery."[89] Even if a humble structure, it sought "in a small way" to "provide a little security and dignity for these men in their old age which America denied them in their youth."[90] In 1970, *El Malcriado* spoke of the coming village "with a future" and its significance: "As the farmworker [movement] moves in the 1970's [it] seeks to build new institutions and structures in order to live in dignity and relative security."[91]

Such values appeared poignantly visible in village meeting notes prior to the completion of Agbayani Village. The latter's first incarnation came in the form of a union-dominated labor camp in Schendley Farms in late 1969 and early 1970—before the victories of 1970. In these bimonthly meetings, Filipino members established a communal garden and distributed labor for the village's upkeep. When residents did not complete the latter, they agreed on a supervisor to hold people accountable, but they insisted on a democratically chosen supervisor—a marked contrast from the rancher-controlled fields in which they labored. In January 1970, they also discussed hospitalized Filipino men who wanted to be part of the new village. Marion Moses was one such person: he had "no family or friends, except those in the strike. He would like to live at the village." Speaking of another hospitalized striker, the UFW stalwart Julian Balidoy said, "He is our brother and should be able to come here to the camp. He likes to be with us."[92] The group also formed a committee to investigate the possibilities for a union clinic to care for these men. In an act that mixed grace with militancy, they agreed to visit the men in hospitals and send village representatives to all funerals, "especially [for] the single men. A wreath could be presented by the Village."[93]

Through such efforts, Filipino farmworkers sought to build the foundations necessary for the new world. They appeared like slivers of potential against a difficult life: a small apartment against the history of racial violence in the U.S. Pacific Coast; a shared garden against the corporate agricultural industry; companionship against the growing disinterest of fellow citizens. For Willie Barrientos, a UFW member from the late 1960s to the late 1970s, Agbayani Village also spoke of a futurity not often associated with the *Manong* generation. Why, he asked in 1978, "is it that we cannot build a village for the Pilipinos, for all the workers in Delano. So that when they cannot work anymore, they have a place to stay." For him, the village represented more than a final resting place. It also sought to care for the younger by demanding what was due to older Filipino laborers. "That's why we demand our share," Barrientos explained, "our share to live as a human being, so that we can also send our children to school and be educated like anybody else. That's why we have this [village]."[94] Like the women unionists in the Coachella Valley, pro-UFW Filipino grape workers made the movement theirs and infused its purpose with their histories and visions, hopes and aspirations—even if the leadership and membership, especially ethnic Mexicans, struggled to see them on their terms.

Conclusion: A Breaking of Dawn

For Coachella Valley grape ranchers, the UFW's labor contracts augured a fundamental change in agricultural power relationships. Long accustomed to commanding as unquestioned law, they became "constitutional monarch[ies]," tethered to contracts that banished contractors and forced new tricks on old supervisors: to hold back anger, to watch words, to speak with forced/feigned respect. Even the contract's seemingly limited demands—field restrooms, cold water, grievance procedures—challenged the workforce's commodification and served as sites for worker power. As Vera Cruz argued in 1970, just as Coachella Valley grape ranchers caved to UFW demands: "[farmworkers] are confronting an absurd society and an unrepresentative government. They want more than a few crumbs from the master's table. They want real change. They want to live in a society where all men are brothers."[95]

In an illustrative grievance, Freedman grape workers filed a grievance in 1971 against Steinberg's supervisor Pete Pilar, who refused to take the union's dispatched members.[96] After learning of Pilar's initial refusal, the local UFW organizers spoke with Steinberg's general supervisor and reminded him of the contract's stipulations. When the general supervisor finally allowed the dispatched workers to join Pilar's crew, Pilar insulted them. In reaction, they *refused to work*.[97] Later in the day, the UFW organizer and the UFW ranch committee met to discuss the incident and decided to give Pilar a "citation," which they planned to serve the next morning. The organizers' notes do not explain the implications of such a citation, or its ultimate effects. But even if ambiguous, the action still spoke of rancher power curtailed and of worker visions for an improved workplace. The rank and file not only engaged in confrontations to subject the supervisor to a common standard, they did so precisely through the very means supervisors had previously maintained worker discipline: the citation and its threat of job termination. Telling of the new dynamics, these laborers went on strike as if to demand the right to *feel insulted*.[98]

For these Coachella Valley grape workers, the UFW contract represented a tool to enforce cooperation onto the rancher, a power seizure that allowed workers to reformulate what to expect in the fields and what to imagine as possible for everyday life. For some, having a contract meant being able to build a space not entirely defined by the field's exploitation—a safe home for children, a private restroom when in need, a secured wage offering life after work. A labor contract also meant farmworkers did not have to look over their shoulders to respond to the boss's unprovoked actions. It meant, too, the increasing recognition that one had allies among coworkers, that one could lead actions to shape the world they wished to inhabit, whether this involved gender equality, a dignified retirement home, or the shared law of "no one walks over no one." "We were fighting for everyone," Ruiz said pointedly, "not just for oneself." "Don't be," she added, "like the short handle hoe," only pulling toward oneself.[99] For many workers, the contract literally promised a different world.

Many of us already know the 1970s did not bring a new day to organized labor—especially to farmworkers. The causes for such disappointment are plural, and they require an accounting of multiple spaces, actors, and forces.

Critically, recent scholarship sees this period as a missed opportunity as UFW neglect and disorganization alienated farmworkers and provided grist for a future Teamsters raid in 1973. There is substance to this critique, as I discuss in chapter 6. For now, I will note that such a declension narrative overlooks what was apparent to Coachella Valley grape workers. For them, these were heady years when they "tasted" contract life, to use Serrano's words, and gained "better things," to use Vera Cruz's words. No one was naïve to think further union progress would come easily, or that ranchers accepted the UFW contracts. As Rosa Olloa told Salandini in 1974, "Yes, Freedman Co. is treating us better, but not because his attitudes toward farm worker changed. Rather it is because he is bound by the contract."

Chapter 5

Chicana/o Coachella and the Civic Retreat of the Rancher Nation

As the 1960s came to an end, year after year, Coachella's boosters announced dreams of an economic and population boom that would turn the city into the "very heart of the Coachella Valley." The "City of Coachella," the *Desert Rancher* wrote in 1967, "is coming to the forefront as a vibrant community with a clear-cut destiny of being the 'hub' of valley development." Two years later, it added, "the Coachella Valley is now settling down to become a boom area once again." Former forecasts had not materialized as imagined, it admitted, for even as the region grew agriculturally the city's commercial projects and population had remained anemic. Still, the monthly stressed the city's record construction growth in 1969, making it "percentage-wise . . . the third fastest growing city in Riverside County." With "proper leadership and planning," the city could even "regain some of its lost stature" in the new decade.[1] The city's boosters imagined a Coachella that finally came into its own, making good on the early settlers' dreams.

The dream was not to be. Since the 1950s, Coachella's sister city, Indio, received the majority of the region's investments, visitors, and tax revenue, while other development took place between Indio and Palm Springs—where date orchards and sand dunes gave way to millionaire country clubs, golf courses, and winter resorts promising a "gracious desert living" of modern amenities and unspoiled nature, one that settled into comforts far removed from the pioneer's labors or the desert's furious heat. In the new city of Palm Desert, the Silver Spur Country Club's marketing typified the promise: "the valley's newest and finest ranch home community: secluded, restricted, sheltered . . . and with magnificent views." As such, the western half's 1970s boom further eclipsed Coachella's farm economy and white pioneer identity.[2]

Two additional developments challenged Coachella's pioneer dreams. First, its postwar demographic change transformed a largely "white" city in the 1940s into a city in the late 1960s with near equal numbers of white and Mexican residents and then one with a Mexican majority in the early 1970s.[3] Second, the increasing visibility of race-justice politics in Coachella led to a dramatic rearticulation of the city's racial future and a critique of the city's pioneer past. As early as 1964, for instance, the *Coachella Valley Sun* had described municipal elections as "scarred" by candidates who alleged the city had underserved ethnic Mexican communities. These early efforts gave way in the late 1960s to United Farm Workers (UFW) strikes and a parallel Chicana/o movement that called for revamping the city's social, political and cultural institutions so as to safeguard Mexican American citizenship. To these Chicanas/os, Coachella did not represent pioneer triumphalism, but instead an emergent Chicana/o home—one that rose into power with other similar communities in the U.S. Southwest.

From 1970 to 1973, while UFW members restructured their relationship to former rancher-kings on the fields, Coachella's Chicana/o activists sought to eliminate the Rancher Nation's racial components in the streets. These activists had worked in agriculture and/or were the children of farmworkers, and many had become politically active through the UFW in the late 1960s. In the early 1970s, they turned to fighting racial inequality in the city, speaking out against police violence and the Vietnam War, against everyday racial discrimination, school mistreatment, and abuse. They led student walkouts and filled school district meetings, ran voter registration campaigns, and formed political parties. They published newspapers that attempted to draw in sympathetic whites and built cultural spaces to articulate a still vague Chicana/o identity. For the most optimistic, these efforts represented the building blocks of a world far removed from the Rancher Nation—a world that, as the local Chicana/o newspaper imagined, finally realized "the ideal of equality, justice and opportunities for all those who live in this country."[4] As implied in the quote, most activists spoke of citizenship to make demands and most demanded far less than the *reconquista* rallying cry of a few young men. But the Chicana/o demand for equal citizenship meant dramatic changes to the region's social relations—akin to the UFW's contract-based constitutional revolution.

For these activists such changes hinted at expected life transformations that echoed the farmworkers' union experiences. The Chicana/o movement had found its focus through the UFW grape strikes of 1968 and 1969. Now, they pushed even further. To most, the two movements were one and the same. But, as we will see in the following chapter, such co-identification carried its own sources of future challenges and unraveling.

Ideal's Vision for the Coachella Valley

In early November 1969, the Coachella Valley's MAPA chapter published the first issue of its bi-monthly and bilingual newspaper, *Ideal*. The UFW had already migrated north and east for the season, promising to return the next year, though farmworker families were mostly back in the Coachella Valley for fall harvests, some after participating in UFW meetings and picket lines. For local MAPA members, November 1969 marked the intensification of their campaigns for Mexican American rights outside the region's agricultural fields, as if spinning off the UFW's momentum to strike at the Coachella Valley's educational, political, and social inequalities.

Emblematic of the next five years, *Ideal*'s first issue mixed accounts of racial injustices and Chicana/o movement victories, while connecting local power dynamics to regional and national social hierarchies. In one article, for instance, *Ideal* lambasted the racist judges in California's rural courts. In San Jose, Judge Chargrin compared Mexicans to animals; in nearby Beaumont, Judge Quitman defended police testimony in cases of police brutality; in Coachella, Judge Cross, with a seventh-grade education, was fired from a police department "for the brutal beating of a Mexican American boy."[5] In the 1968 summer, Cross had handed out jail sentences to MAPA members for protesting a Fourth of July celebration during the UFW Coachella Grape Strike of 1968. As a counterpoint, *Ideal* also knitted together a collection of localized Mexican American struggles against racial marginality in the U.S. Southwest, both documenting and amplifying the voices of a rising Chicana/o movement, and challenging local activists to connect their campaigns to those of others. The Mexican American Legal Defense Fund (MALDEF), for instance, defended Coachella Valley MAPA members while filing court cases against education discrimination in Santa Ana (California), housing and employment discrimination in Los Angeles (California), and false rape charges in Texas. In a profile of Raul Loya, MAPA's jailed president in 1969, the issue similarly traced his organizing spirit to his union days in Arizona mines. Another article showcased San Antonio's MAPA voter registration campaign, and subsequent power transformation, as a model for contesting the Coachella Valley's social relations.

The newspaper would maintain this broad political geography, juxtaposing social marginality with community empowerment. And as a bilingual newspaper, *Ideal* presented itself as a bridge between Spanish and English speakers, and Mexican, Chicana/o and white residents. One Spanish writer summarized the newspaper's aim as introducing "people who do not speak Spanish ... to our way of thinking [and] to establish better relations within the entire community."[6] Similarly, the first editorial reassured potential critics that *Ideal* did not advance radical racial politics, but only "present[ed] the voice of the Mexican American" to "establish dialogue" with "Anglo Americans." The editorial even closed with an expression of confidence in white residents: "We know that [the] racism, discrimination, exploitation[,] and injustice that exist in our country come from a small group of people whose prejudices blur the good name of the American people." To do this, *Ideal* covered local news and reprinted articles from other Chicana/o newspapers. It reserved space for histories of Mexico and ethnic-Mexican working communities, as well as for amateur poems, visual art, and first-person reflections on the "Chicano condition." Lastly, it paired its editorial with letters from readers, local opinion columns, and a political cartoon that mixed kitschy movement slogans with acerbic portrayals of local conservative critics.[7] As the name suggested, *Ideal* aimed to construct a space—or a field—for a multiplicity of stories, those of self and others, of past, present, and future, of struggles and potential—so as to finally realize, as the editors wrote in October 1970, "the ideal of equality, justice and opportunities for all those who live in this country."[8]

The newspaper had other purposes, too. The MAPA editors knew of the Coachella Valley's fervently pro-rancher print culture, which refused to acknowledge the region's racial inequality or the legitimacy of farmworker demands. For them, *Ideal* needed to be a critical intervention in the public sphere, for only the naming of the world as is could build the world as should be. They practiced this intervention in their third issue when they published a letter from Frank Esher, an anti-UFW writer for the *Coachella Valley Sun*, who argued UFW strikers were predatory "outsiders" and local farmworkers had no grievances. Esher wrote: "You talk and talk, or write about racism, that those in the Alamo were only adventurers and traitors, that justice in our country is only a farce. . . . This is the classical language of the radicals who want to destroy our country."[9] The stress on racism, he added, contradicted *Ideal*'s "beautiful name" and showed the editors as "dangerous radicals, and nothing else. I assure it myself who always used to see with sympathy the Mexican Americans trying to overcome themselves."[10] His expression of sympathy and embattled principle reiterated rancher portrayals of the UFW as illegitimate aggression on a harmonious desert of ranchers and workers. His "dangerous radical" accusation also produced the related claims of white innocence and vulnerability, thus presenting *Ideal* and the "dangerous radicals" as the principal, if not only, local social problem.[11] In closing, Esher doubted *Ideal*'s editors would publish his letter given their purported political extremism, explaining his "purpose" as simply "to tell you that you are not fooling all the people."

Perhaps to his surprise, *Ideal* carried his letter after all, but paired it with a sharp retort. "First," the editors countered, "we talk or write about racism, injustices, discrimination, etc., because all this does exist."[12] To deny them was akin to an ostrich with "his head in the sand." It was "cowardice" and did nothing to "resolve these wicked problems." To the "dangerous radicals" charge, *Ideal* countered by accusing Esher with betraying U.S. values and representing the opinions of only a minority of "gringo" "lepers": "the majority of Anglo Americans are decent and just people. The kind of people who made this great country, and have helped so many other countries have liberty and justice." *Ideal* claimed the mantle of American-ness to paint Esher's politics as extreme, unpopular, and historically unrecognizable.

To name and denounce U.S. racism, the editors argued, was the most American thing a citizen could do. It also provided the ground for a diverse society, for the "ideal" of "better relations and dialogue" among different peoples only existed in the counter public of reality, outside the rancher-king's fantasies and ostrich-like middlemen.[13] As evidence, *Ideal* retraced MAPA's Fourth of July protest in 1968 and the jail terms imposed on MAPA members Raul Loya, Alfredo Figueroa, John Kay, and Jim Caswell. Caswell had moved to the Coachella Valley from Canada in the late 1950's, where his liberal politics brought him to Chicana/o and UFW activists in the 1960s and led to his expulsion from the local Democratic Party, whose members included anti-UFW ranchers.[14] In 1968, the four men were tried for disturbing the peace and sentenced by Judge Cross to four months in jail. Older than most MAPA members, Caswell was also diabetic and on medication when incarcerated in the 1969 summer. According to MAPA, guards denied Caswell his diabetes medication despite his protests and swift health deterioration. In three months, he lost one hundred pounds. Shocked and dejected, his friends recalled, Caswell spent days muttering on the jail floor: "This is America. Here in our country, such things cannot happen."[15] With the others, he was released in November 1969, just as *Ideal*'s first issue fanned out across the Coachella Valley. To his MAPA friends, Caswell appeared a broken man, alone in his home, "just laying there [on the sofa], not being able to move.... He wasn't the old Caswell." Ray Rodriguez shared that Caswell had "lost everything, all his enthusiasm, because he believed that in America they could not do that ... He would cry ... he would sit and cry, in jail."[16] Body-wrecked and spirit-exhausted, Caswell died a couple months after his release.

In *Ideal*'s coverage, Caswell stood for the values of a "true American" and died a "victim ... of a few gringos." But *Ideal* also described Caswell as initially incapable of seeing the country's inequalities or the violence deployed against non-white communities. In one article, the Blythe-based MAPA member, Alfredo Figueroa, warned him of the risks in race activism: "Jim, realize that if you get in our fight in order to clear the good name of the American people, they will certainly sacrifice you."[17] If *Ideal* considered Esher a political "coward" and "leper," in other words, it also viewed Caswell as too goodhearted and naive, possibly tinged with white liberalism's conceit: that it knows more about racial inequality than those routinely subjected to its violence. For *Ideal*, Caswell's jail-related death originated in and reflected the country's "wicked problems" and only hinted at the violence that non-white communities faced under white supremacy. This is America, MAPA argued, and here in our country, such things do happen. His death also contradicted

Esher's claims of white innocence, for civic leaders willingly sacrificed an innocent man to fight a race justice movement. *Ideal* aimed to make obvious what Esher painted as "dangerous radical" lies: the Coachella Valley of the early 1970s, like much of the country, remained a racialized, violent, and unequal society that betrayed its social and civic ideals.[18]

For the next five years, *Ideal*'s articles, poems, stories, and columns provided a sober account of such marginality in public schools and popular culture, through police violence and political underrepresentation, in agricultural fields, civic spaces, and psyches. These forces brewed synergistically: migrant labor impeded farmworker children's education and secured a new generation of workers; political underrepresentation led to political violence (e.g., Caswell), and political violence led to political silencing, as the police killing of the Chicano journalist, Ruben Salazar, illustrated. The region had no affordable health care or housing for farmworker families, and few spaces of leisure or positive images for their children. Even the Catholic Church lacked Mexican American leaders, while Coachella's priest considered Mexicans an inferior race.[19] Nationally, a racist popular culture produced advertising like the Frito Bandito brand—a smiling, accented caricature of the Mexican revolutionary, Pancho Villa, who alternated between meek requests for chips and aggressive muggings of white people. Such conditions marked psyches, *Ideal* wrote, and fostered a "schizo-cultural limbo," of being neither "completely American" despite a lifetime in the U.S, and yet, simultaneously, "a displaced gringo" in Mexico.[20]

In contrast to this Rancher Nation worldview, *Ideal* provided a platform for imagining a new society, one that aimed to eliminate its white supremacist structures and the related Mexican American subjugation. In one political cartoon in 1972, for instance, *Ideal* summarized the Chicana/o movement's objectives as:

Chicanos don't:
- Advocate overthrow of government; only participation.
- Advocate overthrow of education; only change.
- Advocate separate societies; only understanding and respect for differences.
- Advocate communistic doctrine; only want a piece of democracy.
- Advocate the elimination of court judicial system; only that the law be applied equally.[21]

The cartoon ended with a man and woman sitting on a park bench discussing the quandary of Chicana/o political philosophy. Summarized in question, the dress-clad woman asked the suited man: "In essence carnal, what we want has already been guaranteed; we just need to get it from those who are reluctant and slow in turning it loose?" Answering in the affirmative, the man added, "Chicanos are truly conservative."[22] Tongue in cheek, the cartoon used the country's rising conservativism-exemplified by Nixon's reelection-to frame their activism as inherent to U.S. values. Chicanas and Chicanos simply wanted what was owed to them: equal citizenship and due process; a right to life, dignity, and safety; a space to shape self and their worlds; a co-existence amidst difference. Much like the UFW's contracts in Coachella Valley grape fields, MAPA's *Ideal* framed U.S. citizenship as a means for filing grievances against the country's social violations and, in the process, for restructuring social relations. In its appropriation of U.S. citizenship, MAPA invalidated its critics as the real political outsiders and extremists—an invalidation that required the ideological intervention of a newspaper.

Critically, and despite the evocation of Chicana/o conservativism, MAPA's demand for equal citizenship entailed a revamped Coachella Valley. It meant social services and resources for all communities, well-paying jobs in agriculture and equal access to other sectors. It meant schools empowering students, politicians addressing community concerns, a self-affirming cultural politics. It meant ending the daily indignities and degradation that led to death, such as the poor housing and health care that Philip Vera Cruz associated with the Rancher Nation's violence. With Caswell in mind, equal citizenship required a judicial and police system that protected and mediated conflicts. It meant, too, cross-racial and cross-ethnic dialogues predicated on social reforms. This "conservative" project, MAPA argued, necessitated relentless Chicana/o activism[23] and the fostering of white allies—those "Anglo Americans" whose sacrifices could uphold American ideals.[24] White allies thus faced the same choice as everyone else: political ideals or political safety, as Caswell showed. What did not exist for *Ideal* was the option of performing political ignorance and naivete, much less racial and national innocence.

Ideal's vision for a just society also called for the transformation of the ethnic Mexican community itself, and here the newspaper deployed much of the movement's masculinist politics that scholars have since critiqued. In their retort to Esher, for instance, *Ideal* accused Mexican residents of aiding racism: "Don't feel embarrassed, Mr. Esher, because even among our own people, there are some persons who have retired their ads from this paper . . . saying that supporting such things is radicalism!" To MAPA, many residents remained politically timid out of fear of retribution and/or desire to appear as respectable. In less-than politically correct terms, one MAPA member described them as "*atonteados, agabachados, y apatronados.*" As chapter 6 discusses, this vision often pivoted on a gendering politics of public confrontation: of brown men fighting white men to bring justice to their feminized and victimized community. Characteristic of the masculinist politics, *Ideal* focused almost exclusively on men. Few articles centered nationally recognized women, and the profiles of local women came under the "Flor del Valle" column, which highlighted promising young women in the language of beauty pageants.[25]

And yet, despite these shortcomings, *Ideal* still presented stories of possibility and empowerment. Like the UFW's *El Malcriado*, it dedicated space to Mexican resistance, both historical and contemporary, local and from afar. Most issues carried biographies of national Mexican leaders, such as the early twentieth century revolutionaries Emiliano Zapata and Pancho Villa, and the 1930s populist president, Lazaro Cardenas.[26] Some provided histories of Aztec life or traced national moments, like Puebla's resistance to French invasion.[27] *Ideal* also profiled Chicana/o activists under its "Raza In Action" column, including Stanford's Mexican American quarterback Jim Plunkett, the New Mexican painter, Patrocinio Barela, and the civil rights lawyer, Gus Garcia, who fought "vigorously for the causes of the Mexican Americans to obtain better jobs and living conditions for his people."[28] These less-known men shared space with Corky Gonzalez, Reyes Tijerina, Bert Corona, and Cesar Chavez. Closer to home, *Ideal* carried brief "human interest" pieces on local "business people, from the professions, students, lay people and politicians" who will "relate their experiences in life in general." Each celebrated their subjects and pointed to schools' racist teaching. Their conclusion was clear: Chicanas/os are more than farmworkers, more than poor and illiterate, more than victims.

It is unclear what this intervention meant to local readers, especially the young people powering the Coachella Valley's Chicana/o movement in the early 1970s. But if we consider the context in which they existed—of Spanish speaking prohibitions in schools, a dearth of Chicana/o teachers and/or local public history, a racist national culture, an ambivalence in self and others—then we can imagine that *Ideal*'s pages, its field of stories, offered abundance. It named the world and its pain, and the world as could be, both in the Coachella Valley and places beyond. Perhaps *Ideal*'s pages validated inchoate feelings and ideas. Perhaps they built bridges between different sets of stories, filling in what had been missing, melding a broader continuity, grafting them to family histories. Perhaps they gave entirely new visions of self and other, of families, neighbors, and home, of places far removed.

Cultural nationalism flickered in and out, but it was less significant than a non-essentialist claim to a defiant past and a present orientation to future possibilities: they were enough of a people, MAPA told readers, shared enough of a history, had enough future promises. This was, in itself, a deeply compassionate and radical intervention. We were more and remain more, they said, than the positions accorded to us today, here, now. The ideal they offered was precisely this embeddedness in history, one of contingency and possibility, one that insisted that as a people with history, the "we" of the Coachella Valley could also claim a new future.

The Chicana/o Movements of the Coachella Valley

The Chicana/o movement's origins in the Coachella Valley are difficult to pinpoint. For some, like Alfredo Figueroa, it began in the mid-nineteenth century, when Mexicans like Joaquin Murrieta fought encroaching white settlers, and in the early twentieth century, when Mexican miners and farmworkers fought for higher wages and safer conditions. For Raul Loya and Ray Rodriguez, it began in Arizona's twentieth century miner strikes, where a unionized Chicana/o community raised children to fight social injustices. For Alfredo Fuller, in contrast, it likely began in the merging of social worlds in his border-straddling Nogales. These different origins did not encompass all MAPA timelines, especially for Coachella Valley locals. They also did not represent the movement origins of those who participated in the Voters League, Brown Berets, United Mexican American Students (UMAS), and *Movimiento Estudiantil Chicana/o Aztlan* (MEChA), or those on organization peripheries, who attended events without formal membership, or became teachers, nurses, and social workers in a movement spirit, or bounced from campaign to campaign. Some residents only entered the Chicana/o movement outside the local desert, often in new college spaces. Like the rest of U.S. Southwest, the Chicana/o movement in the Coachella Valley encompassed a multitude of distinct, if overlapping, trajectories, visions, and effects.

To elaborate this point, consider three cases of early 1970s Chicana activism in the Coachella Valley. For Amalia Uribe Deaztlan, the Chicana/o movement began when she melded her brothers' college organizing with her mother's stories of *ejidataria* and *Purepecha* resistance in Mexico. It crystalized in the UFW Coachella Grape Strike of 1969, where she was a leader, and which encouraged her to attend San Diego State College, a previous impossibility. Once on campus, she felt unprepared and had no mentors to help her navigate her new world.[29] By 1973, she was a mother and living in San Francisco with her husband, where, though removed from the Coachella Valley, she raised feminist daughters and joined the city's gay rights movement.[30] For Clementina Olloque, the early 1970s were politically effervescent. She had not been a grape striker, but the UFW inspired her to lead a vegetable strike in late 1969. Taking notice, the UFW placed her in a local training program, "La Casa de la Raza," where she met UFW volunteers, practiced her English, and recorded contract violations. For someone who had felt "trapped" and "suffocated" by poverty, the new work was lifechanging: she now "felt I was where I needed to be: in the world of justice."[31] For Hilda Rodriguez, in turn, these were arguably more surprising years. She and her family had broken the UFW Coachella Grape Strike of 1968, because she "hungered for a decent education and prayed for a decent job," and feared the strike would derail her.[32] In the next five years, however, she enrolled in San Diego State and joined Teatro Chicana, which triggered a political transformation. In late 1973, she even played her first role in front of San Diego's Mexican community: a UFW striker.[33]

Each person embodied a collection of stories, of past, present, and future, each one navigating imperfect choices, each one both moving with and shaping their own movement, inside or outside the Coachella Valley. This multiplicity has made writing a shared account difficult. What follows then is a collage of Chicana/o movement activities that stresses differences and intersections, while showing three key dynamics. First, the Chicana/o movement signified a diverse collection of egalitarian visions, disruptions, and transformations produced by subjects entering and leaving in different periods. Second, while significant political differences existed, most activists shared a common demand for equal access to resources and opportunities. They used citizenship to articulate an egalitarian future, much like local organizations in the 1950s and 1960s. Third, activists intersected each other in surprising ways and, in the process, helped shape their collective world. MAPA was arguably the most consistent local force for race justice reforms in these years. But their campaigns in education, politics, and police violence existed with, and were often propelled forward by, other activists.

In education, for instance, MAPA identified reforms, mobilized parents and students, and demanded equal citizenship. At Desert Sands Unified School District (DSUSD), they organized workshops to "sensitize" teachers to ethnic Mexican students; called for greater student services and ethnic Mexican teachers and administrators; lambasted "educable retarded" classes and physical punishment.[34] At Coachella Valley Unified School District (CVUSD), where conditions appeared to be worse, MAPA supported Mexican American candidates for board elections and pushed for more hiring ethnic Mexican teachers (*Ideal* counted three in 1970).[35] Reflective of its citizen politics, MAPA pushed for racial integration at DSUSD with a district bussing program and a bilingual-bicultural curriculum for all students, irrespective of race.[36] The latter promised to validate ethnic Mexican student lives while facilitating an equal inter-cultural exchange with white students. As one parent told the DSUSD board, "To remain segregated will not expand on one's knowledge of other people, culture, beliefs, customs and traditions as much like actually being part of it."[37] Critically, the "people" here were white students, not ethnic Mexicans. For this parent and MAPA, equal education entailed white students, in sharing space with non-whites, embracing cultural transformation. For ethnic Mexicans, it meant fighting segregation's impact. As one student told the DSUSD board in late 1970: "The myth that all Chicanos are Americans is a bunch of $&%#&. . . . When you start believing it, you are suddenly reminded [through segregation] that you are nothing but a dirty Mexican."[38]

MAPA also used its newspaper to publicize education racial disparities and celebrate local leaders. In April 1971, for instance, *Ideal* reported on CVUSD's firing of Arnulfo Lucio for teaching "militancy" to his sixth graders.[39] When *Ideal* interviewed the baffled teacher, Lucio explained that he held student discussions and instilled "pride . . . as our heritage, customs and culture are concerned." He organized a successful Christmas event with students and parents and distributed 600 packages of "candy and nuts" just before the holidays—so students "[went] home with the idea that someone cared." He also opened his classroom each morning so students "had a warm place to come into, or to get extra help, play quiet games, play records, or just plain gossip." He even did the "Chicano handshake."[40] What he did not do, *Ideal* reported indignantly, was teach "like the other teachers," "[throw] kids out of the room for disciplinarian purposes," or physically punish students: "I've seen those kids line up . . . and whacked methodically production line style." His colleagues resented the positive rapport, Lucio said, and attempted to undermine him and his career: "For doing this, I was called a militant and a communist."

Others faced backlash, too. In 1972, CVUSD abruptly fired the Oasis elementary director, Robert Luhman, after he built a successful bilingual program with new teachers. In *Ideal*, MAPA accused CVUSD of firing Luhman for his success "in educating Mexican Americans," because the board knew "educated people . . . become better citizens and get better jobs. They fear . . . they might succeed in getting out of the fields and into school boards."[41] Over a hundred parents and community members packed the next district meeting to speak on Luhman's behalf, who they celebrated for supporting bilingual education, building a bilingual faculty, and producing high student results. But the school district's board members, nearly all white and tied to ranchers, refused to change their decision.

Three points can be made about MAPA's activism in these years. First, like its 1960s strategy, MAPA used simultaneous campaigns to advance education equity. It used state pressure for desegregation, trained teachers, mobilized parents, and publicized egregious racist policies. Second, and despite MAPA's self-identified "conservativism," white leaders, educators, and parents mounted unrelenting opposition. In a DSUSD meeting on bussing and desegregation, in fact, a board member filed his nails to ignore students' testimonies on segregation's effects.[42] Like ranchers under UFW contracts, white opposition suggested deep fears of any form of social parity. Third, MAPA was never alone. It played a key role in the region, but as the Lucio and Luhman cases show, trail blazing educators and mobilized parents strengthened their efforts. In some cases, protests came outside MAPA, such as in September 1970, when Chicana/o college students organized a walkout at Coachella Valley High School (CVHS) to protest a ban on Mexican Independence Day celebrations.[43] Some of these college students also studied to become local teachers, such as Socorro Gomez, who began teaching in Mecca's elementary in 1973, when she "felt like things were changing, [that] our community was going to get better and our educational system was going to be better for us."[44] A collection of peoples, in short, each with distinct trajectories, intersected and shaped the context for present and future reform.

Education campaigns also generated their own impacts. Cali Ramos and Larry Salas, whose mothers' activism shaped their own, attended the Coachella Valley's community college, where they instigated a lettuce boycott and mentored high school students. One of the latter, Samuel Maestas, led the 1970 CVHS student walkout and then enrolled at the University of California, Riverside, where he joined Chicana/o organizations and planned for a future clinic in Coachella. Concurrently, Margarita Carrillo, Hilda Rodriguez, and Virginia Rodriguez Balanoff attended San Diego State College/University, where they built Teatro Chicana with mostly Chicanas from the Imperial and Palo Verde valleys. In 1971, they performed their original play, "Chicana Goes to College," for their mothers, who they invited to their campus. The play followed a Chicana's fight for higher education, her academic resilience with other Chicanas, and their collective fight for community needs and gender equality.[45] Through their play, the young students held an inter-generational celebration of Mexican women's struggles and triumphs. As the next section discusses, the theater troupe also helped Coachella Valley Chicanas find an empowered activist identity and a renewed connection to their mothers.[46]

A similar shifting, eclectic, and dynamic field of stories shaped the Chicana/o movement's fight against police violence and political underrepresentation. Again, MAPA played a key role, but it was never alone nor enough to win reforms; the latter, additionally, often came suddenly as multiple forces coalesced unexpectedly. As chapters 1 and 2 discussed, Coachella Valley ethnic Mexican residents had long complained about police abuse, while local newspapers regularly alluded to the police's racial profiling and illegal detentions.[47] So when MAPA began *Ideal* it made sense that its third issue focused entirely on police brutality in the Coachella Valley.[48] In later articles, *Ideal* covered police killings throughout the Southwest, including in Blythe (1972), Denver (1973), and Los Angeles (1971–73). It also tied police violence in the Coachella Valley to the contemporaneous repression of Black activists and to

Border Patrol abuses of Mexican immigrants, including the murder of a pro-union farmworker in California (1972) and the sexual assault of a Mexican woman in San Diego (1972).[49] During the 1970 Chicano Moratorium, moreover, the local MAPA and Brown Beret chapters saw the Los Angeles Police Department tear gas and beat down a peacefully assembled crowd, which led to the police killing of the *Los Angeles Times* journalist, Ruben Salazar. As Salazar showed, MAPA argued, police violence literally silenced Chicanas/os and impeded necessary reforms for equal citizenship.[50]

Chicana/o activists, however, had little early success in regulating the local police. In May 1971, a failed drug-sting led to the killing of Francisco Garcia, a Texas farmworker and father of eleven who worked in Coachella Valley fields before his killing. In *Ideal*, a tired Garcia arrived at his busy family home at dusk, and from there, he and his wife departed to visit a relative and prepare for a godchild's baptism.[51] The couple only drove fifty feet before officers unleashed a barrage of bullets. When the shooting and "terror shrieks" stopped, the police found Garcia bleeding to death, while his wife desperately attempted to help him, in vain. "Hunched over the wheel of his truck," wrote *Ideal*, "the rich brownness draining from his face turning it to a blanched white, dying before the confused and crying eyes of eleven children." To MAPA, the district attorney's subsequent foot-dragging, and then the police officers' exoneration, exemplified the justice system's disregard of Mexican American lives. Even the most unthreatening figures, MAPA argued, such as a family man, farmworker, and tired body, was vulnerable to police violence.[52] In early 1972, moreover, the Coachella Police Department hired James Walter, a former Riverside County Sheriff who had been fired for police brutality–a choice succinctly illustrating Mexican Americans' lack of authority and police officers' general impunity.

Within the formal political system, MAPA argued Mexican Americans had almost no power. *Ideal* mockingly quoted candidates who sought to win over Mexican Americans in 1970 by claiming to "eat tamales and enchiladas!"[53] Mexican Americans, in turn, responded to political marginality with withdrawal, as the U.S. Commission on Civil Rights found in 1971: while Mexican Americans constituted 12 percent of California, they held 2 percent of political positions.[54] In the 1972 elections, MAPA repeated its critique and noted the lack of Chicana/o representatives in the Coachella Valley's school boards, water board, and city and county councils.[55] Their solution was a third political party, writing in *Ideal*, "the present [two party] system has been unfair, unconscious, uninterested, unfaithful, [illegible]. We need to unite and go forward together. The Raza Unida Party is our answer."[56] In 1970, MAPA's Raul Loyal ran as the La Raza Unida Party (LRUP) candidate for California State Assembly, which despite a "poor man's campaign" with "almost impossible to win" odds still promised to "wake-up the Mexican American community to politics.... We knew that very shortly [Loya] was destined for defeat, but we also knew that with time his defeat could be converted to victory."[57]

Perhaps more important than a "wake up" politics, MAPA's LRUP strategy relied on aggressive voter registration of disaffected Mexican American residents in 1970 and 1972.[58] It was these efforts that led to a dramatic change in Coachella's City Council in 1972, converting Loya's defeat into a city council victory two years later. Prior to 1972, rancher-allied politicians still dominated Coachella's city council, which repeatedly rejected Chicana/o demands for police reform, infrastructural investment in Mexican American neighborhoods, and affordable housing for farmworker families. Even after the Voter League's victory in 1966—when its two won by promising equitable distribution of city resources—the Coachella city council kept a pro-rancher majority. But after MAPA's voter registration campaign, Mexican American residents elected two other city councilmembers, Julio Gonzalez and Manuel Rios, who claimed loose ties to the Chicana/o movement.[59] Immediately, the two sided with the Chicano mayor and formed the first Chicano majority in Coachella's city council's history.

A month later, in late May 1972, Chicana/o residents organized a picket of Coachella's city hall to protest police harassment and a spate of police killings in Riverside County.[60] They also called for the firing of James Walter, the officer with a history of abusing residents of color, and Coachella's police chief, Frank O'Neil, who "failed to sensitize his police force so that they may deal effectively with the Chicano community."[61] Lastly, protestors called for firing the city manager, Richard Weiss, who " has expressed no desire to open lines of communication with the Chicano community,"[62] and Judge Cross, who "us[ed] double standards in his administration of justice."[63] To protester surprise, the mayor stated his support for these resignations; when both police chief and city manager refused, the newly constituted city council voted 3-2 to fire them. When *Ideal* asked the mayor why he had not taken this measure beforehand, the mayor's reply marked the extent of the region's shifting political winds: "for years he had noticed the concerns of the majority of the Mexican American community regarding justice in the city," the mayor said he had been "voiceless and powerless to act because of [past council's] composition."[64]

Without question, the firings represented a significant victory for the local Chicana/o movement. Police mistreatment had long marked ethnic Mexicans' second-class citizenship, and their inability to reform it demonstrated their communities' limited political power. The MAPA led-registration effort, initiated for LRUP's 1970 state assembly campaign, built a new political reality that allowed local Chicana/o activists to protest and then check police power, which once appeared invincible. Much like the UFW's grape contracts and their check on "invulnerable" rancher power, Chicana/o activists used citizenship claims to racial inequality. For MAPA, the victory also illustrated the power in an organized Chicana/o community: no longer silenced by fear or racial deference, its members could engage political processes, secure resources, and protect its future. In the process, MAPA argued, Chicanas/os could remake Coachella into the home it already was for so many.

When the Coachella city council voted to fire the police chief and city manager, *Ideal* reported on an exchange between opposing representatives. One of them was Anthony Garcia, a conservative Mexican American leader and an opponent of the firings, and he accused the mayor of turning Coachella into a "Mexican town." "It is already a Mexican town," replied the mayor, "What is so terrible about that?!"[65] In its political cartoon, *Ideal* presented Garcia and his allies as rancher puppets fretting about the rising Chicana/o tide. "Those 8,000 Chicanos demonstrating are outsiders," the cartoonish Garcia said ominously, "They are bad for Coachella. They want to make this a Mexican town. They are militant radicals financed by the communist Party. Please ignore them and let *gabachos* make our decisions."[66] In *Ideal*'s cartoon, the new council members appeared in mid-kick, sending a now-powerless Garcia into exile, embodying the cartoon's succinct message: "Coachella: Love it or Leave It."

To Be in the Movement

The Chicana/o Movement's project remained incomplete, even as late as 1973. The Civil Rights Movement had gained key, recognizable legislative victories, but these did not assure Mexican Americans' equal citizenship in the Coachella Valley. Chicanas/os continued to fight segregation and pushed for education and police reforms and increased political representation. MAPA's *Ideal* also covered national news on the Chicana/o Movement and juxtaposed stories of social marginality and community empowerment, thus creating a counter public that challenged the local pro-rancher newspapers. By late 1971, lastly, the Chicana/o voter registration drive led to a revamped city council in early 1972 and police reform later.[67] But perhaps the greatest changes were those of individual lives. For many of the young, the UFW and Chicana/o movements provided paths to previously inconceivable spaces, such as universities and jobs outside agriculture. These transformations of circumstances and opportunities were a dramatic source of personal growth, much like those described by unionized farmworkers.

The clearest example of this transformation was a young newcomer to the Coachella Valley, Max Huerta. Born in Southern Texas in 1954 and raised in

Delano, Huerta was the middle child in a migrant farmworking household of ten children.[68] His family migrated to California in the late 1950s in search of economic security, but like other Tejanos found the precariousness of the farm labor circuit. From Delano, his family migrated to Stockton and San Jose, and then swung south to the Coachella Valley—arriving for the lucrative grape harvest in May. In his world, poverty and race covered everyone. On Delano's east side, he remembered, poor Blacks and poor Browns lived-in beat-up homes, beat up streets, and beat-up bodies. There, families ran out of money, cars broke down, and illness matured in neglect. There, adults and children stood in hour-long lines for boxes of surplus canned food originally meant for conscripted troops in America's wars against the global red menace.[69]

Deprivations continued to plague his schools, where poverty painted classrooms a dull gray, and left lawns ragged, asphalt crumbling. He remembered his teachers as racists and alcoholics, or racists and abusive, or racists and struggling with personal demons.[70] One, a Mr. Husband, routinely forced him to sit on the soccer field under the sun for entire periods for speaking Spanish in class. Another told to his students, "you are in this class because you Mexicans are not as smart as the other kids." When he dropped a catch in football practice, his coach reacted by throwing a football at his midsection and knocking him to the ground, from where a breathless and writhing Huerta could hear the coach say, "that will teach you, that if someone throws the ball to catch it." For this boy turning into a young man, education meant to be hurt emotionally, intellectually, and physically by unstable and violent white teachers.

The racialized poverty in the community and the racialized abuse in the classroom fed off each other. His parents' poverty, social intimidation, and non-English proficiency meant they did not confront teacher abuse, much less advocate for an empowering education.[71] Family struggles further impeded his education, such as when his father was diagnosed with cancer and twelve-year-old Huerta became responsible for driving his father to chemotherapy treatments in Fresno, fifty miles north of Delano. At the clinic, he translated and scheduled future treatments, and then waited until his chemo-exhausted father reappeared. On the drive home, Huerta sat on pillows to see over the steering wheel and spot hiding cops, all while his father slept next to him. Whatever their emotional weight, the trips (at a minimum) caused classroom absences that increasingly foreclosed the only path for a nonexploitative future.[72] As he moved from middle school to high school, Huerta also became increasingly aware of police harassment and its complement to teacher abuse—with the former's ratio growing in proportion to the student's age.

These interwoven and layered oppressions engulfed his life. For him, poverty meant denial—to a settling for "what poor people eat," "for whatever teacher they give you," for bad neighborhoods, for perpetually feeling like "you don't have access to certain things that others have access." "Things are out of your reach," he said, even basic needs like housing, food, and education: "I'm here and that is waaayyy out there somewhere. That is the feeling."[73] Such poverty also meant psychological effects, such as feeling "like you are in a hole . . . and you want to escape, to get out." But one never gets out, Max remembered: "you feel like ah, I'm almost out. And then suddenly something reminds you of it and you fall all the way in again." Over time, this reality "gets inside you. . . . When you hear, 'You are just a Mexican, you are just a dumb Mexican,' then you start to believe that you are a dumb Mexican."[74] Once admitted, shame settled in. He hated his visible poverty, having to wait for government food, seeing his father work on their perennially broken-down car in the front driveway. He hated walking streets with his shoeshine box—a cube made out of nearby grape planks for the shoes of farmworkers spending their money in Chinatown's pleasures.

Perhaps most devastatingly, Huerta did not know how to speak about these conditions with parents or friends. No one did, he said. Instead, poor people mocked other poor people, poor people failed to hide their poverty from other poor people, poor people remained poor people.[75] In this absence of speaking, Huerta and his friends turned to alcohol and drugs, as if to wash defeat of its despair: "you feel trapped. You know—it's like, okay, so I'm hurting, so I'm poor. What am I going to do about it? Nothing. Nothing. There is nothing I can do about it. Nothing."[76] And so they drank and attempted to take care of each other in their adolescent youth and moved in ways that would eventually suck them back into the hole without escape.

But everything changed with the UFW movement, he said, which erupted in his town when he was eleven years old, a year before the chemo trips that would not save his father. As the UFW strike gained momentum and publicity, as it grew from picket lines in Delano grape fields to downtown marches and then a national consumer boycott campaign, the UFW's presence and demands offered Huerta an entirely new world:

> I came to realize that I was feeling the same sense of injustice that many people were feeling but now the UFW was giving us a voice that we did not have. . . . You couldn't say anything because you'd get punish for it, but now it was being made public. And that was like wow man—to me, there was, man—a sense of being set free in a way. To say what I really felt, what I wanted to say for so long, since I was a kid. You know, and not be punished for it. And instead feel a sense of camaraderie with others who were—with hundreds who were feeling the same way. And now being able to do something about it, which was big part of the

strike, a big part of organizing farmworkers . . . to bring about social change.[77]

For Huerta the UFW movement meant that others had felt the same desperation as he felt; that others dreamt for a new life, like him; that he, too, could have the voice to speak out. His parents may not have been part of the strike, but the UFW movement was part of his world—providing a diagnosis of Delano's racialized, laboring life and presented a militant community that could release him from a world of denial.

For Huerta, the Chicana/o movement represented a natural extension of the UFW's vision, and after the 1968 student "blowouts" and the Brown Berets' increasing visibility, Max and his friends turned their male circle into a Berets chapter.[78] They imposed discipline and eliminated drugs and alcohol from their lives. They organized meetings, read through their organization's manual, and thought about the world they wanted to create. They published a Chicana/o newspaper, assisted key community meetings, and advocated on a range of issues. They also reported police brutality and spoke to adolescents to deter them from joining gangs. When Huerta led a student walkout and was expelled, he continued at a boarding school with Chicana/o teachers, who inspired him for the first time in his young student life. In addition to the UFW and his Brown Berets co-members, these teachers empowered Huerta, taught him to see himself in a positive light, to identify himself as part of a movement. By early 1971, Huerta joined the "La Marcha de la Reconquista," and then settled in Coachella in 1972.[79]

Only six years before, Huerta had been a thirteen-year-old convinced of his (racial) stupidity and ashamed of his poverty, certain of no escape. Much had changed since then. He was still coping, he explained, with the emotional repercussions of his impoverished childhood and his father's death. He was still uncertain about his life and where he was heading. But, he was no longer imprisoned or felt alone.[80] And when he settled in Coachella to join his family, he wanted for his future what had seemed impossible only a few years before: "I didn't want to be poor for the rest of my life. I was tired of being poor. . . . Whatever it would take to get me out of that (!), that is what I wanted. I didn't want to be poor no more. I wanted to help my mom. I wanted to be able to do something to help her."[81] By early 1973, he was a grape worker and union representative in Coachella's Valdora Ranch. Reflecting the union's power, Huerta approached the job as a source of potential life—of respect for him and economic support for his mother, and, perhaps, of a world beyond one of denial.

For others, the Chicana/o movement absorbed them in far removed spaces, all while providing them empowered returns to their childhood homes. Margarita Carrillo, for instance, was set to graduate from Coachella Valley High

School in 1970 and attend San Diego State College.[82] She was the oldest daughter of six in an impoverished, single-parent household. Her mother, born and raised in Texas, had a third-grade education and spent her childhood in fields with her widowed father and eight siblings, all moving along the knitted landscape of the Tejano diaspora. When Carrillo's father left the family, her mother had no familial support and relied on measly welfare rations. Perhaps for these reasons, Carrillo speculated, her Spanish-speaking mother felt intimidated by (white) teachers and gave them the benefit of the doubt. In this context, Carrillo's education achievement defied substantial odds. But, three days before the celebrations, she learned that her counselor had made a course error that resulted in insufficient credits for her graduation and college admission. She felt "dazed," she remembered, "embarrassed and humiliated," saddened further by her mother's refusal to "see the counselor and speak on my behalf."

To Carrillo, this episode exemplified her young life at home and in school in the Coachella Valley. When she was in third grade, her teacher slapped her face for "stealing" classroom paper. "She came towards me," she remembered, "calling my name angrily as I stood there and watched with big terrified eyes and my heart beating so fast I thought it was going to burst." The slap snapped her head back, made her sob, lowered her voiced to a "squeak . . . that I could barely hear myself." Still, Carrillo denied taking the paper, and pointed out that the classroom had three Margaritas—one of whom had presumably been the thief. The teacher immediately gave her twenty-five cents if she promised not to tell her mother, and then changed all the Margarita names to English versions: Margie, Margaret, and Maggie. Like ten years later, her mom did not intervene or "questioned the fact that I became 'Margie' overnight." To Carrillo, alienation and marginalization moved with surprising elasticity and singularity, drawing in multiple people and spaces into a seeming whole that made her feel alone—of poverty in fields and under welfare, of violent teachers and inept counselors and terrified parents, of fleeing fathers and the sense that one may not escape after all—merely because of a mediocre educator making a banal error.

In 1970, however, Carrillo remained determined to attend college. She completed her high school credits in San Diego and immediately enrolled in San Diego State, where she learned about the Vietnam War, farmworker unionization, and women's equality. As an adolescent, she had not participated in Coachella's Chicana/o and UFW movements, so these early college months felt like a wave of unexpected activism. Her new "rebellious" spirit even dismayed her mother, who forced her to drop out of college to return to Coachella—only to return a year later, now married and with an infant. In this second iteration as a college student, Carrillo met the women of "Teatro de las Chicanas," a group that presented minimalist plays on issues related to the Chicana/o student population. Their first play, "Chicana Goes to College," followed the life of a student who fought her boyfriend, father, and mother to attend college.[83] Once on campus, she realized she was academically underprepared in an institution that did not consider her needs or background. To succeed, she studied with and drew sustenance from other Chicanas and from their shared success, they turned to fighting for gender equality and their communities' needs. For Carrillo, the Teatro held up a mirror to her life, offered a warm embrace, and asked her to take an active role. Writing thirty years after her involvement, Carrillo remembered the group's women as "[shining] a new light onto what I wanted in life."[84]

Nearly every theater member came from farmworker families in the Imperial, Coachella, and San Joaquin Valleys, and nearly all fought sexism, racism, and poverty to escape. One of the group's founders was Felicitas Nuñez, the second youngest of nine in a farmworker family from the Imperial Valley.[85] When she had enrolled in San Diego State in 1968, she had already traveled an unlikely path: from farmworker poverty, "Mexican schools," and a patriarchal family to attending a Catholic school full of rancher children (who ostracized her) to coming under the wings of a Mexican American nun who helped her submit a college application. "I wanted to leave," Nuñez said of her high school self, "be independent, away from Brawley [in Imperial Valley]. And when I got accepted, I could not believe it. It was so impossible to believe what was happening." In college, she met other Chicanas with the same drive, wonder, and shock, and together they participated in the social movements surrounding them and lifting them, especially in UFW and Chicana spaces. By the time Carrillo met Nuñez, the latter was already a movement veteran: she had helped found a community center, served as director of student service offices, and was elected the first chairwoman of MEChA in San Diego State.[86]

Carrillo also met Delia Ravelo, whose parents died when she was six years old (in a Ford plant accident, to cancer), and who grew up under a tyrannical uncle in National City.[87] Her uncle "seemed to believe that all women were subhuman," she said, belting her for minor issues with a "sweaty look of intense pleasure." To escape, she gained weight, read books, and "ingratiat[ed]" herself to white adults who could help her get to college.[88] When Ravelo gained admission to San Diego State, she *physically* fought her uncle to move out, while her passive neighbors stared on: "my uncle came out of the house to drag me back . . . pulling my long black hair and everybody part he could grab, leaving his marks." Once on campus, she found a world where her "horizons expanded into rapture." Movements flowed through her school, she discovered, and she through them. She attended rallies and meetings, especially for UFW campaigns, and she joined Teatro Mestizo, a politicized Chicana/o troupe. So, when Carrillo met Ravelo, she saw a person already transformed: as a "firm, but positive person," "intelligent and politically involved," who made "you feel important and wanted."[89]

Nuñez remembered that when she helped found Teatro Chicana in 1971, she'd imagined Chicanas could use theater to "create more roles for ourselves ... to find out why and who we were."[90] Both she and Ravelo had already come to recognize the deep-seated misogyny of their male classmates and movement activists. As Ravelo explained, "The males called for a revolution that did not include women as equals."[91] They also recognized the widening chasm between young women like them and the older women in their lives, especially their mothers. In 1971, they organized a conference for their mothers, where the young women performed "Chicana Goes to College" to explain their college lives and express appreciation for their mothers' support. Later plays also spoke about the UFW movement, gender politics in student Chicana/o groups, and Marxist analysis on ethnic Mexican worker communities. One of Nuñez's favorite plays was adapted from the film, *Salt of the Earth*, which they performed in community parks, college conferences and festivals, in nearby high schools.[92] Through it all, they also fought men's charges of racial betrayal for their feminism and of sexual improprieties for being in an all-women cast.

Other women from the Coachella Valley joined the Teatro. Virginia Rodriguez Balanoff grew up in "the sticks of a desert town, Coachella," where she worked in the fields as a four-year-old, and where she lost Spanish when she entered kindergarten the following year.[93] In high school, she "felt so alone" in college prep classes, where she was the only Mexican student. The Teatro, however, offered "cariño" from women who inspired her—"Wow! They were explosive! Dynamic! Powerful! I liked these women." The Teatro "gave [her] back [her] voice" and "armed [the Mexican community] with knowledge to change their lives for the better." For Hilda Rodriguez, the Teatro offered an unexpected return to Coachella. Rodriguez's family immigrated in 1965 when she was fifteen years old, and like other immigrants her family attempted to scrape an exhausting and humiliating livelihood from field labor.[94] In schools, teachers told her not to expect college and "sentenced her to a life of self-defeat." And when she was about to leave for college in 1968, she remembered breaking the UFW strike and ignoring calls to "join a 'causa justa.'" "I hungered for a decent education," she added, "and prayed for a decent job. Why should I care about the ongoing problem?"[95] In the next five years, she married, moved to San Diego, and then enrolled in the state college, where she saw a Teatro Chicana play—one that first repulsed her, and then drew her in, and then gave her a role to play: that of a UFW striker in a performance to inspire the local Mexican community.[96]

There were more women, of course. There was Peggy Garcia from a conservative Mexican American family in San Diego, who learned to challenge her homophobia, clean broken farmworker restrooms, and slowly embrace a militant politics.[97] There was Laura Garcia from the Imperial Valley, who survived sexual abuse and teacher abuse, who at a young age decided "no one was going to break me, no one." In college, she read Frederick Engels and the history of the *Adelitas* to understand the lives of farmworker Chicanas. The Teatro women, she said, "fought for something bigger than ourselves: justice and equality." And, in turn, the Teatro offered them power and release: "It was a battering ram we used to knock down the walls of our silence. It helped us find our voice, and we intuitively knew that once we had our voice we were closer to our liberation." For Teresa Oyos, these women "began the process of peeling back my layers of protection . . . / My layers of hard ass shell . . . / the shell that has taken so many years of recovery to dissolve."[98] In the process, they "planted seeds" that helped her heal from trauma. Similarly, Guadalupe Beltran survived sexual abuse and child labor, poor medical treatment after she contracted polio, and teacher abuse in schools. But, she wrote, "As a woman I now enjoy life in spite of everything I've gone through. Teatro was a stepping stone to where I am now."[99]

Carrillo slowly learned from these women—about "working class oppression," "equality of the sexes," or the intimacy of shared care, of becoming "each other's mother, sister and *comadre*." They also helped her "understand [her] mother and [their] difficult relationship." Her mother had grown up without a mother herself, she realized, had labored in fields until marriage, and then attempted to survive in a capitalist and patriarchal world. "Basic survival needs," Carrillo wrote, "consumed my mother." "I realize now," she reflected thirty years after her college years, "she did the best that she could under very difficult circumstances."[100]

For these women, the Chicana/o movement provided a community they did not have in the Coachella Valley or in other rural communities.[101] In it, they found courage, confidence, political growth, and self-reflection. They articulated the ways multiple hierarchies affected their lives, how such hierarchies grafted themselves in them, and how, in turn, to undo their impact on their lives. Even their lighthearted moments—like getting lost in a road trip, skinny-dipping in the Pacific, smoking a joint before a play—spoke about a freedom they found through their movement and through each other. Violence and marginality had denied such lightheartedness, they knew, such safety, warmth, and reassurances. There was no need, then, to claim a radical politics to already feel a radical transformation. For as Ravelo remembered, "when Felicitas and I would talk and gaze at the night's canopy of brilliant stars, I knew kindness was reflected everywhere."[102]

Conclusion: Years of "Raza Empowerment"

While Coachella's boosters still hoped for a white population and economic boom, Chicana/o activists directly challenged the region's racialized hierarchies and pressed forward an egalitarian vision. Their efforts involved protests and picket lines, voter registration drives and elections, school walkouts and curriculum reforms, self-reflection, and community formation. These were "year[s] of Raza Empowerment," *Ideal* declared.

For Chicana/o activists, the post-Rancher Nation world meant greater social services and life opportunities for all people in the Coachella Valley. It meant well-paying jobs (even in agriculture), and jobs in many other sectors. It meant ending the everyday indignities and life degradation that often led to death. It meant good schools, responsive politicians, and a self-affirming cultural politics that undermined white supremacist values. It meant profound life transformations and empowering relationships with peers and community members. It meant, too, protesting the Vietnam War's effect on Mexican American families and interrogating the local print culture's racism. As such, even the limited demand of equal citizenship—of voting rights and political representation, of decent schools and student safety, of plays and song and art, of life for itself and camaraderie's warmth—required the wholesale transformation of the Coachella Valley's institutions and social relations. In the process, it held for the possibility of cross-racial and cross-ethnic dialogue—all while stressing those political commitments may require allies to sacrifice their lives, as Caswell's experience showed. White racist inflexibility, Chicanas/os stressed, had made all reforms possible only through concerted mobilization.[103] Their choices were thus between sacrificing political ideals and sacrificing political safety.[104] What did not exist was the option of performing racial and national innocence, as the Rancher Nation had long and repeatedly insisted on.

But not all was well. All social movements come with shortcomings and weaknesses, and the dual Chicana/o—UFW movements of the Coachella Valley had no shortage of both. As the next chapter will show, though activists succeeded in puncturing the Rancher Nation's illusions of forced stability, the power to establish and rebuild the region according to their own vision was still beyond their reach.

PART III

Politics in a Precarious Present

Chapter 6

Insurgent Frailties

Errors, Setbacks, and Fissures, 1970–1973

At the start of 1973, the UFW and Chicana/o movements counted a decade of social antagonism. In 1964, Mexican American candidates led city council campaigns, winning two in 1966, and launching more in later years. In 1965, Filipino farmworkers and members of the Agricultural Workers Organizing Committee (AWOC) led a grape strike in the Coachella Valley, which they followed in September with an inter-racial, Filipino-Mexican strike in Delano. Concurrently, the Coachella Valley's Mexican American Political Association chapter fought school segregation and employment discrimination, while adolescent students spoke of a new Chicana/o identity shaped by the UFW, Black freedom struggles, and the Vietnam War. As the decade closed, a string of rebellions followed: back-to-back UFW grape strikes in 1968 and 1969; roving Brown Beret marches against war and police brutality in 1969 and 1970; Mexican American candidates for local offices and anti-poverty initiatives; new youth organizations mentoring high school students and organizing walkouts; growing tensions that culminated in a police riot in April 1970; and, seismically, UFW grape contracts in the 1970s. For the next three years, as the UFW and Chicana/o movement expanded outside the Coachella Valley, local insurgents worked to solidify their victories.

Some could even imagine a new world just out of reach. And yet, in the very momentum, the two social movements carried significant, widely dispersed, and often unseen frailties. These included the UFW's shortcomings in and out of the Coachella Valley; Filipino rank-and-file mistrust amid strident Filipino leader criticism of Filipino workers; Chicana/o inability to safeguard victories or mitigate divisions, especially among men; local resegregation through white flight and westside luxury development; a national rightward shift in political culture and economics. In chapters 4 and 5, I focused on the changes triggered by the UFW and Chicana/o movements in the Coachella Valley to stress the diversity of participant visions, politics, and experiences. In chapter 6, I turn to both movements' weaknesses and their implications. The chapter argues for seeing the UFW and Chicana/o movements as still-marginal insurgencies vulnerable to reversals and defeats. In doing so, it rejects developmentalist models of social movement history and highlights the many factors shaping future contexts.

Chapter 6 is also the first chapter in the book's third section, which spans from 1970 to 1977 and covers social movement weaknesses, another UFW Coachella Grape Strike (1973), and the 1975–76 state-administered union elections. As in the past, multiple communities shaped the UFW and Chicano/a movement's fortunes. There was no single movement, no a priori end-goal, no shared timeline. Instead, a collection of people swirled in and out of a pulsing field of stories, one that simultaneously held potential, differences, limits, promises, and uncertainties. For this collection of people, freedom work was difficult, vexing, and never linear.

Small Islands in a Vast Sea

Despite the UFW's labor contracts in the Coachella Valley grape fields, its victories remained tenuous. Its industrywide contracts in 1970 triggered a staccato of anti-UFW measures, which drained its resources and undermined campaigns in other regions. In the Salinas Valley, lettuce ranchers reacted to the UFW grape contracts by preemptively signing Teamster Union contracts in the 1970 summer, thereby preventing their lettuce workers from joining the UFW. In doing so, ranchers aimed to re-frame a potential UFW strike as a jurisdictional dispute between two rival unions, and not a campaign for farmworker rights. Such a reframing, they calculated, would dampen the popularity of the UFW boycott among U.S. consumers and blunt its ability to undercut Salinas Valley lettuce profits. The result was another prolonged campaign; another set of strikes, marches, and protests; another round of rancher violence and court injunctions; another fast-weakened Chavez jailed for defying rancher courts. By late 1970, the UFW had won a handful of contracts with boycott-sensitive corporations. But most Salinas Valley lettuce ranchers, like their grape kin, refused to buckle and, by 1971, the UFW's efforts in the region had been reduced to anti-collusion lawsuits.[1]

Overlapping the Salinas Valley strike, multiple state governments with support from the Republican Party attempted to outlaw the UFW's secondary boycott.[2] In 1972 Arizona, the Republican-controlled legislature and governor's office passed such a measure, which prompted the UFW to lead a months-long recall campaign of the state's governor. In California, the measure came as a state proposition in 1972, which forced yet another UFW fight. Similar bills appeared in Washington, Idaho, and Florida, and to each the UFW sent organizers, rallied a base, and often won despite the outsized opposition. In most UFW histories, this period illustrates the union's indefatigable spirit—facing antagonists with disproportionate resources, skipping from one fight to another, still advancing the farmworker movement. Tellingly, the UFW's slogan, "si se puede," was first uttered in the 1972 Arizona campaign—as if rallying the troops against long-odds by tethering the slightly possible to the inevitable.

But each of these campaigns also diluted the UFW's resources and pulled its organizers away from the newly unionized grape fields.[3] In the Coachella Valley, the union's field director, Ray Huerta, only arrived in March 1971, nearly a full year after grape ranchers signed UFW contracts. Like other UFW organizers, Huerta spent the months between the 1970 summer to 1971 spring organizing in the Salinas Valley, while a string of UFW volunteers entered and left the UFW's Coachella office. Huerta also had few assistants, but many responsibilities, including dispatching several hundred workers each morning; visiting fields, resolving contract violations, and communicating with ranchers; leading worker leadership trainings, advocating for the local farmworker community with public agencies, and addressing disgruntled farmworker leaders for what they saw as Delano's imposition on their movement.[4] Overwhelmed, he repeatedly asked UFW leaders for support, writing frantically to Chavez in May 1971: "I find myself inundated with work and problems here in Coachella. I am not the type who cries every time the pressure comes down. In this instance, I am screaming, not just crying."[5] The UFW did send four organizers a couple weeks after this letter, but few had any experience with the Coachella Valley or farmworkers in general.

By then, the UFW's neglect was already apparent. Only Freedman and Karahadian ranches established the contract's mandated worker committees.[6] Other grape ranches may have had some union structure, but these did not have the central office's recognition. The UFW organizers also struggled to build a local membership because they did not know all ranch locations or their workers. One organizer even relied on ranchers for crew information, which he naïvely presented as an organizational strength: a rancher lawyer, he reported to the UFW, "was preparing list[s] of all ranchers with the location and number of crews. Which is good news for us."[7] Similarly, when another UFW organizer visited Coachella Valley grape fields to speak with worker leaders, he found none and merely noted: "He didn't come to ranch," "Outside the region, didn't work," "Nothing known about him."[8] Significantly, the UFW's late collection of worker information came as its attempted to dispatch workers through its hiring hall, a combination Huerta described as a "horrendous job" met by "excellent organizers" without "any experience running a field office."[9]

As Huerta implied, the UFW's tardiness reflected its limited resources. But the UFW also exacerbated its difficulties by sending non-local volunteers with limited organizing skills. In a revealing example, the UFW organizer Andres Gonzalez reported that on his June 1971 visit to a local grape rancher, he *randomly assigned* the crews' union representatives.[10] One worker, Eva Ramos, immediately told Gonzalez the assigned person was the foreman's sister-in-law and thus not a good candidate to lead their union. Agreeing with Ramos, Gonzalez returned the next day to speak to the foreman and select another worker. The foreman, who had a history of anti-union hostility, responded by assaulting and insulting Ramos, who then filed a grievance against the company. In the ensuing letters between the local and central UFW offices, Gonzalez never explained his choice or the lack of worker democracy. He also did not comment on Ramos's view of the incident, though we can imagine she was not particularly impressed with an avoidable grievance, or by Gonzalez's ignorance of the farmworker population and disregard of worker choice.[11]

The Coachella UFW office only completed its union infrastructure in early 1972, when it sent a list of committee members to grape ranchers. This meant UFW members had few chances to form union-based relationships. Most knew their crews, but they did not interact with each other as friends or outside of work. They also did not know union members in other ranches and only met rank-and-file leaders in early 1973, when a looming strike forced them to meet.[12] The Coachella UFW office did begin to organize non-grape fields in late 1972, but beforehand grape workers existed as if an island of unionism in an ocean of unorganized farmworkers.

We can see this "union island" dynamic in the UFW's "History of Union Service" forms. The UFW used these forms in the late summer of 1971 to credit strikers for their contributions.[13] In the Coachella Valley, at least twenty-seven members submitted a form, including Juanita Martinez, who "never stop[ped] helping organize people and enforce our contracts."[14] Arguably, the UFW's victory in the Coachella Valley would have remained an abstraction without worker-leaders like Martinez. And yet, she never discussed farmworkers in the Coachella Valley's non-grape fields nor their relationship to the UFW. Instead, her unionism deepened a revolution in one company while supporting the UFW in campaigns outside the Coachella Valley. Similarly, Irene and Emiliano Treviño wrote they "respect[ed]" the UFW's grape strikes and picketed multiple grape ranchers in the Coachella Valley.[15] But after winning contracts, a near apologetic Treviño said, they returned to work because they had a "family of 12" to support. The Treviños still volunteered in the UFW Coachella office and were "ready to do anything necessary to make this a strong union since it's the only way for us farm workers to get ahead in our goals." But like other strikers, they saw the UFW as an insurgent union built by the rank and file and in need of cross-regional aid. So, when Chavez was jailed in Salinas in December 1970, Coachella Valley unionists like Irene Treviño and her son drove to join pro-UFW lettuce marches. For them, the UFW existed in Coachella Valley grapes, where workers defended their contracts, and in distant lands, where other workers (with Coachella's aid) fought for their own.

Others told the same story.[16] Some joined UFW campaigns in Sacramento and Arizona, and/or fought California's proposition to banning secondary boycotts. Fidela Rivera, "a Ranch Committee-woman representing the sisters and brothers at [Coachella Imperial Distributors]," told *El Malcriado* in April 1972 it was "a great honor to be elected to the Ranch Committee." When asked why she volunteered her time, Rivera said, "I came because it is our duty to defend our union. Yes, I lose one day's pay when I come during the weekend, but it is a great satisfaction to serve my people." Her coworker, Isidoro Nava, explained their "ranch committee vote[d] to decide whether or not we come to struggle in this campaign. Luckily, those of us in favor of coming won overwhelmingly. Next week, more sisters and brothers will come."[17] Critically, both Rivera and Nava stressed their commitment and sacrifice in campaigns outside the Coachella Valley. They did not speak of their neighbors in non-union vegetable, citrus, or date fields, nor share their thoughts on non-union workers or their potential role in a future fight with ranchers. The UFW's membership in the Coachella Valley joined strikers in distant places to form a statewide archipelago of unionism without, however, eliminating the local ocean of rancher power.

The UFW did intend to organize all Coachella Valley farmworkers. In late 1970, Chavez held a press conference in Indio to say the UFW was "prepared to prove that we represent the citrus farmworkers."[18] Such preparation included their ability to organize a strike and boycott, though, Chavez added, they "hoped a boycott would not be necessary." But the Coachella Valley citrus campaign only began in late 1972, when the central UFW office assigned three organizers for eighty crews in thirty-one citrus ranches.[19] In the intervening two years, the UFW focused on other campaigns and failed to make itself central to the local political economy.

Non-grape ranchers, in turn, prepared to prevent such an expansion. After the Coachella Valley grape contracts, a collection of citrus ranchers met with the newly installed member of the State Board of Agriculture, Paul Ames, whose family claimed pioneer status. They discussed the possibility of an immediate UFW fight and the deleterious effects of a UFW boycott on the tangerine market, which depended on Southern Californian consumers. One rancher foreshadowed ominously, "the Los Angeles market is the key to the Tangerine crop and if there is not a free flow of fruit in this market there is real trouble ahead. No one can live with the [grape] contract that have [*sic*] been negotiated."[20] The meeting closed with pledges to fight the UFW at all costs, and with Ames's good news that pro-rancher groups in California planned to introduce a statewide proposition to limit the UFW's boycott, thereby outlawing a key tool. Luckily for them, the UFW turn to the Salinas Valley lettuce strike, and then to the string of anti-boycott campaigns, gave non-grape Coachella Valley ranchers ample time to prepare against unionization.

Arguably, this missed opportunity reflected the UFW's scarce resources as it responded to a multi-pronged attack after 1970. But it also originated in the Coachella Valley's peripheral position in the UFW. It may also have originated in the union's unrestrained optimism after 1970—when some UFW leaders seemed convinced they could, in fact, organize lettuce fields before consolidating their presence in grapes; that they could do so while leading campaigns in other states to protect its secondary boycott; that it could respond to the overlapping farmworker demands in Florida, Texas, and Michigan; and that, almost unhurriedly, it could return to the unattended grape fields to finish the job of dethroning the rancher-king once and for all.

A Minority within a Minority

Perhaps the biggest UFW weakness in the Coachella Valley centered on continued Filipino member mistrust of the union. Since the 1966 merger of the National Farm Workers Association and Agricultural Workers Organizing Committee, Filipino grape workers worried about their status within the new organization. These worries were exacerbated by disgruntled Filipino leaders and contractors, the national framing of the UFW as an ethnic Mexican movement, and Delano's failure to attend to Filipino grievances. In the Coachella Valley, the UFW's late 1960s grape strikes also arrived with a Chicana/o movement, a fortuitous alignment that propelled both, but eclipsed Filipino presence. Filipino invisibility remained in the UFW despite Pete Velasco's intervention in 1969 and it deepened with the Salinas Valley lettuce strike, as nearly all strikers were ethnic Mexican. The UFW's newspaper, *El Malcriado*, printed articles by Filipino leaders and covered the union's multiracial origins and commitment. But most of these articles focused on Larry Itliong and paled in comparison to the union's pervasive use of Mexican symbols.[21] Lastly, Itliong's resignation from the UFW's National Executive Board (NEB) in late 1971, and the initial confusion over his reasons, inflamed further mistrust.[22]

In the Coachella Valley, the discontent revolved around the UFW's hiring hall and its privileging of local farmworkers, who were most likely to hear of and gain dispatches to union fields.[23] When Filipino supervisors attempted to circumvent the hiring hall, the UFW filed grievances against violating ranchers, an act that appeared to validate Filipino suspicions of union discrimination. In May 1971, for instance, the UFW filed a grievance against Bagdasarian Ranches after a supervisor, a longtime Filipino contractor, hired eight Filipino farmworkers outside the hiring hall.[24] The Coachella UFW office demanded Bagdasarian hire its members and pay back lost wages—a response that chapter 4 saw as key to undermining the Rancher Nation's ability to hire and fire workers at will.[25] But the members listed to replace the nonunion Filipino workers were all local Mexicans. Even if the latter had the most seniority, the UFW's action still transferred jobs from Filipino to Mexican laborers—jobs some may have claimed for nearly two decades and now appeared to lose through the union.

In 1972, the Coachella UFW office continued to defend union members in ways that accentuated perceptions of anti-Filipino bias. It filed a grievance against Tenneco for discrimination when a Filipino supervisor offered work to a Filipino-heavy crew while telling an all-Mexican crew the same work was cancelled. The UFW wrote, "The crew #1600 (Simon Matias) is made up by a majority of Filipino brothers with the exception of a few Mexicanos.... The few Mexicanos in crew #1600 were also told that there would not be any work on Saturday."[26] Tenneco contested the allegation and said the workday in question was a non-harvest Saturday for all grape ranchers under a marketing order. The workers employed had only pulled leaves from four acres, a less than lucrative task offered to camp residents on a Friday evening (who happened to be Filipino). The archives do not elaborate on the resolution, but the exchanges hint at the tensions amidst scarcity: there were only so many union jobs in the Coachella Valley and their distribution by a poorly organized office did little to reassure workers who existed in a seemingly zero-sum game.

To be clear, UFW archives do not show explicit discrimination against Filipino workers in the Coachella Valley. The UFW's Coachella office even wrote glowingly of Filipino members in brief autobiographies collected by the Farmworker Movement Documentation Project. In these accounts, Mexican organizers related to Filipino members through a masculine language of militancy opposed to the Coachella Valley's white supremacy and labor exploitation. Of his time in Delano's Filipino Hall, for example, Andres Gonzalez wrote, "I met a lot of beautiful people at Filipino Hall, volunteers as well as farmworkers, diehard strikers like myself. I developed a wonderful relationship with my Filipino brothers, especially Willie Barrientos and Philip Vera Cruz."[27] Other unionists in the Coachella Valley spoke similarly, as did Chicana/o activists in the late 1960s. None noted racial tensions. The obvious disconnect between the two communities—of sparse but positive Mexican views of Filipinos and of Filipino frustration with a Mexican-dominated union—may reflect the blinders inherent to the privileged. For this reason, Itliong argued in 1970 for placing Filipino organizers in grape growing regions, where organizers could address Filipino concerns and fulfill the union's multi-racial commitments. The UFW National Executive Board repeatedly agreed with Itliong, but it never followed through.

Given the Coachella's office's understaffing and the union's limited resources, this failure is not surprising. But the lack of Filipino staff members also reflected the UFW's reliance on volunteers who earned $5 to $10 a week. The volunteer system was both a strategy and a principled stance, presumably lowering costs and attracting only dedicated advocates, those who embraced poverty to aid farmworkers. Whether either calculation was accurate is unclear; it is also less central for understanding Filipino grievances. What is important to note is that most Filipino farmworkers, just like Mexican farmworkers, opted not to volunteer, and the few who did were placed in the San Joaquin Valley, where a large Filipino community existed. In the Coachella Valley, in contrast, UFW volunteers were either local or non-local Chicana/o activists or non-local white liberals, both of whom struggled to resolve Filipino problems. Furthermore, given the smaller size of the Filipino American community, and its relative distance from the UFW movement, there were few Filipino American activists willing and/or capable of volunteering in far-removed places like the Coachella Valley.

The UFW, in short, did not consider how distinct racialized histories and their attendant effects shaped farmworker abilities to volunteer, or how such effects overdetermined the ethnic make-up of its volunteer staff. In this context, Filipino disenchantment grew, especially through everyday actions like meetings held in Spanish, staff members who did not speak English and/or hiring halls that appeared to privilege Mexican farmworkers through the seniority system. This mistrust also grew in the context of multiple anti-UFW challenges, the disorganization of UFW offices, and the constant farmworker poverty, where gaining or losing a job affected the present and near future.

Two other sources of Filipino discontent need to be noted. Neither is specific to the Coachella Valley, but both likely affected Filipino farmworkers' overall relationship to the union. The first originates in the UFW's shortcomings in the San Joaquin Valley and in that region's multi-racial workforce. Like in the Coachella Valley, Filipino members found a chaotic hiring hall in Delano, while also shared fields and camps with Yemeni and Mexican workers. This sharing was often contentious and rife with charges and countercharges of discrimination. Some grape ranchers, furthermore, attempted to fire and replace older farmworkers, many of them Filipino, for labor "inefficiency," a euphemism for older age. Other ranchers closed their migrant housing camps, which disproportionally affected Filipino farmworkers. Lastly, there appears to have been a growing number of young Filipino men who were resistant to UFW contract stipulations or even to unionism. More research is needed on these dynamics, but I suspect Filipino farmworkers found many UFW-related frustrations on the migrant circuit, in which specific troubles in each region accentuated their overall mistrust of the UFW.[28]

The second source centers on Filipino leaders' responses to rank-and-file dissent: they simply demanded more displays of union support. Soon after the UFW won labor contracts in California's table grape industry in 1970, for example, the Filipino leader Philip Vera Cruz wrote in *El Malcriado* on the UFW's uphill battle against the Rancher Nation. Most ranchers, he said, "fight an eternal war against his fellow men," where "a worker cannot talk sense to his boss."[29] Only the UFW could defeat rancher-kings, he argued further, but the UFW depended on "the understanding, quality and honesty of the officers and members," on "people working for it, [those who] pay their dues and fight for its existence and progress." "Make your union strong to fight for you," he said, "Back it up to help you."[30]

Though seemingly reasonable, Vera Cruz's call for member support took a harder tone a couple weeks later. In *"The Farmworkers Union,"* published in November 1970, Vera Cruz summarily dismissed worker complaints about the union's failures by pointing to the UFW lettuce strike in the Salinas Valley. In this embattled context, he said, the UFW could only survive with member sacrifice, such as assisting in meetings, fighting for lettuce workers, and volunteering in the lettuce boycott. To Vera Cruz, the early 1970s were a time for more worker contributions to the union, not vice versa. Intimating dissent, he disciplined: "But, suppose you don't want to be involved because it would cost you your time and gas to fight for your union brother. Do you expect the others (the rest of the union members) to help you when you will be in trouble yourself? If you do, then you are a cheap, unfair and dishonest member to all of us, and we would be a lot better off without you. You want the benefits, but you don't want to help."[31] In his estimation, UFW members needed to transcend their immediate self-interest and fight for the union's strength in local and nonlocal campaigns. Those who only thought of their self-interests thus undermined the rest and illustrated their conditional union status. "We don't get something for nothing," he reminded critics, "We fought, sweated and suffered for over five years to win what we have today. So, we all have to pressure every other union member to help build a better and stronger union." He did not "[intend] to hurt anyone," he added, only "pinpoint the truth" and address "the wrong attitude of some of our brothers and sisters towards the Union."[32]

In this regard, Vera Cruz shared much with other UFW leaders and members. Like them, he was quick to remind critics that most had never given as much as they had to the UFW. Most had broken the Delano Grape Strike of 1965 in the first year and only a small core had sacrificed for five. Hardly real unionists, he implied, they had little right to demand as the UFW continued to fight the Rancher Nation. "Instead of talking against the Union," he chided, "you should get busy helping it. You don't have any right to criticize the others if you don't want to do anything for yourself."³³ In this context, Filipino rank-and-file critiques of UFW failures likely did not receive a sympathetic ear from him or other UFW leaders, whether Filipino or not.³⁴

Other leaders made similar charges. In October and November 1971, Andy Imutan led twenty-three labor camp meetings in the Delano region after Larry Itliong resigned from the UFW. Instead of using this opportunity to reassure Filipino members and/or to introduce union reforms, Imutan chastised them. He said he wanted to determine Filipino commitment to the UFW before he accepted Itliong's former Delano post, starting each meeting with the same blunt accusation: "Larry quit because he did not have the support from you." He also listed his disappointments: they did not go to meetings or rallies; they did not volunteer in campaigns or hiring halls; they did not help Filipino leaders.³⁵ He claimed some dismissed his requests—"The Mexicans are already doing the work!"—and asked accusatorily: "If we build a house and Mexicans did build it—are you not ashamed to live in it?" "That is why Larry felt hurt," he told one camp after another, "because there was no full support," a hurt that grew into shame and union loss: Larry left, he said, because he was "embarrassed when Cesar asked, 'where are the Filipinos?'"³⁶

For Imutan, in other words, the chief problem facing Filipino unionists was self-inflicted. Even if they paid dues and respected union procedures, he found them wanting.³⁷ Others expanded on this. In the first camp meeting, Vera Cruz told the assembled group, "Filipinos have colonial mentality: others make decisions for him."³⁸ At another meeting, Claro Runtal, a Coachella Valley striker in 1969, recounted his union history before vaguely warning dissidents: "Those who do not attend a meeting within 24 hours will swim across the ocean tomorrow." Pete Velasco took a more positive stance, but he still echoed the same demands and occluded Filipino grievances through a political form of obligation: "You started the Union," he said, "you must continue your participation."³⁹

The issue here is not the veracity of Imutan's argument, the legitimacy of his demands, or the reasons behind Itliong's resignation, which were multiple, clouded in confusion, and likely beyond the UFW's control.⁴⁰ What is key, instead, is that these meetings characteristically reflected the UFW's culture of sacrifice, one that conditioned union belonging on contributions. This culture also tended to react to critiques of union shortcomings with threats of exclusion. Imutan thus ended his meetings by demanding members pledge to do better with the UFW. If they did not, he said he would decline the Delano post and leave Filipino unionists without a leader when many already felt like a minority within a minority union. To dissenters—and there were plenty, often young men⁴¹—Imutan pushed Filipinos to assure their interests by "unit[ing]" within a diverse UFW and fulfilling the above expectations.

"Be strong," he said, "to gain respect." In this culture of sacrifice, Filipino grievances had little space for resolution and only seemed to provoke marginalizing reactions.

The story of Filipino discontent in the UFW is a complicated story. It has roots in the Delano Grape Strike's early days, the UFW's national reception, and the Rancher Nation's reliance on Mexican workers, who then become the union's great majority. It also has roots in UFW failings in Coachella and Delano, whether understandable or not, in inter-racial tensions rooted in material scarcity, and in intra-racial Filipino divisions. Such complications make this history difficult to recount, which is compounded further by the archive's limited base, itself a reflection of Filipino marginality in the history of the UFW movement.[42]

These difficulties also likely arise from our relationship to resistance histories, one that expects a determined subject to push into freedom and justice, regardless of costs, implications, and/or probabilities. Most people are not this subject, and most farmworkers in the UFW faced a difficult and ambiguous space of calculating strike days and calculating strike hunger, of holding picket signs and holding children, of hope and realism. This space reflected the Rancher Nation, the same Filipino grape strikers attacked in Coachella and Delano in 1965, and the same requiring attacks in 1966, 1967, 1968, 1969, and 1970, and then, after a brief victory, for the rest of the next two decades. In such accumulated years, choices became more demanding, more deleterious, and more difficult to sustain. How long, we can ask, must one strike to labor in peace? When does one rest, step out of the picket line to live *their* life? When will the new, just world arrive? To these questions, the UFW gave unforgiving answers, as Vera Cruz and Imutan exemplified. And to these, historians must offer answers that transcend simple heroes and simple villains.

The Perils of Brotherhood

Vulnerabilities also riddled the Chicana/o movement. Its initial victories centered on the most egregious forms of discrimination, such as segregated cemeteries. Activists also mentored young students and helped them enroll in regional universities. They built a newspaper counter public, led local and regional political campaigns, and publicized police violence, political underrepresentation, education inequality, and U.S. foreign policy. But such victories did not eliminate ethnic Mexicans' subjected position in the Coachella Valley. And the reasons for this, as with the UFW, were multiple.

In education, for example, Chicana/o activists successfully pushed the Desert Sands Unified School District (DSUSD) to hire more teachers of color, but they failed to revamp curricular approaches to Mexican Americans or de-segregate its student population. They argued a district-wide bilingual and bicultural curriculum would integrate students and improve their learning and well-being. Bilingual education for all would also encourage cultural mixture and exchange among students. But when the DSUSD Board met in May 1972 to discuss bilingual and bicultural education, it unequivocally rejected both. One Board member even filed his nails to ignore the ethnic Mexican parents.[43] Similarly, the Coachella Valley Unified School District (CVUSD) faced walkouts in 1970 and 1972, which participants celebrated as an expression of empowerment. But these failed to increase Mexican representation on the CVUSD Board, revamp its curriculum, or hire of more teachers of color. Some leaders suspected they simply led to a sense of white besiegement that further hardened opposition.[44]

In politics, the Chicana/o movement had even less success. In 1970, MAPA argued that both political parties advanced racist policies, took "Chicanos for granted," and led to Chicana/o underrepresentation in California, where they were 12 percent of the population but only 2 percent of elected officials.[45] Their answer was La Raza Unida Party (LRUP), but for the next three years LRUP lost every local election for seats on school, recreational, and water districts, all of which affected ethnic Mexican residents and remained under pro-rancher politicians. Even when LRUP ran MAPA's Raul Loya for State Assembly in 1970, activists tempered their goals to consciousness raising: "Loya's candidacy," *Ideal* wrote in March 1970, "was to compete, (even though it would be almost impossible to win) to wake-up the Mexican American community to politics, and to make them aware that their indifferent and pessimistic attitude is the reason that many posts are filled with persons that do nothing for us."[46] Such political education, however important, struggled to become political power. By late 1973, LRUP was a fractured party in the Southwest and a non-force locally.[47]

The most illustrative example of Chicana/o movement shortcomings occurred in a recall election of Coachella's first Chicano mayor. The election took place in the summer of 1972, which followed the earlier Chicana/o victories for Coachella city council seats.[48] As chapter 5 argued, the firing of Coachella's police chief and city manager was a profound Chicana/o victory. But conservative Mexican Americans and white residents quickly mounted a recall of the mayor for, as one resident said, "wanting to turn Coachella into a Mexican town."[49] The recall won with a minuscule 572 to 570 majority. For MAPA, the two-vote difference was devastating to the movement and reflected young activists' inability to see the ballot as a critical site of resistance. "Could it be that they only raise hell, but don't take the trouble to vote." "Where were the remaining thousand registered Chicano voters?" they asked accusatorily in *Ideal*, "*Donde estaban vatos locos?*"[50] Whether or not MAPA was correct in its blame, the loss succinctly illustrated the vulnerabilities riving the Chicana/o movement and its struggles to protect victories from a conservative backlash.

These vulnerabilities were not unique to the Coachella Valley or to the Chicana/o movement. All Chicana/o activists in the early 1970s failed to deepen their campaigns—whether in Los Angeles, the San Joaquin Valley, San Diego, Arizona, Texas, New Mexico, and Colorado. A similar set of unconsolidated wins shaped the Civil Rights Movement's southern, northern, and western fronts, as well as the feminist, anti-war, and New Left student movements. Which is to say all movements come with frailties and vulnerabilities, even when seemingly ascendant, and all confront outsized opposition that can reverse their victories. With regards to the Coachella Valley, two key factors need further discussion.

The first is rather paradoxical: early victories may have contained momentum. Young students played a key role in the 1960s manifestations. They were early UFW strikers, faced rancher and supervisor aggression with admirable courage, led spectacular pickets against local anti-UFW businesses, and/or joined rallies against the Vietnam War. They also erupted out of classrooms, fought police rioters, and voted against pro-police politicians. They then entered universities as the first Chicana/o generation in higher education. Many saw college attendance as an attack on the Rancher Nation, for the latter had pegged them as natural brute labor.[51] But this attack also meant young activists were constantly siphoned away from local politics, which could lead to situations like a recall election loss.

A similar weakness in victory developed between the UFW and Chicana/o movements after the 1970 grape victory. The UFW's 1968 and 1969 Coachella strikes spurred Chicana/o activism and offered a springboard for the new decade. But it also contributed to the reception of the UFW as a Mexican/Chicana/o movement, to the chagrin of Filipino unionists. More unexpectedly, the two movements began to compete in political campaigns after 1970: while MAPA pushed LRUP candidates, the UFW allied with Democrats. In 1972, a frustrated *Ideal* editorial criticized Chavez's endorsements and lack of coordination with LRUP,[52] arguing he "creat[ed] mass confusion, particularly in the minds of student organizers who embrace the philosophy of the third party politics coupled with [farmworker] unionization."[53] They accused him further of disregarding Chicano leaders like "Jose Angel Gutierrez, Corky Gonzalez, Bert Corona," and of provoking a backlash among Chicana/o activists: "Chavez has lost many to the Raza Unida Cause and the matter is beginning to look like a confrontation." Some, MAPA suggested, even started to call Chavez a "sell out."[54] Instead of building a coordinated movement, the two wings of a common cause competed with each other.

The second factor in Chicana/o movement frailty was more immanent to activist political culture—and that was their masculinist discourses. MAPA's Ray Rodriguez, for instance, celebrated the farmworker compliments he received during the UFW's 1968 Coachella Grape Strike, in which they compared MAPA's largely middle-class, professional men to Mexican revolutionaries. "They talked so highly of [revolutionaries], that these were men of the people," he said, "and then they put you in almost the same category, well yea, you get pumped up.... That is the ultimate compliment, that people who were striving to better themselves, their futures for their children ... [and they] put you in that light. It ... feels like you are doing something important, and sometimes when you are in, *en una peda*, you know, talking, philosophizing, you say, *Somos chingones. Tu sabes, Tenemos huevos.*"[55] To him, the compliments encapsulated the drive behind their activism and embodied its effect: to resist was to be a man, and to be man compelled fighting for justice. His allusion to genitalia, in turn, highlighted the effects of nonresistance: submission risked a neutered subjectivity. Men who tolerated injustices thus flirted with morphing into a deviant Other—into a subject without the balls that defiance could cup. Like the comparison to Mexican heroes, Chicano anti-racist politics could present resistance as waged to provide better futures for the community at large, *as patriarchs*.

Other activists shared this idealized patriarchy-in-resistance: of stoic sacrifice, righteous anger, authoritative control; of tough men refusing subjugation, of liberating people; *they* protected, *they* led, *they* transformed—*others*.[56] In these narratives, women were invisible or played supportive, passive, and loyal roles.[57] Few *Ideal* articles noted women's independent activism or the patriarchal basis of the agricultural economy. Even when the violence denounced targeted Mexican American women, Chicana/o activists still framed the issue as a social injustice affecting the Chicano community.[58] Unsurprisingly, male activists failed to draw large numbers of Chicanas into their campaigns.[59] As the organizer, Lupe Anguiano, told *Ideal* in 1973: "One reason the Chicano Movement has suffered is because it has not involved women in leadership roles. It's done great harm to our overall effort."[60]

This masculinist discourse also neglected important (though often mundane) organizing labor, what the civil rights organizer, Ella Baker, called "spadework," the everyday, slow, and usually unrecognized work that builds community efficacy. In the Coachella Valley, there was much enthusiasm for protesting police brutality, marching in the *"reconquista"* of the Southwest, storming out of racist classes, and joining UFW strikes—all public actions staging the masculine militant. But, in the invisibility of daily organizing, this subject could falter. In June 1970, for instance, the Movimiento Estudiantil Chicano de Aztlan (MEChA) invited "Chicanos from all over Aztlan" to a "mass junta to end the strike forever." "We must collectively pressure the [oppressors] of our people," the leaders said, and "to this end, we pledge our honor, our strength in numbers and our lives." They echoed the themes in Rodriguez's reference to revolutionaries, and promised a stoic, courageous masculinity that liberated others. But the results were negligible: the initial three thousand "storm troopers" on Saturday fell to four hundred two days later (the strike's first day), of which "twenty percent were hippie types," and then to ten by week's end.[61] A similar absence led to the 1972 recall election— "donde estaban vatos locos?"—and likely deflated gains in education too. Having drawn strength from masculinist discourses, local Chicanos appeared incapable of adopting Baker's view.[62]

To close, while the UFW produced a deep social transformation in Coachella Valley grape fields but failed to expand into all fields, then the Chicana/o movement moved in reverse: it dispersed widely without enough depth to transform the local landscape. Chicanas/os fought racial marginality in education, politics, the judicial system, popular culture, and economy. They built political institutions, led marches, challenged rancher-allied voices, and pushed younger students into a formerly unthinkable option: higher education and careers serving their communities. And yet, their multi-prong drive produced limited wins in all spaces, wins that struggled to dig themselves into some sense of permanence.

On Shifting Ground

The insurgent frailties discussed in this chapter should not be understood as negating the impact of the UFW and Chicana/o movements. Nor should they be the basis for judging either as uniquely deficient, for all such efforts carry frailties, as do power constellations. Nothing is ever sutured into permanence; nothing ever sits outside contingency. Even if ascendant, all remains in flux, and, in such flux, participants move with what they have and with what they can will in spaces shaped by innumerable others, nearby or not, legible or not, allied or not. Which is all to say that what took place in the Coachella Valley in the early 1970s cannot be understood in developmentalist form or as taking place in isolation, as if these towns could be unaffected by the period's churning national dynamics. Of these, four are key: luxury development in the West Coachella Valley; increased immigration to the East Coachella Valley; a concerted attack on organized labor; a rightward turn in national politics.

The first two dynamics occurred locally but signaled trans-local dynamics. In the first, noted briefly in chapter 1, the Coachella Valley's western half grew dramatically after World War II. Palm Springs had a long history as a tourist-oriented city based on Los Angeles's film industry. After World War II, Palm Springs grew into the valley's largest city—from 7,128 people in 1950 to 17,967 and 22,000 in 1970 and 1980, respectively. As Ryan M. Kray writes in "Path to Paradise," the city's planning discouraged middle-class housing and violently evicted poor Black and Latino residents from the Agua Caliente Cahuilla Reservation near the city's downtown. In a 1968 report, the California attorney general described the eviction as a "city-engineered holocaust" that "surpassed federally funded clearance campaigns elsewhere."[63]

A more dramatic transformation took place in the land between Palm Springs and Indio, where sand dunes, date groves, and pioneer towns gave way to luxury tracts housing and resorts. The first of these, Shadow Mountain, was guided by a "central idea": "namely, of a million-dollar family club with a select membership." Each member invested $1 million for their plot of land, and then spent another $2 million in housing construction and $200 annually to cover a sixty-five-person staff, amenities (e.g., pool facilities, tennis courts, a putting golf course), and a "personal calendar of social activities," such as duck hunting and boat racing in the Salton Sea.[64] As a local magazine explained, Shadow Mountain was for those "who love the desert and enjoy the finer things in life."[65] In the two decades after World War II, the formerly unincorporated Palm Desert built more resort clubs, seven churches, five golf courses, two schools, a junior college, three banks, a $50,000 library, and many stores, hotels, and restaurants.[66] Adjacent cities elicited similar "phenomenal growth," and collectively represented a "wonderland," the "winter golf capital of the world." By 1970, the West Coachella Valley counted 48,588 residents, compared to the eastern half's 31,221 residents, which included Indio.[67]

The growth's effect on the UFW and Chicana/o movements were twofold. First, it segregated the Coachella Valley by race, class, and industry, containing Mexican and farmworker poverty in the eastern half and offering rancher-affiliated families a white space in westside cities. Spatial segregation, in turn, muted the effect of Chicana/o electoral victories: the latter now governed racialized poverty with few tools to contest regional inequality. Second, the luxury development served as a base for white reactionary politics. Westside residents joined the John Birch Society and the Barry Goldwater and George Wallace candidacies. They stridently opposed and repeatedly attacked school integration, while rancher wives and westside women formed Women for California Agriculture in 1975, an organization aiming "to give support to the harassed and intimidated grape workers" and "ensure justice for the farmer."[68] The westside's population, wealth, and organizations, in short, posed an often-unseen challenge to those fighting the Rancher Nation in the Coachella Valley.

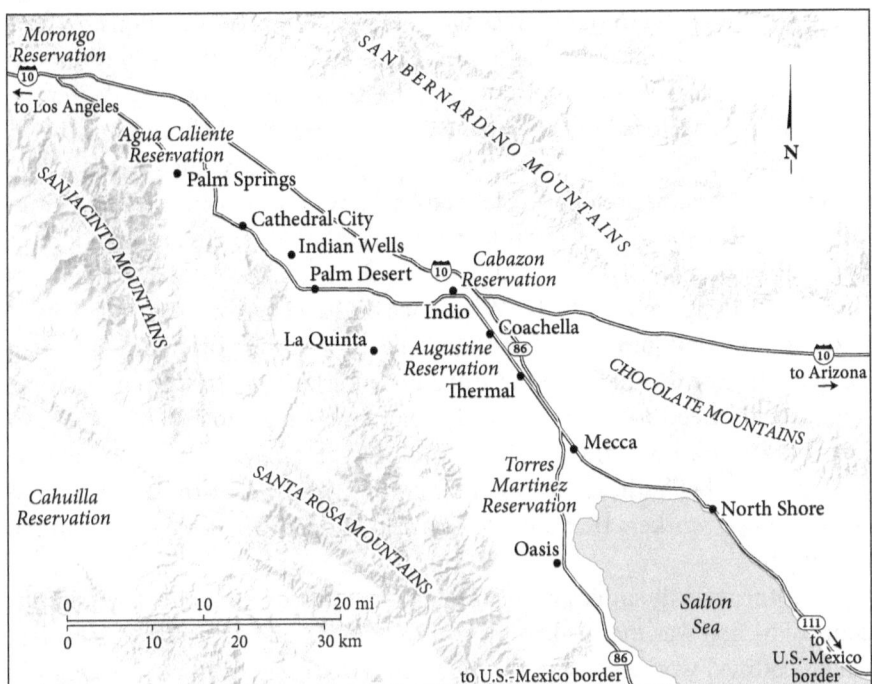

Coachella Valley after 1970: new westside cities.

Simultaneously, the Coachella Valley's eastern half saw a rapid increase in Mexican immigration. As previously discussed, Mexican immigrants played a foundational role in the Coachella Valley's twentieth century development. They also regularly plagued white residents' racially exclusive visions of their communities. The Bracero Program promised to fix the race-labor contradiction by offering ranchers cheap labor during harvests and nonwhite worker invisibility afterwards. But the Bracero Program also stimulated unauthorized immigration, which grew further when Congress ended the Bracero Program in 1964. Some braceros who had previously worked in the Coachella Valley settled in the region with their families, while most engaged in circular migration between Mexican hometowns and a string of farmworker communities in California and the U.S. Southwest. Exact numbers remain elusive, but the national trajectory is clear. In 1967, the Border Patrol reported eighty-six thousand apprehensions; in 1968, 1973, and 1977, apprehensions grew to one hundred thousand, five hundred thousand, and one million, respectively.

For the UFW, which had a troubled history with Mexican immigrants, these numbers posed substantial challenges. Not only did immigrants hold a juridically vulnerable position and face greater losses in a labor strike, but many also had little initial knowledge of the UFW or its campaigns. Arturo Diaz, for instance, immigrated to the Coachella Valley in the early 1970s and learned of the UFW during the Coachella Grape Strike of 1973. When he asked his contractor about the strikers' demands, Diaz believed him when the latter said they were "lazy" and "[full of] lies." Diaz also heard UFW strikes and demonstrations led to lost workdays and violence. "One comes with the idea to work," Diaz said, "not thinking that you're going to join to an organization or anything, until you see the reality."[69] While the scholarship has justly criticized the UFW's stance on strikebreaking immigrants, it is key to note that joining a long-shot strike or fighting powerful bosses in a foreign country was hardly a natural stance for anyone. In this context, the UFW would need to expend already-sparse resources to reach out to and incorporate new immigrants. This is not to suggest immigrants needed to be convinced to be "radical" or pro-worker, but simply that the UFW had to convince new workers that it could win and had, in fact, already won in the recent past.

The other two dynamics were more national in scope but held local significance. The first was the weakening of the National Labor Relations Act (1935), which codified workers' right to unions and arbitrated conflicts through the National Labor Relations Board (NLRB). In the two decades after its passage, unions led a frenetic campaign that peaked in the mid-1950s, when they represented a third of private sector workers and their contracts secured a middle class life.[70] But employers' postwar acceptance of unions reflected self-interest: facing open global markets, they prioritized uninterrupted production lines and agreed to higher wages, benefits, and union recognition to undercut striker sentiment and gain a partner in worker discipline.[71] By the mid-1960s, this model had run its course; increased global competition and costly benefits lowered profits, while new finance structures demanded greater short-term returns. In response, U.S. employers began a two-decade process to weaken unions and lower labor costs. Eventually, they sought the end of unions entirely.[72]

This process began in the early 1960s with businesses pushed anti-union labor law reforms, such as limiting union certification to secret-ballot victories, strengthening employer "free speech," and preventing "improper remedies for" unlawful labor practices. Business did not win these in the 1960s, but Nixon's appointees to the NLRB adopted many of them in the early to mid-1970s.[73] Employers also hired anti-union consultants to guide them in bending and breaking the NLRA, including harassing and firing pro-union workers, threatening plant closures, forcing anti-union meetings, delaying elections, and/or appealing results to cut worker resolve. As Lane Windham has argued, labor law still existed in the 1970s but "its penalties for ... violations were too weak to hold back the assault."⁷⁴ An anti-union consultant agreed: "The probability is you will never get caught [violating the law]," and "if you do . . . the worst thing that can happen to you is you get a second election, and the employer wins 96 percent of those elections." Even when unions overcame employer hostility and won NLRB elections, 40 percent of employers in the 1970s still refused to sign union contracts.

Though the NLRA did not cover farmworkers, its weakening still augured a difficult future for all workers. The UFW movement had relied heavily on AFL-CIO aid in the 1960s and 1970s, which would become rarer as these unions faced a budget crisis in the late 1970s and early 1980s. The UFW movement would also face anti-union politics in local and national spaces, as employers from diverse backgrounds learned from each other and spirited a reactionary base. The defeat of unions among the country's most privileged workers, in other words, undermined union support for the UFW and created precedents for farm employer hostility.

Lastly, and more amorphously, the national political culture made an abrupt rightward turn in the early 1970s. By 1973, white Americans had twice elected a president who refined dog-whistle politics and packed the Supreme Court with conservative judges. White Americans also fought school integration and union-backed politicians. They joined the frantic migrations of suburban white flight and policed racialized urban poverty. Many felt the stings of economic vulnerability, which grew with the onset of the post-1973 stagflation spiral. A majority even held business in higher regard than organized labor. The Coachella Valley's movements against the Rancher Nation, in short, existed in an increasingly unsympathetic national context. Their victories rooted in an earlier period of possibility, appeared to be out of sync with the solidifying political landscape of the 1970s.⁷⁵

For the UFW, this landscape appeared evident after its early 1970s lettuce boycott failed to echo the 1960s. Recent scholarship has argued the UFW's multiple boycotts "confus[ed]" consumers and lowered participation. But as Elizabeth Lamoree argued, the "unfavorable political economic context cast the UFW as 'the historic heir . . . to [union] excesses,'" and "since food purchases were the largest single expense in shoppers' budgets, support for organizations that might increase food prices waned among consumers during the 1970s."⁷⁶ The country's conservative turn also meant racialized hostility to redistributive tax programs, which encouraged migration from the high-tax industrial Northeast and Midwest to the low-tax Sunbelt states. In the early 1970s, California grape ranchers fostered markets in these very states, where racial resentment, neoliberal conservatism, and general union weakness congregated into something like rancher promise. Given the outsized role of the

UFW's boycott in its late 1960s campaigns, the country's rightward turn, and the ranchers' readiness to exploit it, suggested significant challenges for the UFW's future—whether inside or outside the Coachella Valley.[77]

Though often removed from daily confrontations with the Rancher Nation, these local and trans-local dynamics held significant implications for the Coachella Valley's insurgents. They shaped the context for future campaigns and intimated that the local and national victories of the UFW and Chicano movements had taken place in a period that was already being rejected by the rest of America.

Conclusion: Limits and Storms

All insurgencies come with their frailties—with a collection of stumbles and reversals, blind spots, and the accumulation of self-inflicted wounds. In the Coachella Valley, the dual efforts against the Rancher Nation were no different. Theirs included the UFW's woefully unprepared offices and an overall tardiness to organize Coachella Valley's non-grape fields. It also included Filipino farmworkers' long-simmering mistrust of a Mexican-led UFW that often overlooked their contributions and needs, further antagonized by Filipino leaders' unsympathetic responses. Lastly, it included the Chicana/o movement's inability to deepen its victories or transcend a masculinist politics that worsened differences and neglected critical, if invisible, labors.

It is unclear to me, however, whether these frailties are as important as the shifting political and economic landscapes. Or, more to the point, I am not convinced that had the UFW and Chicana/o movements practiced greater diligence, discipline, and foresight, that their efforts could have overcome the challenges already consuming other social movements and well-established labor unions. Another storm, in short, was already brewing, both far away and close at hand, and it was uninterested in the agency of racialized and impoverished insurgents living in a small region far removed from the country's center. As argued in the introduction, agency does not suggest the world moves to one's intention. Agency is shared, contested, and vexing—and it is always less than the desires animating it.

Lastly, I wish to stress a final frailty that can better understood as an "unseeing," and is largely beyond the scope of this book. Both the UFW and Chicana/o movements attempted to form interracial fronts. The UFW consistently identified itself as a multi-racial union and took pains to keep a diverse leadership. Similarly, local Chicanas/os celebrated Filipino workers' masculinity and/or advocated for alliances with African American campaigns, especially against police brutality. But despite these efforts, neither insurgency formed coalitions with the Indigenous Cahuilla, who continued to fight white encroachments and the legacies of settler colonialism. As such, even if the UFW and Chicano movements had successfully led a multi-racial front, and even if they had eventually defeated the Rancher Nation, they still would not necessarily have offered a politics that attacked the Coachella Valley's settler–colonial history and social structure—both of which necessitated and facilitated farmworkers' racialized marginality. Future scholarship would do well to engage this "unseeing" further—and, in the process, to foster an exchange between Native American, Asian American, and Chicana/o/x studies.

Chapter 7

The Battle for Coachella, 1973–1974

Max Huerta, introduced in chapter 5, was twenty years old in early 1973, and already a veteran of the Chicana/o Movement. Since the mid-1960s, he had organized a Brown Berets chapter in Delano, led a high school student walkout to protest conditions and treatment, graduated from a boarding school (after being expelled for the walkout), and then joined a 1971 Chicana/o march through the U.S. Southwest, which sought to bring the Chicana/o movement to the region's small, rural communities. He finally settled in the Coachella Valley in late 1972, when he joined his mother and siblings, who had also recently relocated from Delano.[1] Much had changed in such little time, including what was possible for the young Huerta. "I didn't want to be poor for the rest of my life," he said as recounted earlier. "I was tired of being poor.... Whatever it would take to get me out of that (!), that is what I wanted.... I wanted to help my mom."[2] In January 1973, his ticket out of poverty was unionized grape work at Valdora Ranch, one of the many Coachella Valley grape ranchers who signed United Farm Workers' (UFW) contracts in 1970 and 1971. Unlike his early childhood, Huerta now saw this agricultural job as a potential source of respect for him and economic aid for his mother. Through the UFW, he imagined a farmworker world that existed beyond the death sentence that once seemed inescapable.

But not all was well. The Valdora farmworkers still feared supervisors, failed to demand contract terms, and/or did not know other union members. In early 1973, just a couple months after starting work, Huerta also noticed that Valdora supervisors began a petition drive that said workers wanted the Teamsters Union as their labor representative. Pro-UFW workers like Huerta contested the petition drive in multiple Coachella Valley grape fields, and, in early April, many local grape workers voted for the UFW in an informal election in hopes of settling the issue and avoiding a strike. When it did not, and Coachella Valley grape ranchers unilaterally signed Teamster contracts in mid-April 1973, grape workers like Huerta suddenly faced an open-ended strike that threatened their safety and livelihood. Huerta was used to social movement poverty and danger, he said, but others were not. Some also had grievances against the UFW's local office and/or policies. In a space of uncertainty and scarcity, these workers had to choose (again) their relationship to the UFW and each other.

Taking rank-and-file perspectives, this chapter foregrounds the complex contexts shaping the UFW's Coachella Grape Strike of 1973, a critical moment in the UFW's history and for subsequent union campaigns in and out of the Coachella Valley. The chapter argues that at least half of the region's grape workforce honored the UFW strike in 1973. They did so despite limited resources, a large strikebreaking labor reservoir, and pervasive, relentless rancher–Teamster violence. They also struck at the beginning of the grape thinning season, which meant they forewent harvest wages in the Coachella Valley and, as the strike spread northward, in the San Joaquin Valley. In effect, the Coachella Grape Strike of 1973 initiated a half-year general farmworker strike against California's grape industry—all without as much as a month's warning. Perhaps because of the long odds for success, pro-UFW farmworkers and strikers spoke of both concrete demands, such as a union and a labor contract of their choosing, as well as more abstract goals, such as the reshaping of intra-community relations and the severing of all worker ties to the Coachella Valley's Rancher Nation. Strikebreakers also explained their choices, but these varied significantly. Migrant Filipino and Mexican workers expressed bitter and justified frustration with the UFW's organizational shortcomings. But most strikebreakers simply spoke of need and of the obvious: that grape ranchers could easily replace them and save their harvest, while strikers struggled to survive. Labor strikes and their dynamics, in short, do not easily reflect worker politics.

In the national public sphere, however, the UFW's Coachella Grape strike of 1973 appeared murky and inconclusive. National newspapers failed to see the Teamsters' raid in the Coachella Valley's grape fields as a life raft to a beleaguered Rancher Nation and as a disruption of local and regional farmworker power. Whether intentionally or not, they amplified a false rancher narrative that framed the strike as a jurisdictional dispute between two unions, a framing that ranchers predicted accurately would blunt a UFW consumer boycott. And here we may find the Coachella Grape Strike's real lesson: though the UFW correctly saw the Teamster raid as the Rancher Nation's return, it misjudged the country's political tenor, hopelessly hoping for the consumers' saving grace, all while dissipating the local strike's generative potential.

Hard-Core Arrogant People

Early 1973 brought few reassurances to Coachella Valley ranchers. The anti-UFW California Proposition 22, which sought to outlaw secondary boycotts and harvest strikes, failed in the November 1972 elections, just as the Coachella UFW office assigned crew committees and used the hiring hall to settle grievances with recalcitrant grape ranchers. "Mike Bozac [sic] didn't want to settle some 4 grievances," read one Coachella UFW memo in December 1972, "so they didn't dispatch anyone, and they were settled."[3] The same tactic targeted Carian in early 1973 when he refused to follow UFW dispatch procedures. When four angry ranchers (Mel-Pak, Freedman, Carian, Karahadian) called an emergency meeting to confront the UFW's use of the hiring hall to settle grievances, they uncharacteristically found themselves surrounded by fifteen worker-leaders who lectured them on UFW policies.[4] In late 1972, the Coachella UFW office began organizing onion and citrus fields and demanded that future grape contracts cover the grape ranchers' date and asparagus fields. When one rancher lawyer said there was "no money" in these crops, the UFW sternly said, "we will see about that." To those paying attention, the UFW was consolidating its power in and out of the Coachella Valley's grape fields.

In this context, the Teamsters Union president, Frank Fitzsimmons, offered an alliance to California farmers during their annual association convention in December 1972.[5] Soon afterwards, Teamster organizers informed Coachella Valley grape ranchers of their planned grape campaign and met secretly with fifty local ranchers in late January 1973.[6] In subsequent lawsuits, the UFW leadership alleged Coachella Valley grape ranchers attended the Teamster meeting to collude against the UFW's representation of their grape workers. As evidence, UFW pointed to rancher–Teamster ties, including the Teamster histories of their labor relations lawyers.[7] The UFW also stressed the Teamsters' early efforts to undercut the UFW movement in California and their collusion with Salinas Valley lettuce ranchers in the early 1970s. Coachella Valley grape ranchers, in turn, insisted that these meetings were informal and did not include an agenda, much less a negotiated contract or plan. Conveniently, grape ranchers did not take meeting notes, and no one remembered much of what was said.[8]

In February and March, Teamsters entered nearly every Coachella Valley grape field to gather petition signatures from workers stating their preference for Teamster representation.[9] They faced no opposition from trespass-sensitive ranchers and most received aid from rancher supervisors. In Bagdasarian, Tenneco, CID, Karahadian, Carian, Mel-Pak, and Henry Moreno, Teamster–supervisor duos pressed workers with threats, promises, and deception.[10] They avoided well-known *Chavistas*,[11] pro-UFW workers testified, who also said most workers signed out of ignorance (all petitions were in English) or fear.[12] A minority signed out of conviction, they admitted, while another minority fought the Teamsters. Such was the case with Maria Serrano, who led a crew stoppage when her CID supervisor and former labor contractor, Manuel Alvarado, cooperated with Teamster organizers. "In reaction to the sit-down strike," a UFW memo read, Alvarado threatened the crew, "verbally abuse[d] Mrs. Serrano," claimed to be "organiz[ing] the workers"—to which Mrs. Serrano "replied that she and her fellow workers were already UFW members and as such were already organized."[13]

In later depositions, Coachella Valley grape ranchers would say they signed Teamster contracts because their petitions showed the workers' choice, a claim they used in the subsequent UFW grape strike to portray themselves as victims of a union jurisdictional dispute and as selfless defenders of "their" workers from an abusive UFW office. Though without any basis in reality, this rancher narrative gained a receptive audience from national newspapers and dampened the UFW's grape boycott in 1973 and 1974. Tenneco officials, for instance, said in their deposition that they left the UFW-led contract renegotiations after receiving a Teamster petition with 139 signatures out of their 273 farmworkers. But, under questioning, they admitted their 237 figure was arbitrary, the petition included peach workers, and their supervisors helped Teamsters organizers collect signatures.[14] Most Coachella Valley grape ranchers admitted as much, while one labor relations lawyer accepted that many farmworkers signed Teamster petitions while wanting UFW representation, adding simply: "you never know."[15] The false insistence on farmworker choice, however, did reflect the ranchers' strategy in early 1973: with the Teamsters petitions, ranchers could mount a "war of words" to reframe a UFW strike as a union jurisdiction fight. Such a frame, they predicted, would not "strike the hearts of quite so many people," and thus blunt the national popularity of the UFW's consumer boycott.[16]

For their part, UFW leaders in La Paz and Coachella recognized the Teamster threat while misjudging rancher intentions. La Paz alerted its offices to possible Teamster incursions in December 1972 and, in late January, Coachella UFW organizers reported on the rancher–Teamster meetings in which a model contract was considered.[17] But the local office questioned the latter's prospects because a contract depended on lawyers "get[ting] all the Growers together (fast)," which was not far from assured. The Coachella UFW office also stressed the rank-and-file resistance hampering the Teamster incursion, of pro-UFW workers "kick[ing] [Teamsters] out of fields" and placing "heat on each other if members show[ed] signs of weakening toward [them]."[18] Similarly, when a UFW organizer from La Paz reported on Coachella office issues in mid-February 1973, she noted that the Coachella office director had yet to provide "proof to substantiate [the] claim" of Teamster organizing. To this organizer, other issues were more pressing, including late dues, unapproved fines, and staff turnover.[19] In February and March, the chief UFW negotiator even bragged about telling "growers crying about the threat of Teamsters" to "negotiate with Temos or drop the issue in our negotiation."[20]

As the last quote indicates, the UFW saw rancher references to the Teamsters as a tactic to undercut UFW negotiation demands. The UFW held this view despite increasingly ominous signs, such as rancher refusals to pay into the UFW strike fund, as mandated by the 1970 contract, and a concerted campaign by anti-UFW supervisors and farmworkers for refunds of past union dues a month before the contracts expired.[21] Even in late March 1973, the UFW leadership still spoke of "growers . . . throwing Temo threat in negotiations,"[22] while one rancher lawyer would later testify that Chavez repeatedly responded to his questions of union representation by threatening to "escalate demands" on ranchers "playing" with the Teamsters.[23] The Coachella UFW director would also recall that Chavez "felt [ranchers] would negotiate in good faith [until late March]. Cesar could not see what advantage [ranchers] would have in signing with the Teamsters, that [they] wouldn't be that foolish."[24] And so, when Coachella Valley grape ranchers demanded evidence of workers' pro-UFW sympathies in March 1973, just weeks before the contracts' expiration, Chavez simply promised recalcitrant ranchers a strike–boycott combo, crowing: "We'll show you who represents [your] employees."[25]

If such a threat was meant to cow down grape ranchers, it did not work. As one Tenneco lawyer observed, when Coachella Valley grape ranchers left UFW negotiations in early April 1973, they predicted "workers would not leave fields irrespective of which union asked them to do so . . . guessing the majority . . . wanted to work and would work."[26] Some ranchers insisted their prediction reflected workers' preference for Teamster representation.[27] Nobody admitted the obvious: that strikes meant more than temporary wage losses, for harvest earnings met basic needs in unemployment seasons; that farmworkers knew they had no legal right to their jobs and risked being permanently replaced by strikebreakers if they joined the strike; that local labor contractors could easily find strikebreakers among nonunionized locals and/or nonlocal migrants; that migrant workers also risked losing rancher housing if they joined a strike; that all farmworkers were poor and that the grape harvest was the last local work opportunity in the region; that for all workers, strikes were not abstract exercises in performance politics, but pained wars of attrition; that to not strike, in other words, did not easily reflect worker choice.[28]

In the late 1960s, these factors had encouraged Coachella Valley grape ranchers to oppose to the UFW; they also shaped farmworker skepticism about a possible union victory. The UFW's key weapon then had been the consumer grape boycott and, in 1973, grape ranchers worried again about "a similar period of suffering boycott loss . . . we wanted to avoid that."[29] Perhaps the UFW estimated that such boycott worries would inhibit Coachella Valley grape ranchers.[30] But the country had changed since the late 1960s, as chapter 6 noted. By early 1973, the UFW's lettuce consumer boycott had already failed to force lettuce ranchers into contracts, a failure that was partly rooted in the country's rising conservatism and economic precarity.[31] Since 1970, California grape ranchers had also increased grape demand in export markets and conservative U.S. states, which they hoped would insulate them from pro-UFW consumers in a future altercation. With Teamster contracts and a union jurisdiction narrative, grape ranchers in 1973 thus calculated they stood a good chance of avoiding their previous "traumatic experience."[32]

The UFW leadership finally recognized this calculation when Tenneco left negotiations on April 4, 1973, which was followed four days later by Bagdasarian's firing of its high seniority and pro-UFW crews.[33] Pro-UFW grape workers also reported increased Teamster and supervisor aggression.[34] The UFW responded by holding a grape worker meeting on April 10, where a thousand members voted to strike if ranchers refused to renegotiate their UFW contracts. It also led a non-representative vote on April 10 among pro-UFW crews, in which it won near-unanimous support, to call for renewed contract negotiations. But, on April 11, nearly all Coachella Valley grape ranchers left UFW talks and used the Teamster petitions as a legitimizing fig leaf for unilaterally signing Teamster contracts. No farmworkers were consulted before or during the Teamster-rancher negotiations and contract signatures. The two local exceptions, Freedman and KK Larson ranches, re-signed with the UFW on April 15, 1973. Freedman's owner, Lionel Steinberg, who described UFW worker-leaders as "hard core arrogant people who... started out rank-and-file and gradually became union [professionals] that were anti-grower and more of the [UFW] attitude," said he re-signed UFW contracts because in "an [1973] election my workers would have chosen the [UFW]."[35]

Critically, national newspapers in late March and early April framed a possible UFW strike in the Coachella Valley with "they-said/they-said" accounts, which foreshadowed their skeptical stance toward the UFW for the rest of the year. The *Los Angeles Times*, for instance, paired the April UFW-led worker preference vote with a rancher quote on negotiations "br[eaking] down... on several things, including the fact that the Teamsters claimed to represent a majority of our workers."[36] The newspaper offered no appraisal of either statement, but simply printed yet another rancher assertion: "ranchers might have encouraged the Teamsters to move into grapes, but I don't doubt that they now have a majority of workers in at least some of the companies." The *Los Angeles Times* article then turned to UFW charges of rancher amorality and Teamster collusion before closing with a third rancher quote: "the trouble is that the UFWU is run by $5-a-day reformers and they're like a bunch of new cops who want to hand out so many traffic tickets a day to prove their worth."[37] The *New York Times* and *Washington Post* used the same faux neutrality-pairing UFW charges with Teamster and rancher counter-charges. "This is not the first time," the *New York Times* characteristically quoted the Teamsters' president, Frank Fitzsimmons, "[Chavez] has given farmworkers a side show instead of [a] union."[38]

In the process, early news reports deflected attention from ranchers and laced UFW claims with uncertainty. They did not question rancher opposition to the UFW hiring hall as based on "management prerogatives" and worker preference. They did not note the hall's role in upholding contracts or define "management prerogatives," much less consider the latter's link to rancher power. They failed to highlight ranchers' about-face on unionization or workers' absence in rancher–Teamster negotiations.[39] They simply spoke of "charges and counter-charges," of each union claiming an opaque workforce, whose "typical response," the *Los Angeles Times* reported, came from an unnamed farmworker pruning on the strike's first day: "I just want to work," he demurred, "I'll work with Chavez or with the Teamsters, whoever has the contracts."[40] With such a framework, national newspapers offered a country already tired of social movements the benefit of seeing non-action as solidarity itself. They also offered grape ranchers the prospects of surviving the UFW's once-formidable boycott.

Ranchers, in short, gambled against the UFW's strike and boycott, wagering that neither was threatening *enough* to warrant their resignation to a union intent on snuffing out their former world.[41] The UFW's expansionist plans had made urgent action necessary and, in early 1973, they found an opportunity in the Teamsters and in a national press newly skeptical of UFW narratives. They also likely held less-than-rational reasons for leaving the UFW. Karahadian, for instance, testified in his deposition that his workers were not present in his contract negotiations with the Teamsters, but he stressed that he "negotiat[ed] on behalf of [his] workers." The claim conjures up the absurd scenario of a boss negotiating with the workers' union *on the workers' behalf*. More than absurd, it pithily reflected the Rancher Nation's paternalist generosity before the UFW's 1970 victory.[42] In this nation, ranchers-kings ruled in the absence of worker power, much less the "hard core arrogan[ce]" confronting Freedman's Steinberg. This was the Rancher Nation before the UFW. And, with the Teamsters, ranchers had a chance to return to a time when they (and only they) determined who threatened, ordered, and bestowed generosity.[43]

Who Represents the Workers?

Even today, ambiguities cloud the 1973 Coachella Grape Strike and have produced dramatically different historical accounts. These ambiguities originate in the archival limits—in the "war of words" congealed in news articles, rancher accounts, and union statements, in the spare Coachella Valley paper trails; and in oral history interviewees' insistence that history see the strike through *their* participation, not those on the sidelines. But ambiguities also lie in the strike's sequence, for Coachella Valley grape ranchers forced the UFW into a non-harvest strike when few farmworkers expected either a strike or striker benefits. Many farmworkers also relied on rancher housing, had close and/or important relations with bosses, and knew of the vulnerability a pro-UFW badge brought. In this context, grape workers weighed hopes, needs, and fears, and chose where to stand, a choosing that was itself a form of constraint. The UFW recognized as much and called for union elections within the strike's first week. When ranchers refused, nearly half of the grape workforce went on strike in April. Just as many, however, did not, and the latter's reasons ranged from their precarious social position and critiques of the UFW's failings to the self-interested wish by a few for the privileged scraps of their pre-UFW world.

Critically, this initial mid-April UFW grape strike dwindled during May's labor lull and then sprung up again in the early June harvest. Between the peaks, Coachella Valley grape ranchers secured enough strikebreakers to complete their harvest, while pro-UFW strikers left the region to find work. At the same time, the national press fed itself on spare pickets and abundant labor to speak of ambiguous worker allegiances and questionable UFW boycott claims. Furthermore, in early May, Arvin-Lamont grape ranchers also unilaterally signed Teamster contracts and provoked the UFW grape strike's expansion into California's San Joaquin Valley. This meant that as the Coachella Valley grape harvest began, local grape workers faced an industry-wide, half-year-long strike that magnified their losses while unifying the state's rancher class. In a shifting landscape, farmworkers again chose from options not of their choosing.

We can elaborate on these dynamics with Max Huerta and his Valdora crew. In early April, Huerta's crew voted for the UFW in the latter's poll, hoping to settle the issue of worker union choice, and when it did not, they immediately faced a strike they could not afford. "Oh man," Huerta recalled, "this is not what I was expecting. I thought the growers were going to sign the contract.... The season had just begun, and we were all looking forward to staying in the same crew and going to the different phases... and making some money... and saving what you can."[44] They planned to work four months in the Coachella Valley and more if they migrated north. They all had families, and no one had savings, Huerta explained. "none of us were anticipating a strike... that we were not going to find work."[45] Few of his coworkers had previously joined a labor strike or "knew what to expect." They only knew that "things were going to turn bad with the strike, because... the growers [were] not going to need us because they were going to get labor force through the Teamsters, and these guys don't play around." They predicted pessimistically, "There's going to be some violence here."

And yet, Huerta's crew members went on strike on the first day, as did an estimated half of Valdora's entire workforce in mid-April. The reasons varied and reflected the strike's qualities. Some, like Huerta and his crew leader, Sammy Rodriguez, who would play a key role in the Coachella and San Joaquin valley grape strikes, went on strike out of loyalty to the UFW movement. Others workers simply followed crew leaders, for "whatever the foreman says," Huerta recalled, "people will follow him."[46] Some went on strike despite only having brief interactions with the UFW office and/or despite their frustration with its policies. They did so, furthermore, despite the strike's immediate uncertainty.[47] Huerta's crew, for instance, did not know what to do after leaving Valdora' ranch, so they drove to the Coachella UFW office and joined the growing farmworker assembly in the city's central park. There, they learned that the signed Teamster-rancher contracts meant they faced a long strike of roving picket lines. Several days later, they learned of the measly strike benefits of $50 a week. In between, and as Huerta predicted, grape ranchers found enough strikebreakers and the Teamsters unleashed a wave of violence against pro-UFW farmworkers and residents.

Other UFW leaders echoed Huerta's account of the UFW's 1973 Coachella Grape Strike in their deposition for post-strike lawsuits. In the depositions, rancher lawyers repeatedly tried to contest UFW claims that half of the region's workforce had been on strike in April. But UFW organizers and members remained consistent. The UFW lawyer, Tom Dalzell, said the first week's picket line counted eight hundred to one thousand strikers, which accounted for half the workforce on those days. Of these picketers, he added 95 percent were farmworkers and not outsiders, as ranchers alleged. Like a revolving door, however, strikers picketed for a couple days before leaving to find other jobs. The AFL-CIO (American Federation of Labor and Congress of Industrial Organizations) organizer, Joe Lopez, shared similarly, while the UFW Coachella director, Ray Huerta, likely inflated numbers when he said the strike's first day only saw two hundred strikebreakers out of two thousand workers.[48] Clementina Olloque, who helped lead the Karahadian Ranch strike, said fields were left empty on the first day, while another, Maria Marron, recalled Dalzell's more modest results: 30–40 percent of Karahadian workers did not strike, most of whom were related to supervisors and/or feared rancher retaliation.[49]

Grape ranchers also suggested the same numbers in *their* depositions. Bozick, for example, said his workers chose the Teamsters, but UFW striker violence prevented them from working.[50] He had already fired high-seniority crews before the strike's start and he relied on contractors who managed camps to secure additional labor. For these newly recruited workers, joining the strike during the subsequent harvest meant losing wages and housing.

Still, Bozick testified to facing "instances where work was not performed, and employees left the valley. Left labor camps because of harassment. They would not come to work because they were afraid of getting stopped." When pressed to give a worker shortfall estimate, Bozick said his fifty-person crews fell to thirty in the strike's first week, but that they filled up once a stringent court injunction limited UFW pickets: "when there was nobody harassing them, blocking the driveways, throwing stones, the whole bit." Again, he said UFW violence briefly dissuaded his purportedly pro-Teamster workers from returning to his fields, insisting that there had been no strike among the workers. But when asked to provide his payroll records to determine if his crews returned to their original size with new workers, and thus strikebreakers, his lawyer intervened aggressively and prevented him from doing so.[51]

Similarly, Karahadian said a violent minority of sixty strikers attempted to pull out the rest of his workers (between 120 and 140) on the strike's first days.[52] They broke car windows, he testified, "threatened," did "everything in their effort to make those people afraid." Fear led his farmworkers to flee, he insisted, not their pro-UFW support. But, under questioning, Karahadian's story unraveled: he was "not really sure about" his sixty striker estimate; he did not know the reasons for workers leaving, nor the nature of UFW threats against strikebreakers; his one victim, who was hit with a rock, returned the next day, seemingly undeterred by the alleged violence.[53] He also did not recall the UFW's demand for union elections in late April nor of learning from the labor mediator Reverend Lloyd Saatjian that Karahadian's workers wanted the UFW, as Saatjian testified telling Karahadian in April 1973. Lastly, he admitted to facing a labor shortage in the strike's first "two or three days," but said his supervisors quickly resolved it "without any problems." "It's generally word of mouth ... type of thing," he said, "[supervisors] contact some people ... they know [and] depend on workers to bring other workers with them."[54]

Nearly all other Coachella Valley grape ranchers also admitted in their deposition that they faced disrupted workdays at the strike's start. The Teamster organizer Johnny Macias shared as much to a California state committee in November 1973 when he explained that they brought Teamster "guards" because "the opposition built up very strongly ... after we negotiated the contracts ... things really got big [and] we did not see sufficient law enforcement."[55] But, as Karahadian shared, the Coachella Valley was full of contractors who could immediately replace pro-UFW strikers to complete the pruning and prepare for the harvest. Bozick used Filipino and Mexican contractors—"hardened strikebreakers" from the 1960s, as the UFW organizer Marshall Ganz described them in 1974—to regrow his crews, while Carian brought and housed workers from the Imperial and Mexicali valleys. Peters Ranch's three grape crews included two (one Filipino, one mixed Filipino-Mexican) from the San Joaquin Valley who relied on rancher's housing camps, while Valdora turned to Filipino workers from Delano and Mexican workers from Mexicali, and Tenneco used young Filipino men from Delano and local ethnic Mexican women.[56] The conclusion here is not that migrant farmworkers broke a local strike, but that Coachella Valley ranchers had many sources of labor and that all strikers risked wages and housing for months.

The trained social scientist and Catholic priest, Victor Salandini found similar data when he surveyed Coachella Valley grape workers in the 1975 summer, when passage of California's Agriculture Labor Relations Act predicted a wave of union elections in the state's agricultural landscape. To produce a statistically valid study, Salandini randomly selected forty-two grape workers from a workforce of 2,781 in the twenty-six Teamster grape ranches. Of each, Salandini asked about their union history and union preferences and found that half began working in Teamster grape fields in 1973 or later, which corresponded with pro-UFW organizer and member strike estimates.[57] Half of his interviewees, in other words, appeared to have replaced strikers. The latter may have assembled in Coachella's central park, like Huerta, uncertain about next steps or sources of income. They may have picketed for a couple days, as Dalzell saw, before leaving the strike and/or region to find other jobs. Meanwhile, ranchers revamped their labor force through supervisors. Tellingly, the majority of post-1973 workers told Salandini that they simply wanted to work and would join whichever union won a future election, a refrain the national press then repeated uncritically in 1973 when questioning the UFW's claim to represent the region's grape workers. Strike participation thus became the very evidence for national newspapers of worker disenchantment with the UFW.

This question of strike efficacy and worker union politics is a key concern in the recent and critical UFW scholarship, hence my stress on numbers. This scholarship argues the UFW staffed Coachella Valley picket lines in 1973 with non-farmworker volunteers and failed to gain farmworker backing, much less disrupt the grape harvest. This failure, it adds, reflected farmworker frustration with UFW disorder, not Teamster and rancher violence nor immigrant strikebreaking. The UFW's failure to accept fault, furthermore, prefigured and contributed to its 1980s implosion—for UFW leaders like Cesar Chavez deflected legitimate criticism and led purges that shrunk capacity when the UFW had an uncontested opportunity to unionize all farmworkers.[58] To make this argument, however, the scholarship has relied uncritically on the testimony of UFW leaders with limited history in and knowledge of the Coachella Valley. It also underplays grape ranchers' early use of strikebreakers, the national press's ambivalent framing, and the difficult contexts shaping farmworker choices. Most importantly, it muddles three separate questions in labor history: how many people honored the strike, how many people picketed, and what to deduce from these two numbers about worker politics.

From the sources available, half the Coachella Valley grape workforce participated in the mid-April strike, though the majority, without excess resources, picketed sparingly. The latter also likely reflected the UFW's miscalculation of grape rancher intentions and the related lack of strike preparation. But spare picket lines also mirrored farm labor qualities: for most, to strike and survive as a family meant skipping the picket line to work elsewhere. The strike also appeared as a collection of crew-based stoppages in remote fields where Teamster guards attacked picketers. These crew-based strikes did not occur simultaneously or produce press-friendly picket visuals, but instead mirrored shifting labor needs: for Bozick and Tenneco, the thinning and strike began on Monday, April 16, 1973, but for Karahadian they began two days later, which granted him the weekend to gather strikebreakers. Given the isolated nature of these crew-based strikes and the uncertainty and danger shrouding the first days, honoring the UFW Coachella Grape Strike did not necessarily translate into picketing rural fields. Lastly, the UFW failed to track strikers or offer reassurances about a near-future resolution. For farmworkers like Max Huerta, in short, the early strike's prospects could seem bleak—and yet they went on strike in enough numbers that grape ranchers had to turn to contractors to replenish their crews.

Of the UFW members who broke the Coachella Grape Strike in 1973, their reasons varied dramatically and told a similarly complicated story. In Salandini's 1975 survey, for instance, half of the respondents (twenty-one out of forty-two) had been UFW members since 1970, which suggested they broke the 1973 strike. Of these, twenty-one workers, half (ten) said they wanted the UFW representation and had only worked in 1973 out of necessity. One interviewee, Mr. Rolan, said "he joined the Teamster Union in 1973 because he had to support his family." Romana Pinzon shared simply, "The UFW has more benefits than TU, but one has to work."[59] For these workers, strikebreaking did not signal their union preference but precisely their disempowerment; they had no means to choose their union and maintain their material survival. Their choices, furthermore, existed in and produced an emotionally laden landscape. When another worker spoke of financial need to explain strikebreaking, for instance, their spouse interjected and said "she was ashamed that her husband was a [Teamster] because she and her daughter were members of the UFWA." Some did not offer excuses, but shared that grape ranchers treated them better under a contract and that they planned to vote for the

UFW in a future election.⁶⁰ In fact, only six workers of the forty-two (14 percent) Salandini interviewed said they wanted the Teamsters Union, of which five spoke stridently about UFW errors and disorganization.⁶¹ This minority also spoke against unions in general and protested basic expectations, such as union dues and seniority rules. Some would thus likely remain anti-union regardless of improved UFW offices. Critically, four of the six pro-Teamster workers were Filipino or Puerto Rican, reflecting the ethnic divisions still hampering the UFW movement.⁶²

Rancher-propagated violence further impacted workers' choices.⁶³ Early rumors spread of ranchers and Teamsters carrying guns and rifles, as well as multiple assaults on strikers.⁶⁴ In the first week, for instance, ranchers and Teamsters broke a teenager's cheekbone and permanently injured her eye, led a roadside attack on a father and son, beat strikers visiting a camp, and made life threats and pointed guns at picketers.⁶⁵ The UFW volunteer and organizer, Elizabeth Hernandez, recalled daily harassment that wore down picketers: "every morning the Teamsters would stand side by side . . . [and] taunt, harass, curse, and yell obscenities at the women and just make our day miserable."⁶⁶ From the picket lines, strike violence spilled into public spaces, such as housing camps, supermarkets, and community back streets. "We were afraid," the UFW striker Clementina Olloque recalled, "we felt a terror because we did not know how we were going to finish."⁶⁷ Riverside County sheriffs also arrested several hundred strikers for court injunction violations in the strike's first weeks. In the UFW scholarship, these arrests exemplified the early strike's camaraderie—with jailed strikers singing before their triumphant release. But the situation on the ground was much more troubling and alienating.⁶⁸ Many feared being jailed for striking. Other feared jail-related consequences, such as being framed for drug use⁶⁹ or armed robbery.⁷⁰ Some women strikers also faced threats from their husbands, who "prohibited" their arrests. Just as many brought their children to the picket line only to flee from police tear gas and batons.⁷¹

To strike and to picket, in short, were separate if related concerns, and both differed from workers' union choice. Both were heavily shaped by outsized risks and threats, and neither could directly impact the grape harvest when labor was abundant. Some historians have argued that farmworkers "voted with their feet" by ignoring the UFW's Coachella Grape Strike 1973. But this argument oversimplifies the strike and fails to see that voting with your feet is not voting at all. It is instead a pithy marker of worker political disempowerment. The Coachella Valley's grape ranchers knew this reality when they invited the Teamsters Union, as did the UFW when it called for union elections during the grape strike's first week in late April.⁷² Such an election could have challenged the grape ranchers' narrative of worker union choice and, simultaneously, would have disentangled farmworkers' union politics from life-and-death decisions involved in a labor struggle. Unsurprisingly, the grape ranchers refused to participate in a fair election.

The national media, however, kept its ambiguity-ridden frame. In late April, the *New York Times* reported on the UFW's "administrative problems" and its "losing battle with Teamsters."[73] It quoted UFW officials who, while admitting errors, stressed rancher sabotage and called for union elections. Without addressing either point, the newspaper turned to "the key question at the moment: who represents the workers?" "The Teamsters," it wrote, "contend that many workers are 'fed up' with Mr. Chavez and produced petitions on which several thousand field hands said that they preferred the Teamsters."[74] In other articles, the *New York Times* evenly summarized UFW charges of Teamster petition fraud as well as Teamster charges of UFW poll fraud, offering no resolution of the contradictory claims to its readership, who would soon be called by the UFW to support a new consumer grape boycott.[75] The *Los Angeles Times* and *Washington Post* did the same.[76] Even the pro-labor Harry Bernstein, who accepted rancher–Teamster collusion, refused to imply an equivalent UFW–worker unity, cautioning his readers and potential boycotters: "not all of the guilt or innocence is on either side."[77] By now, one can hope, the UFW's leadership should have realized they existed in a new, more skeptical, and potentially less reliable world.

War of Words

Without recourse to union elections in late April 1973, the UFW could only show Coachella Valley grape worker support through another strike, an already losing proposition for much of U.S. labor in the late 1960s and early 1970s.[78] When the AFL-CIO pledged $1.6 million strike fund to the UFW in mid-May, the *Los Angeles Times* thus wrote, "Chavez in the past has stressed the boycott weapon, saying that because farm workers are poor, they cannot strike since the union has no strike fund."[79] Logic compelled a simple conclusion: without its poverty alibi, a failed strike would expose the UFW as worker abandoned. Whether the UFW felt it had a choice to reject this logic or whether it was confident it could win a hastily organized non-harvest strike after a surprise union raid, it played into the calculation by promising "a real strike for the first time" with AFL-CIO aid.[80]

Before these funds arrived and striker benefits remained $50 a week, the UFW took note of the "hurt feelings" among local grape workers.[81] The latter were upset over "union dues, hiring hall, and Coachella personnel," a picket captain reported on April 26, 1973.[82] "Cesar is good," they told the UFW organizer Marshall Ganz, "but these other problems are bad." Some UFW organizers felt farmworkers' financial need prevented their strike participation. "The majority of the people are with Chavez," the Coachella UFW director Ray Huerta said, "but right now there is need" and the Teamsters had promised them work.[83] Archival traces of late April and early May organizing notes are spare, but the trend was largely pessimistic. By then, the grape workforce had been revamped by ranchers and supervisors, while the UFW struggled with the remaining strikebreakers. Ganz reassured his co-organizers that "pressure will build, and this will prove worth the daily hassle." But skepticism and frustration remained: "Got some workers to stop working," said Frank Ortiz, but "I feel we aren't doing enough."[84]

In early May, the UFW turned from focusing their attention on the Teamsters, who threatened and attacked strikers, and took a "meet-the-problems-of-the-workers-approach."[85] They reached out to farmworkers with meetings, flyers, megaphones, and Friday night rallies.[86] They spoke of past strikes, the source of rancher hostility, and the potential for a unionized future. "There was no job security," they said of their pre-UFW days, "people never knew when they would get fired [and] our children were many times condemned to forget about going to school regularly." "We do not want to go back to the misery of the past," they wrote in *El Malcriado*, "we want to defend our rights and all we have won with so much hard work and sacrifice."[87] Women unionists also recalled of a time before the UFW hiring hall, when job security and gender discrimination grew in inverse proportion—when they "were at the mercy of paranoid labor contractors, neurotic foremen and lecherous supervisors."[88] In Friday night rallies, strikers performed plays about the local strike, dressing Bozick in drag and marrying him off to the Teamsters, all while celebrating "a barbecue for the scabs."[89] Repeatedly, they promised victory with another strike–boycott combination, once-more tethering faint possibilities to the inevitable.[90]

Filipino UFW leaders focused on organizing Filipino grape workers, who had many unaddressed grievances. Claro Runtal stressed the strike's collective good: "Brothers, count the money you make in one year. Yet what are [you] doing for your people. It is important to convince people of our struggle."[91] Similarly, Catalino Millonida tied the strike to Filipino histories of labor exploitation and U.S. colonialism: "We have already been exploited for three generations. We are the ones who made millionaires of the growers. Are they satisfied? No! Instead they now import more illegals and temporary 'green cards' to exploit them in the same way we have been exploited in the past . . . Next year the grower will again ask his rent-a-slave contractors to find more people to replace us."[92] In both, the call to strike was predicated on non-material principles, echoing Velasco's campaign in Coachella in 1969 and Vera Cruz's writings in the early 1970s. They also came with the UFW's deeply problematic and occasionally antagonistic relationship to immigrant strikebreakers. Simultaneously, they warned non-Filipino UFW leaders that union reforms were necessary to avoid a large-scale Filipino defection: "If we do not change our present policy," Runtal told Salandini again in 1975, "we will be lucky to win only three contracts."[93]

But organizers only produced a few converts. The reasons varied and blended the understandable with the self-interested. Filipino workers pointed to dispatch problems and union invisibility.[94] But their strikebreaking also reflected the role of Filipino contractors, who were half of the region's grape contractors, in amassing strikebreakers.[95] Several Filipino contractors also managed housing camps and most faced UFW grievances over labor abuses and living conditions in the early 1970s.[96] Simon Matias, for instance, was "key for [the] H&M [and Tenneco] operation" in 1973, when he ran two camps and employed "young Delano Pinoys."[97] He also managed a Delano camp, where he had hosted Imutan in 1971 and called Filipinos to re-commit to the UFW: "We got to work together," he said then. "This union is yours."[98] His workers' reactions were not recorded, but a couple days later young Filipino men dismissed the "original [1965] strikers" by saying "we young people do not want long speeches—long meetings are boring."[99] It is unclear if similar sentiments animated Matias's young Filipino strikebreakers in 1973 or whether grievances in 1972 affected Matias's relationship to the UFW.[100] What is clear, however, is that in early 1973 Matias led Tenneco's Teamster raid, threatened those who refused to sign petitions, and heralded the "free[dom] . . . of no more dispatches, no more dues." It is likely that a combination of legitimate grievances and self-interest animated Matias and his workers, as both attempted to navigate a labor market structured by worker scarcity, rancher power, and UFW failings.

Other Filipino contractors had more frayed histories with farm labor organizing. Marcelo Tamsi, a 1965 Delano striker who lived in the Filipino Hall strike encampment and made Pete Velasco's favorite mushroom soup, had, according to *El Malcriado*, "sold out his brothers" in 1967, and chafed against the UFW's dispatch system in 1971.[101] In 1973, Tamsi threatened Mel-Pak farmworkers to collect Teamster petition signatures and, by 1975, had become, according to Claro Runtal, "one [of the] worse enemies of the UFWA."[102] Johnny Pader also migrated out of the UFW and was a "hardened scab" by 1973, Marshall Ganz wrote in 1974, while Paul Rubal "didn't even go on strike in 1965."[103] Filipino farmworkers faced real problems in the UFW's offices, but they also existed within and depended on a contractor system that compelled strikebreaking, especially in a precarious present of scarce resources, declining jobs, rising immigration (Filipino and Mexican), and older age.[104]

A similar mixture of legitimate grievances and self-interest existed among Mexican farmworkers and contractors. Some strikebreakers were 1960s strikers marginalized by UFW policies in the early 1970s, such as Maria de Equiveles, who said the UFW denied her a job because she could not pay union dues. She "adamantly" supported the UFW in 1968–69, she said, but the UFW failed her family when "we were desperate for food, work and money."[105] Few members of the 1968–69 Coachella Strike Committee, in fact, appeared in 1973 and their absence may reflect a similar critique. Other workers spoke of unfulfilled promises and of being "treated . . . like animals at the dispatch office." Some wanted to be "free to work" where they wanted without noting this depended on their relationship to labor contractors. Others, such as Margie Meza, said "Chavez sucks the people good. They act just like Pancho Villa. They are only revolutionaries if you didn't pay 3 months of advance."[106] Meza, however, was also a Mel-Pak contractor who said the UFW "demoted" her. In 1973, she and other supervisors returned to their former stature by threatening workers into signing Teamster petitions.[107] The Karahadian contractor Maria Morales similarly described the UFW as "a power union that forces you to do things like pay dues and work where they want but with the Teamsters I can look forward to having my freedom."[108] Her crew disagreed and went on strike. But this crew could not stop Karahadian's contractors from replacing them and safeguarding the grape harvest.[109]

By early May, furthermore, the strike had expanded to Arvin and Lamont and seemed destined to reach Delano. At this point, joining the UFW strike meant foregoing all grape work in California and possibly leaving their work crews and fraying personal relationships. The UFW raised strike benefits to $75 on May 11, but this was (again) a fraction of harvest wages and provided no aid for seasonal unemployment. Workers continued to worry about violence and/or rancher retribution, which discouraged strike participation. On May 10, for instance, armed Teamsters harassed a group of UFW women who were holding a Mother's Day celebration in Coachella's city park.[110] The AFL-CIO organizer, Joe Lopez, later testified the "UFW could only move with fear upon public spaces—in towns, restaurants."[111] Suspicion of pro-UFW sympathies also led to immediate retaliation, such as when one company, Coachella Imperial Distributors sent seventy-three farmworkers home for working too slowly, which the company understood as evidence of workers' UFW sympathies. Similarly, when the Filipino Alberto Dunlao chose to honor the UFW strike on May 14, his coworkers swiftly attacked him and demanded his camp eviction, despite having worked fifteen years in Bagdasarian.[112] By late May 1973, the UFW could organize a five hundred-person picket line in the Coachella Valley's rural and ranch bordering streets, stretching shoulder to shoulder for half a mile. But such a spectacle failed to halt the grape ranchers' collection of strikebreakers, striker migration out of the region, or continued Teamster violence against picketers.

In this context, the UFW's harvest grape strike erupted on June 11, 1973, and continued until it migrated to the San Joaquin Valley on July 4, 1973. In the first week, the UFW claimed 700 workers received the newly increased strike funds ($90 a week), while sheriffs estimated 650 union picketers out of 1,500 workers. In the next week, the picket line grew (900) in tandem with the overall labor force. The UFW volunteer Tom Dalzell estimated the picket line at 1,000–1,500 strikers; most, he said, were local workers and not allies, as the national press suggested when questioning UFW claims of representing grape workers. On Karahadian's picket line, more specifically, 80–90 percent of the 100–120 picketers were Karahadian workers and amounted to more than a minority. As before, Dalzell said strikers picketed for a couple days before leaving to find jobs. Joe Lopez also remembered a picket line of "1,200 strikers and 50–100 supporters," while the local Chicano organizer, Calisto Ramos, said, "I don't think there was a single [strike] crew that was under 100 [people]. And there must have been ten crews, maybe more.... It wasn't a sporadic group of people."[113] The UFW striker Maria Serrano recalled, "There were so, so many people [in strike meetings] that it was impossible to recognize individuals."[114] As chapter 8 will argue, many local and non-grape workers echoed this view and credited the 1973 Coachella Grape Strike as instigating their mid-1970s pro-UFW campaigns.

In reaction, the Teamsters unleashed a wave of violence.[115] On June 20, 1973, they placed a bomb inside a UFW car, which exploded before anyone used it. On the next day, they abducted a man they mistook for a *Chavista*, and then beat him, and stabbed him six times. On the next day (June 22), they drove against a UFW caravan and threw rocks at the car carrying Chavez, breaking the windshield. On the next day (June 23), they burned down a striker's house, nearly killing a young family inside, while at another grape ranch, two hundred Teamsters attacked UFW picketers with metal chains, wooden stakes, and punches.[116] After a Sunday pause, the Teamsters attacked UFW organizers on Monday (June 25), knocked Ganz unconscious on Tuesday, and shot at Ray Huerta's house, where Chavez was staying, on Wednesday. Between April and July, sheriffs counted fifty-eight cases of assault and battery, thirty-seven cases of malicious mischief, and thirty-four cases of assault with a deadly weapon—nearly every single one implicating Teamster organizers.[117] There was nothing remotely comparable from the UFW. In fact, when the Coachella Valley's Farmers Association president, Lee Anderson Jr., told a California state committee that violence was "not one-sided," his *only* example of UFW

El Malcriado images of the UFW's 1973 Coachella Grape Strike against rancher–Teamster collusion. *El Malcriado*, July 13, 1973, 12. Walter P. Reuther Library, Archives of Labor and Urban Affairs, Wayne State University.

violence was a picket line: "We feel that when there's 300 pickets along the roadway," he argued, "it is not freedom of speech but really intimidation."[118]

Inexplicably, the national press kept its ambiguity-laced narrative that questioned UFW claims to represent grape workers. They were uncritical of ranchers' rejection of elections and legitimized rancher charges of UFW mismanagement: "the real problem," the owner of Bagdasarian ranches told the *Los Angeles Times* in early May, "is that in the past three years the [UFW] has just been badly mismanaged."[119] When the grape harvest strike began in June 1973, reporters again tied farmworker politics to the UFW strike's efficacy, as the *Washington Post* wrote: the strike would be "a crucial indicator of how much worker support Chavez can muster."[120] When the UFW announced seven hundred people received strike benefits in early June to show worker support, reporters called for outside verification and quoted Teamsters who pointed to a larger workforce and/or accused the UFW of bribing its strikers. The Teamster leader "[Bill] Grami pointed to the $90 strike fund as evidence that workers don't support the UFW," the *Washington Post* wrote characteristically, because the "UFW had 'exploited the hell out of the workers.'"[121] "Contrary to the claims of Chavistas," the *New York Times* similarly alerted its readers, "not all the grape pickers who are working are there only because they must have the money.... A number of workers interviewed indicated that they wanted no part of Mr. Chavez or 'La Causa,' his almost mystic crusade."[122]

The most egregious newspaper misrepresentation, however, centered on the strike's violence. All papers identified Teamster aggression, including arson, physical and verbal assaults, repeated threats, attempted murder, and attacks on picketers. In contrast, striker violence included foul language, flung rocks and dirt clods, and possibly torching a rancher shed. Yet, newspapers insisted on relative similitude, such as the *Chicago Tribune*'s profile on the sheriff "keep[ing] calm" between the unions, who expressed fear about "what will happen... when this thing hits full swing."[123] In late June, the *Los Angeles Times* similarly reported on a "scuffle" of "300 UFWU pickets [and] 160 Teamsters Union members and farm laborers," which, it claimed, began after a fight between a Teamster organizer and UFW striker provoked others to "join in, swinging fists and shoving." Both camps "battled each other with iron pipes, clubs, belts tire irons and machetes," it continued, just one more episode in the "mad melee of fights and beatings all over the fields." For those with rose-tinted views of the UFW, the *New York Times* prefigured the Coachella Valley Farmers Association president's words to the November 1973 state committee investigating strike violence: "The violence is not one-sided, despite Mr. Chavez's reputation for non-violent methods."

The end effect was a national strike narrative successfully overtaken by Coachella Valley grape ranchers. They remained in the background in a purportedly jurisdictional dispute between two unions, all while gaining a platform to challenge UFW claims, and, by extension, undermine the UFW's looming boycott narrative. In all national newspapers, the coverage ended with what can only be described as the feigned concern of a shrug: "Midway through the six-week harvest," the *Wall Street Journal* wrote in late June 1973, "the impact of the strike is still hard to assess. UFW pickets—not all of them farmworkers—have numbered anywhere from 800 to 1,100 but growers say they haven't had any difficulty recruiting any labor or shipping crops on schedule." The *Wall Street Journal* then recapped rancher claims of UFW mismanagement and farmworker disenchantment with Chavez, especially the "friendly" rancher, Lionel Steinberg. "Up to now," it concluded, "the workers themselves haven't had a voice in determining who represents them."[124] No mainstream national newspaper deviated from this conclusion.

The Kingdom of Heaven

Not everyone in the UFW movement disagreed with the national coverage. In *Trampling out the Vintage*, Frank Bardacke quoted Marshall Ganz in 1978 as chiding the UFW National Executive Board (NEB) when the latter claimed Coachella Valley grape workers went on strike in 1973: "Let's not kid ourselves," Ganz said, "We all know that in Coachella in 1973 we didn't have the workers. We didn't have the members. We shouldn't kid ourselves about that. Those who were there, we know. A lot of them we couldn't even buy for ninety bucks a week."[125] Bardacke did not contextualize Ganz's statement nor provide other board member replies. By 1978, Ganz had spent several years attempting to redirect UFW resources to lettuce workers in the Imperial and Salinas valleys. The 1978 National Executive Board meeting, in which Ganz made his assertion, followed a troubled UFW organizing drive in Coachella Valley grape fields in 1977. Perhaps the latter difficulties reinforced his view that the Coachella Valley's grape workers had abandoned the UFW in 1973 and (thus) that the UFW should prioritize its lettuce workers.

Ganz, however, was not the only witness of the UFW's Coachella Grape Strike of 1973. Others included farmworker leaders like Lupe Murguia, Chicana/o activists like Alfredo Figueroa, Hope Lopez Fierro, Elizabeth Martinez, and Barbara Macri-Ortiz, and white activists like Doug Adair, Rosemary Matson, Terry Vasquez, Pat Hoffman and Pancho Botello. In their brief autobiographies, each recounted seeing Coachella Valley grape workers join the UFW strike in 1973 despite the dire conditions.[126] "The farm workers," wrote Hope Lopez Fierro, "walked out en masse from the grape fields of the Coachella Valley." Lupe Murguia agreed: "The workers stood up against Teamster organizers who were former labor contractors."[127] Terry Vasquez saw "a scene of thousands of farmworkers strung out along the roads lining the grape fields. The workers' spirits were incredibly high; they proudly waved their homemade union flags and sang songs in both Spanish and English to keep up their courage." To the Mexican American Political Association's organizer, Alfredo Figueroa, the "grape strike in the Coachella Valley of 1973 was the most violent that I had experienced since the Imperial Valley AWOC [Agricultural Workers Organizing Committee] strikes of 1960," a view Pancho Botello echoed: "Coachella growers signed behind-the-door contracts with the Teamsters, causing the farmworkers to lose all those contracts. The workers walked off the fields. There was brutality and violence on the part of the hired goons."

These accounts substantiate the post-strike depositions of UFW organizers and Coachella Valley ranchers. They support Salandini's farmworker survey findings in 1975 and align with the assessment of Riverside County's sheriff, Ben Clark, about the UFW's 1973 Coachella Grape Strike. "As a brief comparison," Clark testified to the state committee, "in the peak UFW activity year of 1969, six arrests were made and 83 calls were handled, compared to 500 arrests and 667 calls in 1973."[128] Lastly, the first-hand accounts by pro-UFW organizers and volunteers also reiterate the oral histories of local farmworkers and their allies. All local strike leaders who participated in oral history interviews insisted that a majority of grape workers and the wider community supported and/or participated in the strike. The "Coachella community sid[ed] with the union," Max Huerta recalled, "except for the labor contractors."[129] The strikers Clementina Olloque and Maria Serrano said the same, as did Maria Marron, who understood the year of 1973 as the UFW's "peak" in the Coachella Valley. For the Chicana/o movement activist and founder of the local Brown Beret chapter, Calisto Ramos, 1973 could not have been more different from 1969: in 1969, he felt the UFW's Coachella Grape Strike "had no chance" of success in "a million years," but four years later his view had "changed completely": "I believed they could win, I knew they could win."[130] And for local non-grape farmworkers, as chapter eight will detail, the grape workers' militancy and mobilization in 1973 inspired their own campaigns.

But Ganz's judgment of Coachella Valley grape workers—"A lot of them we couldn't even buy"—also distorts the 1973 Coachella Grape strike in more fundamental ways. It ignores, for instance, the strike's sequence, the conditions mitigating participation, and the austerity of striker benefits. No farmworker would have considered "ninety bucks" the threshold for being bought—if, in fact, as Ganz implied, they could be bought for the right price.[131] The judgment also misses the fact that farmworkers materialized a strike despite the UFW's shortcomings and underpreparation, and without legal protection to jobs in an industry that remained unorganized and outside national labor laws. The strike topped past Coachella Valley campaigns and did not need instigation from UFW or Chicano/a leaders. Most importantly, the notion of bought farmworkers ruts the conversation on body counting, though failing in that, and misses an opportunity to consider what the strike meant to farmworkers, or the lessons we can draw from it. As I have insisted in this book, the Coachella Grape Strike of 1973—like other eruptions—is best seen as producing spaces for community- and self-definition, spaces grappling with past marginality and envisioning future paths, those that lent materiality to stories about what it meant to be part of a community and live outside the rancher's world.

Consider the striker Maria Marron's account of her sister after a Teamster faction took control of Indio's Labor Camp.[132] Her sister, Clementina Olloque, was nineteen years old and worked in the Coachella UFW office and

Karahadian ranches. At some point, Marron said, the Teamsters and county sheriffs prevented pro-UFW farmworkers from entering the labor camp. Undeterred, the two young women arrived at the gates and demanded the stationed officer to let them in. When he refused, Olloque simply sped past him. "Clementina!" a scared Marron yelled, "They are going to shoot us because of you!" "And my sister," Marron continued, "when [Olloque] gets angry, she gets wild, [and Clementina] said: '*Cabrona!* Cowards won't enter the kingdom of heaven!'" Marron said she was already a mother and found the risks too great, so she told Olloque to drop her off at her house. Olloque then drove to the camp's edge where residents congregated to demand the Teamsters' expulsion. The demand led to a physical fight between Olloque and a supervisor's wife, culminating with pro-UFW farmworkers returning triumphantly. "That's how the struggle happened," Marron finished, "The Teamsters outside and the farmworkers inside. Because we were farmworkers. Why would the Teamster stay inside while we were outside?!"[133]

There are many qualities to highlight from this passage. The prospect for violence, for instance, was real and permeated all decisions. Collaboration among the police, ranchers, and Teamsters was apparent to most farmworkers like Marron, and transformed their crew-based strikes into a regional fight against an outsized opposition. The passage also identifies supervisors and contractors as camp residents, their critical role in the Teamster raid, and their likely impact on other farmworkers' choices regarding the UFW Grape Strike. It echoes, moreover, a key argument in chapter 1: farmworkers did not belong to a single community sharing equally in the Rancher Nation's marginality. Instead, they lived and acted in a variegated landscape of power. Those closest to the latter—a contractor's friend, a longtime supervisor, a husband—had accessed benefits a UFW contract could threaten. For these figures, the Teamsters promised their pre-1970 privileges. And for workers like Olloque, the strike necessitated and embodied a new basis for community belonging. In her world, courage, principle, and audacity mixed with righteousness and social potential. Individual action rippled into the texture of community well-being, into life itself, and served as an unwavering measurement for all. No cowards, in other words, in the kingdom of heaven.

Marron did not elaborate on the effects of Olloque's action other than it led to the Teamsters' ouster and the UFW's return to the farm labor camp. But it likely led to other effects, such as the specter of UFW flags in the state-owned camp, of pro-UFW farmworkers talking to ambivalent neighbors about unionization, of anti-UFW bosses confronted in public by local workers, many of them women leaders. Arguably, Olloque helped create the very landscape of possibility through her rebellion. Even if nothing else rippled outward, the fact remained she refused the cowardice (in her view) underpinning the region's misery. Ending the Rancher Nation thus meant establishing new rules on what was allowed and expected from farmworkers and ranchers. It meant taking risks, bearing the collective weight of rebellion, and detaching oneself from the ranchers' world. The UFW's Coachella Grape Strike in 1973 sought a cultural revolution to foster its social equivalent.[134]

Olloque was not the only risk-taker. Her sister, Marron, led the Karahadian strike despite her husband's pro-Teamster politics. Many women strikers contested their husband's authority and pro-Teamster affiliations, which added another layer of repercussions. Other women went on strike despite pregnancies and family demands. Maria Serrano, for instance, noticed her future union ally and friend, Petra Ruiz, in a 1973 strike meeting because Ruiz "was pregnant, and even then, with so much danger she was a very valiant woman, with so much danger she was [still] helping the union by doing her job as a striker ... and not for money, because sometimes they did not even pay us."[135] Each striker also risked violence inside and outside the fields, as Max Huerta had predicted on the strike's first day. Many still took this risk by attaching UFW flags to their cars and homes, by wearing UFW buttons on work clothes and attending Friday UFW rallies—all instances of unapologetically public opposition to the Rancher Nation.[136] The risks began when farmworkers first refused Teamster petitions and they continued every time a worker agreed to meet with a UFW organizer. Even non-grape farmworkers took risks by aiding their striking neighbors, often donating their sacks of flour and beans. "All the other people [did] the same," remembered Virginia Ortega, the pro-UFW farmworker and Indio Labor Camp resident, "the same. They gave what they could."[137]

In addition to establishing a threshold for community belonging, the strike also offered visions of what one could become. Maria Serrano drew inspiration from Ruiz's motherhood and militancy. Ortega did so, as well. She admired the women strikers, she said, and saw them as revolutionaries, as *adelitas* who could teach her: "It was an honor to speak to them, to walk with them, for they were the great figures of the local fight for justice." These women shared her father's radical politics, those that compelled her first pro-UFW action in 1966 Delano, when she told her risk-averse husband to aid the Delano grape strikers. In 1973, Coachella Valley women strikers pushed Ortega further, to be someone who "discovers a cause ... a passion, [who] gives their passion to that cause without caring for the consequences." As before, UFW strikers created collective worlds that reflected the very qualities they aspired to fulfill and embody, those that inspired and fortified. Many would have agreed with Chavez's view of their strike: "Among us is a soul force, a spirit that generates a tremendous force, spreading everywhere. . . . You are more powerful than the ocean."[138]

With Ganz's judgment, in short, we risk not seeing the Coachella Grape Strike of 1973 for what it was: an insurgent field of stories of past, present, and future, self and others, debts and rights, potential, hopes, and fears. In this field, farmworkers moved with pasts as visceral and social facts; with presents layered by risks, calculations, and principles; with the faint outlines of potential futures. They did so in the context of profound vulnerability and uncertainty. As such, for those who embraced the picket line and confronted violence and fear, theirs was a fight against the Rancher Nation writ large, including the farmworkers who sided with ranchers. These were the imperious husbands, the male workers who harassed women, those with ties to contractors, the supervisor and contractor neighbors themselves.[139] Strikers aimed to transform their farmworker community and/to build the kingdom of heaven—where no one could choose to be a coward, an exploiter, or a neutral party amidst structured violence.

Such aims, lastly, help explain the deep animosity dividing the farmworker population during the strike. It explains the unforgiving tone in Mrs. Morales, who told Salandini she was "ashamed that her husband was a [Teamster] member." It explains the common view of strikebreakers as "they make themselves deaf" out of convenience or as "muertos de hambre"—those "starved-to-death" enough to be without a social conscience.[140] It also explains the striker hostility toward supervisors, like Mel-Pak's Margie Meza, who said "the Chavez people call[ed] me a sell-out, a barmaid, a whore for the growers, and a pig!"[141] The Karahadian supervisor, Maria Morales, said the same: "They called me a sellout, a dog. They said that I was going to cry and crawl on my knees in front of them."[142] Neither remarked on Teamster and rancher violence, or the strikers' profound insecurity, or the history of supervisor-facilitated rancher abuse, including their own complicity before the UFW movement. Their testimonies thus arrive from the archives as justifications, self-serving and partial, and yet, I do not doubt the veracity of the intimate hostility the two supervisors felt from strikers.

To be a *Chavista*, in short, was not merely to be a follower of Cesar Chavez, much less to insist on a Mexican-centric view of the UFW movement. It meant instead to be a figure who holds "great courage," as Chavez said, who "struggle[s] and sacrifice[s] to defend their rights and those of all the people."[143] These figures drew from their histories and visions to frame the UFW's Coachella Grape Strike in 1973, their place in it and the strike's place in a shared, just future. They made Chavez theirs, in other words, not vice versa. And, in the process, they called for ending the Rancher Nation and anyone who stood in their way.

THE STRIKE IS RESERVED VERY EXCLUSIVELY TO THOSE MEN AND WOMEN OF GREAT COURAGE WHO ARE COMMITTED TO STRUGGLE AND SACRIFICE TO DEFEND THEIR RIGHTS AND THOSE OF ALL THE PEOPLE.

SISTERS AND BROTHERS, THERE IS NO REASON TO LOSE HEART, NO REASON TO GIVE UP, NO REASON TO BE AFRAID, BECAUSE WE HAVE A GREAT FUTURE. WHAT DID WE HAVE THREE OR FOUR YEARS AGO? NOTHING. AND WHAT DO WE HAVE NOW? WE HAVE A SPIRIT OF STRUGGLE, WE HAVE COURAGE, WE HAVE A CAUSE FOR JUSTICE.

SOONER OR LATER THOSE WHO OPPOSE OUR MOVEMENT, BECAUSE THEY DON'T UNDERSTAND, OR BECAUSE THEY ARE TOO INTERESTED IN MONEY, OR WANT TO GET ALL THEY CAN FROM THE GROWER, ARE IN GENERAL FINALLY DEFEATED AND END UP BEING COMPLETELY REPUDIATED BY THE PEOPLE.

WITH YOUR LOVE AND NON-VIOLENT SACRIFICE, WITH THE SPIRIT OF THE FARM WORKER MASSES, WE WILL FIGHT OUR OPPRESSORS AND DEFEND OUR RIGHTS, SO WE CAN HAVE A TOMORROW OF PEACE, JOY AND SOCIAL JUSTICE FOR OURSELVES AND OUR CHILDREN.

SI SE PUEDE! —CESAR CHAVEZ

Excerpt of Cesar Chavez's speech to Coachella Valley grape strikers in April 1973. *El Malcriado*, May 18, 1973, 15. Walter P. Reuther Library, Archives of Labor and Urban Affairs, Wayne State University.

Again, La Causa; Again, Shortcomings

In critical histories of the UFW movement, the abrupt end to the 1973 Coachella Grape Strike illustrates Cesar Chavez's realpolitik qualities and his future manipulative behaviors. A skilled media figure, it argues, Chavez conned America into seeing the Coachella Valley's grape workers as pro-UFW, as well as the strike's failure as rooted in Teamster and rancher violence and immigrant strikebreaking. But when the Teamster leadership removed their guards in July 1973, those organizers who had produced such chaos in the Coachella Valley, the UFW's David-vs-Goliath narrative suddenly disappeared and threatened to expose Chavez's lie to a newly boycott-skeptical public.[144] The UFW thus unilaterally shifted the strike to the San Joaquin Valley, as if following Teamster violence to maintain the UFW-as-victim farce.

The reality was much simpler and more devastating for the local rank and file. As in the 1968–69 grape strikes, the UFW left Coachella Valley grape workers to face the repercussions as it continued with its state- and nationwide campaign. One can argue that the UFW's strike migration reflected the nature of agricultural unionization: farm strikes matter in harvests, when rancher vulnerability ripens into white humility and union contracts. The UFW thus followed the grape harvests northward to the San Joaquin Valley, where it staged thousand-strong picket lines despite flagrant and pervasive sheriff and rancher violence. It also inspired a series of farmworker strikes in melons, tomatoes, and winter vegetables—each one demanding higher wages and better working conditions, each one drawing more of the UFW's limited attention, each one ending without a clear path to union contracts.[145] The UFW's Delano Grape Strike of 1973 only ended in late August after two strikers were murdered by strikebreakers and police officers. As in the late 1960s, the UFW launched a consumer boycott, mounted lawsuits against Teamster-rancher collusion, and negotiated with the AFL-CIO and Teamsters to settle the jurisdiction dispute triggered by the Teamsters' raid.

In this context, the UFW leadership had few resources to dedicate to the Coachella Valley—other than a couple of white volunteer lawyers and twenty-one-year-old Max Huerta.[146] The latter directed the UFW service center, which helped workers apply for state and federal assistance, get medical attention for strike injuries, and speak with UFW lawyers. He also administered the UFW contracts with Freedman and Larson, including dispatching workers, investigating rancher contract violations, addressing worker grievances, and developing worker leadership. Minimally trained and alone, Huerta quickly felt overwhelmed, as had previous staff members.[147] Coachella Valley grape striker leaders, in turn, found the Coachella UFW office limited and exasperating, and bristled when Huerta helped "esquiroles"—or *scabs*.[148] The

1973 strikers faced blacklists, he explained, as well as debilitating injuries, and mounting medical costs, and they interpreted the union's absence after the strike and Huerta's aid to strikebreakers as betrayal.[149] "They felt that after they had walked out, and they had left their jobs and everything to sacrifice for the union," he said, "now they, themselves, were out of resources, and the union was no longer there for them because the union was busy with the boycott and doing other things, and the union had no resources."[150]

The white volunteer lawyers spent the year filing anti-collusion lawsuits against Coachella Valley grape ranchers, which produced the post-strike depositions that elucidated the local ranchers' defection and the subsequent strike's effect on their operation costs and grape quality. These lawsuits and their paper trail have been invaluable for reconstructing this history. But they offered little compensation to Coachella Valley strikers.[151] The latter complained to Huerta about being unable to reach or communicate with their lawyers. Without job prospects or a clear timeline for the cases, Huerta explained, several hundred strikers found no other recourse than to leave the region and/or find jobs in the Coachella Valley's new westside cities, where luxury resorts hungrily hired at low wages.[152] He, too, was eventually "burned out" by the outsized responsibilities and left the UFW in late 1974.[153]

The UFW's lawyers were also of ambiguous value to the union and gave contradictory reports of Coachella Valley ranchers in the two years after the 1973 Coachella Grape Strike.[154] In October 1973, they reported on the ranchers' "long and gloomy" winter of mounting legal costs, boycott losses, and erratic Teamster behavior. Ranchers were "in general, confused," "gloomy but stuck," susceptible to UFW pressure. But, in January 1974, lawyers reported that the ranchers were suddenly "cocky" and provided few "in roads" for future UFW negotiations. By then, grape ranchers had forced the Teamsters to honor their contracts when the national leadership appeared to waver. They also lowered their labor needs with grape diversion into raisins and wine, and after the invention of a hand tool that deskilled the grape thinning season.[155] In March 1974, UFW lawyers found the ranchers "despondent" again, only to report a month later of newfound swagger.[156] In the November 1973 state hearings on strike violence, furthermore, UFW lawyers appeared unprepared and could not state the status of UFW lawsuits.[157] The latter's eventual settlements, several years after the 1973 strike, only offered farmworkers a couple hundred dollars, a stunningly tiny handful of crumbs after a devastating strike.[158]

With such a skeletal presence, the UFW failed to capitalize on the energy generated by the strike. Besides grape workers, the strike inspired union campaigns in citrus, vegetable, and onion fields; the latter even staged their own strike in the fall of 1973. But the UFW moved slowly. Its volunteers focused on lawsuits, while Huerta guarded for strikebreakers in Freedman and Larson fields. In November 1973, he refused to dispatch Jesus Camacho, a 1973 Coachella grape striker, because he later worked in Delano's grape fields. In his defense, Camacho said he did so after the strike ended and said he needed work to feed his family. But Huerta rejected the appeal and caused a group of rank-and-file leaders, all Camacho's coworkers, to resign in protest. Huerta also found Filipino strikebreakers—"a lot of the Filipinos who broke the strike in Delano are now in the Freedman camp waiting for the pruning"—but the record does not show what followed.[159]

Perhaps most troubling, white volunteers expressed a critical view of Coachella Valley farmworkers. In October 1973, a UFW lawyer wrote on the onion strike and how it paralyzed the harvest and was poised to gain its demands for higher wages. Onion workers also organized a funds collection to pay for a radio segment to explain their goals to potential strikebreakers. But grape ranchers brought their crews to break the strike. Some of the strikebreakers, the white lawyer reported, had been "semi leaders" in the grape strike. How, he asked, can this be? His answer—"$90 strike benefits"—implied the UFW bought its grape strikers in 1973, as ranchers alleged, and as Ganz would argue in 1978.[160] Perhaps the lawyer's answer aired a growing volunteer resentment to the "generous" striker benefits that made the volunteers' $5 a week pay seem especially unfair. Would farmworkers sacrifice enough to win the fight, the would-be allies appeared to ask, or remain near beggars who danced for union alms or scab wages? Of course, privilege is self-referential and self-righteous, blind to the obvious—such as the fact that $90 a week in benefits hardly covered a farmworkers family's basic needs, or that striker families risked and lost their homes, or that many more were blacklisted afterward and thus desperate for work, or, simply, that desperation can make beggars out of anyone.

In the meantime, local strike leaders faced harassment and threats. One such leader, Tereso Rendon, noticed men following him in late January 1974. Fearing for his life, Rendon shared his concern with Max Huerta, but several days after this meeting Rendon was purposely driven off the road and forced into the desert. He escaped, UFW memos summarized, but not before the men shot at him. "The following morning," wrote one lawyer, county sheriffs "found Rendon's truck in the desert, practically completely destroyed by fire."[161] Rendon fled to his relatives across the border and did not return to the Coachella Valley. Similarly, Huerta's crew leader and pro-UFW worker, Sam Rodriguez, received life-threatening phone calls and heard rumors among his Indio labor camp neighbors: "Teamsters are going to get Sammy and all the other Chavista leaders." He, too, fled the Coachella Valley in February 1974, just a few weeks before the grape thinning season, when UFW lawyers reported on widespread public threats against local pro-UFW families: "the Teamsters–growers–contractors," wrote Coachella lawyers, "were telling workers that 'violence' was coming, that guns should be kept . . . that our strike could be stopped like it was in Delano in 1973."¹⁶²

These issues came to the fore in a late March 1974 National Executive Board meeting, when the UFW considered multiple plans for the upcoming grape harvest. The UFW Board weighed the pros and cons of calling off the strike, organizing a "fake" strike, or going "all out on the strike." Chavez called for the latter, while Dolores Huerta disagreed, reminding the group, "last year we put everything into Coachella and had nothing left for Lamont and Delano." Gilbert Padilla, Pete Velasco, and Eliseo Medina sided with Chavez, while Richard Chavez said, "the strike last year really hurt the Coachella growers without much of a boycott to support it." Mark Lyons called for realism, noting they did not have money for more strikes, while Velasco stressed: "the whole world is waiting to see what we will do, expects us to do the same as last year . . . we have to carry on what we did last year." Ganz worried about funds and was ambivalent about Coachella Valley workers, as he would express more forcefully in 1978, and pushed for a stronger boycott. As a compromise, Chavez called for a limited grape strike in 1974 in the thinning season, adding, "he did not agree with the statement that the boycott is what wins the struggle."¹⁶³

Perhaps Chavez took the middle road given the union's limited resources and its goal to organize all farmworkers—not just those in the Coachella Valley's grape fields. The stance also reflected his view of organizing as a love affair—"es como enomorar," Chavez told Coachella Valley organizers in 1973, "se lleva tiempo,"¹⁶⁴ Perhaps he felt they still had time in 1974. But as news arrived of a lukewarm grape boycott, Chavez may have recognized that they did not, in fact, have time.¹⁶⁵ By the mid-1970s, America no longer wished to be courted by past social movements, no longer listened to their demanding love overtures. If there was a great fault to Chavez in this period, it was his inability to see the fickleness of his former allies.¹⁶⁶

Conclusion

The temptation to use farmworker strikes as a measurement of worker politics—and, by extension, to comment on the workers' relationship to specific unions—risks simplifying the dynamics and contexts shaping the strike, such as: the outsized losses for strikers, including housing, wages for a half year, and future unemployment; the common knowledge that strikers would be blacklisted and easily replaced by a large and willing labor force; the cloud of rancher and Teamster violence on picket lines and throughout the region.

The UFW had to mend its relationship with some of its workers, it recognized. But the strike's results did not originate in the UFW's disorganization. It was, instead, a fortuitous victory for ranchers who found a powerful labor ally, an apathetic consumer class, and a newly skeptical national press.

Much of the secondary literature has adopted the rancher story, whether intentionally or not. It stresses the UFW's pre-1973 disorganization, its tardy contract negotiations, its inability to prevent ranchers from defecting to the Teamsters. It argues farmworkers did not strike and voted with their feet by staying put, while the UFW reacted by performing the Teamster-victimized role to avoid explaining to white consumers its failure with local workers. Lastly, the strike's ending illustrates Chavez's increasing madness and authoritarian leadership—for even when the major San Joaquin Valley grape rancher, Guimarra, agreed to UFW contracts in late 1973, Chavez jettisoned the agreement under a torrent of unreasoned profanity: "we have to deal with whores in the camps!" The source for the latter claim, is one former UFW leader and beckons for more substantial evidence and explanation.[167]

Whether or not Chavez "sank the deal with Guimarra" by protesting sexual trafficking, and/or whether a labor leader should play such a moralistic role, and/or whether the use of sex workers in labor camps was a trivial issue, can be studied further by future scholars.[168] For now, what needs to be stressed is that the UFW's 1973 Coachella Grape Strike did not represent an outlier for American unions. Much of labor found itself in straits that transcended undemocratic union leaders or worker timidity. We can understand the UFW's Coachella Grape Strike of 1973, and its conclusion, as instituting a counterrevolution through the violent repression of farmworker power. This took place in the context of a disconnected national audience, who could no longer be wooed to undercut the ranchers' profits through the simple act of boycotting grapes. But, as the next chapter shows, the Coachella Valley's farmworkers and Chicana/o activists were not yet done in fighting for a better world.

Chapter 8

Overlaid Tenses and Trajectories

Movements In and Out of the Coachella Valley, 1974–1977

In 1973, Lorraine Agtang was a twenty-one-year-old farmworker, a wife, and a mother of three school-aged children. Though from a mixed family (Mexican mother, Ilocano father), Agtang and her six siblings grew up in Delano's Filipino community in the 1950s and 1960s. They were born in rancher camps and worked as children in nearby fields, like other farmworker families. Conditions mirrored those elsewhere, too: poverty-level wages; lack of health care or benefits; absent water or restrooms in fields; pesticide exposure; racist ranchers who yelled at parents and their children, called them "stupid," threatened anyone who spoke up. "You could see [workers] were afraid," Agtang recalled many years later, "but what were they going to do? They could lose their jobs. They had to do what they were told."[1] When the Filipino Agricultural Workers Organizing Committee (AWOC) went on strike in Delano in 1965, her pro-union father honored the picket line, which led to her family's abrupt camp eviction—the only home she knew—and to overt hostility from rancher children in her school. The next year, like other farmworker teens, Agtang left school because "you know your future is going to be working in the fields." In 1970, she was eighteen years old, already married and a mother. Despite the UFW's unprecedented victory in California table grapes in 1970, her life remained distant from farm labor unionism and largely shaped by rancher-imposed conditions.

In the late summer of 1973, however, and despite her foreman husband's opposition, Agtang joined the UFW's Delano Grape Strike, which aimed to force grape ranchers to renegotiate UFW contracts. Though without knowing the Coachella Valley's leaders, Agtang participated in and extended their fight against rancher and Teamster collusion in 1973. "I have three kids," Agtang said of her strike involvement, "I need[ed] to have medical benefits. I [wanted] to send my kids to college too, I didn't want my kids to work on the fields when they get older. So, I wanted to go on strike and my husband didn't."[2] After the 1973 Delano Grape Strike ended with two murdered pro-UFW farmworkers, Agtang became a volunteer in the UFW clinic and its new farmworker retirement community, Agbayani Village. She also helped organize union elections under California's Agricultural Labor Relations Act in 1975 (ALRA). This was "the first time I had a job outside of working in the fields," she said, "it was my opportunity to learn." She conducted x-rays and lab work, filed social security benefits for the elder *Manong*, spoke to farmworkers and volunteers about unionization. "All of a sudden, I thought, 'Gee, I'm not so dumb after all.' I was really good at what I did." She felt powerful when they won campaigns, when she faced down ranchers and drew allied support. "I think if I had not been involved," she speculated, "I'd still be in Delano right now, you know, working in the fields. I cannot even imagine what that would be like." The UFW movement "opened the doors to another world that farmworkers don't ever get," and, by 1978, Agtang "thought I could do anything I wanted to do. You know, I believed that."[3]

Agtang's biography and reflections echo many of the themes covered in this book, including the long, intergenerational history of farm labor unionism, especially among Filipino workers, as well as a strike's difficult choices and swift repercussions and the discontinuous quality of movement history. Agtang also illustrates continued Filipino support for the UFW, though in reduced scale, and the gendered cleavages in UFW strikes. Regarding the latter, I have found no example of a pro-UFW husband and pro-Teamster wife, but I have found multiple instances of the opposite. Lastly, Agtang's history gestures to the open-nature of strike demands and their profound implication if won: to give her children, and herself, a life previously impossible. Though Agtang did not organize in Southern California, her trajectory into the UFW serves as a model for thinking of the Coachella Valley's fight against the Rancher Nation in the mid-1970s. As before, the UFW drew farmworkers into its worlds and they, in turn, drew the UFW into theirs. Both moved in flux—as contingent forces working across multiple scales that unpredictably, almost poetically, produced the very contexts sustaining them. The 1973 Coachella Grape Strike, for example, failed to defend UFW grape contracts, but the strike still triggered a wave of farmworker militancy and pressured California to codify farmworker union rights in 1975 (ALRA). Farmworkers in and out of the Coachella Valley then rode a wave of union elections and contract negotiations from 1975 to 1977. Like Agtang, many Coachella Valley farmworkers felt farm unionism's promise for the first time in these elections—all while they sustained the UFW when much of U.S. Labor was already in decline.

As other scholars have stressed, social movements do not move in a linear fashion. They are not merely falling or rising. They often do both, simultaneously—churning in possibility and instability, moving unpredictably across the time and space they help create. This chapter follows the ambivalent and contingent dynamics of the UFW and Chicana/o movements in and out of the Coachella Valley from 1973 to 1977. To illustrate them, the chapter has four parts: the passage and effects of ALRA; the expansion and solidification of the Coachella Valley's farmworker unionism in pro-UFW fields; the continuing

UFW shortcomings and/or rank-and-file skepticism, especially among non-Mexican farmworkers; and the Chicana/o movement's turn to institution building and community service. For some, this was a period of profound transformation and empowerment, as it was for Agtang. But for others, the years came with alienation or ambiguity. Much like a kaleidoscope, the collective/s shaping the UFW and Chicana/o movements shifted and blurred, pulled apart and overlaid each other, collectively attempting to make sense of a world that refused to settle into security.

California's Agricultural Labor Relations Act

With ALRA's passage in June 1975, the UFW's lead lawyer, Jerry Cohen, celebrated "midwif[ing]" the best labor law in the country," if not "the world."[4] The law extended the 1935 National Labor Relations Act's (NLRA) rights and procedures for union recognition, including secret ballot elections and a review board, the Agricultural Labor Relations Board, (ALRB) to address violations in a union election campaign.[5] Unlike the NLRA, however, ALRA did not outlaw all secondary consumer boycotts.[6] It also recognized farm labor's characteristics, such as short harvest timetables, high farmworker turnover rates, and migrant farmworker dependence on rancher housing, to allow union access to fields and camps, an improvement on the NLRA's prohibition of union access to employer property. The ALRA also rejected California ranchers' demand for harvest strike bans or a "cooling off" period, which would have undercut a harvest strike's pressure. It also prohibited ranchers from signing union contracts without a majority vote in an ALRB election, as Salinas Valley lettuce ranchers and Coachella Valley grape ranchers had done in 1970 and 1973, respectively. Like the NLRA, the ALRA tasked its ALRB to review and resolve "unfair labor practices" (ULPs). If the ALRB found that ULPs affected the election, it could call for another election. And if the ALRB certified a union as the employees' labor representative, ranchers were compelled to begin contract negotiations with the union.

At first sight, California's ALRA appears to have effectively subsumed the rancher-king into a common legal framework and granted the UFW a victory despite the union's profound weakness. Only two years before, the UFW movement lost nearly all its table grape contracts, while its ensuing boycotts failed to match the late 1960s successes. The UFW's relationship to the AFL-CIO (American Federation of Labor and Congress of Industrial Organizations), had also been strained by the 1973 grape strikes and by the UFW insistence to lead a boycott despite other union protests. California's ALRA victory also bucked the social, political, and economic trends in the United States. In the mid-1970s, Americans faced the largest postwar recession, a racialized municipal budget crisis, a post-Watergate collapse of political legitimacy, a rapid contraction of union power, and a collection of localized attacks on civil and political rights, especially in public education. The UFW movement thus appeared to have pulled a victory from the jaws of defeat. Most recent UFW histories credit California's governor and the UFW's white lawyers, though the 1973 strikes also pushed California ranchers to "sue for peace."[7] The new labor law, in turn, spirited a frantic wave of union organizing from September to December 1975, when 54,000 workers participated in 354 ALRB elections and 50.2 percent voted for the UFW.[8] Almost no workers opted for "no union," finally giving evidence to what was already known: ranchers lied about their workers not wanting a union.

Some UFW organizers recognized ALRA was hardly a complete victory. Shortcomings included ALRB agents who failed to hold peak-harvest elections, secure accurate employee lists, protect the union's access to ranches, and/or resolve rancher ULPs. ALRB agents also ignored rural California's unequal power dynamics, rancher violence, and farmworker fear of retribution. Some even communicated with ranchers while dismissing UFW complaints.[9] In the Coachella Valley in late 1975, for example, every rancher committed extensive ULPs in ALRA elections, including firing pro-UFW farmworkers, surveilling worker–union meetings, and promising higher wages and benefits in exchange for anti-UFW votes. The same occurred in nearly every other ALRA election in 1975 California. In oral histories, the UFW lawyers stressed their fight for ALRA's enforcement. They confronted agents for erroneous employee lists, helped replace hostile directors, protested farmworker arrests and intimidation, publicized ALRA rights, and recorded rancher violations.[10] In the process, they insisted their efforts pushed the ALRB to enforce the law, concluding it was "the administration of the law, not the law'" itself that produced the anti-union bias.[11]

But they were wrong. Though ALRA improved minimally on the NLRA, it also adopted the latter's anti-labor tenets. Both required a two-step process for union recognition, which gave employers an opportunity to mount anti-union campaigns. Both protected anti-union campaigns as employer free speech, thus legalizing veiled and not-so-veiled threats against pro-union workers. Neither protected economic strikers' claim to their jobs against strikebreakers; only strikers who proved their strike protested anti-union discriminatory behavior could safeguard their jobs. Any other strike, as the AFL-CIO recognized in the 1950s, became a "suicide" pact.[12] Most importantly, neither the NLRA or ALRA contained severe enough repercussions to discourage employers' mass disregard of the law's provisions.[13]

As discussed in chapter 6, the NLRA's weak ULP penalties undercut union elections across the United States in the 1970s. Unfair labor practices doubled between 1970 and 1980, and those pertaining to discrimination or unfair firing of pro-union workers grew at a faster clip.[14] As noted earlier, employers faced almost no repercussions other than reinstating fired workers, paying back wages, and displaying signs admitting a violation. "The probability is you will never get caught," an anti-union consultant reassured employers in 1976, and "if you do get caught, the worst thing that can happen to you is you get a second election, and the employer wins 96 percent of those elections."[15] Union organizers in the 1970s saw the same in their conversations with workers. One organizer recalled: "I would just watch these people go from feeling strong and like we need to do something to feeling like totally terrified to do anything, and paralyzed."[16] Even when unions overcame hostile campaigns and won elections, they still faced employer recalcitrance and failed to gain contracts in two of five cases, "effectively destroy[ing] an organizing effort or, at the very least, signal[ing] to employees the relative ineffectiveness of the union in dealing with management." The NLRA still existed in the 1970s, as the labor historian Lane Windham noted, but "its penalties for labor law violations were too weak to hold back the assault."[17]

Like the NLRA, ALRA's failures were inherent to its formulation. Given the limited repercussions, California ranchers hired anti-union consultants who advised on "bend[ing] and break[ing]" ALRA's rules.[18] Ranchers gave incorrect employee lists and attacked UFW organizers. They unilaterally raised wages and introduced new work benefits for "no union" votes. They fired entire pro-UFW crews, harassed pro-UFW farmworkers, and used the Border Patrol to threaten immigrants. They paid ineligible workers to vote, appealed ALRB decisions to draw out decisions, and used company unions to break and dilute election totals. For this, they received "a mere 'slap on the wrist,'" as Alan Grant, the president of the California Farm Bureau promised ranchers.[19] Despite UFW lawyer claims, in other words, ranchers did not subvert ALRA; they instead used ALRA's weak penalties to subvert the UFW, as industrial capital was already doing to established unions.[20] Even ALRA's celebrated components—a make-whole clause and boycott protections—did little for farmworker unionization: the first died in ALRB litigation in 1979 and the second over-estimated consumer solidarity amidst rising conservative politics and transnational markets.[21]

And yet, it cannot be denied that ALRA provided a shot of union potential in places like the Coachella Valley. As the next section will discuss, "la ley" pulled citrus, row crop, and date workers into the UFW for the first time. To them, ALRA meant possibilities where none existed. Despite its inherent shortcomings, it still sparked a frenetic election season in late 1975, so much so that the ALRB was overwhelmed with ULPs and election appeals. By January 1976, less than six months after its passage, the ALRB had spent its entire allocated funding, which gave anti-UFW and pro-rancher politicians a chance to effectively defund it.

In reaction, the UFW advanced a state proposition in 1976 that strengthened ALRA's weakest components. Proposition 14 replaced ALRA's two-step process of collecting signatures to trigger an election with a one-step signature collection process, thus blunting ranchers' anti-union campaigns.[22] It also tripled fines for ULPs and created a speedy contract mediation process to undercut rancher stalling, which could dissipate worker militancy and union momentum. Lastly, it permanently secured ALRB state funding to bar future rancher attacks through budgetary tactics. Proposition 14 thus represented a labor law that could actually unionize California's farmworker communities, which may explain why ranchers suddenly agreed to refund ALRA while opposing the UFW alternative.

The UFW continued to advance its proposition even after the state refunded ALRA. In critical histories, the UFW's insistence serves as a narrative turning point and dramatizes Cesar Chavez's worst organizer traits. With near-manic faith in his abilities, we learn, Chavez ignored self-identified allies and "political pros" who pleaded with him to abandon the campaign, pointing to the proposition's low chances. These allies also argued the proposition was no longer necessary given ALRA's budget resumption. "Hubris," the historiography argues, animated Chavez's decision, along with a vague propensity for "crusades" of "symbolic" value. In the process, the UFW sacrificed the time it needed to mount another round of ALRA elections, all while Chavez found scapegoats for the proposition's eventual loss in November 1976.[23]

Though attention to Chavez's shortcomings is a welcome change from past accounts, the focus on him can understate the promise of Proposition 14. Though a long-shot gambit, it signified labor rights for farmworkers when the existing ARLA framework offered only false opportunities. Cohen and the other UFW lawyers may have considered ALRA "the best labor law" in the world and country, but this assertion was baseless; it ignored other countries' pro-worker laws and used a non-standard for comparison: the "best" in the United States was hardly indicative of ALRA's value to farmworkers. In fact, public and private sector unions in 1978 pushed for labor reforms that were nearly identical to the UFW proposition.[24] These, too, would fail, and in their failure they would index the country's increasingly anti-labor political culture. Similarly, the defeat of Proposition 14 says less about UFW leaders than the state's racialized electorate, what Martinez HoSang describes as white Californians' "genteel apartheid."[25] The UFW certainly gambled in advancing Proposition 14, as the historiography argues. But the choice facing the UFW in 1976 was between a facile labor law or a long-shot drive to secure farmworker rights as no U.S. labor law had done before—aiming for a victory that could once-again defy history.[26] That the UFW had to defy history (again) was not its choice to make; it was the (imposed) context for making difficult choices.

This historiography has also argued that the loss led to Chavez's unmoored obsession with purging saboteurs. The latter took place in the UFW headquarters and among its volunteers, who then publicized the union's increasing authoritarianism. Like many historians, I am deeply skeptical of psychologizing arguments by non-psychologists, especially when they echo outdated racialized narratives of nonwhite political actors' mental incapacities. Chavez's mental health was also less significant outside the UFW headquarters, such as the Coachella Valley, where the local UFW office and pro-UFW farmworkers led new ARLA elections. The UFW planned to unionize one hundred thousand farmworkers in the late 1970s, and rank-and-file members would play a key role in the campaigns. The next two sections turn to this organizing, beginning with those near the UFW orbit and then to those farther away. The last section returns to the Coachella Valley's mid- to late 1970s Chicana/o movement, which adopted granular campaigns for institutional development and community service—arguably in alignment with the existing political realities.

Movement Currents

Though U.S. unions entered a period of decline in the mid-1970s, this trajectory was not readily apparent among Coachella Valley farmworkers. There, pro-UFW farmworkers spent the years after the Coachella Grape Strike of 1973 building a series of union campaigns. The grape strike itself, though defeated, produced farmworker militancy and raised wages in non-grape fields, as ranchers attempted to address a key source of worker discontent.[27] Some workers also migrated to the Central Valley in late 1973 and early 1974, where they participated in UFW strikes in grape, tomato, cantaloupe, and vegetable fields. When they returned to the Coachella Valley in mid-1974, some began attending local UFW meetings and speaking of union possibilities with their coworkers.[28] With ALRA's passage in 1975, these same farmworkers led union elections in the Coachella Valley's citrus, date, and vegetable ranches, winning most. Simultaneously, Freedman grape workers deepened their union power and challenged farmworker patriarchy. Still other local farmworkers pushed for changes in the Catholic Church and used Liberation Theology to challenge the Rancher Nation. For these men and women, the UFW movement was alive and pulsing with energy: it had bloomed in the 1973 summer and gave scent of new futures for the next four years.

To begin, consider Melecio Sanchez, who migrated to the Coachella Valley as an adolescent during World War II. Born in Hanford, California, but raised in Mexico, Sanchez discovered his U.S. citizenship while applying to the Bracero Program in the early 1940s. Like other men from rural Mexico, he wanted to escape hacienda-based poverty and social inequality. "I was a humble person," Sanchez said, "who wanted to work and find a bit of progress. I always carried a vision that one day I would form a family and live better . . . to find work where they treated me with dignity [and] paid me a fair wage."[29] This vision brought him to the Coachella Valley's lemon fields in the 1950s, when his friends told him of money-growing trees. He found the work satisfying, he said, but resented the exploitation that reminded him of the haciendas he had left in Mexico. Labor contractors skimmed wages and forced speed-ups by choosing the youngest men as crew leaders. They humiliated, chastised, and yelled "so much," and they dismissed complaints with blacklists and threats: "I have extra people who want to work," they crooned. "You feel a sadness," Sanchez said of these years, "you feel impotence because you can't do anything. . . . You tell yourself, 'If I respond, what is my family going to eat, where will I find a job?'"[30]

Possibilities shifted for Sanchez when the UFW movement arrived in the 1960s. Like other skeptical farmworkers, he first dismissed the union as self-serving. But "little by little," he heard of its "ideals," of its demands for "liberty [and] rights in the workplace, laws that protected workers and defended them from injustice," the very visions that animated his migration to the place of his birth. "That was what most pushed me [into the UFW]," Sanchez said, "to add my grain of sand in defense of our rights." After the 1970 UFW contracts in the Coachella Valley grape fields, he and other lemon workers successfully demanded higher wages. They did not win a union, but they remained organized and supported Coachella Valley grape strikers in 1973, when "the people unified itself" to "defend its right," he said. Along the migrant route, Sanchez and other workers also joined a series of strikes in Stockton's vegetable, cherry, onion, and tomato harvests in late 1973 and 1974. In one, seven hundred cars carried four strikers a piece, a "tremendous" force that pushed Stockton's ranchers to negotiate. "We wanted laws to protect our jobs," he said, "a right to salaries, a right to have clinics, to have a [social] security [benefit]."[31] So, when ALRA became law in August 1975, Coachella Valley citrus farmworkers like Sanchez were ready to take the lead in the looming torrent of fall elections.

For his younger nephew, David Perez, the UFW also held possibilities of self-realization. He spent his childhood alone on a family ranch outside the town of Zacapu, Michoacan, where he tended his family's animals and maize field. He spoke to few people in a day, he said, and passed silent nights gazing at stars. When, as an adolescent, he joined his family in Zacapu, he excelled socially and academically and felt a latent ambition: "I wanted to be more," Perez said vaguely, and that wanting meant migrating to the United States, where his brother, father, and grandfather already worked, and where "you had a future." Perez's parents agreed to his migration only after relentless pressure and, at fifteen, he began working in California's fields, including Coachella Valley citrus. "I will never forget my first weekly check was for $25," Perez recalled, the most he had ever held. He even bought his own clothes.[32] As he earned more, he "fe[lt] proud, like I was making it. . . . I thought I can even get married now. I can do this, and this, and this. . . . I felt a fulfillment, I felt self-realized." Still young, Perez gave most of his earnings to his mother and aunts, which fulfilled him even further: "I could help in that way. . . . I had worked it and had earned it."

Unlike his uncle, and perhaps reflective of his youth, Perez did not learn of the UFW movement until the 1973 Coachella Grape Strike. Initially uninterested in the strike because he did not pick grapes, he and other lemon workers became "involved . . . once we saw [the grape strikers]." "If [the union] enters grapes," they reasoned, "why not enter lemons?" He attended Coachella strike meetings, joined pickets with other lemon workers, stood with pride at the sight of a mile-long march in Mecca: "a whole street from top to bottom full of [red] flags . . . you felt powerful. In those days, you saw entire families with their boys and girls, marching. . . . It was a beautiful thing." He entered the union's field of possibility through grape workers' militancy: "We were seeing that something could be done, that *we* could do something."[33]

From 1973 to 1975, Sanchez and Perez organized farmworkers on the migrant route: from their short Coachella Valley stay to the longer period in Stockton and then to their annual vacations in Michoacan. Most had known each other for years and almost all saw or joined the UFW strikes of 1973–74. With ALRA, they mounted and won ten citrus elections in the Coachella Valley in late 1975, covering approximately one thousand farmworkers.[34] "Workers are easy to organize," an outside UFW organizer wrote in 1976, overlooking workers' initiative and self-organization. "[We] did not have someone to direct us," Perez said, "[but] we knew each other and would say, 'Well there is going to be an election.' If we were eighty, we knew seventy were for the Union." Afterwards, Perez and the negotiations committee pressed for higher wages, benefits, and job security. When they signed a contract three months later, they pushed other citrus and vegetable workers to do the same: "We would tell them, 'Hey, don't be dumb/silly. We have this and this and this,' and then they would organize themselves." Though these companies did not have the nationally recognized "great leaders," he said, every crew had effective representatives in union committees: "everything was driven by the workers."[35]

Sanchez and Perez moved on a broad migrant landscape to mount a campaign that culminated in the Coachella Valley—in sharp contrast to the hyperlocality of late 1960s strikes. They also leveraged earlier UFW victories. By 1975, farmworker unionization was enough of a possibility that they and their coworkers could imagine a transformed local economy. In turn, their efforts extended the UFW movement's viability in and out of the Coachella Valley, both relatching the UFW to the local economy and leading another fifteen elections in desert row crops. Though these latter elections were marred more extensively by labor violations and, as a result, less successful than the citrus elections, the Coachella UFW office was still contesting the elections in late 1976; its lawyers spoke optimistically about their future resolution. A couple years after a disastrous loss, in other words, the UFW movement appeared ascendant once more. Arguably, this process began with citrus farmworkers' incorporation into the UFW through local grape strikers, a process sustained by ALRA's passage, which was itself an effect of farmworker strikes in 1973–74. Cause and effect thus materialized each other into potential and contingency, as if suspending the UFW movement in mid-air, ambivalent and promising, breathing still despite the odds and recent history.

For some farmworkers, like Perez, the UFW also alchemized personal ambition into social justice visions. Perez was twenty-five years old in 1976, a married father who counted ten years in the United States. In that year, he was also chosen by his coworkers to represent them in UFW leadership trainings in La Paz. For the former lonely, village boy without schooling, these trainings promised intellectual and professional arrival: "We are going teach you English," the UFW told him, "We are going to teach you laws, we are going to teach everything."[36] With the new skills, Perez imagined organizing the entire Coachella Valley, pressing farmworkers into conversations about "how we can live. With honor and honesty. With dignity and everything." "That is what I envisioned," Perez said, "that one day I would achieve that . . . to help the farmworker, that was my purpose. Nothing else. Just help." Such a purpose glowed with personal fulfillment. He had been chosen by his coworkers, he said proudly, and as an organizer he stood at the cusp of doing "lo que a mi me gusta. Lo que a mi me gusta, yo lo voy a hacer."[37] Union skills also helped him be a better father and husband, he said, and "served him in . . . life, for my own benefit, for my family and others."[38] Like Agtang, Perez entered the union's field of stories, the same he helped create and manifest, the same that opened new worlds for him.

In Freedman Ranch, UFW grape workers deepened the transformations they initiated in 1970. In 1974, the pro-UFW priest, Victor Salandini, interviewed forty-two Freedman workers about their experiences under a UFW contract. The interviewed farmworkers were adults and adolescents, men and women, Filipino and Mexican, migrant and settled. Though social and personal differences shaped some of their answers, the workers nonetheless commonly spoke of the surprising ease living could be, as if a key disruption in their lives had finally been removed. Rosario Gutierrez, for example, merged work conditions, a coming birth, and a general plan for life improvements. "Through the union we work happier," she said, "we cannot be fired ... the foreman doesn't yell at us. The foreman doesn't push us." When asked about the union's work benefits, Gutierrez said she planned to "make use of the Kennedy Medical Plan because I will have a baby," adding, as if an afterthought: "We should make more money. I am going to have a baby soon and I will need more money." In Gutierrez's world, farm labor did not define or disrupt her life. It simply provided the resources she sought and served as the basis for a future that was both vague and nonthreatening—even promising.[39]

This transformation also involved gender relationships in the work fields. In the early 1970s, the local leader Maria Serrano noticed women worked fewer annual hours than men, which resulted in decreased union seniority and absent benefits. After the 1973 Grape Strikes, Serrano saw Delano women pruning grape vines during the winter, an arduous task that the Coachella Valley's grape ranchers had reserved exclusively for men. This reservation, however, contributed to the gendered difference in total annual work hours, and, in the process, weakened women's position within the UFW movement. So, Serrano and a small group of women pushed the UFW to open the Coachella Valley's pruning season to women. The union then held multiple meetings to discuss the matter, each erupting into male protests. In 1974–75, UFW leaders simply overruled local men and opened all jobs to women unionists.[40] Three local farmworkers signed up immediately: Maria Serrano, Petra Ruiz, and Teresa Velez. In the next few years, more added their names. Serrano and Ruiz, discussed at length in chapter 4, were already militant UFW members. The other women, such as Velez, were younger and newer to the UFW, both entering and sustaining the very potential created by an older generation.

Predictably, the men, and some women, fought their challenge. Some mocked them in whisper campaigns; others said their husbands treated them like work mules by allowing them to work in male-only jobs. Bosses also segregated the women into separate crews to visually highlight men's claim of physical superiority and, by extension, male farmworkers' right to these jobs. When the women farmworkers caught up to male crews, Serrano said, the male supervisors turned to helping the men. When the women still did not stop, male farmworkers and their bosses spread rumors about extramarital affairs to provoke their husbands' prohibition—thus leveraging familial patriarchy to sustain workplace patriarchy. "You cannot imagine how much they harassed us," Serrano said, "I think even the company wanted to pressure us to quit. But thank God we did not." Instead, the women unionists learned the tasks, raised their productivity, and, with relentless drive, broke gender barriers in vine planting, ditch digging, and box distribution. "In this way," she said, "we women were able to gain seniority, because women did not have enough hours for seniority, much less . . . to receive the pension plan, the funeral plan, the medical plan, etcetera. . . . It was a very big effort, very exhausting, but thank God we achieved it."[41]

Sanchez, Perez, Gutierrez, Serrano, Ruiz, and Velez: each a history, each a site of and for transformation, each a harnessing of life for life. The point here is not simply to note that more people joined the UFW movement soon after its seeming collapse, or that they did so amidst an increasingly reactionary national political climate, pressing forth despite the odds. That was the case, for sure. But the point I wish to stress here is that their collective histories illustrate the nature of the UFW movement: people built the very movement that built them. They did so in the context of past and present UFW victories inside and outside the Coachella Valley. They did so, too, in the context of community histories, in their dynamics, desires, and aspirations, in their past choices animating visions of better futures. Each farmworker thus moved in a shared space that, in turn, moved with them—contingently and unpredictably, almost magically, like a small stone the size of a child's fist skipping clear across water: so unlikely and yet so real, each skip powering the next.

I am at pains not to include more biographies to further illustrate the uncanny ways people moved through the field of stories they articulated and which, in turn, articulated them. Far from troubled, the UFW churned from the ground up, harboring still a sense of a better world. But this was not the case for everybody, as the next section makes clear.

The Missing Link

For Hilario Torres, the UFW movement arrived in 1976. He first heard of it in late 1975, when his wife gave birth to their child in the UFW Delano clinic, where Lorraine Agtang began her UFW activism in 1973. Torres was young, without health insurance and, as a recent immigrant from Mexico, did not know where to get medical help for his wife. But he learned of the UFW clinic from a crew leader, someone he had met recently, perhaps the only person he felt close enough to ask about aid. To his surprise, the UFW's Delano clinic only charged them $3 for the consultation and birth. Grateful, Torres and his young family migrated out of the region and soon lost contact with the UFW offices until May 1976, when he landed a job with HMS, a Coachella Valley vegetable growing company whose workers voted for the UFW in a late 1975 ALRA union elections. As his wife had gone into labor, these workers entered negotiations. In October 1976, half a year after Torres began working there, HMS signed a UFW contract that included a wage increase and a slew of benefits, including paid holidays, overtime pay, job security, and health care—all conditions he repeatedly described as "muy bonito."

Most strikingly to Torres, the contract followed two successful UFW campaigns in California: the abolishment of the short-handled hoe, which caused debilitating body pain and disability, and the provision of farmworker unemployment insurance, which helped families avoid the migrant route by replacing migrant wages with unemployment benefits. To Torres, the latter led to more farmworker children pursuing higher education, for students could now spend fewer school days on the migrant route and thus improved academically. Migrant farmworker children, Torres said, went to "different schools," "one month here, two more months while finishing the work, and move to another town." But with unemployment benefits, farmworker families could stay longer in one place and their children could "be more constant in school and finish high school and college education. And that was due to the syndicate [UFW]."[42] Through the union's legal advocacy, Torres's newborn could gain what had been unavailable to Agtang and what she wished to offer her children. Like other pro-UFW farmworkers in this period, he was introduced to the UFW through its concrete victories—a key difference from earlier members who acted primarily out of faith and principles. By 1977, he "became involved" in the UFW by volunteering his time to aid the looming grape elections in the Coachella Valley.

Torres's experience, however, was the exception. When ALRA was refunded in 1976, the UFW counted twenty-five elections in the Coachella Valley citrus and vegetables fields. Nearly all were held in 1975, and nine had been certified to cover 623 workers, of which the great majority (511 workers) chose the UFW. The other sixteen ALRA elections, mostly in row crops, remained contested and marred by rancher ULPs.[43] At North Indio Farms, for instance, where the Teamsters Union already held a contract, "the Temos [brought] 2 crews," reported [person] to La Paz "to vote for them." The North Indio Farms election was also held at nonpeak employment, which benefited the company, and after pro-UFW crews were prevented by the company from voting. The UFW contested the results and predicted the election would be set aside, thus allowing them a possible future win. But nearly a year after the election, the contest remained uncertain. Cardinal Distributors, in contrast, challenged fifty-five likely pro-UFW ballots to impede a final decision, while other ranchers fired pro-UFW farmworkers, surveilled union activity, raised wages for no union votes, gave faulty farmworker information, pushed for elections to nonpeak periods, and hired last-minute crews to vote against the UFW. For every election in 1975, the UFW filed ULP complaints against ranchers and began the bureaucratic ALRB process. The UFW did not have such procedures before 1975, but as early as 1976 they already appeared powerless to prevent the rancher stalling that sapped farmworker militancy, encouraging the voices that said the UFW could do little to contest rancher power.

The situation in Teamster-controlled grape fields was also challenging. Persistent Filipino discontent in the UFW movement continued to draw sustenance from a history of union invisibility, Filipino leadership divisions and defections, pervasive difficulties with UFW offices, and Filipino contractor collusion with ranchers in 1973. As an original 1965 striker Claro Runtal told the pro-UFW priest, Victor Salandini, in June 1975, "Filipinos in Coachella Valley were hurt [by] past polic[ies]." These policies included the seniority system, upfront dues payments for dispatches, and stringent penalties. "The UFW will not win," Runtal warned, "if we do not change," stressing "farmworkers do not care so much about the benefits of the contract. They are most concerned in the short run in a job. They WANT A JOB FIRST OF ALL" (emphasis in original). Runtal's comments pointed to the general scarcity shaping farmworker life, while alluding to Filipinos' generation-specific needs. But they also reflected the diversity of worker relationships to unionization—for other members, like Torres and Agtang, valued the UFW benefits—and foreshadowed the challenges the UFW would face in future elections.[44]

Runtal's position also marked a striking political evolution: he no longer deflected criticism of the UFW with unforgiving demands for greater union activism, as he did in the 1971 camp meetings (as discussed in chapter 6).[45] By the mid-1970s, Vera Cruz also moved past his former criticism of rank-and-file workers to critique UFW leaders and their occlusion of Filipino contributions to their movement. To Noel Kent, a student researching Filipino grape strikers, he wrote in early 1975: "In the Coachella-Delano Grape Strike of 1965, the Filipino role is missing in its history" despite the "fact ... [their] strike had set the spark, or triggered the explosion for the Farm Workers Revolution."[46] Filipino strikers faced evictions, Vera Cruz listed, violence, blacklists, and unemployment—for "green carders and illegals took their jobs"—but no one "cared to find out what was happening to Filipino strikers." Even a decade after AWOC's Coachella and Delano Grape Strikes of 1965, no journalist or writer had covered "this missing link in the chain of events." "Ignored," Filipino "dissatisfaction and disappointment" grew and provided an opening for the "disastrous collusion of growers and Teamsters."

Unlike his previous criticism, Vera Cruz now echoed Velasco's warning on the deleterious effect of Filipino invisibility. In the mid-1970s, Vera Cruz worked on "this missing link" by encouraging further studies on Filipino strikers. He helped the Paperworkers' Union writer, William Berg, conduct oral histories of Filipino residents of Agbayani Village for a new history book on the UFW. "Let me remind you again," Vera Cruz told Berg, "that your book about the Grape Strike is important."[47] He said the same to Kent and other students writing on Filipino strikers. He planned to write a book himself, "when I'll be out of the union." "Some people won't like me then," he predicted, "but I don't write just to please them. I'll be looking at the subject from the farm worker's viewpoint."[48] For Vera Cruz, the UFW in the mid-1970s did not represent a new enterprise, or a new set of possibilities and challenges, as it did to new Coachella Valley members, or to new UFW members like Agtang. Instead, it embodied a legacy of ambiguous meaning and of critical but ignored Filipino resistance. As social memory, he approached this missing link as both endangered and salvageable, on that could be leveraged to redraw Filipino workers back into the union and thus to fortify its future and the future of all farmworkers.

This framing would shape his participation in Delano's 1975 ALRA grape elections. He wrote pamphlets detailing rancher attacks on UFW workers and promising effective ALRB mediation.[49] He noted previous UFW errors, listed improvements, and warned against rancher "propaganda ... lead[ing] you to endless oppression and slavery."[50] His former exasperation bubbled up occasionally, such as when he wrote: "By plain common sense, you realize that he wants you to do what is good for him and not for you. He wants you to remain in the dark—groping—and not knowing what to do." But he was mostly compassionate, if at times haunting. When defending the UFW's seniority-dispatch system, for example, Vera Cruz referenced his generation's life knowledge about every worker's fated exhaustion and vulnerability: "Young workers want to move freely without dispatch, but one day they will be the senior citizens who must work to supplement their small social security income. Those workers who are old now, once felt like the young ones feel today, but they didn't accomplish much for themselves individually.... The young of today will be old and helpless tomorrow. The young must help protect the rights of the older workers to their jobs now to ensure their own security for the future."[51] Then Vera Cruz turned to the historical recognition that called for greater labor militancy: "Brothers and Sisters, ten years ago, we Filipino farmworkers went on strike—a strike signaling the birth of our union."

Despite his efforts, however, Vera Cruz did not convince Filipino workers to vote for the UFW in Delano grape elections in 1975. Extensive rancher ULPs marred these elections. But the UFW also simply did not win Filipino support, a failure that reflected the weight of past union errors. Unsurprisingly, when the pro-UFW priest and social scientist, Victor Salandini, conducted a survey study of Coachella Valley grape workers in 1976 he found no pro-UFW Filipino workers. At best, he found Anastacio Rabino, a former UFW member who was now a Teamster and said he was undecided about the two unions. Salandini also met "A. Valdez," a UFW member in Freedman Ranch who planned to vote for the Teamsters. To Valdez, the UFW's seniority system was unfair, dispatchers practiced "favoritism," and union benefits did not justify the higher dues—all views that lined up with Runtal's observations and that Vera Cruz attempted to address in his appeals.[52] Valdez did say he would stay with the UFW if it won a future election, but this was hardly the energy the UFW would need to overcome employer hostility. Perhaps most surprising was Valdez's sense of a secured union future, that the matter was about choosing one union over another, and not what was obvious to Vera Cruz and Runtal: that there was only one real union and that it was endangered.

The rest of Salandini's interviews in 1975 and 1976 reiterated the UFW's challenges in Coachella Valley grape fields. Of the forty-two Teamster grape workers he interviewed in 1975, half had "no union preference," while eleven and ten supported the UFW and Teamsters, respectively. Of the latter, eight farmworkers were Filipino, Puerto Rican, or Japanese, signaling a Mexican/non-Mexican fault line. As chapter 7 noted, Salandini's data pointed to a revamped workforce with limited and/or ambiguous relationships to the UFW. Of the nineteen new hires interviewed in 1975, for instance, four (two Mexicans, one Japanese, one Filipino) planned to vote for the Teamsters and two (one Mexican, one unstated) for the UFW. The rest—thirteen out of nineteen new hires out of forty-two interviewees—said they planned to "join" whichever union won a future election. Few chose "no union" or implied that farm unions were endangered in the Coachella Valley. They simply wished to be amenable and to keep their jobs.

In 1976, Salandini conducted an even larger interview collection of seventy workers from both UFW and Teamster grape fields. Divided equally between the two, Salandini asked workers to speak on their union preferences and experiences under farm labor unions. Among UFW workers, only four (of thirty-five interviewees) did *not* list the UFW as their first choice; three stated no preference and one chose the Teamsters. Perhaps unsurprising today, the UFW's showing in Freedman Ranch (where the majority of pro-UFW respondents worked) still testified to a strong union culture bucking the increasing rate of union decertification in the United States. In Teamster grape fields, the responses were similarly revealing. Of thirty-five workers, five chose the Teamsters, eleven the UFW, and nineteen "no preference" or "not certain," reiterating the 1975 interview findings. Only eighteen (half) Teamster farmworkers had worked under UFW grape contracts, of which nine worked for one year or less. Again, the Coachella Valley grape workers in Teamster-contracted fields in 1975 and 1976 represented a new workforce from that of 1973; even those who worked under UFW contracts in the early 1970s had had limited UFW tenures. Lastly, of the nine who said they worked under the UFW contract for two to three years, eight chose "no preference" and only one chose the Teamsters. Salandini's survey results, in short, suggested the UFW would need ample resources to attract new members and counteract ranchers' anti-union campaigns of some improvements and widespread threats.[53] And yet, at the same time, the UFW could be reasonably content that farmworkers had not expressed explicit hostility toward the union.

Interviews of farmworkers who learned of the UFW in the 1970s suggested similar conclusions. Arturo Diaz, for instance, migrated to the United States in the early 1970s, found work on the California migrant circuit, and slowly began to learn of the UFW during the 1973 grape strikes. He learned more in the subsequent Stockton strikes, where his bosses told him pro-UFW workers had burnt cars and attacked strikebreakers. At the same time, Diaz learned about the union through Melecio Sanchez, who inspired him. He had union "curiosity," Diaz said, but he also feared the repercussions: "I wanted to work" and "any Chavista in that time did not get work." He kept his distance until 1977.[54] Elvia Alicia Castillo shared a similar relationship to the UFW. Castillo migrated from Guaymas, Sonora to Ensenada, Baja California in 1965. She then followed work opportunities in Stockton (1968), Santa Ana (1972), and Coachella (1976). By the mid-1970s, she was a farmworker in the Coachella Valley, a mother of three, and married to an anti-union husband. She was also the main breadwinner for her childhood family in Sonora. She liked the UFW benefits, she said, but her family obligations and undocumented status impeded greater participation: "They wanted to force you to [strike], but that is very difficult when you have your expenses. In a strike, you do not have any rights," she noted perceptively.[55] Both Castillo and Diaz could very well have answered Salandini's questions much like the ambivalent interviewed workers: to choose no preference, or not certain, but stress they will work with whichever union wins a future election.

There are more farmworkers and most expressed the ambiguity shared by Castillo and Diaz. In their interviews, the UFW was neither an immediate source of empowerment nor alienation. For most, it was not even a recognizable model for social organization *in* the United States, where many had limited rights as immigrants. Most considered the UFW through their specific histories and needs, fully conscious of the risks involved. If for Vera Cruz the missing link was the history of Filipino militancy in initiating and advancing the UFW movement, one that (if told) could re-trigger a Filipino return to the UFW vanguard, then for farmworkers like Castillo and Diaz the missing link was the gap between an aspirational, but hazy, future and the vicissitudes of a difficult present. The missing link existed amidst the many other farmworkers making calculations about unions, migration routes, gender relations, and families. They did so in the contexts that some farmworkers had not heard of the UFW or had goals that did not lie in unionizing agriculture, or who were outright anti-unionization, like Castillo's husband. This missing link and the exchange it fostered and forced represented another field of stories, one that often appeared quite distant from a union world. The UFW movement would attempt to address this missing link in 1977 with a tool as inadequate as ALRA.

The Late Chicana/o Movement

The Coachella Valley's Chicana/o movement in the mid-1970s reflected the dynamics explored in this chapter. These included the simultaneity of ambivalent possibilities and resilient insurgencies, the wide-ranging personal trajectories within an overarching, protracted struggle, and the co-constitutive process of individual and community empowerment. Though without their previous visibility, local Chicanas/os continued to mount campaigns to improve the lives of ethnic Mexican residents in the Coachella Valley. Most gravitated to social institutions, such as schools, clinics, and arts organizations. They drew inspiration from past demonstrations and attempted to re-distribute social, political, and cultural resources. But, like the UFW, Chicana/o activists faced an uphill and often solitary battle. Progress was neither steady nor guaranteed in a shapeshifting landscape.

We can begin with the state of the local Mexican American Political Association (MAPA) chapter after the UFW's Coachella Grape Strike in 1973. Soon after the UFW moved its strike to the San Joaquin Valley, the Teamsters Union in the Coachella Valley offered to upgrade MAPA's building in return for office space. The Teamsters approached MAPA, Ray Rodriguez said, to legitimize their raid and foster ethnic Mexican Teamster allegiances by inserting themselves in MAPA's building. To Rodriguez's surprise, a substantial number of MAPA members (especially white allies) supported the Teamsters' offer and ignored counterarguments that such an agreement would irrevocably sever MAPA's ties with the UFW.[56] Concerned, Rodriguez hastily recruited Brown Berets members to join MAPA abruptly to vote against the Teamster proposal. The arguably underhanded effort led to a bitter MAPA split and ended in early 1974 with charges of anti-white racism from white members, compounding the group's earlier divisions and undermining future campaigns.[57] Even its newspaper became a rudimentary shadow of its former self after 1974. Much like the statewide MAPA, the local chapter "was there," Rodriguez admitted, but "only in name."[58]

That said, MAPA members still pushed for education reforms to aid their students. They led workshops on higher education, distributed college scholarships, directed students to Chicano Studies, and pushed parents to allow their children to attend regional universities. They also participated in bilingual education conferences, completed school administration credential programs, and implemented school-wide curriculum reforms. These efforts extended MAPA's education reform campaigns from the late 1960s. With this in mind in 1976, Rodriguez accepted a principal position at Van Buren Elementary, an old, dilapidated school next to Indio's Farm Labor Camp. Nearly all the school's students came from poor, immigrant, and Spanish-speaking farmworker households, many from right next door, where just three years earlier, strike violence had marred the grape harvest. As a principal, Rodriguez hoped to build a school that validated and cared for farmworker children, one that offered options outside farm labor and steered them towards the social mobility that education had given him.[59]

But his ambitions quickly ran into limits. Van Buren had been a "dumping ground," he learned, for district teachers that other schools "did not want." "Maestros mas racista que la chingada, mano," he said, "I mean, I'm telling you, racist." One teacher daily left her students with a teacher's aide, while the only male teacher had a "tendency to always be alone with [first grade] girls." The great majority of the faculty refused pedagogical reforms and told him they "wanted to continue the way" it had been—to be the "queen or king in their classroom."[60] After a year of fighting, Rodriguez filed district paperwork to replace eleven of the sixteen teachers—a task that drew immediate (and outraged) district opposition. Rodriguez's plan also did consider a key question: who, in fact, could serve as the bilingual and bicultural teachers he needed? The local and national history of educational marginalization and neglect, and the impressive tenacity of white supremacy among the country's educators, had led to a shortage of viable candidates for principals like Rodriguez. Recognizing the protracted nature of education reform, he returned to the classroom in 1978, where could at least encourage students to attend college and become teachers, counselors, professionals, and business people—the very figures necessary for building the empowering institutions that the Chicana/o movement envisioned in the 1960s.[61]

Other Chicana/o activists also turned from a politics of protest to one of provision and service. For former students like Amalia Uribe Deaztlan, Tony Reyes, Joe Ceja, Calisto Ramos, Larry Salas, Yolanda Almaraz, and Socorro Gomez, the classroom played a key role in their lives and, as a result, represented for them the foundation for an empowered Mexican American community.⁶² In the mid-1970s, many graduating college students returned to their Coachella Valley communities and took positions in education. "My generation," Ceja noted, "had been encouraged to come back . . . by our parents. It was a whole concept: to come back and continue to support and serve your community."⁶³ His father—a former bracero who joined the Voters League's insurgent campaigns in the 1960s—told him as much just before his death: "Do not forget about your home," he told his son.⁶⁴ For Yolanda Almaraz, her path to teaching in Mecca Elementary in 1973 began with her childhood in the Coachella Valley, her participation in a late 1960s UFW strike, and her student activism in the California State University, San Bernardino. "What inspired me was the children," Almaraz said of her turn to teaching, "they need[ed] a voice. They needed to have someone to be out there . . . [who] treated [them] like human beings." They also "desperately needed a good education."⁶⁵

Other former students turned to complementary institutions. Clementina Olloque enrolled in a nursing program after the Coachella Grape Strike of 1973, in large part because Chavez told her of the union's need for medical workers. In the same period, Sam Maestas envisioned opening a free clinic in Coachella after graduating from University of California, Riverside. The clinic would "help the farmworkers, help the community, help the underprivileged," he said, and serve as an electoral base for progressive candidates.⁶⁶ Still others, like Coachella Valley members of Teatro Chicana at San Diego State, spoke of theater's role in their political evolution and community empowerment. "We wanted to communicate a message," Sandra Gutierrez said, about "the things [we] saw around [us]—poverty, discrimination, sexism."⁶⁷ Art played a similar role for Roy Duarte, who painted murals on public buildings "so the people can see themselves from the struggle of the past to the struggle of today."⁶⁸ More turned to law, business, and public service, or to the construction of public housing or immigrant rights advocacy, all in the name of "serving the people."⁶⁹

For these activists, the UFW movement appeared ascendant in the mid-1970s and did not need their help. They thus turned to the institutions that could fulfill a shared vision of racial egalitarianism—what MAPA's *Ideal* termed as the "conservative" goals of equal citizenship "already . . . guaranteed." Its absence marked and produced their community's racialized subjection. With education, art, law, housing, and health care, Chicana/o activists aimed to help farmworker children escape the exploitative labor cycle maintaining agribusiness—an escape that reflected their own journeys into higher education. These efforts pointed to a future in which the rancher kings could even be starved of its exploited-farmworker lifeblood, one that forced them into a new social context of limited labor and abundant farmworker allies.

Though protests appeared less often, in short, the Chicana/o movement continued to build a world outside the Rancher Nation.[70] But if the Chicana/o movement did not end in the mid-1970s, it also did not reflect a simple story of greater freedom and justice. Much like Rodriguez's struggles at Van Buren Elementary, Chicana/o activists faced daunting conditions and ambiguous resolutions. This was the case in 1976, when Mexican American and white liberal teachers led a walkout from eastern Coachella Valley schools. The walkout was triggered by a case of physical punishment at Dateland Middle School in Coachella, but it quickly gave way to pent up anger over abusive, racist teachers, dysfunctional schools, misspent district funds, and unresponsive district leaders. The latter, for instance, refused to fire a teacher accused of sexually abusing students, while simultaneously portraying the local ethnic Mexican community with racist tropes—as "ignorant" and "undeveloped," and as "parents [who] don't care about their children's education."[71] In response, ethnic Mexican parents and teachers formed the Community Committee for Alternatives in Education (CCAE) and demanded the firing of abusive teachers. When the district refused, the CCAE led a walkout that interlaced the small farmworker towns and drew support from local UFW members and older Chicana/o activists.

Strikingly, the 1976 walkout exemplified this book's approach to social movements as a field of stories—one of difference and syncretism, unpredictable possibilities, and multiple timelines. The trajectory of the teacher-leaders, for instance, began with their family's focus on education and by the efforts of local, regional, and national civil rights groups to open higher education to non-white students. The students' return shared in the Chicana/o pivot to serve communities and adopt national pedagogical reforms. Their 1976 walkout, furthermore, echoed the 1968 East LA Chicano Blowouts and the 1970 Coachella Valley student walkout, which had drawn inspiration from the late 1960s Chicana/o–UFW mobilization, especially in Coachella Valley grapes. For Sandra Gutierrez, the interconnections were biographical and spanned much of the 1970s. She was one of a few Mexican American students in college-bound courses at Coachella Valley High School, she recounted, and then she attended San Diego State College/University, where she joined Teatro Chicana. The latter's politicized plays inspired her to become a UFW organizer in 1975, just as the Coachella Valley held its first union elections, and in 1976 she convinced her Teatro classmates to produce and perform a play on education justice for a meeting of UFW farmworker parents outraged by the Dateland Middle School scandal. After the play, the farmworker parents joined the teacher-led demonstrations against the school district's inaction.[72]

The end results, however, were mixed. The school district grudgingly retired the offending teacher and moved a teacher accused of sexual abuse to nonclass duties. The district also began the first steps toward adopting bilingual education. But these gestures did little to integrate Coachella Valley schools, improve student outcomes, or foster trust between parents and schools. Only two years after the walkout, Rodriguez would leave his Van Buren principal post, and four years later Ceja would find that another school was *also* a dumping ground for egregious teachers. The Coachella Valley Unified School District (CVUSD) board member, Silvia Montenegro (1980–90), said CVUSD board members held racist "attitude[s] towards our *gente*" as late as the 1990s. "As far as [one] was concerned," she said, the Mexicans "were just all farm laborers, and farm laborers were supposed to be stupid." "There are white people," she added, "who believe in . . . power. And how do you control a population? By keeping them ignorant. . . . That's power, that's a lot of power."[73] The 1976 walkouts also negatively impacted the teacher–leaders. They faced hostility from colleagues, threats against their credentials, and local blacklists. Most left the region like workers losing a strike, while one spiraled into tragic and self-destructive behavior. Worse still, Ceja observed, the walkout radicalized the region's "white power complex" into a "siege mentality" that fought any reforms, however measured.[74]

The late Chicana/o movement continued to press for a racially just world—locally and beyond—but it did not do so effortlessly, much less inextinguishably. It also did not exist in a vacuum, without the sober assessments of late 1970s Coachella Valley life. Schools remained largely segregated and violent spaces for non-white students. Wealth remained segregated by race and region, with most in the increasingly resort-based western half of the Coachella Valley. Rising numbers of Mexican immigrants filled low paying agricultural jobs, usually without the recent history of local contestation or even the bare securities of racialized citizenship. And yet, the worse was still to come. The very year Rodriguez left his principal post in 1978, California's white electorate passed an anti-tax proposition that destroyed the state's public and local resources, the same that local Chicanas/os had come to rely on for their campaigns to serve their community.

All of these justice campaigns also exacted a steep price on participants. As Clementina Olloque, a 1973 UFW striker, explained tersely: "young people today need to know what we suffered so that they can have what they have. . . . We were the ones who carried the cross, and a cross that was incredibly heavy, you have no idea."[75] For Max Huerta, who had led Chicana/o campaigns in Delano, joined the Coachella Grape Strike of 1973, and staffed the UFW Coachella office in 1973–74, the price exacerbated emotional wounds rooted in childhood poverty and racism. By the start of 1975, Huerta remembers, he "was already burned out" and likely suffering from post-traumatic stress disorder:

> I was a kid when I thrust myself into the movement. I was fourteen years old. It was a time of a lot of turbulence, and not [a] time to really talk to somebody and understand exactly what I was getting myself involved in. . . . I was involved in a lot of dangerous situations that could have cost me my life, but at that time, I just experienced bouts of fear when it happened, and then just forg[o]t about it. I was just a kid. When I was with the farm workers, they threatened my life, they threatened the lives of my family.[76]

It is likely Huerta was not the only example of such exhaustion and wounding, and it is likely that those who remained in these social movements did so by attempting to carry a cross that weighed against them, against those near them, against their future selves. Like the UFW leaders in the mid-1970s, who increasingly engaged in self-destructive behavior, the narrative here is as much a cautionary tale as it is an homage to activists' valiant efforts.[77] The struggle is for life, not for struggle itself.

Conclusion

All social movements are made up of many people in many places with many positionings. In the Coachella Valley's UFW and Chicana/o movements, these individuals included thousands of farmworkers, both Mexican and Filipino, men and women, migrant and settled, those from Coachella and those from elsewhere. Some counted nearly fifteen years in the UFW movement, and some could trace decades more of union building. Others, however, only counted their first fifteen weeks, or less, and remained cautiously optimistic about its prospects, perhaps naïve still about its cost. The movements also included the farmworkers' children and neighbors, the teachers of these children, those who called themselves Chicanas/os and relished their relentless campaigns against white supremacy. It included first generation college students, with their poetry sessions, street plays, and rallies bouncing between parties, and their attempts to reconnect with younger selves and home communities, and live lives as if they could be carefree and hopeful. It included the new immigrants of the 1970s, people who often claimed to have had a grandparent who followed Zapata or Villa, or said they would have done so themselves if they had only been alive then, or held adolescent dreams of self-realization that meant arrival, and the caretaking of those who once cared for them.

Others did not move as movement participants but had effects, nonetheless. For many Filipino workers, the union had an early heyday followed by years of missteps. Less admitted, however, these years also included worker compromises with the rancher class that undermined autonomous farmworker power. By the mid- to late 1970s, furthermore, the pressing issue for many Filipino workers was not union recognition, as Vera Cruz attempted to leverage, but how to live their last years of life. For Mexican farmworkers, in contrast, the union was most visible in the early to mid-1970s, when contracts, strikes, and elections compelled many to consider their relationship to the Rancher Nation. For many, this period was also shaped by more than the UFW's problems. It included, specifically, their complicated relationships to local bosses, male workers' investments in patriarchy, and the unforgiving hostility of striker families—who, unlike Filipino unionists, offered little community reconsolidation. For the new immigrants trekking north from a country in crisis, the union existed in a different timeline, did not exist at all, or offered little in their aim to build lives in their home country. Lastly, there were Chicana/o activists who felt burned out, moved away from the Coachella Valley, and/or attempted to find some calm from a movement whirlwind that consumed as much as it nourished.

People move in such spaces in distinct form—in and out of campaigns, in and out of commitments, all tugging at individuals who existed, whether or not they wanted to, in and through the collective, who acted in the simultaneity of other people's actions. Each one had to choose their position, their story/ies, their relations to self and other. Each did so in a present tense, each time a/the movement beckoned, and/or inspired, and/or challenged, and/or threatened. They did so, furthermore, in the context of a changing local, regional, and national landscape of power and politics, one that held little of the former decade's claim (however insincere they may have been) of American social progress. Opacity—of the social reality, of social strategy—dominates. How can choices be so solitary, so contained to the individual, and yet so laced with the presence of others? How can such choices be calculated when the ground shifts with the choices of others, who also struggle to measure the costs and benefits, the mixtures of expectation and fear, the weight of that optimism that insists, always, that this time will be different? How does one, in fact, ever puncture into freedom—past the shifting structure that denies?

PART IV

Denials and Afterlives

Chapter 9

Sparks at Dusk

Elections and the (Denied) Promise of Utopian Futures, 1977–1983

For David Perez, 1977 began with much promise. He had spent the last four years immersed in UFW talks and meetings, moving along his migrant circuit while speaking to coworkers about their union benefits and victories, reading about the state's passage of the Agricultural Labor Relations Act (ALRA), even laying the groundwork for a future union vote.[1] In late 1975, he and his uncle had led a successful pro-United Farm Workers (UFW) campaign in Coachella Valley Citrus (CVC), which signed a UFW contract with higher wages, job security, and workplace benefits. For Perez, the CVC contract represented a means for and an attainment of the social mobility and education he envisioned when migrating from his small town in Michoacan, Mexico. During this period, the UFW also began to identify farmworker leaders for the union's expansion through a new round of ALRA elections. To his surprise, and in validation of his labors, Coachella Valley union members elected Perez to represent the region.

Like other UFW delegates from throughout California, Perez traveled to the UFW headquarters in La Paz to begin a year of organizer training, including English language fluency, successful campaign strategies, the minutia of labor law and its implications for ALRA elections, and leveraging local allies and media platforms. He even received training on how to modulate his voice to gain stature among workers and nonworkers alike. As he set off to La Paz, Perez imagined returning to the Coachella Valley—not yet his home, but increasingly his future—as the UFW's official representative for the final unionization push. In a matter of a few years, he believed, all farm workers would be covered by UFW contracts with job security, higher wages, and benefits, including those of intangible quality, like respect from bosses and "gusto" in labor. Perez's vision of political economic transformation also mixed with existential purpose: "I wanted to help and work for farmworkers," he said, "to help the people.... I was not interested in fame or anything like that ... I just wanted to help. That's what I imagine.... One day, I told myself, one day I'll be able to accomplish that. I will be able to help the farmworkers. That was my life purpose."[2]

But, after six months in La Paz, Perez questioned the viability of his social dream. Their ALRA election wins did not assure contracts with ranchers, who flouted their legal obligations to undercut farmworker militancy and UFW strength. In the Coachella Valley in 1977, the UFW's grape elections faced such brazenly illegal behavior from grape ranchers that Perez doubted the UFW movement would ultimately prevail. The worst part of his realizations, Perez said, was the fact that the UFW appeared helpless and in denial—incapable of seeing its weaknesses, much less to chart a path forward. When he tried to voice his concerns to UFW leaders in La Paz, they unconvincingly told him not to worry about the union's future. In his doubts, he felt like he was betraying his coworkers by keeping up with the organizing when he was convinced of the union's bleak future. So he resigned in late 1977 and returned to the Coachella Valley, where (to his surprise) co-unionists did not believe him and began to suggest he had "sold out."[3]

Critically, Perez continued to work under a UFW contract until the mid-1980s, a half decade of job protections, strong wages, and much-needed benefits.[4] In this regard, his UFW membership and the UFW's contract with Coachella Valley Citrus meant a relatively good life inside the Rancher Nation. But this was a far cry from Perez's social dream of an egalitarian and just agricultural economy. As he had recognized in 1977, his last years as a union farmworker were the exception to the UFW's challenging fortunes in the late 1970s and 1980s—not so much as running against the grain of union defeat but as an exception that appeared like a union pocket *not yet* reconsumed by the Rancher Nation. It was just a matter of time, Perez said, before the desert's ranchers eliminated even this.[5]

Using Perez's observations, this chapter delves into the UFW's ALRA campaigns in the Coachella Valley grape fields in 1977, which were part of the UFW's ambitious goal of one hundred thousand members by 1980. As Perez intuited, the UFW's 1977 campaign in the Coachella Valley illustrated ALRA's ineffectiveness as a farm labor law. It failed to prevent grape ranchers' flagrantly illegal behavior and, by extension, to protect farmworkers' right to choose their labor representative. In every election, Coachella Valley grape ranchers' waged relentless and often violent anti-union campaigns, which included promises of higher wages and work benefits for "no union" votes, surveillance of farmworker political affiliations, harassment and discriminatory termination of pro-UFW workers, stuffing ballot boxes with anti-UFW votes, and a range of physical assaults. Most importantly, the Agricultural Labor Relations Board (ALRB) failed to provide timely decisions after the UFW filed complaints. Most final decisions came in late 1979 and late 1980, when the prospects of a union future had been largely defeated throughout the country, and when the ALRB could offer little more than validate the UFW's charges in 1977.

For most UFW members, the UFW's defeat appeared to come much later—as late as the mid-1980s, if not after Cesar Chavez's death. But, like Perez, these farmworkers existed in union pockets amidst an anti-union economy—less vanguardist than anachronistic, as exceptions to the rule of a re-ascendant Rancher Nation.

"A Harsh and Vindictive . . . Program"

For an illustrative example of the Coachella Valley's ALRA elections in 1977, we can turn to the three-hundred-acre Carian Ranch and its mixed Filipino and Mexican workforce. During the UFW's 1969 Coachella Grape Strike, Harry Carian had framed his opposition to the UFW as a principled stand for the country's "silent majority," a politics that made his UFW tenure (1971–73) bitter and contentious, culminating with the Coachella UFW office's refusal to dispatch farmworkers to his fields until Carian addressed a backlog of grievances.[6] In April 1973, Carian joined the Coachella Valley's grape rancher rush into the Teamsters' hands, and in 1974 he invented a grape thinning tool that undercut UFW sabotage of the thinning season. From 1973 to 1976, Carian also removed all known *Chavistas* from his crews to prevent a future union campaign.[7] He thus embodied the local rancher class, even if his opposition to the UFW surpassed that of his rancher kin.

In this context, the UFW movement began its ALRA union campaign in the Coachella Valley's grape fields in January 1977, when UFW organizers visited the Mayo Vitalino crew. The Vitalino crew was from the San Joaquin Valley and had taken rooms in Carian's camps after he offered them work for six months, which meant the crew planned to complete Carian's harvest before migrating to Delano. They were one of three crews in Carian's operation and they reflected the company's ethnic composition: a third of the crew was ethnic Filipino and the rest were ethnic Mexican. Some had already learned about and participated in UFW activities in Northern California's Yuba City and enthusiastically welcomed the UFW campaign. In January and February of 1977, the crew met secretly with UFW organizers, attended union meetings, and spoke to one another about the union's future election.[8]

By the start of the thinning season in March 1977, the Vitalino crew represented the core of the Carian operation, with UFW organizers estimating their 85 percent support.[9] In March, the crew also began to visibly flaunt its allegiances. They spoke openly to UFW organizers during and after work, organized pro-UFW meetings with other workers in Carian's housing camps, and collected the UFW card signatures to trigger an ALRB election. Some even put up pro-UFW paraphernalia in common and private spaces; the crew's cook, for instance, posted a UFW flag in Carian's housing camp kitchen, while farmworkers covered their private rooms with UFW pamphlets, wore UFW buttons during and after work, lent their cars to UFW organizers, and/or collected money to pay for a radio announcement on the UFW's upcoming Mecca-to-Coachella march on March 27, 1977. The march concluded the UFW's early organizing efforts and kicked off the more concerted and more public campaign. At least four Vitalino workers marched front and center, including the Philippines' flag-waving Danny Lopez, a Coachella Valley grape worker since 1952 and a voice in the UFW's Coachella radio ad, where he "presented himself as a Harry Carian Philippine worker." Though some farmworkers were just learning of the UFW, the 1977 march represented only the most recent manifestation of the UFW's history in the Coachella Valley: four years earlier, for instance, the UFW had lost nearly all its grape contracts; three years before then, Steinberg had triggered a statewide unionization of grape workers; five years before that, AWOC's Filipino organizers and members had planned a surprise grape strike. Now, nearing the end of another decade, the UFW movement appeared ready to finish their union drive, once and for all.

In reaction, Carian unleashed an anti-union campaign the ALRB later described as a "harsh and vindictive . . . program of illegal coercion and interference."[10] He first refused to give farmworker information to the UFW, as ALRA mandated, to prevent communication between the UFW and his employees. He then attempted to identify farmworkers' union support by requiring his employees fill out information cards asking their opinion on the UFW. The Vitalino crew instantly accused Carian of surveillance and refused to participate. The UFW followed with a formal ALRA complaint and the ALRB subsequently found Carian's cards to be "unlawful interrogation." Carian then instructed his supervisors to surveille the Vitalino crew, especially their contact with UFW organizers, who were then entering his ranches as protected by ALRA. Other supervisors also surveilled their crew's UFW-worker meetings and threatened workers against signing UFW cards or expressing pro-UFW sympathies. All supervisors, furthermore, kept notes on crew productivity levels to provide legal cover for a future mass dismissal. Carian, the ALRB would later concluded, engaged in a "clear pattern of 'outrageous' and 'pervasive' misconduct" that "severely interfered with the election."[11]

And then, in a moment of intensified anti-union hostility, Carian simply fired the *entire* Vitalino crew a few days after the Mecca-to-Coachella march—a first, the ALRB discovered, in Carian's history. Carian followed the firing with a forty-five cent hourly wage increase for the two other crews, as well as a company commitment to match future UFW wages and improve on the outgoing Teamster insurance plan. Under ALRA, all of Carian's actions were unfair labor practices (ULPs) that, as the ALRB would recognize, undermined farmworkers' right to union choice. The combined dismissal of an entire pro-UFW crew and the bestowing of benefits to presumably anti-UFW or union-neutral crews exemplified the NLRB's "fist in a velvet glove" principle, in which an employer signaled "the source of benefits now conferred [was] also the source from which future benefits must flow and which may dry up if it [was] not obliged."[12] The company's benefits, in other words, were predicated on farmworkers' opposition to the UFW, and thus violated their right to union representation of their choosing.

But the ALRB's decisions only came after the UFW filed complaints and triggered its bureaucratic processes. The final decisions were finally determined in 1980. As such, the ALRB did not stop Carian's actions *during* the ALRA campaign nor rectify his actions' effects on the remaining workforce after March 1977.[13] In fact, Carian continued to surveil his workers and then laid off another thirty-five *Chavistas* in early April. He later claimed these dismissals had nothing to do with farmworkers' union sympathies: by then, he said, his ranches simply did not need a large workforce. The ALRB disagreed with him, however, and upheld the multiple UFW organizer testimonies that traced growing pro-UFW sympathies among Carian's other workers after he fired the Vitalino crew. More damning, the ALRB pointed to Carian's payroll, which showed he hired replacements in mid-April 1977. "These layoffs could not have been better timed to devastate the union organizational plan," the ALRB agent concluded, for "there would be no peak period until the harvest season as the UFW activists scattered in search of available work, and [thus] the winter campaign would have gone for nought."[14] In the two weeks after the UFW's Mecca-to-Coachella march, Carian had thus fired over eighty farmworkers for their pro-UFW politics. His peak harvest total, meanwhile, was estimated at two hundred.

And yet, Carian was just getting started. In the two months before the June 1977 election, the UFW's organizers entered Carian's property during lunch to speak to farmworkers about the coming election, as protected by ALRA. In response, Carian became even more hostile. He and his supervisors followed UFW organizers as the latter entered Carian's grape fields and they made themselves visible as they listened to farmworker–UFW organizer conversations. They also photographed farmworkers near organizers and repeatedly threatened both. Some even yelled at workers against signing the authorization cards that would trigger an ALRB election.[15] In a telling moment, the Carian farmworker Antonio Bielma responded to UFW entreaties by asking the rhetorical question: "How do you think we can sign with Robert Carian [Carian's son] applying pressure?"[16] In a similar incident, a supervisor's yelling stopped a group of farmworkers from speaking to UFW organizers.

The same supervisor told another group that if he had known they were *Chavistas* he would never have hired them.

Carian workers also faced employer violence and sexual harassment. In June 1977, and less the three weeks from the ALRB-administered election, Carian's son literally drove his truck against four UFW cars to prevent organizers from reaching farmworker crews in Carian's three hundred acres, which was (again) protected by ALRA. After this incident, Carian prohibited the UFW from parking its cars inside Carian's ranch, a prohibition that flirted with violating ALRA's workplace access rule. When the UFW ignored the prohibition, Carian's son returned to attacking organizers, such as driving a tractor against a parked UFW car and forcing the UFW organizer to run back from the fields, where he had been speaking to workers, and move the vehicle to prevent further damage. In another incident, Carian's son drove up to a UFW car heading to a working crew, and then *veered against* it to cause the organizer to crash into a pole. On the very same day, Harry Carian confronted a group of UFW group organizers, pushed one aside, and tried to approach Chavez, before a UFW bodyguard stepped in. A couple weeks later, Carian physically assaulted the bodyguard in a yet another incident.

To undermine UFW momentum, Carian also engaged in rampant sexual harassment. They accused women organizers and sympathizers of being sex workers, promiscuous, and morally tainted. Carian's son and supervisors, for instance, repeatedly asked the UFW organizers, Lucy Crespin and Elizabeth Sullivan, for sexual favors ("how much... for a trick?"), speculated on their sexual behavior ("said she would make a good bed partner"), and promised to "satisfy her" sexually.[17] Carian also distributed a pamphlet that portrayed pro-UFW women as promising male workers (who purportedly had no interest in the UFW) sexual benefits for their pro-UFW votes. "Why don't we go to your house..." the pamphlet's woman worker asked, "I am sure I can teach you the benefits you do NOT have now."[18] To the ALRB, these depictions constituted illegal rancher behavior for they had a "reasonable tendency to discourage woman employees and UFW organizers from continuing organizing activities for the UFW [out of fear] of embarrassment and ridicule, especially so among the Mexican-American and Mexican employees."[19]

Amid all this, Carian laid off another seventeen pro-UFW farmworkers in mid-June 1977, just a week before the ALRB elections. Again, Carian relied on his labor lawyers to justify the firings as reflecting the company's declining labor needs. To maintain impartiality, Carian said, the company decided to dismiss farmworkers who were not living in one of his housing camps. Carian did not note that camp workers, precisely because of their housing dependence, would be more susceptible to his threats and further removed (physically and socially) from UFW organizers. Again, the ALRB found Carian's testimony unreliable and a "pretext for weeding out those employees most sympathetic to the UFW." By this point, Carian had dismissed over *one hundred workers* for pro-UFW sympathies when his peak harvest workforce never surpassed two hundred. He also dismissed farmworkers while threatening the rest. "At the first scarcity of work," his supervisors told the workforce, "all the *Chavistas* [will] be kicked out . . . we know you are illegal, and the rancher will get you out or fire you. If not, immigration will get you, or we will get immigration to take care of you."[20] Still, the UFW ALRA campaign gained more and more farmworker interest, forcing Carian and his supervisors to engage in what can only be described as a union whack-a-mole frenzy.

Unsurprisingly, these dynamics did not end on the election day itself, which fell on June 24, 1977. On the night before, Carian gave a speech to his employees where he "[made] it clear . . . he preferred no union because he thought the [company] and its employees were a harmonious family and that the union would bring problems. He recited the benefits, including medical benefits, that the workers were already enjoying." The UFW organizer present in the meeting tried to contest Carian's claims and to share the union's positions with the farmworker audience. But Carians' supervisor and a handful of anti-UFW farmworkers—almost all male—silenced him. By the late 1970s, the employer practice of forcing workers into employers' anti-union meetings had been effective in diminishing workers' pro-union resolve, and the same intention appears to have shaped Carian's election eve meetings. On election day, furthermore, he instructed his son to hire two busloads of anti-UFW farmworkers to illegally vote against the UFW in Lamont, California, where a simultaneous Carian election took place because the initial organizing unit included his Lamont and Coachella Valley grape fields. In Mecca, Carian's supervisors stood by the voting booths, which violated ALRA rules, to intimidate pro-UFW farmworkers. When the UFW demanded their removal, one Carian supervisor reacted so angrily that he threw a wild punch at a UFW organizer, which mistakenly landed on an ALRB agent.

The end effect of four months of unrelenting illegal behavior was a contested election. Carian received 88 "no union" votes, while the UFW received 80 votes, and 140 ballots were challenged for further review by the ALRB. The UFW filed complaints against Carian's ULPs and, to resolve them, the ALRB spent over three years collecting farmworker, union organizer, and employer interviews, investigating accusations, holding court appearances, and hearing appeals. In October 1980, the ALRB finally provided its decision, which found Carian's actions so egregious that it ruled out the possibility for holding another election. Instead, it adopted the agent's recommendation to set aside the 1977 election and use the initial UFW authorization cards to certify the UFW as the workers' representative. It also ordered Carian to immediately begin contract negotiations, using National Labor Relations Board (NLRB) precedents that similarly ordered contract bargaining after "serious unfair labor practices [interfered] with the election process and tend[ed] to preclude holding a fair election."[21]

There Is No Alternative

Arguably, the ALRB's Carian decision marked a turning point in the Coachella Valley's Rancher Nation. Carian used verbal and physical violence, mass firings, credible threats, and paternalism to keep his farmworkers subjected and pliable—in keeping with his past and the rancher-king's impulse to rule as sovereign.[22] But the ARLB's ruling suddenly denied him his former impunity and flattened the agricultural landscape into a neutral juridical space for farmworkers, ranchers, and union organizers. Like the UFW's 1970 table grape contracts, the Board's decision implied a "constitutional revolution" in Californian agriculture, where the *patron* no longer ruled as "an absolute monarch" with "his private security guards" and "private judges and enforcement system." Now, under state orders to negotiate a UFW contract, Carian again faced the prospects of no longer embodying "life and death" to his employees. Not for nothing, we can note, does the recent scholarship insist on portraying ALRA as the most progressive labor law in the country—as a pro-union tool that could resolve its initial shortcomings.[23]

But such conclusions are woefully disconnected from the dynamics on the ground. Consider ALRA's bureaucratic timeline. The UFW submitted complaints against Carian's unfair labor practices (ULPs) during the thinning season in late March 1977. The administrator law officer (ALO) submitted their first findings in August 1977, held hearings in May 1978, and then completed a second set of findings in December 1978. In each instance, the UFW and Carian appealed the ALO's findings and the ARLB's decisions and ultimately received the ALRB's final order in October 1980, three and a half years after the Carian election and four years after the UFW began the ALRA campaign. In the interim years, the pro-UFW farmworkers who risked and lost their Carian jobs saw no benefits for or potential value in their union involvement. In fact, not one pro-UFW farmworker fired by Carian in early to mid-1977 had a right to their jobs in Carian Ranches until early 1981. By then, UFW organizers discovered, formerly pro-UFW farmworkers questioned the value and efficacy of future UFW campaigns, including negotiating a contract. In turn, those who voted against the UFW—regardless of their motivations—could be imagined as appearing discerning, as being right about unionization's dim odds, or in accepting the boss's paternalism, or in their cynicism about organizer's true intentions.[24]

Only the most egregious ALRA violations, furthermore, received Carian's treatment in the Coachella Valley. Every Coachella Valley grape rancher who faced UFW elections in 1977 perpetrated significant, if not violent, ULPs to undercut pro-UFW support among employees before and during the ALRB elections. For example, Karahadian and his supervisors did not attack UFW organizers; they did not sexually harass pro-UFW workers or call UFW organizers prostitutes, or dismiss entire pro-UFW crews, or pay ineligible crews to vote illegally. But in mid-April 1977, or two weeks after the UFW announced its grape election campaign with a very public march, Karahadian did promise his employees a generous health plan and higher wages (from $2.70 to $3.50). The ALRB's ALO found these actions to be ULPs because they interfered with farmworkers' right to choose a union through "allurement rather than coercion."[25] Citing a bevy of NLRB and ALRB precedents, the ALO pointed to the "fact that wages were raised *exactly* to union scale for that area." The increase was unusually large (30 percent) and paired with the company's anti-union statements.[26] Quoting from *National Labor Relations Board v. Exchange Parts Co.* (1964), the ALO elaborated: "The danger inherent in well-timed increases in benefits is the suggestion of the fist inside the velvet glove . . . [in which] the source of benefits now conferred is also the source from which future benefits must flow and which may dry up if it is not obliged."[27]

This "allurement," furthermore, paralleled Karahadian's legal and illegal anti-union behaviors. As to the former, Karahadian hired the Associated Farmers' consultant, Tony Mendez, in December 1976 to coordinate his campaign and instruct supervisors on avoiding unlawful acts. Among anti-union consultants, this coordination entailed the strategic breaking and bending of labor laws to break worker resolve. Mendez thus organized farmworker meetings that unlawfully connected Karahadian's wage increase and health benefits to a "no union" vote in the upcoming election. The ALO also found Karahadian's supervisors illegally interrogated employees about their union affiliation and/or preference, threatened pro-UFW leaders, and created an atmosphere of surveillance in Karahadian's labor. In June 1977, or two weeks before the grape elections, Karahadian Ranches also fired Maria Elena Ferrel, a key pro-UFW worker–leader who wore pro-UFW buttons, distributed flyers, and publicized her support in a local radio broadcast. Due to Ferrel, a Karahadian supervisor said indignantly, though revealingly: "people were 'losing respect' for her as crew-boss, and 'becoming disorderly.' . . . Before there had been 'no complaints' about anything and now they were 'always complaining about every little thing.'"[28] If Ferrel's presence fostered greater farmworker insubordination in Karahadian fields, as the supervisor lamented, we can imagine that her sudden absence two weeks before the ALRA elections also impacted the workforce's sense of the rancher's power and the risks involved in unionization.

Again, the ALO found Karahadian's behavior undermined the ALRB election's integrity and ALRA's stated purpose to grant farmworkers the right to choose their labor representative, if any. To show how Karahadian's behavior undermined ALRA's purpose, the agent summarized NLRB precedents and academic debates on employers' deleterious impact on unionization, noting how union elections were already "uphill battles" and required more effort from unions and pro-union workers than from employers. These efforts included "getting people to meetings, getting people to sign cards, getting people to read something, and ultimately getting people to make a commitment." Past studies also showed a correlation between workers' lack of union knowledge and their pro-company vote, as well as the rather sobering conclusion that "a substantial majority of undecided and switchers vote company." Even when successful, union vote totals indicated union losses from previously committed votes. In this context, employer behavior played a key role in shaping an election's integrity, thus requiring vigilant regulation from state agencies. Karahadian was not Carian, in other words, but he did not need to be to have undermined the election of June 1977.

The ALRB, however, overruled the ALO's most significant findings. Regarding Karahadian's promise of benefits for anti-UFW votes, the ALRB found they "were declared approximately three months prior to holding a representation election" and did not represent behavior intent on interfering with farmworker rights. The ALRB also disagreed with the ALO's finding that Karahadian's supervisors discriminated against Ferrel for her pro-union politics. It agreed with the ALO's report that Karahadian engaged in illegal farmworker surveillance and harassment, and that he illegally fired Ferrel. But its final order only called for ending the employer's illegal behavior and reinstating Ferrel with backpay. It is unclear what the ALRB expected with verbalizing prohibitions already stated in ALRA's architecture or whether Ferrel would want her job back. What is clear, however, is that the ALRB's final order came in *May 1979*, two entire years after Karahadian's unfair labor practices. The Karahadian ALRA vote, furthermore, remained disputed in late 1979. The ALRB recorded 175 votes for "No Union," 128 votes for the UFW, and 48 challenged ballots, all of whom were grape strikers from 1973. The UFW needed every challenged ballot to win the election, so when the ALRB sustained Karahadian's challenges to four challenged ballots, it automatically spelled the UFW's defeat. The ALRB's final decision in November 1979 stated the obvious: "in view of our finding that a majority of the valid votes were cast for 'No Labor Organization,' and because more than one year has lapsed since the election, we hereby dismiss the objections to the election as moot."

At Mel-Pak Vineyards, the ALRB similarly found an extensive list of employer ULPs, including worker surveillance, discriminatory dismissals of pro-UFW workers, and "granting, promising and announcing . . . increased wages, a new medical plan, an employee party, refreshments in the field, a new break time and a new recall system [for supervisors]."[29] The UFW also competed against *two* company unions *and* a "no union" campaign. And yet, the results remained tantalizingly close with a tally of 142 pro-UFW votes out of 292. The rest broke down as fifty-five for "no union," ninety for the two company unions combined, and five pro-UFW ballots challenged by Mel-Pak. Again, the UFW needed all challenged ballots to win the election and the ALRB's decision in one reflected the latter's failure to consider agriculture's distinctiveness. In the case of Beatriz de Bautista's challenged vote, the ALRB ruled against counting the ballot because she had attempted to return to Mel-Pak weeks after participating in the UFW's 1973 Coachella Grape Strike. De Bautista said she made the job solicitation as a "joke" and did not gain it. Under ALRA, grape strikers from 1973 could participate in elections involving their former employers. De Bautista's claim to be joking when requesting her former job sought to safeguard her right to vote in the Mel-Pak election. Still, the ALRB ruled against her and cited National Labor Relations Act (NLRA) precedent recognizing an economic striker's vote only if they solicited their former jobs to "protect . . . unemployment benefits."[30]

Agriculture, however, was not industry. The ALRB, for instance, did not consider farmworkers' lack of unemployment insurance in 1973 or that the impulse behind the NLRB case—namely, economic survival and not political choice—also shaped de Bautista's attempt to regain her job after striking in 1973. Given farmworkers' underemployment and the below-industry wages, the lack of social provisions and the greater costs related to migration, one could argue that such economic survival tactics (i.e., strikebreaking) rang truer for farmworkers than for the industrial laborers informing the ALRB's decision. When the ALRB decided against de Bautista in late 1979, it also ruled that the UFW failed to gain an outright majority and called for a runoff election among the most current workforce between the UFW and one of the company unions. That is, the ARLB called for a 1980 harvest election (three years after the initial vote) without the pro-UFW farmworkers who were fired by Mel-Pak in the 1977 ALRA campaign.

Every single union election in Coachella Valley grape ranches in 1977 had similar numbers and types of rancher ULPs.[31] Each election was an uphill battle driven by courageous women and men, each one an interplay between workers and organizers, workers and bosses, and workers and workers. Each was also an elaboration of the ranchers' tenacious impunity. The ALRB's failure to prevent unlawful behavior in the campaigns themselves meant it only resolved the 1977 elections between late 1979 and 1981, anchoring the UFW movement to a lethargic and toothless bureaucratic structure. In the interim period, the UFW could not gain certification as the workers' labor representative nor negotiate a contract to prove its value to those who risked unionization. Pro-UFW farmworkers fired by anti-union grape ranchers, furthermore, could not return to their former jobs until the ALRB provided its final decisions, which meant that many pro-union rank-and-file leaders left agricultural jobs to work in the region's growing westside tourism industry. As it approached the new decade, the UFW thus faced waning farmworker militancy, a dearth of new union dues, and limited means for gaining a labor contract. A decade later, the ALRB also limited the UFW's right to mount boycotts when it was not the certified labor representative, regardless if past elections had been lost due to rancher ULPs.[32] The result was that the much-vaunted ALRA failed to secure fair elections for farmworkers or provide an avenue to effectively contest rancher power.

Recent critical histories have argued the UFW's ALRA fortunes in the Coachella Valley reflected the union's internal weaknesses, especially Chavez's leadership. The UFW, for instance, could only trigger ALRA elections among 40 percent of the Coachella Valley's grape fields because of purportedly widespread anti-UFW grape worker sentiment. The UFW still chose to organize Coachella Valley grapes, the histories continue, because an autocratic Chavez held an irrationally sentimental relationship to grape workers as the UFW's original membership. He also sought a Chavez-alinged grape-member region to counterweight the increasingly assertive lettuce farmworkers in the Salinas and Imperial valleys, whom Chavez saw as aligned with Marshall Ganz, a potential union rival. In this scholarship, in other words, the Coachella Valley grape election defeats in 1977 did not illustrate ALRA failures, but instead an increasingly weak UFW due to its lack of union democracy and Chavez's cultish leadership. The UFW, especially Chavez, only had itself to blame for its failed mission. In one account, the historian simply said the Coachella Valley grape elections were "all in all . . . relatively free elections."[33]

Several points need to be made in this respect. First, the grape workers who participated in ALRB elections represented 40 percent of the Coachella Valley's nonunionized grape workers, who were themselves two-thirds of the region's entire grape workforce. The other third were the pro-UFW farmworkers in Steinberg's Freedman Ranch, the largest grape employer in the region. In other words, the purported anti-UFW animus in the Coachella Valley was smaller than implied by the scholars' statistics. Second, it remains unclear if the UFW failed to hold more grape elections because of local anti-union animus or because of its limited capacity. In 1977, the UFW was engaged in a frenetic number of ALRA elections, which cumulatively stretched its limited volunteer corps.[34] Third, the UFW rationale for advancing an ALRA grape campaign in the Coachella Valley involved more than Chavez's nostalgic authoritarianism. The Teamster contracts expired in 1977, offering the UFW an opportunity to regain their former fields. More importantly, the year was the last opportunity for 1973 grape strikers to vote in ALRA elections involving their former employers, as mandated by ALRA specifications.[35] Fourth, the argument that the local anti-UFW animus originated in the early 1970s failings oversimplifies workers' complex relationship to unionization and to the workforce's diversity. It also simply ignores the fact that Coachella Valley grape ranchers purged their *Chavista* employees in 1973.

But, even if we were to grant the scholarship's criticism, ALRA's fundamental failures remained and over-determined the UFW's presence (or non-presence) in the Coachella Valley and in California. The law failed to deter ranchers' flagrantly illegal behavior and impeded workers' choice, which ALRB agents readily and repeatedly recognized. Critically, this failure had systemic consequences. It meant the UFW movement could not gain contracts to then court the presumably anti-UFW fields in the late 1970s. Even when it won an "uphill" election, the UFW's overall weak position empowered ranchers to stonewall subsequent contract negotiations. At the same time, and still without new union dues, the UFW's lettuce workers led a series of strikes in 1979 and 1980 that hobbled the union with a budget crisis. Like the rest of organized labor, this budget crisis undercut the UFW's ability to service its remaining contracts, much less expand into other fields.[36] So, when the ARLB released its final decisions in the early 1980s, the UFW faced the prospects of re-starting their grape campaign in the Coachella Valley from ground zero— or less than zero given the deteriorating economy, a spectacularly anti-union government, and an AFL-CIO membership in free fall. Even if the UFW had enough hubris to embark on another round of grape elections, it knew Coachella Valley ranchers would commit the same ULPs in a context of less worker militancy, less union resources, or higher rancher odds—all for elections involving relatively small, single ranches out of many more ranches in one small valley in a very large state. By the early 1980s, the election results sang the same old threat: there is no alternative to the Rancher Nation.

"A Vicious Cycle": U.S. Labor Before and After Reagan

The UFW's fate in the Coachella Valley had echoes throughout the state and reflected the fate of all U.S. unions in these years. To address this, however, I need to extend the above discussion on the critical scholarship. In the latter, the UFW declined in proportion to Chavez's deteriorating psychology after the defeat of Proposition 14 (1976). Chavez, it argues, refused to take responsibility or admit his "crusade" exhausted the UFW resources prior to ALRA elections in 1977.[37] Instead, he purged boycott volunteers, who he said sabotaged the proposition.[38] He also jettisoned the legal department in 1978 when UFW lawyers requested salary raises. Against the counsel of advisors, Chavez abolished the sector that could contest ULPs and facilitate future elections. Chavez thus undermined UFW strengths at the very moment the Teamsters abandoned field organizing and California re-funded the ALRB. He also instituted a cult-like "game," where friends, relatives, and coworkers attacked each other with shockingly personal insults. Chavez even led an attack on his only critic on the National Executive Board, Philip Vera Cruz, forcing Vera Cruz's resignation and serving as a model for disciplining other rivals. In the next four years, Chavez attacked Eliseo Medina, Marshall Ganz, Jessica Govea, Gil Padilla, and Jerry Cohen. All left the UFW by 1981 and all were allegedly replaced with Chicana/o sycophants. Finally, when the UFW's independent Salinas Valley members had the temerity to nominate two of their own for National Executive Board positions, Chavez led an all-out assault that further weakened the union.[39]

The scholarship, in short, finds the UFW's central problem as organizational: without democratic locals, the UFW movement unmoored itself from farmworker accountability and became susceptible to Chavez's authoritarian impulses. Much like a mad king surrounded by a corrupt (Chicana/o) nobility, a manic Chavez tore away at everything he and others had built, unconsciously killing the very prospect of a farmworker union to save his position within it. As the title of the leading historical account argues, Chavez grabbed defeat "from the jaws of victory."

Whether the scholarship's description of Chavez is accurate needs to be addressed by other scholars. For now, however, we must separate Chavez's purported behavior from its effect on the UFW movement. Chavez may very well have behaved in such authoritarian forms. But we would do well to recognize that such authoritarianism shaped the UFW movement since its inception. It was widely shared among strikers in 1965 and it was legitimized by strikers' years of sacrifices. In fact, it characterized the very leaders Chavez would subsequently purge, such as Philip Vera Cruz.[40] It also served as a form of community discipline, with union stalwarts pushing coworkers to sacrifice more to strengthen their union and receive union benefits. In the early 1970s, for instance, Coachella Valley militants instituted fines on co-unionists for missing UFW meetings. They also disregarded member complaints about dues, and took to calling those averse to greater sacrifice as being mere "members of convenience"—who only appeared when promised union handouts. In these instances, they were very much Vera Cruz's political kin. Most would likely have agreed with his damning assertion about critical members: "we are better off without you."⁴¹ But this early authoritarianism did not lead to the union's implosion, or to any leader dissent, or to an effective rank and file rebellion.⁴²

To hold this authoritarianism/union-weakness argument, the scholarship has also overlooked the secondary literature on U.S. union decline in the 1970s and 1980s. In *Knocking on Labor's Door*, Lane Windham found that U.S. unions triggered as many NLRB elections as in the previous two decades, illustrating union enthusiasm among workers who were increasingly non-white, women, immigrants, and younger. But, employers also intensified anti-union tactics, including the hiring of anti-union consultants, engaging in pervasive and egregious unfair labor practices, and relying on weak NLRB provisions to isolate workers and push for "no union."⁴³ One in three NLRB elections included the discriminatory firing of at least one pro-union worker and nearly all contained barely legal employer speech that equated a pro-union vote with a future company bankruptcy or a worker-debilitating strike.⁴⁴ Without repercussions, these anti-union campaigns dropped the union election victory rate from 80 percent in the 1940s, when they were either illegal or less common, to less than 50 percent in 1977.⁴⁵

American employers' anti-union hostility had roots in the 1960s, when they became increasingly active in political campaigns and advanced anti-labor reforms to undercut unions.⁴⁶ But what was initially piecemeal, Windham showed, became a concerted effort to weaken the NLRA, install pro-employer NLRB members, and isolate all unions. This concerted effort took place during the economic, political, and cultural whiplash of the 1970s and 1980s. Critically, anti-union employers defeated union campaigns in the entire United States.⁴⁷ Even when unions managed to overcome employer hostility in private-sector elections, and won an election majority, nearly *two of out five election victories* failed to gain a union contract, deflating worker militancy and union power.⁴⁸ The UFW's fortunes echoed U.S. labor history, which offered little evidence that "democratic" and "radical" unions could leverage good politics into better contracts.

The AFL-CIO also understood it needed to reform the NLRA's anti-labor provisions, such as employers' free speech (e.g., tacit bankruptcy threats), permanent striker replacement, and the lack of repercussions for using strikes to destroy unions. Labor leaders wanted to simplify the arduous two-step process for union certification because it aided employer counter-organizing. To stress, the NLRA was not especially worse than ALRA.⁴⁹ Furthermore, the labor reforms the AFL-CIO pushed in 1977–78 echoed the UFW's Proposition 14, including quick elections, access to workplaces, double back pay for discriminatory firing, greater repercussions for labor violations, and a larger NLRB to expedite cases.[50] The AFL-CIO's bill, however, failed to get a majority in Congress after corporations presented small businesses as potential victims of Big Labor's power-hungry and antidemocratic maneuver—echoing grape rancher assertions in 1973. "Corporate leaders," Windham dryly noted, "who once sought to reshape labor law now defended it, because it was so weak."[51] Feeling betrayed, many industrial unions asked in a *Wall Street Journal* ad, "Why? What is your motivation? . . . where is the moral basis for your attacks? . . . Do you want to destroy American trade unionism?"[52]

Of course, the answer was yes. Committed to ending an effective labor law, U.S. capital and its political allies prepared for an opportunity to fully undermine unions. That came in 1980 with Ronald Reagan's election to the presidency and a decade-long debilitating budget shortfall that limited union campaigns to expand their base. For Windham, the latter hastened a "vicious [downward] cycle," in which the NLRA's weak provisions pushed unions away from new elections and, as a result, further weakened them by isolating their members in an increasingly anti-union and union-free political economy.[53]

By early 1980s, this vulnerable position gave way to unions' all-out decimation. The 1981–1982 recession wiped out entire industrial union densities, heightened the public budget crises, and triggered another vicious downward cycle. Ronald Reagan's NLRB appointments halted the Board's reviews, while the much-publicized attack on the air controllers' strike of 1981 led to a labor "chill."[54] To John Logan, the U.S. replacement of air controller strikers "represented a watershed moment that . . . legitimized the use of permanent replacements" to rid companies of their unions. For the rest of the decade, employers repeatedly used the bargaining table to goad unions into strikes and then used the strike to "replace economic striker[s] [and] unload unwanted unions."[55] From their 1954 peak of 35 percent, union percentages declined to 30 percent in 1960, 23 percent in 1980, 15 percent in 1985, and 12 percent in 1990.[56] As Windham concluded, "It is not enough to blame lousy labor leaders or an individualistic working-class culture for labor's decline. Employer resistance to organizing was a far more effective culprit, coupled with U.S. policies and laws that enabled . . . this employer behavior."[57]

Arguably, the downward spiral of nonagricultural unions marked their relative privilege vis-à-vis California's farmworkers. The former had gained labor protections in the 1930s and grew their numbers in the near-client state of the World War II period. They also achieved their greatest social mobility in the postwar giddy affluence predicated on military industries, global economic hegemony, and Keynesian economics. Their members were primarily white, male, and citizens, and with close (if less than ideal) ties to New Deal politicians. They had enough social height, in other words, from which to spiral downward. In contrast, the UFW movement won contracts in California's table grapes when U.S. employers had already perfected their anti-union practices and amidst a rising revanchist political culture. For the next decade, the UFW faced wars of attrition in every field and constant opposition in contracted fields and in local, state, and national governments. Like other unions, the UFW confronted an economic recession in the early 1980s; but unlike them, it also sought to organize an extra-marginalized workforce, whose outsized poverty reflected generational and structural racism, state neglect and/or repression, and transnational economic disruption.[58] The UFW elections in places like the Coachella Valley were thus the stifled attempts to spiral upwards, attempts instantly halted by the same forces decimating formerly powerful unions. In a few years, little of the UFW movement's brief promise could be felt in many parts of California's agricultural landscape.

Two additional factors differentiate the UFW's efforts from those of industrial labor and highlight the sources of the UFW's defeat. First, the UFW faced a mobile and variously positioned labor force, one that was primarily Mexican immigrant, increasingly undocumented, and cyclically migratory. We do not need to engage in xenophobic depictions of immigrants to note that many could not readily join UFW strikes or join unions for fear of strikes, because of their juridical vulnerability and/or commitments to families and communities in Mexico—much like the braceros of chapter 2. But, even if Mexican immigrants in the late 1970s and early 1980s held a decontextualized radicalism, it still meant the UFW movement had to extend nonexisting resources to draw immigrants into its campaign—to visit their homes and share plans, to speak of past campaigns and make promises of risk-managed strikes. In this regard, industrial unions faced easier prospects and most were still largely destroyed.

Second, the UFW movement faced a near-Sisyphean project of organizing a shape-shifting industry in one state in a national economy increasingly shaped by transnational trade. Even if the UFW won its late 1970s ALRA elections, it still contended with agribusiness's ownership schemes. In Oxnard, for instance, the UFW leader Eliseo Medina led a campaign against the Coastal Growers Association and won a sweeping victory in the late 1970s.[59] But, just as sweepingly, ranchers simply left the association and turned to labor contractors, who offered union-free labor.[60] In Santa Cruz, strawberry ranchers adopted sharecropping in the late 1970s and 1980s to make the UFW an irrelevant force.[61] Throughout California, agribusiness fought UFW contracts with phony bankruptcies, sales to subsidiaries, and greater mechanization. The UFW attempted to respond, but the whack-a-mole quality of organizing agriculture without state allies or an effective union law challenged any potential efficacy.[62] If this does not dampen spirits, questions remain. What would the UFW need to do in Reagan's America to organize all of agriculture, given that ranchers claimed UFW contracts placed California at a competitive disadvantage? How would the UFW respond to rising numbers of imported and exported crops? How would the UFW regain legal protections and consumer support when both had already declined? How would it do so in states outside California?[63]

Organized labor's overall losses in the late twentieth-century United States challenge us to abandon arguments that place the UFW's defeat squarely in the hands of a mad king. We can certainly fault Chavez's behavior, speak of our dismayed discoveries, even sympathize with victimized white volunteers. But if we wish to speak of cause and effect, of contexts and contingency, then we must move beyond the abusive paternal figure who beats his figurative children and upholds his racialized community's oppression. Admittedly, the UFW did manage to win some elections and contracts in these years, as did all labor. But, these victories were only the exceptions to a rancher victory—the last sparks of promise in a dusk already giving way to night, engulfing the whole country as much as the Coachella Valley.

"I'm Tired of Fighting"

In late 1970s Coachella Valley, as in the state, UFW membership remained anemic, only to decline further in the early 1980s. And yet, oral histories generally could not point to a moment when the union's fortunes turned for the worse, when loss was apparent and unavoidable. If pressed, interviewees usually spoke of Chavez's death in 1993, a surprise event that shook many to their core. It was then, many said, that the UFW's leadership appeared disappointing, though they readily admitted the union had already lost much of its strength.

Most strikingly, oral histories recounting this period almost always expressed confidence that the UFW would remain a permanent staple of Coachella Valley life. Union contracts still protected them from rancher abuses, paid wages higher than previously imagined, and provided a host of benefits. These contracts also improved all grape worker wages and conditions in the Coachella Valley, as local ranchers attempted to avoid unionization by matching UFW gains.[64] In an interview in 1978, the Filipino leader Willie Barrientos shared as much when he recounted the UFW's history and listed the benefits they had won since 1965: work restrooms, daily rests, higher wages, shade structures. "Why do we have these things," he asked rhetorically, "because of the Union. The people get together. And still, we are fighting, I hope."[65] In this same period, women like Maria Serrano and Petra Ruiz continued to fight for leadership positions in Freedman Ranch, contesting both male coworkers and supervisors. Even in 1980, when the UFW haphazardly renegotiated its Freedman contract, and in the process provoked rank-and-file criticism, farmworkers still won a near $5 hour wage and expanded employer benefits. The wage increase marked a fourfold wage increase in a decade and forced the Coachella Valley's anti-union ranchers to match it.[66] For some union grape workers, the Rancher Nation could appear increasingly tamed, even if not defeated, in the new decade.

Similar conditions continued to shape farmworker life in the UFW's non-grape fields. David Perez had already lost faith the UFW could organize the Coachella Valley, but he still worked under a UFW contract that secured higher pay, job security, and benefits.[67] He served as a UFW representative until 1986, he said, in a "good job" where he felt "respected." For Hilario Torres, these years also represented his greatest involvement in the UFW. Besides higher wages and job security, contracts also restrained supervisors' behavior: they treated workers carefully, he said, in the late 1970s and early 1980s.[68] Similarly, Leonor Suarez only entered the UFW in 1978, after migrating from Washington state, where she had worked since childhood. For the next ten years, Suarez and her husband worked in Coachella Valley Citrus and earned a living wage for less than eight hours a day. The work was difficult, Suarez said, and the periodic UFW stoppages initially frustrated her. But then she gave birth to her youngest child in 1979 and the UFW health insurance covered their medical bills. "From there," she said, she and her husband "started to learn what the union was about [and] I realized the union was good." She dived into union life, used her English to speak to supervisors, took union classes to replace her interrupted schooling, and joined negotiations, where "the boss was here, and I was here [next to him]."[69] "I learned a lot," she said, "it opened my eyes." For workers like Suarez and Torres, UFW contracts in the late 1970s and early 1980s continued to offer dignified work, one that spurred personal and political growth, fostered their leadership, and reshaped what they once considered possible.

Similar stories appeared in the oral histories of other UFW workers during these years, including those of Salvador Ramirez, Filogonio Angel, Remedios Martinez, Federico Vargas, Antonio Puga Torres, and Arturo Diaz. I have not introduced most of these workers for lack of space, but they collectively expressed a continued sense of possibility that echoed farmworkers in the mid-1960s, grape union members in the early 1970s, or the Coachella strikers of 1973. As a field of stories, the UFW movement still drew farmworkers into its worlds, while farmworkers (in turn) continued to sustain the union when all U.S. labor faced an unprecedented attack.

In this union potential, few spoke of apparent decline, much less of a future without the UFW. Arguably, such a sense of union permanence already existed when Victor Salandini interviewed Coachella Valley grape workers in the mid-1970s, when most spoke of unionization as a fact of life regardless of their union preference. Perhaps the real growth in union contracts in the Coachella Valley following ALRA elections in 1975 had substantiated such assumptions. And perhaps, having just been introduced to union protections and to a coterie of co-unionists and events outside the Coachella Valley, or having just joined union actions after several years of sitting on the sidelines, or having just taken a position of leadership that defied what was once considered possible—perhaps in such a moment of transition and possibility, local UFW members could not consider the possibility that such victories existed within a plane of union decline. Even Perez's attempt to alert his co-unionists of such a reality only provoked charges of betraying their still-growing revolution, of having lost the faith.

But as with U.S. labor, UFW members in the Coachella Valley existed in a bifurcated space, one in which their union immersion may have denied them the means to see union losses in the economy, and which would eventually undermine their isolated union. For Hilario Torres, the bifurcation became apparent in 1979 when coworkers elected him ranch committee president. From that position he saw the union's unevenness. His employer grew citrus, row crops, and dates, Torres noticed, which meant the UFW represented workers with varying levels of bargaining power. Date farmworkers were the most powerful because their work made replacing them difficult and thus strengthened their ability to mount strikes. Such power became visible when the company stalled negotiations in 1980 and date farmworkers reacted by planning a strike during the date pollination season. An arduous and critical process, the pollination season was the company's Achilles' heel, which workers could exploit to force the company to change its tune and sign another UFW contract that covered more than the date fields.

But not all companies had such vulnerabilities, Torres added. While his employer signed new contracts, other citrus and vegetable companies without date workers undermined the UFW by using labor contractors, bankruptcies, and company sales. Local labor contractors drew from a large workforce from the Mexicali Valley, approximately 90-minutes' drive away, and from the rising numbers of immigrants fleeing Mexico's economic downturn in the early 1980s. In need and with few resources, these workers became a malleable force in rural California and the Coachella Valley—both socially vulnerable to labor contractor disciplining while also culturally indebted to labor contractor aid in an otherwise stark economy. By the mid-1980s, the Coachella Valley membership remained anemic, even if unionized fields continued to provide empowering spaces to UFW members. The latter were increasingly reduced to contracts with Freedman and a few citrus and vegetable ranchers, incapable of stopping ranchers' union evasion scheme or expanding with a weak labor law. The local chapter, weak and isolated, could no longer imagine restructuring the Coachella Valley's political economy, as it once did. It was increasingly invisible to the new families entering its fields.

At the end, Torres concluded, the UFW movement could not "outlast the rancher."[70] Despite its ALRB victories in 1979–81, and despite the enthusiasm of many rank-and-file workers like Suarez and Torres, the UFW no longer represented a threat to the Rancher Nation. Instead, its few victories were faint traces of promise already defeated—much like smoke from contained fire, already less than glowing embers. This defeat took place just as the rest of the UFW's membership declined in the early 1980s, when it found itself reduced to boycotting the very legal structure that was supposed to be farmworkers' Magna Carta.

Such a reality of limits, defeats, and exhaustion confronted Luciano Crespo when he arrived in the Coachella Valley in 1983 as the UFW's final (and ninth since 1970) office director for its Coachella office.[71] Originally from Delano and of mixed Filipino Mexican background, Crespo literally grew up in the UFW movement. He was ten years old when he joined his grandmother on their first NFWA meetings in late 1962 and early 1963. He was twelve when his grandmother and mother, and many of his impoverished neighbors, joined the 1965 Delano Grape Strike and stayed on the migrating picket line for the next five years, in poverty and social ostracism. In adolescence, Crespo celebrated the UFW's 1970 contract victory in California table grapes and then chose UFW union organizing over college attendance after the Teamsters raided the San Joaquin Valley table grape fields in 1973. In the next decade, he organized in nearly every corner of California; led boycott campaigns on the east coast, New York City, and Canada; learned how to fundraise, negotiate contracts, and lobby wayward politicians. The UFW tested him, challenged him, exhausted him, denied him stability or small luxuries. But it gave him a radical education, took him to many towns and cities, and introduced him to a loving union family, where he would meet his future wife, Lupe Crespo. It also made him feel powerful, capable, and valuable. "I wasn't told I was smart," he said, by way of examples, "until I joined the UFW."[72]

Assigned to the Coachella Valley in 1983, Crespo immediately took over the unfinished ALRA campaigns in table grape ranches. The UFW still had contracts with two small grape companies (300–350 workers) and Freedman (1,000 workers), which collectively accounted for nearly a third of the local grape harvest workforce. Crespo was tasked with negotiating contracts with four companies where the UFW had been certified as the labor representative, but where ranchers had also stalled negotiations. When he arrived, Crespo discovered the dynamics already visible before the 1977 ALRB elections.

He learned pro-UFW worker-leaders in ALRA campaigns never returned to their jobs after they were illegally fired by ranchers. They found work elsewhere and "moved on," he said. Those who had not been fired, but who weathered a hostile election and then five years of apparent union inaction, were discouraged and embittered with the UFW. Some simply did not want to fight any more: "I'm tired of fighting," they told him. The rest, almost all new farmworkers, were largely unaware of former campaigns and often did not know about the UFW certification. Most also did not know of the UFW's role in raising local wages and work benefits, even when ranchers adopted them as anti-union tactics. Still, Crespo organized new leaders and restarted their campaigns. As before, ranchers blocked worker access, threatened and/or demoted pro-union leaders to undercut worker resolve, and provoked the necessary questions: why get involved, what do you gain with speaking out?[73]

Crespo did get traction among the workers of Cardinal Distributors, which grew grapes, row crops, and citrus. He identified former campaign leaders, who he moved from bitterness to renewed ambition. Together, they created a bargaining committee, organized coworkers (who appeared receptive), and pressured the company to negotiate a contract. But then the UFW moved him abruptly (though temporarily) to another campaign—very much in keeping with the union's history. La Paz assured him somebody would be assigned to the Cardinal campaign. But when he returned, he discovered to his utter disappointment that nothing had been achieved in his six-month absence, a period that ended the workers' tentative hope.

It is unclear what possibilities existed for Crespo in 1983. By then, local, regional, and national shifts in culture, politics, and economics made any vision of a unionized agricultural landscape in the Coachella Valley (or anywhere in California) increasingly far fetched, at best. Already defeated, the UFW moved in a deflated desperation—pushing forth legal cases, reanimating campaigns in certified fields, speaking still of a union future—that convinced no one, neither workers, nor ranchers, nor union organizers like Crespo. "I'm tired of fighting," Crespo heard, "I'm tired of fighting." He did not share their social and existential exhaustion in 1983, but he would in 1987, when he and his growing family packed up their few possessions and left the UFW's run-down apartment, envisioning a life of social justice outside unionized agriculture.

Conclusion: The Rancher-King's Body

In 1974, Fausto Figueroa was a twenty-one-year-old newlywed and a new immigrant to the United States. He grew up in a small town in Michoacán, Mexico, and was the second oldest of fourteen children; he had only known work by the time he immigrated, he said, from a childhood of caring for animals and the family's *ejidos* to an adolescence in construction and a mechanic shop. There was little school in his life or the lives of his friends, though Figueroa still had vague memories of having small school books when he was a boy. When he married in late 1973, the young couple made plans to build their house and establish a mechanic shop, where Figueroa could be his own boss. He immigrated to the United States with such expectations and obligations, not unlike young Filipino men a half century before and the many Mexican immigrant families since. And, like both, he found mostly difficulties; less jobs and pay than he imagined, he said, and more Border Patrol raids and a quicker than expected deportation.

His second trip in 1976 was more successful. His older brother, who had already found work in KK Larson's grape ranch, secured Figueroa housing and employment. The supervisor, Jesus Contreras, was known for helping undocumented immigrants. Figueroa did not know Contreras's relationship to the UFW or Contreras's previous treatment of his employees. He only knew he had finally found a life opportunity—"si vienen las oportunidades, entonces que aprovechar"—and began to expand his visions of possibility back home: a restroom inside the house he still had not built, an extra set of rooms, more money to help his twelve younger siblings. When asked what he thought of the UFW in the mid- to late 1970s, he said he never learned much about the union. He knew there was a rivalry between the UFW and Larson, but he did not know its origin or points of contention. Contreras and other contractors kept UFW organizers out of the ranch and kept workers away from organizers. When workers asked about the union and its message, the bosses said workers did not need a union—that they were already paid well, that they had jobs, and that they were protected from immigration raids.

There was truth to the contractors' claims. In the late 1970s, Figueroa made more than he had in his life; he also had free housing and felt safe from the Border Patrol; he even brought his family to the Coachella Valley. And when Figueroa became near fatally ill in the early 1980s and required surgery from his neck to his pelvis, the Larson health plan covered all the medical costs. If some farmworkers first became acquainted with the UFW movement through its member benefits, especially its health insurance and near-free clinics, then Figueroa's near-death experience validated his assessment of Larson as a generous employer. Without the region's local history, he could not see Larson's benefits and wages as an attempt to prevent unionization by making it obsolete. He also saw no ill will, or exploitation, when Larson subsequently asked him to repeatedly show his surgery-scarred body to grape buyers. "Show them my famous body," Larson would instruct. Figueroa said that he did not understand the ritual, but we can imagine that these buyers may have wished to address lingering criticism of worker exploitation, and that for them Figueroa's body evidenced rancher generosity. At the end of each harvest, he would thus unbutton and remove his work shirt and then peel off his undershirt to show the scar down his torso. His famous body, his and the rancher's.

In January 1986, the UFW's former head lawyer, Jerry Cohen, wrote an opinion piece for the *Los Angeles Times* on the state of farmworker living and working conditions in California, calling for the UFW to "return to the basics": "only day-to-day organizing by the farm workers' union can help these people assert their legal right in an effective manner." While recognizing that California's conservative government had sided with ranchers, Cohen still insisted the UFW had "the capability to ensure that [it] fulfills its potential." Besides the boycott and the picket line, the UFW had "ALRA, which is quite simply the best labor law in America." He listed ALRA's "elements," for which "most unions would gladly give their eye-teeth," and which the UFW had discarded before the hostile governor was sworn in. If anyone was responsible for the "UFW's failure as yet to fulfill its promise," it was Chavez. Cohen had left the UFW in 1981; it is unclear what he hoped to achieve with his column. What is clear is that he did not understand ALRA's limitations, the multiple challenges facing the UFW in the mid-1980s, or labor leaders' assessment of all U.S. labor law. No one, in other words, would have paid with their "eye-teeth" for ALRA, and no one would have celebrated its elements. Only Cohen, who like a white father blinded by pride and self-regard, insisted he had given California's nonwhite farmworkers a critical "asset" for their movement: "the best labor law in America."

As Figueroa's life attests, the real world was far less encouraging for the UFW than Cohen believed. Like all U.S. labor law, ALRA was deeply flawed, both toothless and glacial. It was, in effect, a godsend to ranchers and consumers: the former could break the law with abandon and face no repercussions; the latter could pretend they cared about farmworkers and offer nothing. By the 1980s, the Rancher Nation in the Coachella Valley had managed to reconstitute itself enough that even former allies like Cohen could only find fault with the UFW leadership, while ranchers like Larson could display a person's body to undercut unionization—and be praised for it.

Chapter 10

Here Is Where We Meet

In October 1990, Cesar Chavez visited the Coachella Valley to dedicate the first school named after him, Cesar Chavez Elementary, near Coachella's newer housing. The name was the work of United Farm Workers (UFW) members and Chicana/o activists, and the students slated to attend were Mexican and Mexican American, the great majority the children of farmworkers. In his dedication speech, Chavez spoke about his family's history in migrant labor in the 1930s and the dozen schools he attended before the eighth grade, a reality that still shaped the lives of many students in the Coachella Valley. Chavez then turned to the history of farmworker sacrifice in the UFW movement to advocate for an education that transcended "teach[ing] our young people to be successful."[1] "We cannot," he said, "seek achievement for ourselves and forget about progress and prosperity for our community. Our ambitions must be broad enough to include the aspirations of others. For their sakes *and* for our own" (emphasis in original). He also rejected "discourage[ment]" and "pessimis[m]" despite the UFW's emaciated membership in 1990. "The future is ours!," he exclaimed, predicting that in "twenty and thirty years, the great cities and valleys of our state . . . will be dominated by farm workers and not by [ranchers] . . . History and inevitability are on our side."[2]

I was seven years old in 1990, the eldest of two and soon-to-be three children. My parents worked, and would work for the rest of their lives, in the Coachella Valley's fields and packing houses, golf courses, retail stores, and country clubs. They had met in 1983 in a Thermal packinghouse when both were nineteen years old, but from disparate worlds: my father, a tattooed, English-speaking Mexican American with at least four family generations in the United States; my mother, a Spanish-speaking immigrant from Mexico, highly educated and ambitious, part of an undocumented immigration wave in the 1970s and 1980s.[3] When Chavez gave his speech, our family lived in Thermal's public housing, a collection of simple two-story buildings and ample green space for fifty families. Though far from perfect, our community was a stark contrast to the substandard housing available to most farmworkers in the Coachella Valley. Nearly all our neighbors were Spanish-speaking Mexican immigrants working in nearby fields and packinghouses. I knew already, at seven years old, that my family and neighbors did not have money for anything. I even credited my early math skills to childhood worries over money: having learned multiplication tables in the second grade, I spent entire days calculating what a five cent, ten cent, twenty-five cent raise would mean for our family and our neighbors.

Because I lived in Thermal, I would not attend Cesar Chavez Elementary, which was just as well for my young self because I thought the school was named after the Mexican boxer, *Julio* Cesar Chavez, and I was not impressed.[4] If my parents had been at the school's dedication, they also would not have known about Chavez or the UFW movement. My parents, like nearly all our neighbors, moved in a world without the UFW and Chavez's sense of inevitability. Most adults, I imagine, would have agreed with his vision for education. But a future that was ours? By 1990, not only were rancher-kings as strong as ever, but the Coachella Valley's westside luxury development added another layer of poverty-paying jobs to service a politically regressive community that refused to relinquish its hold on rural California.[5] Today, thirty years after Chavez's speech, neither the Coachella Valley nor the rest of rural California is dominated by farmworkers and their children. Instead, the Rancher Nation breathes and pulses with an unrelenting vigor, even if occasionally overshadowed by rural resorts and their luxury leisure.

In this final chapter, I wish to consider the afterlives and implications of the UFW and Chicana/o movements, as well as the longed-for combination of "history and inevitability." I caution against memorialized utopias, those tired visions of boundless resistance, as well as single villain narratives, and museums eliding the contradiction between history and inevitability. This book, if anything, insists that no future is inevitable, that it never was, that possibilities are not guarantees, that we are left, today, to ourselves, to each other, and to our shared and often fragmented stories. Without a history that can assure our future, we are left in/with the present, with our sense of what is right and wrong, what is possible and not, what can be sacrificed and what must be held dear. If there is a concise lesson, then it is that History offers us nothing more than the reminder that nothing is permanent, and that, without grasping for guarantees, we can still move to each other today and to the world we wish to inhabit.

What's Left for Me

It is unclear to me whether Chavez's optimism at the dedication was sincere. Perhaps he thought of earlier times when possibilities seemed similarly dismal, such as when he left his stable job in 1962 to organize farmworkers with few resources or clear paths. He had worried about his family's well-being then, as did his wife, Helen.[6] The other National Farm Worker Association (NFWA) organizers, Dolores Huerta and Gilbert Padilla, also worried, as did the San

Joaquin Valley families who joined these early efforts, when risks overwhelmed potential.[7] Perhaps Chavez imagined a similarly unlikely trajectory for the Coachella Valley at the end of the twentieth century. In 1965, he had written in *El Malcriado* that social movements erupted when "a group of people begins to care enough that they are willing to make sacrifices."[8] He spoke of sacrifices because he knew the risks involved, and he knew the farmworkers he often admonished knew the risks too. But he also knew that worker realism could be an alibi for complacency, and that movements could appear, as if alchemy, from nothing more than sacrifice.[9]

By 1990, Chavez had lived a long movement life. He had organized farmworker meetings in the early 1960s that a seven-year-old Luciano Crespo recalled as somber affairs in packed homes lit by green kerosene lamps.[10] He had followed the Filipino Agricultural Workers Organizing Committee (AWOC) Delano Grape Strike in 1965, in an act of solidarity driven by rank-and-file workers. He also survived the early strike months through Filipino generosity and food.[11] As their harvest strike became a multiyear movement, Chavez had elicited ideas from the strikers' eclectic community, such as the March to Sacramento in 1966 and the National Consumer Grape Boycott of the 1960s.[12] He connected with allies in colleges, churches, and union halls, and he met farmworker movement builders in many places, including the Coachella Valley. He spoke often of victory, and he likely felt a joyful confidence each time early sacrifices appeared to be on the cusp of triggering great change in California.[13] And yet, shortcomings always haunted them, enemies amassed resources and repeatedly struck with force, allies offered unreliable aid. The rancher–UFW stalemate in the mid-1970s should have taught Chavez that he had not changed the country for the better, as he seemed to believe, that it remained hopelessly regressive, self-absorbed, easily violent, and entitled, and that it was likely incapable of actualizing farmworker justice, or any sort of social justice.

Perhaps such a recognition, and its lining of humility, could have prevented his worst behaviors in the late 1970s and early 1980s, when the Agricultural Labor Relations Act (ALRA) failed the union and when a difficult lettuce strike sprouted few sustainable wins.[14] Both ALRA and strike shortcomings led to caustic rifts within the UFW movement, much of it allegedly instigated by Chavez, and produced a wave of UFW leadership resignations in the early 1980s. Perhaps as Chavez looked at the Coachella Valley crowd in 1990, many of whom organized with leaders he drove out, he considered the union's history, his past choices and actions, and the avenues not taken.

He would have certainly noted the headwinds they faced in the 1980s. In that anti-labor decade, California ranchers thwarted the UFW by restructuring their companies and associations, declaring bankruptcies, adopting sharecropping arrangements, importing Mexican harvests, and developing boycott-insulated markets inside and outside the United States.[15] California's Republican governor, George Deukmejian, furthermore, weakened ALRA's already tepid protections by packing the Agricultural Labor Relations Board (ALRB) with anti-union members, a process that mimicked the National Labor Relations Board's conversion into an anti-union institution.[16] The economic recession of the late 1970s and early 1980s devastated rural communities and magnified farmworkers' strike-related concerns: why risk unionization, in other words, when it could lead to strikes made vulnerable by an unemployed population?[17] Not to be outdone, white Californians spent the century's last two decades waging a war on non-white residents by slashing social services to lower property taxes and passing a slew of racist propositions.[18] Just four years after the 1990 school dedication, Californians voted for a draconianly anti-immigration bill—aptly named, "Save Our State"—that inspired a wave of xenophobic laws across the United States.[19] Union leaders certainly played key roles in labor's fortunes in the 1980s, as Chavez and others did in the UFW movement. But they did not act in a vacuum.[20] Often, they could only give speeches of unlikely futures in the hopes of loosening the stranglehold of an overdetermined present.

The UFW's decline in the Coachella Valley reflected this broader trajectory. The contested elections of 1977, and the ALRB's multi-year review process, blunted the UFW's growth in the region and state. Local ranchers with UFW contracts sold to anti-union companies, declared bankruptcies, or simply refused to renegotiate. Each loss withered the UFW's ability to expand into non-union local fields. Meanwhile, the Coachella Valley's tourist-driven western cities grew significantly and concentrated political power among wealthy, white residents. In 1982, they elected Patricia "Corky" Larson to Riverside County's Board of Supervisors, which covered the eastern Coachella Valley's agricultural and largely ethnic Mexican towns. Larson was married to K. K. Larson, the rancher who used Figueroa's scarred body to sell grapes in the 1980s. She was also a founding member of California Women for Agriculture (CWA), a group of white women and rancher spouses who "g[a]ve support to the [UFW-] harassed and intimidated grape workers in the Coachella Valley."[21] Palm Springs residents formed the first CWA chapter in 1975; seven years later, when Larson was elected to the county board, they counted ten chapters and 4,822 members statewide, all ready to "mobilize for action when necessary to insure justice for the farmer."[22]

More research is needed on Supervisor Larson's impact on the UFW's prospects in the Coachella Valley. But her election, and the policies she pursued, suggest a difficult climate. When Riverside County faced pressure to improve farmworker housing, for instance, Larson proposed "a complex of 'shade' shelters" that consisted of "concrete slabs with metal roofs, communal bathrooms and barbecue pits."[23] The complex had no walls to protect farmworker families from the wind, heat, rain, and cold, but Larson lauded the proposal as "novel" and "visionary," especially its "low cost compared to more permanent dwellings," and its leisure-like qualities: "it is like camping out in our state parks."[24] Among farmworker families, Larson's proposal was insulting and startling. "How can we live without walls?" asked Leonel Favela, a farmworker, father, and resident of a "crude encampment of plywood shacks." The Coachella chapter of California Rural Legal Assistance (CRLA) denounced it as "pathetic," "second-rate housing for agricultural workers," and as a denial of farmworker rights. They sued the county to produce a better housing plan and, in response, Larson described CRLA as "typical [of] fuzzy-headed, liberal thinking" preferring to "see people stay in unsanitary conditions." In 1992, a Superior Court judge paused the project, calling it "worse than nothing at all."[25]

The UFW and Chicana/o movements had helped reshape the Coachella Valley; naming a school after a man once branded a menace and charlatan testified to these changes. But much remained of the old world in the 1980s and 1990s. Larson's defense of wall-less housing by referencing camping even recalled the common farmworker homelessness before the UFW, when families lived under mesquite trees or in desert shacks made from leftover wood. Since the 1970s, the Coachella Valley also faced the national trends undercutting labor's ability to restart its movement, including the miseries of an extended economic recession, pervasive reactionary politics, and a dismantled safety net. Though nothing was inevitable, all U.S. unions confronted a discouraging future with little of Chavez's optimism.

In oral history interviews, farmworkers recognized as much and identified several reasons for the UFW movement's decline in the Coachella Valley and California. The most ardent union members saw a decline only after Chavez's death, three years after his 1990 speech.[26] Others pointed to the UFW refusal to pay salaries and its dependence on "fanatic" farmworkers and naïve white volunteers.[27] Still others blamed their coworkers, those who refused to strike, pay union dues, or build the base for a new world—one that made rancher bribes and threats irrelevant.[28] A minority blamed UFW leaders, including Chavez, but no one suggested the UFW's decline was primarily self-inflicted.[29] Despite their different diagnoses, they all stressed local and nonlocal structural problems, like unrelenting rancher hostility, white racism, an economic recession, a large and under-employed labor force, and social movement exhaustion.[30] To a small minority, the decline arguably hollowed the union's value and meaning for them. "I helped a lot, you know," Evangelina Mendoza said in 2014, in a spare, and noisy nursing home near the fields she picketed, months before her death. "Now today, now, now, nothing is left for me," she said, extending her arms dejectedly, pointing to her surroundings.³¹

For many more local farmworkers in the 1980s, however, the UFW movement simply had not existed. As in the previous chapter's conclusion, farmworkers like Fausto Figueroa lived in a region largely devoid of UFW visions and history, even if they worked and lived under conditions reflecting the UFW's impact. This was especially true for the Mexican immigrant community. Like past farmworkers, newcomer families carried stories of potential and restraint, of hopes, community, and realism, of resistance and accommodation. Most also moved in the United States under heightened vulnerability and with family obligations in Mexico.³² They found a desert mostly without strikes, contracts, and elections, nor the generative union spaces earlier farmworkers created and lived in, spaces that could alter what was possible and necessary. Instead, most toiled with only bits and pieces of union hearsay, if that, in a union narrative spareness that occluded the region's once shimmering visions.

The poet and writer, Rigoberto Gonzalez, provided such a portrait in his coming-of-age memoir, *Butterfly Boy: Memories of a Chicano Mariposa*.³³ In 1990, Gonzalez was a twenty-year-old sophomore at the University of California, Riverside, where he studied English and Philosophy. He was born in Zacapu, Michoacan, Mexico, in the small city that fostered David Perez's ambitions a couple decades earlier. Gonzalez was born into a "culture of work," he said; his great grandparents and grandparents migrated cyclically to labor in U.S. fields throughout the twentieth century, and, in the early 1970s, his parents and extended family did the same.³⁴ They ultimately settled in the Coachella Valley in the late 1970s and early 1980s. There, they held to dreams, interests, and identities that transcended field labor. His father was a boxer, musician, aspiring electrician, and UFO (Unidentified Flying Object) enthusiast. His mother alternated between workday scarves to protect from pesticides and evenings of perfume, nail polish, and make-up. They were loving parents, but like all parents, they were human, fragile, flawed, and under relentless marginality. His mother, for instance, comforted Gonzalez in his childhood but failed to protect and embrace his budding queerness. She also fought and tolerated her husband's alcoholism, became ill, felt cursed, and died at thirty-one. Gonzalez was twelve years old then, his younger brother, barely ten. A year later, in 1983, their father left the two boys with their paternal grandparents, who lived in Indio's labor camp. Ten years earlier, UFW strikers like Clementina Olloque, Maria Marron, Maria Serrano, and others fought Teamster "goons" in the camp. There, "locked up," Gonzalez wrote, he entered adolescence.³⁵

The memoir follows Gonzalez and his father as they traveled to Zacapu to visit his mother's grave in 1990—two months before Chavez's speech in Coachella. Along the grueling bus ride, Gonzalez recalled his childhood and adolescence, his mother and father, siblings, cousins, aunts, uncles, and grandparents, their brief hopes and extended grief. In his world, the UFW was nearly invisible: an unnamed strike that upended the family's livelihood; prescription glasses and hospital bills paid by workplace insurance; his brother's name, *Beneficio*—or Benny, for short—to honor work benefits; a grandfather who cooked the Filipino dishes he learned in his migrant farm working youth. Otherwise, the Rancher Nation was fervently, almost a-historically present. Its wages kept Gonzalez's family in poverty and in substandard, overcrowded housing. Its fields continued to expose them to pesticides, sexual harassment, wage freezes, child labor, and heat stroke.[36] Conditions outside the fields cultivated violence, alcoholism, drug use, racial shame, cockroaches, patriarchy, and homophobia. The Rancher Nation is "violence," Vera Cruz wrote in 1970. To Gonzalez in 1990, it remained.

Gonzalez's memoir also pointed to the UFW's erasure among residents. In the 1970s, worker–leaders like David Perez envisioned an egalitarian farmworker world. But in the mid-1980s, and while living in the same camp, an adolescent Gonzalez could only imagine escape through higher education—one without a return, as Chicana/o activists once advocated.[37] For the nineteen-year-old narrator, the erasure also shaped his life in ways he did not know but perhaps felt. His journey to Mexico, for example, was prompted by a hope to remember his mother and, through her, his younger life. Once in Zacapu, Gonzalez's maternal grandparents gave him a box with his mother's pictures and documents, including UFW paraphernalia and photos of the Coachella Grape Strike of 1973. In one picture, his toddler-self carried the union's red flag, the stark black eagle the size of his face. Until then, he had not known his mother as a striker, nor the "entire history that unfolded even before my brain began to store memory." "Suddenly," he wrote, "I have this image of a political woman raising her fist up in the air, demanding better working conditions and better pay. I see her marching in synch with the other farmworkers, their bodies linking together to create one palpable force plowing through the stunned avenue."[38]

The newly discovered archive thus made a previously inconceivable past possible for the young Gonzalez. It also gave feeling to a social and personal loss he had not noticed before, a loss shaping much of his life, one snuffed into numbness; in its resurfacing, the loss appeared to spirit new social and personal possibilities for him. But, critically, Gonzalez made this discovery in Zacapu, Mexico, not in the Coachella Valley, where the Rancher Nation felt as pervasive as ever. The discovery of a militant mother also did not suggest

Gonzalez shared Chavez's 1990 prediction of a farmworker-ruled rural California. I doubt most other farmworkers did either. Too many were simply too tired and removed to envision the power of earlier times. Thirty years later, after an extended global pandemic and nationwide farmworker vulnerability, built on thirty years of farmworker marginality, the magnitude of Chavez's miscalculation is all too obvious.[39]

Residues of Utopia

This erasure also shaped much of my young life in the eastern Coachella Valley and the lives of those around me, including my parents and siblings, immediate and extended family, school friends, and neighbors, those I knew well and those I did not. It also shaped the impulses driving this book, which began as an attempt to rethread a past to envision new futures, a past that was barely hidden around us, from us, *once seen*—a past that I hoped could elicit new possibilities, like Gonzalez's photos, and help us imagine the unlikely trajectory Chavez called inevitable. In these final pages, I wish to make a rather unconventional turn by writing about my life, the choices and circumstances that led to researching the Coachella Valley's UFW and Chicana/o movements, and about my sense of history's modest and vexing utility for present-day readers.

I will begin with my parents. By the time my mother crossed the fictive line on the sand in 1982 for a fictive American Dream, much of the UFW presence in the Coachella Valley had faded into a handful of contracts, which it would soon lose. For a nineteen-year-old, immigrant worker like my mother, the desert's fields existed as any other place of oppressive employment: under the boss's impunity and in the hurried labors to make rent; against the unsettled desires for more while shrouded in the feeling that everyone was on their own. She decided to migrate after her mother's death coincided with Mexico's economic collapse. She was also pregnant, and she decided to leave her university education to offer her future son U.S. citizenship. Like other immigrants, my mother envisioned a country with social opportunities and a steady plane on which to build a life of one's choosing. But, like others, she found poverty and body crushing labor, smirking white men in Border Patrol trucks, and Mexican men running farmworker crews ragged. She once heard of a union, she said in her interview, but what it did and why it did it, or who founded it and when, or what sustained it when victories were few or unlikely, were opaque to her and her coworkers. In only a few years, farmworkers like her could live outside the UFW's visionary frame, as if it had not affected the very world in which she now toiled.

My father's story was significantly different, though in many respects it was quite similar. He was born in Indio, California, to a Mexican American family that counted four or possibly five generations in the United States, an uncertainty that marked the family's inter-generational marginality: though American citizens, they, too, toiled in Southwestern fields and lived in the poor *barrios* of Yuma, Arizona. Yuma was also Chavez's childhood home and a key UFW movement target in the early 1970s. Yet, I do not have a single memory of my father speaking about Yuma's social movements, nothing on campaigns affecting his early life, much less improving it. Instead, his stories told of a life overdetermined by his father's abandonment, his mother's early death, and a foster home that neglected and abused him. At fifteen, he fled to the Coachella Valley to search for his father, a trek his older sisters had already completed, and one ending in the same precarity: low-wage work in the desert's fields and packinghouses, substandard homes in *colonias*, halted education, alcohol and substance use, police harassment, unresolved trauma, tattooed and scarred bodies.

My parents met in a packinghouse in Thermal in 1983. They did not speak each other's language, but they still managed to build a relationship and form a young family. They soon left field work for jobs in the poverty-paying service sector, in retail stores for my mother and in manual labor for my father, including in the westside's golf resorts. They also secured an apartment in Thermal's public housing, which was adjacent to an elementary school built in the early 1900s, when it was part of the early settler-colonizers' claim to civilizing the "wasteland." There, in the 1980s and 1990s, I grew up among farmworker families and attended bilingual classes. Of these years, I remember every single adult toiling in the innumerable fields; countless hours, it seemed to my young self, for such little pay. Malaise also seemed to suffocate all—a malaise that felt like exhaustion grating into bitterness, or exhaustion in a disemboweled resignation, or exhaustion numbed into the grooves of despair. And as a child, I knew that if I did not want to feel this, then I needed to leave—a rather typical prescription (I was to learn) for "the promising" of any oppressed community.[40]

Years later, I would come to see my childhood home as more than afflicted. Like the Filipino and Mexican communities in the early-to-mid twentieth century, marginality often yielded to pockets of resistance and humanity, to caretaking, accompaniment, and joy. Every spring, for example, my father and his friends organized our baseball little league, which doubled as a town center for several months, months that gave us a safe space, a bit of athletic drama, endless nachos. My mother and aunts also volunteered at our school; they fundraised, chaperoned, and built bridges between our homes and our classrooms.

Our public housing neighbors hosted birthday parties, first communion parties, wedding parties, graduation parties, Christmas parties, just regular parties—each one a flurry of children, plates of food, a tenor of familiarity I have yet to feel again. All of this could be leveraged to aid each other, such as when new families moved into an apartment without any furniture and their new neighbors shared their extra items. One mother cried, I remember distinctly. I was ten years old and so accustomed to this generosity that her tears confused me. Women also used this community to protect their families from violent husbands. Neighbors used it to keep an eye on all children, to borrow money, or to get advice on work, heartache, and migration. Everyone was a poet and philosopher in my community, each one attempting to make sense of their world and the world of others, to shape it, to render it meaningful. So, I readily recognize now, there was more than the malaise I felt as a boy and young man. And yet, what was there, and what shaped me and those near me, was often the social equivalent of triage—a clinging to each other for life.

I doubt my childhood neighbors shared the UFW and Chicana/o movements' visions of an altered landscape, of socialized dignity as ordinary as the act of neighbors caring for each other. The spoken alternative to poverty was higher education, to which, as a bookish, unathletic, and queer boy, I was particularly well suited. I was fortunate to have had caring teachers, too, who guided me as my family faced uncertainty and tragedies, including my father's untimely death—which was much like the untimely deaths of many of my neighbors. I was fortunate to learn our poverty had not been our doing, that our work was dignified, that we deserved more, could fight for more. But these lessons often felt like uncommon visions and as situated outside my home. So, when I left for college in 2001, I was set on learning about other people's freedom struggles to return to my home as a teacher with liberation stories. I hoped these could fill the discursive void I felt in my community. With them, I reasoned, we could begin to see past our present of denial and spur visions of life-affirming futures. To my fortune, a new high school opened to serve the eastern Coachella Valley's farmworker communities, and there I began teaching. In a brief four years, I entered a world of dedicated teachers and school leaders, proud and determined parents, much like my own, and a spirited student gaggle that makes you believe in possibility.

In this context, a colleague gave me a copy of the UFW's 1974 documentary, "The Fight for Our Lives," which followed the Coachella Grape Strike of 1973.[41] As summarized in chapter 7, the UFW movement claimed grape ranchers and the Teamsters Union colluded to undermine farmworker power in California. The UFW also claimed economic need prevented farmworkers from striking, that rancher greed exploited immigrants and children alike, that white allies were again necessary for other people's freedoms. I was conscious then that the documentary was a limited retelling. And yet, it still felt like a near-revelation. I felt stunned in fact. Here was my seemingly desolate home in a fierce confrontation with those controlling the political economy, speaking with pride and self-assuredness, demanding a better society. It was foreign to my world and sense of history, and to those around me; no one I knew, for instance, spoke of a UFW or Chicana/o movement in our home. A school named after Chavez had done little to recount this history.

Years later, I came across Jose Muñoz's *Cruising Utopia: The Then and There of Queer Futurity* and found the language to explain my reaction to the film.[42] In *Cruising Utopia*, Muñoz framed queerness as pointing to utopian worlds—to the "not-yet-conscious" and "not yet here."[43] To imagine the latter, Muñoz turned to history and its "residue of utopian impulse," to the faint traces of past visionary gestures that existed in present quotidian spaces. He asked readers to engage this residue to deny the status quo's claim of permanence. With Muñoz in mind, I saw the UFW documentary as the residue of a past utopian moment, as a faint "no-longer-conscious" in my community of farmworker poverty. In its residue, however, it produced the cognitive dissonance he called political potential. To use his words, I imagined "look[ing] back to a fecund no-longer-conscious in the service of a [Coachella Valley] futurity," one that "resists the various violent asymmetries that dominate our present moment."[44]

I also drew inspiration from the historian Robin D. G. Kelley and his appeal for utopian histories, on visions "fashioned mainly by those marginalized . . . activists who proposed a different way out of our constrictions."[45] He labeled these "freedom dreams" and saw them as the "many different cognitive maps of the future, of the world not yet born," all forged "in the poetics of struggle and lived experience." Like Muñoz, Kelley saw freedom dreams as guides for a future past the present—as maps to an expansive and dialogic horizon. And, like Muñoz, Kelley found freedom dreams "in the utterances of ordinary folk, in the cultural products of social movements, [and] in the reflections of activists." Neither suggested uncritical adoptions. Instead, they argued that by thinking of utopia without naïveté that marginalized communities could begin to build the intellectual and cultural levees to guard against the pervasive sense of defeat. Such stories also provided strength to press forward on the long trek to the mountaintop of freedom.

With Muñoz and Kelley, I imagined this book as a critical history of hope and tenacious dreaming, one that could help fight the defeat and exhaustion that had long wrapped itself against my childhood community. I wanted to offer this history to my students, too, as sustenance for when prospects appeared dim, as dim as those in the early twenty-first century.

Given the paucity of archival material, I turned to oral history interviews to begin this study. I knew oral histories were imperfect and defined by their unsettled elements, especially the morphing of memory and event. But I also knew that no archive escaped such imperfections. What I did not expect was for the interviews to echo, if not embody, the very appeals made by Muñoz and Kelley, *for the people I interviewed sought me as much as I sought them.* The reasons for their participation varied, but most settled on the political exchange of tenses: to intervene in the present's understanding of the past to shape the future. They spoke of a past latent with urgent significance for younger people. Like Muñoz's utopian residue and Kelley's freedom dreams, they insisted on a "fecund no-longer-conscious" and sought to steal/steel the young into a future past the present.

No one spoke of utopia, per se. Instead, they spoke of everyday changes that rippled into a world beyond what they had known or considered possible. Their demands reflected distinct histories and conditions and the immanent nature of most politics. But once achieved, these demands also produced new and unexpected horizons, such as militant friendships among co-unionists, especially for women farmworkers, or union roles that sharpened intelligence, or attending college, a once-impossible dream for the children of farmworkers. Some spoke of feeling meaningful, of being proud of oneself, of others' generosity, courage, and love. The "not-yet-conscious" often appeared in, with, and through others. Taken together, the oral history participants insisted their world had not been well, that what they had was not enough or right, that they deserved more, *wanted* more, that more was, in fact, possible. For many, these were days when they felt the palpable weight of freedom against their hands, when they joined and labored in the communal effort that is to hold up the sky of new tomorrows.

They also spoke of militant aspirations that served as self-defining ethics and political strategy. Whether Filipino or Mexican, women or men, local or not, the most militant activists argued freedom and potential originated in people's interiority, in the thoughts and sensibilities shaping their behavior and in the actions that sprang from social convictions. They said some version of: one feels it in one's skin; one acts from one's heart; one does what one must do. Like Chavez's editorial earlier, they argued moralized actions produced new contexts of possibility, which then propelled new visions, gained adherents, and grew capacity to make change.[46] Succinctly expressed in the UFW mantra, "Si Se Puede," they rooted freedom in our lives' intimate spaces. Justice beckons us, they seem to say, it does not simply protect us.

If the UFW and Chicana/o movements had a "poetics of struggle," to use Kelley's phrase, then it came as a deeply impassioned historical romance. Historical romances, David Scott writes in *Conscripts of Modernity: The Tragedy of Colonial Enlightenment*, are "narratives of overcoming" that depend "on a certain (utopian) horizon toward which the emancipationist history is imagined to be moving."[47] In similar fashion, oral history interviewees spoke of great struggle, of the collective's courage and conviction birthing epochal change: gross social inequalities met their challenge; agriculture began a militant reformulation; racialized citizenship met its egalitarian contrast. Like a dawn, they narrated their efforts as a social overcoming that transformed and clarified their world. Like most romance narratives, they offered their history as a gift for fighting despair: they historicized their victory to speak of human capacity, insisting we can reach the horizon if we simply keep marching to it.

Here then, I thought, I have found the story I have been searching for, a story fighting the sense of permanent marginalization, a story that, like Muñoz and Kelley imagined, spoke of future possibility by turning to our rebellious and often forgotten pasts—a story I could share with my students to mobilize their lifelong contributions for a better world.

Movement Afterlives

An important, though largely submerged, concern in the book has been an ambiguous relationship to this romance narrative. The world I experienced as a child, and the world that continues to haunt families in the Coachella Valley, insisted on making a pointed question: if the interviewees were right in what they achieved and could still be achieved, then what happened? How exactly could my childhood experiences and community conditions be reconciled with UFW and Chicana/o narratives? A contradiction soon appeared between the interviewees' message and the interviews' purpose. The former spoke of a rebellious past filled with possibility, of a beloved community shaping their world, but the latter spoke of a "fecund no-longer-conscious," of the need to collect traces so "the young" can press into possibilities. Both came in the romantic register—of heroic struggle and epochal change—but the interviews' purpose questioned their insistence: that freedom was, in fact, felt and built, once.

Generally, participants responded to this contradiction with three moves. First, they answered the question—what happened?—by speaking about the forces arrayed against them. They pointed to rancher recalcitrance and labor contractors, to the Teamster raids in 1970 (lettuce) and 1973 (grapes), which dissipated resources, and the state's 1970s right-wing politics. They also spoke about the troubles of the much-famed ALRA elections and the string of UFW leaders brought from the outside. Some spoke bitterly of their neighbors who refused to go on strike, took the union for granted, did not vote, and/or made no demands from bosses or from themselves. In UFW parlance, these were

Para Cual Cosa

Los trabajadores campesinos por
se y demandar una vida y salario
sus familias. Algunos, como los
era pagina, han trabajado toda su
Ahora solo pidemos solo lo que e
mejores condiciones, poca dignid
tros, pero mucho mas... para n

--Para darles mejor educacion y opor-
tunidad para una mejor vida.

--Para darles comida que necesitan,
buena ropa, y medecina cuando estan
enfermos.

...amos Peleando?

...do de California empiezan a parar-
...usticia social para si mismo y
...s describidos en foto en la prim-
...do a los racheros y este valle rico,
...erecemos, para un buen sueldo,
...seguridad en la vida. Para noso-

--Para que ellos nunca llegen a sufrir
lo que nosotros sufrimos.

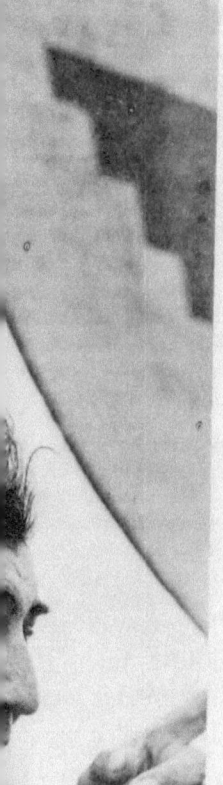

--Para darles orgullo en sus padres y
en su gente. Y en la raza.

UFW movement demands in June 1966: "Today we only ask what is rightfully ours, for a good wage, better conditions, some dignity, and greater security in life. For ourselves, but much more so . . . for our children." *El Malcriado*, June 2, 1966, 12–13. Walter P. Reuther Library, Archives of Labor and Urban Affairs, Wayne State University.

"union members of convenience," men and women who joined when it was safe, when union goods had been won, by others, when nothing was asked in return.[48] A similar view existed among some Chicana/o activists.

Second, some interviewees challenged the argument my life experiences questioned their triumphs, that there was a contradiction in the oral histories' message and purpose. They identified the very interview as testament of their victories. How do you think you became a professor, they asked, if not for the programs and relationships we instituted? The affordable housing you lived in, the head start that introduced you to school, the Spanish classes that shaped your early education, the Mexican American teachers in middle school and college readiness workshops in high school—who do you think created it? Now, they added with a near scoff, you are here as a researcher and writer, as an historian, with questions about the UFW and Chicana/o movements, an *unthinkable* statement when we were your age, and you ask about the supposed world we did not achieve? We may not have completed our utopian world, they insisted, but we started the long task of building it, including what was needed to hold this very conversation.

The third point brought these two responses together by extending the time frame into the future, as if to say: if perhaps we did not win, then know *we have not yet lost*. For them, the interviews embodied the traces of past utopian worlds, the conditions afforded by past efforts, and the very material in a transitory present for building a utopian future. As if passing a justice baton to a younger generation, they tied the past, present, and future in a contested but singular movement to emancipation. Inherent to this pass, they identified achievements and failures and pointed not so much as forward, but to the existence of forward. This temporal move thus reasoned away the contradiction of message and purpose—which was to say, that heroic struggle today, like in the past, can still find, build, and feel freedom in the future.

They were not wrong, I had to admit. Even if the Rancher Nation survived in places like the Coachella Valley, it had been fundamentally challenged and circumscribed. In the fields, the UFW banned the short-handle hoe and gained unemployment insurance, which granted farmworkers greater geographic stability and encouraged higher education among farmworker children. It also directed attention to pesticide use and working conditions. Not all ranchers improved conditions, they noted, but regulations were still won, and their very existence improved on pre-UFW days, when blatant farmworker marginality—dangerous pesticides, relentless work without water or restrooms, child labor—drew minimal societal concern. The fact they fought and won reforms testified to what was possible, and that sense of possibility could be leveraged to the fight against the Rancher Nation today. Nothing was the same, they insisted, and nothing was in vain.

Interviewees also spoke of the multiple organizations they created and joined in the 1980s and 1990s. In 1988, for instance, a group of farmworker women leaders, and the daughters of farmworker women, formed *Mujeres Mexicanas* to address women's issues in the eastern Coachella Valley's farmworker communities. The organization soon become a statewide network, *Lideres Campesinas*, that led workshops on pesticide protection, workplace sexual harassment, and domestic violence. They also organized farmworkers to improve work conditions, provided language translation for Spanish and Mixtec speakers, and promoted pro-farmworker policies in California's capital. Illustrative of the field of stories, the organization was founded by the college-educated daughter of local pro-UFW farmworkers, Mily Treviño Sauceda, who met the local UFW women already championing these issues.[49] In the same period, Coachella Valley families joined Father Patricio Guillen and Sister Rosa Marta Zarate in Catholic conferences on Liberation Theology, community studies on rural California, and social reform campaigns.[50] A central figure in this space was Virginia Ortega, who joined the Delano Grape Strike in 1966 and participated in the Coachella Grape Strike of 1973 before turning to Catholic organizing with Sister Zarate. The latter figure had also been inspired to dedicate her life to farmworker justice by the UFW's Imperial Valley lettuce strikes in early 1970s.[51] Both women, like other UFW women, moved along the broad, curving rivers of justice visions, coalescing repeatedly into deltas of possibility.

Among Chicana/o activists, post-movement mobilization was also significant. Chicana/o educators at the Desert Sands Unified School District and Coachella Valley Unified School District (CVUSD) pushed for bilingual teachers and curriculum and for greater respect of their students' farmworker, Spanish-speaking, and ethnic-Mexican families. After the Mexican American Political Association collapsed in the mid-1970s, former MAPA members guided their students in college applications, distributed scholarships, and mentored Chicana/o student organizations.[52] The latter played a key role in the 1994 Coachella Valley and Indio high school walkouts against California's Proposition 187, which sought to deny undocumented immigrant families access to health care, education, and public services.[53] Chicano activists like Al Fuller, Calisto Ramos, and Larry Salas also taught English and citizenship classes to a new generation of immigrants, like my mother, who became a U.S. citizen and English speaker in the 1990s, the very moment of California's xenophobic frenzy.[54] My own education reflected their wins: I attended Spanish classes until the fourth grade, when, already literate in one language, I entered an English class taught by Mrs. Ceja, where I then learned a second.[55] Mrs. Ceja's husband, Joe Ceja, spent the 1980s and 1990s as a CVUSD principal, where he hired a legion of dedicated, bilingual teachers. At the turn of century, he and other education leaders built a state-of-the-art elementary to high school campus for farmworker families in the east Coachella Valley, where I began my teaching career in 2006.[56]

Outside education, some turned to offering health services and building health institutions. Clementina Olloque, Irene Gonzalez, and Felicitas Nuñez became nurses and worked with farmworker families.[57] Nuñez continued to lead the Teatro Chicana troupe, which, by the 1980s, had become collective of teachers, translators, counselors, union officials, and health care providers, each offering "their *granito de arena*—their own contribution—for a better society."[58] In 1981, Sam Maestas founded the free Coachella clinic, *El Progreso del Desierto*, which provided full medical and pre-natal care, optometry, and dental services. It also had social and youth components and tended to AIDS patients and undocumented immigrants in the 1980s.[59] In a characteristic flash of confidence, Maestas assured me my mother received prenatal care at *El Progreso*, and then challenged me to ask her. She had, as he predicted. She said she learned of the clinic through a network of family and friends because everyone went there. And though she worried about her immigration status when she first visited, she was quickly and respectfully assigned to her obstetrician. She was nineteen, a new immigrant and farmworker, and a soon-to-be mother with few financial resources: the very person the clinic wanted to serve. Still others, like the UFW organizer from Delano, Luciano Crespo, turned to mental health advocacy and founded Coachella's Esperanza Youth and Family Center, a substance abuse rehabilitation clinic that pioneered a family-centered approach.[60]

Movement participants attempted to address other key areas of marginalization. Some built affordable housing in Coachella, Thermal, and Mecca, each more substantial than Larson's wall-less proposal. I grew up in one of these, and though imperfect, it offered my family and our neighbors a dignified home, one I never took for granted.[61] Another UFW organizer, Lupe Crespo, used her union skills to organize and lead Coachella Valley Unified School District bus drivers.[62] The former Brown Berets and UFW organizer, Max Huerta, established a Christian missionary church in Indio, which still serves Coachella Valley families.[63] Huerta's brother, Israel Huerta, a 1973 UFW striker in the Coachella and San Joaquin valleys, served as a career counselor in the Coachella Valley's Center for Employment Training (CET), an office that trained farmworkers to enter non-agricultural industries, where job security and higher wages are more common.[64] Whatever the limits of such programs, its vision of non-agricultural alternatives contrasted with pre-movement stories of feeling trapped, of having no options, of being, in Amalia Uribe Deaztlan's words, *expected* to be farmworkers.[65]

The UFW and Chicana/o movements' legacies could also appear in less visible, though significant, forms. Leonor Suarez, for instance, joined the UFW as a citrus worker in the mid-1970s and continued until their company declared bankruptcy in the mid-1980s. Having already experienced unionized work, she said, she only applied to union jobs, which brought her to a local Safeway. Her new position provided an economic base for her children and a career path for one of her sons, Gabriel Suarez, who today organizes with United Food Commercial Workers (UFCW).[66] In two decades, Suarez has led campaigns in grocery stores, slaughterhouses, and pharmacies, and participated in immigration reform and local progressive candidacies.[67] The children of Evangelina Mendoza, Maria Serrano, Amalia Uribe Deaztlan, Simon Machuca, Pablo Carrizales, Virginia Ortega, Remedios Martinez, Ray Rodriguez, Joe Ceja, and Larry Salas, to name just a few, serve in state agencies, public schools, hospitals, universities, and other critical institutions. Still other children expressed more personal goals, like Petra Ruiz's son, Francisco Ruiz, who cared for his mother until her last days and who continues to safeguard her memory, especially her contributions to the UFW movement.[68]

Admittedly, there is an element of the cursory in this retelling of social movement afterlives. In part, this reflects the topic's extensiveness and its need for another history—one of the afterglow, of past potential dimmed but not extinguished. This history continues today in relationships, institutions, and stories, in unseen traces nonetheless felt. Fortunately, scholars are beginning to trace these legacies, including their roles in California's revived labor movement and its diverse electorate, or in progressive labor and non-labor campaigns outside California.[69]

There is a final union afterlife that warrants special attention, and that is the lives of Filipino UFW members in their final days in Delano's Agbayani Village. Agbayani Village was the UFW's farmworker retirement home. It was named after the AWOC striker, Paulo Agbayani, an "original" striker who refused to follow Filipino contractors out of AWOC's strike in late October 1965.[70] Though opened to fanfare in 1974, historians have since stressed the project's unaffordable rent, policing of commercial sex, and cynical display to promote UFW interests. These critiques may be true, though far more research is needed.[71] In the 1974 commemoration, for instance, Philip Vera Cruz described Agbayani Village as the first phase of a statewide housing system "for the discarded and poorest elderly farm workers who made U.S. agriculture a multibillion-dollar business." With few resources to retire, Vera Cruz said, farmworkers must "work to survive, but ironically, some of them just fall down and die on the job. Out of poverty and frustration, perhaps this belated way of committing suicide is the surest and instant exit from the racial discrimination and suffering in this blessedly rich society."[72] "That is why we build this building, this Agbayani Village," Willie Barrientos said in 1978, "cause when [farmworkers] retire, they could come here and retire."[73]

The UFW failed to achieve its ambitious plan, but it nonetheless attempted to decouple rights and needs—such as housing—from the calculus of labor value and rancher profits. For older Filipino men, who had long fought to more than labor, the retirement home offered the prospects of autonomy and humanity in their final years. "It is," Vera Cruz said, "the most beautiful expression of gratitude and care for the farmworker, who feed and clothe the world."[74] In 1973, months before its opening, Sebastian Sahugan shared similarly while writing on his generation's exposure to discrimination and exploitation. They had relied on rancher housing, Sahugan said, to cobble together work on the migrant circuit, and now, "when many of us are old and cannot work as well," ranchers treated them "like old clothes or shoes to be burned or thrown away because we've passed our usefulness."[75] "To me," he wrote, "this is the most beautiful home in the whole world," built by "the strong, beautiful hands of men and women whose hearts are filled with love, spirit of unity and a determination to remake this world into a better place to live in."

In the late 1970s and early 1980s, Agbayani Village was home to mostly Filipino retirees who had been UFW organizers since 1965. They ate meals together, watched shows together, played cards, and wagered on fighting roosters together. They planted a garden of "eggplants, tomatoes, beans and so many types of vegetables," Willie Barrientos reported in 1982. "We plant so many trees, like oranges, grapefruits, little grapes in the surrounding," which meant a "very busy claiming during spring when the weather got hot."[76] They also hosted young visitors from across the country and globe, including the Philippines. They were especially attentive to college students, such as the twelve Minnesota visitors in January 1983, who stayed in the village, toured the clinic, service station, and a nearby camp, and learned to prune grapes.[77] In one evening, the students also learned about AWOC's Delano Grape Strike in 1965, "a day long remembered," the retirees said, "in the History of the United Farm Workers AFL-CIO." The Agbayani Village leaders then "gather[ed] all our Brothers, every-one," so they had "a chance to tell their names, ages and the kind of work they have experience in 20 years, 25 years to 50 years."[78] For a community repeatedly erased—from an industry they built and a movement they initiated—such visits offered an opportunity to tell their stories and, in the process, to re-tell the story of the world they shared with visitors.

For many village residents, safeguarding these stories became a central preoccupation.[79] They met with historians, gave community talks, wrote letters and entire books to each other.[80] Many of these sources are now available in the Welga! Digital Archive and the Farm Worker Documentation Project,

A group of the Manongs who will live at the Agbayani Village are shown here at the Schenley labor camp where they have been living, awaiting the completion of the Village. These Pilipino men were in the forefront of farm worker strikes for many years, including the Delano Grape Strike of 1965 which led to the formation of the United Farm Workers of America.

El Malcriado - June 24, 1974 - Page 9

Former AWOC members and Agbayani Village residents in June 1974. Many lived the rest of their years in the UFW's retirement community. *El Malcriado*, June 24, 1974, 9. Walter P. Reuther Library, Archives of Labor and Urban Affairs, Wayne State University.

both indispensable for future histories. Agbayani Village residents also advocated commemorating Filipino strikers in UFW spaces, such as their 1983 proposal for a "statue and flame, to honor the Un-known Filipino farm workers who started the Great Delano Grape Strike and Boycott of 1965."[81] They sustained their memory work with visitors, especially young activists.[82] As Linda Ogawa Ramirez reported for *Philippine News* in 1980, "Asian and Pacific students and community activists saw [the Agbayani Village] as a symbol not only of the farmworkers' struggle but also, specifically for Filipinos, as a tribute to the early immigrants who left the Philippines in the 1930s."[83]

Lastly, and perhaps most importantly, the Agbayani Village offered company and care in their final years. As lifelong organizers, the residents formed a committee that, as Barrientos summarized in 1982, "[saw] to that if anyone don't come for breakfast we go and knock his door whether he is in good health. If he is sick, we will take him to the doctor. If he is very sick, we take him to the Emergency Hospital.... Anytime of the day or night. If he wants to go to the social security office, we also take him there. If anyone dies, we also take care of arranging his papers to the mortuary of Delano, that his body [is] well buried in a peaceful and decent manner."[84] So, when the eighty-four-year-old Antonio Racimo suffered a stroke in 1983, the committee quickly took him to Delano's hospital and then brought him "back [to] his room." "We take care of his food," Barrientos reported, "whatever is necessary for him to get well. That is our job ... we are like one family."[85] The committee cared for Leonardo Daus, whose "legs and feet are very tired to walk and also his hands are very stiff," and rushed a wounded Justantino Lecorte to the emergency room after he accidently started a fire in his room. Lecorte died soon afterwards, but not alone: "At fifteen minutes to 9:00 A.M., the dr. told me my friend passed away."[86] By then, Barrientos had taken to listing the friends who had passed, taking brief notes on their lives, collecting their wills.[87] One belonged to Isidro Taay, who mentored young Luciano Crespo, and who left his car, television, clothes, and shoes to "Maximo Jacildone[,] who has been my dear and caring friend for the past thirty odd years."[88]

I imagine these men would have found each other even if they had not initiated and then remained in the UFW movement for nearly two decades. They had been part of each other's lives since their adolescence, or had been part of the lives forced on them since their migration to the United States when many were in their adolescence. They had worked together, migrated together, grieved and dreamt together. They had seen their fortunes fluctuate, especially after World War II, and they had gambled repeatedly with well-timed labor strikes. For some of these men, the UFW movement's strikes and boycotts took them to cities and towns across the country and introduced them to many people who shared their labor politics. Like the UFW members and Chicana/o activists of the Coachella Valley, they built the movement that built them in return, and they did so for more than personal material goods. As Claro Runtal wrote to his lifelong friend, Fred Abad in the 1980s: "If my life experiences in labor struggles may ever come to a written book, I wish ... [it] may remain to guide our off-springs for their success of life for a better tomorrow.... Let us not forget brothers and sisters that we farm workers are born soldiers of the soil to help one another to move the crop which everyone serves on the table.... Rest assured that my spirit is always with all of you brothers and sisters to continue our struggle."[89]

More needs to be written. More needs to be read. More needs to be connected. But what is evident now is that social movements are never in vain, even when they fall short of their visions; that everything has an effect, whether seen or not; that afterlives remain, even if only as dying among dear friends or as traces insisting on another world. Know we have not yet lost.

To Stutter Together

In the introduction to this book, I wrote about the tendency to write about unions and social movements as a train on tracks moving on a single timeline to an a priori endpoint. I argued this model risked conflating the differences and opacities shaping much of history, and that it limits the question we ask about unions and social movements. I suspected a reason for this model's popularity was rooted in a desire to resolve contingency's unruliness, to manage it, and, in the process, to map a path out of our constrictions. More than a map, in fact, this model suggests that there is a map, a possible way out, that we can gain an assurance, a process towards the freedom and justice that our communities deserve. Kelley offered such vision in his conclusion to *Freedom Dreams*, where he imagined "fantastic, futuristic tale of a group of 'Maroon poets'" who transformed "a local struggle over police brutality into a full-fledged revolution rooted in love, creativity, and cooperation over the course of seven hundred years."[90] The time frame of thirty-seven generations aimed to encourage those considering justice work on the human scale. Like the people I interviewed, Kelley suggested that even those who experienced the valley's dark centuries, those who saw and felt the fog of despair and uncertainty, still moved toward the mountaintop's resolution and clarity. It is this story I hoped to offer my students about our home, and it is this story I imagine the oral history participants wanted from me.

But, as this book has argued, when we turn to the UFW's rank-and-file membership, we see a stunning level of contingency, one that shaped the union's origins, dynamics, and ends, and one that was produced by multiple actors interacting in local and trans-local spaces in multiple time periods. This contingency also involved the forces outside farmworkers' control, such as an anti-union Teamster raid, a hostile social and political climate, a tepid commitment from self-identified allies. The contingency of all history, in short, overflows human designs. It builds and undermines efforts. It denies predictions and unravels trajectories. It inspires, it suffocates, it surprises and surprises, again. And it challenges all well-intentioned prescriptions through history—through the suggestion that *this* error or strategy or politics was the key, that this key offers us a path to building a better world, that there is, in fact, a path, that we just need to stay on it. The contingency in this book makes this untenable; there is no reassured future path available to History. There is no train track and there is no train. Even if they/we have not yet lost, as my friends and oral history participants insisted, and even if valiant efforts for human dignity continue, as they do throughout rural California today, no History can assure us that we will ever know if we will win the world we deserve. Contingency denies any assurances.

The end goal here is not despair. If we abandon the desire for assurances, even for the humbling seven-hundred-year framework, then we can better glean the political lessons from this history, which largely come in ethical form. If there is anything to learn, then it is to emulate the farmworker strikers who joined their picket line without knowing if they would win, much less when or with whom. Two examples come to mind, and with these I will close the book. The first involves Pete Velasco, who kept a strike journal from December 1965 to March 1966, a period of considerable uncertainty in the union's history, when victory was far from assured. And yet, Velasco's co-strikers woke up each cold morning in Delano to picket the nearby grape fields, and to organize camps, reach out to unions, and keep the strikers' spirits high. "They have madness in their hearts," Velasco wrote of his compatriots, "They have patience.... They have also laughter, and humor." It would take another five years before the UFW gained its 1970 victory. The latter did not create a utopian world; in fact, it led to increased Filipino alienation. Velasco still stressed the strike's inherent value. Delano grape workers went on strike in 1965 expecting a short conflict, yearning to see the "light at the end of their journey." But it was in that journey that strikers met each other, picketed with each other, cared for each other, for themselves. For many, the strike—as exhausting and debilitating as it was—opened an unexpected space for new life, a space of stories, one they entered, one that entered them.

The UFW movement's implicit "lesson" beckons and demands from us. It calls us to become, as Velasco wrote, a "striker true at heart," a person who fulfills their "promise to come back to picket till victory is won," someone who stays on the "firing line" with others, and who contributes with new friends and new kin for the strike's hoped-for victory. To Velasco, such "strikers true at heart" internalized the union's values of solidarity and dedication, and secured the entire (striking) community's survival. These strikers stayed on the picket line despite the thick fog of uncertain futures, many with a politics that begins with the present and avoids the fantasies of a past that says our future holds our dawn—a politics, in short, that rebels for just principles.

The second story comes from Evangelina Mendoza, who shared that her husband attempted to repress her independence throughout their lives and even prohibited her from attending UFW meetings and demonstrations.[91] When I asked her if she participated in the UFW to defy her his authority, she clarified she became a UFW member and leader "so that he would believe/see that we could we win." "And," Mendoza added, "we won." When Coachella Valley farmworkers participated in union elections in the mid-1970s, Mendoza took an active role in her company. And when they won, her husband continued to say their victory was a lie. He was especially upset the local news stations credited Mendoza's leadership for one of the election wins. For good measure, her husband sneered, "*You're* going to win? You don't even know how to talk." By this point, I doubt Mendoza was shocked by her husband's statements, much less intimidated. She had already built a life of her own, migrated to a new country, raised healthy children, and helped lead an unprecedented labor insurgency in California's agricultural spine. It did not surprise me, then, that Mendoza shot back at her husband: "I told him, 'Look—I may not know how to talk, but at least we can stutter together.'"[92]

We may not know how to talk, too, and we may not know how to find the worlds we deserve. But we have each other in our imperfections, in our limited visions and knowledge, in the stutters implying difficulties but also commitment. Like Velasco and Mendoza, we do not need to know the path forward. But we do need to be with each other, to attempt to see each other, to build relentlessly, justly, with each other.

May we love as much as we have been loved. May we fight for others as much as others have fought for us. May we know that nothing has ever been or ever will be in vain. And as we face a present of looming difficulties, may we always remember that better worlds are possible, that we have each other to build them, that we deserve them. Here is where we meet.

Acknowledgments

When I first envisioned this project, I had just turned twenty-six years, a few years past college, when I was still teaching in my hometown. Thirteen years have since passed and, along with the gathering gray hair, I have met a community I had not anticipated to find. This community reminds me that all knowledge is collective.

This project began in earnest with the aid of the library director in Mecca, California, Miguel Rodriguez, who introduced me to many of the oral history interviewees in this book—each of whom then offered coffee, cookies, and pictures, and guided me through their lives. They encouraged me when I grew tired, and they read my writing when I first began to complete dissertation chapters. After nearly a decade, many became close friends, both mentors and kindred spirits, who I visited long after we stopped recording our conversations. I am deeply grateful for this experience, so unexpected and yet so foundational to who I am today. Thank you for your generosity, honesty, and kindness, and for trusting me with your histories. The interviewees include Stella Acuña, Doug Adair, Filogonio Angel, Guillermina Arredondo, Manuel Arredondo, Eliseo Arrellano, Silveria Beltran, Ruben Cancino, Guadalupe Carrizales, Elvia Alicia and Armando Castillo, Joe Ceja, Carmen Celaya, Fernando Chavez, Luciano and Lupe Crespo, Arturo Diaz, Alfredo and Demesia Figueroa, Fausto Figueroa, Mike Figueroa, Alfredo Fuller, Ruben Gonzalez, Israel and Max Huerta, Raul and Sherrie Loya, Tony Lopez, Simon Machuca, Sam Maestas, Maria Marron, Remedios Martinez, Evangelina Mendoza, Flora and Tony Mendoza, Silvia Montenegro, Isabel and Constantino Moreno, Louise Neely, Felicitas Nuñez, Clementina Olloque, Virginia Ortega, Gilbert Padilla, Sophie Paiz, David Perez, Salvador Ramirez and Maria Teresa, Calisto Ramos, Irene Reyes, Enrique Rodriguez, Ray Rodriquez, Fred Ross Jr., Marcos and Catalina Ruiz, Petra Ruiz, Larry Salas, Alfonso Sanchez, Melecio Sanchez, Gilda Guitron-Sandsness, Maria Serrano, Leonor and Rodolfo Suarez, Antonio Puga Torres, Hilario Torres, Amalia Uribe Deaztlan, Federico Vargas, and Juan Venegas.

I also have received support from many scholars, starting with my graduate advisors, George Sanchez, William Deverell, Marjorie Becker, Juan De Lara, and the late Maria Elena Martinez. Benny Andres, Deborah Cohen, Daniel HoSang Martinez, Pablo Mitchell, Mae Ngai, Steve Pitti, and Devra Weber helped me begin transforming the dissertation into a book. The participants of the Bancroft Latinx History Seminar at UC Berkeley spent an entire afternoon with an earlier version of this book. They included Mark Brilliant, Margaret Chowning, Raul Coronado, Brian Delay, Edward Escobar, Ramon Gutierrez, Lisbeth Haas, David Montejano, Ignacio Ornelas-Rodriguez, Lorena Oropeza, Ivon Padilla-Rodriguez, and Juana Maria Rodriguez. My close friend, Max Felker-Kantor, read the manuscript and offered much needed suggestions. My good friends' parents translated texts in Ilocano and Tagalog. Thank you, Nicanor Gangano Ramos and Joy Tabaranza Francisco. My mother, Sandra Paiz, repeatedly translated Spanish texts—and all without reminding me to practice my Spanish!

In the last decade, I have crossed paths with many wonderful scholars—each offering revisions and encouragements, cocktails in conferences, phone calls in pandemics. They included Lauren Araiza, Eric Avila, Aaron Bae, Rick Baldoz, Allyson P. Brantley, Antonia Castañeda, Lori Flores, Max Felker-Kantor, Dorothy Fujita-Rony, Rudy Guevara, Felipe Hinojosa, Max Krochmal, Patricia Limerick, George Lipsitz, Rosina Lozano, Kelly Lytle-Hernandez, Gordon Mantler, Sarah McNamara, Ana Minian, Natalia Molina, Carlos Parra, Rhacel Parreñas, Nic Ramos, Robyn Magalit Rodriguez, Ana Rosas, Jenn Tran, and Chris Zepeda-Millan. Dear Jenn, so much of USC reminds me of you and your spirit, generous and boundless. Thank you for being part of my life. The late Dawn Buholano Mabalon, whose scholarship allowed for mine, sat with me, bought me food and advised me when I found myself overwhelmed by the UFW archives in Detroit in the 2011 summer. You are deeply, deeply missed, Dawn. In Detroit, a warm community invited me into their homes and showed me life outside my California. Thank you, Luke Polcyn (and family!), Gabriel Guerrero, Robert Orler, and Danielle Daguio. Lastly, I am grateful to my editor, Brandon Proia, who shepherded this project and reminded me, repeatedly, to keep writing.

At the University of California, Berkeley, I am thankful to the institution builders, scholars, and teachers who remind me every day of what drew me into this profession. Thank you, Cristina Mora, Kris Gutierrez, Angela Marino, Lisa Garcia Bedolla, Cybelle Fox, Tianna Paschel, Leti Volp. Lisbeth Haas and David Montejano, our writing group has been one of the best experiences I have had in the academy; I miss them already. Brian Delay and Mark Brilliant, you offered a much needed second home. Christina and Kris—what could I have done without you? I am grateful to my colleagues in the Ethnic Studies Department, whose scholarship and organizing has offered a path for my own. Thank you, Jesus Barraza, Juan Beruman, Thomas Biolsi, Michael Chang, Catherine Choy, Greg Choy, Carolyn Chen, Raul Coronado, Harvey Dong, Keith Feldman, Pablo Gonzalez, Ramon Grosfoguel, Maria Heredia, Shari Huhndorf, Jeannie Imazumi, Laura Jimenez-Olvera, Keyva Kendall, Enrique Lima, Salar Mameni, Latonya Minor, Peter Nelson, Laura Perez, Beth Piatote, Sandra Richmond, Victoria Robinson, Juana Rodriguez, Lok Siu, Dewey St. Germaine, Ray Telles, Lis Tsuchitani, and Khatharya Um. To Chris Zepeda-Millan, who went to sunny Los Angeles, thank you for helping me land on my feet those first couple years.

Last, but not least, I am indebted to my students at UC Berkeley. Our seminar discussions, talks over coffee, the occasional rant while walking—what a gift to be a teacher. Thank you, Joshua Aragon and Martin Mercado for conducting archival research. Thank you, Joelle de Leon, Julissa Espinoza, and Osirus Polachart for transcribing interviews. Gregoria Gibson, Giselle Perez-Leon, Lisa Ng, and Anayeli Nuñez Almengor—your enthusiasm for your scholarship energizes mine.

This project has been supported by the Ford Foundation, the Provost Fellowship at the University of Southern California, the Jack Henning Fund for Labor Culture and History, the Institute for Research in Labor and Employment, and the Humanities Research Fellowship at UC Berkeley. It builds on the labors of countless scholars in ethnic studies and social history, and on the often-unseen labors of librarians and archivists—such as those in the Walter Reuther Library, Welga! Archives-Bulosan Center for Filipino Studies, Farmworker Movement Documentation Project, and Coachella Valley History Museum. Professor Robyn Magalit Rodriguez, your work at the Bulosan Center allowed for the Filipino voices in this book. Thank you for all your academic leadership, institution building, and activism.

Much of this book, however, lived and grew outside the academy. It was largely inspired by the educators and students at Desert Mirage High School, with whom I grew as a thinker and person. Morelia Baltazar, Joe Ceja, Erasmo Cisneros, Christina Endres, Dora Flores, Roy Garza, John Gonzalez, Brian Katz, Mo Martin, Luis Pinedo, Shane Reyes, Yuridia Rochin, Alfonso Taboada—I carry you with me still. The book was also shaped by the wine-flowing conversations with my life-long friend, Crystal Gonzalez, and our often-stubborn but always generous comrade-teacher, Michael Rosenfeld. It gained warmth through the many friendships I gathered in beautiful Los Angeles—where days and evenings brought cumbias, poetry readings, and backyard asados, morning pâté with leftover wine, impulse food drives to Koreatown, and those citrus-pungent evening streets. Thank you, Heather Ashby, Yina Chapa, Yousef Crownhead, Yago Cura, Amanda Duran, Max Felker-Kantor, DJ Gonzalez, Patricia Gonzalez, Kip Austin Hinton, Nadia Kanagawa, Vanessa Mancia, Elizabeth Martinez, Karla Morel, Mona Navarro, Amalia Leticia Ortiz, Carlos Parra, Monica Pelayo, Jesus Perez, Ivy Quicho, Nic Ramos, Jenn Tran, and Jessica Viramontes for having been part of this journey. And Stacey Greene—we met as I was leaving Los Angeles, but I am so fortunate to have you in my life. Every single sentence in this book has been written with you—whether in unreasonably early morning hours or in my preferred late evenings, in cafés, my office, or new home, in New York, Los Angeles, Berkeley, and Mexico City. Even during pandemics. Thank you for every one of these years—for your brilliance, your kindness, your care. Haruki and Fidelito just meowed at you.

Lastly, my family—my political and personal home base. I was raised by loving and ambitious parents, Sammy and Sandra, who dreamt for their children what was impossible for them, parents who do what so many other poor parents do—work and work to create a space of possibility for their children, for the world they should have had, as well. Gracias, ama. Thank you, dad. I hope always to make you proud. I was also raised in a rambunctious community of uncles and aunts, *tias* and *tios*, cousins and *primos*, neighbors, godparents, teachers, and mentors. Each one guided me, each one encouraged me, each one lightened me. Thank you. To my wonderful brother and sisters, Sammy, Marlene, and Litzy, and my cousin-sister, Ana. I am proud of everything we achieved, despite the damn odds, and overjoyed we continue to gravitate to each other. Sammy and Glenda, thank you for your hospitality and food (those lambchops!), and for raising such a kind, happy, and generous daughter. Anita, Litzy, and Marlene, you saved this book countless times—from finding my computer, transcribing notes, and recommending writing songs to joining me on cocktail adventures because the writing gods demanded it. We have much celebrating to do!

To my dear students at Desert Mirage High School—I think often of our campus, of reading Zinn and Takaki with you, of watching our soccer teams win everything, of your beautiful love for your families. I hope you see your joy and curiosity in these pages. I sometimes wish, too, that the people in this book had met you. I know they would be inspired by you, as I was. Thank you.

Appendix
Oral History Project: United Farm Worker Movement in the Coachella Valley

Participant Name	Interview #	Date	Interview Length
Stella Acuña	1, p.1	4.18.17	6:28
Stella Acuña	1, p.2	4.18.17	1:17:23
Doug Adair	1	2.2.15	1:44:51
Doug Adair	2	2.7.15	1:35:01
Doug Adair	3	2.15.17	1:09:12
Filogonio Angel	1	4.16.17	1:29:04
Filogonio Angel	2	4.19.17	1:43:02
Filogonio Angel	3	4.19.17	33:32
Guillermina Arredondo	1	2.12.17	1:36:49
Manuel Arredondo and Joe Ceja	1	2.06.15	2:01:18
Eliseo Arrellano	1	2.06.15	1:15:27
Silveria Beltran	1	4.16.17	28:45
Silveria Beltran	2	4.19.17	1:31:58
Ruben Cancino	1	4.17.17	52:55
Maria Carmona	1	1.31.14	48:35
Maria Carmona	2	1.31.14	47:01
Maria Carmona	3	2.10.17	53:43
Maria Carmona	4	2.10.17	39:39
Guadalupe Carrizales	1	3.01.14	1:01:56
Elvia Alicia and Armando Castillo	1	4.17.17	1:12:32
Elvia Alicia Castillo	2	4.17.17	1:07:51
Elvia Alicia Castillo	3	4.18.17	1:02:46
Joe Ceja	1	11.20.13	1:25:05
Joe Ceja and Manuel Arredondo	2	2.06.15	2:01:18
Joe Ceja	3	4.15.17	1:45:02
Joe Ceja	4	2.9.18	1:14:48
Carmen Celaya	1	10.15.13	2:06:58
Fernando Chavez	1	11.15.13	1:17:17

(continued)

(*continued*)

Participant Name	Interview #	Date	Interview Length
Luciano Crespo	1	1.30.14	0:32:07
Luciano Crespo	2	2.1.14	2:24:00
Luciano Crespo	3	2.8.14	2:14:27
Luciano Crespo	4	4.17.17	1:21:49
Luciano Crespo	5	5.08.20	51:27
Luciano Crespo	6	5.30.20	1:10:54
Arturo Diaz	1	1.31.15	1:15:37
Alfredo Figueroa	1, p.1	10.3.13	0:23:50
Alfredo Figueroa	1, p.2	10.3.13	0:54:54
Alfredo Figueroa	2, p.1	10.5.13	0:5:49
Alfredo Figueroa	2, p.2	10.5.13	0:41:47
Alfredo Figueroa	2, p.3	10.5.13	0:1:25
Alfredo Figueroa	2, p.4	10.5.13	0:2:43
Alfredo Figueroa	2, p.5	10.5.13	0:31:41
Alfredo Figueroa	3	10.12.13	1:33:16
Alfredo Figueroa	4	11.09.13	1:50:18
Alfredo Figueroa	5	10.25.14	57:58
Demesia Figueroa	1, p.1	10.5.13	0:49:31
Demesia Figueroa	1, p.2	10.5.13	0:25:44
Demesia Figueroa	1, p.3	10.5.13	0:21:28
Demesia Figueroa	1, p.4	10.5.13	0:59:53
Demesia Figueroa	2	11.09.13	2:02:43
Demesia Figueroa	3	5.20.20	59:36
Fausto Figueroa	1	4.19.17	1:43:02
Mike Figueroa	1	1.23.15	1:25:57
Ray Rodriguez and Alfredo Fuller	1	10.8.13	1:46:29
Ray Rodriguez and Alfredo Fuller	2	10.10.13	2:26:21
Ray Rodriguez and Alfredo Fuller	3	10.15.13	2:16:58
Ray Rodriguez and Alfredo Fuller	4	10.17.13	2:45:52
Ray Rodriguez and Alfredo Fuller	5	11.12.13	2:02:39
Ray Rodriguez and Alfredo Fuller	6	11.14.13	2:02:14
Alfredo Fuller and Ray Rodriguez	7	1.22.15	2:43:35
Alfredo Fuller and Ray Rodriguez	8	2.11.17	1:40:21
Ray Rodriguez	9	5.05.20	1:08:38
Ray Rodriguez	10	5.06.20	51:19
Ray Rodriguez	11	5.07.20	57:28
Ray Rodriguez	12	5.08.20	1:08:20
Alfredo Fuller	13	5.20.20	1:05:06

(*continued*)

Participant Name	Interview #	Date	Interview Length
Ruben Gonzalez	1	10.23.13	0:57:07
Israel Huerta	1	11.21.13	1:27:37
Max Huerta	1	3.18.15	2:40:00
Max Huerta	2	1.30.15	3:10:12
Max Huerta	3	3.18.15	2:45:46
Max Huerta	4	4.17.17	1:16:00
Ray Huerta	1 p.1	11.14.13	0:15:25
Ray Huerta	1 p.1	11.14.13	0:15:25
Tony Lopez	1	2.27.18	2:19:04
Tony Lopez	2	2.28.18	1:29:41
Raul and Sherrie Loya	1	11.8.13	0
Simon Machuca	1	11.05.13	1:30:04
Simon Machuca	2	11.26.13	2:15:19
Simon Machuca	3	2.11.17	1:04:51
Sam Maestas	1	2.13.17	2:06:15
Maria Marron	1	1.31.14	0:47:01
Maria Marron	2	1.31.14	0:48:35
Maria Marron	3	2.7.14	0:27:11
Maria Marron	4	10.31.14	
Remedios Martinez	1	1.30.14	0:30:51
Remedios Martinez	2	4.13.17	1:07:51
Remedios Martinez	3	4.17.17	59:15
Evangelina Mendoza	1, p.1	2.8.14	0:32:23
Evangelina Mendoza	1, p.2	2.18.14	0:06:23
Flora (Avila) and Tony Mendoza	1	10.11.13	1:27:23
Flora (Avila) and Tony Mendoza	2	10.14.13	2:36:44
Silvia Montenegro	1	2.1.15	1:08:19
Silvia Montenegro	2	5.28.20	55:10
Silvia Montenegro	3	5.29.20	1:17:26
Isabel and Constantino Moreno	1	2.10.17	1:43:34
Louise Neely	1	10.13.13	3:27:06
Felicitas Nuñez	1		Not recorded
Felicitas Nuñez	2	6.01.20	1:01:29

(*continued*)

(continued)

Participant Name	Interview #	Date	Interview Length
Clementina Olloque	1	11.25.12	0:24:38
Clementina Olloque	2	8.12.14	1:38:23
Clementina Olloque	3	8.13.14	1:23:05
Clementina Olloque	4	8.14.14	1:15:45
Clementina Olloque	5	2.1.15	38:19
Clementina Olloque	6	2.11.17	1:00:06
Clementina Olloque	7	2.11.17	7:59
Clementina Olloque	8	5.08.20	47:47
Virginia Ortega	1	1.21.15	2:13:00
Virginia Ortega	2	1.30.15	1:52:43
Virginia Ortega	3	2.11.17	57:57
Virginia Ortega	4	2.11.17	1:45:42
Virginia Ortega	5	4.18.17	1:44:42
Virginia Ortega	6	4.19.17	1:28:15
Virginia Ortega	7	5.05.20	1:47:02
Virginia Ortega	8	5.06.20	1:46:46
Virginia Ortega	9	5.07.20	1:26:29
Gilbert Padilla	1	1.15.15	0:47:08
Sophie Paiz	1	4.15.17	1:09:50
Sophie Paiz	2	4.16.17	1:29:36
David Perez	1	2.14.17	3:43:38
David Perez	2	4.15.17	1:32:25
David Perez	3	4.18.17	1:36:38
David Perez	4	6.01.20	56:07
Maria Teresa and Salvador Ramirez	1	4.15.17	34:40
Calisto Ramos and Larry Salas	1	10.22.13	1:46:44
Calisto Ramos and Larry Salas	2	10.29.13	2:01:56
Calisto Ramos and Larry Salas	3	11.12.13	0:49:45
Calisto Ramos and Larry Salas	4	11.14.13	1:52:53
Calisto Ramos and Larry Salas	5	11.19.13	1:27:39
Calisto Ramos	1	2.10.17	53:44
Calisto Ramos	2	4.18.17	1:36:38
Calisto Ramos	3	5.21.20	1:01:54
Calisto Ramos	4	5.28.20	1:10:33
Irene Reyes (Gonzalez)	1	1.14.15	2:04:13
Tony Reyes	1	2.27.14	
Enrique Rodriguez	1	3.1.14	1:22:26

(continued)

Participant Name	Interview #	Date	Interview Length
Miguel Rodriguez	1	1.31.15	58:29
Fred Ross Jr.	1	2.14.15	46:15
Marcos and Catalina Ruiz	1	11.19.13	1:11:20
Petra Ruiz	1 p.1	10.4.13	1:00:25
Petra Ruiz	1 p.2	10.4.13	0:18:50
Petra Ruiz	2	1.30.14	1:23:58
Alfonso Sanchez	1	11.18.13	0:48:11
Melecio Sanchez	1	2.14.17	1:40:07
Melecio Sanchez	2	2.15.17	1:32:42
Gilda Guitron Sandsness	1 p. 1	10.3.12	0:14:28
Gilda Guitron Sandsness	1 p. 2	10.3.12	0:12:05
Gilda Guitron Sandsness	2	10.7.13	1:19:16
Gilda Guitron Sandsness	3	10.14.13	0:20:28
Maria Serrano	1	11.27.13	3:15:09
Maria Serrano	2	11.28.13	2:26:16
Maria Serrano	3	1.31.14	2:22:37
Maria Serrano	4	2.7.14	0:18:16
Maria Serrano	5	2.10.17	2:06:29
Maria Serrano	6	2.13.17	1:42:10
Maria Serrano	7	5.04.20	29:21
Maria Serrano	8	5.07.20	1:10:16
Maria Serrano	5	2.10.17	2:06:29
Leonor and Rodolfo Suarez	1		
Leonor and Rodolfo Suarez	2	2.14.17	1:35:42
Antonio Puga Torres	1	2.13.17	1:23:56
Antonio Puga Torres	2	4.19.17	1:02:14
Hilario Torres	1	11.22.13	1:27:37
Hilario Torres	2	2.12.17	1:48:29
Hilario Torres	3	5.31.20	56:05
Amalia Uribe Deaztlan	1	1.22.15	1:29:56
Amalia Uribe Deaztlan	2	3.18.15	1:35:02
Amalia Uribe Deaztlan	3	2.12.17	1:45:37
Amalia Uribe Deaztlan	4	5.21.20	49:35
Federico Vargas	1	2.12.17	1:40:42
Federico Vargas	2	2.14.17	1:10:13
Juan Venegas	1	11.16.13	1:13:23

Notes

Introduction

1. "The Strikers of Coachella," *El Malcriado*, July 1, 1969, https://libraries.ucsd.edu/farmworkermovement/ufwarchives/elmalcriado/1969/July%201-15,%201969%20No%207_PDF.pdf.

2. "Cesar E. Chavez: Model Curriculum," California Department of Education, accessed December 14, 2021, https://chavez.cde.ca.gov/ModelCurriculum/Intro.aspx.

3. Li Fellers, "Stamp Honors Chavez," *Los Angeles Times*, April 24, 2003; "New Stamp Honors Labor Leader," *NPR Morning Edition*, April 23, 2003, https://www.npr.org/templates/story/story.php?storyId=1240971; "First UFW Headquarters," National Park Service, accessed December 14, 2021, https://www.nps.gov/places/ooo/first-ufw-headquarters.htm.

4. Armando Ibarra, "Symbolic Tribute to Chavez Isn't Enough," *Progressive Magazine*, January 26, 2021.

5. Jay Newton-Smalls, "Obama's 'Si Se Puede,'" *Time Magazine*, January 15, 2008; Garance Franke-Ruta, "Obama Honors the Coiner of a Slogan," *Washington Post*, March 31, 2009.

6. In order of publication, Marco G. Prouty, *Cesar Chavez, the Catholic Bishops, and the Farmworkers' Struggle for Social Justice* (Tucson: University of Arizona Press, 2006); Miriam Pawel, *The Union of Their Dreams: Power, Hope, and Struggle in Cesar Chavez's Farm Worker Movement* (New York: Bloomsbury, 2009); Marshall Ganz, *Why David Sometimes Wins: Leadership, Organization and Strategy in California's Farm Worker Movement* (Oxford: Oxford University Press, 2010); Randy Shaw, *Beyond the Fields: Cesar Chavez, the UFW and the Struggle for Justice in the 21st Century* (Berkeley: University of California Press, 2010); Frank Bardacke, *Trampling Out the Vintage: Cesar Chavez and the Two Souls of the United Farm Workers* (London: Verso, 2011); Matt Garcia, *From the Jaws of Victory: The Triumph and Tragedy of Cesar Chavez and the Farm Worker Movement* (Berkeley: University of California Press, 2012); Miriam Pawel, *The Crusades of Chavez: A Biography* (New York: Bloomsbury, 2015); Luis D. Leon, *The Political Spirituality of Cesar Chavez: Crossing Religious Borders* (Oakland: University of California Press, 2015); Gabriel Thompson, *America's Social Arsonist: Fred Ross and Grassroots Organizing in the Twentieth Century* (Oakland: University of California Press, 2016); LeRoy Chatfield with Jorge Mariscal, *To Serve the People: My Life Organizing with Cesar Chavez and the Poor* (Albuquerque: University of New Mexico Press, 2019). Outside books, see *Delano Manongs*, documentary, directed by Marisa Arroy, Media Factory, 2014; *Cesar Chavez: History Is Made One Step at a Time*, biography/drama, directed by Diego Luna, Canana Films, 2014; *Dolores: Portrait of a Labor and Feminist Icon*, biography/drama, PBS, 2018.

7. Eugene Nelson, *Huelga! The First Hundred Days of the Great Delano Grape Strike* (Delano, CA: Farm Worker Press, 1966); John Gregory Dunne, *Delano* (New York: Farrar,

Straus & Giroux, 1967); Peter Matthiessen, *Sal Si Puedes: Cesar Chavez and the New American Revolution* (New York: Random House, 1969); Sam Kushner, *Long Road to Delano: A Century of Farm Workers' Struggle* (New York: International Publisher Press, 1975); Ronald B. Taylor, *Chavez and the Farm Workers: A Study in the Acquisition and Use of Power* (Boston: Beacon, 1975); Susan Ferris and Ricardo Sandoval, *The Fight in the Fields: Cesar Chavez and the Farmworkers Movement* (San Diego, CA: Harcourt Brace, 1997); Craig Scharlin and Lilia V. Villanueva, *Philip Vera Cruz: A Personal History of Filipino Immigrants and the Farmworkers Movement* (Seattle: University of Washington Press, 2000).

8. Garcia has noted that the farmworker absence in United Farm Workers (UFW) histories reflects methodological limits: "all systematic collection of oral histories and documents from farm workers during the heyday of the UFW remains to be done." Garcia, *From the Jaws of Victory*, 10. This absent frame contrasts significantly from pre-UFW farmworker histories. For Mexican farmworkers in California, for instance, see Devra Weber, *Dark Sweat, White Gold: California Farm Workers, Cotton, and the New Deal* (Berkeley: University of California Press, 1994); Gilbert G. Gonzalez, *Labor and Community: Mexican Citrus Worker Villages in Southern California County, 1900–1950* (Chicago: University of Illinois Press, 1994); Jose M. Alamillo, *Making Lemonade Out of Lemons: Mexican American Labor and Leisure in a California Town 1880–1960* (Chicago: University of Illinois Press, 2006); Frank Barajas, *Curious Unions: Mexican American Workers and Resistance in Oxnard, California, 1898–1961* (Lincoln: University of Nebraska Press, 2012); Benny J. Andres Jr., *Power and Control in the Imperial Valley: Nature, Agribusiness, and Workers on the California Borderland, 1900–1940* (College Station: Texas A&M University Press, 2016); Lori Flores, *Grounds for Dreaming: Mexican Americans, Mexican Immigrants and the California Farm Worker Movement* (New Haven, CT: Yale University Press, 2016).

9. For an exception, see Margaret Rose, "Traditional and Nontraditional Patterns of Female Activism in the United Farm Workers of America, 1962 to 1980," *Frontiers: A Journal of Women Studies* 11, no. 1, Las Chicanas (1990): 26–32. New scholarship promises to foreground rank-and-file workers. See Neama Alamri, "Long Live the Arab Worker: A Transnational History of Labor and Empire in the Yemeni Diaspora" (PhD diss., University of California, Merced, 2020); Ivon Padilla-Rodriguez, "Undocumented Youth: The Labor, Education and Rights of Migrant Children in Twentieth Century America" (PhD diss., Columbia University, 2021).

10. Five books guided and shaped *The Strikers of Coachella*. They are: Tera W. Hunter, *To 'Joy My Freedom: Southern Black Women's Lives and Labors after the Civil War* (Cambridge: Harvard University Press, 1998); Dawn Bohulano Mabalon, *Little Manila Is in the Heart: The Making of the Filipina/o American Community in Stockton, California* (Durham: Duke University Press, 2013); Charles M. Payne, *I've Got the Light of Freedom: The Organizing Tradition and the Mississippi Freedom Struggle* (Oakland: University of California Press, 1995); Vicky L. Ruiz, *Cannery Women, Cannery Lives: Mexican Women, Unionization, and the California Food Processing Industry, 1930–1950* (Albuquerque: University of New Mexico Press, 1987); *Migrant Imaginaries: Latino Cultural Politics in the U.S.-Mexico Borderlands* (New York: New York University Press, 2008).

11. For an incisive critique of this model, see John D. Marquez, *Black-Brown Solidarity: Racial Politics in the New Gulf South* (Austin: University of Texas Press, 2013), 33–39. For a critique of historical "empty time"—which allows for the train on tracks model—see Walter

Benjamin, "Theses on the Philosophy of History," in *Illuminations: Essays and Reflections*, ed. Hannah Arendt, trans. Harry Zohn (New York: Schocken Books, 1968), 260–64.

12. For a discussion on the intellectual and political shortcomings of these questions, see Robin D. G. Kelley, "Preface" and "'When History Sleeps': A Beginning," in *Freedom Dreams: The Black Radical Imagination* (Boston: Beacon Press, 2002), 1–12. See also Jose Esteban Muñoz, "Introduction: Feeling Utopia," in *Cruising Utopia: The Then and There of Queer Futurity* (New York: New York University Press, 2009), 1–18.

13. Linda Chavez and Pete Velasco, interview by Ray Telles, 1995/1996, audio recording available under "Paradigm Productions Farmworker Interviews—1995–96," Oral History Collection, Farmworker Movement Documentation Project (henceforth, FMDP), https://libraries.ucsd.edu/farmworkermovement/media/oral_history/paradigm/lchavez-SR%2002%2003.mp3.

14. "Pete Velasco Ilocano Letter, nd," Folder 4, Box 4, UFW Administration Collection, Part III, Archives of Labor and Urban Affairs (henceforth, ALUA).

15. Amalia Uribe Deaztlan, interview by Christian Paiz, January 22, 2015.

16. For photos of the UFW Coachella Grape Strike of 1969, see "Coachella March, May 1969" Photo Collection by Hub Segur, Media Gallery, Farmworker Movement Documentation Project (FMDP): http://libraries.ucsd.edu/farmworkermovement/gallery/index.php?cat=18.

17. For a nuanced discussion, see Walter Johnson, "On Agency," *Journal of Social History* 37, no.1 (Autumn 2003): 113–24.

18. Lowell J. Bean, *Muskat's People: The Cahuilla Indians of Southern California* (Berkeley: University of California Press, 1974); Lowell J. Bean, *The Cahuilla Landscape: The Santa Rosa and San Jacinto Mountains* (Menlo Park, CA: Ballena Press, 1991); Deborah Dozier, *The Heart Is Fire: The Worlds of the Cahuilla Indians of Southern California* (Berkeley: Heyday Books, 1996); Theodore Gordon, *Cahuilla Nation Activism and the Tribal Casino Movement* (Reno: University of Nevada Press, 2018); Harry C. James, *The Cahuilla Indians* (Banning, CA: Malki Museum, 2011); Ambrose I. Lane Sr., *Return of the Buffalo: The Story Behind America's Indian Gaming Explosion* (Westport, CT: Praeger, 1995); Traci Brynne Voyles, *The Settler Sea: California's Salton Sea and the Consequences of Colonialism* (Lincoln: University of Nebraska Press, 2021).

19. Christian Paiz, "Essential Only as Labor: Coachella Valley Farmworkers and Covid-19," *Kalfou* 8, nos. 1 & 2 (Spring and Fall 2021): 31–50; Jonathan London, Teri Greenfield, and Tara Zagofsky, "Revealing the Invisible Valley," Eastern Coachella Valley Data Project, California Institute for Rural Studies, June 2013.

20. The quotations attributed to Cesar Chavez come from Douglass Adair, a long-time volunteer for the NFWA and subsequent iterations of the UFW movement. For Adair's references to the Rancher Nation, please see Douglass Adair, interview by Greg Truex, March 10, 1995, transcript, p. 33, California State University, Northridge.

21. For this reason, the book refers to California's growers as "ranchers" and "rancher-kings."

22. Philip Vera Cruz, "Editorial: Of Violence and Non-Violence," *El Malcriado*, April 15, 1970.

23. Philip Vera Cruz, "Union Protection and Power," *El Malcriado*, November 1, 1970.

24. Vera Cruz, "Union Protection and Power."

25. For a classic portrait of early twentieth-century Californian agriculture, see Carey McWilliams, *Factories in the Field: The Story of Migratory Farm Labor* (Berkeley: University of California Press, 1999). For a complementary account, see Cletus Daniel, *Bitter Harvest: A History of California Farmworkers, 1870–1941* (Berkeley: University of California, 1982). The studies on Mexican American agricultural communities in California, see Alamillo, *Making Lemonade*; Matt Garcia, *A World of Its Own: Race, Labor, and Citrus in the Making of Greater Los Angeles, 1900–1970* (Chapel Hill: University of North Carolina Press, 2001); Gonzalez, *Labor and Community*. For transnational labor organizing before World War II, see Camille Guerin Gonzales, *Mexican Workers and American Dreams: Immigration, Repatriation, and Californian Farm Labor 1900–1939* (New Brunswick, NJ: Rutgers University Press, 1994); Weber, *Dark Sweat, White Gold*; Deborah Cohen, *Braceros: Migrant Citizens and Transnational Subjects in the Postwar United States and Mexico* (Chapel Hill: University of North Carolina Press, 2011). For Filipino-American and Japanese American agricultural communities, see Eiichiro Azuma, *Between Two Empires: Race, History, and Transnationalism in Japanese America* (Oxford: Oxford University Press, 2005); Rick Baldoz, *The Third Asiatic Invasion: Empire and Migration in Filipino American 1898–1946* (New York: New York University Press, 2011); Dawn Bahulano Mabalon, *Little Manila Is in the Heart: The Making of Filipina/o American Community in Stockton, California* (Durham, NC: Duke University Press, 2013).

26. On the Coachella Valley's westernmost point, settlers founded the resort-based city of Palm Springs, which quickly became a key destination site for filmmakers, actors, and artists from Los Angeles. See J. Sweaton Chase, *Our Araby: Palm Springs and the Garden of the Sun* (New York: J.J. Little & Ives, 1928); Ryan Kray, "Second Class Citizen at a First-Class Resort: Race and Public Policy in Palm Springs" (PhD diss., University of California, Irvine, 2009).

27. The phrase comes from Edith Carlson, "Palm Desert: America's Third Way of Life," 1950s Growth, Folder I, Drawer 4, Palm Desert Collection, Palm Desert Historical Society (henceforth, PDHS), Palm Desert, CA. See also PDHS's collection on early luxury development for more news clippings.

28. Lawrence Culver, *The Frontier of Leisure: Southern California and the Shaping of Modern America* (Oxford: Oxford University Press, 2010); Ryan Kray, "The Path to Paradise: Expropriation, Exodus, and Exclusion in the Making of Palm Springs," *Pacific Historical Review* 73, no. 1 (February 1, 2004): 85–126.

29. "Our Desert Valley Grows 8,000 Acres of Grapes," *Desert Rancher*, July 1952; "Valley Growers Key to Grape Industry Market," *Desert Rancher*, June 1955; "Grapes May Still Top Record," *Desert Rancher*, June 1964.

30. My approach to submerged stories draws heavily from Robin D. G. Kelley's observations in "'We Are Not What We Seem': Rethinking Black Working-Class Opposition in the Jim Crow South," *Journal of American History* 80, no. 1 (June 1993): 75–112.

31. In her history of the 1960s and 1970s Coors boycott, Allyson P. Brantley emphasized the "vibrancy, creativity, and persistence of leftist activism in the late twentieth century." *Brewing a Boycott: How a Grassroots Coalition Fought Coors and Remade American Consumer Activism* (Chapel Hill: University of North Carolina Press, 2021), 5. In similar fashion, Chicana/o politics continued to shape Coachella Valley life in the 1970s and 1980s, even as it faced daunting forces.

32. The quote is the title of Garcia's history, *From the Jaws of Victory*. Other histories pivoting on Chavez's failings include Bardacke, *Trampling Out*; Ganz, *Why David*; Pawel, *The Union*.

33. Lane Windham, *Knocking on Labor's Door: Union Organizing in the 1970s and the Roots of a New Economic Divide* (Chapel Hill: University of North Carolina, 2017), 8.

34. I made no effort to interview Coachella Valley ranchers for three reasons. First, local and national newspapers diligently amplified their views and interests, especially in the 1970s, when the national tenor become more skeptical of UFW claims. Second, pro-rancher leaders conducted oral history interviews, such as Coachella's Father Humphrey in 1974: "'The Farm Labor Issues: A Searching for the Truth,' by Father Humphrey," which interviewed and presented the views of K.K. Larson, Ben Laflin, and Lionel Steinberg. See "Salandini Notes on 1974 Coachella Priest Meeting on Strikes," Folder 10, Box 8, Victor Salandini Papers, Special Collections, Stanford University. Third, the post-1973 strike lawsuits produced a trove of rancher depositions. See chapter 7. As such, available archives provided rancher views with depth and complexity. Regarding anti-UFW farmworkers, I interviewed a handful of workers who were anti-UFW and then UFW stalwarts, which explained their willingness to participate in the oral history project. I paired these interviews with interviews of non-farmworker Mexican Americans, of which some shared they were initially anti-UFW. But, most importantly, I draw heavily from archival collections, such as pro-Teamster farmworker testimonies in 1973 and Victor Salandini's farmworker surveys of 1974, 1975, and 1976. See chapters 7 and 8.

35. For Filipino oral histories, see the collections in the Welga Archive-Bulosan Center for Filipino Studies at the University of California, Davis, https://welgadigitalarchive.omeka.net/items/browse?search=&advanced%5B0%5D%5Belement_id%5D=&advanced%5B0%5D%5Btype%5D=&advanced%5B0%5D%5Bterms%5D=&range=&collection=&type=4&user=&tags=&public=&featured=&exhibit=&submit_search=Search+for+items&sort_field=added&sort_dir=a. See also the FMDP at the University of California, San Diego, https://libraries.ucsd.edu/farmworkermovement/medias/oral-history/. For bracero oral histories, see the Smithsonian's Bracero History Archive, http://braceroarchive.org/. For Mexican American pioneers, see the interviews conducted by the historian Sarah Seekatz, available in the Coachella Valley History Museum, https://www.cvhm.org.

36. For a brief introduction to oral history, see Sally Chandler, "Oral History Across Generations: Age, General Identity and Oral Testimony," *Oral History* 33, no. 2 (Autumn 2005): 48–56; Sean Field, "Beyond 'Healing': Trauma, Oral History and Regeneration," *Oral History* 34, no. 1 (Spring, 2006): 31–42; Gary Y. Okihiro, "Oral History and the Writing of Ethnic History," *The Oral History Review* 9 (1981): 27–46. For Mexican American oral history, consider the very helpful *US Latina and Latino Oral History Journal*.

Chapter 1

1. Historians of Californian agriculture have documented the Rancher Nation's history. Since early colonization, ranchers claimed land through war and exploited racialized laborers to harvest. For profits, they paid misery wages, pitted workers against each other, and crushed unions with mobs and police batons. For whiteness, ranchers segregated workers into racialized spaces on town edges, where they bore substandard housing, social services,

and infrastructure. The rancher embodied virility and civilization and spoke of their responsibility to provide and the right to rule with the king's impunity. See citations at note 24 in the introduction.

2. "Introducing: Desert Rancher, Valley's First Farm Magazine," *Desert Rancher*, July 1950. The *Desert Rancher* profiled over seventy-five Coachella Valley ranchers in two decades, covering operations, domestic life, and community contributions. All issues are available in the Coachella Valley History Museum (henceforth, CVHM), Indio, California.

3. White settlers founded Hagerty's town in the early twentieth century. Though initially bustling, it suffered devastating fires that dimmed ambitions by the 1930s. In the *Desert Rancher* profile, Hagerty promised to stem the town's decline. "Typical Valley Farm Family: Meet Your Neighbors, The Hagerty's of Thermal," *Desert Rancher*, July 1950.

4. Patriarchy and heteronormativity undergirded this world. See "Charlie Cast's Dream of 1918 Is Edna's 'Garden of the Setting Sun,'" *Desert Rancher*, September 1950; "Busy Life and Interesting Background Is Story of Codekas Family," *Desert Rancher*, June 1958; "Doug and Madelyn Nance Happy on the Farm After Early Misgivings," *Desert Rancher*, November 1958; "Mr. and Mrs. Ben Laflin Jr. Are Enthusiastic Members of Pioneer Date Family," *Desert Rancher*, June 1961.

5. The *Desert Rancher* credited the region's development to rancher initiative: "Coachella has always been closely allied to the agriculture of Coachella Valley and, similarly, agriculture has played an important role in the city's amazing growth." See "Commercial Development of Coachella Linked Closely to Valley's Farming," *Desert Rancher*, May 1960.

6. One of the earliest, Smeaton Chase's *Our Araby: Palm Springs and the Garden of the Sun* (New York: J.J. Little & Ives, 1928), wrote on Palm Spring's virgin land and bourgeoning white colony alongside "friendly Indians." See also Wayland A. Dunham, *It's a Date!* (Los Angeles: Publication Press, 1948) and Ole J. Nordland's *Coachella Valley's Golden Years* (Los Angeles: Coachella Valley Water District, 1972). Dunham wrote: "the desert waited—sullen, hot and fierce in its desolation, holding its treasures under the seal of death against the coming of the strong ones," 1. The CVHM also holds amateur settler histories, such as Paul Wilhelm, "The Coachella Valley Story, Saga of a New Frontier: Being the History of the Colorado Desert and the Coachella Valley from Earliest Times" (unpublished manuscript) and Ralph E. Pawley, "The History of the Coachella Valley" (unpublished manuscript). Wilhelm's chapters followed the reclamation story: "Before Spaniards," "Indian Remembered Land," "Make Dry Sand Bloom," "Pioneer Bootstrap Legacy," "By Their Own Free Enterprise."

7. See Nevada C. Colley, *From Maine to Mecca* (Indio, CA: Nevada C. Colley, 1967), Nina Paul Shumway, *Your Desert and Mine* (Los Angeles: Westernlore Press, 1960), and Josephine Morse True, *Painted Rocks* (San Diego, CA: Arts and Craft Press, 1965). Each portrayed the Indigenous Cahuilla as de-evolving, which (the writers argued) prevented them from reclaiming the desert.

8. The *Date Palm*'s masthead (1910s) read: "A landless man for a manless land." By the third issue, the newspaper changed it to the boosterish: "Send this paper to a landless man!" In "The Story of Read Dates," the *Date Palm* wrote characteristically on October 30, 1914: "The story of this Date Garden is a simple record of perseverance in the face of many difficulties and the pioneering of a new industry that will change the whole of the Coachella Valley." The same issue carried summaries of each town's development and modernity, which Nina Paul Shumway repeated for the *Coachella Valley Submarine: Development Edition* (Coachella, 1923), Local History Collection, Indio Public Library, Indio, CA.

9. In the 1930s and 1940s, the Coachella Valley's Riverside County Date Fair paired the region's date-based orientalism (an "America's Arabia") with cowboy days, gold hunts, and frontier nostalgia. As Sarah Seekatz explained: "Whether gawking at Indians or pretending to be Arabs, the engagement with the exotic became a crucial component of the Fair." Sarah Anne Seekatz, "America's Arabia: The Date Industry and the Cultivation of Middle Eastern Fantasies in the Deserts of Southern California" (PhD diss., University of California, Riverside, 2014), 197–99. Newspapers commemorated "early pioneers" in the 1930s to 1940s. See "Annual Meeting of Coachella Valley Pioneers," *Coachella Valley Submarine*, March 13, 1936; "Pioneer Meeting a Success," *Coachella Valley Submarine*, April 3, 1936. See also "Echoes from the Past," *Date Palm*, May 13, 1945. "Frontier Days Fete Start Saturday," *Date Palm*, November 8, 1945.

10. *Stories of Pioneer Families of the Coachella Valley: As Told by Coachella Valley Union High School Alumni from the Classes of 1937–1946* (Coachella Valley Pioneer Society, 2004), Local History Collection, Palm Desert Public Library, Palm Desert, CA.

11. Lowell J. Bean, *Muskat's People: The Cahuilla Indians of Southern California* (Berkeley: University of California Press, 1974); Lowell J. Bean, *The Cahuilla Landscape: The Santa Rosa and San Jacinto Mountains* (Menlo Park, CA: Ballena Press, 1991); Deborah Dozier, *The Heart Is Fire: The Worlds of the Cahuilla Indians of Southern California* (Berkeley, CA: Heyday Books, 1996); Theodore Gordon, *Cahuilla Nation Activism and the Tribal Casino Movement* (Reno: University of Nevada Press, 2018); Harry C. James, *The Cahuilla Indians* (Banning, CA: Malki Museum, 2011); Ambrose I. Lane Sr., *Return of the Buffalo: The Story Behind America's Indian Gaming Explosion* (Westport, CT: Praeger, 1995); Traci Brynne Voyles, *The Settler Sea: California's Salton Sea and the Consequences of Colonialism* (Lincoln: University of Nebraska Press, 2021).

12. True, *Painted Rocks*, 45.

13. Shumway, *Your Desert*, 241.

14. Wilhelm, "The Coachella Valley Story."

15. Chase, *Our Araby*; Ryan M. Kray, "The Path to Paradise: Expropriation, Exodus, and Exclusion in the Making of Palm Springs," *Pacific Historical Review* 73, no. 1 (February 2004): 85–126.

16. John Mack Faragher, ed., *Rereading Frederick Jackson Turner: The Significance of the Frontier in American History, and Other Essays* (New Haven, CT: Yale University Press, 1994); Patricia Nelson Limerick, *The Legacy of Conquest: The Unbroken Past of the American West* (New York: W. W. Norton, 1987).

17. For an early case study, see William Cronon's *Changes in the Land: Indians, Colonists, and the Ecology of New England* (New York: Hill & Wang, 2003). For discourses sanctioning land theft before and after the U.S. Revolution, see Alan Taylor, *William Cooper's Town: Power and Persuasion on the Frontier of the Early American Republic* (New York: Vintage Books, 1996). Even opponents of settler violence spoke of Indigenous peoples as children needing civilization. See Margaret Jacob, *White Mother to a Dark Race: Settler Colonialism, Maternalism, and the Removal of Indigenous Children in the American West and Australia, 1880–1940* (Lincoln: University of Nebraska, 2011), Pablo Mitchell, *Coyote Nation: Sexuality, Race, and Conquest in Modernizing New Mexico, 1880–1920* (Chicago: University of Chicago Press, 2005), and Laura Wexler, *Tender Violence: Domestic Visions in an Age of U.S. Imperialism* (Durham: University of North Carolina Press, 2000). For a history of Indigenous resistance, see Nick Estes, *Our History is the Future* (London: Verso, 2019).

18. See chapter 1 in Jose M. Alamillo, *Making Lemonade Out of Lemons: Mexican American Labor and Leisure in a California Town 1880–1960* (Chicago: University of Illinois Press, 2006) and Matt Garcia, *A World of Its Own: Race, Labor, and Citrus in the Making of Greater Los Angeles, 1900–1970* (Chapel Hill: University of North Carolina Press, 2001). For the Imperial Valley, see Benny J. Andres, *Power and Control in the Imperial Valley: Nature, Agribusiness and Farm Workers on the California Borderland* (College Station: Texas A&M University Press, 2016). For California's early twentieth century racialized nostalgia, see William F. Deverell, *Whitewashed Adobe: The Rise of Los Angeles and the Remaking of its Mexican Past* (Berkeley: University of California Press, 2004) and Phoebe Kropp, *California Vieja: Culture and Memory in a Modern American Place* (Berkeley: University of California Press, 2008).

19. For desert reclamation see Donald Worster, *Rivers of Empire: Water, Aridity, and the Growth of the American West* (Oxford: Oxford University Press, 1985).

20. Settled by white entrepreneurs in the 1890s, locals boasted thousands of resident-settlers on "reclaimed" land by the 1910s, reaching sixty thousand irrigated acres in 1930. Andres, *Power and Control*, 40–67; Worster, *Rivers of Empire*, 194–212.

21. I found Kelly Lytle Hernandez's definition particularly useful: "Settlers invade in order to stay and reproduce while working in order to remove, dominate, and ultimately, replace the Indigenous populations.... Even as many settler societies depend on racialized workforces, settler cultures, institutions, and politics simultaneously trend toward excluding racialized workers from full inclusion in the body politic, corralling their participation in community life, and, largely shaped by rising and falling labor demands, deporting, hiding, or criminalizing them or otherwise revoking the right of racialized outsiders to be within the invaded territory." Kelly Lytle-Hernandez, *City of Inmates: Conquest, Rebellion, and the Rise of Human Caging in Los Angeles, 1771–1965* (Durham: University of North Carolina Press, 2017), 7–8.

22. This characterized nearly all early newspapers, local histories, and postwar coverage of the irrigation-based expansion. The exception came in the 1960s in white women's memoirs that insisted on their contributions to the region's civilizational project.

23. See Bureau of Reclamation, Department of Interior, "Contributions of the All-American Canal System, Boulder Canyon Project, to the Economic Development of the Imperial and Coachella Valleys, Calif., and to the Nation" (Washington: Government Printing Office, 1956), xiii–xiv, Special Collections, University of Southern California, Los Angeles, CA.

24. The original crop, dates, continued to offer a regional identity, as evident in the towns named Oasis and Mecca, high school mascots of Arabs and Rajahs, and an annual county fair production of *A Thousand and One Nights*. See Seekatz, "America's Arabia."

25. Bureau of Reclamation, "Contributions of the All-American Canal," 4–7. By the late 1950s, the *Desert Rancher* boasted, "with proper care and water there is little the Valley can't produce, one of the most diversified agricultural areas in the nation." "Rich Harvest...," *Desert Rancher*, February 1958; "Desert Land Productive of Many Crops," *Desert Rancher*, March 1957.

26. "1964 C.V. Crops Top 42 Million," *Desert Rancher*, January 1965.

27. "Fabulous Valley," *Desert Rancher*, March 1956; "Valley Growers Are among the Most Modern and Efficient in the World," *Desert Rancher*, January 1964.

28. The *Desert Rancher*'s September cover in 1957 was an imposing aerial shot of an unspecified region. The upper half was covered in dark, grainy shrubs, marking the "raw

desert." The other was even "smooth crop land" anticipating development. "Coachella Valley Story: Raw Desert... One Day. Smooth Crop Land... The Next," *Desert Rancher*, September 1957.

29. "Ranchers Favor New Grapes for Their Earliness," *Desert Rancher*, March 1952; "Coachella Valley Grapes Are Often Nation's First Fruit of Spring," *Desert Rancher*, March 1963.

30. By the mid-1950s, Bagdasarian's "Mr. Grape" brand was a local quality leader and earned him the presidency of the Coachella Valley Grape Grower's League. "Mr. Grape Makes His Debut This Season," *Desert Rancher*, April 1954. Another example was Ed Kandarian, whose parents were San Joaquin Valley growers. "Ed and Dorothy Kandarian Have Full and Active Life in Coachella Valley," *Desert Rancher*, May 1960.

31. "New Trend, City Boys Head for the Farm," *Desert Rancher*, April 1955; "Jimmy Gimian Learns Which End of the Shovel Makes Good Vineyard," *Desert Rancher*, July 1958; "Mecca Grape Rancher Has a Colorful Background with 'Greats' of Aviation," *Desert Rancher*, July 1957.

32. For early date and grape harvests (1920s), see "Desert Ranching Not So Different in Years Past, Submarine Proves," *Desert Rancher*, July 1950. For post-1920s grape history, see "Our Desert Valley Grows 8000 Acres of Grapes," *Desert Rancher*, March 1952; "CV Grape Cooperative is Valley's Oldest Plant," *Desert Rancher*, July 1954; "Loyalty, Efficiency Synonymous at Johnson Ranch," *Desert Rancher*, July 1955.

33. In 1952, the *Coachella Valley Sun* celebrated Henry Briggs, "a farmer at heart, and a successful one, as well as a good businessman" who saved the region from an "acute" labor contraction in 1942 by forming the Coachella Valley Farmers Association (CVFA) and securing Mexican Nationals through the Bracero Program. The paper also stressed his community service: "I realize that careful planning and intelligent and progressive thinking in the administration of civic affairs are essential in order to make this a city that will continue to grow." "Henry Briggs, Long Active in Valley Farm Affairs, Seeks Civic Office," *Coachella Valley Sun*, April 3, 1952. See also "Valley Crops Hit New Peak," *Desert Rancher*, February 1961 and "Wide Variety of Crops," *Desert Rancher*, March 1962.

34. "Modernist Homes," *Desert Rancher*, March 1955.

35. Coachella had "modern stores, an expanding elementary school, one of Riverside County's finest halls," the region's first bank, a high school with "modern classroom structures," a fire department, three churches, a ballpark and theater, and a medical center. "Coachella—The Hub of the Valley: Progress Seen in All Phases of Coachella's Life," *Desert Rancher*, March 1952; "Coachella is a Friendly City," *Desert Rancher*, March 1954.

36. "Indio Moves with Progress as CV Grows," *Desert Rancher*, March 1954; "Indio Grew From Rail Stop to Key City of Fabulous Coachella Valley," *Desert Rancher*, March 1956; "Indio Blossomed as Business and Residential Center of CV," *Desert Rancher*, March 1961; "Indio, New Valley's Commercial Center," *Desert Rancher*, February 1967; "Climate, Location Have Made Indio a Real Life 1963 Boom Town," *Desert Rancher*, March 1963.

37. "Land Developing Around Mecca," *Desert Rancher*, March 1952; "Coachella Is Nerve Center for Valley," *Desert Rancher*, March 1955.

38. "Origin of New Perlette, Delight Grapes," *Desert Rancher*, March 1952; "Research on Packing, Packages Use Fiberboard as Wood Substitute," *Desert Rancher*, October 1954; "75 Years of Grape Research Celebrated at Davis," *Desert Rancher*, July 1955; "Desert Citrus Problems Under Study" and "New Quarantine for Citrus May Allow Import of New

Varieties," *Desert Rancher*, June 1956; "Citrus Station to Trace 50 Year Research," *Desert Rancher*, January 1957; "Researchers Link Root Stocks to Spread of Citrus Fungus," *Desert Rancher*, November 1957.

39. Estes, *Our History*, 112, 119, 133–68; Limerick, *The Legacy*, 78–96; Worster, *Rivers of Empire*, 131–43.

40. Tanis Thorne, "The Death of Superintendent Stanley and the Cahuilla Uprising of 1907–1912," *Journal of California and Great Basin* 24, no. 2 (2004): 233–58.

41. In 1912, the resistance against abusive agents led to Superintendent William Stanley's death. In the subsequent investigation, another federal official explained Cahuilla grievances: they want "a nation within a nation and be absolutely free of any control of the United States or of the State of California." Quoted in Thorne, "The Death," 17.

42. "Indian Land Right of Way: Indians Still Plan to Collect Toll for Entering Palm Canyon," *Coachella Valley Submarine*, September 13, 1930; "Indians Get Their Price: Pale Face Officials Capitulate to Demands of Palm Springs Redskins," *Coachella Valley Submarine*, October 24, 1930.

43. Dozier, *The Heart*, 77. See also Gordon, *Cahuilla Nation*, 136–48; Lane, *Return of the Buffalo*.

44. Dozier, *The Heart*, 25. At least 550 Cahuilla lived in reservations in or near the Coachella Valley in the late 1950s.

45. By the late 1940s and the early 1950s undocumented immigration ranged from five hundred thousand to one million annually in the United States. For bracero data, see Leland Yost Testimony, Subcommittee on Migratory of the Committee on Labor and Public Welfare, Senate, U.S. Congress, S. 1129: *A Bill to Stabilize the Domestic Farm Labor Force*, 87th Cong., 2nd sess., February 8–9 (Washington: Government Print Office, 1962), 711. For a brief history, see "The Bracero Era: 1942–1964," in Timothy J. Henderson, *Beyond Borders: A History of Mexican Migration to the United States* (Oxford: Wiley Blackwell, 2011), 58–88.

46. The examples come from Pawley's "History of Coachella," unnumbered pages but references under sections "Early Farming in Coachella Valley," "Coachella Valley Farmers Association," "Date History," and "Grapes." Wilhelm's history noted the 1,800 men hired from Yuma and Cahuilla reservations for the New Liverpool Salt Refinery Company and the owner's use of "Indians to build his ranch house in Indio" in 1896. Likewise, Nordland noted "men stomp[ing] upon the Coachella Valley to harvest in a single generation a community which has leapt into astonished life with outstanding vigor." Nordland, *Golden Years*, 14.

47. "Saund Still Sings Ballad of Abuse," *Desert Rancher*, August 1960; "Average Wage Scale of Nationals Far Above Prevailing Minimums," *Desert Rancher*, December 1960; "Grower Sponsored School for Children of Migrant Workers in Not Appreciated," *Desert Rancher*, September 1961; "Conversational English Classes for Braceros Are Well-Received," *Desert Rancher*, August 1962; "Yost Hits 'Off-Base' Charges of Labor Leaders Regarding Braceros," *Desert Rancher*, June 1963; "Bracero World's Most Successful 'Peace Corps' GOP Candidates Say," *Desert Rancher*, November 1964.

48. In "Fabulous Dunlap Ranch" (1961), the *Desert Rancher* gushed over rancher citrus practices, which allowed a "crew of 80 men [to] double plant 80 acres with 9,000 trees in 32 hours, a feat impossible with the conventional type of nursery tree." In the article's presentation, the workers appeared indistinct from inanimate tools, while worker errors highlighted the critical value provided by overseeing rancher expertise.

49. "Huge Losses Forecast in Farm Economy," *Coachella Valley Sun*, February 4, 1965; "End of Bracero Program Not Just Concern of Cal Farmers," *Coachella Valley Sun*, August 19, 1965. See also *Desert Rancher* articles on braceros in late 1964 and 1965.

50. "Braceros are not wetbacks; Braceros are not cheap labor," it explained, "The Bracero program is an ideal foreign aid–mutual assistance program." "These Hands Are Important to You," *Desert Rancher*, September 1961.

51. Given the rancher's role in establishing membership, labor's erasure and commodification situated workers outside the community. It made them external to its history and identity and denied them standing to level grievances.

52. Maria Marron, interview by Christian Paiz, January 31, 2014. Hilario Torres spoke of similar physical injuries. Hilario Torres, interview by Christian Paiz, November 22, 2013. In an oral history interview in 1978, Willie Barrientos, a 1965 Delano Grape Striker and Agricultural Workers Organizing Committee (AWOC) member, turned his attention away from the interviewer and toward a group of farmworkers, adding, "All these people that you see here they could hardly walk. They work[ed] in the fields [for] most of their lives." Willie Barrientos, interview by Linda Mabalot, March 21, 1978, transcript, p. 1, Linda Mabalot Collection, Welga Archive-Bulosan Center for Filipino Studies (henceforth, Welga).

53. In June 1945, the *Date Palm* reported the "Wage ceiling for grapes set" at 70 to 85 cents an hour. In "Agricultural Wage Rates," *Indio Daily News*, January 6, 1950, reported wages had dropped from 80 cents to 65 cents since World War II, while "some aliens" received only 45 cents. In the early 1960s, AWOC reported $1 hourly wages among its members in the Coachella Valley, though nonmembers earned less than 90 cents an hour. For wage fluctuations in central California, see Matt Garcia, *From the Jaws of Victory: The Triumph and Tragedy of Cesar Chavez and the Farm Worker Movement* (Berkeley: University of California Press, 2012), 15–16.

54. "[Que] ni vamos a sacar para el chivo." Maria Serrano, interview by Christian Paiz, November 28, 2013.

55. Uvaldo Palomares, "A Study of the Role of Mobility in the Acculturation Process of Rural Migrant and Non-Migrant Disadvantaged Mexican Americans in the Coachella Valley" (Thesis, University of California, Los Angeles, 1966), Special Collections, University of Southern California, Los Angeles, CA.

56. U.S. Census, household income 1960, generated by Christian Paiz using data.census.gov.

57. Margaret Breed MacKaye, "A Historical Study of the Development of the Bracero Program, with Special Emphasis on the Coachella and Imperial Valleys" (Thesis, University of Southern California, 1954), 21, Special Collections, Santa Clara University Library, Santa Clara, CA.

58. For a national history of migrant farmworker education, see Ivon Padilla-Rodriguez, "Undocumented Youth: The Labor, Education, and Rights of Migrant Children in Twentieth Century America" (PhD diss., Columbia University, 2021).

59. Clementina Olloque, interview by Christian Paiz, August 12, 2014. In the next interview, Olloque added: "There were no doors for me, to continue forward.... I felt the depression in our home, in the form of food, we were too many, there was no expression in schools, you had to stay quiet.... I felt sad because many whites laughed at us, we were completely humiliated." Clementina Olloque, interview by Christian Paiz, August 13, 2014.

60. "You can't go to a school where people aren't poor," he said, "You can't live in certain areas because you're poor. You can't wear certain clothes because you're poor.... You

can't eat in certain places because you are poor." "There was a part of us that wanted to fight for our rights," he added, "but there was a part of us that wanted to numb the memory, forget the memory of what you went through school." Max Huerta, interview by Christian Paiz, January 30, 2015.

61. The rancher "fights an eternal war against his fellow men," he added, and views the world through the prism of "survival of the fittest." Philip Vera Cruz, "Union Protection and Power," *El Malcriado*, November 1, 1970.

62. Douglass Adair, interview by Greg Truex, March 10, 1995, transcript, p. 34, California State University, Northridge.

63. All schools practiced some form of racial segregation. Most elementary schools dedicated a classroom for Mexican students and few high schools expected many. Calisto Ramos and Larry Salas, interview by Christian Paiz, October 29, 2013; Joe Ceja, interview by Christian Paiz, November 20, 2013; Clementina Olloque, interview by Christian Paiz, August 13, 2014; Flora and Tony Mendoza, interview by Christian Paiz, October 11, 2013; Louise Neely, interview by Christian Paiz, October 13, 2013; Ray Rodriguez and Alfredo Fuller, interview by Christian Paiz, October 15, 2013; Gilda Guitron Sandsness, interview by Christian Paiz, October 3, 2013; Amalia Uribe Deaztlan, interview by Christian Paiz, January 22, 2015.

64. The description of farmworker conditions is drawn from original oral history interviews with Coachella Valley residents and farmworkers. All interviews are digital recordings in author's possession unless otherwise noted. Alfredo Figueroa, interview by Christian Paiz, October 5, 2013; Ray Rodriguez and Alfredo Fuller, interview by Christian Paiz, October 15, 2013; Calisto Ramos and Larry Salas, interview by Christian Paiz, November 19, 2013; Maria Serrano, interview by Christian Paiz, November 28, 2013; Maria Marron, interview by Christian Paiz, January 31, 2014.

65. Gilda Guitron Sandsness, interview by Christian Paiz, October 7, 2013; Flora and Tony Mendoza, interview by Christian Paiz, October 11, 2013; Louise Neely, interview by Christian Paiz, October 13, 2013.

66. Calisto Ramos and Larry Salas, interview by Christian Paiz, October 29, 2013; Joe Ceja, interview by Christian Paiz, November 20, 2013; Ray Rodriguez and Larry Fuller, interview by Christian Paiz, October 15, 2013.

67. "Mexicans Embroiled in Stabbing Scrape," *Coachella Valley Submarine*, May 15, 1931. It also reported on a Mexican and Cahuilla teenage boy fight that ended with one death. "Death Closes Boy's Quarrel," *Coachella Valley Submarine*, June 24, 1931.

68. Even when the obvious culprit was white, such as when a white woman ran over a five-year-old Mexican boy, the *Coachella Valley Submarine* wrote: "While the accident was unfortunate, Mrs. Roberts was exonerated from all blame as she did all that was possible to avoid the accident. Several drivers . . . have stated since that they have narrowly avoided striking these same children as they darted out in front of their cars." "Little Joe Ruiz Struck by Auto," *Coachella Valley Submarine*, November 22, 1929.

69. "Mexican Storks," *Coachella Valley Submarine*, November 8, 1929.

70. "Mexican Storks," *Coachella Valley Submarine*, November 8, 1929.

71. "Run Filipinos Out of Valley: Gang of Whites and Mexicans Start 'Roughhouse' Proceedings," *Coachella Valley Submarine*, February 13, 1931. "Labor Troubles Are Over Now: Sheriff Makes Report to Supervisors on Valley Labor Situation," *Coachella Valley Submarine*, February 20, 1931.

72. Louisa Sprenger Ames, "A Program of Relief for Coachella Valley" (Thesis: University of Southern California, 1933): 46–47, Special Collections, University of Southern California, Los Angeles, CA.

73. In "Mexicans to Be Returned—Movement of Aliens Given Endorsement by Supervisors at Monday Meeting," *Coachella Valley Submarine* reported on August 29, 1931, that forty adults and children "solely or partially" dependent on county relief were repatriated to Mexico. Unfortunately, the repatriated included Coachella Valley High School's star quarterback, which prompted the football coach to search for him in Mexico and bring him back to lead the school's winning season. His family stayed behind. See Benjamin Montoya, *Coachella Valley Union High School: The First 50 Years, 1910–60* (CVHS Alumni Association, 2010), 53–54, available in CVHM.

74. While Mexican families represented 27 percent of aid recipients in 1931, they represented only 18 percent of recipients the following year. Ames, "A Program of Relief," 34–37.

75. Ames, "A Program of Relief," 37.

76. MacKaye, "A Historical Study," 19.

77. In 1957, the CVFA director, Leland Yost, estimated the number of braceros as 3,700, which represented a quarter to a third of the region's labor force. U.S. Congress, Senate, Subcommittee on Migratory of the Committee on Labor and Public Welfare, *S. 1129: A Bill to Stabilize the Domestic Farm Labor Force*, 87th Cong., 2nd sess., February 8–9 (Washington: Government Print Office, 1962), 711.

78. Like other places with braceros, the region also employed undocumented immigrants, though their numbers remain elusive. By the late 1940s and 1950s, annual undocumented immigration to the United States ranged from five hundred thousand to one million. See "The Bracero Era: 1942–1964," in Henderson, *Beyond Borders*, 58–88.

79. Israel Huerta, interview by Christian Paiz, November 21, 2013; Irene (Gonzalez) Reyes, interview by Christian Paiz, January 14, 2015; Tony Reyes, interview by Christian Paiz, February 27, 2014; Manuel Arredondo, interview by Christian Paiz, February 6, 2015; Louise Neely, interview by Christian Paiz, October 13, 2013; Gilda Guitron Sandsness, interview by Christian Paiz, October 7, 2013. Filipino migrants were the only postwar exception to the Mexican-as-poor-farmworker rule. They worked the grape harvest, lived in rancher camps, and interacted minimally with institutions (e.g., schools, hospitals).

80. By the 1960s, almost no ethnic Mexican resident held office, while white leaders supported policies that marginalized ethnic Mexicans, such as expanding bracero labor, funneling children into Mexican classrooms, and maintaining housing segregation and hiring discrimination. The local court was led by a white man, who had been fired from the local police force for "brutally beating" a Mexican adolescent. Joe Ceja, interview by Christian Paiz, November 20, 2013; Calisto Ramos and Larry Salas, interview by Christian Paiz, October 29, 2013; Ray Rodriguez and Alfredo Fuller, interview by Christian Paiz, October 15, 2013; Flora and Tony Mendoza, interview by Christian Paiz, October 11, 2013; Louise Neely, interview by Christian Paiz, October 13, 2013; Gilda Guitron Sandsness, interview by Christian Paiz, October 7, 2013. On the Post Office, Alfredo Figueroa, interview by Christian Paiz, October 12, 2013; Ray Rodriguez and Alfredo Fuller, interview by Christian Paiz, October 17, 2013. On the water district, Calisto Ramos and Larry Salas, interview by Christian Paiz, November 12, 2013; on the service sector, see Amalia Uribe Deaztlan, interview by Christian Paiz, January 22, 2015. Alfredo Figueroa said the local judge had a seventh-grade

education, which symbolized the court's lack of preparation and discriminatory practices. Alfredo Figueroa, interview by Christian Paiz, October 5, 2017; Ray Rodriguez and Alfredo Fuller, interview by Christian Paiz, October 17, 2013; "Father Murdered," *Ideal*, June 1–15, 1971, 1.

81. In 1962, six candidates ran for Coachella's city council; none were Mexican American. See "5 or 6 Candidates for Council," *Coachella Valley Sun*, February 15, 1962. For Coachella Valley High School Board, see "CV High Board," *Coachella Valley Sun*, April 12, 1962. See also "Oasis Rancher Appointed to Oasis School Board," *Coachella Valley Sun*, May 31, 1962; "Tenure Awarded to 15 Teachers," *Coachella Valley Sun*, May 21, 1964 (all teachers were white). In "School Updates," *Indio Daily News*, January 6, 1950, a district-contracted consultant had to tell the Thermal Parent Teacher Association (PTA) it needed to include Mexican American parents, which were entirely absent from even the PTA.

82. See the entire issue of *Coachella Valley Sun*, December 6, 1962. "Other Areas Now Involved in Sidewalk Controversy," *Coachella Valley Sun*, March 5, 1964; "Fix Sidewalks or Else . . . City to Tell Owners," *Coachella Valley Sun*, April 9, 1964; "Coachellita Is Finally Getting Gutters and Curbs," *Coachella Valley Sun*, September 7, 1967.

83. "Velasquez Cleared on Charge of Using Car as Weapon," *Coachella Valley Sun*, March 29, 1962. Young women were also not safe from police officers, as illustrated by the Coachella Police Chief's request in 1962 that the overseeing judge dismiss the case against an officer who had sexually propositioned a seventeen-year-old girl. "Police Chief Asks Judge," *Coachella Valley Sun*, August 30, 1962; "Candidates," *Coachella Valley Sun*, April 2, 1964. In "2 Mexican Brothers Resisted Arrest," the *Coachella Valley Sun*, June 18, 1964, reported on two brothers who were interned in the arrest of a third Mexican man, whom the police officer arrested because he was "annoying him." In opposition to the farm labor camp, the rancher Chuchian said, "He'd talked to lots of property owners around Avenue 52 'and they don't want these winos around. A camp would make land values go way down.'" "Citizens Protest Farm Labor Camp," *Coachella Valley Sun*, March 3, 1966. In the same issue, columnist Gale Ellis argued that the families living "in the mesquite brushland all over the lower part of the Valley" were "bums and transients" who only worked one or two days a week to "finance wine." See also "Residents Again Pack Council Room to Protest Farm Labor Camp Idea," *Coachella Valley Sun*, March 17, 1966; "Coachella Mayor: Farm Labor Camp 'A Dead Issue,'" *Coachella Valley Sun*, March 24, 1966.

84. For detailed testimonies of teacher mistreatment in the Coachella Valley, see Laura E. Garcia, Sandra M. Gutierrez, and Felicitas Nuñez, eds., *Teatro Chicana: A Collective Memoir and Selected Plays* (Austin: University of Texas Press, 2008). In 1966, the Mexican American Political Association pushed four candidates for the Coachella Valley High School Board: "Board to Ponder Two High School Budget Proposals," *Coachella Valley Sun*, April 28, 1966.

85. Palomares, "A Study of the Role of Mobility in the Acculturation Process of Rural Migrant and Non-Migrant Disadvantaged Mexican Americans in the Coachella Valley." See also Padilla-Rodriguez, "Undocumented Youth."

86. In the early 1970s, tenants led a rent strike to improve camp conditions and asked county officials why the camp had not been painted, to which officials answered by saying the housing was low income. Maria Marron, interview by Christian Paiz, October 31, 2014. Joe Ceja remembered his camp home as a sixteen square foot room with plywood walls without insulation. It allowed for two small beds and a propane stove. They did not have private restrooms, running water, or heat or cooling systems. Joe Ceja, interview by Christian Paiz,

November 20, 2013. For a history of California migrant housing, see Greg Hise, *Magnetic Los Angeles: Planning the Twentieth-Century Metropolis* (Baltimore: Johns Hopkins University Press, 1997), 86–116.

87. In summer of 1955, Indio School District leaders planned to sell "Lincoln Elementary," which was located in Indio's oldest section, in the "hopes to abandon the substandard building as soon as other school facilities are available." The district appraised the school's value at $80,000, but the highest offer did not reach $60,000. "Sale of Lincoln School Discussed," *Coachella Valley Sun*, June 16, 1955. Lincoln Elementary was also the "Mexican school," plus African American children, and covered only the first three grades. For subsequent grades, students attended the white school, Roosevelt Elementary, which ran from first to eighth grades. According to Flora Mendoza, most Mexican children at Lincoln Elementary could not transition to Roosevelt because they were held back early for teacher claims of limited English proficiency. Eventually, much older students became despondent about still being in first or second grade and refused to attend school. Flora and Tony Mendoza, interview by Christian Paiz, October 14, 2013. In his oral history interview for the Mexican American Pioneer Project, Art Preciado recalled that "I never felt that, I know a lot of people feel that way but never, never entered our minds that we were you know different because we were Hispanics. We were treated just like anybody else would . . . we never really had an impact, you know, on being kind of looked down on." But, a couple sentences later, Preciado shared that he "didn't realize it when we came here [that] they had segregation here. They had a school here, Lincoln School, right here on, what's the name of the street? Bliss and Oasis Street, there was a little school there called Lincoln School. And all the Mexican kids went to that school. I didn't know that. Of course, like I said, when we came here I was twelve years old." Art Preciado, interview by Sarah McCormick, August 20, 2007, transcript, p. 13, CVHM. For more on school segregation, see Gilda Guitron Sandsness, interview by Sarah McCormick, July 16, 2007, transcript, pp. 2–3, CVHM; Mary Carmona, interview by Sarah McCormick, August 23, 2007, transcript, pp. 2–3, CVHM. George Sicre recalled that he "was transferred to the Lincoln School" while his light-complexion brother was assigned to Roosevelt School. The latter was built on his mother's family's land claims after the city took the property through eminent domain. When school officials then tried to bar George Sicre from attending the school on his family's former land, his mother confronted the district: "This was our property at one time where the school is," she told them. "This property used to be our [sic] it was taken from us and you're telling me now that my child cannot attend your school?" George Sicre, interview by Sarah McCormick, July 19, 2007, transcript, p. 13, CVHM.

88. Laura E. Garcia, Sandra M. Gutierrez, and Felicitas Nuñez, eds., "Margarita Carrillo," chap. 10 in *Teatro Chicana: A Collective Memoir and Selected Plays* (Austin: University of Texas, 2008), 82–83.

89. "Second Generation Farmer Typifies Growth of Oasis to Salad Bowl Title," *Desert Rancher*, May 1957; "Background Colorful in Story of Shibata Family," *Desert Rancher*, February 1959; "Ray and Cherry Ishimatsu Have Enjoyed 13 Years of Living, Working on Desert," *Desert Rancher*, July 1962.

90. "Ben Peralta, "Letter to Editors," *Coachella Valley Sun*, October 29, 1965. For reactions to Peralta, see "Ellis," *Coachella Valley Sun*, November 19, 1964.

91. "Local Labor Needs the Work: Shippers Being Requested to Employ Local Labor Only in Carrot Harvest," *Coachella Valley Submarine*, January 2, 1931. For histories of

anti-Filipino racism, see Rick Baldoz, *The Third Asiatic Invasion: Empire and Migration in Filipino America 1898–1946* (New York: New York University Press, 2011) and Mae M. Ngai's "From Colonial Subject to Undesirable Alien: Filipino Migration in the Invisible Empire," in *Impossible Subjects: Illegal Aliens and the Making of Modern America* (Princeton, NJ: Princeton University Press, 2014), 91–126.

92. Edith Carlson, "Palm Desert: America's Third Way of Life," 1950s Growth, Folder I, Drawer 4, Palm Desert Collection, Palm Desert Historical Society, Palm Desert, CA.

93. See Kray, "The Path to Paradise."

94. MacKaye, "A Historical Study," 19.

95. Manuel Arredondo, interview by Christian Paiz, February 6, 2015; Luciano Crespo, interview by Christian Paiz, January 30, 2014; Max Huerta, interview by Christian Paiz, January 30, 2015; Simon Machuca, interview by Christian Paiz, November 26, 2013; Clementina Olloque, interview by Christian Paiz, August 12, 2014; Calisto Ramos and Larry Salas, interview by Christian Paiz, November 19, 2013.

96. The labor contractor's position also meant less labor and greater authority, symbolized by his large truck: he drove to the fields where he checked on workers.

97. One oral history participant elaborated on this point: "[The contractor] would say [to the farmworkers he hired] but you need to give me ten percent. [You are] not going to come work for free! . . . You have 150 people in your crew, and imagine everyone is giving you ten percent on payday—every week, they come and give you ten percent of their checks, because you gave them a job." Calisto Ramos and Larry Salas, interview by Christian Paiz, November 19, 2013.

98. Luciano Crespo, interview by Christian Paiz, January 30, 2014; Simon Machuca, interview by Christian Paiz, November 26, 2013; Clementina Olloque, interview by Christian Paiz, August 12, 2014; Maria Serrano, interview by Christian Paiz, November 28, 2013.

99. Garcia, *From the Jaws*, 18–19; Jacques E. Levy, *Cesar Chavez: Autobiography of La Causa* (Minneapolis: University of Minnesota Press, 1975), 46–47, 60–63, 68–69; Daniel Rothenberg, *With These Hands: The Hidden World of Migrant Farmworkers Today* (Berkeley: University of California Press, 1998), 17, 55–57, 91–120; Stephen H. Sosnick, *Hired Hands: Seasonal Farm Workers in the United States* (Charlotte, NC: McNally & Loftin, 1978), 95–105. For a more measured account of labor contractors in South Texas, see Cristina Salinas, *Managed Migrations: Growers, Farmworkers, and Border Enforcement in the Twentieth Century* (Austin: University of Texas Press, 2012), 117–29.

100. Simon Machuca, interview by Christian Paiz, November 26, 2013; Calisto Ramos and Larry Salas, interview by Christian Paiz, November 19, 2013.

101. Simon Machuca, interview by Christian Paiz, November 26, 2013; Calisto Ramos and Larry Salas, interview by Christian Paiz, November 19, 2013; Luciano Crespo, interview by Christian Paiz, January 30, 2014; Clementina Olloque, interview by Christian Paiz, August 12, 2014; Maria Serrano, interview by Christian Paiz, November 28, 2013.

102. I am indebted to Vicki L. Ruiz for this analysis. In *From Out Of the Shadows: Mexican Women in the Twentieth Century*, Ruiz compared twentieth century racist representations of ethnic Mexican farmworker families, which characterized Mexican women as following the "traditions of feminine subservience," with Chicana/o Studies' "rosy notions of happy extended families." Ruiz wrote, "I too may be guilty of casting a fairly uncritical eye on extended family networks in *Cannery Women, Cannery Lives*. . . . We must move beyond a celebration of *la familia* to address questions of power and patriarchy, the gender politics of

work and family." Vicki L. Ruiz, *From Out of the Shadows: Mexican Women in Twentieth Century America* (Oxford University Press, 1998), 13. See also, "Gloria Arrellanes," in Mario T. Garcia, *The Chicano Generation: Testimonios of the Movement* (Oakland: University of California Press, 2015); Ines Hernandez-Avila, "Manifesto de Memoria: (Re)Living the Movement Without Blinking," in Dionne Espinoza, Maria Eugenia Cotera, Maylei Blackwell, *Chicana Movidas: New Narratives of Activism and Feminism in the Movement Era* (Austin: University of Texas, 2018): 355–74. On contemporary Latinx gender relations and politics, see Aida Hurtado and Mrinal Sinha, *Beyond Machismo: Intersectional Latino Masculinities* (Austin: University of Texas, 2016).

103. Demesia Figueroa shared that her husband, though he fought for farmworker and Chicana/o rights, was a "Mr. Macho, a Mr. Macho Man." He believed "the woman ha[d] to stay at home and take care of the kids," demanded she complete all household labor, and, once, when she mistakenly served him oatmeal instead of the requested rice cream, flung the plate at her. She came into her own through her adolescent daughters, who challenged constraining gender norms and encouraged her to be more assertive. "I became a fighter," Figueroa said, "I became a fighter." Demesia Figueroa, interview by Christian Paiz, November 9, 2013. Male interviewees shared similar memories. Tony Reyes, for instance, shared that when he married his wife in the late 1960s, his father-in-law offered him just one piece of advice: he reminded Reyes that he was now a husband and thus the authority within the household: "su palabra es la ley" or "your word is law." Tony Reyes, interview by Christian Paiz, February 24, 2014. See also Joe Ceja, interview by Christian Paiz, November 20, 2013; Ray Rodriguez and Alfredo Fuller, interview by Christian Paiz, October 10, 2013; Calisto Ramos and Larry Salas, interview by Christian Paiz, November 14, 2013.

104. Guadalupe Carrizales, interview by Christian Paiz, March 1, 2014; Virginia Ortega, interview by Christian Paiz, January 21, 2015.

105. In addition to Carrizales, Figueroa, Ortega, see Maria Marron, interview by Christian Paiz, January 31, 2014; Clementina Olloque, interview by Christian Paiz, August 12, 2014; Tony Reyes, interview by Christian Paiz, February 24, 2014; Petra Ruiz, interview by Christian Paiz, October 4, 2013; Maria Serrano, interview by Christian Paiz, November 28, 2013; Amalia Uribe Deaztlan, interview by Christian Paiz, January 22, 2015.

106. When I asked if men bragged about spending their family's money, Serrano said yes, "as if they were competing [with each other]." Maria Serrano, interview by Christian Paiz, November 28, 2013.

107. Virginia Ortega, interview by Christian Paiz, January 21, 2015. For Maria Marron, such control came after her father forced her, her sisters, and mother to leave Guadalajara, where they had built an independent life. Marron suspected her father wanted their earnings, a practice she saw as common in the Coachella Valley. When she confronted him about this, he said she owed him for the money he spent on her migration. Maria Marron, interview by Christian Paiz, January 31, 2014.

108. Maria Serrano, interview by Christian Paiz, November 28, 2013.

109. In "Chicanas and Mexican Immigrant Families 1920–1940: Women's Subordination and Family Exploitation," Rosalinda M. Gonzalez explained, "The organization of farm labor reinforced patriarchal tendencies within families. Women could labor for the *patron* at work and the *patron* at home." Lois Scharf and Joan M. Jensen, eds., *Decades of Discontent: The Women's Movement, 1920–1940* (Lebanon, NH: Northeastern University Press, 1983). For a Midwestern Mexican farmworker account, see Fran Leeper Buss, ed.,

Forged Under the Sun/Forjada Bajo el Sol: The Life of Maria Elena Lucas (Ann Arbor: University of Michigan Press, 1993).

110. The very hiring process reflected and reified patriarchal relationships, which originated with the male rancher and male contractor. The latter culled contacts, which were usually patriarchal family heads. Women depended heavily on men's work hours to survive economically and may have tolerated their husband's abuse to avoid worse conditions. Petra Ruiz, interview by Christian Paiz, October 4, 2013.

111. The rancher families' gendered inequalities were visible in the titles of profile articles, such as "Doug and Madelyn Nance Happy on the Farm After Early Misgivings," *Desert Rancher*, November 1958. Rancher spouses were not powerless; they joined religious and charity groups, the local Elks chapter, the Women's Club of Indio, and PTAs—all actions that domesticated the settler-colonial project. Some also labored in the ranches and advocated for local harvests. But, at least as local newspapers reflected, male ranchers had the first and final say in their families, and their spouses' agency was limited to supportive roles.

112. Patricia Zavella, *I'm Neither Here Nor There: Mexicans' Quotidian Struggles with Migration and Poverty* (Durham, NC: Duke University Press, 2011), 8–10.

113. Quoted in Dawn Bahulano Mabalon, *Little Manila Is in the Heart: The Making of the Filipina/o American Community in Stockton, California* (Durham, NC: Duke University Press, 2013), 73–74.

114. Craig Charlin and Lilia V. Villanueva, *Philip Vera Cruz: A Personal History of Filipino Immigrants and the Farmworkers Movement* (Seattle: University of Washington Press, 2000), 9.

115. Charlin and Villanueva, *Philip Vera Cruz*, 15.

116. Charlin and Villanueva, *Philip Vera Cruz*, 45–47.

117. Charlin and Villanueva, *Philip Vera Cruz*, 109–10.

118. The son of a Filipino farmworker, Jose Jazmin, recalled in 2015: "You got to understand, some of the Filipinos there were very much into the administration part. A lot of them were foremen . . . [and had] inroads with the farmers." Jose Jazmin, interview by Robyn Rodriguez, February 13, 2015, transcript, Welga, https://welgadigitalarchive.omeka.net/items/show/176. Douglass Adair said UFW contracts disempowered Filipino contractors. "Douglass Adair Interview, Part 1," Cal State University Northridge Oral History Collection, FMDP, https://libraries.ucsd.edu/farmworkermovement/media/oral_history/music/CSUN%20TAPES/Adair,%20Doug.mp3. In the Coachella Valley, Vera Cruz found Filipino supervisors headed crews. See "Chapter 1: The Farm Workers Struggle in Delano," Folder 18, Box 8, Philip Vera Cruz Collection, ALUA.

Chapter 2

1. "They saw the fields," Isabel's son said, "and went to work, because that is what they knew." Joe Ceja, interview by Christian Paiz, February 9, 2018.

2. For similar *colonias*, see Jose M. Alamillo, *Making Lemonade Out of Lemons: Mexican American Labor and Leisure in a California Town 1880–1960* (Chicago: University of Illinois Press, 2006); Matt Garcia, *A World of Its Own: Race, Labor, and Citrus in the Making of Greater Los Angeles, 1900–1970* (Chapel Hill: University of North Carolina Press, 2001). Gilbert G. Gonzalez, *Labor and Community: Mexican Citrus Worker Villages in Southern California County, 1900–1950* (Chicago: University of Illinois Press, 1994).

3. Local newspapers regularly reported on segregated classrooms and language prohibitions, such as the *Coachella Valley Submarine*'s "Coachella Grammar School Notes," October 20, 1933: "No Spanish is to be spoken on the school grounds this year. We feel that children understand English and can do much better work when forced to speak it at play as well as work. The Mexican building is much better at obeying the rule than those in the American school." The Parent Teacher Associations were also segregated. See "Local Mexicans for PTA," *Coachella Valley Submarine*, October 13, 1933; "Coachella Mexican PTA Meets," *Coachella Valley Submarine*, November 10, 1933.

4. Jose also worked the tomato harvest for a Japanese American rancher, a standard practice among local workers with near year-round employment to supplement their incomes. Joe Ceja, interview by Christian Paiz, February 9, 2018.

5. See the "Mexican American Pioneers Project," Oral History Collection conducted and transcribed by Sarah (McCormick) Seekatz in the 2007 summer. The collection includes nine interviews and covers various facets of Mexican American life in the Coachella Valley before and after World War II (WWII). The participants included Onesimo and Ruben Arias, Mary Carmona, Priscilla Garcia, Louise Neely, Art Preciado, Charlotte Salazar, Gilda Sandsness, Alex Sicre, George Sicre. All transcripts are available in the Coachella Valley History Museum (henceforth, CVHM) in Indio, CA.

6. On labor and racial violence, see "Juan Ortiz Released," *Coachella Valley Submarine*, October 27, 1933; "Will Discuss Farm Problems," *Coachella Valley Submarine*, November 3, 1933; "Fatal Ending of Beer Brawl," *Coachella Valley Submarine*, November 10, 1933.

7. Emblematic of this ambivalent position, the *Date Palm* carried articles in early 1945 that listed Mexican American enlistment into the U.S. military while reporting on "zoot-hoodlum[s]." "Zootsuiter Fined in Theater Disturbance" and "Zoot Hoodlum Knife Wielder Again in Jail," *Date Palm*, January 18, 1945. Local hybrid identities appeared visible in "Coachelese," *Indio Daily News*, January 29, 1949, which announced a new local language: "Coachelese," a "mutilated Spanish with English in it." For oral histories, see the contrasting accounts offered by the brothers, Alex Sicre, interview by Sarah McCormick, July 19 and 23, 2007, transcript, CVHM, and George Sicre, interview by Sarah McCormick, July 19, 2007, transcript, CVHM. See also Mary Carmona interview by Sarah McCormick, August 23, 2007, transcript, CVHM, and Priscilla Garcia, interview by Sarah McCormick, August 20, 2007, CVHM.

8. On high school numbers, the *Indio Daily News* estimated ethnic Mexican students constituted 23 percent of the high school population. "Local Schools Growing," *Indio Daily News*, March 20, 1948. On positive newspaper coverage, see *Indio Daily News*, "Spanish Column New Exclusive Feature in News," November 25, 1948, which explained that "in recognition of the important past [roles] Coachella Valley's Mexican American [community] played in the development of this area, the *Indio News* this week is introducing a column specifically for those who speak and read in Spanish."

9. Businesses included bars and restaurants, migrant labor camps, and small shops, such as clothing and groceries. Louise Neely, for instance, found employment in processing braceros for local ranchers. Louise Neely, interview by Christian Paiz, October 13, 2013. See also Mary Carmona, interview by Sarah McCormick, August 23, 2007, transcript, pp. 9–11, CVHM, where she discusses her father's restaurant, El Charro, and the clientele of "braceros, servicemen, a lot of the people that were noted [sic] for Indio," p. 10.

10. In the four May issues of 1956, the *Coachella Valley Sun* carried articles on two youths "convicted on dope," the firing of a police officer for inappropriate arrests of "'celebrating' farm workers," fights between Mexican men in Indio's restaurant and bar row, an incomprehensible letter by "a bracero," and an example of Mexican farmworker bestiality. For 1960–62, see this collection: "Coachella Police Quell Jungle Riot," *Coachella Valley Sun*, February 15, 1962; "Coachella Police Do Big Job; Transients Major Problem," *Coachella Valley Sun*, March 8, 1962; "Five Mexican American Men in Coachella Brawl," *Coachella Valley Sun*, April 2, 1964; "Mexican Accused of Fatal Drugs," *Coachella Valley Sun*, April 30, 1964; "Two Mexican Brothers Resisted Arrest," *Coachella Valley Sun*, June 18, 1964; "Dope Smuggling Charge Jails 5," *Coachella Valley Sun*, December 3, 1964.

11. For emblematic examples, see Mary Carmona, interview by Sarah McCormick, August 23, 2007, transcript, CVHM; Priscilla Garcia, interview by Sarah McCormick, August 20, 2007, transcript, CVHM; Art Preciado, interview by Sarah McCormick, August 20, 2007, transcript, CVHM.

12. "Club of Mexican American Voters," "Pan American Politics," and "New Club— United Americans' Voters' Club," *Indio Daily News*, April 9, 1950; "Farm Labor Camp Children Seek for Eggs at Egghunt," *Coachella Valley Sun*, April 22, 1954; "Pan American Day," *Coachella Valley Sun*, April 19, 1956; "Largest Cinco de Mayo," *Coachella Valley Sun*, May 6, 1960; "Mexican Society to Have Benefit Dinners," *Coachella Valley Sun*, April 26, 1962. On July 24, 1958, for instance, the *Coachella Valley Sun* carried an article, "Valley Council of LULAC Is Organized Here," that identified LULAC as a "service club" and "not a social club." Participants in the 2007 Mexican American Pioneer Project Oral History shared a similar emphasis on charity work. See Gilda Sandsness, interview by Sarah McCormick, November 16, 2007, transcript, pp. 22–23, CVHM; Louise Neely, interview by Sarah McCormick, July 19, 2007, transcript, pp. 19–20, 29–30, CVHM.

13. "Mexican Progresista Society Organize BBQ," *Coachella Valley Sun*, September 27, 1962; "Coachella Sept 16 'Fiesta,'" *Coachella Valley Sun*, September 6, 1962; "Cinco de Mayo a big event," *Coachella Valley Sun*, May 3, 1962. For oral history accounts of Mexican American involvement in the Riverside County Date Fair, see Priscilla Garcia, interview by Sarah McCormick, August 20, 2007, transcript, pp. 8–9, CVHM; Louise Neely, interview by Sarah McCormick, July 19, 2007, transcript, pp. 26–27, CVHM; Alex Sicre, interview by Sarah McCormick, July 19, 2007, transcript, pp. 12–13, CVHM.

14. In 1962, the *Coachella Valley Sun* reported on "CV Farmers Association Will Help Crippled Son of Bracero," August 30, 1962: "Ramon's benefactors are a large number of farmers of the Coachella Valley, employers of his father and more than 900 other braceros from Mexico." In 1964, it carried a series on ranchers paying for heart surgery for a farmworker's child: "Paiz Youngster Recovering from Heart Surgery," *Coachella Valley Sun*, May 7, 1964. See also "Three Local Agencies Aid Indigent Families Stranded in Our Valley," *Coachella Valley Sun*, July 9, 1964; "Coachella Valley Rotary, Operation Mercy Drugs," *Coachella Valley Sun*, July 30, 1964; "CV Friendly Aid Takes Care of Needy Transient Families," *Coachella Valley Sun*, December 30, 1964.

15. "Gay 5 de Mayo Fete Planned in Coachella," *Coachella Valley Sun*, April 24, 1952; "Coachella Is Scene of Gala 5 de Mayo Festivity," *Coachella Valley Sun*, May 1, 1952; "Queen to Reign Over Gala Mexican Holiday Festivity," *Coachella Valley Sun*, August 21, 1952; "Cinco de Mayo Celebrated by More Than 2,000 in Coachella Sunday," *Coachella Valley Sun*, May 8, 1958.

16. On May 27, 1954, the *Coachella Valley Sun* quoted the recently naturalized Castulo Rivera in "Newest Citizen": "I'm very proud to become a citizen of such a great country as the United States, where I have been treated fairly and have been very happy."

17. "To Our Good Neighbors of Coachella Valley," *Coachella Valley Sun*, April 8, 1954.

18. "Mexican Society to Have Benefit Dinner," *Coachella Valley Sun*, April 26, 1962; "Mexican Progresista Society Organize BBQ," *Coachella Valley Sun*, September 27, 1962. The Progresistas planned to send proceeds to Coachella's community building fund and pay for Indio baseball lights. In 1967, the Progresista Lodge (PL) also fundraised for and installed benches in the city park. Both white columnists and PL members understood the project as a Mexican American contribution to local development—one tinged with the frontier's shared labors, and one that preconditioned Mexican American visibility on their contributions. The PL member Eleanor Williams Lopez celebrated such efforts in her letter to the editor:

> This valley has been my home for 28 years and Coachella my favorite City. As in all growing communities we have had our growing pains, but now I believe pains are something of the past. Through the efforts of the Committee of Civic & Patriotic Affairs, the City Park took on a new life. The city . . . built a roof over a bare platform and restrooms to both parks. Also recently a wall was built on the platform. The Sociedad Progresista Mexicana No. 63, this past year, have held dances twice a month and because of their great success, an idea was born. They built benches around the dance area for the comfort of persons attending. Congratulations to Mr. Dolores Arrietta, a member of the construction of these sturdy benches. This donation to the City was a wonderful gesture of appreciation and a great improvement to the park.

"Eleanor Williams Lopez: Letter to the Editor," *Coachella Valley Sun*, January 5, 1967.

19. "Ben Peralta: Letter to Editor," *Coachella Valley Sun*, October 29, 1964. For a brief discussion on local reaction to Peralta's letter, albeit dismissive toward any critique of Peralta, see "Gale Ellis," *Coachella Valley Sun*, November 19, 1964.

20. Calisto Ramos and Larry Salas, interview by Christian Paiz, October 29, 2013.

21. Manuel Arredondo and Joe Ceja, interview by Christian Paiz, February 6, 2015.

22. "Candidates," *Coachella Valley Sun*, April 2, 1964.

23. "Saiz's Position," *Coachella Valley Sun*, April 9, 1964.

24. To the *Coachella Valley Sun*'s columnist, Gale Ellis, the organization's presence "was proof" of American freedom, where "anyone can effectively participate in local politics . . . and make a real impression on any community." "Gale Ellis" and "WHG Editorial," *Coachella Valley Sun*, April 16, 1964.

25. "This isn't the way councilmen are appointed," Ellis wrote in his column. "Matter of Opinion by Gale Ellis," *Coachella Valley Sun*, October 6, 1966.

26. As a 1960s high school student, Joe Ceja was questioned by police officers who wanted to know if Voters League members included communists. Ceja said, "I'm looking at him, and thinking, he's wondering if members like my dad are communists—Well, hell yeah! [Laughs]. He's from Michoacan, you know? He's a Lazaro Cardenas guy, he's going to expropriate everything and give it back to the people!—But I said, 'No, no.'" Joe Ceja, interview by Christian Paiz, November 20, 2013.

27. Members included: the older David Hernandez, a barber with a shop on main street Indio, and who played the "father" role of the local Chicano Movement; Joe Narvaez, who

was responsible for the organization's finances; Tony Avalos, who was always thinking of economics for "la Raza," and Enrique Viveros, the organizer of vivacious fiestas. The list continues: Joel Perez, the younger David Hernandez, and others. Alfredo Fuller and Ray Rodriguez, interview by Christian Paiz, November 14, 2013.

28. At the age of eight, he said, he refused to be cowed down by a white teacher who demanded the flag pledge every morning. Seventy years after the fact, Figueroa recalled it with a barking laugh, white teeth gleaming a boyish boastfulness. As an adult, he worked his family's mine and participated in Chicana/o and farmworker campaigns. In 1962, he helped found a Mexican American Political Association chapter in Southern California and in 1963 became the first Chicano to sue a police station for police brutality in California. When the National Farm Workers Association initiated a small boycott of targeted companies after the 1966 Pilgrimage to Sacramento, Figueroa led carloads of Blythe sympathizers to picket Coachella Valley stores with boycotted goods. Alfredo Figueroa, interview by Christian Paiz, October 12, 2013.

29. Originally from Arizona mining towns, Ray Rodriguez and Raul Loya arrived in Coachella in late 1965 with teaching degrees paid by football scholarships. Like Figueroa, Rodriguez and Loya lived a life of Chicano self-assertion and bristling masculinity. Rodriguez grew up in Globe, Arizona, a mining town where unionized Mexican families prepared for strikes every three years, refused meek negotiations, and practiced worker solidarity. At twenty he led a wildcat strike that further politicized him. Many families also counted two generations in the region, which meant they could advocate for their children's educational future; some, like Rodriguez and Loya, even earned postsecondary degrees. At twenty-five, Rodriguez was committed to his "protective wild cat" mother's command: "no te dejes de los gringos." Alfredo Fuller and Ray Rodriguez, interview by Christian Paiz, October 10, 2013.

30. Fuller's father was from Savannah, Georgia, who, at sixteen, fled to New Orleans to escape an authoritarian father and racist society. Enlisting in World War I, he spent six weeks in France before being shipped to Arizona to chase after the Mexican revolutionary, Pancho Villa. Fourteen years later, Fuller's father decided to spend the rest of his life in Central Mexico. But after crossing the border into Nogales, Sonora, he met his future wife and had a son. Alfredo Fuller and Ray Rodriguez, interview by Christian Paiz, October 10, 2013.

31. Alfredo Fuller and Ray Rodriguez, interview by Christian Paiz, October 15, 2013.

32. June Namias, "Willie Barrientos: Filipino Farmworker," in *First Generation: In the Words of Twentieth Century American Immigrants* (Boston: Beacon Press, 1978), 81–82.

33. Linda Mabalot, "Willie Barrientos Oral History Transcript, Interview 2," Welga Archive-Bulosan Center for Filipino Studies (henceforth, Welga), https://welgadigitalarchive.omeka.net/items/show/13.

34. Namias, "Barrientos," 85.

35. Vera Cruz said stories of migrant success "impressed" him: "Back then, America was the 'land of opportunity,' no doubt about it. We hear friends tell stories from letters they received from relatives in the U.S. telling them how much they were earning, and photographs of these people abroad were always passed around." See Craig Scharlin and Lilia V. Villanueva, *Philip Vera Cruz: A Personal History of Filipino Immigrants and the Farmworkers Movement* (Seattle: University of Washington Press, 2000), 53. For another account, see Mabalot, "Willie Barrientos." On the Philippines' conditions, see Ronald T. Takaki, *Pau*

Hana: Plantation Life and Labor in Hawaii, 1835–1920 (Honolulu: University of Hawaii Press, 1984), 49–52; Dawn Mabalon, *Little Manila Is in the Heart: The Making of the Filipina/o American Community in Stockton, California* (Durham, NC: Duke University Press, 2013), 46–57.

36. Mabalon, *Little Manila*, 46–48.

37. On white teachers, see Vicente L. Rafael, "Colonial Domesticity: Engendering Race at the Edge of Empire, 1899–1912," chap. 2 in *White Love and Other Events in Filipino History* (Durham, NC: Duke University Press, 2000).

38. Scharlin and Villanueva, *Philip Vera Cruz*, 61–63. For an autobiographical account, see Carlos Bulosan, *America Is In* (Seattle: University of Washington Press, 1973).

39. For Filipino experiences in Stockton, see Mabalon, *Little Manila*, 101–50. For Los Angeles, see Linda España-Maram, *Creating Masculinity in Los Angeles's Little Manila: Working-Class Filipinos and Popular Culture, 1920s–1950s* (New York: Columbia University Press, 2006), 16–21.

40. Rick Baldoz, *The Third Asiatic Invasion: Empire and Migration in Filipino America 1898–1946* (New York: New York University Press, 2011), 21–35, 156–93; Kramer, *The Blood of Government: Race, Empire, the United States, and the Philippines* (Chapel Hill: University of North Carolina Press, 2006), 159–228; Mae M. Ngai, *Impossible Subjects: Illegal Aliens and the Making of Modern America* (Princeton, NJ: Princeton University Press, 2014), 97–101; Veta Schlimgen, "The Invention of 'Noncitizen American Nationality' and the Meanings of Colonial Subjecthood in the United States," *Pacific Historical Review* 89, no. 3 (Summer 2020): 317–46.

41. For a devastating fictional rendering, see Carlos Bulosan, "Life and Death of a Filipino in America," in *On Becoming Filipino: Selected Writings of Carlos Bulosan*, ed. E. San Juan Jr. (Philadelphia: Temple University Press, 1995), 85–89. See also Cecilia M. Tsu, *Garden of the World: Asian Immigrants and the Making of Agriculture in California's Santa Clara Valley* (Oxford: Oxford University Press, 2013), 184–86.

42. Carlos Bulosan, *American Is In*, 146.

43. Baldoz, *Third Asiatic*, 156–94.

44. For a comparative account, see Tsu, *Garden of the World*. On census data, see Ngai, *Impossible Subjects*, 103–5; Mabalon, *Little Manila*, 61–76.

45. For conditions and wages, see Mabalon, *Little Manila*, 61–100; Dorothy B. Fujita-Rony, *American Workers, Colonial Power: Philippine Seattle and the Transpacific West, 1919–1941* (Berkeley: University of California Press, 2003), 79–115; Linda España-Maram, *Creating Masculinity in Los Angeles's Little Manila: Working-Class Filipinos and Popular Culture, 1920s–1950s* (New York: Columbia University Press, 2006), 15–50. For Magnos and other testimonies, see Fred Cordova, *Filipinos: Forgotten Asian Americans* (Dubuque, IA: Kendall Hunt, 1983), 22–56. For labor's emotional toll, see Takaki, *Pau Hana*, 102–05.

46. Scharlin and Villanueva, *Philip Vera Cruz*, 5–6.

47. Fujita-Rony, *American Workers*, 98–104; Cordova, *Filipinos*, 63–71.

48. España-Maram, *Creating Masculinity*, 42–50.

49. España-Maram, *Creating Masculinity*, 51–104.

50. Bulosan, *America Is In*, 194–210; España-Maram, *Creating Masculinity*, 44–50; Mabalon, *Little Manila*, 88–99; Takaki, *Pau Hana*, 152–77.

51. On Alaskan canneries, see Fujita-Rony, *American Workers*, 79–116; Cordova, *Filipinos*, 73–82.

52. Larry Itliong exemplified labor's role in community formation. In 1915, he joined a solidarity strike with Washington cannery workers. Though the strike failed, it introduced him to unions and older Filipino leaders, such as veterans of Hawaiian strikes. He remained an organizer for the rest of his life. "A Man of Dedication: Larry Itliong," *El Malcriado*, October 21, 1966, 15–16. For Filipino labor organizing and radical politics, see Fujita-Rony, *American Workers*, 150, 164–66, 175, and Tsu, *Garden of the World*, 186–96.

53. Takaki, *Pau Hana*, 168

54. Ngai, *Impossible Subjects*, 107

55. Fujita-Rony, *American Workers*, 169–99; quoted in Mabalon, *Little Manila*, 91.

56. For a detailed account on gender and unionism among Filipino farmworkers in the Northwest, from where I borrow the term "union men," see Fujita-Rony, *American Workers*, 171.

57. For postwar political rights, see Baldoz, *Third Asiatic*, 194–236; Mabalon, *Little Manila*, 244–54.

58. Scharlin and Villanueva, *Philip Vera Cruz*, 26.

59. Mabalon, *Little Manila*, 238.

60. Lorraine Agtang, interview by Ray Telles, no date, digital recording, "Growing Up in a Migrant Worker Family: 8 Oral History Accounts," Farmworker Movement Documentation Project (henceforth, FMDP), https://libraries.ucsd.edu/farmworkermovement/media/oral_history/music/docFilmInt/Agtang-Greer-01.mp3.

61. On this issue, Vera Cruz reflected, "All the people who worked in these stores and all the shoppers were lily-white, and too many were arrogant and sarcastic towards Filipinos." Scharlin and Villanueva, *Philip Vera Cruz*, 8–9.

62. For an account on older parenting, because of racist anti-miscegenation laws, see "Bacerra (Max) Oral History Interview," Welga, https://welgadigitalarchive.omeka.net/items/show/177.

63. "To a great extent," the United Farm Workers (UFW) leader Pete Velasco said, "the [Coachella Valley's] rich green vineyards are part of [Filipino workers'] history. Most of the vines were planted by Filipino hands and most of the prized fruit has been developed through his skill." See "'Filipino' Speech: April 13, 1969," Folder 4, Box 4, UFW Administration Collection, Part III, Archives of Labor and Urban Affairs (henceforth, ALUA).

64. Abad migrated to continue his education and planned to return in three years. But he "never went back to school" and "never went back [home]." "Letter to Tom Dalzell from Fred Abad," January 21, 1982, "The Filipino Brothers Oral History 1981" Collection, FMDP, https://libraries.ucsd.edu/farmworkermovement/media/oral_history/FRED%20 ABAD%20ESSAY.pdf, 3.

65. Mabalon, *Little Manila*, 217–68.

66. "'Soldiers of the Soil,' Letter from Claro Runtal to Fred Abad," December 16, 1981, The Filipino Brothers Oral History Collection, FMDP.

67. Mabalon, *Little Manila*, 254–58.

68. Philip Vera Cruz, interview by Albert S. Bagdayem, December 30, 1989, digital recording, Box 36, Tape 192a, "The Filipino Brothers Oral History 1981," FMDP, https://libraries.ucsd.edu/farmworkermovement/media/oral_history/jan09/PHILIP%20 VERA%20CRUZ%20INTERVIEW/01%20Box%2036%20Tape%20192%20A%20(JS).mp3; Scharlin and Villanueva, *Philip Vera Cruz*, 33.

69. The Bracero Program was a collection of U.S.–Mexico agreements that, in two decades after WWII, imported five million Mexican nationals under short-term labor contracts. Marshall Ganz, *Why David Sometimes Wins: Leadership, Organization and Strategy in California's Farm Worker Movement* (Oxford: Oxford University Press, 2010), 53–54, 60–74, 80–82, 93–99.

70. Ganz, *Why David*, 98–99.

71. Quoted in Mabalon, *Little Manila*, 260.

72. Organizer Activity Log: Benjamin Gines, July 13–15, 1963, Folder 12, Box 16, Agricultural Workers Organizing Committee (henceforth, AWOC) Collection, Part II, ALUA.

73. "Organizer Activity Log: Ramon Gutierrez, Feb. 8, Feb. 15, 1965," Folder 14, Box 16, AWOC Collection, Part II, ALUA.

74. "Organizer Activity Log: Sam Miramontes, Feb. 9, 1965," Folder 7, Box 17, AWOC Collection, Part II Collection.

75. "Organizer Activity Log: Sammy Torda, July 6–13, 1965," Folder 11, Box 16, AWOC Collection, Part II, ALUA.

76. Bulosan, *America Is In*, 163.

77. Torda, July 6–13, 1965.

78. Leland Yost Testimony, Subcommittee on Migratory of the Committee on Labor and Public Welfare, Senate, U.S. Congress, *S. 1129: A Bill to Stabilize the Domestic Farm Labor Force*, 87th Cong., 2nd sess., February 8–9 (Washington: Government Print Office, 1962), 711.

79. For an introduction to the inherent relationship between capital and working-class differentiation, see Elizabeth Esch and David Roediger, "'One Symptom of Originality': Race and the Management of Labor in US History," in David R. Roediger, *Class, Race, and Marxism* (London: Verso, 2017), 115–55.

80. For recordings and transcripts of bracero oral history interviews, see the collection at "Bracero History Archive," http://braceroarchive.org/, accessed March 24, 2016.

81. For an in-depth description of braceros and their families, Ana Rosas, *Abrazando El Espíritu: Bracero Families Confront the US–Mexico Border* (Oakland: University of California Press, 2014).

82. Rosas, *Abrazando El Espíritu*, 19–48. Criticism of the Bracero Program included worker exploitation, detrimental impact on bracero families, and worsening agricultural conditions in the United States. But for many braceros, the differences between the two national economies translated into perceived potential in Mexico. In this potential, braceros related to the Coachella Valley as other locations: as a short-term, potentially lucrative, and always-exhausting contract.

83. From the sixty bracero interviews with ties to the Coachella Valley, only three spoke of some labor organizing. Most said they did not want trouble and/or did not remember union campaigns. These interviews echo Rosas's framing of the Bracero Program as a transnational disciplining of laborers and families. Other historians have suggested greater braceros unionism, however. See Mireya Loza, *Defiant Braceros: How Migrant Workers Fought for Racial, Sexual and Political Freedom* (Chapel Hill: University of North Carolina Press, 2016), 97–134; Deborah Cohen, *Braceros: Migrant Citizens and Transnational Subjects in the Postwar United States and Mexico* (University of North Carolina Press, 2011), 145–72; Frank Bardacke, *Trampling Out the Vintage: Cesar Chavez and the Two Souls of the United Farm Workers* (London: Verso, 2011), 95–107.

84. Louise Neely, interview by Christian Paiz, October 13, 2013. Louise Rodarte Neely, interview by Sarah McCormick, July 16, 2007, transcript, CVHM.

85. The estimate was five years of contracts. See Rosas, *Abrazando El Espiritu*, 66–81.

86. Mateo Murillo Lamas worked as a bracero before, during, and after WWII in California, Arizona, and Colorado. He emphasized his positive relationships with employers and bracero contributions to Mexico and the United States. He also noted that conditions worsened over time and that he did see braceros fired routinely. When asked if he knew or participated in any labor organizing efforts, he said no, "yo me dedicaba a mi trabajo"—I focused on my job. Mateo Murillo Lamas, interview by Denise Loya and Mario Sifuentez, no date, digital recording, Bracero History Archive, https://braceroarchive.org/items/show/371. Juan Aguilar Lopez said he and other braceros were comfortable with the living conditions they found: "uno no viene a buscar por comodidades," he said—One does not come searching for comfort. They were content with having work and a place to live. If a worker was unhappy, he added, they still did not leave; no one organized protest or heard, much less interacted, with union organizers. Juan Aguilar Lopez, interview by Alma Carrillo and Juan Aguilar Lopez, May 20, 2006, digital recording, Bracero History Archive, https://braceroarchive.org/items/show/336.

87. Adam Goodman, *The Deportation Machine: America's Long History of Expelling Immigrants* (Princeton, NJ: Princeton University Press, 2020); Timothy J. Henderson, *Beyond Borders: A History of Mexican Migration to United States* (Oxford: Wiley Blackwell Press, 2011), 58–88; Jessica Ordaz, *The Shadow of El Centro: A History of Migrant Incarceration and Solidarity* (Chapel Hill: University of North Carolina Press, 2021); Cristina Salinas, *Managed Migrations: Growers, Farmworkers, and Border Enforcement in the Twentieth Century* (Austin: University of Texas Press, 2021). In the Coachella Valley, newspapers reported on rising undocumented immigration, usually involving a crime or deportation. In the late 1940s and early 1950s, the *Coachella Valley Sun* also published a Spanish language column titled, *Noticiero Mexicano Americano*, which discussed undocumented Mexican immigration. Referring to immigrants as "wetbacks" and "wires" (an allusion to the border's chain-link fence), it reported on June 8, 1950: "In the last few weeks, great numbers of 'wires' or 'wetbacks' have been repatriated. From places as north in the United States as Chicago, the Immigration and Naturalization Service have sent to Mexico as little as 670 illegal Mexican immigrants by airplane and recently sent 800 by train to Laredo, Texas . . . from the Coachella Valley, nearly 100 'wires' are repatriated daily to Mexico." On June 22, 1950, the column reported, "During May, the Border Patrol returned 32,000 'wires' (wetbacks) to Baja California. This compares to the 20,000 returned 'wires' during the month of April."

88. On rancher law breaking, MacKaye said, "The rancher sympathized with the wetback, who only wanted to work and be left alone. He might shop for food for him, throw out a blanket or an old stove where the wetback could find it, but in practice he never openly admitted that he 'knew' he had wetbacks on his ranch. Or he might pass a warning along to his foreman, if he learned in time, that the Border Patrol car was on its way. One moment a field might be full of cotton pickers, but when the patrol arrived, all would have vanished like morning mists." Margaret Breed MacKaye, "A Historical Study of the Development of the Bracero Program, with Special Emphasis on the Coachella and Imperial Valleys" (Thesis, University of Southern California, 1954), 41.

89. MacKaye credited Floyd Conway, the former manager of the Coachella Valley Farmers Association, for the region's workers. He took "[trips] into central Mexico after good

workers," she wrote, and "spoke the language of the people fluently and he wasn't above looking at a man's hands to see if he'd done manual labor." MacKaye, "A Historical Study," 27–28.

90. MacKaye, "A Historical Study," 41.

91. In an exception, locals formed the "Concilio Coordinado Mexicano del Valle de Coachella" in the 1949 summer to address problems affecting the ethnic Mexican community, such was the division between the local community and Mexican migrant laborers, especially braceros. By October 1949, the committee hosted English language classes for braceros. "Noticiero Mexicano Americano," *Coachella Valley Sun*, October 23, 1949. The more common dynamic can be gleaned by articles, such as "Wetback Robbed After Telling He Had Money," *Coachella Valley Sun*, June 17, 1954, and "Four Braceros Get in a Fight in Local Tavern," *Coachella Valley Sun*, June 24, 1954. Flora and Tony Mendoza, and Alfredo Figueroa remembered local men attacking braceros or using derogatory language. Flora (Avila) and Tony Mendoza, interview by Christian Paiz, October 14, 2013; Alfredo Figueroa, interview by Christian Paiz, October 3, 2013.

92. For the Midwest, see Marc Simon Rodriguez, *The Tejano Diaspora: Mexican Americanism and Ethnic Politics in Texas and Wisconsin* (Chapel Hill: University of North Carolina Press, 2014). For the Northwest, see Mario Jimenez Sifuentez, *Of Forests and Fields: Mexican Labor in the Pacific Northwest* (New Brunswick, NJ: Rutgers University Press, 2016). For Texas agriculture and anti-Mexican politics, see David Montejano, *Anglos and Mexicans in the Making of Texas, 1936–1986* (Austin: University of Texas Press, 1987), Cristina Salinas, *Managed Migrations: Growers, Farmworkers, and Border Enforcement in the Twentieth Century* (Austin: University of Texas Press, 2018), and Monica Muñoz Martinez, *The Injustice Never Leaves You: Anti Mexican Violence in Texas* (Cambridge: Harvard University Press, 2018).

93. Fifteen years after the Coachella Extension of the All-American Canal, Huerta's family found an Eden-like land. "Here, there was tangerines," he marveled, "there were grapefruit, there were lemons, there were dates, there were vegetables, and uh, like Indio, it was the hub of the valley, because all around Indio there were a lot of date groves, a lot of citrus groves, and around there, there were a lot of vegetables, onions, radishes, carrots, parsley, . . . oh my god . . . our parents taught us they would tell us, if you want to get ahead you had to work." Israel Huerta, interview by Christian Paiz, November 21, 2013.

94. "Agricultural Workers Organizing Committee, AFL-CIO Weekly Activity Report of Benjamin Gines, November 17, 1962 to November 20, 1962," Folder 11, Box 16, AWOC Collection, Part II, ALUA.

95. Joe Ceja, interview by Christian Paiz, November 20, 2013.

96. Amalia Uribe Deaztlan, interview by Christian Paiz, January 22, 2015.

97. In his interview, Huerta said,

When we came, we were living under some trees. . . . We had no place to live. . . . When we were working, [my parents] talked to a foreman out in a ranch and he said, "Look, I don't have a house, but you can stay at the ranch and sleep out in the open, or in your cars, but you can park your cars there and you can sleep there." So we went up there and my dad and my mom slept—the little kid slept in the car, and the rest of us slept out there on the ground, you know. And I'm going to tell you something—it goes with that because my sister-in-law is named Lupe and married to my brother Max, and she used to say, "You know, my mom used to make sandwiches and she used to make burritos and she would have my dad sell them to the workers in the fields . . . but one day we went out and saw some people living under the trees and my dad felt so sorry for them he just went over there and gave them all the sandwiches and the burritos, he just gave them away to them." And my brother starts laughing and crying at the same time, and she said, "Why are you laughing?" [Brother]: 'That was us. That was us. That was my family. I remember your dad came over there and he and my dad became good friends after that.

Israel Huerta, interview by Christian Paiz, November 21, 2013. The *Coachella Valley Sun* covered "transient" families by focusing on white generosity. They never discussed agriculture's role, such as the systemic lack of affordable housing, stable employment, or livable wages. See "Three Local Agencies Aid Indigent Families Stranded in Our Valley," *Coachella Valley Sun*, July 9, 1964; "CV Friendly Aid Takes Care of Needy Transient Families," *Coachella Valley Sun*, December 30, 1964.

98. Mexican youth faced police harassment in proportion to their age, such as when the teenage Velasquez was charged in 1962 for using a car as weapon against a police officer. The incident took place when police officers answered a report that fifty Mexican youth were drinking alcohol in a neighborhood at night. Despite their questioning, they found no illicit drinks. In the process, one got pinned between two vehicles when Velasquez's car lost its emergency brake. "Velasquez Cleared on Charge of Using Car as Weapon," *Coachella Valley Sun*, March 29, 1962. Mexican girls and young women were also not safe from police officers, as suggested by the cases of police sexual abuse of young ethnic Mexican women in Coachella and the surrounding townships. See chapter 1, note 83. "Police Chief Asks Judge to Dismiss Case," *Coachella Valley Sun*, August 30, 1962. For school testimonies, see Laura E. Garcia, Sandra M. Gutierrez, and Felicitas Nuñez, eds., "Felicitas Nuñez," in *Teatro Chicana: A Collective Memoir and Selected Plays* (Austin: University of Texas Press, 2008), 167.

99. Ray Rodriguez and Al Fuller, interview by Christian Paiz, November 14, 2013. In a less extreme case, Amalia Uribe Deaztlan was placed in a middle school classroom with mediocre white students because she was considered a "smart Mexican." Though spared the worst indignities, her teachers still made racist remarks, such as insinuating Mexican immigrants (like her) were indirectly responsible for President Kennedy's assassination in 1963. Amalia Uribe Deaztlan, interview by Christian Paiz, January 22, 2015.

100. Uvaldo Palomares, "A Study of the Role of Mobility in the Acculturation Process of Rural Migrant and Non-Migrant Disadvantaged Mexican Americans in the Coachella Valley" (Thesis, University of California, Los Angeles, 1966), 64; Ivon Padilla-Rodriguez, "Undocumented Youth: The Labor, Education, and Rights of Migrant Children in Twentieth Century America" (PhD diss., Columbia University, 2021), 62–111.

101. Manuel Arredondo, interview by Christian Paiz, February 6, 2015; Irene (Gonzalez) Reyes, interview by Christian Paiz, January 14, 2014; Israel Huerta, interview by Christian Paiz, November 21, 2013; Louise Neely, interview by Christian Paiz, October 13, 2013; Tony Reyes, interview by Christian Paiz, February 27, 2014; Gilda Guitron Sandsness, interview by Christian Paiz, October 7, 2013.

102. "Ben Peralta, Letter to Editors," *Coachella Valley Sun*, October 29, 1965. For reactions to Peralta, see "Gale Ellis," *Coachella Valley Sun*, November 19, 1965.

103. In November 1962, Gines reported visiting the Coachella and Imperial Valleys, where he came across pro-union Mexican workers: "we could have held a meeting except for the language barriers. We informed them we would return with a Spanish speaking representative." In April 1963, he again met "unorganized locals [who] are mainly Spanish speaking." He requested Spanish speaking organizers, which he received a couple days later, but subsequent meetings were never recorded. His requests appear to have received little further attention. See "Organizer Activity Log: Ben Gines," Folder 11, Box 16, AWOC Collection, Part II, ALUA.

104. Amalia Uribe Deaztlan, interview by Christian Paiz, January 22, 2015.

105. "Everyone that moved from Michoacan that they knew, or from Colima, their first stop was our home, where they would be fed and clothed. They would help them wash their clothes. And then eventually they would come across the border." Even in her eighties, she remembered, "there was always that spirit of helping the poor, it was important for my mother." Amalia Uribe Deaztlan, interview by Christian Paiz, January 22, 2015.

106. Amalia Uribe Deaztlan, interview by Christian Paiz, January 22, 2015; Ramses Noriega, interviewed by Denise Lugo, transcript, pp. 5, 8, 11, Institutional Repository, John Spoor Broome Library, California State University Channel Islands.

107. Amalia Uribe Deaztlan, interview by Christian Paiz, January 22, 2015.

108. Guadalupe Carrizales, interview by Christian Paiz, March 1, 2014.

109. Guadalupe Carrizales, interview by Christian Paiz, March 1, 2014.

110. Maria Marron, interview by Christian Paiz, January 31, 2014.

111. "Grape Workers Back at Work," *Coachella Valley Sun*, May 13, 1965, 1.

112. "Chapter 1: 'The Farm Workers Struggle in Delano,'" Folder 18, Box 1, Philip Vera Cruz Collection, ALUA, Walter Reuther Library, Detroit. For a corroborating account, see "Andrew G. Imutan 1965–1974," Essays by UFW Volunteers Collection, FMDP, https://libraries.ucsd.edu/farmworkermovement/essays/essays/015%20Imutan_Andrew.pdf.

113. Vera Cruz referred to the Coachella Strike as "a half-victory" because they "didn't get a contract, and in a labor negotiation, the salary is really secondary to a contract." Scharlin and Villanueva, *Philip Vera Cruz*, 39. Imutan was similarly critical, "Andrew G. Imutan, 1965–1947," Essays by UFW Volunteers Collection, FMDP, 1.

Chapter 3

1. "Andrew G. Imutan 1965–1947," Essays by UFW Volunteers Collection, Farmworker Movement Documentation Project (henceforth, FMDP), https://libraries.ucsd.edu/farmworkermovement/essays/essays/015%20Imutan_Andrew.pdf, 1.

2. "Andrew G. Imutan 1965–1974," Essays by UFW Volunteers Collection, FMDP, 2.

3. "Andrew G. Imutan 1965–1947," Essays by UFW Volunteers Collection, FMDP, 2; Andy Imutan, interview by Rachel Goodman, Part I, no date, digital recording, "The Filipino Brothers Oral History Collection—1981," FMDP, https://libraries.ucsd.edu/farmworkermovement/media/oral_history/music/new/Imutan01.mp3.

4. Florence V. Bryant, "The Union Makes Us Strong," *Trends* 5 (April 1973): 33–40, UC Davis Asian American Studies Files Collection, Welga Archive-Bulosan Center for Filipino Studies (henceforth, Welga), http://welgaproject.ucdavis.edu/.

5. Bryant, "The Union Makes Us Strong," 33–40.

6. Linda Mabalot, "Willie Barrientos Oral History Transcript, Interview 2," Welga, https://welgadigitalarchive.omeka.net/items/show/13.

7. June Namias, "Willie Barrientos: Filipino Farmworkers," *First Generation: In the Worlds of Twentieth Century American Immigrants* (Boston: Beacon Press, 1978), 84.

8. Esther Uranday, interview by Leroy Chatfield, June 12, 2008, digital recording, "Huelgistas: Delano Grape Strikers Oral History 1965," Collection, Oral History Media, FMDP, https://libraries.ucsd.edu/farmworkermovement/media/oral_history/uranday/1.%20Audio%20Track.mp3.

9. Frank Bardacke, *Trampling Out the Vintage: Cesar Chavez and the Two Souls of the United Farm Workers* (New York: Verso, 2011), 193–96, 215–17, 308–40; Marshall Ganz, *Why David Sometimes Wins: Leadership, Organization, and Strategy in the California Farm Worker Movement* (Oxford: Oxford University Press, 2009), 136–54, 213–14, 222–24; Matt Garcia, *From the Jaws of Victory: The Triumph and Tragedy of Cesar Chavez and the Farm Worker Movement* (Berkeley: University of California Press, 2012), 46–74; Miriam Pawel, *The Union of Their Dreams: Power, Hope, and Struggle in Cesar Chavez's Farm Worker Movement* (New York: Bloomsbury Press, 2009), 17–21, 28–36.

10. For a popular account, see the 2014 motion picture by Diego Luna, *Cesar Chavez: History Is Made One Step at a Time*, biography/drama, directed by Diego Luna, Canana Films, 2014. For an academic account, see Susan Ferris and Ricardo Sandoval, *The Fight in the Fields: Cesar Chavez and the Farmworkers Movement* (Boston: Houghton Mifflin Harcourt, 1997). Even critical histories may reproduce this narrative shorthand by focusing on pro-United Farm Workers (UFW) grape farmworkers and volunteers and then pivoting to pro-UFW lettuce workers after the 1970 grape victory. The reader may then not see the farmworker ambivalences and/or losses due to the UFW's campaign, nor the pessimism shaping many farmworker views of the union's likely success—all of which existed prior to the UFW's organizational failures in its three-year contract (1970–73).

11. "I knew the union was good for the workers," Vera Cruz said of the Agricultural Workers Organizing Committee (AWOC) and the Delano Grape Strike of 1965, "The only thing I didn't know back then was how difficult the struggle would get." Craig Scharlin and Lilia V. Villanueva, *Philip Vera Cruz: A Personal History of Filipino Immigrants and the Farmworkers Movement* (Seattle: University of Washington Press, 2000), 35; Bardacke, *Trampling Out*, 161–64; Ganz, *Why David*, 128–36; Jacques E. Levy, *Cesar Chavez: Autobiography of La Causa* (Minneapolis: University of Minnesota Press, 1975), 187–94.

12. Levy, *Cesar Chavez*, 195–200. Regarding the reference to volunteers, see "FW Initiative De-Briefing Minutes," no date, Folder 16, Box 2, Philip Vera Cruz Papers, Archives of Labor and Urban Affairs (henceforth, ALUA). In the latter minutes, Cesar Chavez said:

> The other thing was people—how do you do it? And we said, "Well hell—the farm workers' problem is not only my problem, it's the problem of everyone in society. They're responsible and we'll make them responsible." And so we started the strike in September and by May of 1966 there were hardly any farm workers left. All the farm workers went back to work, they had too many bills, they were afraid—they had gone through the experience so many times of loosing [sic] strikes. So, we were on picket lines with students and the growers were saying, "you don't have any farmworkers, all you have is students," and we would say, "we have 100s of farm workers, picketing and marching," ... [Farm workers] weren't prepared ... so we used students on the picket lines, sometimes 100% students, no farmworkers. ("FW Initiative De-Briefing Minutes," 2)

13. "Rudy Reyes 1965–1980," Essays by Author Collection, FMDP, http://libraries.ucsd.edu/farmworkermovement/essays/essays/018%20Reyes_Rudy.pdf.

14. Levy, *Cesar Chavez*, 269–71, 288–93. See also Luciano Crespo, interview by Christian Paiz, January 30, 2014 and February 8, 2014.

15. "Editorial: Luming Imutan," *El Malcriado*, June 1967.

16. For additional biographies, see "A Man of Dedication: Larry Itliong," *El Malcriado*, October 21, 1966; "Dolores Huerta: A Picture of Our VP," *El Malcriado*, October 1, 1970. The Filipino crew leader, Fred Abad, relinquished his higher paying position to join the Delano striker community full time. Initially, however, Abad "was torn between the needs of my family and the needs of the union." He only returned to the picket line after being inspired by the "people who were so dedicated to the union, who also were sacrificing." "Fred Abad Interview," interviewed by Ray Telles, Paradigm Production Interview Transcripts 1995/1996, Oral History Collection, FMDP.

17. Andy Imutan, interview by Rachel Goodman, Part 2, no date, digital recording, "The Filipino Brothers Oral History Collection—1981." FMDP, https://libraries.ucsd.edu/farmworkermovement/media/oral_history/music/new/Imutan01.mp3. See also, Scharlin and Villanueva, *Philip Vera Cruz*, 19, 36, 41–42, 47.

18. Scharlin and Villanueva, *Philip Vera Cruz*, 44–51. Philip Vera Cruz, interview by Albert S. Bagdayem, December 30, 1989, digital recording, Box 36, Tape 192a and b; "The Filipino Brothers Oral History—1981," FMDP. In Levy's *Cesar Chavez*, Chavez fired AWOC's Filipino organizers and crew leaders for refusing to accept the union's five dollars a week salary (Levy, *Cesar Chavez*, 242–43).

19. In October 1966, *El Malcriado* replied to the defections with heroic portraits of Filipino leaders, such as Larry Itliong and Paul Agbayani, while calling Ben Gines a "judas" who "betrayed AWOC and the Filipinos for a big Teamster salary." "A sinister new element has appeared in Delano," *El Malcriado* reported, "the worst of all, because they are like Judas, who sold his soul to the devil for a handful of coins. KNOW THIS ENEMY! DENOUNCE HIM! We are talking about the ones who have betrayed their own people: The Teamsters, the Scabs they have brought in: and even some former strikers who betrayed their brothers." "The Enemy," *El Malcriado*, October 7, 1966. For a measured discussion on Filipino perspectives on the AWOC–NFWA (National Farm Workers Association) merger, see Philip Vera Cruz, interview by Albert S. Bagdayem, December 1989 to January 1990, interviews #1 and #2, digital recording, "The Filipino Brothers Oral History—1981," FMDP, https://libraries.ucsd.edu/farmworkermovement/medias/oral-history/.

20. See "Philip Vera Cruz to Bill Berg: December 2, 1972," Folder 4, Box 1, Philip Vera Cruz Papers, ALUA, where Vera Cruz explained,

> You know our problem of leadership started with the AWOC. The struggle for power had ruined the opportunity to organize and consolidate the Filipinos more within the union. The leadership at that time was very aggressively selfish and over-protective in a factional way that confused many of our people. That was why I was passive in [my] personal role because competing with them would only complicate more misunderstanding and fighting within our group. Though Larry [Itliong] was not the ideal Filipino leader, perhaps his resignation might had caused some Filipinos to be suspicious of our Mexican brothers' intentions. They really didn't know why he left the union. To add more confusion, he said different reasons to different groups and places.

See also "Philip Vera Cruz to Segor Hub: January 15, 1975," Folder 8, Box 1, Philip Vera Cruz Papers, ALUA, and Philip Vera Cruz interview by Albert S. Bagdayem, December 1989 to January 1990, interviews #1 and #2, digital recording, "The Filipino Brothers Oral History—1981," FMDP. To Vera Cruz, Gines worked hard for AWOC's membership, but he still considered Gines as drawing too heavily from past Filipino union models that could challenge a multiracial organization. Vera Cruz, in contrast, imagined a multiracial coalition: "There were some [Filipino leaders] that told me that 'they [Mexicans] are greater in numbers, and we are few in comparison with their numbers,' you know. Then they said, and Ben said to me, 'some day when they will be in control, we will not have any chance, because we will have to follow what they say. Because they'll run it [union], you know.' So that was the argument. And then, as for me, of course, it could be true but the principle of togetherness in a union is stronger for me." Interview #2 continues this discussion. For Imutan, see "Andrew Imutan to Patty Enrado: October 25, 2003," Patty Enrado Collection, Welga, where Imutan called Ben Gines and Pete Manuel scabs after the union merger.

21. Quoted in Scharlin and Villanueva, *Philip Vera Cruz*, 107.

22. "Philip Vera Cruz to Noel Kent: January 16, 1975," Folder 8, Box 1, Philip Vera Cruz Papers, ALUA. Vera Cruz also placed blame for the Filipino erasure on "Anglos who wrote the story [and] didn't know all the facts." Scharlin and Villanueva, *Philip Vera Cruz*, 92. In "Andrew Imutan to Patty Enrado: October 25, 2003," Patty Enrado Collection, Welga, Imutan blamed the erasure on "Filipinos who were active in the UFWOC [and] did not have the initiative and desire to make sure that history is preserved." This argument is contradicted by the rank-and-file voices now available in the FMDP and Welga Archives.

23. Pro-UFW organizations, such as the Mexican American Political Association (MAPA), joined "the UFWOC in opposition to farms using illegal immigrants to pay lower wages and use non-union labor. They accuse the government of allowing powerful growers to influence border patrol policies." "Mexican American Group Objects to Use of Wetbacks," *Los Angeles Times*, April 29, 1967.

24. "Melons in Texas," *El Malcriado*, October 7, 1966. See also "12 Farm Workers Jailed in Texas," *New York Times*, October 25, 1966; "Mexico Arrests 3 Texans Who Block Border Bridge," *New York Times*, November 1, 1966; "Strikers Urged to Be Tolerant," *Los Angeles Times*, November 28, 1966. In "Chavez Confers with Mexico Labor Leaders," *Los Angeles Times*, December 4, 1966.

25. When it came to "remedies" for "wetbacks, greencards, out-of-state workers," two solutions appeared: "political pressure is needed" and "get greencards' names and subpoena and scare the hell out of them." "Strike & Boycott: November 7, 1967," Notes, Folder 3, Box 2, Philip Vera Cruz Papers, ALUA.

26. The first *Dolce Vita* cartoon was published in March 1967 and appeared in each subsequent *El Malcriado* issue for several months. See the *El Malcriado* Collection, FMDP.

27. "Dolce Vita," *El Malcriado*, July 19, 1967.

28. In 1966, for instance, Coachella's council rejected plans for building a farmworker housing complex inside the city, which led to a series of acrimonious council meetings. "Coachella Council in Busy, Active Session Tuesday," *Coachella Valley Sun*, January 20, 1966. As recounted earlier, the local rancher Chuchian opposed the city's development of farmworker housing because, he claimed, it would only attract "winos" to their residential community. "Citizens Protest Farm Labor Camp," *Coachella Valley Sun*, March 3, 1966. In the same issue, the newspaper's columnist Gale Ellis discounted concerns over houseless

families living in the desert by describing these people as roving bands of alcoholic men. In "Residents Again Pack Council Room to Protest Farm Labor Camp Idea," *Coachella Valley Sun*, March 17, 1966, a local resident, R. B. Van Blaricum also argued against a farmworker childcare program because it was unnecessary: "their parents want them out in the fields working." See also "Coachella Mayor: Farm Labor Camp 'A Dead Issue,'" *Coachella Valley Sun*, March 24, 1966.

29. Since incorporation, white ranchers and sympathizers dominated every city election. For election coverage, see "Candidates Speak Their Piece: How They Stand on Four Issues," *Coachella Valley Sun*, March 31, 1966; Gale Ellis, "Matter of Opinion," *Coachella Valley Sun*, March 31, 1966; "Coachella and Indio Council Elections Tuesday; 10 Running," *Coachella Valley Sun*, April 7, 1966; "Heavy Council Vote in Coachella, Indio," *Coachella Valley Sun*, April 14, 1966; "Strictly Personal," *Coachella Valley Sun*, April 14, 1966.

30. "Candidates Speak Their Piece," *Coachella Valley Sun*, March 31, 1966.

31. Gale Ellis, "Matter of Opinion," *Coachella Valley Sun*, March 31, 1966.

32. Gale Ellis, "Matter of Opinion," *Coachella Valley Sun*, April 7, 1966.

33. Palomares's quote appears in the paper's column written by Gale Ellis, "Matter of Opinion," *Coachella Valley Sun*, June 16, 1966.

34. "Grape Strikers Rap Brown, Who Spends Day with Family," *Los Angeles Times*, April 11, 1966. Alfredo Figueroa, interview by Christian Paiz, October 5, 2013; Ray Rodriguez and Alfredo Fuller, interview by Christian Paiz, October 15, 2013; Ray Rodriguez and Alfredo Fuller, interview by Christian Paiz, November 14, 2013.

35. The local newspaper said the crowd totaled 350 people. The union's newspaper totaled 600. "Gale Ellis: Matter of Opinion," *Coachella Valley Sun*, May 19, 1966; "Gale Ellis: Matter of Opinion," *Coachella Valley Sun*, June 2, 1966; "Desert Workers Demand Justice," *El Malcriado*, June 2, 1966, FMDP.

36. The newspaper accused MAPA men of attacking the white women employees. "The performance of these three 'men' [against] the girls," Ellis wrote, "is enough to make any male's blood boil." These men lacked "anything resembling decency" and displayed a "cowardly attitude." Even if "polished 'gentlem[en]' on the outside, [they were] uncouth, woman baiting, loudmouth [underneath]," a crowd from whom "you can expect a 'hate' campaign quicker than intelligent attempt to convince." See Gale Ellis, "Matter of Opinion," *Coachella Valley Sun*, April 7, 1966. "Strictly Personal," *Coachella Valley Sun*, April 7, 1966.

37. "Weekend Should About End 'Good' Perlette Season," *Coachella Valley Sun*, June 9, 1966.

38. "Matter of Opinion," *Coachella Valley Sun*, May 19, 1966.

39. In preparation, Coachella passed a "no foolishness" policy that involved maintaining an ancillary police force to prevent "local spillover of current race riots." Regarding the Detroit rebellion, Ellis advocated draconian measures: "strength is universally respected. Weakness is scorned everywhere." "Gale Ellis: Matter of Opinion," *Coachella Valley Sun*, August 3, 1967. See also "Gale Ellis: Matter of Opinion," *Coachella Valley Sun*, October 12, 1967; "Gale Ellis: Matter of Opinion," *Coachella Valley Sun*, December 7, 1967.

40. "Chavez Has Become a Hero but Accomplished Very Little," *Desert Rancher*, September 1967; "Matter of Opinion," *Desert Rancher*, November 1967.

41. "Coachella Paving Project Approved," *Coachella Valley Sun*, February 16, 1967.

42. "Coachella Approves of Low-Income Housing," *Coachella Valley Sun*, March 23, 1967; "Fed Funds for Low-Income Housing," *Coachella Valley Sun*, July 6, 1967.

43. Gale Ellis on "Community Action Committee Elections for OED," *Coachella Valley Sun*, January 19, 1967; "Anti Poverty Officials Chosen," *Coachella Valley Sun*, July 13, 1967; Ray Rodriguez and Alfredo Fuller, interview by Christian Paiz, October 15, 2013; Ray Rodriguez and Alfredo Fuller, interview by Christian Paiz, October 17, 2013.

44. For quote, see "Tears for a Man Who Cared: Chicanos Weep for a Man Who Cared and Tried," *Los Angeles Times*, December 18, 1969. For MAPA activities, see Ray Rodriguez and Alfredo Fuller, interview by Christian Paiz, October 8, 2013; Ray Rodriguez and Alfredo Fuller, interview by Christian Paiz, November 14, 2013; Alfredo Fuller and Ray Rodriguez, interview by Christian Paiz, February 11, 2017.

45. "Tears for a Man Who Cared: Chicanos Weep for a Man Who Cared and Tried," *Los Angeles Times*, December 18, 1969.

46. "Tears for a Man Who Cared: Chicanos Weep for a Man Who Cared and Tried," *Los Angeles Times*, December 18, 1969.

47. Calisto Ramos and Larry Salas, interview by Christian Paiz, October 29, 2013.

48. For the political implications of these actions, see Dionne Espinoza, María Eugenia Cotera, and Maylei Blackwell, eds., *Chicana Movidas: New Narratives of Activism and Feminism in the Movement Era* (Austin: University of Texas, 2018), 1–30.

49. For a similar inter-generational dynamic in Boyle Heights, see George J. Sanchez, *Boyle Heights: How a Los Angeles Neighborhood Became the Future of American Democracy* (Oakland: University of California Press, 2021), 190–92.

50. Ramses Noriega, interviewed by Denise Lugo, transcript, pp. 9–10, Institutional Repository, John Spoor Broome Library, California State University Channel Islands.

51. Newspapers reported the first casualties in September 1967. In "Wounded Sergeant," the *Coachella Valley Sun* reported on Jack Alvarez, who enlisted in March 1966 and whose leg was "shattered" by a bullet (September 14, 1967). The next week, it sparsely profiled Thermal resident Guadalupe Gonzalez (twenty-three years old) and Indio resident Cruz Gomez. On November 23, 1967, it carried three tiny profiles of new soldiers. For histories on the interplay between the Chicana/o and anti-Vietnam War movements, see Ernesto Chavez, *My People First! "Mi Raza Primero!": Nationalism, Identity, and Insurgency in the Chicano Movement in Los Angeles, 1966–1978* (Berkeley: University of California Press, 2002), 61–79; Lorena Oropeza, *Raza Si! Guerra No!: Chicano Protest and Patriotism During the Viet Nam War Era 1978* (Berkeley: University of California Press, 2005).

52. Rodriguez said there was also a lot of attention on "the anti-Vietnam War [Movement].... It was an unjust war. We really had no business there. So, it carried over to the young people." Ray Rodriguez and Alfredo Fuller, interview by Christian Paiz, October 15, 2013.

53. Amalia Uribe Deaztlan's parents insisted their older sons attend college to avoid the military draft. As a result, fourteen-year-old Deaztlan left school to work with her farmworker parents, where her wages supplanted her brothers' labor and where she learned of her mother's politics. Amalia Uribe Deaztlan, interview by Christian Paiz, January 22, 2015. Joe Ceja, a high school student in the late 1960s, attended the funerals of friends and neighbors who died in the Vietnam War. "Going to college," he said, "was a way to avoid the Vietnam War—everybody aimed for this." Joe Ceja, interview by Christian Paiz, November 20, 2013.

54. Rodriguez estimated Chicanos were "28%" of all casualties when they were only "7–9%" of soldiers. Ray Rodriguez and Alfredo Fuller, interview by Christian Paiz, October 17, 2013.

Similarly, Larry Salas's "concern [in 1968] was the disproportionate number of people going off to war in Vietnam.... My cousin had gone. Two of my cousins went. First cousins." Calisto Ramos and Larry Salas, interview by Christian Paiz, November 12, 2013.

55. Calisto Ramos, interview by Christian Paiz, February 10, 2017.

56. Virginia Ortega, interview by Christian Paiz, January 21, 2015; Virginia Ortega, interview by Christian Paiz, January 30, 2015.

57. Virginia Ortega, interview by Christian Paiz, January 21, 2015 and January 30, 2015.

58. Virginia Ortega, interview by Christian Paiz, January 21, 2015 and January 30, 2015.

59. Virginia Ortega, interview by Christian Paiz, January 21, 2015.

60. While still in the fields, Ortega called out to him: "Come outside and sign.... That they want to fight for more dignity for the farmworker, for rights, for a contract." Virginia Ortega, interview by Christian Paiz, January 21, 2015.

61. Virginia Ortega, interview by Christian Paiz, January 21, 2015.

62. Pablo Carrizales, "The Constitution and the Farmworker," *El Malcriado* (Delano, CA), January 13, 1967.

63. Carrizales, "The Constitution and the Farmworker."

64. On the boycott, see "Capitalism in Reverse" in Garcia, *From the Jaws*, 44–74; Bardacke, *Trampling Out*, 308–13.

65. Ray Rodriguez and Alfredo Fuller, interview by Christian Paiz, November 14, 2013.

66. Alfredo Figueroa, "Corrido de Cesar Chavez: La Llegada al Valle de Coachella," available in "Media Music Archive: Alfredo Figueroa and Family," FMDP.

67. In contrast, the Coachella Valley's ranchers appeared like Mexico's "latifundistas," the estate owners who used debt to control peasants and were targets in Mexico's Revolution. Figueroa, "Corrido de Cesar Chavez."

68. Bardacke, *Trampling Out*, 293. Kenney's campaign would also draw from the Mexican American optimism in the 1960 "Viva Kennedy" campaign. See Ignacio Garcia, *Viva Kennedy! Mexican Americans in Search of Camelot* (Austin: Texas A&M University Press, 2000).

69. By 1968, MAPA had led small campaigns, such as picketing the Postal Office for hiring discrimination and organizing pro-UFW actions. The 1968 RFK campaign would be its biggest project yet. Ray Rodriguez and Alfredo Fuller, interview by Christian Paiz, October 15, 2013.

70. The quote attributed to Carrizales comes from Rodriguez in Ray Rodriguez and Alfredo Fuller, interview by Christian Paiz, October 17, 2013. For a longer discussion on farmworkers' constrained choices, see Ray Rodriguez and Alfredo Fuller, interview by Christian Paiz, November 12, 2013. Rudy Reyes's question from the 1965 Delano strike remained relevant: "Who wants to hear about the 'Great Farmworkers' Struggle' when your wife and kids are asking for money?" "Rudy Reyes 1965–1980," Essays by Author, Essays Collection, FMDP, https://libraries.ucsd.edu/farmworkermovement/essays/essays/018%20Reyes_Rudy.pdf.

71. Alfonso Sanchez, interview by Christian Paiz, November 18, 2013.

72. "History of Service: Juanita Martinez," Folder 29, Box 27, UFW Administration Collection, Part II, ALUA. In 1971, UFWOC asked local leaders to fill out "History of Union Service" forms. Martinez submitted hers, as did her husband. His form was in English and in trained penmanship, suggesting local office support. Coachella Valley UFW leaders, such as Tereso and Vivian Rendon, Mary Lou and Rafael Torres, Armando Sanchez,

Nicasio Campos, and Irene and Emiliano Treviño, filled and submitted approximately twenty-seven forms.

73. Similarly, Emiliano Treviño "respected" the 1968 Grape Strike despite not being a grape worker. He gave up his job in the okra harvest "to donate my time (including my family) to picket" and stood "ready to do anything necessary to make this a strong union since it's the only way for us farm workers to get ahead in our goals." "History of Service: Irene Treviño; Emiliano Treviño," Folder 29, Box 27, UFW Administration Collection, Part II, ALUA.

74. Twenty-three-year-old Tony Lopez grew up in a former bracero household and learned of the Delano strikers in 1966 while working with his immediate and extended family on the migrant farm labor circuit. Lopez said he felt the strikers' oppression on his "carne propia," on his own being, and was moved to join them: "algo lo lleva hacerlo," "something compels one to do it." He also knew that Mexican unions had empowered workers and he wanted to improve working conditions in California. He was especially conscious of the treatment his parents had endured. Tony Lopez, interview by Christian Paiz, February 27, 2018.

75. Tony Lopez, interview by Christian Paiz, February 28, 2018.

76. In Jerry Cohen's summary, the Coachella ranchers calculated that "if [the UFW's] boycott works and they hurt us in the pocketbook then we'll have to do something." "Jerry Cohen to Cesar, Larry, Jim, Leroy: May 25, 1968," Folder 2, Box 26, Office of the President Collection, Series III, ALUA.

77. Grape ranchers also knew farmworkers faced a context of surveillance, blacklisting-as-exile, and uncertain worker allegiances. As discussed in the first two chapters, divisions, separation, and collusions divided the labor force.

78. "Grape Harvest Underway with 'Good Prospect,'" *Coachella Valley Sun*, May 16, 1968; "Grape Strike Tension Eased After Meeting," *Coachella Valley Sun*, May 30, 1968.

79. Deaztlan joined MAPA's campaign only after quizzing her night school teacher and a MAPA leader, Rodriguez, on his knowledge of the United Farm Workers Organizing Committee's (UFWOC) Chavez. Deaztlan's friend and peer, Irene Reyes, joined UFWOC while her brother, still a student at UC Riverside, joined MAPA. The intergenerational dynamic built on MAPA's earlier attempts to create a Chicano youth leadership centered on the War on Poverty grants. Ray Rodriguez and Alfredo Fuller, interview by Christian Paiz, October 15, 2013; Ray Rodriguez and Alfredo Fuller, interview by Christian Paiz, November 14, 2013; Irene Reyes, interview by Christian Paiz, January 14, 2015; Amalia Uribe Deaztlan, interview by Christian Paiz, January 22, 2015.

80. The strike committee planned to kick off the campaign on June 7 with an Indio-to-Coachella march and a Coachella rally. Even if late in the season, some reasoned, the strike could prepare them for the following year and leverage a new president for legislation. Ray Rodriguez and Alfredo Fuller, interview by Christian Paiz, October 17, 2013.

81. "The Triumph and the Tragedy," *El Malcriado* (Delano, CA), June 15, 1968. "His assassination was the death of our future," Huerta reflected in 2018, "Civil rights would have been at the forefront of his agenda." "How RFK's Assassination Set Back Latino Civil Rights: A Talk with Activist Dolores Huerta," *NBC NEWS*, June 6, 2018, https://www.nbcnews.com/news/latino/how-rfk-s-assassination-set-back-latino-civil-rights-talk-n880156.

82. "Kennedy Shooting May Have Stopped Chavez 'Parade,'" *Coachella Valley Sun*, June 6, 1968.

83. Alfredo Figueroa, interview by Christian Paiz, October 12, 2013 and November 9, 2013.

84. "Strike in Coachella," *El Malcriado*, July 1, 1968; "Strike Shifts from Coachella to Valley," *El Malcriado*, July 15, 1968.

85. "Strike Imminent in Coachella," *El Malcriado*, July 1, 1968; "Strike in Coachella," *El Malcriado*, July 1, 1968; "Strike Shifts from Coachella to Valley," *El Malcriado*, July 15, 1968; "Violence in Coachella: An Example," *El Malcriado*, July 15, 1968.

86. "Strike in Coachella," *El Malcriado*, July 1, 1968.

87. "April 1969 Coachella UFW Meeting Notes," Folder 4, Box 4, UFW Administration Collection, Part III, ALUA.

88. "Chavez Gone: Grape Harvest Completed—Grape Volume and Price Much Better Than Early Estimated," *Coachella Valley Sun*, July 11, 1968.

89. Flora and Tony Mendoza, interview by Christian Paiz, October 14, 2013.

90. Louise Neely, interview by Christian Paiz, October 13, 2013.

91. Some of these wrote to the *Coachella Valley Sun* in support of its pro-rancher reporting and said, "they resented people they didn't even know telling them what to do." "Strictly Personal," *Coachella Valley Sun*, August 15, 1968. See also "City Park Usage by Union Causes Citizens' Protest" and "Noriega Arrested Released on Bail," *Coachella Valley Sun*, July 4, 1968. In the latter event, the local activist and UCLA student, Ramses Noriega, was arrested for picketing Eleanor Lopez's newsstand. Lopez was a leader of the more conservative Progresista Lodge and publicly opposed the UFW movement. Strikingly, not one of the nine participants in the Mexican American Pioneers Oral History Project (2007) discussed their views of the local UFW or its effects. There are likely many reasons for the omission, but one may be a negative view of or active opposition to the union. The latter suggestion comes from Ray Rodriguez and Alfredo Fuller, interview by Christian Paiz, October 15, 2013.

92. Alfredo Figueroa, interview by Christian Paiz, October 12, 2013 and November 9, 2013.

93. "Growers generally stated Chavez's efforts to 'talk' workers out of their fields were unsuccessful, 'but he did slow down the work somewhat with continued harassment.'" "Chavez Gone: Grape Harvest Completed—Grape Volume and Prices Much Better Than Early Estimates," *Coachella Valley Sun*, July 11, 1968. The same conclusions appeared in the *Desert Rancher*, which reported in June 1968: "In some fields, many [workers] did [strike]. In others, very few. Total effect to the overall harvest to date anyway—has been nil." "Chavez 'Pickets' Move into Valley Fields," *Desert Rancher*, June 1968. See also, "Chavez 'Grape Strike' Not Successful," *Desert Rancher*, July 1968.

94. In a common local argument, pro-rancher leaders argued that the UFW grape strike only harmed farmworker families because it prevented them from earning the brief harvest's high wages. Local farmworkers, pro-rancher leaders insisted, knew enough to think for themselves and not be manipulated by an outsider. To them, the UFW movement's subsequent inability to curtail the late harvest gave further evidence that the strike's limited impact signaled low pro-UFW sympathies among local farmworkers.

95. Gale Ellis, "A Matter of Opinion," *Coachella Valley Sun*, June 20, 1968.

96. "Tunney 'Clap Down' Leaders Start 120 Days Sentence," *Coachella Valley Sun*, May 29, 1969; "Tunney 'Clap Down' Trio Jailed; Loya Granted Stay," *Desert Rancher*, June 1969.

97. "Chavez May Pull Out Because of 'Violence,'" *Coachella Valley Sun*, July 4, 1968; Gale Ellis, "Matter of Opinion," *Coachella Valley Sun*, July 11, 1968.

98. The strike ultimately only hurt farmworkers, ranchers said, for "this is the time of year they make their money, and any effort to keep them from working will be just as unfair to them [farmworkers] as it is to the grower." "Chavez 'Sets Up Shop' in Coachella," *Coachella Valley Sun*, June 13, 1968.

99. "Chavez 'Sets Up Shop' in Coachella," *Coachella Valley Sun*, June 13, 1968. Anti-UFW residents also collected a petition against UFWOC's use of Coachella's park, "City Park Usage by Union Causes Citizen's Protest," *Coachella Valley Sun*, July 4, 1968.

100. "Noriega Arrested, Released on Bail," *Coachella Valley Sun*, July 2, 1968; "Ramses Noriega Fined $125 for Picket Incident," *Coachella Valley Sun*, August 1, 1968.

101. "Pickets Threat in Coachella," *Coachella Valley Sun*, July 25, 1968.

102. "'Pray in' Group Hits 'White Racism,' Support Dr. Hiebert," *Coachella Valley Sun*, July 25, 1968.

103. "'Liberal' Demos Will Still Try to 'Candidate,'" *Coachella Valley Sun*, August 1, 1968.

104. "Gale Ellis: Matter of Opinion," *Coachella Valley Sun*, August 15, 1968.

105. In August, Democratic presidential candidates McCarthy and Humphrey pledged support, as did the National Association for the Advancement of Colored People (NAACP). At the end of the month, the *Los Angeles Times*'s Harry Bernstein speculated the boycott may bankrupt ranchers. Ranchers responded with a lawsuit against UFWOC, but courts tossed it out in late October. See "McCarthy Backs Boycott," "Grape Boycott Spreads," and "NAACP Endorses Strike and Boycott," *El Malcriado*, August 1, 1968. See "Humphrey, Chavez Meet in LA," "Growers May Be 'Crippled,'" and "Humphrey Endorses Boycott," *El Malcriado*, August 15, 1968.

106. "La Huelga Becomes La Causa," *New York Times*, November 11, 1968; "Want Laborers to Go When Work Is Finished," *Los Angeles Times*, November 11, 1968; "Sacramento Report: The Mexican American Farm Worker," *Los Angeles Sentinel*, July 4, 1968; "Hip Shoot in the Vineyards," *Los Angeles Times*, August 23, 1968; "Grape Growers Loss at $3–4 Million," *Los Angeles Times*, October 17, 1968. The San Antonio Bishop ("San Antonio Bishop Supports Boycott," *El Malcriado*, September 1, 1968) and Filipino American Political Association ("FAPA Endorses Boycott," *El Malcriado*, October 1, 1968) also sent endorsements.

107. "Cesar Chavez to Mike Bozick," Folder 4, Box 31, Office of the President Collection, Part II, ALUA.

108. "Letter to Editor: Gordon H. James, Minister of Indio's First Methodist Church," *Coachella Valley Sun*, October 10, 1968; "Letter to Editor: Patricia Laflin," *Coachella Valley Sun*, October 24, 1968. The Progresista's Eleanor Lopez wrote an impassioned letter in January 1969, where she thanked her "many friends" who came to her aid when local Chicano and Chicana students picketed her store. The pickets were stressful, she wrote, but they also reminded her that the Coachella Valley was a place "where people are very loyal and happy" and where she had wide-spread community support. She also wrote at length about the region's equal opportunities for Mexican Americans, who have access to "richer" lives with "two heritages," especially the much-maligned Tejano newcomers. But after the strike and demonstration, Lopez continued, she and her neighbors "realize that a group could come in and change their peaceful town." "Letter to the Editor: Eleanor Williams Lopez," *Coachella Valley Sun*, January 30, 1969.

109. "'Grape Boycott' Hassle Continues," *Coachella Valley Sun*, August 15, 1968.

110. Gale Ellis, "Matter of Opinion," *Coachella Valley Sun*, November 7, 1968.

111. "Editorial" and "Election Results Spell Trouble," *El Malcriado*, November 15, 1965; "Sacramento Eyes Farm Labor Legislation," *El Malcriado*, December 15, 1968; "Veysey Proposes Farm Labor Law," *Coachella Valley Sun*, December 12, 1968; "Senator Murphy Will Speak on Farm Bill," *Coachella Valley Sun*, May 22, 1969.

112. "MAPA Threatens School Trustees with Bond Veto," *Coachella Valley Sun*, January 16, 1969; "Gale Ellis: A Matter of Opinion," *Coachella Valley Sun*, February 20, 1969; "Gale Ellis: A Matter of Opinion," *Coachella Valley Sun*, February 27, 1969; "'Legal' Election This Friday for Poverty Officers," *Coachella Valley Sun*, March 6, 1969; "Gale Ellis: A Matter of Opinion," *Coachella Valley Sun*, March 6, 1969.

113. Chavez made this direct argument in a public letter to Bozick, referring to farmworkers as Americans and melding boycotters and strikers with U.S. exceptionalism tropes. Regarding the latter, he said the UFW would negotiate solely on pesticide use because "we will be damned—*and we should be*—if we permit human beings to sustain permanent damage . . . from economic poisons." "Cesar Chavez to Mike Bozick," Folder 4, Box 31, Office of the President Collection, Part II, ALUA.

114. The UFW usually claimed ranchers "us[ed] the poorest of the poor of another country to defeat the poorest of the poor in this country. That's about as low as you can get." But in other instances, *El Malcriado* simply announced, "Wetbacks Flood California," November 15, 1968. National newspapers echoed this narrative. See "La Causa Becomes La Huelga," *New York Times*, November 17, 1968; "CRLA Challenges Immigration Policies," *Los Angeles Times*, July 1, 1968; "Farm Union Leader Urges End to California Strike," *New York Times*, July 3, 1968.

115. "Grape Growers Face Subpoena," *Los Angeles Times*, August 16, 1968.

116. For Carrizales, the boycott represented the next logical step given that power (and victory) existed elsewhere. He took his family to El Paso, where he led the boycott from the fall of 1968 to the summer of 1969. Lopez went to Chicago.

117. Irene Reyes, interview by Christian Paiz, January 14, 2015.

118. Reyes added: "The majority of people were from Coachella, yes. We did have some white people, who came." Irene Reyes, interview by Christian Paiz, January 14, 2015.

119. "Clipping: *Coachella Valley Sun*: 'Organizers for Chavez Union Set Up Shop,'" March 27, 1969, Folder 4, Box 4, UFW Administration Collection, ALUA.

120. "Chavez Threatens to Step Up Use of Boycott," *Coachella Valley Sun*, April 17, 1969.

121. The aforementioned "Clipping: *Coachella Valley Sun*" presented an article in which the accompanying photo presented union leaders surrounded by Mexican workers.

122. Velasco argued this view took hold after the 1966 AWOC–NFWA merger. Summarizing Filipino critiques of the UFW, he wrote, "After the [1966] merger, all publicity is Mexican. There is no mention of Filipinos, yet they were the ones who started the strike. Why?" "Pete Velasco to Gilbert Padilla: 'Suggestions for Winning Filipinos to la Causa,'" Folder 4, Box 4, UFW Administration Collection, Part III, ALUA.

123. "Pete Velasco to Gilbert Padilla: 'Suggestions for Winning Filipinos to la Causa,'" Folder 4, Box 4, UFW Administration Collection, ALUA.

124. Velasco knew that many of the Coachella Valley's Filipino grape workers in 1969 had participated in earlier farm labor strikes. He also knew that not all strikes overcame their loses nor inspired assurances about future prospects. Some of these grape workers

may very well have participated in AWOC's 1965 Grape Strikes in Coachella, Arvin-Lamont, and Delano. For them, like for most people, being pro-union did not automatically mean being pro-strike. They needed to be persuaded, too.

125. On April 21, for instance, the lawyer-organizer David Averbuck reported he was writing a "long narrative about how Filipinos were screwed" by the abrupt closure of labor camps. In meetings, organizers also addressed Filipino concerns, such as when Paul Pastor spoke to Tomsey, a Filipino crew leader. Meeting notes read: "Long conversation with Tomsey. Tomsey angry with Larry, Cesar, and now Pete. Why? . . . Badly hurt pride. This man lost three times . . . DiGiorgio, Goldberg, P-M." Like Pete's prototypical foreman, Tomsey's relationship to the UFW reflected a pained history of union failures. With this in mind, the organizers "agreed that Paul should stay on him, find out what bugs him." "Coachella UFW Meeting Notes: April 21–29, 1969," Folder 4, Box 4, UFW Administration Collection, Part III, ALUA.

126. "Coachella UFW Meeting Notes: April 21–29, 1969," Folder 4, Box 4, UFW Administration Collection, Part III, ALUA.

127. Carrizales later wrote to Chavez a scathing letter defending local authority: "I write to you this letter to tell you the surprise and disillusionment I felt when I learned that Mr. Gilbert Padilla came from the general offices and behaved arrogantly and abolished the committee that we established democratically, basing his decision on opportunistic and shameless legalism." "Pablo Carrizales to Cesar Chavez: November 25, 1969," Folder 4, Box 4, UFW Administration Collection, Part III, ALUA.

128. "Picket Line Lists," Folder 9, Box 4, UFW Administration Collection, Part III, UFW Archive; "Strike Records, 1969," Folder 31, Box 27, UFW Administration Collection, Part III, UFW Archive.

129. "Pete Velasco Ilocano Letter, nd," Folder 4, Box 4, UFW Administration Collection, Part III, ALUA.

130. Velasco also never used the words "Mexican," "Chicano/a," or "Chavistas," referring to them as "our fellow workers," "other nations," "other poor nations," and "our other poor workers"—de-Mexicanizing the strike and framing Mexican workers through Filipino history.

131. "March to Mexico Builds: 100 Mile March in 110 Heat," *El Malcriado*, May 1–31, 1969, 2–3.

132. "Coachella Growers Ignore Wage Law," *El Malcriado*, April 1–15, 1969. In "Coachella Growers on the Run," a rancher in drag even danced frantically to escape UFWOC's strike—in contrast to the jovial community of three male strikers. "Coachella Growers on the Run," *El Malcriado*, April 1–15, 1969.

133. "Workers Leave Field, Grower Flips Out," *El Malcriado*, June 1–30, 1969. See also, "Growers' Game Endangers Lives," *El Malcriado*, July 15–31, 1969. Strikebreakers "know what we are trying to do, and they are with us," *El Malcriado* wrote, but "they are desperately poor and need the money." With "no insults, no threats," organizers met these pre-supporters and convinced strikebreakers "to leave the strike zone and find work elsewhere." "The Strike in Coachella," *El Malcriado*, June 1–30, 1969, 3, 10–11.

134. "Soldiers of the Soil," "The Filipino Brothers Oral History—1981" Collection, FMDP, https://libraries.ucsd.edu/farmworkermovement/media/oral_history/clarorundalessay.pdf, 4.

135. "Sit-Ins Slam Coachella," *El Malcriado*, June 1–30, 1969, 2; "Growers Offer Negotiations," *El Malcriado*, June 1–30, 1969, 3.

136. Amalia Uribe Deaztlan, interview by Christian Paiz, March 18, 2015.

137. Deaztlan recalled multiple conversations with Larry Itliong and Pete Velasco. In one, Deaztlan said Itliong encouraged her to attend college and offered to pay for her tuition. She remembered this as evidence of Itliong's generosity but did not realize the offer was also rooted in Filipino American history, in which racist prohibitions dashed education aspirations. Amalia Uribe Deaztlan, interview by Christian Paiz, March 18, 2015.

138. "It is hard to single out the turning point in this year's Coachella strike. Certainly, the unity of the Filipino and Mexican-American workers was a crucial factor in victory. Certainly, the historic march from Indio to Mexicali and the rising support of the Union by Mexican citizens was a high point. Certainly, the historic sit-in by Filipino workers at Bagdasarian Camp #2 was the high point of the strike." "Coachella Strike Ends Victoriously," *El Malcriado*, July 15–31, 1969, 2.

139. "Grape Profits, Production in Tail Spin," *El Malcriado*, June 1–30, 1969, 13; "Camp-Outs, Muu-Muu Picketing and Rotting Grapes," *El Malcriado*, July 15–31, 1969, 2.

140. "The Strike in Coachella," *El Malcriado*, June 1–30, 1969, 3, 10–11.

141. Craig Charlin and Lilia V. Villanueva, *Philip Vera Cruz: A Personal History of Filipino Immigrants and the Farmworkers Movement* (Seattle: University of Washington Press, 2000), 107–13.

142. Calisto Ramos and Larry Salas, interview by Christian Paiz, November 12, 2013.

143. "Council Calls Park Use Moratorium: Riot Aftermath Finds City Cautious," *Coachella Valley Sun*, April 9, 1970; "Strictly Personal," *Coachella Valley Sun*, April 9, 1970; Frank Adams, "Running Open," *Coachella Valley Sun*, April 9, 1970. Calisto Ramos and Larry Salas, interview by Christian Paiz, November 12, 2013.

144. Calisto Ramos and Larry Salas, interview by Christian Paiz, November 12, 2013.

145. Calisto Ramos and Larry Salas, interview by Christian Paiz, November 12, 2013.

146. "Council Calls Park Use Moratorium: Riot Aftermath Finds City Cautious," *Coachella Valley Sun*, April 9, 1970; "Strictly Personal" *Coachella Valley Sun*, April 9, 1970; Frank Adams, "Running Open," *Coachella Valley Sun*, April 9, 1970.

147. Calisto Ramos and Larry Salas, interview by Christian Paiz, November 12, 2013.

Chapter 4

1. "The Farmworker in the 1970's: Review of the Past . . . Hopes for the Future . . . ," *El Malcriado*, January 1–31, 1970.

2. "Bulletin: More Growers to Sign with UFWOC," *El Malcriado*, June 15, 1970.

3. "New Contracts Net 17,000 Acres: 3,400 Workers Are Protected New UFWOC Contracts with Their Employers. They Cover Grapes and Other Crops in 15 Ranches," *El Malcriado*, July 1, 1970.

4. "Editorial: Ray of Hope," *El Malcriado*, April 1, 1970.

5. With the Coachella victories the UFW promised a *permanent* "better future" for agricultural communities in California—for, as the newspaper celebrated, the "farmworker movement [was] here to stay." "Editorial: Ray of Hope," *El Malcriado*, April 1, 1970.

6. Tony Lopez, interview by Christian Paiz, February 27, 2018.

7. Philip Vera Cruz, "Union Protection and Power," *El Malcriado* (Delano, CA), November 1, 1970.

8. Douglass Adair, interview by Greg Truex, March 10, 1995, transcript, p. 34, California State University, Northridge.

9. Douglass Adair, interview by Greg Truex, March 10, 1995, transcript, p. 34, California State University, Northridge.

10. In another two camps, both run by Bozick foremen, the UFW found the same "filthy" rooms and restrooms. "Richard Bagdasarian Grievances," Folder 27, Box 20, UFW Administration Collection, Part III, Archives of Labor and Urban Affairs (henceforth, ALUA).

11. "Richard Bagdasarian Grievances," Folder 27, Box 20, UFW Administration Collection, Part III, ALUA.

12. "Union Notes on Bagdasarian: June 17, 1971," Folder 27, Box 20, UFW Administration Collection, Part III, ALUA.

13. "Gonzalez to Bozick: March 25, 1972," Folder 27, Box 20, UFW Administration Collection, Part III, ALUA.

14. "Richard Bagdasarian Grievances," Folder 27, Box 20, UFW Administration Collection, Part III, ALUA.

15. "Richard Bagdasarian Grievances," Folder 27, Box 20, UFW Administration Collection, Part III, ALUA.

16. "Karahadian Grievances," Folder 30, Box 21, UFW Administration Collection, Part III, ALUA. For "cochinero" reference, see "Villegas Organizer Notes," Folder 33, Box 27, UFW Administration Collection, Part II, ALUA.

17. "Ray Huerta Organizer Notes: May 8, 1971" and "Jesus Villegas Report: May 13, 1971," Folder 33, Box 21, UFW Administration Collection, Part II, ALUA. For UFW grievances against Coachella Valley grape ranchers from 1972 to 1973, see Boxes 96 to 98 in the UFW Administration Collection, Part II, ALUA.

18. In 1972, Salandini interviewed the Coachella Office director of 1971, Jesus Villegas, who said Larson and Freedman did not follow UFW rules for pesticide use: "They do not advise the worker when they will spray and what they will spray. We have a regular monthly meeting with the union members. In regard to the pesticide problem above, we first try to inform the grower of the infraction of the contract. Then, in no luck, we ask the workers what they want to do." "Salandini Interview of Jesus Villegas, 1972," Folder 6, Box 8, Victor Salandini Papers, Stanford University.

19. In a subsequent letter to Coachella Imperial Distributors, the UFW threatened to "take immediate steps to remove this element" if this behavior continued. "Coachella Imperial Distributors (CID) Grievances," Folder 13–14, Box 21, UFW Administration Collection, Part III, ALUA.

20. "Richard Bagdasarian Grievances," Folder 27, Box 20, UFW Administration Collection, Part III, ALUA.

21. "Ray Huerta to Milton Karahadian: November 23, 1971," Folder 30, Box 21, UFW Administration Collection, Part III, ALUA. In December of 1971, the UFW also filed similar grievances against Beckman and Bender, when foreman Alex Tonogdo hired six non-UFW members. "Ray Huerta to Bobaba Ranch: December 27, 1971," Folder 38, Box 20, UFW Administration Collection, Part III, ALUA.

22. For Coachella Vineyards, for instance, the UFW filed grievances between February and March of 1972 for hiring three, then seventeen, and then two workers not dispatched from the UFW's hiring hall. "Coachella Vineyard Grievances," Folder 20, Box 21, UFW Administration Collection, Part III, ALUA.

23. "Vicente Ponce to Moreno: February 24, 1972," Folder 9, Box 22, UFW Administration Collection, Part III, ALUA.

24. "Frank Ortiz to Herbekian: June 23, 1972," Box 20, Folder 38, UFW Administration Collection, Part III, ALUA.

25. "Ray Huerta to Richard Peters, January 12, 1972," Folder 19, Box 22, UFW Administration Collection, Part III, UFW ALUA.

26. "Ray Huerta to Milton Karahadian: November 23, 1971." For other grievances, see "Ray Huerta to Bobaba Ranch: December 27, 1971" and "Tenneco Grievances," Folder 29, Box 22, UFW Administration Collection, Part III, ALUA.

27. "David Valdora Grievances," Box 22, Folder 41, UFW Administration Collection, Part III, ALUA.

28. Frank Bardacke, *Trampling Out the Vintage: Cesar Chavez and the Two Souls* (London: Verso, 2011), 396–409; Matt Garcia, *From the Jaws of Victory: The Triumph and Tragedy of Cesar Chavez and the Farm Worker Movement* (Berkeley: University of California Press, 2012), 118–23; Miriam Pawel, *The Union of Their Dreams: Power, Hope, and Struggle in Cesar Chavez's Farm Worker Movement* (New York: Bloomsbury Press, 2009), 84–85, 108.

29. To overlook hiring violations, the UFW also risked weakening its presence in Coachella—for ranchers could arguably show farmworkers that they still determined who was hired and fired regardless of union representation. UFW passivity also risked outraging UFW stalwarts and granting ranchers loyal/dependent workers. When ranchers did not resolve these violations in 1972, Coachella wrote to the Central Office: "it is a necessity that, the Union should arbitrate this case, because the Ranchers must learn to respect every Clause of the Agreement." "Andres Gonzalez to Nancy Klieber: March 6, 1972," Folder 20 "Coachella Vineyard Grievances," Box 20, UFW Administration Collection, Part III, ALUA.

30. "Ray Huerta to Harry Carian, Re: Meeting: February 2, 1972," Folder 3, Box 21, UFW Administration Collection, Part III, ALUA.

31. "Ray Huerta to Harry Carian, Re: Meeting: February 2, 1972," Folder 3, Box 21, UFW Administration Collection, Part III, ALUA.

32. Carian's lawyer, David English, added "I have taken the liberty to assure Mr. Carian that your organizations would also follow [the] contract . . . would not instruct your people to be hostile to Mr. Santos." "David English (Labor Relations Consultant for Carian) to Ray Huerta: April 10, 1972," Folder 3, Box 21, UFW Administration Collection, Part III, ALUA.

33. "Ray Huerta to Harry Carian," Folder 3, Box 21, UFW Administration Collection, Part III, ALUA.

34. "Ray Huerta to Carian: December 19, 1972," Folder 3, Box 21, UFW Administration Collection, Part III, ALUA.

35. "Field Office Conference: December 15–17, 1972," Folder 1, Box 62, UFW Administration Collection, ALUA. Six months earlier (June 1971), Coachella wrote to Coachella Imperial Distributors about a supervisor: "Workers no longer care to work under his supervision and will be dispatched elsewhere." "Ray Huerta Memorandum to Reider (CID),"

File "Coachella Imperial Distributors," Box 23, UFW Administration Collection, Part III, ALUA.

36. Ranchers insisted, "All problems between Union and growers can be solved within the contract. Threatened work stoppage is just words. Refusing to dispatch is not in order." "Ray Huerta to Harry Carian, Re: Meeting: February 2, 1972," Folder 3, Box 21, UFW Administration Collection, Part III, ALUA.

37. Douglass Adair, interview by Greg Truex, March 10, 1995, transcript, p. 34, California State University, Northridge.

38. Serrano's family migrated to the San Joaquin Valley and from there moved into the Stockton region or further west into the San Jose–Santa Cruz agricultural zone.

39. Maria Serrano, interview by Christian Paiz, November 27, 2013.

40. Maria Serrano, interview by Christian Paiz, November 27, 2013.

41. Maria Serrano, interview by Christian Paiz, November 27, 2013.

42. Maria Serrano, interview by Christian Paiz, November 28, 2013.

43. The direct quote in Spanish was: "[Que] ni vamos a sacar para el chivo." Maria Serrano, interview by Christian Paiz, November 28, 2013.

44. Maria Serrano, interview by Christian Paiz, November 28, 2013.

45. Maria Serrano, interview by Christian Paiz, November 28, 2013.

46. Maria Serrano, interview by Christian Paiz, November 28, 2013.

47. Maria Serrano, interview by Christian Paiz, November 28, 2013.

48. "Coachella Valley Workers Interviews 1974," Folder 10, Box 4, Salandini Papers, Special Collections, Stanford University.

49. "Coachella Valley Workers Interviews 1974," Folder 10, Box 4, Salandini Papers, Special Collections, Stanford University, pp. 31–35.

50. "Coachella Valley Workers Interviews 1974," Folder 10, Box 4, Salandini Papers, Special Collections, Stanford University, pp. 73–75.

51. "Coachella Valley Workers Interviews 1974," Folder 10, Box 4, Salandini Papers, Special Collections, Stanford University, pp. 38–41.

52. Salandini noted Ramirez "owns an acre of land. His place looks like a small farm, lots of fruit trees, chickens, etc. He is in the process of building a new home. He has eight children." "Coachella Valley Workers Interviews 1974," Folder 10, Box 4, Salandini Papers, Special Collections, Stanford University, pp. 52–54. Julio Delgadillo's two rambunctious sons "broke their arms," as well, but the health plan covered their treatment. "Coachella Valley Workers Interviews 1974," Folder 10, Box 4, Salandini Papers, Special Collections, Stanford University, pp. 62–65.

53. "Coachella Valley Workers Interviews 1974," Folder 10, Box 4, Salandini Papers, Special Collections, Stanford University, pp. 71–73.

54. "Coachella Valley Workers Interviews 1974," Folder 10, Box 4, Salandini Papers, Special Collections, Stanford University, pp. 1–4. One worker, who began in Freedman in 1974, said that his ranch committee had not been elected by his crew and complained of UFW demands, such as giving crews less than twenty-four hours to participate in a San Diego rally—which meant leaving Coachella at 3 A.M.

55. "Two of the workers said that maybe Teamster's Union could do more for farm workers than Chavez." "Coachella Valley Workers Interviews 1974," Folder 10, Box 4, Salandini Papers, Special Collections, Stanford University, p. 22.

56. See chapter 3.

57. Adair added, "It might not have lasted for long, but it was a vision and a dream that when *El Malcriado* said 'the land should belong to the people,' right on!.... There was still the dream to win. To win meant the land, to win meant more than five cents an hour, to win meant a lot more than," Adair, interview by Greg Truex, March 10, 1995, transcript, p. 13, California State University, Northridge.

58. Maria Serrano, interview by Christian Paiz, November 28, 2013.

59. In Spanish: "palabras terminantes y seguras." Serrano interview #2, November 28, 2013.

60. Maria Marron, interview by Christian Paiz, January 31, 2014.

61. Maria Marron, interview by Christian Paiz, January 31, 2014.

62. Ruiz first heard of the UFW when it organized a 1971 funeral procession for Mexicali-based farmworkers killed in a bus accident. For her, the UFW's effort to dignify victims reflected the humanitarianism she learned from her mother, who taught her to "never be abusive" and always to aid those in need. She decided to "join Cesar, in the procession taking the bodies to Mexicali, and there I never let him go ... that was the beginning." Within months, Ruiz worked in multiple UFW campaigns under Rosario Pelayo, a UFW leader Ruiz referred to as "my commandant." For a description of Pelayo, see Bardacke, *Trampling Out*, 463. Petra Ruiz, interview by Christian Paiz, October 4, 2013.

63. Petra Ruiz, interview by Christian Paiz, October 4, 2014.

64. Petra Ruiz, interview by Christian Paiz, October 4, 2014.

65. Petra Ruiz, interview by Christian Paiz, October 4, 2014.

66. Ruiz said many male coworkers "didn't see us with good eyes.... No, no nothing pleasing." They also questioned "a woman [who was] on her own" and asked, "Why isn't she in her house?" Petra Ruiz, interview by Christian Paiz, October 4, 2014.

67. See chapter 7.

68. Petra Ruiz, interview by Christian Paiz, January 30, 2014.

69. When I asked her to explain this sexual harassment, she said, "usted sabe quel el hombre es asi, verdad? Le gusta mucho ... de la nada pensar que cualquiera se deja burbuñiando, que por que le diga, 'mira vente pa' aca' y no—eso no." "You know how men are, right? They like to ... for no reason think that anyone will let themselves be harassed, to be told, 'hey, come over here,' and no-not that." Petra Ruiz, interview by Christian Paiz, January 30, 2014.

70. Petra Ruiz, interview by Christian Paiz, January 30, 2014.

71. Petra Ruiz, interview by Christian Paiz, January 30, 2014.

72. To put it differently, for women like Ruiz, the UFW's victory after 1970 made Coachella Valley's farmworker patriarchy akin to labor exploitation: both were holdovers of the pre-UFW era, and both were to be eliminated by the farmworker movement.

73. *El Malcriado*'s first two covers were of "Don Sotaco," the demurring worker who believes the labor contractor is his friend, and "Don Coyote," who exploits and mocks farmworkers. In its first year, *El Malcriado* printed a series of political cartoons that presented the two characters as deviant masculinities, where their interlocking relationship sustained the region's agricultural inequality. For digital copies of most *El Malcriado* issues, see FMDP collection, https://libraries.ucsd.edu/farmworkermovement/archives/. For physical copies, see Boxes 14 to 19, UFW Publications Collection, ALUA.

74. For an emblematic example, see "The Valdez Family Leads the Cincinnati Lettuce Boycott," *El Malcriado*, December 1970.

75. Serrano became a steward after male leaders failed to address worker concerns. At first, she had to draw "inner courage" to confront ranchers. But as she acquired skills and experience, she developed functioning relationships with powerful ranchers *and* safeguarded worker interests. Maria Serrano, interview by Christian Paiz, January 31, 2014. Marron would play a key role in the UFW's 1973 Karahadian Ranch strike, while her sister, Clementina Olloque, worked in the UFW Coachella office. Olloque said she chose nursing school at Chavez's personal request and as a means to serve her community needs. For another voice, see Salandini's 1974 interview of Rosa Ulloa, who was a steward in Freedman in 1974. "Coachella Valley Workers Interviews 1974," Folder 10, Box 4, Salandini Papers, Special Collections, Stanford University.

76. Evangelina Mendoza, interview by Christian Paiz, February 18, 2014.

77. Maria Serrano, interview by Christian Paiz, January 31, 2014.

78. Petra Ruiz, interview by Christian Paiz, January 30, 2014.

79. Prior to the UFW movement, Serrano said women farmworkers worked in silence and in isolation from each other. Their silence, she suspected, reflected their husband's authority in their home—or, as Ortega said, the "lion's den." But as union members, women farmworkers now met for crew and ranch committee meetings. The UFW also organized leadership trainings, reviewed the contract with workers (to teach its different facets and procedures), and asked workers to help in national campaigns. In these spaces, women interacted with each other outside the patriarchal home and formed new connections with other women.

80. Virginia Ortega, interview by Christian Paiz, January 21, 2015.

81. Virginia Ortega, interview by Christian Paiz, January 21, 2015.

82. Evangelina Mendoza, interview by Christian Paiz, February 8, 2014.

83. Evangelina Mendoza, interview by Christian Paiz, February 8, 2014.

84. "Agbayani Village: A Monument to Working People," *El Malcriado*, May 18, 1973.

85. "Agbayani Village: A Monument to Working People," *El Malcriado*, May 18, 1973.

86. "Agbayani Village: A Monument to Working People," *El Malcriado*, May 18, 1973.

87. "Agbayani Village: A Monument to Working People," *El Malcriado*, May 18, 1973.

88. "Filipino Retirement Village Being Planned," *El Malcriado*, August 1–15, 1969.

89. "Filipino Retirement Village Being Planned," *El Malcriado*, August 1–15, 1969.

90. "Filipino Retirement Village Being Planned," *El Malcriado*, August 1–15, 1969.

91. Regarding the history: "Agbayani Village will hopefully close a sad chapter of California history—the inhumane treatment of Filipino farmworkers. It promises him a place to live in dignity and harmony with his fellow workers. This promise was made but never kept by the industry that enslaved him for so long." "Agbayani: A Village with a Future," *El Malcriado*, May 1, 1970.

92. "Minutes of Agbayani Village Meeting, Feb. 5, 1970," Folder 6, Box 4, Philip Vera Cruz Papers, ALUA.

93. "Minutes of Agbayani Village Meeting, Jan 27, 1970," Folder 6, Box 4, Philip Vera Cruz Papers, ALUA.

94. Willie Barrientos, interview by Linda Mabalot, March 21, 1978, interview #2, transcript, Linda Mabalot Papers, Welga Archive-Bulosan Center for Filipino Studies, https://welgadigitalarchive.omeka.net/items/show/9.

95. Philip Vera Cruz, "Editorial: Of Violence and Non-Violence," *El Malcriado*, April 15, 1970.

96. "Villega Organizer Notes: May 24, 1971," Folder 33, Box 27, UFW Administration Collection, Part II, ALUA.

97. "Villega Organizer Notes: May 24, 1971," Folder 33, Box 27, UFW Administration Collection, Part II, ALUA.

98. Similarly, in 1971, a group of UFW workers assigned to David Valdora "brought a statement" to the UFW office detailing their foreman's anti-union actions; they also gathered declarations on Alvarez's history. When Alvarez committed another violation, the UFW organizer pressed the central office to follow the workers' lead: "The time has come to act because [Alvarez] is not a good member of standing if he continues to subvert the union." "Andres Gonzalez to Ray Huerta: June 13, 1971," Folder 41, Box 22, UFW Administration Collection, Part III, ALUA.

99. Petra Ruiz, interview by Christian Paiz, October 4, 2014.

Chapter 5

1. "Coachella's Role Is Important One," *Desert Rancher*, March 1963; "Communities Growing Rapidly: Coachella's Roll Vital," *Desert Rancher*, February 1967; "Coachella City Population Boost Third Fastest in Riverside County," *Desert Rancher*, February 1969; "Even Brief History of Valley Intriguing," *Desert Rancher*, February 1969.

2. Edith Carlson, "Palm Desert: America's Third Way of Life," 1950s Growth, Folder I, Drawer 4, Palm Desert Collection, Palm Desert Historical Society, Palm Desert, CA.

3. Oral history participants remember 1940s Coachella as largely "white," but by the late 1950s and early 1960s, it changed to 50–60 percent white and 40–50 percent Mexican. Joe Ceja, interview by Christian Paiz, November 20, 2013; Evangelina Mendoza, interview by Christian Paiz, February 18, 2013; Calisto Ramos and Larry Salas, interview by Christian Paiz, November 12, 2013.

4. "Editorial," *Ideal*, October 1–15, 1970. The *Ideal* archives are digitized and available in the California Newspaper Project, http://cnp.ucr.edu/.

5. "Against All Justices of the Peace," *Ideal*, November 1–14, 1970; "Judge Makes Racist Comment," *Ideal*, March 13–31, 1970; "Gerald Chagrin Censured," *Ideal*, July 1–14, 1970.

6. Pablo Carrizales, "Ideal y Realidad," *Ideal*, February 15–28, 1970.

7. In the first issue, for instance, the political cartoon presented a triumphant Raul Loya confronting Coachella's white elected leaders, who—it claimed—had failed to jail the Chicana/o movement. The cartoon also celebrated the local Chicana/o community's political awakening and imminent liberation, while crediting the idea of jailing MAPA's leaders to racial traitors, or "sell outs" and "tio tacos" fawning for white approval.

8. "Editorial," *Ideal*, October 1–15, 1970.

9. Frank Esher, "Letter to the Editor: This Radical Newspaper," *Ideal*, December 1–16, 1969.

10. Esher, "Letter to the Editor: This Radical Newspaper," *Ideal*, December 1–16, 1969.

11. Esher's critique reiterated local coverage on the UFW movement in 1968 and 1969, which rooted the grape strike to "outsiders'" and their predatory agitation for nonlocal power struggles. Esher similarly argued *Ideal*'s publishers were political extremists who posed a danger to the existing community, a danger Esher took to unmasking.

12. "Answer to this Letter," *Ideal*, December 1–16, 1969.

13. On Chicana/o counter publics, see Randy L. Ontiveros, *In the Spirit of a New People: The Cultural Politics of the Chicano Movement* (New York: New York University Press,

2014); Monica De La Torre, *Feminista Frequencies: Community Building Through Radio in the Yakima Valley* (Seattle: University of Washington Press, 2022); Lorena Oropeza, "Introduction: 'Viviendo y Luchando: The Life and Times of Enriqueta Vasquez," in Lorena Oropeza and Dionee Espinoza, ed., *Enriqueta Vasquez and the Chicano Movement: Writings from El Grito del Norte* (Houston: Arte Publico Press, 2006).

14. Caswell played a mentorship role for the younger Loya and Fuller, who remembered him as providing them with a "global" perspective of labor and social movements. In late 1969, *Ideal* carried several Caswell biographies, which said he was initially skeptical of the Chicana/o insistence that a two-tier racial caste defined the 1960's Coachella Valley. For Caswell, the United States was a land of opportunity accessible to immigrants (like himself) and to racial minorities (like Chicanas/os). Over the course of a few years, however, Caswell came to agree with his Chicana/o friends and dedicated his energy to fight against racial exclusion. Thus, when Governor Brown fled to Palm Springs to avoid the UFW's 1966 March to Sacramento rally, Caswell joined a small Chicana/o group picketing the governor at his Palm Spring residence. And when the UFW called for a boycott of an Indio supermarket, Caswell joined the group organized by Alfredo Figueroa. He also provided financial support to start *Ideal*, and he helped students enroll in nearby colleges. As *Ideal* explained, Caswell was "our brother and our champion"—for "when Mexican Americans needed funds for their struggle, Jim opened his pocket generously. When his advice was sought, he gave it. When his presence was required, there he was in the front lines. . . . ." See, Miguel Soldevilla, "Requiem for a Champion: Jim Caswell, The American," *Ideal*, December 1–16, 1969; "Tears for a Man Who Cared: Chicanos Weep for a Man Who Cared and Tried," *Los Angeles Times*, December 18, 1969; James Drake, "Jim Caswell: A Brother Who Gave Everything," *El Malcriado*, November 15–30, 1969. Alfredo Fuller and Ray Rodriguez, interview by Christian Paiz, January 22, 2015.

15. Soldevilla, "Requiem for a Champion: Jim Caswell, The American," *Ideal*, December 1–16, 1969.

16. "He didn't deserve to go that way," Rodriguez reflected, "[the movement] died right there. It died right there in jail. *Perdio todo. Todo el animo*, [He lost everything. All his will,] because he believed that in America they could not do that. He took it very hard. *Llorraba, Raul decia, se sentaba, y lloraba*, in jail. [He would cry, Raul said, he would sit, and cry, in jail]. Alfredo Fuller and Ray Rodriguez, interviewed by Christian Paiz, January 22, 2015.

17. Soldevilla, "Requiem for a Champion: Jim Caswell, The American," *Ideal*, December 1–16, 1969.

18. "Against All Justices of the Peace," *Ideal*, November 1–14, 1970; "Boycott Against Theater," *Ideal*, January 15-February 1, 1970; "Editorial," *Ideal*, February 15 to March 1, 1970; "Theater Protest Successful," *Ideal*, March 1–15, 1970; "Judge Makes Racist Comment," *Ideal*, March 13–31, 1970; "Gerald Chagrin Censured," *Ideal*, July 1–14, 1970.

19. "Against Catholic Churches," *Ideal*, January 16–31, 1970; "Catolicos Por la Raza," *Ideal*, February 15-28, 1970; "Church Awakens," *Ideal*, August 1–14, 1970. For a national history of Latinx religious activism, see Felipe Hinojosa, *Apostles of Change: Latino Radical Politics, Church Occupations, and the Fight to Save the Barrio* (Austin: University of Texas Press, 2021). For a history on the Catholic Church and the United Farm Worker Movement, see Marco G. Prouty, *Cesar Chavez, the Catholic Bishops, and the Farmworkers' Struggle for Social Justice* (Tucson: University of Arizona, 2006).

20. "Advertisement and Racism," *Ideal*, March 1–15, 1970; "NMAADC [National Mexican American Anti-Defamation Committee] and the Mass Media," *Ideal*, May 5, 1971; "Editorial," *Ideal*, May 15–31, 1971; "Bandits or Heroes: Pancho Villa," *Ideal*, May 15–31, 1971. For a history of the Chicana/o Movement and its relationship to mass and mainstream media, see Randy J. Ontiveros, *In the Spirit of a New People: The Cultural Politics of the Chicano Movement* (New York: New York University Press, 2014).

21. "Cartoon: Are Chicanos Radical?" *Ideal*, December 5–20, 1972.

22. "Cartoon: Are Chicanos Radical?," *Ideal*, December 5–20, 1972.

23. In a letter to the editor in late 1970, one sympathizer wrote, "The only thing that we can advice [sic] is what we have been advising along. Unification of Chicanos through political and economic power. At this time the only organization doing anything in this area is MAPA. If you do not belong to MAPA contact your local president and join." See, "Filiberto Reyes: Letter to the Editor," *Ideal*, September 15–30, 1970. See also, "Cartoon: Protests Lead to American Dream," *Ideal*, February 15–March 1, 1971; "Theater Protests Successful," March 1–15, 1971.

24. "We believe in the American people," the paper announced, "and for them is our message directed." "The Ideal of Justice and Equality," *Ideal*, November 2–16, 1969.

25. Over its five-year run, *Ideal* carried only five articles that profiled ethnic Mexican women activists and leaders: Dolores Huerta, "the unsung heroine of the farmworker movement"; Alicia Escalante, "the controversial head of the Welfare Rights Organization"; Margaret Cruz, the Mexican American Political Association's (MAPA) first statewide president (elected in 1973); Lupe Angiano, a UFW member who credited Cesar Chavez with her feminist politics; and Raquel Welch, a star Hollywood actress identified as a potential race traitor. "Dolores Huerta: Heroine of la Causa," *Ideal*, July 1–15, 1970; "Raza Women Seek Greater Role," *Ideal*, March 20–April 5, 1972; "Raza in Action: Lupe Anguiano," *Ideal*, February 20–March 5, 1973; "Raza in Action: Alicia Escalante," *Ideal*, May 20–June 5, 1973; "Woman, Margaret Cruz, Chosen as President," *Ideal*, July 20–August 5, 1973.

26. "Cardenas Succumbs at 75," *Ideal*, May 15–31, 1970. "Editorial: True Villa History," *Ideal*, November 1–15, 1971; "Bandits or Heroes," *Ideal*, May 15–31, 1970; "Emiliano Zapata," *Ideal*, April 5–20, 1972.

27. "Struggle Begins 16 of September," *Ideal*, September 15–30, 1970; "Fifth of May," *Ideal*, May 1–15, 1971; "Cuahtemoc," *Ideal*, February 1–15, 1972.

28. "Raza in Action by Jose Chacon: Gus Garcia," *Ideal*, October 20–November 5, 1972.

29. Amalia Uribe Deaztlan, interviewed by Christian Paiz, January 22, 2015.

30. Amalia Uribe Deaztlan, interviewed by Christian Paiz, March 18, 2015.

31. Clementina Olloque, interviewed by Christian Paiz, August 12, 2014, digital recording in author's possession.

32. "Hilda Rodriguez," 92. Rodriguez's family immigrated in 1965 when she was fifteen years old, and like other immigrants her family attempted to scrape an exhausting and humiliating livelihood from field labor. One day, her sister refused to work and said: "I feel very humiliated. Look at the way we have to dress in order to protect ourselves from the overbearing heat and dirt, I feel we are the smallest and poorest creatures of the world." In schools, teachers told her not to expect college and "sentenced her to a life of self-defeat." And when she was about to leave for college in 1968, she remembered breaking the UFW strike and ignoring calls to "join a '*causa justa*.'" Besides wanting an education, she asked herself: "Why should I care about the ongoing problem?" Laura E. Garcia, Sandra M. Gutierrez, and

Felicitas Nuñez, eds., "Hilda Rodriguez," chap. 11 in *Teatro Chicana: A Collective Memoir and Selected Plays* (Austin: University of Texas, 2008), 89–96.

33. "Now," she reflected, "I was acting with remorse, pleading for sympathy and teaching the importance of UFW grape boycott from my stage to a live audience." Garcia, Gutierrez, and Nuñez, "Hilda Rodriguez," 93.

34. At Desert Sands Unified, which served the western cities of Indio to Palm Desert, ethnic Mexican students were a fourth of the student population but most attended schools near Indio's labor camp, which bordered the City of Coachella. At Coachella Valley Unified, segregation existed within schools: the children of ranchers and contractors attended honor courses while the rest did not. These racial imbalances were rooted in early twentieth century segregation and, in the postwar period, continued to fail to provide Mexican American students with "the basic fundamentals of education." "School Discrimination against Mexican Americans," *Ideal*, February 10–March 1, 1971; "S.F. District Sued," *Ideal*, December 15, 1970–January 1, 1971. "Editorial: Bussing or Education," *Ideal*, March 13–31, 1970.

35. By 1971, Coachella Valley Unified School District had a couple of Chicano teachers in its faculty, though its student body population was 95 percent ethnic Mexican. "For a Chicano to get a job in this district," *Ideal* claimed, "is like trying to become president of General Motors. They defend their racist hiring practice by using the age-old argument that 'there aren't any Mexican Americans that qualify.'" "Editorial," *Ideal*, March 15–April 1, 1970; "C.V. Teacher Fired!," *Ideal*, March 15–April 1, 1973.

36. "Conference in Indio to help the Chicano Student," *Ideal*, November 2–16, 1969. See also "A Constitutional Right: Bilingual, Bicultural Education," and "The Right Education??? Maybe," in *Ideal*, January 20–February 5, 1972. "Bandits or Heroes," *Ideal*, May 15–31, 1971; "Cartoon: Chicano Studies and Aztlan University," *Ideal*, April 20–May 5, 1972; "Cartoon: Chicano Enlightenment Views 16th Century Differently," *Ideal*, September 5–20, 1972.

37. When officials said Mexican American students received a good education in any school (and did not need to be integrated with white students), the 150-parent crowd replied that school segregation always led to inequality, and that it was a reminder of Mexican Americans' racialized marginalization. "Editorial," *Ideal*, March 20–May 5, 1973.

38. "Editorial: Big Circus on Integration Issue," *Ideal*, February 15–28, 1970; "Dignity Restored," *Ideal*, November 1–15, 1970.

39. "Mexican American CV Teacher Fired," *Ideal*, March 15–April 1, 1973.

40. "I can't see where this handshake involves any militancy," Arnulfo said, nearly incredulous, "Its no different in meaning than the peace sign and probably more relevant than those crazy secret handshakes that fraternities and other organizations practice." "Mexican American CV Teacher Fired," *Ideal*, March 15–April 1, 1973.

41. "Editorial," *Ideal*, February 1–15, 1972.

42. "Editorial," *Ideal*, March 20–May 5, 1973.

43. Sam Maestas, interviewed by Christian Paiz, April 13, 2017.

44. Socorro Gomez Potter, interview by Matt Garcia, March 4, 2004, transcript, Brown University, https://repository.library.brown.edu/storage/bdr:105543/HTML/.

45. See Laura E. Garcia, Sandra M. Gutierrez, and Felicitas Nuñez, eds., "Chicana Goes to College," in *Teatro Chicana: A Collective Memoir and Selected Plays* (Austin: University of Texas, 2008), 175–90.

46. "My mother later met the *teatro* women and saw me perform with them," Margarita Carrillo wrote in her short memoir in the early twenty-first century, "She told me that she

saw something in me that she lacked herself. We then talked about the changes that women were making in society. She loved talking to Delia, Cubanita, and Hilda. My mother told me that she liked seeing how we interacted with our children, teaching them and explaining things to them. My mother and I can now sit down like good friends and talk about women's liberation or why women should be equal to men. . . . I believe she is proud of me, too." Laura E. Garcia, Sandra M. Gutierrez, and Felicitas Nuñez, eds., "Margarita Carrillo," chap. 10 in *Teatro Chicana: A Collective Memoir and Selected Plays* (Austin: University of Texas, 2008), 81–89.

47. In perhaps the most egregious example, the *Coachella Valley Sun* reported on a police officer accused of propositioning paid sex to an ethnic Mexican minor, though the newspaper insisted on the officers' claim to innocence and the Police Chief's later request for court leniency. In the early 1960s, Mexican American organizations complained about police abuse during cultural and fundraising events. These incidents contributed to the Voter League's formation in 1964 and served as a key issue for one Mexican American city council candidate in 1966. Lastly, when the UFW movement led the Coachella Grape Strike in 1968 and 1969, police officers reacted by interrogating community leaders for their alleged affiliations with communists. See chapters 1 and 2.

48. "Police Harassment," *Ideal*, January 16–31, 1970. In March 1971, *Ideal* summarized the United States Commission on Civil Rights Report, which found region-wide police mistreatment of Mexican Americans and police interference with Mexican American organizing. For the next three years, it reported on police harassment, like the police attack on the Los Angeles Chicano Moratorium in August 1970 and February 1971. See, "LA Police Violence: 1 Killed, 50 Injured, 60 Arrested," *Ideal*, September 1–14, 1970; "East LA Protest Police Brutality," *Ideal*, January 15–February 1, 1971; "'Another's Hands' Killed Salazar," *Ideal*, October 1–15, 1970. "Police and the People," *Ideal*, July 1–15, 1971; "Officers cleared in 'Garcia's' Murder," *Ideal*, July 1–15, 1971.

49. Blythe Resident murdered by Police," *Ideal*, May 20–June 5, 1972; "Blythe Cop Charged with Murder," *Ideal*, June 5–20, 1972; "Police kill Chicano in Denver," *Ideal*, March 20–May 5, 1973; "Police Indicted by Study," *Ideal*, March 1–15, 1971; "How Romilo Died," *Ideal*, February 15–March 1, 1972; "Border Patrol Man Accused of RAPE," *Ideal*, July 20–August 3, 1972; "Forty Ladies Abused Physically by Immigration Dept. Officers," *Ideal*, December 1–16, 1969.

50. "Salazar's Killing," *Ideal*, October 1–15, 1970; "East LA Protest Police Brutality," *Ideal*, February 1971; "Editorial: Police call Chicanos Radical," *Ideal*, February 1971.

51. Editorial," *Ideal*, June 1–15, 1971; "Sandy Valenzuela and the Thermal Massacre," *Ideal*, August 1–15, 1971. "Officers cleared in 'Garcia's' Murder," *Ideal*, July 1–15, 1971.

52. "Was Garcia," *Ideal* asked, "another one of the recalcitrant Mexicans who openly demanded their rights? NO. Frank Garcia spent too much of his life just struggling to stay alive to become involved in 'LA CAUSA.' He worked the fields from dawn to dusk then retired to an all too small 'house' and too little food, and love, and sleep to prepare to struggle again for survival the next day." "Editorial," *Ideal*, June 1–15, 1971.

53. "Raza Unida Party Abandons Democrats," *Ideal*, August 1–15, 1971. MAPA accused both parties of participating in ethnic Mexicans' racial subjugation. The local Democratic congressman John Tunney—and his 1968 refusal to support the UFW strike—best embodied the limitations of the more progressive party of the two available options.

54. "Findings," *Ideal*, March 1–15, 1971.

55. The few Chicanas/os invited to Republican and Democrat party meetings, it added, traded community concerns for glitter and coins: "After the party we will all get up with the whale of a hangover. Some of us will wake up with a few quarters securely placed in our pockets or hands." "If we clear our heads after eating some hot menudo," it mocked, "we will recall the mountains of promises made during our weakened moments." "Editorial: 1972 Elections," *Ideal*, December 1–15, 1971.

56. "La Raza Unida Party," *Ideal*, August 1–14, 1970.

57. "The Spectator," *Ideal*, August 1–14, 1970.

58. "Chicano Power: Electoral Block Power," *Ideal*, December 1–15, 1971; "Editorial: 16 Candidates for Coachella," *Ideal*, March 21–April 1, 1972.

59. "Indentured Servitude of Coachella Chicanos," *Ideal*, July 20–August 3, 1972.

60. "Coachella Police Picketed," *Ideal*, June 20–July 1, 1972.

61. "Also," they added, "much harassment and intimidation is practiced by the force under O'Neil's orders." "Coachella Police Picketed," *Ideal*, June 20–July 1, 1972.

62. "Coachella Police Picketed," *Ideal*, June 20–July 1, 1972.

63. "City Manager and Police Chief Asked to Resign," *Ideal*, July 5–20, 1972.

64. "City Manager and Police Chief Asked to Resign," *Ideal*, July 5–20, 1972.

65. "Coachella City Manager Fired," *Ideal*, July 20–August 3, 1972.

66. "Indentured Servitude of Coachella Chicanos," *Ideal*, July 20–August 3, 1972.

67. In this context, "La Marcha de la Reconquista" passed through the Coachella Valley in May 1971. Marchers drew attention to Chicana/o conditions in the U.S. Southwest, moving in a group of thirty to one hundred Brown Berets from California to Arizona, New Mexico, and Texas, and then back to California, where they spent a month in Catalina Island. In each city, they met up with local Chicana/o activists and organized rallies against police and Border Patrol abuse. One of the marchers, Max Huerta, remembered that they did not wish to overturn society, but believed they needed to tell Chicanas/os to fight against multiple forms of oppression: "Our hope was that it would give people an encouragement to at least start maybe being more vocal about some of these issues that they were confronting and that some of their friends in the area were confronting but were not standing up to them." Max Huerta, interview by Christian Paiz, January 30, 2015. For other testimonies, see Calisto Ramos and Larry Salas, interview by Christian Paiz, October 29, 2013; Calisto Ramos and Larry Salas, interview by Christian Paiz, November 12, 2013; Calisto Ramos and Larry Salas, interview by Christian Paiz, November 14, 2013.

68. Max Huerta, interview by Christian Paiz, January 30, 2015.

69. Max Huerta, interview by Christian Paiz, January 30, 2015.

70. Max Huerta, interview by Christian Paiz, January 30, 2015.

71. Max Huerta, interview by Christian Paiz, January 30, 2015.

72. Max Huerta, interview by Christian Paiz, January 30, 2015.

73. Max Huerta, interview by Christian Paiz, January 30, 2015.

74. As noted earlier, Max Huerta recalled that despite their activism he and his friends attempted to forget their traumatic school experiences, numbing the memories until it felt distant, even foreign: "You know, you want to numb, you want to forget, there are stuff you don't want to remember, and the way you try to cover from remembering is by numbing your brain, you know? Numb yourself." Max Huerta, interview by Christian Paiz, January 30, 2015.

75. "[Poverty] was something you don't really talk about.... You know, you make fun of each other, because you want to feel a little superior than somebody else, even though you may be in the same class. But you want to feel a little different." Max Huerta, interview by Christian Paiz, January 30, 2015.

76. Max Huerta, interview by Christian Paiz, January 30, 2015.

77. Max Huerta, interview by Christian Paiz, January 30, 2015.

78. Max Huerta, interview by Christian Paiz, January 30, 2015.

79. On the "Marcha de la Reconquista Caravana," see "La Caravana de la Reconquista: The Brown Berets Contest Memories of Conquest," Omar Valerio-Jimenez, in Mario T. Garcia and Ellen McCracken, eds., *Rewriting the Chicano Movement: New Histories of Mexican American Activism in the Civil Rights Era* (Tucson: University of Arizona Press), 2021: 71–91. For a more critical account of the Brown Berets, see David Montejano, *Quixote's Soldiers: A Local History of the Chicano Movement, 1966-1981* (Austin: University of Texas Press, 2010).

80. Max explained he and other activists encouraged "people to speak up if things happen. [To] come let us know so that we can help you and do something about it. Help people understand that they were not alone because we knew that feeling—or that the law is greater than you and you're under some kind of authority, you feel alone. Sometimes you have a loved one who was incarcerated, you feel alone. You don't feel good, you don't feel like there is a way out of the situation." Max Huerta, interview by Christian Paiz, January 30, 2015.

81. Max Huerta, interview by Christian Paiz, January 30, 2015.

82. Laura E. Garcia, Sandra M. Gutierrez, and Felicitas Nuñez, eds., "Margarita Carrillo," chap. 10 in *Teatro Chicana: A Collective Memoir and Selected Plays* (Austin: University of Texas, 2008), 81–89.

83. See Garcia, Gutierrez, and Nuñez, eds., "Chicana Goes to College," in *Teatro Chicana*, 175–90.

84. Garcia, Gutierrez, and Nuñez, "Margarita Carrillo," 84.

85. Garcia, Gutierrez, and Nuñez, eds., "Felicitas Nuñez," chap. 17 in *Teatro Chicana*, 137–71; Felicitas Nuñez, interview by Christian Paiz, November 8, 2013.

86. Garcia, Gutierrez, and Nuñez, "Felicitas Nuñez," 144–49.

87. Garcia, Gutierrez, and Nuñez, eds., "Delia Ravelo," chap. 1 in *Teatro Chicana*, 3–16.

88. But, she reflected, "the price I had to pay was swallowing my pride and being my teacher's little Mexican peon throughout high school." Garcia, Gutierrez, and Nuñez, "Delia Ravelo," 5.

89. Garcia, Gutierrez, and Nuñez, "Margarita Carrillo," 84.

90. Garcia, Gutierrez, and Nuñez, "Felicitas Nuñez," 167.

91. Garcia, Gutierrez, and Nuñez, "Delia Ravelo," 9.

92. Garcia, Gutierrez, and Nuñez, eds., "Salt of the Earth," in *Teatro Chicana*, 205–28.

93. Garcia, Gutierrez, and Nuñez, eds., "Virginia Rodriguez Balanoff," chap. 8 in *Teatro Chicana*, 65–72.

94. After each workday, Rodriguez described "ach[ing] all over and [having] to use body ointment and pills to reduce the pain so I could go to sleep at night. We all worked with the dust and juice of the plant, producing a terrible smell that clung." Garcia, Gutierrez, and Nuñez, eds., "Hilda Rodriguez," chap. 11 in *Teatro Chicana*, 89–96.

95. Garcia, Gutierrez, and Nuñez, "Hilda Rodriguez," 92.

96. Rodriguez credited the theater group with her political and intellectual growth: "now I was learning and understanding with eyes from my heart."

97. Garcia, Gutierrez, and Nuñez, eds., "Peggy Garcia," chap. 2 in *Teatro Chicana*, 27–42.

98. Garcia, Gutierrez, and Nuñez, eds., "Teresa Oyos," chap. 5 in *Teatro Chicana*, 47–53.

99. Garcia, Gutierrez, and Nuñez, eds., "Guadalupe Beltran," chap. 13 in *Teatro Chicana*, 53–60.

100. Garcia, Gutierrez, and Nuñez, "Margarita Carrillo," 86–87.

101. I know have quoted extensively from *Teatro Chicana: A Collective Memoir and Selected Plays*. In part, this has to do with my approach to the book as a field of stories, much like the oral history interview participants' relationship to their histories and their hope that it aids in building more egalitarian and just futures. The introduction to the memoir suggests this is appropriate: "The book project was started in 1999, and can perhaps be called a collective memoir. It contains the reminiscences of the strong women typical of the group, women who are today engaged in a variety of professions. . . . This compendium invites readers into their lives and into the realm of the *teatro*. There are lessons to be derived from both excursions." Garcia, Gutierrez, and Nuñez, eds., *Teatro Chicana*, xxix–xxx.

102. Garcia, Gutierrez, and Nuñez, "Delia Ravelo," 15.

103. See "Filiberto Reyes: Letter to the Editor," *Ideal*, September 15–30, 1970; "Cartoon: Protests Lead to American Dream," *Ideal*, February 15 to March 1, 1971; "Theater Protests Successful," *Ideal*, March 1–15, 1971.

104. "We believe in the American people," the paper announced, "and for them is our message directed." "The Ideal of Justice and Equality," *Ideal*, November 2–16, 1969.

Chapter 6

1. Frank Bardacke, *Trampling Out the Vintage: Cesar Chavez and the Two Souls* (London: Verso, 2011), 359–91; Miriam Pawel, *The Union of Their Dreams: Power, Hope, and Struggle in Cesar Chavez's Farm Worker Movement* (New York: Bloomsbury Press, 2009), 69–79.

2. Bardacke, *Trampling Out*, 359–91; Pawel, *Union of Their Dreams*, 69–79.

3. See Elizabeth Anne Lamoree's insightful dissertation, "The Managed Crisis: Labor Relations and Management in California Agriculture, 1930–1980" (PhD diss., University of California, Santa Barbara, 2012), especially chapter 4, 253–334.

4. On office demands and protesting workers, see "Ray Huerta to Cesar Chavez: May 20, 1971," Folder 15, Box 36, Office of the President Collection, Series III, Archives of Labor and Urban Affairs (henceforth, ALUA).

5. "Ray Huerta to Cesar Chavez: May 20, 1971," Folder 15, Box 36, Office of the President Collection, Series III, ALUA.

6. "Ray Huerta to Cesar Chavez: May 20, 1971," Folder 15, Box 36, Office of the President Collection, Series III, ALUA.

7. "Daily Reports 1971," Folder 33, Box 27, UFW Administration Collection, Part II, ALUA.

8. Each organizer was assigned a set of ranchers. UFW organizer Jose Luna was assigned to Bianco (four crews), Coachella-Imperial Distributors (six), Mouradick (two), and Coachella Vineyards (two). Jesus Villegas had Freedman (eight), Karahadian (four), and H&M (four). Huerta had Bagdasarian (five), Mel-Pak (four), and Bobara/Kay Kas (one each). Lastly, Adrian Gonzalez had a collection of growers (Laflin, Kandarian, Bender/

Becker), including eight crews under R. A. Glass. "Field Office Correspondence 1970 to 1973," Folder 13, Box 29, UFW Administration Collection, Part II, ALUA.

9. Rey Huerta, "Rey Huerta 1968–1975: The Most Memorable Times of Our Lives," Essays by Authors, Essays Collection, Farmworker Movement Documentation Project (FMDP), http://libraries.ucsd.edu/farmworkermovement/essays/essays/053%20Huerta_Rey.pdf. In 1972, the teenage volunteer, Pilar Pederson, found the task so emotionally traumatizing that she left the union the next year. See Pilar Pederson, "Pilar Pederson 1971–1973," Essays by Authors, Essays Collection, FMDP, chrome-extension://efaidnbmnnnibpcajpcglclefind mkaj/https://libraries.ucsd.edu/farmworkermovement/essays/essays/097%20Pedersen _Pilar.pdf.

10. "Andres Gonzalez to Ray Huerta: June 13, 1971," Folder 41, Box 22, UFW Administration Collection, Part III, ALUA.

11. "Andres Gonzalez: Organizer Notes, May 20, 1971," Folder 33, Box 27, UFW Administration Collection, Part II, ALUA.

12. Maria Serrano, interview by Christian Paiz, January 31, 2014.

13. Archives hold twenty-seven forms for Coachella Valley leaders. These forms were likely not filled out by farmworkers without local UFW supervision and mediation. Most were written in English and in three similar penmanship styles. Nancy Elliot explained to Huerta the forms were for gaining information on local leaders: for "many of them [were] unknown to us [UFW central office]." "Nancy Elliot to Ray Huerta: July 26, 1971, Re: History of Union Service," Folder 29, Box 27, UFW Administration Collection, Part II, UFW Archive.

14. "History of Service: Juanita Martinez," Folder 29, Box 27, UFW Administration Collection, Part II, ALUA.

15. Emiliano noted that he did not work in grapes prior to the strike. He worked in the okra harvest, but he said that he gave up that job to picket grape ranchers: "I left this grower to donate my time (including my family) to picket grape fields in the Coachella Valley." "History of Service: Irene Treviño; Emiliano Treviño," Folder 29, Box 27, UFW Administration Collection, Part II, ALUA.

16. See "History of Service: Julian Rico," Folder 29, Box 27, UFW Administration Collection, Part II, ALUA; "History of Service: Isidoro Nava," Folder 29, Box 27, UFW Administration Collection, Part II, ALUA.

17. "Why Our Sisters and Brothers Give Their Weekend to La Causa," *El Malcriado*, April 28, 1972.

18. "UFWOC Ask Recognition from Citrus," *Ideal*, October 1–15, 1970.

19. "Coachella Report: Field Office Conference, December 12–19, 1972," File 1, Box 62, UFW Administration Collection, Part III, ALUA.

20. "Doug Adair to Jim Rutkowski Re: Citrus Grower Meeting," Folder 7, Box 28, UFW Administration Collection, Part III, ALUA.

21. The UFW's mouthpiece did carry the occasional article written by Filipino leaders and on Filipino members. The latter, however, was primarily entirely on the UFW's retirement home in Delano, Agbayani Village.

22. "Stockton UFW Office to Cesar Chavez," Folder 16, Box 36, Office of the President Collection, Series III, ALUA.

23. In the Coachella Valley, this meant migrant farmworkers faced fewer job opportunities after the 1970 contracts. Matt Garcia, *From the Jaws of Victory: The Triumph and*

Tragedy of Cesar Chavez and the Farm Worker Movement (Berkeley: University of California Press, 2012), 116–26.

24. The hiring supervisor was a longtime Filipino grape worker, John Pader. The workers he hired were all Filipino: Andy Aquino, Paulina Della, Placido Lozaro, Javier Verduzco, Juana Villareal, Francisco Ila, Maria Ila, Lucrecio Pader. "UFW Coachella to Bagdasarian: May 21, 1971," Folder 27, Box 20, UFW Administration Collection, Part III, ALUA.

25. "UFW Coachella to Bagdasarian: May 21, 1971," Folder 27, Box 20, UFW Administration Collection, Part III, ALUA.

26. "Andres Gonzalez to Tenneco: June 6, 1972," Folder 29, Box 22, UFW Administration Collection, Part III, ALUA.

27. Andres Gonzalez, "Andres Gonzalez 1970–1972," Essays by Authors, Essays Collection, FWDP, chrome-extension://efaidnbmnnnibpcajpcglclefindmkaj/https://libraries.ucsd.edu/farmworkermovement/essays/essays/073%20Gonzales_Andres.pdf. Ray Huerta expressed similar sentiments of Filipino strikers—usually with a tinge of masculinist identification.

28. Primary sources on these issues are quite limited. But the following are a good place to start for future scholarship. On racial tensions, see Douglass Adair, interview by Greg Truex, March 10, 1995, Part II, California State University, Northridge; "National Executive Board Meeting, Day 3: October 14, 1974," Folder 5, Box 3, Philip Vera Cruz Papers, ALUA. On migrant camp closures, see "Tenneco, Felipe Campo Meeting: November 17, 1971" and "A. Caratan Meeting: November 22, 1971," Folder 15, Box 2, Pete Velasco Papers, ALUA; "Meeting with workers over 65 years old: May 1, 1971," Folder 3, Box 2, Philip Vera Cruz Papers, ALUA. Regarding the latter, Philip Vera Cruz's meeting notes read: "[Tenneco] company would not hire workers over 65 years but left their bosses in the field to decide." On Filipino difficulties with the UFW in the San Joaquin Valley, see "Vera Cruz to Berg: December 2, 1972, Folder 4, Box 1, Philip Vera Cruz Papers, ALUA; "News clip: Philippino [sic] Farm Labor, 1973," Folder 24, Box 2, Pete Velasco Papers, ALUA.

29. Philip Vera Cruz, "Union Protection and Power," *El Malcriado*, November 1, 1970.

30. A strong union required the "principles that attracted worldwide attention and invited donations, personal knowledge, skills and sacrifices *must be all applied to all* whom the Farm Workers Union touches. Principles and actions must coincide, or the union crumbles on its foundations" (emphasis added). Vera Cruz, "Union Protection and Power."

31. Philip Vera Cruz, "The Farm Worker's Union," *El Malcriado*, November 15, 1970.

32. Vera Cruz, "The Farm Worker's Union."

33. Regarding union services, Vera Cruz began by briefly noting the UFW's stretched budget: "In six weeks of operations in the Santa Maria and Salinas Valleys, the Union spent $208,000. In return, we won contracts with Inter-Harvest, Freshpict, Brown and Hill and Pic N Pac." Given this, Vera Cruz argued, "it's obvious that the Union cannot afford to even pay a minimal salary, or wage to any of the volunteers in the Union. How, then, can the Union hire more office workers? I suggest that you ask yourself the questions: how much time and money have I offered, or given to help my Union." Vera Cruz, "The Farm Worker's Union."

34. In oral history interviews, Vera Cruz also spoke obliquely about the tensions between him and Filipino members after the Delano victory in 1970. See Philip Vera Cruz, interviewed by Albert S. Bagdayem, December 30, 1989, digital recording, Box 36, Tape 192 B,

"The Filipino Brothers Oral History—1981," FMDP, https://libraries.ucsd.edu/farmworker movement/media/oral_history/jan09/PHILIP%20VERA%20CRUZ%20INTERVIEW/01%20 Box%2036%20Tape%20192%20A%20(JS).mp3. The quote appears approximately at minute 15:00.

35. The quote comes from the Joe Escalona camp meeting on October 31, 1971: "Issue is to organize ourselves; a. get Filipinos be interested; b. Leadership has to be earned," and "Larry quit because he did not have the support from you . . ." "Camp Meeting Notes, 1971," Folder 15, Box 2, Pete Velasco Papers, ALUA. Imutan gave specific but varying statistics to show the lack of Filipino support for the UFW. He noted that UFW meetings routinely involved "10 Pinoys to 1,000 Mexicans" and that "7 thousand Mexicans [joined demonstrations] in Salinas last year, [but] only 1 Filipino [was present] on a bicycle." "Armington Camp Meeting Notes, 1971," Folder 15, Box 2, Pete Velasco Papers, ALUA. In another camp, Imutan said three thousand Mexicans and seven Filipinos participated in anti-boycott rally in Sacramento in 1971. The Sacramento rally reference appeared again in the Jack Radovich meeting on November 23, 1971, when the statistics were nine thousand Mexicans and twenty-seven Filipinos. "Simon Camp Meeting Notes, 1971," Folder 15, Box 2, Pete Velasco Papers, ALUA. In other meetings, he said there were *no* Filipino volunteers in any dispatch office ("Pando Pete Quadra Camp Meeting Notes, November 2, 1971," Folder 15, Box 2, Pete Velasco Papers, ALUA) or only in two offices out of fourteen ("Frank Duleich, Alex Felduero Camp Meeting Notes, November 5, 1971," Folder 15, Box 2, Pete Velasco Papers, ALUA).

36. "Tenneco Camp Meeting Notes, November 12, 1971," Folder 15, Box 2, Pete Velasco Papers, ALUA.

37. To Imutan, these unifying actions were more important than union dues: "your dues are important; our unity is more important." "Andy Imutan Meeting Notes for Simon's Camp, October 30, 1971," Folder 15, Box 2, Pete Velasco Papers, ALUA.

38. Vera Cruz then compared the Filipino workers in the meeting unfavorably to the Japanese and Chinese workers. "First Camp Meeting, October 26, 1971," Folder 15, Box 2, Pete Velasco Papers, ALUA.

39. "Armington Camp Meeting Notes, 1971," Folder 15, Box 2, Pete Velasco Papers, ALUA.

40. In early 1972, Vera Cruz listed several reasons for Itliong's departure, including differences with Chavez, the union's low salary, frustration with white volunteers, and anger at the UFW's slow progress in building a retirement community for Filipino strikers. "[Itliong] threatened to quit the union once before the merger," Vera Cruz noted wryly to Ray Pascua in 1972, "and three times afterwards. For the fifth and last time, he was not bluffing." "Philip Vera Cruz to Ray Pascua, January 14, 1972," Folder 4, Box 1, PVC Collection, ALUA. A year later, Vera Cruz wrote to his friend and New York unionist, Bill Berg: "Though Larry was not the ideal Filipino leader, perhaps his resignation might had [sic] caused some Filipinos to be suspicious of our Mexican brothers' intentions. They really did not know why he left the union. To add more confusion, he said different reasons to different groups and places." "Philip Vera Cruz to Bill Berg, December 12, 1972," Folder 4, Box 1, PVC Collection, ALUA.

41. Philip Vera Cruz directly told younger men they could only build union power by participating in it, while Imutan summarized the first generation's struggles in the United

States as a cautionary tale against young workers' anti-union politics. "First Camp Meeting, October 26, 1971," Folder 15, Box 2, Pete Velasco Collection, ALUA. At the Armington Camp, Armington stressed older Filipino sacrifices and younger workers' obligation to build the Union's strength (October 28, 1971). The young men in the meeting, however, replied: "We young people do not want long speeches, long meetings are boring." In the Pando-Pete Quadra camp (November 2, 1971), Imutan reminded younger workers they also needed a union, or risked being fired in older age, as several older Filipino men had already experienced in the early 1970s. See "Camp Meeting Notes, 1971," Folder 15, Box 2, Pete Velasco Collection, ALUA.

42. For relatively new collections, see ALUA (Walther Reuther Library, Detroit), the Farmworker Movement Documentation Project (University of California, San Diego) and the Welga Archive-Bulosan Center for Filipino Studies (University of California, Davis).

43. "Editorial: Desert Sands Unified School District Ignored Parents," *Ideal*, March 20 to May 5, 1973.

44. Joe Ceja remembered that a siege mentality gripped local white leaders in the early to mid-1970s. When he returned to the Coachella Valley in 1975, he explained, Coachella Valley and Desert Sands school district officials refused to offer him a position as a teacher despite their need and his academic training. They refused, he later learned, because they considered Ceja a "radical" activist, a view based on very little. Manuel Arredondo and Joe Ceja, interview by Christian Paiz, February 6, 2015.

45. The 1970 elections, furthermore, threatened to worsen these statistics for the new representatives could (and to MAPA, *would*) reapportion districts to undermine future Chicana/o political candidates. "Findings," *Ideal*, March 1–15, 1970.

46. "Plan Strategy for Coming Election," *Ideal*, March 13–31, 1970; "The Spectator," *Ideal*, August 1–14, 1970.

47. As Chicana/o historians have shown, the League of Latin American Citizens' victory in Crystal City, Texas, did not entail a strategy for replication. See Ernesto Chavez, "'The Voice of the Chicano People': La Raza Unida Party," chap. 4 in *My People First! Mi Raza Primero! Nationalism, Identity, and Insurgency in the Chicano Movement in Los Angeles, 1966–1978* (Berkeley: University of California Press, 2002), 80–97. See also Carlos Muñoz Jr.'s "The Rise and Fall of La Raza Unida Party," chap. 4 in *Youth, Identity, Power: The Chicano Movement*, 2nd ed. (New York: Verso, 2007), 123–52.

48. "Coachella City Manager Fired," *Ideal*, July 20 to August 3, 1972.

49. After the local Chicano election victory, *Ideal* had drawn these "yes-men" as literally kicked out of Coachella by the "brave Chicanos" following the community's wishes. "The Recall of a Mayor Thru Chicano Apathy," *Ideal*, November 20 to December 5, 1972.

50. "MAPA State President Warns Chicano," *Ideal*, November 5–20, 1972; "The Recall of a Mayor Thru Chicano Apathy," *Ideal*, November 20 to December 5, 1972.

51. Amalia Uribe Deaztlan, interview by Christian Paiz, January 22, 2015.

52. Enrique Ramirez, "Politics: McGovern, Chavez and the Raza Unida Party," *Ideal*, June 20–July 5, 1972.

53. Ramirez, "Politics: McGovern, Chavez and MAPA."

54. Ramirez, "Politics: McGovern, Chavez and MAPA."

55. "We are badasses. You know, we have balls." Alfredo Fuller and Ray Rodriguez, interview by Christian Paiz, November 12, 2013.

56. For a similar view, see Ramses Noriega, interviewed by Denise Lugo, 1980, transcript, John Spoor Broome Library, California State University, Channel Islands, https://repository.library.csuci.edu/handle/10139/5033?show=full. Ramses explained, "the spirit of our people had been castrated... The soul of our people [had been ripped out] by the Spanish; they went after our spirit," p. 8. Calisto Ramos and Larry Salas remembered a martial-like debate with their white community college professors on the issue of Cesar Chavez's purported communist politics. Calisto Ramos and Larry Salas, interview by Christian Paiz, November 14, 2013. *Ideal* also provided profiles of the masculine-resistant Chicano subject under the recurring columns, "Raza in Action" and "Informes del Valle," and its Johnny Sabe political cartoons. Its news articles did the same. In a characteristic discussion, *Ideal* reported on the Coachella Chicano Conference of 1970 by crediting the all-male leadership with masculine prowess and virility, of political leadership via (male) courage. Bert Corona was thus "a robust-virile Chicano who has been struggling for Chicano liberation much longer than any Chicano alive." "Chicanos Unite," *Ideal*, July 1–14, 1970.

57. As mentioned earlier, Ideal ran only five articles profiling women political leaders during its time of publication, two on farmworkers (Dolores Huerta, Lupe Anguiano), two on other Chicana leaders (Alicia Escalante, Margaret Cruz), and one critical of actress Raquel Welch. And the only profiles of *local* women came under the "Flor del Valle" column, which highlighted promising young women in the language of beauty pageants. "Dolores Huerta: Heroine of la Causa," *Ideal*, July 1–15, 1970; "Raza in Action: Lupe Angiano," *Ideal*, February 20 to March 5, 1973; "Raza in Action: Alicia Escalante," *Ideal*, May 20 to June 5, 1973. As noted earlier, the newspaper largely portrayed women as victims of racial discrimination or as pupils of Chicano politicization. This gendered lens and its limits was not unusual. The UFW's newspaper, *El Malcriado*, similarly personified the social positions shaping California's Central Valley exclusively as men: the gluttonous and racist white rancher, "Don Ranchero"; the cunning, amoral, and sexually deviant ethnic Mexican labor contractor, "Don Coyote"; and the spineless and failed farmworker patriarch, "Don Sotaco." To *El Malcriado*, the only normative masculinity came in the UFW striker, "El Malcriado."

58. See "In Coming Election Threat to Mexican Americans," *Ideal*, January 1–16, 1970; "Border Patrol Man Accused of Rape," *Ideal*, July 20 to August 3, 1970; "El Chicano en Washington," *Ideal*, July 1–15, 1971; Elizabeth Martinez, "La Chicana," *Ideal*, September 9–20, 1972.

59. In oral history interviews, Chicanos insisted they welcomed women, but felt that women were less interested in joining them. The membership of all local Chicana/o organizations in the 1960s and 1970s (outside the UFW) was almost entirely male. The Brown Berets had no women members. The local MAPA chapter, which represented the largest chapter in the state, had two to three members—in a sea of two hundred male members. Alfredo Fuller and Ray Rodriguez, interview by Christian Paiz, November 12, 2013. The Coachella Voting League, which was responsible for expanding Mexican American voting rolls, was heavily male. Calisto Ramos and Larry Salas, interview by Christian Paiz, October 29, 2013. Even the 1968 student generation, presumably less tied to the "irrelevant" Mexican tradition of machismo, remained predominantly male. The cohort's few women included Amalia Uribe Deaztlan, Irene Reyes, and the daughters of pro-UFW farmworker and MAPA member, Pablo Carrizales. In the Coachella UFW

office, Ray Huerta's organizing team in 1971 and 1972 included male and female volunteers. But the latter oversaw office paperwork and work permit distribution, the former "enforced" the grape contracts.

The local movement politics also had excluded women in seemingly banal ways. Calisto Ramos and Larry Salas, for instance, said women did not join because fathers did not allow them to participate in evening meetings, when organizations hashed out strategies and dispensed with roles. For Ramos and Salas, if patriarchy militated against women's activism it was a patriarchy found in women's homes—a patriarchy akin to the "irrelevant tradition" of a backward Mexico. Here, the specter of sexual impropriety and the double standard (as well as the patriarch's unlimited power) was evident. That said, these organizations did little to respond to this context, such as holding meetings in the day and/or in women's homes. In fact, the very structure of their meetings reflected male privileges within these patriarchal norms and provided a space for the actualization of their masculine identities. Calisto Ramos and Larry Salas, interview by Christian Paiz, November 14, 2013.

60. "Raza in Action: Lupe Anguiano," *Ideal*, February 20–March 5, 1973.

61. Ybarra noted that the experience provided "a valuable lesson about 'activists and self-proclaimed leaders.'" Richard Ybarra, "Richard Ybarra: 1970–75, 1980–82," Essays by Authors, Essays Collection, FWDP, http://libraries.ucsd.edu/farmworkermovement/essays/essays/087%20Ybarra_Richard.pdf.

62. For an in-depth portrait of this "slow and respectful work," see Charles M. Payne's magisterial *I've Got the Light of Freedom: The Organizing Tradition and the Mississippi Freedom Struggle* (Berkeley: University of California Press, 1995), 236–64.

63. Ryan Kray, "The Path to Paradise: Expropriation, Exodus, and Exclusion in the Making of Palm Springs," *Pacific Historical Review* 73, no. 1 (February 1, 2004): 87.

64. "Shadow Mountain Club Factual Statement," Shadow Mountain Club 1950–54, Folder III, Development Drawer, Palm Desert Historical Society (henceforth, PDHS); "Luau in the Desert Is Many Splendored," Shadow Mountain 1955–59, Folder III, Developments Collection, PDHS. In his oral history interview, Alex Sicre recounted a school trip to Shadow Mountain, where he was allowed on the premises because he has a light complexion, while his twin brother was darker.

> I'm *guero* [he began], which means you look like an Anglo, but you're not, okay. And then my brother was dark. So [my brother] encountered early on more discrimination than I did. Because when people saw me I could go anywhere and fit in anywhere, no questions asked. In fact, I remember one time when we, after a softball game, we were just kids, and the Shadow Mountain Club in Palm Desert was the big club of the Valley, you know. . . . Mr. Hokey took us . . . to the Shadow Mountain to go swimming, that was our treat for, I don't know, winning so many games or something. And I was the first one through the gate, you know there's, the rest of the boys walked through, and I'm coming through and I go through, and my brother's right behind me. And next thing you know, I hear, Alex, Alex! And I turn around and my brother's not through the fence yet; some guy stopped him, you know. And so I went back there, and I says, Come on. Well he won't let me through. And I looked at the man and I says, why can't he? Well he can't come, he's of huh, he's Mexican he can't come here. Well, so am I, I'm a Mexican. No you're not. Yes I am; he's my brother and he's coming with me.

Alex Sicre, interview by Sarah Seekatz, July 19, 2007, transcript, p. 17, Mexican American Pioneer Oral History Project, Coachella Valley History Museum, Indio, CA.

65. "Something New Under the Sun," 1940s, Folder I, Growth Drawer, PDHS.

66. Several reporters speculated about Palm Desert's population growth, as many as eighty thousand residents by 1980. Gloria Greer, "Desert Boom: Blue Strip, College of the Desert Lure Top Construction, More Residents," 1960s Growth, Folder 1, Palm Desert Growth Drawer, PDHS. For newspaper accounts, see 1950s Realtors & Escrow, Folders I–III, Business and Industry Drawer, Palm Desert Collection, PDHS; 1960s Realtors & Escrow, Folders I–IV, Business and Industry Drawer, Palm Desert Collection, PDHS.

67. Quoted in Greer, "Desert Boom." For newspaper accounts, see 1950s Realtors & Escrow, Folders I–III, Business and Industry Drawer, Palm Desert Collection, PDHS; 1960s Realtors & Escrow, Folders I–IV, Business and Industry Drawer, Palm Desert Collection, PDHS. Examples include "Hours More Sun, Lots More Fun," Palm Desert Chamber of Commerce, 1960s Tourist Trade, Folder I, Business and Industry Drawer, PDHS;

68. "Brief History of CWA," published in California Women for Agriculture (CWA) 1991 annual newsletter, no folders, Box 1, CWA Collection, Coachella Valley History Museum, Indio, CA.

69. Arturo Diaz, interview by Christian Paiz, January 31, 2015.

70. Nelson Lichtenstein, *State of the Union: A Century of American Labor* (Princeton, NJ: Princeton University Press, 2002); Jack Metzgar, *Striking Steel: Solidarity Remembered* (Philadelphia: Temple University Press, 2000); Kevin Boyle, *The UAW and the Heyday of American Liberalism, 1945–1968* (Ithaca, NY: Cornell University Press, 1998); Robert H. Zieger, *The CIO: 1933–1955* (Chapel Hill: University of North Carolina Press, 1997).

71. In *The Most Dangerous Man in Detroit: Walter Reuther and the Fate of American Labor* (Champaign: University of Illinois Press, 1997), Nelson Lichtenstein noted the contradictory and limited nature of organized workers' power in post–World War II (WWII) United States. The much celebrated 1950 "Treaty of Detroit," for instance, represented both an unequivocal material advance for unionized auto workers, but also the United Auto Workers' inability to gain managing rights or to fundamentally reshape the national political economy.

72. In a review of post-WWII corporate relations with organized labor, John Godard explains:

If there was a change, it was the adoption by large corporate bureaucracies of a sales and marketing conception of management. This conception emphasized not only sales growth, but also—in order to take advantage of growing market opportunities—certainty and stability (for example, Galbraith 1967; Pfeffer and Salancik 1978). Progressive management, under which firms sought to accommodate labor unions and agreed to share the gains from ongoing productivity improvements, was considered to be necessary in order to achieve such stability and growth. But this doctrine was little more than an adaptation of the earlier "personnel management" school, which was based on the premise that treating employees benevolently was consistent with, and had to be justified in terms of, long-run profitability (Harris 1996;56, Kaufman 2004: 136).

John Godard, "The Exceptional Decline of the American Labor Movement," *ILR Review* (October 2009): 82–108, p. 93. For a detailed and illuminating history of U.S. employers' increasing aggression against labor unions in the 1960s and 1970s, see Lane Windham, "Employers Close the Door," chap. 3 in *Knocking on Labor's Door: Union Organizing in the 1970s and the Roots of a New Economic Divide* (Chapel Hill: University of North Carolina, 2017), 57–84.

73. Windham, *Knocking on Labor's Door*, 64, 135. Godard roots the increasing weakness of the National Labor Relations Act, and the National Labor Relations Board anti-labor decisions, in postwar Supreme Court decisions. Godard, "The Exceptional Decline," 96–98.

74. "Unfair labor charges against employers soared exponentially during the 1970s," Windham noted, "Though the number of workers who tried to form unions remained steady at about half a million a year, those workers faced far more employer lawbreaking. All ULP charges against employers rose sevenfold between 1950 and 1980, and the number of the most severe type of charges—those dealing with discrimination or unfair dismissal for union support—rose nearly sixfold," Windham, *Knocking on Labor's Door*, 65. Godard offered a similar conclusion: "Unions were thus virtually defenseless against management attacks, freeing employers from the need to engage in the 'realism' of the postwar era and allowing them to pursue a more openly anti-union and in many cases anti-worker agenda. Second, and in tandem, the United States had seen the growth of a sophisticated union avoidance industry (see Logan 2006), one that remains unparalleled elsewhere." Godard, "The Exceptional Decline," 99. In a review of U.S. labor history, Larry G. Gerber, emphasizes Sanford Jacoby's observation that "analyses of American labor exceptionalism have too often tended to ignore the crucial role played by management in shaping the nation's industrial relations system. He argues quite persuasively that the most distinctive feature of the American system of industrial relations has been the 'exceptionally high degree of employer hostility' toward unions." Larry G. Gerber, "Shifting Perspectives on American Exceptionalism: Recent Literature on American Labor Relations and Labor Politics," *Journal of American Studies* 31, no. 2 (August 1997): 253–74, p. 264.

75. For overviews, see Jefferson Cowie, *The Great Exception: The New Deal and the Limits of American Politics* (Princeton: Princeton University Press, 2016); Ruthie Gilmore, *Golden Gulag: Prisons, Surplus, Crisis, and Opposition in Globalizing California* (Berkeley: University of California, 2007); Andrew Hartman, *A War for the Soul of America: A History of the Culture Wars* (Chicago: University of Chicago Press, 2015); Elizabeth Hinton, *From War on Poverty to War on Crime: The Making of Mass Incarceration in America* (Cambridge: Harvard University Press, 2016); Lisa McGirr, *Suburban Warriors: The Origins of the New American Right* (Princeton: Princeton University Press, 2001); Bethany Moreton, *To Serve God and Wal-Mart: The Making of Christian Free Enterprise* (Cambridge: Harvard University Press 2009); Michelle Nickerson and Darren Dochuk, eds., *Sunbelt Rising: The Politics of Space, Place, and Region* (Philadelphia: University of Pennsylvania, 2011); Manuel Pastor, *State of Resistance: What California's Dizzying and Remarkable Resurgence Means for America's Future* (New York: The New Press, 2018); Rick Perlstein, *Nixonland: The Rise of a President and the Fracturing of America* (New York: Scribner, 2008); Robert O. Self, *All in the Family: The Realignment of American Democracy Since the 1960s* (New York: Hill and Wang, 2012).

76. Elizabeth Lamoree, "Gambling on Grapes: Management, Marketing, and Labor in California Agribusiness," *Agricultural History* 86, no. 3 (Summer 2012): 104–27, pp. 121–22.

77. Lamoree, "Gambling on Grapes," 120–21.

Chapter 7

1. Max Huerta, interview by Christian Paiz, January 30, 2015, and March 18, 2015.
2. Max Huerta, interview by Christian Paiz, March 18, 2015.
3. "FO Conference 12/15/72-12/17/72," in "Plaintiffs Witnesses: Ray Huerta," Folder 1, Box 62, UFW Administration, Archives of Labor and Urban Affairs (henceforth, ALUA).
4. "Caplan & UFW Meeting Re: Grievance—December 28, 1972," Folder 38, Box 20, UFW Administration Collection, Part III, ALUA. See also, "Ray Huerta to Carian: December 19, 1972," Folder 3, Box 21, UFW Administration Collection, Part III, ALUA.
5. Frank Bardacke, *Trampling Out the Vintage: Cesar Chavez and the Two Souls of the United Farm Workers* (London: Version, 2011), 424–25.
6. "Ray Huerta Deposition 1976," Folder 2, Box 62, UFW Administration Department Records, Part III, ALUA.
7. In 1970, David Smith moved to the Coachella Valley to represent half the grape ranchers. When Teamsters offered "sweetheart" contracts to Salinas Valley, Smith wrote to them to organize Coachella. "Dave Smith Deposition V.1, May 2, 1974," Folder 5, Box 58, UFW Administration Department Records, Part III, ALUA; "David Eason Smith," Folder 8, Box 23, UFW Administration Department Records, Part III, ALUA. For other connections, see "Al H. Caplan . . . From Labor Official to Union Buster, The Story of an Opportunist in the U.S.A," Folder 3, Box 23, UFW Administration Department Records, Part III, ALUA; "Caplan Deposition V. 2, July 30, 1976," Folder 3, Box 58, UFW Administration Department Records, Part III, ALUA; "David Valdora Deposition," Folder 2, Box 58, UFW Administration Department Records, Part III, ALUA.
8. The grape rancher David Valdora said he heard of the meeting by word of mouth, though he did not recall who invited him. He also attended because there was nothing to do in the Coachella Valley. "David Valdora Deposition," Folder 2, Box 58, UFW Administration Department Records, Part III, ALUA.
9. Bardacke, *Trampling Out*, 426–27.
10. At Bagdasarian, Henry Maggaco and Matis Quezon recalled Bozick-led meetings pushing the Teamster's contract. See "Richard Bagdasarian Declarations," Folder 24, Box 20, UFW Administration Department Records, Part III, ALUA. Rodolfo Garcia reported working for Bagdasarian, Mel-Pak, and Moreno in the thinning season; in all, supervisors led meetings to push Teamster signatures. "I was told that Silvia Villalobos [Carian] and Amelia Rodriguez [Bagdasarian] were also *mayordomas* who did these things on other ranches, and a friend of mine who worked at Mouradick told me that Petra Gonzalez, a *mayordoma*, also was working with the Teamsters on that ranch." The supervisors mixed reassurances about wage increases with threats: "Three days before the strike, Margie Meza told us that when the Teamsters took over, the foremen could run their jobs any way they wanted—they could fire anyone, push those who get behind, and make people sign with the Teamsters or be fired." "Rodolfo Garcia Declaration," Folder 38, Box 21, UFW Administration Department Records, Part III, ALUA. For similar declarations for each of the Coachella Valley's grape ranchers, see Boxes 20 to 22 in the collection.
11. In Carian Ranch, the forewoman Silvia Villalobos connected Teamster organizers with workers and promised "medical, unemployment benefits and no dispatch system." "Incidents of Grower–Teamster Collusion: Carian," Folder 40, Box 20, UFW Administration Department Records, Part III, ALUA. At Mel-Pak, supervisor Margie Meza promised

farmworkers new benefits, no dues, and work wherever they wanted, while supervisors Tamse and Castañeda threatened anyone who refused to sign the Teamster petitions. "Incidents of Collusion: Melpak-Melkisian," Folder 38, Box 21, UFW Administration Department Records, Part III, ALUA.

12. In early May, two Mel-Pak workers, Paulino Cruz and Aurelio Ramirez, stated "we signed only because we did not want to lose our jobs and our homes. We signed under pressure for a union that we do not support or want in any manner . . . we want it to be known that we are still loyal Chavistas, who were forced to sign against our will." "Declarations: Paulino Cruz and Aurelio Ramirez," Folder 38, Box 21, UFW Administration Department Records, Part III, ALUA. In the same ranch, Guadalupe Agcaoli said she signed the petition after supervisor Meza pressured her, though she did not know what the petition stated. "Declarations: Guadalupe Agcaoli," "Incidents of Collusion: Melpak-Melkisian," Folder 38, Box 21, UFW Administration Department Records, Part III, ALUA. For summaries of worker declarations for nine ranchers, see "Coachella 1973_1973 Declarations," Folder 15, Box 27, UFW Administration Department Records, Part III, ALUA.

13. "Maria Serrano: Background," Folder 10, Box 20, UFW Administration Department Records, Part III, ALUA.

14. "Deposition of Henry Weatherholt," Folder 1, Box 55, UFW Administration Department Records, Part III, ALUA. In the strike, Tenneco attempted to use its petitions to request a court injunction against UFW pickets, alleging that the UFW did not represent its workers and was thus engaging in illegal disruptions. When the UFW filed worker affidavits of forced signatures, Tenneco withdrew its injunction request.

15. "Caplan, Grami, Cotner Meeting, Early 3/73," Folder 29, Box 28, UFW Administration Department Records, Part III, ALUA. The lone rancher to reject the petitions, Karahadian, led a "survey" of his "key employees." The survey began with a negotiations update—he "didn't believe a contract could be reached with the [UFW]"—and ended with one question: "The Teamsters [say] they represent you fellows and I want to know what you feel about the Teamsters." Karahadian did not recall how many people he questioned nor their names. He felt language barriers did not pose a problem for the survey (though he did not know Spanish), and he doubted workers felt intimidated to answer truthfully: "I was very careful to not make my feelings, you know, partial. . . . I felt that they were able to express freely what they felt." "In general," he found, "they indicated that they did like the Teamsters." When Karahadian was asked if he considered worker fears, he said "I don't know what fear exists normally between an employer and an employee. . . . Whether that was [opting for a Teamster contract] because they just wanted a union, for whatever reason, or whether that was because they were just so adverse to the UFW, I cannot tell you." "Karahadian Deposition," Folder 14, Box 57, UFW Administration Department Records, Part III, ALUA.

16. Elizabeth Lamoree, "Gambling on Grapes: Management, Marketing, and Labor in California Agribusiness," *Agricultural History* 86, no. 3 (Summer 2012), 121.

17. "Cesar to Field Offices: December 6, 1972," Folder 1, Box 62, UFW Administration Department Records, Part III, ALUA. "Ray Huerta to Chavez: January 30, 1973," in "Oasis Gardens Grievances," Folder 19, Box 22, UFW Administration Department Records, Part III, ALUA.

18. "Ray Huerta to Chavez: January 30, 1973," in "Oasis Gardens Grievances," Folder 19, Box 22, UFW Administration Department Records, Part III, ALUA. "Coachella Area

Report by Ray Huerta," in "Transcription of Teamster Brainstorming Conference: March 23, 1973," Folder 37, Box 28, UFW Administration Department Records, Part III, ALUA.

19. "Barbara [Macri] to Cesar [Chavez]: February 26, 1973," Folder 12, Box 62, UFW Administration Department Records, Part III, ALUA.

20. "Coachella Area Report by Ray Huerta," in "Transcription of Teamster Brainstorming Conference: March 23, 1973," Folder 37, Box 28, UFW Administration Department Records, Part III, ALUA.

21. "Bill E. to Chavez: February 10, 1973," Folder 26, Box 28, UFW Administration Department Records, Part III, ALUA. Bill learned that before he arrived in the Coachella Valley, the rancher lawyer Dave Smith had told ranchers not to pay into the UFW Defense Fund, as mandated by the 1970 UFW contract.

22. "Coachella Area Report by Ray Huerta," in "Transcription of Teamster Brainstorming Conference: March 23, 1973," Folder 37, Box 28, UFW Administration Department, Part III, ALUA.

23. "Meeting Notes: March 20, 1973," Folder 4, Box 23, UFW Administration Department, Part III, ALUA.

24. "Ray [Huerta] said he really didn't think they got into it [strike planning] as far as policy and hard core decisions until 2–3 weeks before contracts expired." "Summary Deposition: Ray Huerta Volume III," Folder 2, Box 62, UFW Administration Department, Part III, ALUA.

25. In his deposition, Karahadian quoted Chavez on representation. "Karahadian Deposition," transcript, p. 32, Folder 14, Box 57, UFW Administration Department, Part III, ALUA. Al Caplan testified that the UFW representative Dave Burciaga told him the UFW would submit to union elections if ranchers agreed to statewide elections. "Al Caplan Deposition V. 1: July 29, 1976," transcript, p. 118, Folder 3, Box 58, UFW Administration Department Records, Part III, ALUA. See also, "Deposition of David Smith: May 2, 1974," transcript, p. 33, Folder 2, Box 58, UFW Administration Department Records, Part III, ALUA.

26. "Lee Shaw Deposition: Summary," transcript, p. 121, Folder 6, Box 58, UFW Administration Department Records, Part III, ALUA.

27. Milton Karahadian said that prior to signing with the Teamsters he did not expect to "have trouble getting an adequate workforce." He said he was proved correct in 1973, which he took as evidence of worker union preference. "Milton Karahadian Deposition: March 24, 1976," Folder 14, Box 57, UFW Administration Department Records, Part III, ALUA.

28. Given these dynamics, Filipino workers framed the 1965 strike as a near-painless strike, where rancher vulnerability and worker unity could overcome the challenges. It explains Itliong's opposition to a late strike in 1968 Coachella—with Filipino strikers facing job losses without a clear union victory—and Velasco's 1969 caution against seeing Filipino strikebreakers as anti-union. They also explain why UFW members prior to 1970 emphasized ethics: one went on strike out of political conviction, not because victory was assured.

29. "Alfred H. Caplan Deposition Volume II: July 30, 1976," Folder 3, Box 58, UFW Administration Department Records, Part III, ALUA.

30. In a Delano meeting two months before the expiration of grape contracts in 1973, Ray Huerta reported on the Teamster organizer presence in the Coachella Valley. Though ranchers remained intransigent, Huerta expected "growers most likely will renew contract" because they "don't want no problem with boycott." "Field Office Meeting: February 11, 1973," Folder 14, Box 1, Pete Velasco Papers, ALUA.

31. Lamoree, "Gambling on Grapes," 104–27.

32. For some agricultural employers, Lamoree noted, "relinquishing control over the distribution and recruiting of workers represented a traumatic experience." Lamoree, "Gambling on Grapes," 119.

33. "Summary of Deposition: Ray Huerta V. III," Folder 2, Box 62, UFW Administration Department Records, Part III, ALUA. See also, "Summary of Incidents of Chicanery and Hornswoggling: Richard Bagdasarian," Folder 24, Box 20, UFW Administration Department Records, Part III, ALUA.

34. Max Huerta said their Valdora supervisors openly organized with Teamsters in mid-March 1973. "Deposition of Max Huerta: September 8, 1976," Folder 17, Box 61, UFW Administration Department Records, Part III, ALUA.

35. "Lionel Steinberg," interview by Ray Telles, 1995/1996, audio recording available under "Paradigm Productions Farmworker Movement Interviews," Farmworker Movement Documentation Project (henceforth, FMDP), https://libraries.ucsd.edu/farmworkermovement/medias/oral-history/.

36. "Teamsters Claim to Represent Majority of Vineyard Workers," *Los Angeles Times*, April 11, 1973.

37. Also, ranchers refuted the UFW's claim of the grape industry's profitability ("good years despite of, not because of, the UFWU") and leveled the rancher.

38. "Meany Criticizes Teamster Drive," *New York Times*, April 19, 1973. See also "Meany Backs Chavez Against Teamster Bid," *Wall Street Journal*, April 19, 1973; "Meany Rips Teamster in Farm Fight," *Washington Post*, April 18, 1973.

39. As the UFW's Tom Dalzell noted, when the "Coachella strike began against AWOC in 1965, some growers didn't sign until six years . . . [of] constant strike and boycott pressure." But in 1973, "Growers sign with Teamos after no pressure from latter at all." "Dalzell Deposition Summary V. 2," Folder 8, Box 62, UFW Administration Department Records, Part III, ALUA.

40. "200 Chavez Pickets Appear at Fields," *Los Angeles Times*, April 16, 1973. On April 15, 1973, the *Los Angeles Times* reported on a thousand-strong UFW meeting in Coachella, where workers voted unanimously to strike. It then reported the harvest workforce totaled 3,000–4,000 and repeated the Teamster claim of holding 2,500 worker signatures. "Chavez Farm Union in All-Out Fight for Life," *Los Angeles Times*, April 15, 1973. On the following day, the *New York Times* reported on the "displayed stack of [Teamster] petitions" and their claim to represent "4,000 of the 5,000 workers," and concluded with a strike–boycott prediction from Chavez. "Teamsters Gain California Farms," *New York Times*, April 16, 1973. The *Chicago Tribune* and *Wall Street Journal* repeated the same, with the latter pairing Chavez's vague existential comment ("If we lose here, we lose our identity") with the Teamsters' (political) promise, "grapes will be harvested by [a] labor union." "Grape Growers Sign Pact with Teamsters; Chavez Boycott Seen," *Wall Street Journal*, April 16, 1973; "Chavez Orders Vineyard Strike," *Chicago Tribune*, April 17, 1973.

41. For a similar argument, see Elizabeth Lamoree, "The Managed Crisis: Labor Relations and Management in California Agriculture, 1930–1980" (PhD diss., University of California, Santa Barbara, 2012).

42. "Karahadian Deposition," Folder 14, Box 57, UFW Administration Department Records, Part III, ALUA.

43. Like Karahadian, Coachella Valley grape ranchers universally claimed to respect their employees' choice when they unilaterally signed Teamster contracts. They also claimed to share their farmworkers' victimized position between two rival unions. Maria Marron, however, remembered a Karahadian supervisor celebrating the Teamster contract by saying the workers' "honeymoon" was over. Maria Carmona, interview by Christian Paiz, February 10, 2017.

44. Max Huerta, interview by Christian Paiz, March 18, 2015.

45. Maria Teresa Ramirez said her family almost lost their home because they could not pay the mortgage for three months. They were spared what many strikers faced only after a UFW letter secured them a grace period from their lending bank. Maria Teresa and Salvador Ramirez, interview by Christian Paiz, April 15, 2017.

46. Max Huerta, interview by Christian Paiz, March 18, 2015; "Summary Deposition Maximo Huerta, V. III," Folder 18, Box 61, UFW Administration Department Records, Part III, ALUA.

47. Salvador Ramirez said he went on strike because he wanted higher wages and better treatment. Some farmworkers did not leave the fields, he recalled, and he was unsure why. He suspected some made themselves "deaf to the union," while his daughter (who was present in the interview) said a lot of people simply followed others. Maria Teresa and Salvador Ramirez, interview by Christian Paiz, April 15, 2017.

48. "Lopez Deposition Notes," Folder 9, Box 62, UFW Administration Department Records, Part III, ALUA; "Ray Huerta Deposition Summary Vol. III," in "Plaintiffs Witnesses: Ray Huerta '76," Folder 2, Box 62, UFW Administration Department Records, Part III, ALUA.

49. Clementina Olloque, interview by Christian Paiz, August 13, 2014; Maria Marron de Carmona, interview by Christian Paiz, January 31, 2014; Maria Marron interview by Christian Paiz, February 10, 2017. In meetings, Max Huerta said he learned half the farmworkers in Bagdasarian, Mouradick, and Coachella Vineyards also went on strike. Max Huerta, interview by Christian Paiz, March 18, 2015.

50. Conducted in 1974 and 1975, these depositions covered Teamster meetings, strike participation and violence, and the question of worker preference. The exception was Bozick; his deposition originated in his lawsuit against the UFW for business losses due to an unfair strike. "Bagdasarian v. UFW Deposition: November 21, 1973," Folder 19, Box 54, UFW Administration Department Records, Part III, ALUA. The depositions are organized by rancher across Boxes 57 to 62 in the UFW Administration Department Records, Part III, ALUA.

51. "So," the UFW's lawyer asked, "we would be able to determine then who was working at what time over a several week period in 1973 to see the rise and fall in the level of employment, and then if we have the energy, and resources, and if the parties are willing, we might then question those persons as to the reasons for their not working at that time?" "Counsel, I made the objection, and he's not going to answer the question." "Bagdasarian

v. UFW Deposition: November 21, 1973," Folder 19, Box 54, UFW Administration Department Records, Part III, ALUA.

52. "Summary Karahadian Deposition: March 24, 1976," transcript, p. 4, Folder 14, Box 57, UFW Administration Department Records, Part III, ALUA. Karahadian's estimates were also contradicted by his anti-UFW workers. In her April 1973 declaration, Louisa Velasquez said she was working at Karahadian Ranch when 250 people came with red flags and forced her out of the fields. Similarly, Mary Morales said at least 100 picketers pulled her out of Karahadian Ranch. "Louisa Velasquez Declaration," Folder 1, Box 55, UFW Administration Department Records, Part III, ALUA; "Declaration Mary Morales," Folder 1, Box 55, UFW Administration Department Records, Part III, ALUA.

53. Two other crews thinned a second Karahadian Ranch, where fifteen Teamsters—who "could not have been anything else other than a motorcycle gang," said Eloisa Amador, a Karahadian striker—verbally abused picketers. "Declaration of Eloisa Amador: April 19, 1973," Folder 27, Box 21, UFW Administration Department Records, Part III, ALUA.

54. Karahadian said: "I discussed [the labor shortage] with my general supervisor and I discussed with all my crew foremen . . . [and] I told them, 'We should make every effort to build our crews back to full strength.'" "Karahadian Deposition: March 24, 1976," Folder 14, Box 57, UFW Administration Department Records, Part III, ALUA, pp. 146–49.

55. See Johnny Macias testimony in "An Examination of Violence in the Farm Labor Dispute," Palm Springs, CA, November 26, 1973, California Legislature, Assembly Select Committee on Farm Labor Violence, transcript, p. 132, Folder 64, Box 28, UFW Administration Department Records, Part III, ALUA.

56. "As you can see," Ganz told Manuel Chavez in 1974, "and as you know, it ain't at all like Imperial Valley, with five or six key contractors." "Marshall Ganz to Manuel Chavez Memo," no date, Folder 29, Box 5, Marshall Ganz Papers, ALUA.

57. "42 Teamster Interviews: Coachella Summer 1975 Research," Folder 9, Box 10, Victor Salandini Papers, Special Collections, Stanford University. For a rancher survey by the anti-UFW priest, Father Humphrey, see "The Farm Labor Issues: A Searching for the Truth by Father Humphrey," Folder 10, Box 8, Victor Salandini Papers, Special Collections, Stanford University. For a critical description of Father Humphrey, see Silvia Montenegro, interview by Christian Paiz, February 1, 2015.

58. Miriam Pawel, *Union of Their Dreams: Power, Hope and Struggle in Cesar Chavez's Farm Worker Movement* (New York: Bloomsbury, 2009), 117. Bardacke, *Trampling Out*, 432.

59. "42 Teamster Interviews: Coachella Summer 1975 Research," Folder 9, Box 10, Victor Salandini Papers, Special Collections, Stanford University.

60. Ramon Torres said, "I have been a farm worker for 30 years in California. I joined with Chavez in 1970 and when Teamsters won in 1973 I joined them." But, he added, "I prefer the UFW. I have only heard of the abuses of the UFW, but it is still a good union." Seven (16.5 percent) workers settled on joining whichever won elections—a position reporters stressed. "42 Teamster Interviews: Coachella Summer 1975 Research," Folder 9, Box 10, Victor Salandini Papers, Special Collections, Stanford University.

61. Presumably, these are the workers that Karahadian, Carian, Bozick, and others "overheard" when deciding to switch unions in 1973.

62. Though Salandini aimed to collect statistically valid data by randomly selecting workers from the entire Coachella Valley Teamster membership, his forty-two interviews

fall short of what he needed. For a definitive account, his total needed to be double. That said, his interviews provide an invaluable insight into worker perspectives, especially when paired with other sources. They suggest that how many people honor a strike is different from how many people picket, and what to deduce from the two is a complicated affair.

63. Clementina Olloque described the first day of the Karahadian Ranch strike in harrowing terms: police helicopters flew low to the ground to intimidate strikers; police officers beat strikers before arresting them; general mayhem ensued; "everyone was crying." Olloque's recollections contradicted Karahadian's deposition and suggests that the pall of violence settled before and/or as soon as the strike began, shaping the very context of subsequent worker choices regarding the strike. Clementina Olloque, interview by Christian Paiz, August 13, 2014.

64. On April 9, 1973, the UFW organizer Carlos Fierros reported, "Lorenzo de los Santos, supervisor at Harry Carian, drove by on the road at the outskirts of the field, perpendicular to the one where we were.... I moved up onto the bank of the road in order to be out of his path. Santos came along the road, and when he saw me, accelerated the car, veered towards me, and hit me with the pick up.... As I was unconscious, I was taken to the Valley Memorial Hospital in Indio by Santos, at the insistence of the workers in the crew." "Declaration of Carlos Fierros: April 9, 1973," Folder 40, Box 20, UFW Administration Department Records, Part III, ALUA. "Coachella Farm Workers Support Union!" *El Malcriado*, April 20, 1973.

65. "Francisco Diaz Declaration: April 23, 1973," Folder 16, Box 2, UFW Administration Department Records, Part III, ALUA; "Jeffrey Lewis Declaration: June 14, 1973, Folder 16, Box 2, UFW Administration Department Records, Part III, ALUA. In November 1973, Esperanza Sauceda testified on the violence on the Karahadian picket line: "One man that's in here, Roberto Hernandez, [was] carrying a gun, threatening pickers and it was pretty bad. I mean I was really scared to go out in the picket line because of those guys, staring at you, calling you names and everything." "An Examination of Violence in the Farm Labor Dispute," Palm Springs, CA, November 26, 1973, California Legislature, Assembly Select Committee on Farm Labor Violence, transcript, p. 106, Folder 64, Box 28, UFW Administration Department, Part III, ALUA.

66. "The worst place that I picketed was in the Coachella Valley in the early spring of 1973," Elizabeth Hernandez recalled, "The grape growers had hired goons (Teamsters) to keep us off the fields.... This was a long, hot summer where temperatures were often over 100 degrees." "Elizabeth Hernandez, 1971–1977," Essays by Authors (1970s), Essay Collection, FMDP, https://libraries.ucsd.edu/farmworkermovement/essays/essays/103%20Hernandez_Elizabeth.pdf.

See also "Eloisa Amado Declaration: April 19, 1973, which describes Teamsters' use of "nasty" and "gross" language that "our people are not used to," "Delbert Adams Declaration: April 24, 1973," which recounts being spit at and pushed by Teamster guards, next to apathetic police officers, and the "Reinaldo Bermes, Salvador Alvarado, Armendia Garcia Declaration: April 14, 1973," which recounted supervisors ripping UFW flags from pro-UFW farmworker cars and laughing at the protesting workers. All three declarations are just a handful of examples the UFW filed in its lawsuit against Karahadian Ranches. All three are under Folder 27, Box 21, UFW Administration Department Records, Part III, ALUA, Pro-UFW farmworker submitted similar, if not starker and more violent, declarations for all Coachella Valley grape ranchers in 1973.

67. Olloque stressed the fear strikers felt each morning, in the drives to the fields, at the end of the strike day, and while attending to everyday activities, like going to church or buying groceries. Clementina Olloque, interview by Christian Paiz, August 14, 2014. Arturo Diaz, Silvia Montenegro, and Eliseo Arrellano recalled similar violence. Arturo Diaz, interview by Christian Paiz, January 31, 2015; Silvia Montenegro, interview by Christian Paiz, February 1, 2015; Eliseo Arrellano, interview by Christian Paiz, February 6, 2015.

68. See striker testimonies in "Striker Ignore Court Injunctions," *El Malcriado*, May 4, 1973; "They Can Jail a Man but Not His Spirit," *El Malcriado*, May 4, 1973. Clementina Olloque recalled children crying, women demanding water and access to restrooms, and police hostility. The only redeeming quality of this experience came in her co-strikers, who sang outside the jail and kept her company. Clementina Olloque, interview by Christian Paiz, August 14, 2012. For a UFW organizer account, see "Barbara Macri-Ortiz 1969–1990," Essays by Authors (1960s), Essays Collection, FMDP, https://libraries.ucsd.edu/farmworkermovement/essays/essays/068%20Macri%20Ortiz_Barbara.pdf. Bardacke, *Trampling Out*, 430–32.

69. Martha Vasquez, Olga Hernandez, and Catalina C. Vasquez found a "paper bag [with] some pills" in their jail room. They feared police officers "had put the pills there just so that they could catch us with the drugs, or whatever they were. We flushed the pills down the toilet. In just a few minutes, the matron came into our cell, and she began looking. The first place that she went to was exactly where pills had been, but of course she did not find them." "Martha Vasquez, Olga Hernandez, Catalina Vasquez Declaration: April 20, 1973," Folder 38, Box 21, UFW Administration Department, Part III, ALUA.

70. Barbara Macri-Ortiz said she "was falsely accused of having committed an armed robbery at a liquor store in Indio, after an eyewitness identified my mug shot as the 'Mexican woman wearing a bandana' who drove the getaway car. I was never so scared in my life, thinking that some grower agent had framed me. Thanks to my lawyer, Sandy Nathan, and several young farmworker women who appeared in the lineup with me, I was finally allowed to leave the county after the eyewitness was unable to pick me out of the lineup. I was lucky." "Barbara Macri-Ortiz 1969–1990," Essays by Authors (1960s), Essays Collection, FMDP, https://libraries.ucsd.edu/farmworkermovement/essays/essays/068%20Macri%20Ortiz_Barbara.pdf

71. "[The police] didn't care that the children were small," Jose Perez told *El Malcriado*, "The cops jailed them along with everyone else. We later had to send the children to stay with their relatives because they were so frightened. We will stay on the picketline." "They Can Jail a Man but Not His Spirit," *El Malcriado*, May 4, 1973.

72. On April 20, 1973, at the end of the strike's first week, Chavez telegrammed Coachella Valley grape ranchers calling for a union election before the UFW mounted a national boycott of table grapes. "Good Friday," *El Malcriado*, May 4, 1973.

73. "Chavez and Union Fight for Lives: Administrative Problems, Hiring Hall Eliminated, They Seem to Be Losing in Battle with Teamsters," *New York Times*, April 29, 1973.

74. "Chavez and Union fight for Lives: Administrative Problems, Hiring Hall Eliminated, They Seem to Be Losing in Battle with Teamsters," *New York Times*, April 29, 1973.

75. In its neutrality posture, the *New York Times* also overlooked the very nature of the fight: the UFW demanded elections, while ranchers opposed them. It also foregrounded

Steinberg, the "friendly rancher," who described Chavez as "the world's worst administrator" and repeatedly presented the strike in muddled terms: "All the Chavez people are not wearing 'the white hats,'" he stressed, "and all the Teamsters are not wearing the 'black hats.'" "Chavez Tackles the Teamsters: That National Farm Workers," *New York Times*, April 22, 1973

76. See "Chavez Asks Vote on Union," *Washington Post*, April 21, 1973; "Teamsters Deny Chavez Jurisdiction Elections," *Washington Post*, April 26, 1973.

77. For the *Los Angeles Times*, Harry Bernstein stressed that "not all of the guilt or innocence is on either side," quoting rancher complaints of a UFW that failed its workers by behaving like a "revolutionary movement" with "5-dollar-hot-shots . . . more interested in thumbing their noses at the rich [rancher] than in settling a grievance." Even "friendly" ranchers, like Steinberg, said "It is hard to work with a man who believes he is a saint." "Coachella Strike Analysis," *Los Angeles Times*, April 24, 1973.

78. Joseph A. McCartin, "Re-Framing US Labour's Crisis: Reconsidering Structure, Strategy, and Vision," *Labour/Le Travail* 59 (Spring 2007): 133–48; John Logan, "Permanent Replacements and the End of Labor's 'Only True Weapon,'" *International Labor and Working-Class History* (Fall 2008): 171–92; Windham, *Knocking on Labor's Door: Union Organizing in the 1970s and the Roots of a New Economic Divide* (Chapel Hill: University of North Carolina, 2017), 75, 182. In the 1960s, California growers argued that union preference among workers could be determined with strike participation; if workers did not go on strike, they argued, then the UFW did not represent the workers. Lamoree, "Gambling on Grapes," 116.

79. "AFL-CIO Will Give Chavez $1.6 Million to Fight Teamsters," *Los Angeles Times*, April 10, 1973.

80. "AFL-CIO Will Give Chavez $1.6 Million to Fight Teamsters," *Los Angeles Times*, April 10, 1973.

81. John Banks, "Coachella Valley Grape Strike Newsletter," May 7, 1973, Folder 36, Box 28, UFW Administration Department Records, Part III, ALUA.

82. "Picket Captains' Report on Coachella Grape Strike, April 26, 1973," Folder 26, Box 28, UFW Information & Research Department (henceforth, IRD) Collection, ALUA.

83. "Picket Captains' Report on Coachella Grape Strike, April 26, 1973," Folder 26, Box 28, UFW IRD Collection, ALUA.

84. A small contingent of primarily older Filipino grape workers remained pro-UFW. On April 24, 1973, the Filipino organizer Pancho Caliente helped organize Filipino workers. "Reorganized Picket Captain Meeting, April 24, 1973," Folder 26, Box 28, UFW IRD Collection, ALUA.

85. John Banks, "Coachella Valley Grape Strike Newsletter," May 8, 1973, Folder 36, Box 28, UFW Administration Department Records, Part I, ALUA. In mid-May, Banks reported Chavez participated in a local radio program where he said the UFW would address "problems with the union." "Coachella Valley Grape Strike Newsletter," May 12–14, 1973, Folder 36, Box 28, UFW Administration Department Records, Part I, ALUA.

86. John Banks, "Coachella Valley Grape Strike Newsletter," May 8, 1973, Folder 36, Box 28, UFW Administration Department Records, Part I, ALUA.

87. "Why We Fight," *El Malcriado*, May 4, 1973.

88. "Farm Worker Women for Equality," *El Malcriado*, April 20, 1973.

89. John Banks, "Coachella Valley Grape Strike Newsletter," May 4, 1973, Folder 36, Box 28, UFW Administration Department Records, Part I, ALUA.

90. Reverend Chris Hartmire, "Boycott Will Win Again," *El Malcriado*, May 18, 1973. The "boycott will win again," Hartmire, Director of the National Farm Worker Ministry, said: "it's just a matter of time."

91. "42 Teamster Interviews: Coachella Summer 1975 Research," Folder 9, Box 10, Salandini Papers, Special Collections, Stanford University.

92. Millonida's reference to Mexican immigrant strikebreakers reiterated the UFW movement's 1960s discourse on immigrant workers and their seeming incapacity to join labor unions (see chapter 3). Millonida was not the only person who blamed Mexican immigrants for weakening the UFW's Coachella Grape Strike in 1973. This was a consistent theme and it grew further in 1974, when the UFW led a xenophobic campaign against immigrants in the San Joaquin Valley. John Banks, "Coachella Valley Grape Strike Newsletter," June 11, 1973, Folder 36, Box 28, UFW Administration Department Records, Part III, ALUA.

93. "42 Teamster Interviews: Coachella Summer 1975 Research," Folder 9, Box 10, Salandini Papers, Special Collections, Stanford University.

94. Carlos Masip, for instance, told Salandini: "Chavez is a good man, but the administration is bad. . . . Illiterate people have been placed in charge of the administration. . . . Strict fines offended many." Masip noted "despite all this the union has improved our lives. The problem has been with administration." Masip's Filipino coworkers, Vicente Tijan and Themistocles Abeno, were not so sure: they "thought maybe Teamsters' union could do more for farm workers than Chavez." "1974 Interviews in Coachella Valley," Folder 9, Box 8, Salandini Papers, Special Collections, Stanford University. The following year, Runtal highlighted the same problems: "The Filipino workers who objected to these three above policies [seniority system, dues for dispatch, late fines] were never present at meetings where these policies were decided upon by majority vote." Manueto Duldulao said the same. "42 Teamster Interviews Summer 1975: Coachella Summer 1975 Research," Folder 9, Box 10, Salandini Papers, Special Collections, Stanford University.

95. Some Filipino workers interviewed by Salandini in 1975 had migrated to the United States in 1973–74, such as Ruel Granada and Isabelita Caluya. Neither had worked under a UFW contract and both found employment through Filipino contractors.

96. For a detailed breakdown of Coachella Valley grape contractors, Filipino or Mexican, as well as their sources of labor and the number of housing camps under their direction, see "Marshall Ganz to Manuel Chavez Memo," no date, Folder 29, Box 5, Marshall Ganz Papers, ALUA.

97. "Marshall Ganz to Manuel Chavez Memo," no date, Folder 29, Box 5, Marshall Ganz Papers, ALUA.

98. See "Simon's Camp October 30, 1971" under "Camp Meeting Notes, 1971," Folder 15, Box 2, Pete Velasco Papers, ALUA.

99. See "Armington Camp October 28, 1971" under "Camp Meeting Notes, 1971," Folder 15, Box 2, Pete Velasco Papers, ALUA.

100. See chapter 4. See also "Andres Gonzalez to Tenneco: June 8, 1972," Folder 29, Box 22, UFW Administration Department Records, Part III, ALUA.

101. For Velasco reference, see "Velasco Journal: Entry December 1, 1965," Folder 12, Box 12, Agricultural Workers Organizing Committee Papers, ALUA. For 1971 dispatch, see "Gene

Redovich and M. Tamsi, November 10, 1971" under "Camp Meeting Notes, 1971," Folder 15, Box 1, Pete Velasco Papers, ALUA. For "sold out" quote, see "Scabs!" *El Malcriado*, January 13, 1967.

102. On Mel-Pak, see "Incidents of Collusion," Folder 38, Box 21, UFW Administration Department Records, Part III, ALUA; on Runtal, see "42 Teamster Interviews: Coachella Summer 1975 Research," Folder 9, Box 10, Salandini Papers, Special Collections, Stanford University.

103. "Marshall Ganz to Manuel Chavez Memo, nd," Folder 29, Box 5, Marshall Ganz Collection, ALUA.

104. Consider Runtal's frustrated entreaties to strikebreakers: "When scabs on the picket line say, 'we have a union and we don't want your union' Claro answers 'We simply want to educate you about our union.' When scabs yell out 'you strikers are lazy people,' Claro answers, 'Brothers count the money you make in one year. Yet what are you doing for your people? It is important to convince people of our struggle." "42 Teamster Interviews: Coachella Summer 1975 Research," Folder 9, Box 10, Salandini Papers, Special Collections, Stanford University.

105. "Maria de Esquiveles Declaration: April 19, 1973," Folder 9, Box 26, UFW Administration Department Records, Part III, ALUA.

106. "Margie Meza Declaration: April 19, 1973," Folder 9, Box 26, UFW Administration Department Records, Part III, ALUA.

107. "Guadalupe Agcaoli Declaration: June 19, 1973," Folder 38, Box 21, UFW Administration Department Records, Part III, ALUA; "Declaration of Maria Agcaoili, Paula Archeto, Flora Morelos, Fecilitas Perez, Cortes: June 25, 1973," Folder 38, Box 21, UFW Administration Department Records, Part III, ALUA. In 1974, Marshall Ganz summarized what he thought of Meza to Manuel Chavez, who was tasked with organizing a limited harvest strike: "We talked to her last year. Useless. You know her story." "Marshall Ganz to Manuel Chavez Memo, nd," Folder 29, Box 5, Marshall Ganz Collection, ALUA.

108. "Maria Morales Declaration: April 20, 1973," Folder 9, Box 26, UFW Administration Department Records, Part III, ALUA.

109. For Morales's crew strike, see "Marshall Ganz to Manuel Chavez Memo, nd," Folder 29, Box 5, Marshall Ganz Collection, ALUA. Karahadian's other contractors were Henry Pugal and Pancho Cadiente, both Filipino. In his pro-Teamster declaration in 1973, Cadiente spoke of his "boys," their fear of *Chavista* violence, and Teamsters' good treatment. Pugal shared similarly: "my people don't like Chavez one bit. With him they have to wait, wait, wait.... My workers are happy now with Teamsters.... *Crew Boss* of 12 years." For both, see "Pro-Teamster Declarations," Folder 9, Box 26, UFW Administration Department Records, Part III, ALUA.

110. The women called the police after they noticed Teamster men carrying guns, which the police later found inside a picnic cooler in a Teamster car. John Banks, "Coachella Valley Strike Newsletter: May 10, 1973," Folder 36, Box 28, UFW Administration Department Records, Part I, ALUA.

111. "Joe Lopez Deposition Notes," Folder 9, Box 62, UFW Administration Department Records, Part I, ALUA.

112. "Alberto Dunlao Declaration: May 15, 1973," Folder 24, Box 20, UFW Administration Department Records, Part III, ALUA.

113. Calisto Ramos, interview by Christian Paiz, April 18, 2017.

114. Maria Serrano, interview by Christian Paiz, February 10, 2017.

115. "Teamster Violence: Personal Injury Declarations," Folder 67, Box 28, UFW Administration Department Records, Part II, ALUA.

116. "An Examination of Violence in the Farm Labor Dispute," Palm Springs, CA, November 26, 1973, California Legislature, Assembly Select Committee on Farm Labor Violence, transcript, p. 106, Folder 64, Box 28, UFW Administration Department, Part III, ALUA.

117. "Between April and July," local Sheriffs said, "the six most frequently reported cases were disturbing the peace, we had 161; violations of court injunctions, 70; trespassing, 64; assault and assault and battery lumped together, 58; malicious mischief, 37; assault with a deadly weapon, 34 . . . [plus] 14 bookings for felony assault." "An Examination of Violence in the Farm Labor Dispute." "An Examination of Violence in the Farm Labor Dispute," Palm Springs, CA, November 26, 1973, California Legislature, Assembly Select Committee on Farm Labor Violence, transcript, p. 137–140, Folder 64, Box 28, UFW Administration Department, Part III, ALUA. See also the accompanying testimonies of Juan Arredondo and Lorenzo Patino.

118. "An Examination of Violence in the Farm Labor Dispute," Palm Springs, CA, November 26, 1973, California Legislature, Assembly Select Committee on Farm Labor Violence, transcript, p. 137–140, Folder 64, Box 28, UFW Administration Department, Part III, ALUA. Quoted in Lamoree, "The Managed Crisis," 311. For a similar discussion on strike-related violence in the Coachella Valley, see Lamoree, "The Managed Crisis," 303–10.

119. "My people want the Teamsters," Bozick told the *Los Angeles Times*, "you people [UFW] are irresponsible." "Set Farm Labor Election Now, Bishop Pleads," *Los Angeles Times*, May 5, 1973. A month later, the newspaper compared Bozick and Steinberg to present the former as a reasonable, self-made businessman with a miner-union history. When asked about elections, Bozick said, "There is no point to an election. The workers have already decided, I saw the cards they signed myself. I'm satisfied. They're satisfied. It's done. We don't need no election." In the same article, Steinberg complained: "The UFWU and Chavez have acted arrogantly, irresponsibly," they "just didn't understand the people." "Two Rival Growers Hold Fate of Chavez Union in Their Hands," *Los Angeles Times*, June 7, 1973.

120. "Farmworkers Union Faces Test," *Washington Post*, June 4, 1973. The *Chicago Tribune* added: "The big question here is whether Chavez and his UFW can lure Mexican and Filipino laborers out of vast ranches without serious battles." Replaying earlier themes, it quoted ranchers and strikebreakers who "insist[ed] Chavez and his followers made shambles of the union," Teamsters who claimed to protect "workers who are fed up with Chavez," and the UFW who blamed injunctions for early strike's struggles. "Teamsters, AFL-CIO Gird for Battle on Farmworkers," *Chicago Tribune*, June 4, 1973; "Union's Battle Lines Form as Grape Harvest Begins," *Chicago Tribune*, June 5, 1973.

121. "Chavez Union Struggling to Survive," *New York Times*, June 27, 1973.

122. "Chavez Union Struggling to Survive," *New York Times*, June 27, 1973.

123. "Union's Battle Lines Form as Grape Harvest Begins," *Chicago Tribune*, June 5, 1973. On June 8, 1973, and after the Seafarers' Union offered to aid the UFW's pickets, the *Los Angeles Times* wrote "the picket and Teamster guards have been involved in a number of minor incidents." "Seafarers Union to 'Guard' Chavez Pickets in Strike," *Los Angeles*

Times, June 8, 1973; "2 Unions in Dispute Bring Out 'Guards,'" *Washington Post*, June 9, 1973; "Teamsters Hit Use of Guards by Farm Union," *Los Angeles Times*, June 12, 1973; "Spitting Incident: Teamster Aid Seized in Strike," *Los Angeles Times*, June 14, 1973.

124. "Struggle in Fields: Chavez Union Fights for Survival as the Teamsters Mount a Strong Drive to Represent Farm Laborers," *Wall Street Journal*, June 29, 1973.

125. Bardacke, *Trampling Out*, 443.

126. See the historical reflections of Jose Guadalupe "Lupe" Murguia, Doug Adair, Alfredo Figueroa, Hope Lopez Fierro, Pancho Botello, Rosemary Matson, Barbara Macri-Ortiz, Pat Hoffman, Elizabeth Martinez, Terry Vasquez: Essays by Author, FMDP, https://libraries.ucsd.edu/farmworkermovement/essay/.

127. "The workers," he added, "we had been organizing and working with in previous years stood up against the teamsters and demanded elections. It was a violent summer with many beatings and arrests." Jose Guadalupe Murguia, "Jose Guadalupe Murguia, 1963–1991," Essays by Author, FMDP.

128. "An Examination of Violence in the Farm Labor Dispute," Palm Springs, CA, November 26, 1973, California Legislature, Assembly Select Committee on Farm Labor Violence, transcript, p. 67, Folder 64, Box 28, UFW Administration Department, Part III, ALUA.

129. Max Huerta, interview by Christian Paiz, March 18, 2015.

130. "It was very encouraging," Ramos said, "You felt a sense of unity. A sense that you belonged with this group. You no longer had doubts that they could win. You realized at that point that they did have a good chance to win.... You saw it all over the place. People were actually not afraid to fly the union flag. They were putting it on their ... little union flags, as small as handkerchiefs, ... and no one would go there to do anything to them, tear them down, take them down. And you got to see that throughout Coachella and in '73—I don't think there was a single crew that was under 100. And there must have been ten crews, maybe more." Calisto Ramos, interview by Christian Paiz, April 18, 2017.

131. Olloque recalled strikers suffered deprivation from the start. They did not have enough money, so they collected donations from other farmworkers, as well as aluminum cans to recycle. Clementina Olloque, interview by Christian Paiz, August 14, 2014. The Ramirez family almost lost their home, while Virginia Ortega first noticed the local UFW leader Maria Serrano precisely when Serrano was collecting donations for the grape strikers among Indio's farm labor camp residents.

132. Maria Marron, interview by Christian Paiz, January 31, 2014.

133. Maria Marron, interview by Christian Paiz, January 31, 2014.

134. Serrano said that she and Petra Ruiz had "tasted" the contract, hence she fought for her union. Arguably, the Coachella Grape Strike of 1973 offered another instance of a "taste" for a better life for many workers and strikers. Maria Serrano, interview by Christian Paiz, February 10, 2017.

135. Maria Serrano estimated she received $25 a week for her family and said her family could not have survived on that. Maria Serrano, interview by Christian Paiz, February 10, 2017.

136. "Grower Repression: Workers Fired for Participating in Pro-Chavez Marches," *El Malcriado*, May 18, 1973, 5.

137. Virginia Ortega, interview by Christian Paiz, May 6, 2020; Clementina Olloque, interview by Christian Paiz, August 14, 2014; David Perez, interview by Christian Paiz, February 14, 2017.

138. "Good Friday," *El Malcriado*, May 4, 1973, 14.

139. Clementina Olloque said the strike strained families and led to splits. She also emphasized the women's role in the strike and the strike's role in challenging patriarchal authority in families. The strikers also faced public insults and hostility, she said, and the majority of strikebreakers were boss-associated families or people outside the Coachella Valley. Clementina Olloque, interview by Christian Paiz, August 14, 2014.

140. Salvador Ramirez, interview by Christian Paiz, April 15, 2017. Clementina Olloque said strikebreakers did not know they were breaking the strike and/or they pretended not to hear the strikers. Clementina Olloque, interview by Christian Paiz, August 14, 2014.

141. "Margie Meza Declaration: April 19, 1973," Folder 9, Box 26, UFW Administration Department Records, Part III, ALUA.

142. "Maria Morales Declaration: April 20, 1973," Folder 9, Box 26, UFW Administration Department Records, Part III, ALUA.

143. Cesar Chavez, "Untitled," *El Malcriado*, May 18, 1973.

144. Bardacke, *Trampling Out*, 437.

145. Bardacke, *Trampling Out*, 439–52

146. "I think the whole union was in shock, because of all the loss of contracts, and everything that happened, and the people were getting shot up in Delano, and people were trying to recover from their injuries here in the Coachella Valley, and there was just too much." Max Huerta, interview by Christian Paiz, April 17, 2017.

147. Max Huerta, interview by Christian Paiz, April 17, 2017.

148. Strikers "hadn't gotten over the whole strike thing, so they were still upset," Huerta said, "they would come and tell me, 'How come you're helping that person out?' . . . They [were] like, 'Those guys stayed over there, and we got beat up, and now they want to come over here? Now they want to get services from you, they want you to go help them to the welfare office and all that, and you shouldn't be helping them. You should tell them to go with the Teamsters so that they can help them.'" Max Huerta, interview by Christian Paiz, March 18, 2015.

149. Max Huerta, interview by Christian Paiz, April 17, 2017.

150. Max Huerta, interview by Christian Paiz, April 17, 2017.

151. Huerta noted that after facing death threats for five years, which were exacerbated by his participation in the UFW lawsuits, he received a check for $500.

152. "A lot of them went to work in the other industries like gardening, or the hotel industry, and they said they'd never go back to the grape fields, because of all the pain and everything that they've endured with during the strike." Max Huerta, interview by Christian Paiz, March 18, 2015. "You don't want to be considered a scab, and then betrayal to your family. So, a lot of that would create a, just get out of the whole dispute, go work somewhere else, a total different kind of work." Max Huerta, interview by Christian Paiz, April 17, 2017.

153. Max Huerta, interview by Christian Paiz, April 17, 2017.

154. The Coachella Legal reports begin from October 31, 1973 to April 1974, and they include case summaries, conversations with key ranchers, and speculations about possible rancher motivations and future decisions. See "Coachella Reports 1973–1974," Folder 11, Box 27, UFW Administration Department Records, Part III, ALUA.

155. "Coachella Legal to Cesar and Manuel: April 18, 1974," Folder 11, Box 27, UFW Administration Department Records, Part III, ALUA.

156. "They do not know how they are going to beat the boycott," Coachella Legal reported on April 7, 1974, "but they think that the Teamsters will provide some kind of blanket protection." "Coachella Legal to Cesar & Jerry: Conversation with Charlie K.: April 7, 1974," Folder 11, Box 27, UFW Administration Department Records, Part III, ALUA.

157. "An Examination of Violence in the Farm Labor Dispute," Palm Springs, CA, November 26, 1973, California Legislature, Assembly Select Committee on Farm Labor Violence, transcript, pp. 94–106, Folder 64, Box 28, UFW Administration Department, Part III, ALUA.

158. As noted earlier, ranchers paid only a pittance for their anti-union collusion, with plaintiff Max Huerta receiving only $500. Max Huerta, interview by Christian Paiz, April 14, 2017.

159. "Max Huerta to Cesar Chavez: November 11, 1973," Folder 1, Box 98, UFW Administration Department Records, Part III, ALUA. Union disappointment with 1973 grape strikers also existed outside the Coachella Valley. On October 14, 1974, the UFW's National Executive Board said "a lot of people on strike last year went back to work this year; we are mad with them but try not to show it—they are ashamed and hide from us." "National Executive Board Meeting: Day 3, October 14, 1974," Folder 5, Box 3, Philip Vera Cruz Papers, ALUA.

160. "Coachella Legal Report to National Executive Board: November 17, 1973," Folder 11, Box 27, UFW Administration Department Records, Part III, ALUA.

161. "Coachella Legal to Chavez: Re: Teamsters and Grower Violence: March 17, 1974," Folder 11, Box 27, UFW Administration Department Records, Part III, ALUA.

162. "Coachella Legal to Chavez: Re: Teamsters and Grower Violence: March 17, 1974," Folder 11, Box 27, UFW Administration Department Records, Part III, ALUA.

163. "Minutes of National Executive Board Meeting: March 29, 1974," Folder 12, Box 37, Office of the President II, ALUA.

164. It is like falling in love: it takes time.

165. On boycott troubles, see Lamoree, "The Managed Crisis," 318–22. Lamoree notes rancher organizations found consumers were less aware of the grape boycott in 1973 (p. 318). Food retailers also resisted UFW pressure to remove grapes, a development Mike Bozick cheered: "It wasn't the consumer who really stopped buying grapes that hurt growers the last time, it was the chain stores which didn't buy grapes as a result of UFW pressure. Since both the UFW and the Teamsters claimed the right to represent farm workers, retailers classified the second table grape boycott a product of a 'jurisdictional dispute'" (p. 321). As the economy worsened in 1974, and as employer discourses blaming unions for inflation gained currency, the "UFW's boycott lost some of its efficacy as an economic weapon." Lamoree, "The Managed Crisis," 327. For Chris Hartmire, the Executive Director of the National Farm Worker Ministry, public support for the UFW had "grow[n] stale" in 1974. A year later, and after a tour of boycott offices, he found dwindling boycott support: "there was an awful lot of whatever it is out there, an awful lot of desire to back away from this issue to do other things; to assume that the law is solving the problem; to want to not boycott anymore because it is complicated now." Pawl, *The Union*, 140, 174–75. See also Bardacke, *Trampling Out*, 461, 467–68.

Max Huerta recalled Coachella Valley farmworkers joined the grape boycott in 1973 and "came back disillusioned because they heard from the different people that were organizing the boycott that it wasn't the same like it had been in years before. They weren't getting the same support that they got at one time, from the churches, from the other unions." Max Huerta, interview by Christian Paiz, April 14, 2017.

Coachella Valley grape ranchers noticed the weak boycott support. The UFW legal team in Coachella described them in April 1974 as "cocky" and hoping to survive the boycott with Teamster contracts. "Coachella Legal to Cesar and Jerry: April 7, 1974," File 11, Box 27, UFW Administration Records, Part III, ALUA. Lastly, the UFW's National Executive Board (NEB) meetings in June and October 1974 echoed similar grape boycott difficulties. In October 1974, for example, UFW leaders reported on their boycott cities' challenges. "National Executive Board Meeting: Day 2, June 12, 1974," Folder 1, Box 3, Philip Vera Cruz Papers, ALUA. "National Executive Board Meeting: Day 1, October 12, 1974," Folder 5, Box 3, Philip Vera Cruz Papers, ALUA.

166. Not everyone agrees with this assessment. In *From the Jaws of Victory: The Triumph and Tragedy of Cesar Chavez and the Farm Worker Movement* (Berkeley: University of California Press, 2012), Matt Garcia writes: "The lettuce boycott never really succeeded in getting off the ground; however, the experience of boycotting grapes and the public's memory of the first grape boycott allowed the union to achieve a degree of success" (138). Garcia's source is an interview with the UFW lawyer, Jerry Cohen. Further scholarship is needed here.

167. Garcia, *From the Jaws*, 139–40, 143.

168. Garcia's sole source on Chavez's "whores in the camp" spectacle was Jerry Cohen, again. Future scholarship needs a more substantial source base, such as rancher correspondence during these negotiations that corroborates or contradicts Cohen's memory.

Chapter 8

1. In one instance, a rancher's son-in-law called them "stupid" and said "we were not picking the banana colored grapes, that someone blind with one arm that they could do a better job than all the workers." Lorraine Agtang-Greer, interview by Ray Telles, no date, Part 1 & 2, digital recording in "Filipino Brothers Oral History—1981," Oral History Media Collection, Farmworker Movement Documentation Project (henceforth, FMDP), https://libraries.ucsd.edu/farmworkermovement/media/oral_history/music/docFilmInt/Agtang-Greer-01.mp3 and https://libraries.ucsd.edu/farmworkermovement/media/oral_history/music/docFilmInt/Agtang-Greer-02.mp3.

2. Welga Project, "Agtang (Lorraine) Oral History Interview," Welga Archive-Bulosan Center for Filipino Studies (henceforth, Welga), accessed July 14, 2021, https://welgadigitalarchive.omeka.net/items/show/1.

3. Lorraine Agtang-Greer, interviewed by Ray Telles, no date, Part 1 & 2, audio recording in "Filipino Brothers Oral History—1981," Oral History Media Collection, FMDP, https://libraries.ucsd.edu/farmworkermovement/media/oral_history/music/docFilmInt/Agtang-Greer-01.mp3 and https://libraries.ucsd.edu/farmworkermovement/media/oral_history/music/docFilmInt/Agtang-Greer-02.mp3; Welga Project, "Agtang (Lorraine) Oral History Interview," Welga, accessed July 14, 2021, https://welgadigitalarchive.omeka.net/items/show/1.

4. "Midwifed" is quoted from Miriam Pawel, *The Union of Their Dreams: Power, Hope, and Struggle in Cesar Chavez's Farm Worker Movement* (New York: Bloomsbury, 2009),

155. "World" is quoted from Frank Bardacke, *Trampling Out the Vintage: Cesar Chavez and the Two Souls* (London: Verso, 2011), 487.

5. The process began with a union filing a notice of intention to organize a field with the Agricultural Labor Relations Board (ALRB), which required ranchers to provide their employee list with contact information. After gaining signatures from 50 percent of workers expressing a desire to hold a union election, the ALRB organized the election during the peak workforce season. The Agricultural Labor Relations Act (ALRA) forbade intimidation or bribery of workers, and it tasked the ALRB with reviewing allegations of "unfair labor practice." If the ALRB found that unfair labor practices affected the election, then it had the power to set aside the election and call for another. Lastly, if the ALRB certified a union as receiving a vote majority, the employer was compelled to begin bargaining a labor contract.

6. Matt Garcia, *From the Jaws of Victory: The Triumph and Tragedy of Cesar Chavez and the Farm Worker Movement* (Berkeley: University of California Press, 2012), 147–49.

7. Bardacke, *Trampling Out*, 484.

8. The historian Matt Garcia has provided a succinct summary of the early ALRA results in California:

The UFW won all of its elections where it held contracts, whereas the Teamsters lost 58 percent of the workers they had held under contract on 177 ranchers prior to the elections in 1975. Finally, in spite of the growers' vigorous campaigns against unions among employees, only six ranches involving 938 workers switched from either the UFW or the Teamsters to no union at all. In fact, growers succeeded in convincing only 4 percent of the workers to vote for no representation in twenty elections.

Garcia, *From the Jaws*, 161; Bardacke, *Trampling Out*, 522.

9. Garcia, *From the Jaws*, 148–57.

10. Pawel, *The Union*, 162–65; Garcia, *From the Jaws*, 151–56.

11. Quoted in Garcia, *From the Jaws*, 148. The quote belongs to the UFW volunteer Sandy Nathan. Before Nathan's assessment, Garcia also quoted a United Auto Worker attorney, Jerry Goldman, who called ALRA "one of the most anti-union laws I have ever seen" (148). Garcia did not offer a resolution, but he argued "the UFW kept growers honest [in elections] and consumers informed by maintaining a strong boycott of Gallo wine, California grapes, and lettuce" (157) and "the threat of a boycott and the aggressive action by Cohen and the UFW legal team helped the union win far more elections than it lost" (160). Garcia did not provide evidence of a strong boycott nor of its role in promoting election integrity and UFW successes. The latter may very well have occurred *despite* a weak boycott and dishonest growers. For Chris Hartmire, the Executive Director of the National Farm Worker Ministry, the boycott-election relationship was the opposite: former UFW allies "assume[d] that the law [ALRA] is solving the problem" and did "not boycott anymore because it is complicated now." Pawl, *The Union*, 140, See also Elizabeth Lamoree's account of growers' "defeat" of ALRA in "The Managed Crisis: Labor Relations and Management in California Agriculture, 1930–1980" (PhD diss., University of California, Santa Barbara, 2012), 399–420.

12. Immanent to the early National Labor Relations Act (NLRA), the lack of job protection became more prominent in postwar National Labor Relations Board decisions. John Logan, "Permanent Replacements and the End of Labor's 'Only True Weapon,'" *International Labor and Working Class History* (Fall, 2008): 175.

13. See chapters 6 and 9.

14. Lane Windham, *Knocking on Labor's Door: Union Organizing in the 1970s and the Roots of a New Economic Divide* (Chapel Hill: University of North Carolina, 2017), 65.

15. Windham, *Knocking on Labor's Door*, 24.

16. Windham, *Knocking on Labor's Door*, 76.

17. "By the 1970s," Windham noted, "the courts had so constrained the NLRA that many unions thought the National Labor Relations Board was an obstacle to their expansion and effectiveness." Windham, *Knocking on Labor's Door*, 72. See also Elizabeth Lamoree, "Gambling on Grapes: Management, Marketing, and Labor in California Agribusiness," *Agricultural History* (Summer 2012), 120.

18. In *Trampling Out*, Bardacke argued the ALRB's general counsel, Walter Kintz, did not intervene effectively to "prevent this open defiance of the law," 513. To Bardacke, ALRA's shortcomings reflected past UFW failures and Kintz's administration, not so much the regressive nature of the law itself. The reference to "bend and break" comes from Windham, *Knocking on Labor's Door*, 65.

19. For "slap on wrist," see Bardacke, *Trampling Out*, 513.

20. In *Trampling Out*, Bardacke made the opposite argument: "But the fact that in the long run the UFW was defeated in the California fields cannot be blamed on the new labor law; although the law on its own did not guarantee success, it provided the framework within which a healthy union, leading a farm worker movement, could have thrived" (485).

21. Regarding the make whole clause, see Philip L. Martin, *Promise Unfulfilled: Unions, Immigration, & the Farmworkers* (Ithaca, NY: Cornell University Press, 2003), 157.

22. In this regard, Proposition 14 mimicked far more progressive labor laws in Canada, Sweden, and Germany. On Sweden and Germany, see Windham, *Knocking on Labor's Door*, 22. On Canada's card-check process, see John Godard, "The Exceptional Decline of the American Labor Movement," *ILR Review* (October 2009): 82–108. Godard writes:

> The Canadian version of Wagnerism, as adopted in both the federal and all ten provincial jurisdictions by the close of the 1940s, was considered to be weaker than the initial version of the NLRA. But it was gradually strengthened throughout the postwar era (see Logan 2002 for a fascinating account), typically in ways that restricted aggressive electioneering by either labor or management and protected against employer intimidation. By the mid-1980s, it generally contained most of the characteristics initially associated with the Wagner model (that is, prior to 1939), including provision for card certification in all but one jurisdiction, a prohibition on the use of permanent striker replacements in all jurisdictions, and de facto bans on open shop arrangements.

Godard, "Exceptional Decline," 98.

23. "Sandy understood that the union's political capital was at an all-time high," Pawel observed, "but he would have preferred they use the cachet to enforce the law and expand their base rather than engage in a fight that was more symbolic than substantive. He was unhappy about the initiative but did not feel it his place to voice doubts." Pawel, *The Union*, 194.

24. Joseph A. McCartin, "'A Wagner Act for Public Employees': Labor's Deferred Dream and the Rise of Conservatism, 1970–76," *Journal of American History* 95, no. 1 (June 2008): 123–48; Windham, *Knocking On Labor's Door*, 76–81.

25. See Martinez HoSang's discussion of California's "genteel apartheid. Daniel Martinez HoSang, *Racial Propositions: Ballot Initiatives and the Making of Postwar California* (Berkeley: University of California Press, 2010), 5–9.

26. In *From the Jaws*, Garcia provides a necessary account of the Nisei farmer, Harry Kubo, and his reasons for opposing Proposition 14. After experiencing Japanese American internment, Kubo was "distrustful of the government and vigilant about protecting his rights" (170), such as his private property rights as a small farmer. More research, however, is needed here. In April 20, 1973, more than three years before Proposition 14, *El Malcriado* carried a tiny article on the "Nisei Farmers League president Harry Kubo, whose organization spent most of its time last fall trying to break the strike at White River Farms." The newspaper added: "Kubo underscored his main concern as a conspiracy among a small faction of Mexican-Americans driven by the belief that California once belonged to Mexican Americans and will one day revert back to them" (14). Garcia may be right in his view of Kubo's reasons for opposing Proposition 14, but future research may consider the role of interracial tensions in the San Joaquin Valley and the rather common, unfounded fears of a potential racial takeover. See Jim Horgan, "Cowpies from the Growers," *El Malcriado*, April 20, 1973.

27. David Perez, interview by Christian Paiz, February 14, 2017.

28. David Perez, interview by Christian Paiz, February 14, 2017.

29. "You want money?" an acquaintance asked him rhetorically: "It's there, in the [lemon] trees." Melecio Sanchez, interview by Christian Paiz, February 14, 2017.

30. Melecio Sanchez, interview by Christian Paiz, February 14, 2017.

31. Melecio Sanchez, interview by Christian Paiz, February 14, 2017.

32. David Perez, interview by Christian Paiz, February 14, 2017.

33. Emphasis in original. David Perez, interview by Christian Paiz, February 14, 2017.

34. Marc Coleman, "Citrus Research Strategy," July 5, 1976, Folder 2, Box 3, Marshall Ganz Papers, Archives of Labor and Urban Affairs (henceforth, ALUA).

35. David Perez, interview by Christian Paiz, February 14, 2017.

36. David Perez, interview by Christian Paiz, April 18, 2017.

37. Translation: ". . . what brings me joy. What brings me joy, I will do." David Perez, interview by Christian Paiz, April 18, 2017.

38. David Perez, interview by Christian Paiz, April 18, 2017.

39. "Coachella Valley Interviews: 1974," Folder 9, Box 8, Victor Salandini Papers, Special Collections, Stanford University.

40. Maria Serrano, interview by Christian Paiz, February 10, 2017. On December 2, 1974, the Coachella Field Office reported to La Paz on this transition: "On 11/27 Ted Enochs said they weren't going to hire any more women. He mentioned only 1 case where they had a problem teaching a woman to prune. He said the company had met any requirement by hiring a few women. He complained they weren't strong enough, too short and weren't doing the work. All the workers, including men, have said they saw no problems with the women." "Coachella FO Weekly Report: 12/2/74," File 20, Box 35, Office of the President (OOP), Part II, ALUA.

41. Maria Serrano, interview by Christian Paiz, February 10, 2017.

42. Hilario Torres, interview by Christian Paiz, November 22, 2013.

43. "Elections, Coachella 1976," Folder 5, Box 5, Marshall Ganz Papers, ALUA.

44. "42 Teamster Interviews: Coachella Summer 1975 Research," Folder 9, Box 10, Victor Salandini Papers, Special Collections, Stanford University.

45. "Camp Meeting Notes, 1971, (Camp Armington Meeting Notes, October 28, 1971)," Folder 15, Box 2, Pete Velasco Papers, ALUA.

46. "Philip Vera Cruz to Noel Kent: January 16, 1975," Folder 8, Box 1, Philip Vera Cruz Papers, ALUA.

47. Berg had become friends with many 1965 Agricultural Workers Organizing Committee strikers and he intended to write a book on the Filipino UFW movement by interviewing Filipino strikers living in Agbayani Village. Berg told Vera Cruz he began transcribing the interviews in the mid-1970s. It is possible that transcripts of these oral history interviews may exist in an archive or a private family collection. Unfortunately, I was not successful in locating them. Regarding the chapter's themes, Berg's Paperworkers' Union was also facing "a very vicious anti-union campaign." "Bill Berg to Philip Vera Cruz: February 28, 1975," Folder 8, Box 1, Philip Vera Cruz Papers, ALUA.

48. "Philip Vera Cruz to Bill Berg: March 11, 1975," Folder 8, Box 1, Philip Vera Cruz Papers, ALUA.

49. "Philip Vera Cruz Open Letter: Pandol Arrests, 1975," Folder 17, Box 1, Philip Vera Cruz Papers, ALUA.

50. "Philip Vera Cruz Open Letter on Elections," Folder 17, Box 1, Philip Vera Cruz Papers, ALUA.

51. "Philip Vera Cruz Open Letter on Dispatches," Folder 17, Box 1, Philip Vera Cruz Papers, ALUA.

52. "Coachella Farmworker Survey: 1976 Elections," Folder 11, Box 8, Victor Salandini Papers, Stanford University.

53. "Coachella Farmworker Survey: 1976 Elections," Folder 11, Box 8, Victor Salandini Papers, Stanford University.

54. Arturo Diaz, interview by Christian Paiz, January 31, 2015.

55. Elvia Alicia Castillo and Armando Castillo, interview by Christian Paiz, April 17, 2017; Elvia Alicia Castillo, interview by Christian Paiz, April 17, 2017; Elvia Alicia Castillo, interview by Christian Paiz, April 18, 2017. The quote is from the second interview.

56. Alfredo Fuller and Ray Rodriguez, interview by Christian Paiz, February 11, 2017.

57. See chapter 6.

58. Alfredo Fuller and Ray Rodriguez, interview by Christian Paiz, February 11, 2017. As an aside, Mexican American Political Association (MAPA) members already counted a decade of activism by 1975, which had exposed them to threats and constant criticism. Perhaps for these reasons, too, MAPA's increasingly older members appeared less likely to engage in the public demonstrations.

59. Ray Rodriguez, interview by Christian Paiz, May 8, 2020.

60. Ray Rodriguez, interview by Christian Paiz, May 8, 2020.

61. Alfredo Fuller and Raul Loya did the same. The three identified education as a key part of their social mobility and political participation and saw its potential for their students. Alfredo Figueroa, who led the UFW in Blythe, founded an autonomous Chicana/o school. When I asked Ray Rodriguez in 2013 what progress he saw in the Coachella Valley, he said: "I see the changes that have come about for the betterment all occurred because of education. I see a congressman. I see a state assembly man. I see a mayor. I see lawyers. I see superintendents. I see business people. Just almost representing all of the different professions that earned the respect of all Americans.... And I think all this happened ... even though they might not understand why, is because there was a struggle in the past, in the

60s, 70s and forward—that promoted education so strongly, almost bible like—'you have to educate yourself,'" Ray Rodriguez and Alfredo Fuller, interview by Christian Paiz, October 17, 2013.

62. "Mr. Reyes feels that there are many things that need to be done," *Ideal* wrote. "There are many people in need of professional services in his opinion. He wants to establish a precedent and that is to have the native professionals return to Coachella upon graduation and become part of its future growth." "Informes del Valle: 'Tony Reyes,'" *Ideal*, December 20, 1973. See also Yolanda Almaraz, interview by Matt Garcia, April 2, 2004, online transcript, *Education for Change: Latina Activism and the Struggle for Educational Equity*, Brown University, https://library.brown.edu/htmlfiles/1139260446516000.html; Yolanda Almaraz and Gilberto Esquivel, interview by Matt Garcia, September 15, 2004, online transcript, *Education for Change: Latina Activism and the Struggle for Educational Equity*, Brown University, https://library.brown.edu/cds/catalog/catalog.php?verb=render&id=1139260494194558&colid=15.

63. His close friend and coeducator, Manuel Arredondo added, "If you want to make an impact in any society, it starts with education. Education is the key. . . . Because that is the first thing—if you want to enslave a people, you take their education." Manuel Arredondo and Joe Ceja, interview by Christian Paiz, February 6, 2015.

64. Joe Ceja, interview by Christian Paiz, April 15, 2017.

65. For quote, see Yolanda Almaraz, interview by Matt Garcia, April 2, 2004, online transcript, *Education for Change: Latina Activism and the Struggle for Educational Equity*, Brown University, https://library.brown.edu/htmlfiles/1139260446516000.htmled. See also Yolanda Almaraz and Gilberto Esquivel, interview by Matt Garcia, September 15, 2004, online transcript, *Education for Change*, https://library.brown.edu/cds/catalog/catalog.php?verb=render&id=1139260494194558&colid=15.

66. The clinic aimed "to help the farmworkers, help the community, help the underprivileged. Of course, we had higher sights. Eventually we were looking at taking over the city of Coachella, the school board . . . but we needed a base. . . . We had dental services, optometry, full medical, pre-natal care, social service component, a youth service component, we were the first medical unit in Riverside County that provided services to aids patients. . . . We had the largest amnesty program in the country." Sam Maestas, interview by Christian Paiz, February 13, 2017.

67. Laura E. Garcia, Sandra M. Gutierrez, and Felicitas Nuñez, eds., "Sandra M. Gutierrez," chap. 9 in *Teatro Chicana: A Collective Memoir and Selected Plays* (Austin: University of Texas Press, 2008), 78.

68. "Murals for his People," *Ideal*, June 5–20, 1973.

69. "Informes del Valle: 'Chema,'" *Ideal*, October 5–20, 1973; "Informes del Valle: 'Charlie Garcia,'" *Ideal*, May 5, 1974; "Informes del Valley: 'Henry Martinez Nieto,'" *Ideal*, March 25, 1974; "Conference on Low-Income Family Homes," "Spanish Speaking Bishops Gaining," "Parents: Teach Your Children to Learn," *Ideal*, September 3, 1974.

70. The Chicana/o movement can be understood as a periodic table element, one that does not lose its nature despite different states. In the classic period (1960s and early 1970s), the movement came in solid form—a dense and visible object to break barriers and provide the foundation for a new society. In the 1970s, it turned to a liquid and entered institutions, aiming to transform them and to circulate their life force to the wider community. We can think of Chicana/o Studies—whether in elementary classrooms, community

plays, popular culture, and/or academia—as the movement's gaseous form, offering breadth that deepens and softens and fortifies.

71. Socorro Gomez Potter, interview by Matt Garcia, March 4, 2004, transcript, Brown University, https://repository.library.brown.edu/storage/bdr:105543/HTML/.

72. Garcia, Gutierrez, and Nuñez, "Sandra M. Gutierrez," 73–80. For an example of Coachella Valley teacher abuse experienced by one of these theater activists, see Garcia, Gutierrez, and Nuñez, eds., "Margarita Carrillo," chap. 10 in *Teatro Chicana*, 81–88.

73. Silvia Montenegro, interview by Christian Paiz, May 29, 2020.

74. White locals feared Chicanas/os would lead a rebellion, he explained, a fear rooted in the UFW strikes. His first job in the area was in Palm Springs in 1975, because, as the Palm Springs superintendent told him: "[Coachella] people are afraid that you are too radical to hire." He laughed in this moment in the oral history and said, "All I did was get a degree." Joe Ceja, interview by Christian Paiz, April 15, 2017.

75. Clementina Olloque, interview by Christian Paiz, August 12, 2014.

76. Max Huerta, interview by Christian Paiz, April 17, 2017. With Huerta's resignation, the Coachella Field Office reported "a major setback" as it closed its "Service Center because there is only 1 staff person to handle social services and field office work." "Coachella Field Office: September 30, 1974," Folder 14, Box 1, Philip Vera Cruz Papers, ALUA.

77. Karen L. Ishizuka, *Serve the People: Making Asian America in the Long Sixties* (London: Verso, 2016), 195–97.

Chapter 9

1. David Perez, interview by Christian Paiz, April 18, 2017.

2. David Perez, interview by Christian Paiz, April 18, 2017.

3. David Perez, interview by Christian Paiz, April 18, 2017.

4. By 1986, he joined the growing exodus of farmworkers to the golf resort industry—where nonunion jobs still paid higher wages and provided much more secure year-long employment.

5. Perez's solution was to abandon the UFW's volunteer system, as some UFW leaders advocated too. Perez felt the volunteer system prevented worker-leaders from participating in the union's leadership, and that it made the union reliant on fanatics, who he did not consider the best organizers. Whether the UFW could have transitioned to a paid staff—when it already struggled to afford its campaigns—remains to be determined by future researchers. Windham's review of unions' budgetary crises in the late 1970s and early 1980s, suggests the UFW faced an uphill battle in its transition. Lane Windham, *Knocking on Labor's Door: Union Organizing in the 1970s and the Roots of a New Economic Divide* (Chapel Hill: University of North Carolina, 2017), 180–85.

6. See chapter 4.

7. See chapters 7 and 8.

8. Harry Carian Sales, 6 ALRB 55 (1980).

9. In the ALRB report for Harry Carian Sales, the UFW organizer Liz Sullivan testified that Vitalino crew members "signed authorization cards, took part in UFW projects, donated funds for radio spots, passed out leaflets, and displayed posters and bumper stickers." Harry Carian Sales, 6 ALRB 55 (1980), 46.

10. Harry Carian Sales, 6 ALRB 55 (1980), 41.

11. Harry Carian Sales, 6 ALRB 55 (1980), 41.

12. The Board's agent elaborated: "I find that the grant of benefits announced at the peak of the pre-election campaign, one day after the firing of an entire crew, two days after a widely publicized UFW march, and presented in an employer propaganda speech and leaflet was made to induce employees to vote against the union. See Anderson Farms Company, supra. The conduct amounted to substantial inference with employee rights and constituted an unfair labor practice in violation of Section 1153 (a). The 'velvet glove had worn thin' and was notable to 'veil the clenched fist of unlawful activity.'" Harry Carian Sales, 6 ALRB 55 (1980), 92–93.

13. Windham makes this same observation with regards to NLRB complaints and investigations in the 1970s and 1980s:

> [Pro-union workers] would have to endure what was a typically an eight to twelve-week campaign period in which employers campaigned against the union, routinely pulling employees off their jobs and forcing them to listen to antiunion propaganda. Their employer could even prohibit them from speaking in these meetings. The union, meanwhile would be barred from entering the workplace. By the [late 1970s], 30 percent of employers facing a union campaign fired at least one worker. Yet such employers did not incur large fines or penalties if caught—they simply had to rehire the worker, pay the lost wages, and hang a sign in the break room stating they had broken the law.

Windham, *Knocking on Labor's Door*, 23.

14. Harry Carian Sales, 6 ALRB 55 (1980), 137.

15. Additional examples abound. On June 2, the UFW organizer, David Martinez, spoke to a group of workers in Carian's Campo de Oro when the supervisor Hilario Castro yelled at Martinez and told him he should not be there. On June 6, pro-UFW worker Jesus Muñoz attempted to speak to two workers and both left as soon as Carian approached them. On June 10, pro-UFW worker Federico Vargas spoke to workers while a supervisor told them not to sign authorization cards. On June 16, pro-UFW worker Maria Serrano spoke to a woman from Mexicali while supervisor Hilario Castro came from behind to watch them. Harry Carian Sales, 6 ALRB 55 (1980), 178.

16. Harry Carian Sales, 6 ALRB 55 (1980), 171.

17. Harry Carian Sales, 6 ALRB 55 (1980), 148.

18. Harry Carian Sales, 6 ALRB 55 (1980), 189.

19. The Board's agent summarized the effect on one pro-UFW worker organizer: "Maria Serrano, an active UFW supporter was working in the Beas-Medrano crew and Medrano, a foreman, gave her a copy of this leaflet. She also observed him passing these leaflets out to the other members of the crew. She read it and interpreted it to mean that as a woman organizer for the UFW she would have to submit her body. She felt angry about the leaflet and felt that she would be embarrassed among the workers." Harry Carian Sales, 6 ALRB 55 (1980), 189–90.

20. Harry Carian Sales, 6 ALRB 55 (1980), 9.

21. Harry Carian Sales, 6 ALRB 55 (1980), 29–31.

22. Carian's paternalism also reflected the Rancher Nation's patriarchal authority and came with limits; it did not extend to the approximately one hundred workers he fired during the UFW campaign.

23. See chapter 8.

24. Luciano Crespo, who served as UFW's Coachella field director in the early to mid-1980s, said the great majority of pro-UFW workers did not get their jobs back after they were fired. Even if the UFW was certified as the labor representative in a field he was organizing, Crespo only found farmworkers who had voted against the UFW, did not know about the UFW, and/or felt betrayed by earlier failed UFW campaigns. In the latter instance, pro-UFW grape workers had faced years of mockery from others for aligning with the UFW. Luciano Crespo, interview by Christian Paiz, April 17, 2017.

25. Karahadian Ranches Inc., 5 ALRB 37 (1979), 46.

26. Emphasis in original. Karahadian Ranches Inc., 5 ALRB 37 (1979), 64.

27. Even if Karahadian claimed a history of wage increases—and thus presented the 1977 spike as company practice and not unlawful interference—the agent argued that precedent placed the burden of proof on employers to show such action did not violate the law, which Karahadian did not address. Karahadian Ranches Inc., 5 ALRB 37 (1979), 49.

28. The Board's agent further added that "[the supervisor] thought [Ferrel] was 'trying to prove a point to the people that we were afraid of her'" and that when the supervisor temporarily demoted Ferrel, Ferrel testified that she heard the "'[supervisor] laughing sarcastically and stating to [an assistant], within hearing of the crew: 'Nobody around here has got seniority.'" Both testimonies illustrated the contentious nature of Karahadian's anti-union campaign and evidenced the supervisor's violations. Karahadian Ranches Inc., 5 ALRB 37 (1979), 33.

29. Mel-Pak Vineyards, Inc., 5 ALRB 61 (1979).

30. For the NLRB case, see *Pacific Tile and Porcelain Company*, 137 NLRB 1538 (1962): https://www.nlrb.gov/cases-decisions/decisions/board-decisions?search_term=PACIFIC+TILE+AND+PORCELAIN+COMPANY&op=Search&volume=-1&slip_opinion_number=&page_number=&items_per_page=100&form_build_id=form-6QVU6pmFoQf7dgnKPEkx4iPsYhJo8NNpNoTRVZEw3oA&form_id=board_decisions_form. For the Mel-Pak elections, see Mel-Pak Vineyards, Inc., 5 ALRB 61 (1979).

31. For ALRA election decisions, visit the Agriculture Labor Relations Board (ALRB) digital collection at https://www.alrb.ca.gov/legal-searches/search-decisions/. In *From the Jaws of Victory: The Triumph and Tragedy of Cesar Chavez and the Farm Worker Movement* (Berkeley: University of California Press, 2012), Matt Garcia cited an unnamed study that reported "the UFW could have won 15 to 20 percent more votes in elections if the ALRB had enforced the law and policed distortions in lists of eligible voters" (157). If this is accurate, then we can imagine that the UFW's ALRA campaign in Coachella Valley grape fields in 1977 would have won nearly every election, given the close vote tallies.

32. Philip L. Martin, *Promise Unfulfilled: Unions, Immigration, and the Farm Workers* (Ithaca: Cornell University Press, 2003), 149–51.

33. Quoting Doug Adair, Bardacke, 567.

34. Eliseo Medina, who led the Coachella ALRA grape elections of 1977, expressed frustration with the UFW's lack of volunteer support. Many of its volunteers had been reserved for other campaigns and miscommunication between Chavez and Marshall Ganz prevented the transfer of volunteers from the Imperial Valley to the Coachella Valley.

35. In Coachella Valley Distributors, 5 ALRB 18 (1979), the ALRB ruled that the eighteen-month window for economic striker participation in union elections had to consider the half-year hiatus due to the Board's 1976 budget crisis. For Coachella Valley, the 1977 har-

vest was the last chance for 1973 strikers to participate in a union election for companies they had been on strike. For the UFW movement, the 1977 elections also meant they could illustrate to striker leaders and the workforce that it followed through with its campaigns. Without contesting the Teamsters in 1977, furthermore, the UFW ran the risk of letting existing company unions solidify and pose future challenges.

36. Windham, *Knocking on Labor's Door*, 180–85.

37. See Matt Garcia, *From the Jaws*, 163–77.

38. From late 1976 to late 1977, the UFW fired one hundred volunteers.

39. See "Civil War: November '80 to October '81," in Frank Bardacke, *Trampling Out the Vintage: Cesar Chavez and the Two Souls of the United Farm Workers* (London: Verso, 2011), 688–720.

40. In its first year, *El Malcriado* blamed agribusiness's inequality on male farmworkers' cowardly stupidity—a language the National Farm Workers Association shared with Agricultural Workers Organizing Committee leaders, including Larry Itliong and Philip Vera Cruz. See chapter 3.

41. Philip Vera Cruz, "The Farm Worker's Union," *El Malcriado*, November 15, 1970.

42. After the UFW won the 1970 contracts, the Delano leadership removed Coachella Valley leaders who criticized Delano policies, dismissing them as "scabs." Simultaneously, Vera Cruz responded to Filipino critiques with *El Malcriado* articles conditioning their union membership. Union democracy, he wrote, began with members' disciplined sacrifice, not in union benefits. Imutan repeated the message in the 1971 fall camp meetings in the San Joaquin Valley. See chapter 6.

43. In *Knocking on Labor's Door*, Windham quotes a labor organizer who recounted the effectiveness of employers' anti-union campaigns: "I would just watch these people go from feeling strong and like we need to do something to feeling like totally terrified to do anything, and paralyzed." Windham, *Knocking on Labor's Door*, 76.

44. The most striking element of this percentage is how it pales in comparison to discriminatory firing in the 1977 Coachella grape elections: every election included the illegal firing of multiple pro-union workers.

45. Windham, *Knocking on Labor's Door*, 4.

46. See chapter 6. This was also a period, to boot, in which Americans consistently reported to hold corporations in higher esteem than labor unions.

47. In "Permanent Replacements and the End of Labor's 'Only True Weapon,'" John Logan explains, "the 1960s and the 1970s saw the emergence of a new generation of strike management firms, which often had a close working relationship with union avoidance consultants and law firms . . . maintain production during strikes by providing workplace security and replacement workers and transporting replacements across picket lines." John Logan, "Permanent Replacements and the End of Labor's 'Only True Weapon,'" *International Labor and Working Class History* (Fall, 2008): 171–92, p. 180.

48. The only (telling) exception was the public sector, which only faced the determined hostility from municipal and state governments later. And yet, as Joseph A. McCartin argues, "The failure of public employee unions to win their own Wagner Act also boded ill for labor unions in general as they headed into the 1980s. By almost every measure, the 1970s were disastrous for private sector unions. . . . Private sector unions found it increasingly difficult to organize amid 1970s stagflation. Although unions had won a majority of workplace representation elections each year since the passage of the Wagner Act in 1935,

their luck abruptly turned in 1974. Thereafter and through the 1980s, they lost the majority of representation elections each year." See Windham, *Knocking on Labor's Door*, 24–25, 57–84; Joseph A. McCartin, "'A Wagner Act for Public Employees': Labor's Deferred Dream and the Rise of Conservatism, 1970–76," *Journal of American History*, 95, no. 1 (June 2008): 123–48.

49. Differences included ALRA's access to workplaces, a "make whole remedy" for discriminating against pro-union workers, a constrained secondary boycott, and the agricultural-labor specificities that ruled out immediate "redo" elections in case of labor violations. As to the first, ranchers fought UFW access through lawsuits, violence, and intimidation and performed impunity—even when the ALRB reiterated union access. As to the "make whole remedy," Phillip L. Martin argues ALRB weakened the provision in 1979 and 1987. It also entangled the UFW in litigation. See Phillip L. Martin, *Promise Unfulfilled: Unions, Immigration, & Farm Workers* (Ithaca, NY: Cornell University Press, 2003), 156–60.

50. Prior to their compromise with the Carter administration, the AFL-CIO proposed labor reform that eliminated the two-step authorization process, repealed the Taft-Hartley Act's prohibition against union shops, and protected unions in the case of company sale. Again, these reforms reiterated or mimicked the UFW's Proposition 14. For the reform law, see Windham, *Knocking on Labor's Door*, 77–78. For a discussion on a similar failure among public sector unions, see McCartin, "A Wagner Act for Public Employees."

51. Windham, *Knocking on Labor's Door*, 78.

52. Quoted in Windham, *Knocking on Labor's Door*, 80.

53. The downward cycle also blunted overall union efficacy (whether real or perceived), because union workers were less willing to risk certain turmoil for uncertain ends. See "Employers Close the Door" and "Conclusion" in Windham's *Knocking on Labor's Door*.

54. For Reaganism's anti-UFW roots, see Todd Holmes, "The Economic Roots of Reaganism: Corporate Conservatives, Political Economy, and the United Farm Workers Movement, 1965–1970," *Western Historical Quarterly*, 41, no. 1 (Spring 2010): 55–80.

55. Logan, "Permanent Replacements."

56. Joseph A. McCartin, "Re-Framing US Labour's Crisis: Reconsidering Structure, Strategy, and Vision," *Labour/Le Travail* (Spring 2007): 133–48.

57. Windham, *Knocking on Labor's Door*, 8.

58. See Ana Minian's *Undocumented Lives: The Untold Story of Mexican Migration* (Cambridge, MA: Harvard University Press, 2018) for an in-depth discussion of these conditions.

59. Bardacke, *Trampling Out*, 583–86.

60. Bardacke, *Trampling Out*, 725–28.

61. See Miriam J. Wells, *Strawberry Fields: Politics, Class, and Work in California Agriculture* (Ithaca, NY: Cornell University Press, 1996).

62. For a summary of 1970s and 1980s ALRA cases, and of agribusiness strategies, see Martin, *Promise Unfulfilled*.

63. On the question of labor organizing in the post 1970s economy, the long-time UFW organizer, Jim Drake, emphasized that U.S. unions were in a "different economic situation" and "there's not going to be more major labor movements in America in at least this century... it's over." He added: "You can be airline pilots now [laughs]... airline traffic controllers and they'll replace you in a couple of years. That's not just because they have an ideological force, Ronald Reagan, but because it is possible. There's an excess of all labor now. We live in a time of excess of all labor. In the 60s we lived in a time of fatness, where

the grape industry was expanding, and they needed more workers and they wanted to plant more grapes. And they did not want any problems because they were going to grow. Today, they are shrinking, and if you take some workers out [in a strike] there's already a line of workers ready to take their jobs." James Drake, interviewed by Patricia Hoffman, 1985, interview #2, https://libraries.ucsd.edu/farmworkermovement/media/oral_history/music/new/JimDrake2.mp3.

64. At Freedman in 1977, the UFW's Coachella director, Eliseo Medina, negotiated a new union contract that served as a standard for non-UFW fields, which met UFW contract wins to avoid unionization. See Miriam Pawel, *The Union of Their Dreams: Power, Hope, and Struggle in Cesar Chavez's Farm Worker Movement* (New York: Bloomsbury, 2009), 229–32.

65. Linda Mabalot, "Willie Barrientos Oral History Transcript, Interview 1," Welga Archive - Bulosan Center for Filipino Studies, accessed February 9, 2022, https://welgadigitalarchive.omeka.net/items/show/9.

66. Bardacke, *Trampling Out*, 679–81.

67. David Perez, interview by Christian Paiz, April 15, 2017.

68. Hilario Torres, interview by Christian Paiz, February 12, 2017.

69. Leonor Suarez, interview by Christian Paiz, February 14, 2017.

70. Hilario Torres, interview by Christian Paiz, February 12, 2017.

71. The other organizers had been Marshall Ganz, Jesus Villegas, Ray Huerta, Max Huerta, Ruth Shy, Eliseo Medina, and Saul Martinez. Not one was from the Coachella Valley. The summary of Crespo's life represents a synthesis of oral history interviews conducted in 2013 and 2014. See chapters 4 and 7.

72. Luciano Crespo, interview by Christian Paiz, February 1, 2014.

73. Luciano Crespo, interview by Christian Paiz, April 17, 2017.

Chapter 10

1. "Statement by Cesar Chavez: School Dedication," October 19, 1990, Coachella, CA. Document in author's possession.

2. "Statement by Cesar Chavez: School Dedication," October 19, 1990, Coachella, CA.

3. See Ana Raquel Minian, *Undocumented Lives: The Untold Story of Mexican Migration* (Cambridge, MA: Harvard University Press, 2018), especially chapters 3, 4, and 6.

4. John Marquez shared as much when he wrote, "The most famous Latino/a civil rights leader, Cesar Chavez, was an unknown figure to me until I enrolled in those aforementioned Chicano/a studies courses in college. When I first heard of him, I thought one of my favorite professional boxers, Julio Cesar Chavez, had retired from the sport and was now working as an activist on behalf of immigrant rights." John D. Marquez, *Black-Brown Solidarity: Racial Politics in the New Gulf South* (Austin: University of Texas Press, 2013), 9.

5. See Lawrence Culver, "Making the Desert Modern: Palm Springs after World War II," chap. 6 in *The Frontier of Leisure: Southern California and the Shaping of Modern America* (Oxford: Oxford University Press, 2010).

6. See Jacques E. Levy, "How Will We Eat?" chap. 2 in *Cesar Chavez: Autobiography of La Causa* (Minneapolis: University of Minnesota Press, 1975), 157–65.

7. Jacques E. Levy, *Cesar Chavez: Autobiography of La Causa* (Minneapolis: University of Minnesota Press, 1974), 166–78.

8. "Editorial: Our Social Movement," *El Malcriado*, no date, no. 1, 1965.

9. To the respondents who said they would join the social movement once everyone stood up simultaneously, *El Malcriado* mocked: "There will never be such a thing as all rising in protest. When you hear that phrase, remember that the uttering lips do so out of fear. A man who wants to protest does not wait for others to do it. Such a man goes forward and protests without [waiting]." "Editorial: *Viva la Causa—Si Todos Unidos Reclamaramos!*" *El Malcriado*, no date, no. 18, 1965.

10. Luciano Crespo, interview by Christian Paiz, February 8, 2014.

11. In a strike journal that ran from December 1965 to March 1966, Pete Velasco documented several instances of Mexican strikers eating in Delano's Filipino Hall. Velasco's journal is found in Folder 2, Box 12, AWOC II, Archives of Labor and Urban Affairs (henceforth, ALUA). See also Philip Vera Cruz, interview by Albert S. Bagdayem, December 30, 1989, digital recording, Box 36, Tape 192 B, "The Filipino Brothers Oral History—1981," Farmworker Movement Documentation Project (henceforth, FMDP).

12. Marshall Ganz, *Why David Sometimes Wins: Leadership, Organization, and Strategy in the California Farm Worker Movement* (Oxford: Oxford University Press, 2009), 127–36, 139–44, 146–68.

13. In early 1969, Chavez wrote a four-page letter to the Coachella Valley's Desert Grape Growers League President, Mike Bozick, to call for negotiations and to convince Bozick that he fought the inevitable: the UFW's "international boycott [had] reached a critical stage of its development," he wrote, from a haphazard project to a well-orchestrated "machinery" of labor, church, and civil rights groups, and rancher opposition to unionization would only extend their financial pain. "Cesar Chavez to Mike Bozick," Folder 4, Box 31, Office of the President Collection, Part II, UFW Archive, Walter Reuther Library, Detroit.

14. The Imperial and Salinas Valley lettuce workers went on strike in 1979 despite the National Executive Board's opposition. The lettuce workers were unconvinced by Chavez's view that strikes offered few rewards for the steep costs, and that more promise existed in another boycott. The lettuce strikers did defend some of their UFW contracts. But their success was partly due to a heat wave that forced some to meet their demands. Just as many companies, however, held out, which meant their strike failed to keep all pre-strike UFW contracts. In the process, the strike exhausted union funds and may have limited UFW campaigns in other regions, like the Coachella Valley. See "'*Esta Huelga Esta Ganada*,'" in Frank Bardacke, *Trampling Out the Vintage: Cesar Chavez and the Two Souls of the United Farm Workers* (New York: Verso, 2012), 620–54. For references on the strike's costs, see pp. 642–44. For references to fortuitous weather, see pp. 653–54. For references to companies who refused to re-sign with the UFW, see pp. 655 and 660–62. For a discussion on labor's budget crisis in the late 1970s and early 1980s, and its constraining impact on new union campaigns, see Lane Windham, *Knocking on Labor's Door: Union Organizing in the 1970s and the Roots of a New Economic Divide* (Chapel Hill: University of North Carolina Press, 2017), 183–87.

15. For an account on strawberry ranchers' adoption of sharecropping to avoid unionization, lower labor costs, and externalize market risks, see Miriam J. Wells, *Strawberry Fields: Politics, Class, and Work in California Agriculture* (Ithaca, NY: Cornell University Press, 1996). "Sharecropping," Wells explained, "offered growers crucial benefits in the post-1960s political climate. These had to do with the way that the organization and incentive structure of sharecropping undercut the solidarity and oppositional leverage of

workers, and with the way that the legal status of sharecropping enabled growers to avoid the restrictions and costs of labor-protective laws" (Wells, *Strawberry Fields*, 243). For transnational corporate structures, see Heidi Tinsman, *Buying into the Regime: Grapes and Consumption in Cold War Chile and the United States* (Durham, NC: Duke University Press, 2014). For a discussion on farm acquisitions and revamping, see Philip L. Martin, *Promise Unfulfilled: Unions, Immigrations, and the Farm Workers* (Ithaca, NY: Cornell University Press, 2003), 169–72. "In 1984," Martin noted, Sun Harvest "gave up its leased farmland, signaling the exit of companies that hired large numbers of workers directly and were vulnerable to union-called boycotts.... Many [other] farmers turned to labor contractors who hired unauthorized workers, and a unionized harvesting association that had fifteen hundred UFW members was disbanded" (Martin, *Promise Unfulfilled*, 182).

16. As chapters 8 and 9 argue, the Agricultural Labor Relations Board (ALRB) was already ineffective before Deukmejian's appointments. For a detailed discussion on the ALRB's shortcomings, see Elizabeth Lamoree, "The Managed Crisis: Labor Relations and Management in California Agriculture, 1930–1980" (PhD diss., University of California, Santa Barbara, 2012). For ALRB appointments in the 1980s, see Philip L. Martin, *Promise Unfulfilled*, 172–75. Regarding the National Labor Relations Board (NLRB), Windham observed that corporate leaders came to defend the NLRB because it did so little to protect workers' interests. Windham, *Knocking on Labor's Door*, 79. See also Windham's discussion on Reagan's conservative NLRB appointments (Windham, *Knocking on Labor's Door*, 182–84).

17. For California's late twentieth century economic and political crisis, especially in rural and agricultural California, see Ruth Wilson Gilmore's "Crime, Croplands, and Capitalism," chap. 4 in *Golden Gulag: Prisons, Surplus, Crisis, and Opposition in Globalizing California* (Berkeley: University of California Press, 2007), 128–80.

18. For California's propositions and the "genteel apartheid" they consolidated, see Daniel Martinez HoSang, *Racial Propositions: Ballot Initiatives and the Making of Postwar California* (Berkeley: University of California Press, 2010). For California's racialized carceral system, see Gilmore, *Golden Gulag*, especially chapters 1 and 2. In Manuel Pastor, *State of Resistance: What California's Dizzying Descent and Remarkable Resurgence Means for America's Future* (New York: New Press, 2018), Pastor writes on California's 1978 tax reform: "While this 'immigrant shock' would soon feed into a more targeted anti-immigrant fervor, the immediate shot across the bow was Prop 13 and its attempt to symbolically pull up the drawbridge just as new guests were arriving" (Pastor, *State of Resistance*, 51). For a succinct account of California's illiberal disarray in the 1980s and 1990s, see chapter 3 of Pastor's *State of Resistance*, "Things Fall Apart." For racialized anti-immigrant politics among white Californians, see Otto Santa Ana, "Proposition 187: Misrepresenting Immigrants and Immigration," chap. 3 in *Brown Tide Rising: Metaphors of Latinos in Contemporary American Public Discourse* (Austin: University of Texas Press, 2002).

19. Kevin R. Johnson, "Proposition 187 and Its Political Aftermath: Lessons for U.S. Immigration Politics After Trump," *UC Davis Law Review* (April 2020): 1859–905.

20. Windham notes: "When we shine the historical spotlight on the working people who tried to form unions in the 1970s, it becomes clear that it is not enough to blame lousy labor leaders or an individualistic working-class culture for labor's decline. In fact, employer resistance to organizing was a far more effective culprit, coupled with U.S. policies and laws that encouraged and enabled this employer behavior." Windham, *Knocking on*

Labor's Door, 8. Reviewing a generation of Chicana/o labor historians, Vicki Ruiz found a similar set of conclusions: "These authors, among others, note that in the 1980s and 1990s, the transformation of women's work networks into effective union representation seems more elusive than ever. In recent years, run-away shops, anti-labor campaigns, and high-priced union-busting consultants, participative management styles, police harassment, mechanization, unemployment, and even the NLRB have stymied labor activism." Vicki Ruiz, *From Out of the Shadows: Mexican Women in Twentieth-Century America* (Oxford: Oxford University Press, 2008), 167.

21. "Brief History of CWA," published in California Women for Agriculture's (CWA) 1991 annual newsletter, no folders, Box 1, CWA Collection, Coachella Valley History Museum, Indio, CA.

22. "Brief History of CWA," CWA 1991 annual newsletter, no folders, Box 1, CWA Collection, Coachella Valley History Museum, Indio, CA

23. Patrick J. McDonnell, "Worse Than Nothing at All: Judge to Rule on Shelters for Migrant Workers," *Los Angeles Times*, July 7, 1992.

24. McDonnell, "Worse Than Nothing at All."

25. McDonnell, "Worse Than Nothing at All."

26. Arturo Diaz, interview by Christian Paiz, January 31, 2015; Simon Machuca, interview by Christian Paiz, February 11, 2017; Maria Marron, interview by Christian Paiz, January 31, 2014; Petra Ruiz, interview by Christian Paiz, January 30, 2014.

27. David Perez offered the most stringent criticism of the UFW's volunteer system. David Perez, interview by Christian Paiz, April 15, 2017. Like other volunteers, Remedios Martinez and her husband, Saul, found the union's demands to be too exhausting. In 1987, after nearly a decade of UFW organizing, they decided "they needed to do something for themselves." Remedios Martinez, interview by Christian Paiz, January 30, 2014.

28. Antonio Puga Torres, for instance, blamed "brown nosers" and "dumb" workers who did not see the UFW's value. Antonio Puga Torres, interview by Christian Paiz, February 13, 2017. Leonor and Rodolfo Suarez blamed workers who opposed the UFW because they wanted to bring relatives without seniority into high paying jobs. Other families, they added, simply needed to work, and could not join UFW campaigns. Leonor and Rodolfo Suarez, interview by Christian Paiz, February 14, 2017. Perhaps more forgivingly, Simon Machuca explained, "Hubo un tiempo que [la union] estuvo muy fuerte, pero no se pudo aproverchar"—"There was a time when the union was strong, but it was not taken advantage of." Simon Machuca, interview by Christian Paiz, November 26, 2013; Petra Ruiz, interview by Christian Paiz, January 30, 2014; Federico Vargas, interview by Christian Paiz, February 14, 2017.

29. Luciano Crespo felt the UFW could have reconnected with their 1960s allies in the 1980s to retrigger their movement, but that the UFW instead "chose to go political," in reference to the union's attempt to affect local and statewide representative elections. Crespo argued this was a key mistake. Luciano Crespo, interview by Christian Paiz, February 8, 2014. Crespo added that internal fissures undermined intra-union trust and "put us back in terms of vitality and organization." Luciano Crespo, interview by Christian Paiz, April 17, 2017. Alfredo Figueroa, a key early supporter from Blythe, California, said the UFW fell after 1980 because it prioritized nonorganizing labors. Alfredo Figueroa, interview by Christian Paiz, November 9, 2013.

30. Hilario Torres, who joined the UFW in the late 1970s and continues to organize pro-UFW activities in the Coachella Valley, noted with succinct clarity the limits of farmworker action in this period. He summarized ranchers' constant threats to close their union companies unless workers gave in to their demands and of contractors' turn to vulnerable labor to undercut union workers. He also found that the Agricultural Labor Relations Act offered few protections and state regulators were often ineffective in preventing labor violations, such as wage theft. "It is very difficult to want to fix the world when you do not have the strength to do it." Hilario Torres, interview by Christian Paiz, November 22, 2013; Federico Vargas, interview by Christian Paiz, February 14, 2017. See chapters 7 and 8 for a discussion on movement exhaustion. See also chapter 9 for Crespo's account of grape worker union exhaustion in the late 1970s and early 1980s, when the contested 1977 elections led to years of anti-union worker and rancher harassment.

31. Evangelina Mendoza, interview by Christian Paiz, February 8, 2014. Maria Marron noted a similar sense of dismay when she said she feels defrauded when she thinks that farmworkers continue to face harmful conditions, but "bureaucrats" get a day off on Chavez's birthday. "These people have not suffered the exhaustion [*el cansancio*] of the fields," she added. Maria Marron, interview by Christian Paiz, January 31, 2014.

32. See Ana Raquel Minian, "The Intimate World of Migrants," chap. 3 in *Undocumented Lives: The Untold Story of Mexican Migration* (Cambridge, MA: Harvard University Press, 2018), 77–130.

33. Rigoberto Gonzalez, *Butterfly Boy: Memories of a Chicano Mariposa* (Madison: Wisconsin University Press, 2006).

34. Gonzalez, *Butterfly Boy*, 55.

35. Gonzalez, *Butterfly Boy*, 133.

36. When Gonzalez received his first glasses, after a young lifetime of poor sight, he finally noticed the effects of farm labor on his grandfather's body: "When I watched my grandfather behind the wheel of the pickup, I traced the definitions of his age and the damage of his numerous strokes on his face—wrinkles, flabby chin, the squinting right eye and its fan of deep groves reaching out from its corner. He had been dyeing his hair, eyebrows, and mustache for years now to hide the outgrowths of white. The job was painfully obvious." Gonzalez, *Butterfly Boy*, 132.

37. In the 1990 summer, while riding a bus to the Coachella Valley, Gonzalez saw "the same beat-up trucks and cars with dented doors that the farmworkers drive and for the agricultural fields. The long lines at the [gas station] pumps could only mean that the crews have stopped working for the day. Any of these people scrambling about for water to quench their thirst could be someone I'm related to. Any of these bodies wincing at the trappings of their hot clothing could have been me. I feel lucky that this was not my fate." Gonzalez, *Butterfly Boy*, 11.

38. Gonzalez, *Butterfly Boy*, 181.

39. Christian Paiz, "Essential Only as Labor: Coachella Valley Farmworkers during COVID-19," *Kalfou: A Journal of Comparative and Relational Ethnic Studies*, 8, no. 1–2 (Spring and Fall 2021): 31–50. *The Other Side of Coachella*, Public Broadcasting Service, November 14, 2018, https://www.pbs.org/video/the-other-side-of-coachella-0cxp6r/. Manuel Gomez, *To Live For the Harvest*, OC World, February 22, 2022.

40. John D. Marquez wrote similarly of his journey out of his community: "I fled Baytown in the early 1990s, scarred psychologically and physically by its streets and violence,

exhausted by the routine of death, mourning, and hopelessness, and not wanting to submit to life at a refinery or in a prison cell." John D. Marquez, *Black–Brown Solidarity: Racial Politics in the New Gulf South* (Austin: University of Texas Press, 2013), 7.

41. "The Fight for Our Lives," produced by Glen Pearcy, Peter Matthiessen, and Luis Valdez in 1973 and 1974. For media coverage on the Coachella Valley labor struggle, see Folders 36, 40, 43, Box 95, UFW Central Administration Collection, Part III, UFW Archive.

42. Jose Muñoz, *Cruising Utopia: The Then and There of Queer Futurity* (New York: New York University Press, 2009).

43. Regarding utopia's radicalism, Muñoz cautioned, "I am also not interested in a notion of the radical that merely connotes some notion of extremity, righteousness, or affirmation of newness. My investment in utopia and hope is my response to queer thinking that embraces a politics of the here and now that is underlined by what I consider to be today's hamstrung pragmatic gay agenda." Muñoz, *Cruising Utopia*, 10.

44. Muñoz, *Cruising Utopia*, 84.

45. Robin D. G. Kelley, *Freedom Dreams: The Black Radical Imagination* (Boston: Beacon, 2003), xii.

46. Strikingly, the UFW's mouthpiece, *El Malcriado*, made a similar argument in its first two years of publication (1965 and 1966). The paper presented movement participants, for instance, as being engaged in a personal and social evolution, and described victories as both achieved and discovered. From each victory, participants discovered conclusions that were to be integrated into their lives as a "life rule": "When a campaign's conclusion has been discovered, it is necessary to know not to have it on one's lips and pointed to outside; instead, and always active, it is necessary to transform that conclusion into a life rule." "Editorial: Our Social Movement," *El Malcriado*, no date, no. 1, 1965.

47. David Scott, *Conscripts of Modernity: The Tragedy of Colonial Enlightenment* (Durham, NC: Duke University Press, 2004), 8.

48. "There were many [UFW members]," Petra Ruiz recalled, "but few who truly felt what they fought for.... The others waited in case the supervisor gave them a small piece of bone." Petra Ruiz, interview by Christian Paiz, January 30, 2014.

49. Maylei Blackwell, "Lideres Campesinas: Grassroots Gendered Leadership, Community Organizing, and Pedagogies of Empowerment," prepared for NYU/Wagner Research Center for Leadership in Action, no date. See also Ruiz, *From Out of the Shadows*, 174–75; Amber Amaya, "Lideres Campesinas: Fighting for Farmworker Women," *Coachella Unincorporated: Youth Media*, March 28, 2015, https://coachellaunincorporated.org/2015/03/28/lideres-campesinas-fighting-for-farmworker-women/.

50. Louis Sahagun, "One Nun's Fight: San Bernardino Diocese Sued for $1.5 Million Over Job Refusal; Sex Discrimination Charged," *Los Angeles Times*, July 10, 1988. For a brief account, see Ruiz, *From Out of the Shadows*, 171–72. In the latter, Ruiz explained, "As a labor historian, I will try to resist the temptation of privileging the workplace as *the* locus of claiming public space. Mexican women have relied on others as well, including, historically, the Roman Catholic Church." Ruiz, *From Out of the Shadows*, 168. For an introduction to Liberation Theology, see Gustavo Gutierrez, *A Theology of Liberation: History, Politics, and Salvation* (Maryknoll, NY: Orbis Books, 1988). For a recent account of the Chicana/o movement's church-based activism, see Felipe Hinojosa's *Apostles of Change: Latino Radical Politics, Church Occupations, and the Fight to Save the Barrio* (Austin: University of Texas Press, 2021).

51. Virginia Ortega, interview by Christian Paiz, February 11, 2017; Virginia Ortega, interview by Christian Paiz, April 18, 2017.

52. Alfredo Fuller and Ray Rodriguez, interview by Christian Paiz, January 22, 2015.

53. Mexican American Political Association organizers helped organize the first Chicana/o graduation ceremony at Indio High School in 1979. Education continued to play a key role in politicization. Ray Rodriquez and Alfredo Fuller, interview by Christian Paiz, October 17, 2013.

54. Ray Rodriguez and Alfredo Fuller, interview by Christian Paiz, October 8, 2013; Calisto Ramos, interview by Christian Paiz, April 18, 2017.

55. Joe Ceja's parents organized the Voter's League, who the Coachella Valley Unified School District hired as the first local Mexican American teacher, and whose cousin helped lead the middle school student walkout in 1976.

56. The Coachella Valley Unified School District also named one of its Mecca elementary schools after a former UFW organizer and California Highway Patrolman, Saul Martinez, who died in 1997 after sustaining injuries from saving his partner. See "Community remembers fallen CHP officer, Saul Martinez, 20 years later," *News Channel 3*, March 19, 2017, https://kesq.com/news/2017/05/19/community-remembers-fallen-chp-officer-saul-martinez-20-years-later/. For related topics, see Mauricio Peña, "Death in the Fields: Maria de Jesus Bautista Died from the Heat," *Desert Sun*, November 19, 2015; Chad Powers, "La Quinta Teen Wants to Repay Elementary School that Shaped Her with School Supplies," *Desert Sun*, September 30, 2020; Raymond Bondad, "Reporter Feels Press Conference Lacked Sincerity," *Coachella Unincorporated*, June 8, 2011.

57. Felicitas Nuñez also participated in Teatro Chicana, which published a collective memoir in 2008 "to help us understand the significance of Chicana women banding together to speak about social injustice." Laura E. Garcia, Sandra M. Gutierrez, and Felicitas Nuñez, eds., *Teatro Chicana: A Collective Memoir and Selected Plays* (Austin: University of Texas Press, 2008), xxix.

58. Garcia, Gutierrez, and Nuñez, *Teatro Chicana*, 170–71.

59. Sam Maestas, interview by Christian Paiz, February 13, 2017.

60. Luciano Crespo, interview by Christian Paiz, April 17, 2017.

61. Silvia Montenegro, interview by Christian Paiz, May 29, 2020. "Policy Brief: East Coachella Valley Housing," *Eastern Coachella Valley Data Project*, California Institute for Rural Studies, 2013. Jonathan London, Teri Greenfield, and Tara Zagofsky, "Revealing the Invisible Valley," *Eastern Coachella Valley Data Project*, California Institute for Rural Studies, June 2013.

62. Unrecorded conversation with Lupe Crespo, April 17, 2017.

63. Max Huerta, interview by Christian Paiz, April 17, 2017. Huerta said that though the UFW and Chicano movements aimed to provide for their community's social and physical needs, he also wanted to provide for their spiritual needs, which he considered central for addressing self-destructive behaviors.

64. Israel Huerta, interview by Christian Paiz, November 21, 2013; see also the Center for Employment Training's website, https://cetweb.edu/location/coachella-ca/.

65. On limits, see Lola Fadulu, "Why Is the U.S. So Bad at Worker Retraining?" *The Atlantic*, January 4, 2018, https://www.theatlantic.com/education/archive/2018/01/why-is-the-us-so-bad-at-protecting-workers-from-automation/549185/. Amalia Uribe Deaztlan, interview by Christian Paiz, January 22, 2015. Career training served an empowering role in the lives of Clementina Olloque, who worked in a Coachella leadership center in the late

1960s and early 1970s, and Remedios Martinez, who worked in the UFW Coachella office in the late 1970s. See Remedios Martinez, interview by Christian Paiz, April 13, 2017; Clementina Olloque, interview by Christian Paiz, August 12, 2014.

66. Leonor and Rodolfo Suarez, interview by Christian Paiz, February 14, 2017.

67. Unrecorded phone conversation Gabriel Suarez, January 10, 2022.

68. Unrecorded conversation with Francisco Ruiz, January 30, 2014.

69. Randy Shaw, *Beyond the Fields: Cesar Chavez, the UFW, and the Struggle for Justice in the 21st Century* (Berkeley: University of California Press, 2010); Ignacio Ornelas Rodriguez, "The Struggle for Social Justice in the Monterey Bay Area: Mexican and Mexican American Political Activism 1930–2000" (PhD diss., University of California, Santa Cruz, 2017). Fran Leeper Buss, ed., *Forged Under the Sun/Forjada bajo el sol: The Life of Maria Elena Lucas* (Ann Arbor: University of Michigan Press, 1993). Jim Drake, who was originally from the Coachella Valley, and joined the early National Farm Workers Association's efforts, organized workers in South Texas and Mississippi after he left the UFW. See Jim Drake, interview by Pat Hoffman, 1985, parts 1–3, digital recording, "Patt Hoffman: 33 interviews 'Impact of Farmworker Movement on Churches and Church Leaders,'" FMDP, https://libraries.ucsd.edu/farmworkermovement/medias/oral-history/.

70. For a discussion of Agbayani Village, see chapter 4. For a reflection on Agbayani Village's meaning to one Filipino UFW member, see Willie Barrientos, interview by Linda Mabalot, March 28, 1978, transcript, Oral History collection, Linda Mabalot Papers, Welga Archive-Bulosan Center for Filipino Studies (henceforth, Welga).

71. For a critique of Agbayani Village by a retired unionist, see "Rudy Reyes 1965–1980: July 15, 2003," in "Filipino Brothers Oral History—1981," Media Collection, FMDP, https://libraries.ucsd.edu/farmworkermovement/essays/essays/018%20Reyes_Rudy.pdf.

72. Philip Vera Cruz, "The Agbayani Retirement Village," Folder 5, Box 4, Philip Vera Cruz Papers, ALUA.

73. Willie Barrientos, interview by Linda Mabalot, March 28, 1978, transcript, Linda Mabalot Papers, Welga, https://welgadigitalarchive.omeka.net/items/show/13.

74. Vera Cruz, "The Agbayani Retirement Village."

75. Sebastian Sahugan, "Letter from a Manong," December 15, 1973, Ang Katipunan, Welga, https://welgadigitalarchive.omeka.net/items/show/53.

76. "Record of Agbayani Village: How the Manong have their exercise," Folder 2, Box 4, Philip Vera Cruz Papers, ALUA.

77. "Record of Minnesota Students: January 12, 1983," Folder 2, Box 4, Philip Vera Cruz Papers, ALUA. In the tour, the students learned of the "many high offices of this nation [who] visited the Filipino Community of Delano. Hundreds and thousands of different races visited that Filipino Hall." See "Records of Visitors—Agbayani Village July 14, 1982," Folder 2, Box 4, Philip Vera Cruz Papers, ALUA, for a list of other visitors, including organizers and relatives from Philippines.

78. Students also worked on the village to grasp the union's goal: "It is a combination of hope, working together, better understanding with all kinds of races the same common goal." "Record of Minnesota Students: January 12, 1983," Folder 2, Box 4, Philip Vera Cruz Papers, ALUA.

79. Filipino leaders had already fought for Filipino visibility within the UFW movement, such as Pete Velasco in the Coachella Valley in 1969 and Philip Vera Cruz's aid to

Filipino oral history projects. Greg Morozumi reflected on Philip Vera Cruz in 2015: "I think that was something that was very particular about [Philip Vera Cruz] that his wasn't just the immediate struggle or the lives of the brothers that he was with right now, but he saw it as an international thing.... [He] was adamant that we don't erase the memory of the Filipino struggle." Greg Morozumi, interview by Allen Jason Sarmiento, March 26, 2015, transcript, Welga, https://welgadigitalarchive.omeka.net/items/show/93.

80. See "Agbayani Village 1982 Orientation Packet," Folder 2, Box 4, Philip Vera Cruz Papers, ALUA. Letters and brief autobiographies are conveniently organized under "The Filipino Brothers Oral History—1981," Media Collection, FMDP, https://libraries.ucsd.edu/farmworkermovement/medias/oral-history/.

81. "Record: Willie Barrientos," no date, Folder 2, Box 4, Philip Vera Cruz Papers, ALUA.

82. See "Agbayani Village 1982 Orientation Packet," Folder 2, Box 4, Philip Vera Cruz Papers, ALUA. See also Isao Fujimoto, interview by Robyn Rodriguez, April 27, 2015, transcript, Welga, https://welgadigitalarchive.omeka.net/items/show/99. Fujimoto shared that Filipino farmworker history played a central role in the construction of Asian American studies and Asian American identity. See also Lillian Galedo, who discusses a memorial she organized for Philip Vera Cruz after his death. Lillian Galedo, interview by Alaina Kyra Cagalingan and Miggy Cruz, June 5, 2015, transcript, Welga, https://welgadigitalarchive.omeka.net/items/show/178.

83. Linda Ogawa Ramirez, "Agbayani Village: For the Manongs, a Home at Last," *Philippine News*, September 6–12, 1980, Folder 2, Box4, Philip Vera Cruz Papers, ALUA.

84. "Record: Our Responsibility in the Village," no date, Folder 2, Box 4, Philip Vera Cruz Papers, ALUA.

85. "Record: Sick Person," February 1983, Folder 2, Box 4, Philip Vera Cruz Papers, ALUA.

86. "Record: December 16, 1983," Folder 2, Box 4, Philip Vera Cruz Papers, ALUA.

87. In 1982, Barrientos listed eighteen deaths, including Justantino Lecorte, Tony Armington (throat trouble), Isidro Taay (operation), Paulo Dundalao (natural), Henry Adsura (heart attack), Art Racimo (suicide), Marcos Ramos (heart trouble), Leo Mangba, Moreno Mabalot (suicide), Barry Quclinderin (heart attack), Cerico Bautislal, Rudy Urbe, Basilio Gaspi (operation), Candido Feliciano (pd), Mariano Santiago (pd), Martin Salesport (pd), Anastasio Pulmano, Francisco Schileng. "Record: Died in the Agbayani," Folder 2, Box 4, Philip Vera Cruz Papers, ALUA. For an example of an obituary, see "Record: Marco Ramos, April 2, 1983," Folder 2, Box 4, Philip Vera Cruz Papers, ALUA.

88. "Last Will and Testament of Isidro Taay," Folder 2, Box 4, Philip Vera Cruz Papers, ALUA. For a biography of Isidro Taay, see Luciano Crespo, interview by Christian Paiz, May 30, 2020.

89. "'Soldiers of the Soil': Letter from Claro Runtal to Fred Abad," "The Filipino Brothers Oral History 1981" Collection, FMDP, https://libraries.ucsd.edu/farmworkermovement/media/oral_history/clarorundalessay.pdf, 5.

90. Kelley, *Freedom Dreams*, 196–98.

91. Evangelina Mendoza, interview by Christian Paiz, February 8, 2014.

92. In Spanish, "Pos le digo, 'Mira—no sabemos hablar pero tartamuramos.'" Evangelina Mendoza, interview by Christian Paiz, February 8, 2014.

Index

Abad, Fred, 58, 60, 75, 115, 276, 314n64, 321n16
Abeno, Themistocles, 115, 362n94
Adair, Douglass (Doug), 106, 111, 116, 194, 293n20, 308n118, 335n57
AFL-CIO, 6, 208, 245–46, 378n49; decline in 1980s, 243; support for AWOC, 59; support for UFW, 77, 171, 187; and 1973 Coachella Strike, 182, 219; and Teamsters, 200
African American Farmworkers, support for UFW, 7
African American rights; and interracial solidarity, 138; campaigns, 172; and MLK Jr., 86; influence on Chicana/o movement, 153
African Americans, displacement in Palm Springs, 39, 168
African Americans, school segregation, 305n87
Agbayani Village, 122–24, 205, 219, 273–76, 336n91, 372n47
Agbayani, Paulo (Paul), 123, 273, 321n19
Agricultural Labor Relations Act (ALRA), 7, 18–19, 205–14, 217, 219, 231–45, 252, 254, 258, 383n30, 369n5; efficacy of, 232–39, 369n11, 370n18, 378n49; elections, 208, 210, 217, 231–44, 247, 250. *See also* Agricultural Labor Relations Board
Agricultural Labor Relations Board (ALRB), 207–11, 244, 258, 369n5, 381n16; response to unfair labor practices, 218, 219, 232–43, 370n18, 376n31, 376n35, 378n49
Agricultural Workers Organizing Committee (AWOC), 6, 47, 59–61, 74, 153, 205, 301n53, 377n40; coordination with NFWA, 76–77; Filipino membership/leaders, 15, 47, 59–61, 66, 218, 234, 321n20;

merger with NFWA, 158; strikes, 47, 68–70, 75–76, 194, 257. *See also* Vera Cruz, Philip
Agtang, Lorraine, 58, 205, 216
Aimes, Jimmy, 75
Alaska, Filipino workers in, 56, 57
All-American Canal, Coachella extension, 15, 29, 317n93
Almaraz, Yolanda, 223, 224
ALRA. *See* Agricultural Labor Relations Act
ALRB. *See* Agricultural Labor Relations Board
Alterado, Henry, 107
Alvarado, Manuel, 176
Amador, Eloisa, 358n53
American Federation of Labor and Congress of Industrial Organizations. *See* AFL-CIO
Ames, Paul, 157
Angel, Filogonio, 249
Anguiano, Lupe, 166
Aquino, Andy, 346n24
Arizona: Chicana/o movement in, 165, 342n67; Filipino workers in, 56; Mexican workers in, 19, 20, 52, 53, 263, 316n86; outlawing boycotts, 154; UFW campaigns in, 157; union miners in, 129, 135, 312n29, 312n30
Armington, Bob, 75, 123, 347n41
Armington, Tony, 387n87
Arredondo, Manuel, 66, 373n63
Arvin-Lamont, California: grape ranchers, 181; AWOC/UFW in, 6, 190
Avalos, Tony, 312n27
Averbuck, David, 330n125
AWOC. *See* Agricultural Workers Organizing Committee

Bagdasarian Ranch, 158–59, 176, 179, 190, 299n30, 344n8, 353n10, 357n49; Bagdasarian sit-in, 331n138
Bagdasarian, Richard, 30, 192
Baker, Ella, 166
Balanoff, Virginia Rodriguez, 138, 147
Balidoy, Julian, 124
Barrientos, Willie, 59, 60, 75–76, 90, 301n52, 387n87; and Agbayani Village, 124, 273, 274, 275, 276; and Delano Filipino Hall, 159; immigration to US, 54–55; on union accomplishments, 248
Bautista, Beatriz de, 241
Bazua, Porfi, 62
Becerra, Amalia, 66–67
Beckman and Bender Ranch, 332n21
Beltran, Guadalupe, 148
Benzon, Salvador, 60
Berg, William (Bill), 219, 347n40, 372n47
Bernstein, Harry, 187, 328n105, 361n77
Bielma, Antonio, 235
Border Patrol (United States), 35, 63, 139, 169, 209, 253, 316n88, 342n67
Botello, Pancho, 194
Bozick, Mike, 92, 97, 182, 183, 185, 188, 329n113, 332n10, 353n10
Bozick, Richard, 107, 109, 110
Bracero Program, 15, 31–34, 37, 43, 50, 61–64, 169, 303n77, 303n80, 315n69, 315n82, 317n91; cancellation of, 34, 60, 69; and union organizing, 59, 60, 69; vulnerability of braceros, 62, 316n86
braceros. *See* Bracero Program
Briggs, Henry, 299n33
Brown and Hill Ranch, 346n33
Brown Berets, 6, 135, 139, 153, 174, 342n67, 349n59; chapter in Coachella Valley, 91, 144, 195; protest in Coachella, 100; recruitment to MAPA, 22
Brown, Edmund Gerald (Pat, Governor of California), 323n34, 338n14
Bulosan, Carlos, 56
Burciaga, Dave, 355n25

Cahuilla Nation, 11, 27, 33, 300n41, 300n44; lack of support from unions, 172; resistance, 31–32; in workforce, 15, 32, 33, 300n46; white views of, 15, 27, 296n7
Cahuilla reservation(s), 31–32, 39; expansion of Palm Springs, CA, 32, 168
Caliente, Pancho, 361n84
California Agricultural Labor Relations Act of 1975. *See* Agricultural Labor Relations Act
California Farm Bureau (CFB), 209
California Proposition 14 (1976), 210–11, 244, 245, 371n26, 378n50
California Proposition 187 (1994), 271
California Proposition 22 (1972), 154, 157, 175
California Rural Legal Assistance (CRLA), 259
California Women for Agriculture (CWA), 258
Camacho, Jesus, 202
Campos, Nicasio, 87, 326n72
Cardinal Distributors, 217, 252
Carian Ranch, 233, 353n11, 359n64, 374n9
Carian, Harry, 109–10, 233; anti-union activity, 176, 183, 234–39, 375n15; grievances against, 109; sexual harassment, 236
Carian, Robert, 235, 236
Carrillo, Margarita, 38, 138, 144–47, 148, 340n46
Carrizales, Guadalupe, 41, 67, 83
Carrizales, Pablo, 67, 84–85, 87, 93, 273, 329n116, 330n127
Castillo, Elvia Alicia, 221
Caswell, James (Jim), 82, 83, 91, 100, 131–32, 133, 149, 338n14
Catalan, George, 75
Ceja, Joe, 223–24, 226, 271–72, 273; farmworker conditions, 304n86; and police, 311n26, 324n53; racism in Coachella schools, 348n44, 374n74
Ceja, Jose, 49, 52
Ceja, Maria, 271
Center for Autonomous Social Action, 92
Cesar Chavez Elementary School, 255
Chavez, Cesar, 4, 18, 19, 20, 95, 248, 255, 257–59; and boycott, 92; and California

390   Index

Proposition 14 (1976), 210–11; in Coachella valley, 85, 89, 157, 191, 255; concern for pesticides, 329n113; conflict in UFW, 184, 211, 244, 330n127, 347n40, 376n34; criticism of, 200, 203, 204, 210–11, 242, 244, 254; and Democratic candidates, 165; fasts, 1, 86, 154; founding of NFWA, 76; jailing of, 154, 156; Media presentation of, 179, 187, 193, 327n93, 360n75, 364n119, 364n120; in negotiation, 178, 360n72, 380n13; and RFK, 86, 89; and student support, 77, 320n12; union strategy, 203, 242, 243, 380n14; union victories, 98–99; and women in the union, 121

Chavez, Manuel, 363n107

Chavez, Richard, 203

Chicana/o movement, 9, 15–17, 19, 86, 92, 95, 129, 132, 145, 206, 273, 374; in Coachella Valley, 128, 134–41, 149, 163–65, 222–28, 259; masculinist discourse in, 166; support for LRUP, 164; and UFW, 97, 100–101, 144, 153, 158, 160, 165; women in, 148, 166. *See also* Brown Berets; Mexican American Political Association

Citizens United for Social Justice, 91

citizenship-based politics, 47–48, 51, 61, 65–66, 68–69, 128, 139, 149; and Filipinos, 47, 55, 57–60; and Mexican Americans, 15, 47, 49, 50, 52, 133, 136, 141, 224; and UFW, 80, 92–93, 95

Coachella City Council, 37, 52, 53, 81, 82, 140, 141, 164

Coachella grape strikes:

—1965 AWOC, 16, 68–70;

—1968 UFW, 1, 16, 86, 89–90, 136, 166, 341n53, 355n28; Robert F. Kennedy and, 86, 89; MAPA and, 86–87, 129; rancher response, 88;

—1969 UFW, 1, 9–10, 16, 91–98, 135, 341n47; 100-mile march, 95; rancher opposition, 233;

—1973 UFW, 9, 18, 170, 174, 179–208 passim, 215, 264, 360n72, 362n92, 365n134; rancher reaction, 176–78, 180–83; Teamster raid, 174, 176–78, 182, 184, 186, 191; media representation of, 192–93, 356n40, 360n74

Coachella Valley Citrus (CVC), 231, 232, 249

Coachella Valley Farmers Association, 32, 63, 62, 90, 193, 310n14, 316n89

Coachella Valley Grape Growers Association, 107

Coachella Valley High School, 50, 67, 138, 145–46, 225, 303n73

Coachella Valley Submarine (newspaper), 32, 36, 302n68, 309n3

Coachella Valley Sun (newspaper), 53, 69, 81–82, 88–89, 127, 130, 299n33, 310n14, 316n87, 318n97, 327n91, 341n47; protest against, 91

Coachella Valley Unified School District (CVUSD), 100, 136–37, 164, 226, 271, 272, 340nn34–35, 348n44, 385nn55–56

Coachella Vineyards, 109, 333n22, 344n8, 357n49

Coachella-Imperial Distributors (CID), 108, 157, 190, 332n19, 333n35, 344n8

Coastal Growers Association, 247

Cohen, Jerry, 207, 210, 244, 254, 326n76, 368n166, 368n168, 369n11

Community Committee for Alternatives in Education (CCAE), 225

Community Service Organization (CSO), 76

Contreras, Jesus, 253

Conway, Floyd, 316n89

Corona, Bert, 89, 134, 165, 349n56

Crespin, Lucy, 236

Crespo, Luciano, 251–52, 257, 272, 276, 376n24, 382n29

Cruz, Paulino, 354n12

Dalzell, Tom, 182, 184, 191, 356n39

date industry/dates, 15, 31, 39, 69, 250; and ALRA, 209, 211; and grape ranchers, 176

Date Palm (newspaper), 296n8, 309n7

Dateland Middle School, 225–26

Daus, Leonardo, 276

Deaztlan, Amalia Uribe, 10–11, 67–68, 83, 87, 273, 318n99, 324n53; and Chicana/o movement, 135, 223; and Filipinos, 94, 96, 331n137; and MAPA, 326n79; women in union, 121, 349n59

Delano grape strikes:
—1965 AWOC, 1, 6, 7, 9, 16, 75–77, 82, 161, 218, 251, 257, 274, 278, 355n28; MAPA and, 81;
—1966 AWOC-NFWA Delano grape strike, 54, 80, 84;
—1967 UFWOC Delano grape strike, expansion to Coachella, 85, 143;
—1968–1969 UFW, 1;
—1973 UFW, 200, 205
Delano, California, 142, 144; ALRA grape elections, 219; AWOC in, 9, 54, 69, 74, 205; Filipino Hall, 74, 159, 380n11; Filipino workers, 58, 74, 95, 97, 122, 123, 158, 160, 162, 163, 189, 202, 218, 321n16; MAPA in, 82, 87, 90; NFWLU in, 59; Reagan gubernatorial campaign and, 82; tensions with Coachella UFW, 155, 377n42; UFW in, 93, 94, 95, 97, 98, 162, 197, 203, 216; white media coverage of Delano strikes, 80. *See also* Agbayani Village; Delano grape strikes
Delvo, Cipriano, 57, 59
Democratic Party, 52, 131, 165, 328n105, 341n53, 342n55
Desert Grape Growers League (DGGL), 92, 380n13
Desert Rancher (newspaper), 26–27, 29, 30, 42–43, 296n2, 296n5, 300n48, 308n111; and farmworkers, 33; and Japanese Americans, 38
Desert Sands Unified School District (DSUSD), 91, 136, 163–64, 271, 340n34, 348n44
Diaz, Arturo, 170, 221–22, 249
Drake, Jim, 378n63, 386n69
Dunlao, Alberto, 190

education: bilingual, 164, 226, 271; Cesar Chavez vision for, 256; farmworker opportunities and conditions, 12, 25–26, 34, 37–38, 49, 62, 65, 132, 134, 142, 145, 168, 188, 217, 225, 263, 270, 372n61; racial inequality in, 10, 31, 37–39, 65, 129, 171, 223, 302n63, 309n3, 331n137; 340n34, 340n37; and Chicana/o Movement, 16, 92, 128, 132, 141, 163, 165, 167, 224;

Mexican Americans and, 15, 86, 138; and MAPA, 54, 83, 91, 92, 133, 136–37, 139, 153, 223. *See also* Farmworker experience: visions/hopes
El Malcriado (newspaper), 1, 4, 6, 7, 9, 80, 89, 134, 161, 321n19, 380n9, 384n46;and immigrant workers, 329n114; masculinist discourse in, 120, 335n73, 377n40, 377n42; and multiracial UFW, 158; and Proposition 14, 371n26; and strikes/strikebreakers, 95–97, 330n133; utopian vision, 102, 335n57
Equiveles, Maria de, 190
Esher, Frank, 130, 131, 132, 133
Esperanza Youth and Family Center, 272
Espinoza, Ramon, 93

farmworker experience:
—life conditions, 25, 34, 36, 42, 45, 54–55, 65, 102, 143, 205, 262–64, 296n1; education, 10, 36, 37, 48–49, 50, 65, 132, 147, 217; housing, 36, 38, 49, 56, 65, 107, 255, 259; patriarchy in, 41–42; poverty, 34, 50, 77; social marginality, 8, 12, 15, 19, 26, 33, 48, 50, 59–60, 120, 270, 298n21;
—visions/dreams, 4–5, 10, 59–60, 69, 88, 102, 111–12, 125, 144, 174, 197–98, 205, 212, 224, 264, 266–67; education, 149, 217, 256, 373n63. *See also* Agbayani Village, Chavez, Cesar; Vera Cruz, Philip
—working conditions, 25, 33–34, 40–41, 54–56, 58, 108, 111–16, 205, 249, 262–63, 296n1; wages, 34, 36, 64, 65, 249; gender discrimination and sexual harassment, 41, 113, 117–20, 215–16, 236, 239; structural unemployment, 34, 50. *See also* UFW contracts and benefits
Favela, Leonel, 259
feminists, 135, 147, 165, 307n103; and UFW, 117, 119–22. *See also* patriarchy: and UFW; UFW: women in
Ferrel, Maria Elena, 239–40, 376n28
Fierro, Hope Lopez, 194
Fierros, Carlos, 359n64
Figueroa, Alfredo, 53, 85, 89–91, 131, 135, 194, 312n28, 317n91, 338n14, 372n61, 382n29
Figueroa, Demesia, 307n103

Figueroa, Fausto, 252–54, 258, 260
Filipino Agricultural Labor Association (FALA), 57, 75
Filipino American farmworkers, 7, 9, 15, 32, 39, 44–45, 47, 54–58, 69, 75, 86, 90, 123–24, 257, 330n125; and AWOC, 6, 15, 58–59, 66, 355n28; bachelorhood and anti-miscegenation laws, 6, 55, 56, 58, 94, 122; grape workers, 1, 15, 26, 38, 58, 61, 65, 80, 108, 183–84, 202, 233, 314n63, 331n138, 347n41; interracial solidarity, 77; masculinist discourse, 56–60, 95; separation from Mexican farmworkers, 43, 77, 93, 100; and UFW, 9, 16, 17, 44, 74, 77–78, 90, 93–96, 100, 115, 122, 153, 158–63, 165, 172, 188–90, 218–20, 228, 278, 329n122, 347n35, 364n120, 377n42, 386n79; and unions, 57–58, 68, 75, 206, 221, 322n20. *See also* Agbayani Village, Agricultural Workers Organizing Committee
Filipino American Labor Union, 59
Filipino Hall, Delano, California, 74, 77, 380n11, 386n77
Fitzsimmons, Frank, 176, 179
Freedman Ranch, 108, 112–25 passim, 155, 176, 179, 242; and pesticides, 332n18; and strikebreakers, 202; and UFW, 112–25 passim, 155, 179, 200, 211, 215, 220, 242, 249, 250, 251, 379n64
Freshpict (ranch), 346n33
Fuller, Alfredo (Al), 53, 54, 135, 271, 338n14

Ganz, Marshall, 183–203 passim, 242, 244, 363n107, 376n34, 379n71
Garcia, Anthony, 141
Garcia, Francisco, 139, 353n52
Garcia, Gus, 134
Garcia, Laura, 148
Garcia, Peggy, 148
Garcia, Rodolfo, 353n10
gender relations. *See* farmworker working conditions: gender discrimination and sexual harassment; feminists; patriarchy; UFW, women in
Gines, Ben, 59, 60, 68, 77, 319n102, 321n19, 322n20

Gomez, Cruz, 324n51
Gomez, Socorro, 138, 223
Gonzalez, Adrian, 344n8
Gonzalez, Andres, 155–56, 159
Gonzalez, Corky, 134, 165
Gonzalez, Estella, 114
Gonzalez, Guadalupe, 324n51
Gonzalez, Irene, 272
Gonzalez, Julio, 140
Gonzalez, Petra, 353n10
Gonzalez, Rigoberto, 260–62
Govea, Jessica, 244
Grami, Bill, 193
Grant, Alan, 209
Guillen, Father Patricio, 271
Guimarra (ranch), 204
Gutierrez, Jose Angel, 165
Gutierrez, Rosario, 215, 216
Gutierrez, Sandra, 224, 225

H&M Ranch, 108, 189, 344n8
Hagerty, Horace, 26–28, 30, 296n3
Hawaii, Filipino workers in: 54, 55, 57, 75
Henry Moreno (ranch), 109, 176, 353n10
Herbekian (ranch), 109
Hernandez, Elizabeth, 186, 359n66
Hernandez, Olga, 360n69
HMS (ranch), 217
Hoffman, Pat, 194
Huerta, Dolores, 76, 203, 256, 326n81, 339n25, 349n57; and Robert F. Kennedy, 89
Huerta, Israel, 64, 65, 66, 272, 317n93, 317n97
Huerta, Max, 35. 142–44, 174, 181–202 passim, 226, 227, 272, 342n67, 345n9, 356n34, 366n148, 366n151, 367n158, 367n165, 374n76, 379n71, 385n64
Huerta, Ray, 155, 182, 188, 191, 345n13, 350n59, 355n24, 356n30, 379n71

Ideal (newspaper), 128–35, 141, 224, 337n11, 338n14; and education, 137, 340n35; and police brutality, 138, 141, 341n48; and politics, 139, 164, 348n49; and UFW, 165; and women/gender relations/patriarchy, 166, 349nn56–57

Index   393

immigrants/immigration, 15, 37, 63–64, 139, 147, 167–70, 209, 223, 228, 273; as farmworkers, 37, 61, 80, 226, 245, 253, 260; as strikebreakers, 89, 92, 184, 189, 200, 362n92; undocumented immigrants, 43, 63, 64, 253, 262, 271–72, 303n78, 316n87; and UFW, 80, 89, 93, 96, 169–70, 221, 247, 362n92. *See also* Border Patrol; California Proposition 187

Immigration and Naturalization Service (INS), 80, 316n87

Imperial Valley, 25, 29, 33, 114, 146, 148, 319n103, 358n56, 376n34; Coachella strikebreakers from, 183; lettuce workers, 7, 194, 242, 271, 380n14; MAPA in, 53

Imutan, Andy, 77, 162, 163, 189, 347n35, 347n37, 347n41, 377n42

Imutan, Luming, 77

Indigenous Nations: erasure of, 29, 33, 43, 297n17, 298n21; Mexican Americans and, 52; U.S. seizure of land, 31. *See also* Cahuilla Nation

Indio High School, 271, 385n53

Indio school district, 305n87

Indio, California, 15, 28, 30, 37–39, 42, 51, 81, 127, 168, 272, 305n87; farmworker camp, 36, 49, 65, 84, 90, 195, 202, 223; schools, 50, 223, 271, 340n34, 385n53; UFW in, 93, 94, 157, 326n80, 331n138, 338n14

Inter-Harvest (ranch), 346n33

International Brotherhood of Teamsters. *See* Teamsters Union

Itliong, Larry, 57, 59, 69, 74, 75, 158, 159, 162, 314n52, 321n19, 321n20, 331n137, 347n40, 355n28

Jacildone, Maximo, 276

Japanese Americans, 57; farm workers 32, 56, 57, 220, 347n38; ranchers, 38, 309n4, 371n26

Karahadian Ranch: anti-union activity, 109, 176, 180, 183, 190, 198, 239–40, 354n15, 355n27, 357n43, 358n53, 376n27, 376n28; compliance with union, 155, 344n8; conditions at, 108; strikes at, 182–83, 185, 190–91, 197, 358n52, 359n63, 359n65

Karahadian, Milton, 355n27

Kay, John, 131

Kennedy, Robert F., 86, 88–89

Kent, Noel, 218, 219

Kintz, Walter, 370n18

KK Larson (Ranch), 108, 179, 200, 202, 253–54. *See also* Larson, Patricia (Corky).

Kono, Ed, 38

Kubo, Harry, 371n26

La Raza Unida Party (LRUP), 139–40, 164–65, 341n53

Lamas, Mateo Murillo, 316n86

Larson, Patricia (Corky), 258–59, 272

Lecorte, Justantino, 276, 387n87

Lideres Campesinas, 271

Lopez, Danny, 234

Lopez, Eleanor, 311n18, 327n91, 328n108

Lopez, Joe, 182, 190, 191

Lopez, Juan Aguilar, 316n86

Lopez, Tony, 88, 93, 104–06, 107, 111, 326n74

Los Angeles Police Department, 138, 139, 341n48

Los Angeles Times, 179, 180, 187, 193, 364n123

Los Angeles, California, 86, 129, 157

Loya, Raul, 53, 54, 91, 100, 129, 131, 135, 140, 164, 312n29, 337n7, 338n14, 372n61

Lozano, Bernie, 85

Lozaro, Placido, 346n24

Lucio, Arnulfo, 137, 138

Luhman, Robert, 137, 138

Luna, Jose, 344n8

Lyons, Mark, 203

Machuca, Simon, 273, 382n28

Macias, Johnny, 183

Mackaye, Margaret, 34, 37, 39, 63, 316nn88–89

Macri-Ortiz, Barbara, 194, 360n70

Maestas, Samuel (Sam), 138, 224, 272, 373n66

Maggaco, Henry, 353n10

Mangaoang, Ernesto, 57

Manuel, Pete, 59, 60, 77, 322n20

MAPA. *See* Mexican American Political Association
Marron, Maria, 33, 116–17, 182, 260, 357n43, 383n31; and patriarchy/gender relations, 42, 67–68, 120, 307n107; women in UFW, 121, 195–97
Martinez, David, 375n15
Martinez, Elizabeth, 194
Martinez, Juanita, 87–88, 156, 325n72
Martinez, Remedios, 249, 273, 382n27, 386n69
Martinez, Saul, 379n71, 385n56
masculinist discourse: among farmworkers, 33, 42, 119–20, 159, 335n73; in Filipino community, 56–60, 95; in Mexican/Mexican American community, 67, 133–34, 166–67, 312n29, 349n56, 349n59; in rancher nation, 29–30. *See also* feminists; patriarchy; UFW: women in
Masip, Carlos, 115, 362n94
Matias, Simon, 159, 189
Matson, Rosemary, 194
Mecca, CA, 28, 34, 213, 237, 272, 298n24; Filipino migrant workers in, 43, 59; UFW office in, 94
Medina, Eliseo, 104, 203, 244, 247, 376n34, 379n64, 379n71
Mel-Pak Ranch, 176, 189, 190, 198, 241, 344n8, 353n10, 353n11, 354n12
Melgoza, Ramon, 87
Mendez, Tony, 239
Mendoza, Evangelina, 121–22, 259, 273, 278–79
Mendoza, Flora, 90, 317n87
Mensalvas, Chris, 57, 59
Mexican American community, 15, 47, 49–50, 52–53, 68, 95, 100–101, 132, 149, 223; citizenship claims and political/social marginality, 16, 47, 50–53, 68, 73, 81, 86, 128–29, 136, 139–41, 149, 153, 164, 304n81, 340n34, 340n37, 341nn47–48, 349n59; conservatives in, 38, 51–53, 65, 82, 90–91, 100, 141, 164, 311n18; displacement by whites, 39; locals and migrants, 44, 50, 62, 64–65, 328n108; non-farmworkers, 26; as teachers, 37, 136–37, 163, 270, 340n35, 385n55. *See also* Mexican American Political Association; Progresista Lodge; Voters League
Mexican American Legal Defense and Education Fund (MALDEF), 92, 129
Mexican American Political Association (MAPA), 6, 52, 53, 54, 65–66, 81–82, 128, 134, 136, 224, 323n36, 326n79; conservative Mexican American opposition to, 91, 100, 133; cooperation with UFW, 85–87, 89; education reform, 91, 92, 136–38, 139, 223, 271; *Ideal* newspaper, 128, 130, 133, 141; John V. Tunney protest, 91, 92, 100, 131; negotiations with Teamsters, 222–23; and police violence, 138–39; political organizing, 81–83, 86, 88, 89, 139–41, 164–66, 341n53; and Robert F. Kennedy, 89, 325n69
Meza, Margie, 190, 198, 353n11, 354n12, 363n107
migrant farmworkers, 34, 36, 61, 64; in Coachella Valley, 9, 15, 32, 317n91, 345n23; grape workers, 37, 39, 43, 55, 58; in Pacific West, 6, 56, 213; as strikebreakers, 178; and UFW, 94–95, 175; vulnerability/precarity of, 26, 37, 80, 132, 184, 217, 255. *See also* Bracero Program; Filipino farmworkers
migrant worker camps, 309n9; from labor contractors, 40; rancher camps, 160, 178, 207. *See also* farmworker: living conditions
Millonida, Catalino, 188, 362n92
Mission Indian Federation (MIF), 32
Montenegro, Silvia, 226
Morales, Maria, 190, 198
Morales, Mary, 358n52
Moses, Marion, 124
Mouradick Ranch, 344n8, 353n10, 357n49
Movimiento Estudiantil Chicana/o Aztlan (MEChA), 135, 146, 166–67
Mujeres Mexicanas, 271
Muñoz, Jesus, 375n15
Murello, Herman, 115
Murguia, Jose Guadalupe (Lupe), 194, 365n127
Murshed, Mohammed, 107

Nathan, Sandy, 360n69
National Consumer Grape Boycott.
    See UFW boycotts
National Farm Workers Association
    (NFWA), 6, 76–77, 81, 312n28, 377n40;
    merger with AWOC, 9, 77, 329n122;
    Mexican base, 6, 76
National Farmworkers Labor Union, 59
National Labor Relations Act (NLRA), 170,
    171, 207–09, 238, 239, 241, 245, 246,
    352n73, 369n12, 370n17, 370n22, 375n13,
    381n16, 381n20
National Labor Relations Board (NLRB).
    See National Labor Relations Act
Nava, Isidoro, 157
Neely, Louise, 52, 90, 309n9
New York Times, 179, 187, 193, 356n40,
    360n75
NFWA. *See* National Farm Workers
    Association
Nixon, Richard M., 92, 133, 170
NLRA. *See* National Labor Relations Act
NLRB. *See* National Labor Relations
    Board
Noriega, Ramses, 83, 327n91
Nuñez, Felicitas, 146–47, 272, 385n57

Oasis Gardens (ranch), 109
Oasis, California, 15, 28, 34, 298n24;
    Japanese Americans in, 38; schools, 137
Olloa, Rosa, 126
Olloque, Clementina, 35, 195–97, 224, 226,
    301n59, 385n65; other career, 224, 272; as
    UFW leader, 135, 182, 186, 260, 359n63,
    360nn67–68, 365n131, 366nn139–40
Ortega, Guadalupe, 114
Ortega, Virginia, 41, 42, 84, 87, 121, 197, 271,
    273, 336n79, 365n131
Ortiz, Frank, 188
Oyos, Teresa, 148

Pader, Johnny, 75, 189, 346n24
Padilla, Gilbert (Gil), 76, 82, 93–94, 112, 203,
    244, 256, 329n124, 330n127
Palm Desert, California, 39, 127, 168,
    340n34, 350n64

Palm Springs, California, 15, 28, 39, 81,
    167–68, 258, 296n6, 338n14; and Cahuilla
    people, 31–32; displacement of people of
    color; 39
Palomares, Uvaldo, 34, 81
Pastor, Paul, 330n125
patriarchy: among farmworkers, 40–43, 62,
    67–68, 117–18, 216, 228, 307n109, 308n110;
    in Chicana/o Movement, 166; in Mexican
    American families, 9, 121–22, 308n102,
    349n59; ranchers and, 15, 42–43, 91, 100,
    108, 110–11, 375n22; and UFW, 9, 119–21,
    211, 335n72, 336n79, 366n139
Paular, Jerry, 44
Paulo Agbayani Village, Delano, CA.
    See Agbayani Village
Pederson, Pilar, 345n9
Pelayo, Rosario, 117, 335n62
Perez, David, 212–14, 216, 231–33, 249, 250,
    261, 374n5
Perez, Henry, 83
Perez, Jose, 360n71
Perez, Roger, 81
pesticide use: farmworker exposure, 33, 205,
    260, 261; Lideres Campesinas workshops,
    271; rancher violations, 332n18; UFW
    bans on, 102, 105, 106, 112, 270, 329n113
Peters Ranch, 183
Philippines: anti-imperialism in, 54;
    farmworker remittances to, 57; migration
    from, 55; U.S. relations with, 56, 123;
    visitors to Agbayani Village, 274
Pic N Pac, 346n33
Pilar, Pete, 125
Pilgrimage to Sacramento (1966), 1, 81,
    312n28, 338n14
Pinzon, Romana, 185
police: in Coachella, 81, 100–101, 139–40;
    differential treatment of Mexicans, 37, 50,
    65, 133, 140, 303n80, 310n10, 318n98;
    harrassment of Voter's League, 53; as
    rancher allies, 12, 35, 59, 96, 196, 359n66;
    reform efforts, 136, 138–41, 144, 153,
    163–66, 277, 312n28, 342n67; violence by,
    53, 129, 132, 139, 186, 200, 304n83,
    341nn47–48, 359n63; 360n69

396   Index

Progresista Lodge (PL), 51, 100, 311n18, 327n91
Proposition 14. See California Proposition 14 (1976)
Proposition 187. See California Proposition 187 (1994)
Proposition 22. See California Proposition 22 (1972)
Puerto Rican farmworkers, 186, 220

Rabino, Anastacio, 220
Racimo, Antonio, 276
racism/racial discrimination, 9, 12, 15, 32, 35–59 passim, 65, 80, 94, 102, 130–32, 149, 169, 247, 259; accusations of anti-white racism, 91, 222; denials of, 129, 130; among Mexican Americans, 133. See also education: racial inequality in
Ramirez, Aurelio, 354n12
Ramirez, Edmundo, 114
Ramirez, Maria Teresa, 357n45
Ramirez, Miguel, 114, 334n52
Ramirez, Salvador, 249, 357n47
Ramos, Cali, 138
Ramos, Castilo (Cali), 83–84, 138, 191, 195, 223, 271, 349n56, 349n59, 365n130
Ramos, Eva, 155–56
Ramos, Marcos, 387n87
Ravelo, Delia, 146–47, 148
Reagan, Ronald, 82, 246, 248, 378n63
Rendon, Tereso, 87, 202, 325n72
Rendon, Vivian, 87, 325n72
Republican Party, 154, 258, 342n55
Reyes, Irene, 87, 93, 121, 326n79, 329n118, 349n59
Reyes, Isabel, 48–49, 52
Reyes, Rudy, 77
Reyes, Tony, 223, 307n103, 373n62
Rios, Manuel, 140
Rivera, Fidela, 157
Riverside County, CA, 60; arrests of strikers, 186, 195; police killings in, 140; supervisor Patricia Larson, 258–59
Rodriguez, Amelia, 353n10
Rodriguez, Hilda, 136–37, 138, 147, 339n32
Rodriguez, Juan, 107–08

Rodriguez, Nabor, 53, 81
Rodriguez, Porfiria, 114
Rodriguez, Ray, 53–54, 83, 131, 135, 166, 222–23, 226, 273, 312n29, 324n52, 326n79, 372n61; on Caswell, Jim, 338n16
Rodriguez, Sam (Sammy), 182, 202
Rodriguez, Virginia. See Balanoff, Virginia Rodriguez
Rubal, Paul, 189
Ruiz, Francisco, 273
Ruiz, Petra, 117–21, 125, 197, 215, 216, 248, 273, 335n62, 335n66, 335n72, 365n134
Runtal, Claro, 59, 60, 96, 162, 188, 189, 218, 220, 276, 362n94, 363n104

Saatjian, Lloyd, 183
Sacramento, California, 1, 6, 61, 157, 347n35; AWOC asparagus strike 1965, 60; Filipino workers in, 58, 59
Saiz, Ben, 53
Santos, Lorenzo de los, 109, 359n64
Sauceda, Esperanza, 359n65
Sauceda, Mily Treviño, 271
Schendley Farms, 123
Serrano, Maria, 111–14, 126, 191, 195, 260, 273, 365n134, 365n135; as union leader, 116, 121, 176, 248, 336n75, 375n15, 375n19; and gender relations, 42, 120, 307n106, 336n79; women in union, 197, 215–16, 365n131
Serrano, Ramon, 108
Servin, Elodia, 114–15
settler colonialism, 25–33, 35, 45–46, 52, 73, 98, 173, 263, 297n17, 298nn20–21, 308n111
sexual harassment of farmworkers, 12, 34, 41, 118, 261, 271, 335n69; targeting of UFW members, 236, 239; and UFW, 16, 113, 118, 119
Shy, Ruth, 379n71
Sicre, Alex, 309n5, 350n64
Sicre, George, 305n87, 309n5
Silva, Alvino, 32
Silva, Rudy, 107
Simo, Enriqueta, 114
Smith, David Eason (Dave), 353n7, 355n21
South Asian farmworkers, 15, 32, 56

Index 397

Steinberg, Lionel, 100, 112, 113, 125, 179, 180, 193, 234, 242, 361n75, 364n119,
Stockton, CA, 55, 57, strikes in, 59, 69, 212, 221
strikebreakers, 40, 175–91 passim, 198, 200–202, 208, 241, 330n133, 363n104, 364n120, 366nn139–140; Filipinos, 189, 202, 355n28; Mexican immigrants as, 89, 92, 184, 200, 362n92; UFW and, 96, 170, 183, 221
Strikes: air controllers, 246; Cannery and Agricultural Workers International Union, 57; 1937 FALA asparagus, 75; 1948 Filipino American Labor Union, 59; Hawaii, 57, 75; Sacramento, 60; Salinas, 158, 161; Stockton, 69, 212, 221. *See also* Coachella grape strikes; Delano grape strikes
student activism, 76, 77, 85, 86, 100, 128, 135, 138, 144, 165, 174, 224; and UFW, 320n12, 386n78. See also Teatro Chicana
Suarez, Gabriel, 273
Suarez, Leonor, 249, 251, 273, 382n28
Sullivan, Elizabeth (Liz), 236, 374n9

Taft-Hartley Act (1947), 59, 378n50
Tamsi, Marcelo, 189
Teamsters Union, 17, 126, 174–204, 217–22, 233, 234, 243–44, 376n35; cooperation with MAPA, 222; cooperation with ranchers, 114, 154, 174–205, 217–18, 234, 264, 267, 353n7, 353n10, 353n11, 354n15, 355n27, 357n43, 367n156, 367n165; Filipinos and, 218, 321n19, 362n94, 363n109; media representations, 175, 179–80, 187, 193, 356n40, 361nn74–75, 364n119, 364n120, 364n123; and UFW boycotts, 367n165; violence, 175, 181–204 passim, 358n53, 359n66, 363n110; worker views of, 115, 174, 180–206 passim, 220–21, 358n60, 365n127, 366n148, 369n8
Teatro Chicana, 136, 138, 145–48, 224, 225, 272, 340n46, 385n57
Teatro Mestizo, 146
Tejanos, 32, 64, 65
Tenneco Ranch, 109, 159, 176–79, 184, 185, 189, 354n14
Texas, 64, 65, 67; UFW in, 80, 82, 158

Thermal, California, 15, 26, 28, 34; public housing, 255, 272
Tijan, Vicente, 115, 362n94
Tijerina, Reyes, 134
Torda, Sammy, 59, 60, 61
Torres, Hilario, 216–17, 218, 249, 250, 251, 383n30
Torres, Mary Lou, 87, 325n72
Torres, Rafael, 87, 325n72
Torres, Ramon, 358n60
Treviño, Emiliano, 87, 156, 326n72, 326n73, 345n15
Treviño, Irene, 87, 156, 326n72
Tunney, John V., US Representative, 90–92, 341n53
Turner, Frederick Jackson, 28, 29; pioneer story, 27–29, 31, 73. *See also* settler colonialism

UFW boycotts, 1, 6, 7, 85, 91–102 passim, 154, 157, 187, 200–201, 203, 380n13; and ALRA, 207, 242; anti-boycott campaigns, 157, 158, 175, 177; decreasing efficacy of, 171–72, 178, 180, 258, 367n165, 368n166, 369n11; and *El Macriado*, 120
UFW contracts, benefits, and other victories, 98, 100, 102, 104–15, 119, 121, 124–25, 174, 185, 206, 215, 217, 232, 248, 249, 259, 270; health clinic, 216–17. *See also* Agbayani Village
UFW management/leadership, 89, 98, 110, 121, 155–62, 172–90 passim, 194, 200–204, 210–11, 227, 231–32, 242–54 passim, 257, 333n29, 377n42, 382n29; limited resources/dependence on volunteers, 155, 156, 158, 160, 200–202, 218, 244, 247, 259; 346n33, 374n5, 376n34, 377n38, 380n14, 382n27; non-violence, 86, 193. *See also* Chavez, Cesar; Huerta, Dolores; Itliong, Larry; Velasco, Pete; Vera Cruz, Philip
UFW public presentation, 92, 95, 96, 97, 102–04, 120, 384n46; masculinist discourse, 95, 120, 166; citizenship rights, 92. *See also El Malcriado*
UFW strategy/political action, 88–89, 207–08, 210; justice, 116; equality, 117;

Mecca-to-Coachella March, 234–35; support for Democratic party, 165. *See also* Agricultural Labor Relations Act; California Proposition 14 (1976)

UFW strikes. *See* Coachella grape strikes; Delano grape strikes, strikes

UFW, race relations in, 9, 44, 93–96, 100, 122, 153, 158–59, 162–63, 172, 188–90, 198, 219, 329n122; 347n35, 386n79; and Mexican immigrants, 80, 169–70, 329n114, 362n92

UFW, women in, 10, 113, 115, 117–22, 188, 206, 215, 278, 335n72, 336n75; sexual harassment of, 236. *See also* Dolores Huerta

UFWOC. *See* UFW

unemployment benefits, 217, 241, 270, 353n11

United Farm Worker Organizing Committee (UFWOC). *See* UFW

United Farm Workers. *See* UFW

United Mexican American Students (UMAS), 6, 86, 135

United States imperialism in Philippines, 54, 55, 123. *See also* settler colonialism

Uranday, Esther, 76

Valdora Ranch, 144, 174, 181–82, 184, 356n34
Valdora, David, 109, 337n98, 353n8
Van Buren Elementary School, 223, 226
Vargas, Federico, 249, 375n15
Vasquez, Catalina C., 360n69
Vasquez, Martha, 360n69
Vasquez, Terry, 194
Velasco, Pete, 9–10, 59, 94–97, 203, 278, 279, 329n124; Filipino concerns, 162, 314n63; interracial solidarity in UFW, 380n11; perception of UFWOC as Mexican, 93, 94–96, 329n122, 330n130, 387n79; tensions with Coachella UFW, 94

Velez, Teresa, 215, 216

Vera Cruz, Philip, 12, 59, 347n40; and Agbayani Village, 123, 228, 273–74; calls for sacrifice by union members, 161, 346n33; 347n41, 377n42; and Coachella UFW, 159; concerns about Filipino voice in UFWOC, 77, 80, 218–19, 221, 321n20, 322n22, 386n79; concerns within Filipino community, 44, 162; criticism of UFW leaders, 218; and farmworker precarity/living conditions, 12, 56, 125, 133, 273; and immigrant labor, 80, 218; power and violence of ranchers, 35, 106, 111, 161, 261; and NFLU, 59; and 1975 UFW elections, 219–20; resignation from UFW, 244; on UFW resources, 33; and white racism, 58, 314n61

Vietnam War, 73, 83–84, 86, 149, 324nn52–54; anti-war protests, 100, 165; and Chicana/o Movement, 128, 145, 153, 324n51

Villalobos, Silvia, 353n10, 353n11
Villegas, Jesus, 332n18, 344n8, 379n71
Vitalino, Mayo, 233–35, 374n9
Voters League (VL), 52–53, 81–82, 85, 86, 88, 135, 140, 224, 311n26, 341n47, 385n55

Walter, James, 140
Washington Post, 179, 187, 192, 193
Weiss, Richard, 140

Yap, Nick, 75, 76
Yemeni farmworkers, 7, 160
Ytom, Felicing (Felix), 74, 115

Zarate, Sister Rosa Marta, 271

www.ingramcontent.com/pod-product-compliance
Lightning Source LLC
Chambersburg PA
CBHW031750220426
43662CB00007B/342